Fodor's

SWITZERLAND

44th Edition

Where to Stay and Eat for All Budgets

Must-See Sights and Local Secrets

Ratings You Can Trust

Fodor's Travel Publications   New York, Toronto, London, Sydney, Auckland
www.fodors.com

FODOR'S SWITZERLAND

Editors: Robert I. C. Fisher, Amanda R. Theunissen

Editorial Production: Bethany Cassin Beckerlegge

Editorial Contributors: Nancy Coons, Katrin Gygax, Jennifer McDermott, Marton Radkai, Sharon-Anne Wilcox, Kay Winzenried

Maps and Illustrations: Henry Columb and Mark Stroud, Moon Street Cartography; David Lindroth Inc.; William Wu; Bob Blake and Rebecca Baer, *map editors*

Design: Fabrizio La Rocca, *creative director;* Guido Caroti, *art director;* Ann McBride, *designer;* Melanie Marin, *senior picture editor*

Cover Photo (Lake high above the town of Zermatt on the Matterhorn, Valais Alps): Patitucci-Photo/Outdoor Collection/Aurora Photos

Production/Manufacturing: Angela McLean

COPYRIGHT

Copyright © 2007 by Fodor's Travel, a division of Random House, Inc.

Fodor's is a registered trademark of Random House, Inc.

All rights reserved under International and Pan-American Copyright Conventions. Published in the United States by Fodor's Travel, a division of Random House, Inc., and simultaneously in Canada by Random House of Canada, Limited, Toronto. Distributed by Random House, Inc., New York.

No maps, illustrations, or other portions of this book may be reproduced in any form without written permission from the publisher.

Forty-Fourth Edition

ISBN 978–1–4000–1782–9

ISSN 0071–6553

SPECIAL SALES

This book is available for special discounts for bulk purchases for sales promotions or premiums. Special editions, including personalized covers, excerpts of existing books, and corporate imprints, can be created in large quantities for special needs. For more information, write to Special Markets/Premium Sales, 1745 Broadway, MD 6-2, New York, New York 10019, or e-mail specialmarkets@randomhouse.com.

AN IMPORTANT TIP & AN INVITATION

Although all prices, opening times, and other details in this book are based on information supplied to us at press time, changes occur all the time in the travel world, and Fodor's cannot accept responsibility for facts that become outdated or for inadvertent errors or omissions. So **always confirm information when it matters,** especially if you're making a detour to visit a specific place. Your experiences—positive and negative—matter to us. If we have missed or misstated something, **please write to us.** We follow up on all suggestions. Contact the Switzerland editor at editors@fodors. com or c/o Fodor's at 1745 Broadway, New York, New York 10019.

PRINTED IN THE UNITED STATES OF AMERICA

10 9 8 7 6 5 4 3 2 1

Be a Fodor's Correspondent

Your opinion matters. It matters to us. It matters to your fellow Fodor's travelers, too. And we'd like to hear it. In fact, we *need* to hear it.

When you share your experiences and opinions, you become an active member of the Fodor's community. That means we'll not only use your feedback to make our books better, but we'll publish your names and comments whenever possible. Throughout our guides, look for "Word of Mouth," excerpts of your unvarnished feedback.

Here's how you can help improve Fodor's for all of us.

Tell us when we're right. We rely on local writers to give you an insider's perspective. But our writers and staff editors—who are the best in the business—depend on you. Your positive feedback is a vote to renew our recommendations for the next edition.

Tell us when we're wrong. We're proud that we update most of our guides every year. But we're not perfect. Things change. Hotels cut services. Museums change hours. Charming cafés lose charm. If our writer didn't quite capture the essence of a place, tell us how you'd do it differently. If any of our descriptions are inaccurate or inadequate, we'll incorporate your changes in the next edition and will correct factual errors at fodors.com *immediately.*

Tell us what to include. You probably have had fantastic travel experiences that aren't yet in Fodor's. Why not share them with a community of like-minded travelers? Maybe you chanced upon an off-the-beaten-track village in the Val d'Entremont or a tempting cheese factory in Appenzell that you don't want to keep to yourself. Tell us why we should include it. And share your discoveries and experiences with everyone directly at fodors.com. Your input may lead us to add a new listing or highlight a place we cover with a "Highly Recommended" star or with our highest rating, "Fodor's Choice."

Give us your opinion instantly at our feedback center at www.fodors.com/feedback. You may also e-mail editors@fodors.com with the subject line "Switzerland Editor." Or send your nominations, comments, and complaints by mail to the Switzerland Editor, Fodor's, 1745 Broadway, New York, NY 10019.

You and travelers like you are the heart of the Fodor's community. Make our community richer by sharing your experiences. Be a Fodor's correspondent.

Happy Landings!

Tim Jarrell, Publisher

CONTENTS

CONTENTS

ABOUT THIS BOOK

Our Ratings

Sometimes you find terrific travel experiences and sometimes they just find you. But usually the burden is on you to select the right combination of experiences. That's where our ratings come in.

As travelers we've all discovered a place so wonderful that its worthiness is obvious. And sometimes that place is so experiential that superlatives don't do it justice: you just have to be there to know. These sights, properties, and experiences get our highest rating, **Fodor's Choice,** indicated by orange stars throughout this book.

Black stars highlight sights and properties we deem **Highly Recommended,** places that our writers, editors, and readers praise again and again for consistency and excellence.

By default, there's another category: any place we include in this book is by definition worth your time, unless we say otherwise. And we will.

Disagree with any of our choices? Care to nominate a place or suggest that we rate one more highly? Visit our feedback center at www.fodors.com/feedback.

Budget Well

Hotel and restaurant price categories from ¢ to $$$$ are defined in the opening pages of each chapter. For attractions, we always give standard adult admission fees; reductions are usually available for children, students, and senior citizens. Want to pay with plastic? **AE, D, DC, MC, V** following restaurant and hotel listings indicate if American Express, Discover, Diner's Club, MasterCard, and Visa are accepted.

Restaurants

Unless we state otherwise, restaurants are open for lunch and dinner daily. We mention dress only when there's a specific requirement and reservations only when they're essential or not accepted—it's always best to book ahead.

Hotels

Hotels have private bath, phone, TV, and air-conditioning and operate on the European Plan (aka EP, meaning without meals), unless we specify that they use the Continental Plan (CP, with a continental breakfast), Breakfast Plan (BP, with a full breakfast), or Modified American Plan (MAP, with breakfast and dinner) or are all-inclusive (including all meals and most activities). We always

list facilities but not whether you'll be charged an extra fee to use them, so when pricing accommodations, find out what's included.

Many Listings

★	Fodor's Choice
★	Highly recommended
✉	Physical address
✛	Directions
✍	Mailing address
☎	Telephone
🖷	Fax
🌐	On the Web
✎	E-mail
🎫	Admission fee
☉	Open/closed times
⚑	Start of walk/itinerary
Ⓜ	Metro stations
☰	Credit cards

Hotels & Restaurants

🏠	Hotel
⇴	Number of rooms
⚲	Facilities
❍⎮	Meal plans
✕	Restaurant
⚲	Reservations
🎩	Dress code
↘	Smoking
⚟	BYOB
✕🏠	Hotel with restaurant that warrants a visit

Outdoors

⛳	Golf
⛺	Camping

Other

☺	Family-friendly
⑧	Contact information
⇨	See also
✉	Branch address
☞	Take note

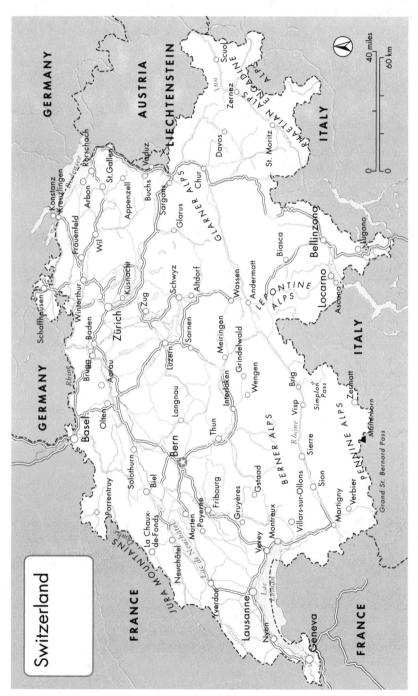

Switzerland

Switzerland is a very small country indeed. Nature here has been lavish only in the bestowal of beauty. Though it is the size of a postage stamp on a map of Europe, Switzerland continues to offer far more mileage per tourist euro than many a larger country. With such diversity in the Swiss scene—four national languages (German, French, Italian, and Romansch), 22 Catholic and Protestant member cantons, and the heavy cultural influences from its border neighbors of Germany, France, and Italy—it is astonishing that there should be a Swiss way of life. But as you tour Switzerland (or, to use the four main dialects: Die Schweiz, La Suisse, Svizzera, Svizra), you'll find that its 7,250,000 residents all adhere to the country's motto: *Unus pro omnibus, omnes pro uno* ("One for all, all for one"). Because the country is as packed as a Lionel model village and overflows with Mother Nature's scenic masterpieces, fascinating museums, and postcard-pretty villages, here is a so-much-scenery-so-little-time distillation of the sightseeing best bets, region by region. The geographic organization of the following paragraphs mirrors the organization of the book. Beginning with Zürich, the coverage follows a roughly clockwise path around the country, finishing in Geneva.

ZÜRICH

Given that it is one of the world's leading financial centers, Zürich is surprisingly small, but its wealth of cultural and material riches more than makes up for its size. Straddling the Limmat River, Zürich's center is made up primarily of medieval churches, guildhalls, and town houses, today providing homes for a charming mix of restaurants and hotels. The former moat-turned-main-road, the Bahnhofstrasse, boasts an array of luxury shops leading to the pristine lake, where residents and tourists alike cool off on hot summer afternoons. The city has shaken off most of its Old World cobwebs in favor of a young and refreshing air. Its social venues are varied and numerous—from the renowned opera to outdoor techno parties held on the surrounding hilltops; from see-and-be-seen cafés and sidewalk barbecues to the starched linens of the guilds' dining halls; from outdoor flea markets to the stylish haute couture boutiques in the Old Town. Snow-clad peaks in the distance oversee the hustle and bustle below. After touring the small but luxuriously gentrified **Altstadt** (Old Town), window-shop along the famous **Bahnhofstrasse,** visit the famed Asian art on view in the **Museum Rietberg,** and take in the delicate **Fraumünster.** Cross the river over to bustling Oberdorf and Niederdorf areas to see the hulking **Grossmünster** and the modern masterpieces of the **Bührle Collection,** then hop a tram to nearby Winterthur to gaze at some of Europe's most beautiful old master paintings on view at the **Oskar Reinhart Collection.**

WHAT'S WHERE

EASTERN SWITZERLAND	East of Zürich, the Rhine snakes through and around the cantons of Glarus, Schaffhausen, Thurgau, St. Gallen, and Appenzell, as well as the independent principality of Liechtenstein. The eastern cantons make up one of the quietest and most untouched regions of Switzerland, which is nevertheless chockfull of Baroque churches, monasteries, and a wide variety of museums. In tiny towns and small cities, you'll find everything from wood-shingle farmhouses to town houses adorned with oriel windows and frescoes. Hills dotted with fruit trees and munching cows rise upward from the Bodensee toward Mt. Säntis, an imposing 8,000-foot peak with views of nearby Germany and Austria. No one will want to miss the old Rhine city of **Schaffhausen**, known for its medieval frescoes and Baroque oriel windows, or **Neuhausen am Rheinfall**, the city known for its broad, dramatic series of falls. Tiny **Stein-am-Rhein** is a medieval gem situated on the river. Then dip south to **St. Gallen**, a busy textile center with an active Old Town beside its grand Baroque cathedral, finishing up in picture-pretty **Appenzell** before crossing the border over to storybook **Liechtenstein**.
GRAUBÜNDEN	It's the stark geography of what used to be called Rhaetia in the Middle Ages that has determined the spirit of Graubünden and its people. The mountains made the region difficult to conquer, while the passes reaped profits from Europe's south–north traffic. Emperors, kings, and lesser lieges attempted to woo or coerce the Rhaetians for centuries, but they remained fiercely independent, thanks in part to clever alliances between noblemen and yeomen, notably the *Graubünden,* or "Grey Confederation," founded in 1395. Economic decline followed the Napoleonic wars, especially after the opening of new trans-Alpine routes. But by the mid-19th century, the romantic landscapes were attracting new conquerors: tourists. And the Rhaetians have been giving them the warmest of welcomes ever since.

From the north, everyone starts out in the capital, **Chur**, taking the gorgeous train ride to **Arosa**. Or opt for a detour north to "Heidi-Country" in **Maienfeld**. Famed writers love **Klosters** for its peace and quiet; billionaires and CEOs favor posh **Davos**. In the Engadine, the **Parc Naziunal Svizzer** is a magnificent federally protected nature reserve, set near the calendar villages of **Guarda** and **Scuol** (don't miss the fairytale castle of Tarasp). The grand finale is **St. Moritz**, where "attitude, not altitude" can be yours in the chic winter season. |

THE TICINO

Italian in language, culture, and spirit, the Ticino is an irresistible combination of Mediterranean pleasures and Swiss efficiency. With its yacht-filled waterfront promenades of Locarno and Lugano and its constantly sunny climate, the Ticino is a canton set apart. Its hills preserve UNESCO World Heritage sites—such as the 15th-century castles of **Bellinzona**—whereas its vibrant piazzas draw ever more aficionados to a variety of cutting-edge film and music festivals. The region's sinuous lakes, perhaps its greatest attraction, extend the promise of a relaxing stroll along fashionable waterfront promenades or a drawn-out lunch in a secluded grotto reachable only by boat. The local tradition of playing cards may have been overshadowed by a more sophisticated, touristic gallivanting, but the rustic feel, relaxed mood, and *italianità* (Italian flair) of the Ticino have not lost their hold. Concentrate on beauteous **Lugano,** hopefully from a lakeside hotel balcony. Not far away is the serene hillside city **Locarno** and the adorable village of **Ascona,** both on the shore of Lago Maggiore. Also memorable is tiny **Campione,** an Italian enclave on Swiss territory, or one of the Ticino's many "movie-set" villages.

LUZERN & CENTRAL SWITZERLAND

Blessed with a sophisticated transportation system that easily gets you into almost every little town and onto every mountain, central Switzerland is the most visited region in the country. No wonder: lush green hillsides dotted with cows and chalets surround the **Vierwaldstättersee,** the "lake of the four forest cantons," famous for its 19th-century paddleboat steamers, which cruise past some of the most beautiful (and bluest!) lakeside vistas in the world.

But this lake is also steeped in history for it is here that you will find the **Rütli Meadow,** the "birthplace" of Switzerland. The Oath of Eternal Alliance was renewed here, and it's also the home of the legend of Wilhelm Tell—just across the lake is the stunningly picturesque waterside chapel devoted to the 13th-century hero.

Luzern itself, with its medieval Old Town so cleanly refurbished that it could be mistaken for a museum exhibit, is one of the country's major draws. As you stroll along the city's magnificent lakefront promenade, many Alpine views will look familiar, as this is where all those travel poster photos originate. Overlooking the city is **Mt. Pilatus,** where you can feast on fabulous mountaintop panoramas.

WHAT'S WHERE

BASEL 	Its position at the corner of three countries, the so-called *Dreilaendereck* where Switzerland meets Germany and France, puts Basel at the very center of Europe. This German-speaking city's motto, "Basel beats differently," is a reference to the drums of its infamous carnival. Every year during *Fasnacht,* the city shows a boisterousness unrivaled by other Swiss towns. And it's not just during this festival that the population pours out into the streets. In the 15th century, the city won the right to hold an unlimited number of fairs (including the hyperchic **Art Basel**), and has been doing its best to throw a year-round party ever since. Basel's **Old Town** is noted for its **Münster** and the sweeping views from the terrace overlooking the Rhine. Art enthusiasts will head to the **Kunstmuseum** and the **Museum Tinguely** but don't forget to organize a day trip to Riehen, where the **Fondation Beyeler**'s stunningly well-rounded (and beautifully presented) collection of 20th-century art can be reached in a mere 20 minutes by tram. Return to the city center to enjoy a leisurely late-afternoon walk across the Mittlere Rheinbrücke and upstream along the sunny **Kleinbasel riverside promenade** (Oberer Rheinweg)—a good way to see the town in its best light.
FRIBOURG & NEUCHÂTEL 	Largely undiscovered, the cantons of Fribourg and Neuchâtel represent two very different worlds in western Switzerland. Fribourg, part German and part French, is overwhelmingly rural, its hills divided into a checkerboard of fields with a neatness only the Swiss can achieve. The abundance of castles and walled medieval villages attest to its less peaceful past, the ubiquitous religious buildings to Roman Catholic determination in the face of Protestant Bern. Neuchâtel, fiercely French in language and culture, exudes a sunny, holiday atmosphere, with its yellow sandstone buildings, stunning views of the alps and a pristine lakefront promenade. If you're coming from Bern, Basel, or Zürich, start with **Neuchâtel**'s Altstadt and lakefront promenade. Next up is the medieval lakeside town of **Murten** and the fountain-studded, Gothic-flavored city of **Fribourg.** No one can afford to miss stunningly picturesque **Gruyères,** with one of Switzerland's most camera-ready castles posing over this centuries-old village. If you have time, travel northwest through watchmaking country to **La Chaux-de-Fonds.**

BERN 	Humble and down-to-earth, Bern is a city of broad medieval streets, farmers' markets, and friendly, slow-spoken people. A dominant political center since the 12th century, Switzerland's federal capital sits in the country's largest canton (state) sharing name and coat of arms. Its size and influence mirror the pride, and on occasion, the boastfulness of its citizens. As a World Cultural Heritage city, its sandstone arcades, painted fountains, and performing mechanical clock, the **Zytglogge**, are as ardently protected as the country's neutrality. A walk to the site of Bern's founding at the **Nydeggkirche** will take you past several of the city's famous fountains and to the climb uphill to the **Rosengarten** for one of the best views of the city, or double back to the **Münster**, for panoramic city views, and the **Bundeshaus**, both must-sees. Art lovers will make a bee line for the new **Zenturm Paul Klee**.
BERNER OBERLAND 	Reach for the sky in this hyper-magical provence, among the most popular destinations in Switzerland, and with good reason. Here you'll find panoramas of the towering **Eiger, Mönch, and Jungfrau mountains**; gorgeous eagle's-nest towns like **Mürren** and **Wengen**—just the place to live life literally on the edge (it is a wonder Mürren just doesn't tumble off its skyhigh cliff-face); **Interlaken,** which, thanks to the tons of public transporation lines, is the Penn Central of the region (let's not forget its wide array of lovely hotels); crystalline lakes and waterfalls; emerald slopes dotted with cattle and gingerbread chalets; some of the best skiing in the world—not to mention the Swiss "Shangri-la," the **Lauterbrunnen Valley**—our choice for the most beautiful spot in the entire country. More must-dos: the **Freilichtmuseum Ballenberg**—a Williamburg-like open-air museum of nearly 80 historic houses—and the taste of the high life (in more ways than one) you can get in **Gstaad**, getaway of the rich and famous (Liz still owns the chalet she bought there with Richard Burton). In addition, there are cultural events on offer, from world-class tennis matches and classical music concerts to Switzerland's largest folkloric festival, the Unspunnen (held, however, only once every 10 years in Interlaken—the last was in 2006).

WHAT'S WHERE

VALAIS	This is the Switzerland of tumbledown huts, raclette eaters, winemakers, and yodelers—not to mention alpine villages, world-class resorts like Zermatt, and, oh, yes, the **Matterhorn**. This valley of the Rhône is one of the country's most fertile plains, where fruit production and grape cultivation make full use of the intensely sunny environment and keep elevating the reputation of Valaisan wines. Romans and other travelers through the ages have breached the mountain passes and settled in this region leaving ruins and artifacts, dialects and bloodlines. You'll feel unsated if you miss Switzerland's most photographed icon, the Matterhorn, so strike out for its lovely home, **Zermatt**, and a few days of shutter-snapping and stuffing yourself with raclette. Visit the Gianadda museum in **Martigny**, explore the citadel and Old Town of **Sion**, or take luxury to new heights in the three fabled resorts like **Saas-Fee, Verbier,** and **Crans-Montana,** all magnificently sited and stuffed with important restaurants and elegant hotels.
VAUD	Lausanne, Montreux, and the Alpes Vaudoises constitute one of Switzerland's most diverse regions. Centered around **Lac Léman (Lake Geneva),** this French-speaking canton harbors some of the country's most famous cathedrals and castles, as well as Alpine villages, balmy lake resorts, gastronomic restaurants, and above all, its verdant vineyards. A heritage built on Roman foundations is evident in tumbledown ruins and restored fortifications strung along the waterfront. Territorial conflicts and Reformation struggles left their brand on the individual—slightly contrarian to the dictates of central authority and resistant to groupthink. Outside the commercial and academic centers, the rhythm of life remains tied to the cycles of the vineyards previously under the domain of monastic orders. But if time is limited? Drive the shore highway through **Coppet** to **Nyon's** Roman museum and medieval castle then immerse yourself in the sights, shops, and streetside cafés of glamorous **Lausanne,** taking in the Old Town, museums, and hyperactive waterfront. Escape along the winding Corniche de la Vaud to visit a *vignoble* (vineyard) or two in **Lutry.** The harbor-front town of **Vevey** deserves a leisurely visit, especially its older section. A night's rest in **Montreux** will ready you to take in the glitzy, Riviera-like city's highlights before touring its fabled **Château de Chillon.**

As the birthplace of Calvinism and the International Red Cross, home to the European headquarters of the United Nations, and a stronghold of private banks and exclusive boutiques, Geneva is, in many ways, a paradox.

It's geographic positioning early on established the city's outsize importance; originally the guardian of a river crossing, then a market town straddling major trade routes, then a safe haven for Protestant refugees, now a neutral space where governments meet to negotiate everything from disarmament to the politics of AIDS, it is, today, home to only 185,000 people.

Its manageable size is a blessing for visitors—any point in the city is accessible on foot from almost anywhere else.

Spend your first morning exploring the downtown waterfront, with its boats, swans, 15-foot-wide flowered clock face, and feathery **Jet d'Eau**—Geneva's "Eiffel Tower."

Then up in the **Vieille Ville** (Old City), visit the starkly beautiful **Cathédrale St-Pierre**, the cavelike archaeological ruins underneath it, and the **Musée International de la Réforme**.

Don't forget the contemplative **Auditoire de Calvin**; the **Monument de la Réformation** sums it all up. The International Area is famed for the **Palais des Nations** and the **Musée International de la Croix-Rouge et du Croissant-Rouge**.

Watch the sun set over the city from the Auberge du Lion d'Or or the bottom of the hill, and then wander home along the quays.

QUINTESSENTIAL SWITZERLAND

Cheese: The Swiss Cure

It was Swiss cheese that put the apples in the cheeks of the hardy little mountain girl named Heidi, the heroine earth-child who inspired Victorians to leave dark city streets for clear Alpine air; to rise early, work hard, and—first and foremost—eat cheese three times a day. For Heidi and Clara—for whom daily meals of cheese and goat's milk worked a mountain miracle—butterfat was a virtue; cholesterol, a concept unborn.

Today, cheese is still a way of life in Switzerland so every visitor has to try the famous *fondue* at least once (it may be a winter fixture but tourists are allowed to eat it year-round). Once the Gruyère, Emmental, or Appenzeller is melted and skillfully mixed with a soupçon of garlic, a teaspoon of flour, and some white wine, the richly aromatic whole is brought to table in the pipkin and placed on a spirit lamp. Guests armed with long-handled forks then spear small squares of bread or meat into the steaming dish. But the eating of fondue is a fine art: each guest who fails to withdraw his morsel is called upon to offer a bottle of wine to the company—a lady, they say, pays with a kiss to whom she chooses. Fondue is rendered all the more convivial by the tradition of downing a shot of 90-proof kirsch halfway through the pot: the *coup du milieu.*

What Makes Them Tick?

It lies on the beveled-glass countertop of Vacheron Constantin's Geneva store: centuries of technology compressed into a miniature of gold and glass, its second hand sweeping to a point within 10 seconds of when it reached the same point last month—Swiss precision in microcosm. The fact that Vacheron is the world's oldest manufacturer of watches (it sold its

If you want to get a sense of contemporary Swiss culture and indulge in some of its pleasures, start by familiarizing yourself with the rituals of daily life. These are a few highlights—things you can take savor with relative ease.

first sober design in 1755) underscores that these mechanical gems, as they were, are also Swiss history. During the Reformation Calvin banned gilded crucifixes and chalices, leaving scores of brilliantly skilled goldsmiths with idle hands. Before long, an industry was launched, which, to this day, makes you believe in national stereotypes: the Swiss are precise and persevering. You can see this when a factory worker neatly drops into place a minute hand the size of an eyelash; or in the gradations of firewood stacked from finest kindling to fattest logs with the geometric complexity of inlay at a country inn; or as you step off a train in Lausanne just as the second hand on the station clock hits the arrival time. Yes, Swiss watchmaking is a science but visit Geneva's Patek Phillipe Museum to be wowed by fantastical creations, brilliant colors, and awe-inspring detail. Clearly, Swiss watchmaking is about much more than time.

How Now, Brown Cow?

Snow-clad peaks reach defiantly into an azure sky, green valleys sway with wild flowers, "toothpick"-paneled chalets dot the Alpine meadows: surely this is the Switzerland of the imagination. But one element is missing—the sound of cowbells tinkling in happy indiscipline. This is a sound many travelers often later hear in their dreams. Get up close to these pretty brown-and-white livestock and you can smell their sweet breath—testament to all the succulent grasses (which also go in many of the world's top perfume) they've munched. Newspapers recently reported that Switzerland's cows were "stressed," so these days many of them get to go on "vacations" from factories to spend summers up in the hills. After all without the milk of these cash cows, Swiss cheese and chocolate would be half as famous. Now if they could only create a breed that produces *chocolate* milk!

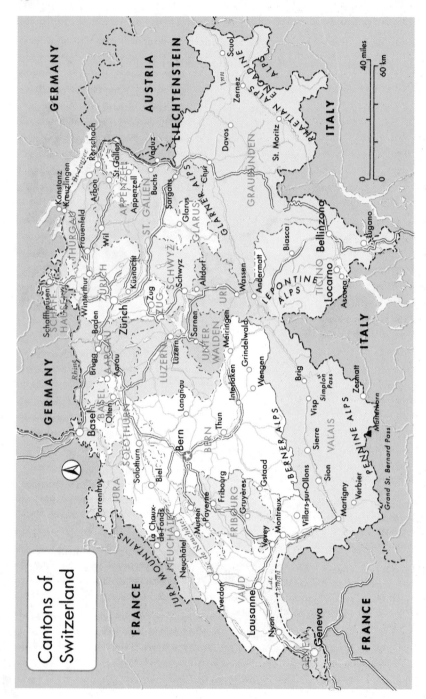

Cantons of
Switzerland

GERMANY

AUSTRIA

LIECHTENSTEIN

ITALY

ITALY

FRANCE

FRANCE

FRANCE

GERMANY

40 miles
60 km

RHAETIAN ALPS

Scuol
Zernez
ENGADINE
Inn

Davos
GRAUBÜNDEN
St. Moritz

Konstanz
Kreuzlingen
Bodensee
Rorschach
THURGAU
Arbon
St. Gallen
APPENZELL
Appenzell
Buchs
Vaduz
Sargans
Chur

Schaffhausen
SCHAFF-
HAUSEN
Frauenfeld
Wil
Glarus
GLARUS ALPS
GLARNER ALPS
Biasca

Rhine
Winterthur
ZÜRICH
Baden
Küsnacht
Zug
ZUG
SCHWYZ
Schwyz
Altdorf
Wassen
Andermatt
LEPONTINE
ALPS
TICINO
Bellinzona

Bragg
AARGAU
Aarau
Zürich
Luzern
LUZERN
Sarnen
UNTER-
WALDEN
URI
Meiringen

Basel
BASEL
Olten
SOLOTHURN
Langnau
Grindelwald
Wengen
Brig
Simplon
Pass
Locarno
Ascona
Lugano

Porrentruy
JURA
Solothurn
Biel
BERN
Bern
Thun
Interlaken
BERNER ALPS
Visp
Sierre
VALAIS
Zermatt
Matterhorn

JURA MOUNTAINS
La Chaux-
de-Fonds
NEUCHÂTEL
Neuchâtel
Lac de Neuchâtel
Murten
Payerne
FRIBOURG
Fribourg
Gruyères
Gstaad
Sion
PENNINE ALPS
Verbier
Martigny
Grand St. Bernard Pass

Yverdon
VAUD
Lausanne
Vevey
Montreux
Villars-sur-Ollons

Nyon
GENEVA
GENÈVE
Geneva
Lac Léman

IF YOU LIKE

Great Food

La Cuisine? Die Kockkunst? La Cucina? Like the patchwork that is Switzerland, fine Swiss food is a culinary trifecta drawn from three countries: France, Germany, and Italy. French areas like Vaud and Neuchâtel still seduce with *cuisine bourgeoise* and such delights as beef entrecôte and *truite meunière*. Over in German cantons such as Schwyz and Luzern, Teutonic nature conquers Gaul with servings of sausage and schnitzel in nearly Wagnerian proportions. Heading south, Italian risotto and gnocchi appear virtually unscathed in the Ticino. Today, however, a bevy of superstar chefs have begun to strike a diplomatic balance between French, German, and Italian styles. In the process, they are giving centuries-old favorites like fondue and raclette a newer-than-now-nouvelle spin.

Restaurant de l'Hôtel de Ville–Phillippe Rochat, Crissier, Vaud. Rochat spent nearly 20 years with legendary chef Freddy Giradet and he maintains a creative level that vies with the best chefs of Paris.

Petermann's Kunststuben, Zürich. Listed as one of Forbes's most expensive restaurants in the world, set in a 1879 house hung with modern paintings ("Kunststuben" means art studio), this is the stage for Horst Petermann, whose Tuscan dove with pine nuts or salmon in caviar crème are so strikingly arranged on the plate you feel you should hang the main course on the wall, not eat it.

Waldhotel Fletschhorn, Saas-Fee, Valais. Crowned Gault-Millau's "Chef of the Year" in 2007, Markus Neff has been wowing foodies with his lobster dim sum and bison tournedos. To learn how he mix-masters Alpine foods with exotic styles, sign up for one of the cooking classes given by this red-haired wunderkind.

"Peak" Experiences

"Mountains are the beginning and end of all scenery," the great 19th-century writer John Ruskin once observed. And if mountains have a "home" it is truly Switzerland—a summit of summits. View-collectors flock to that big schlock candy mountain, the Matterhorn. Adventurers are seduced by the "sheer" excitement of the Jungfrau. "Social climbers" head to the chic villages of Wengen and Mürren, which seem to levitate at either end of the Lauterbrunnen valley, while daredevils worship at the foot of the Eiger's notorious north face. No matter where you head, you'll find hillside footpaths can be almost as crowded as supermarket checkout lines (remember: the higher the trail, the less "conversation"—you need to concentrate!). Here are some places that will leave you with that top-of-the-world feeling.

Matterhorn, Valais. From the summit station of Gernergrat, this snaggle-toothed mountain steals the thunder from all surrounding peaks.

Jungfraujoch, the Berner Oberland. From the top of the 11,395-foot-high Jungfraujoch, the Aletsch Glacier looks like a vast sea of ice.

Neuhausen am Rheinfall, Eastern Switzerland. With its mists, roaring water, jutting rocks, and bushy crags, the Rheinhall, from the Neuhausen side, appears truly Wagnerian.

Lauterbrunnen Valley, the Berner Oberland. Looking more like a painting than real life, the jaw-dropping vista of this shangri-la valley is spectacularly threaded by 72 waterfalls that plummet from sky-high cliffs.

Glacier 3000, Les Diablerets, Vaud. A two-part lift to the top of the Alpes Vaudoises is filled with nonstop, spine-tingling, 360-degree vistas.

Traveling Through Time

Wander the slopes of Klewenalp above the Vierwaldstättersee on a still spring day, gaze across the placid waters beneath, and it is easy to identify Switzerland as a land of peace. Wander on a mile or so and you are reminded that for much of its time Switzerland has been nothing of the kind. Here is the Rütli, the meadow where legend avers that the men of the three forest cantons, Uri, Schwyz, and Unterwalden, met in 1291 to plot the overthrow of their Habsburg landlords (thereby creating the world's first democracy). But move beyond this spot—hallowed by Wilhelm Tell—and you'll find Switzerland is practically crawling with history from border to border.

Old Town, Basel. When the sound of fife-and-drum music drifts from upstairs windows of guild houses of Basel's Old Town, you'll think the Middle Ages have dawned again.

Tellfreilichtspiele, Interlaken, Berner Oberland. For a festive evening, rent a lap blanket and settle in to watch a grand retelling of the life of Wilhelm Tell, perfomed under the stars.

Site Archéologique, Geneva. An underground warren of excavated stone walls, mosaics, and metal walkways meanders through history underneath the Cathédrale St-Pierre.

Monument de la Réformation, Geneva. The complex history of the Protestant Reformation as it unfolded across Europe is boldly rendered in granite.

Stiftsbibliothek and Kathedrale, St. Gallen. For Rococo splendor and opulence, nothing beats this complex of Abbey Library and Cathedral, adorned with spectacular excesses of 18th-century wedding-cake trim.

The Most Beautiful Villages

Whatever town or valley you pick, you'll have a battle on your hands insisting that your favorite spot in Switzerland *is* the (only/best/unique) top place in the country. The *whole* of Switzerland is undeniably beautiful. But there are certain places where the needle would fly right off the scale if they were rated on a beauty-measuring gauge. Oozing half-timbered houses and sgraffitoed chapels, these once-upon-a-timefied places have a sense of tranquillity not even tour buses can ruin. Some are so small they seem your own personal property, others rise out of Swan Lakes, and some are backdropped by mountains crowned in snowy ermine. Nearly everyone has a mind's-eye view of the perfect Swiss village—and here are some candidates.

Guarda, Graubünden. This federally protected hamlet in the Lower Engandine is full of architectural photo-ops, with cobblestone streets and flower boxes filled with red geraniums.

Stein-am-Rhein, Eastern Switzerland. A nearly perfectly preserved medieval village, this is replete with shingled, half-timber town houses boasting ornate oriels and flamboyant frescoes.

Gandria, the Ticino. Clinging vertiginously to a hillside, its flower-filled balconies overlooking Lake Lugano, the tiny town of Gandria retains the ambiance of an ancient fishing village.

Murren, Bernese Oberland. A Noah's Arc village pasted 5,400 feet up a mountainside, Murren offers a so-close-you-can-touch-it vista of the Jungfrau and the Eiger.

Gruyéres, Fribourg. Right out of a Brothers Grimm fairy tale, this storybook village is crowned with one of the most picture-perfect castles in Switzerland.

GREAT ITINERARIES

SWISS GASTRONOMY

9 Days

This food-intensive itinerary offers aficionados an opportunity to travel from one great dining experience to another, sampling the very finest *haute gastronomie* at one stop, the most authentic regional classics—even the earthiest peasant cuisines—at another. Incidental pleasures—wandering in the Alps, for example, or strolling through medieval town centers in Switzerland's greatest cities—can be squeezed in between meals. Remember that reservations must be made well in advance.

Geneva

2 nights.

Your first night, indulge in a hearty Lyonnaise meal at the Bistrot du Bœuf Rouge. For lunch the next day, head out into the vineyards for exquisite seasonal cuisine at the Domaine de Châteauvieux. Back in Geneva, have a relatively light Ticinese supper at La Favola. Fill the time between meals with a brisk stroll along the quais or a visit to one of the city's many museums. ➪ *Chapter 12.*

Lausanne

1 night.

Testing Phillipe Rochat's mettle at Restaurant de l'Hôtel de Ville in nearby Crissier may be the triumph of the trip—but reserve judgment for after Basel and Zürich. At night, head down to the waterfront at Ouchy and have a chic, light supper at the Café Beau-Rivage. ➪ *La Côte & Lausanne in Chapter 11.*

Basel

1 night.

Two hours north, lunch at Bruderholz, which gives Phillipe Rochat a run for his money. Then, after visiting, say, the Münster and the history museum, relax in the downstairs bistro at the Teufelhof: the light specialties are prepared by Michael Baader, who is chef for the top-notch restaurant upstairs as well. ➪ *Chapter 6.*

Zürich

2 nights.

Have lunch at Petermann's Kunststuben, in the suburb of Küssnacht, where the gastronomy vies for the title "best in Switzerland." Then, after a thorough walking tour of Zürich's Old Town, you can settle in for an atmospheric, old-world evening at the Picasso- and Matisse-lined Kronenhalle. ➪ *Chapter 1.*

Luzern

1 night.

For a total contrast and perhaps the most authentically *Swiss* meal of your tour, head for Galliker and a lunch of real farm food. Having absorbed the Lion Monument, crossed the Kapellbrücke, and toured the history museum, you can think about the evening meal: a light, sophisticated river-fish meal at Rotes Gatter, in Des Balances hotel, affords waterfront views. ➪ *Chapter 5.*

Saas-Fee

1 night.

From Luzern allow for a full day's scenic mountain drive south over the Brünigpass, then on over the Grimselpass and down the Rhône Valley to Brig and the spectacular little resort of Saas-Fee. Once there, retreat to the isolated Waldhotel Fletschhorn for a sophisticated dinner by rising star Markus Neff (Gault-Millau's Chef of the Year 2006) and a bare minimum of one night to take in the mountain air. ⇨ *Zermatt & Saas-Fee in Chapter 10.*

Verbier

1 night.

Following the Rhône back west toward Geneva, take one more Alpine side trip up to this famous ski resort to feast and sleep at Rosalp, the popular rustic-chic inn in the village center. ⇨ *Val d'Entremont to the Col du Grand St-Bernard in Chapter 10.*

By Public Transportation

Each of the stopovers is accessible by train, though some of the restaurants may require cabs or tram rides; a rental car will give you more flexibility for reaching country inns.

CASTLES & CATHEDRALS
8 Days

Romantics, history buffs, and architecture fans can circle western Switzerland to take in some of the country's best medieval and Gothic landmarks.

Geneva

1 night.

The excavations below the 12th-century Cathédrale St-Pierre, open to the public as the *site archéologique,* have yielded two 4th-century sanctuaries, Roman mosaics, and an 11th-century crypt. ⇨ *Chapter 12.*

Montreux

1 night.

The Château de Chillon, partially surrounded by the waters of Lake Geneva, may be the most completely and authentically furnished in Switzerland. Lord Byron signed the pillar where his "Prisoner of Chillon" was manacled. ⇨ *Lavaux Vignobles & Montreux in Chapter 11.*

Gruyères

1 night.

This magnificently beautiful castle-village draws crowds to its central street, souvenir shops, quaint inns, and frescoed castle, complete with dungeon and spectacular views. ⇨ *Fribourg in Chapter 7.*

Fribourg

1 night.

This bilingual city is the last Catholic stronghold of western Switzerland, rooted in its single-tower Cathédrale St-Nicolas. The cathedral's Last Judgment tympanum and Art Nouveau stained-glass windows deserve attention—but leave time to explore the Old Town, with its multilevel fortifications constructed for the ubiquitous Zähringens. ⇨ *Fribourg in Chapter 7.*

Thun

1 night.

If you're driving, cut across Fribourg toward Thun (by train, connect through Bern), where you'll see the Bernese Alps in all their splendor. Schloss Zähringen, which dates from 1191, features a knights' hall, tapestries, local ceramics, and an intimidating collection of weapons. ⇨ *Thunersee in Chapter 9.*

Bern

1 night.

The Zähringens fortified this gooseneck in the River Aare; its 15th-century Münster features a restored (full-color, painted) main portal. ⇨ *Chapter 8.*

Basel

1 night.

In this historic, cosmopolitan city is a Münster with a lovely Romanesque portal and the tomb of the great humanist Erasmus. ⇨ *Chapter 6.*

By Public Transportation

The complete itinerary works by rail, with most sites accessible on foot from the station; Gruyères has bus connections to the elevated castle and the Old Town.

WHEN TO GO

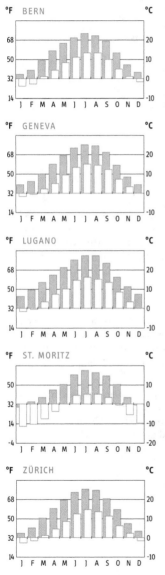

In July and August Switzerland's best weather coincides with the heaviest crowds. June and September are still pleasant, and hotel prices can be slightly lower, especially in resorts. In May and June the mountains are at their loveliest, with Alpine flowers blooming and the peaks capped with snow; however, as ski season is over and high summer hasn't begun, this is often considered low season, and many resort hotels close down. Those that remain open reduce their prices considerably. Another low-season disadvantage: some cable car and cogwheel train operations take a break between the midwinter and midsummer rushes; some must wait for snow to clear before reopening. The most prestigious ski resorts charge top prices during the Christmas–New Year holidays but reduce them slightly in early January. February through Easter is prime time again. Late autumn—from mid-October through early December—is the least appealing season for visiting the Alps because there's usually little snow, no foliage, and a tendency toward dampness and fog. If you're sticking to the cities to shop and tour museums, you won't notice the doldrums that take over the resorts. The exception to the above rules of thumb: the Ticino, the only portion of Switzerland south of the Alps, boasts a Mediterranean climate and declares high season from April through October. Many of its hotels close down altogether from November through March.

Climate

Summer in Switzerland generally lasts from July to September and tends to be mild, although night temperatures can be chilly in some locations. At high altitudes, the air remains crisp through the hottest summer days. Beautiful fall foliage begins to lose its grip on the trees by the end of October, when the autumn rains usually sweep through the country. Snow can make its first appearance in November, which is usually foggy. Cold temperatures kick in from January to March, often dropping below freezing.

🛈 Forecasts **Weather Channel Connection** (☎ 900/932–8437 95¢ per minute from a Touch-Tone phone ⊕ www.weather.com).

ON THE
CALENDAR

Top events in Switzerland include Fasnacht celebrations in February and March, the Landsgemeinde open-air vote in Appenzell in April, the glittering Art Basel modern art fair in Basel in mid-June, the Montreux International Jazz Festival in July, the Menuhin Festival in Gstaad from mid-July through early September, Luzern's International Festival of Music from mid-August to mid-September, and the Fête de l'Escalade in Geneva in December. Events are named below as publicized by the host region, usually in the local language.

SPRING

March–May

The Lugano Festival is an annual spring concert series.

Villages throughout the Engadine and the Albula and Mustair valleys celebrate the Chalanda Marz children's festival on the first day of the month. Kids in costume parade and sing, ringing bells to chase away winter.

The Engadine Ski Marathon covers the 42 km (26 mi) between Zuoz and Maloja.

During St. Moritz's Snow & Symphony Music Festival, top classical and jazz musicians perform in luxury hotels and on mountaintops.

April

Sechseläuten, in Zürich, shows all its medieval guilds on parade and climaxes in the burning of the Böögg, a straw scarecrow representing winter.

Small towns throughout the Valais hold a Combat de Reines, or cow fight, where female cows are pitted against each other in a head-butting contest to choose the "queen" who will lead the herds to higher pastures for the summer.

Good Friday processions take place in several southern villages, including Mendrisio in the Ticino, where the procession derives from a medieval Passion Play that is performed on Maundy Thursday as well.

Luzern's Osterfestspiele celebrates Easter with sacred music. International music stars perform at the Spring Festival in Samnaun.

The lovely lake town of Morges draws a crowd to its annual Fête de la Tulipe (Tulip Festival).

Landsgemeinde takes place in the town of Appenzell on the last Sunday of the month punctually at noon, with all citizens voting on cantonal issues by a public show of hands.

ON THE CALENDAR

May	The International Jazz Festival—Bern lasts five days in the federal capital.
SUMMER June–August	In Interlaken, an outdoor play about *Wilhelm Tell* is an epic-scale production with a huge cast of locals. For more than six weeks, the Yehudi Menuhin Festival in Gstaad showcases world-class musicians. Lugano's Blues to Bop Festival brings authentic blues to the lakefront.
June	The Grindelwald Country-Festival brings American country-and-western groups to this mountain resort. The Zürich Festival hosts dance, opera, theater, and more in several venues throughout the city.
July	World-class artists perform at the Montreux International Jazz Festival. In Leukerbad, the Clown & Cabaret Festival is an international congregation of clowns and street performers. The British Classic Car Meeting brings antique- and classic autos to St. Moritz. During the Paléo Festival Nyon, international musicians play a multistage outdoor concert. The Shepherds Festival is a gathering of shepherds and their flocks at the Daubensee in Leukerbad. Engadiner Concert Weeks bring outdoor classical music events to resorts throughout the region. The Festival International de l'Orgue Ancien, at Valère in Sion, honors the 13th-century instrument within the church. In Vevey, the Marchés Folkloriques (Folkloric Markets) feature wine tasting. For more than two weeks the Verbier Festival & Academy hosts a classical music festival with an impressive guest roster.
August	Swiss National Holiday celebrates the confederation's birth in 1291 with fireworks and bonfires on the first of the month. Locarno's International Film Festival unveils top new movies in the Piazza Grande. The Fêtes de Genève packs Geneva's waterfront for 10 days of food and entertainment plus fireworks.

	In Zürich, the Street Parade, a huge techno music party, thumps its way through Zürich's lakefront district.
	The International Folklore Festival occurs in Fribourg.
	Zürich's Theaterspektakel showcases avant-garde and mainstream playwrights as well as theater troupes from around the world.
	The world-renowned Internationale Musikfestwochen in Luzern, combines concerts, theater, and art exhibitions.
	Davos's Young Artists in Concert features tomorrow's classical music stars.
	The Vevey-Montreux Music Festival invites important artists to these twin lake resorts.
FALL June–August	The multimedia Images festival in Vevey features cinema, video, and photography.
September	Knabenschiessen takes place in Zürich with a folk festival and fair.
	Bénichon, a traditional autumn Fribourg feast, is held during the second week of September.
	The Neuchâtel Wine Festival is the biggest in the country.
	L'Etivaz Cheese Sharing celebrates the division of spoils from the cheese cooperative with yodeling, wrestling, and other activities.
	Fribourg Braderie combines a citywide sidewalk sale, folk festival, and onion market.
	The small Vaud town of St-Cergue has an annual Fête Désalpe, a ritual for the cows coming down from the mountains. It lasts all of a Saturday morning, allowing hundreds of cows to parade the streets in amazing floral headgear. Another *désalpe* festival is held in October in Charmey, near Gruyères in Fribourg.
October	In Lugano a traditional Wine Harvest Festival is held at the Piazza della Riforma and on the lakeside.
	On the middle two Saturdays, horse races are held in Maienfeld.
	Olma Schweizer Messe für Land- und Milchwirtschaft (agricultural and dairy fair), in St. Gallen, gathers representatives of the farming industry from across Switzerland.

ON THE CALENDAR

November	Bern's **Zwiebelemärit** (Onion Market) celebrates the open market established for area farmers in gratitude for aid they gave Bern after the great fire of 1405.
WINTER December	Geneva's **Fête de l'Escalade** commemorates the city's 1602 defeat of the Duke of Savoy. Local myth has it that one woman fought off the soldiers scaling the walls by dumping hot soup on their heads.
January	**Vogel Gryff Volksfest** is a colorful Basel tradition, with a costumed Griffin, a Lion, and a Wild Man of the Woods floating down the Rhine and dancing on the Mittlere Rheinbrücke. Winter golf tournaments happen in Silvaplana, Vulpera, and Disentis. **Schlittedas Engiadinaisa** is an Engadine tradition in which couples ride horse-drawn sleighs from village to village. The **Château-d'Oex Hot-Air Balloon Week** showcases the Vaud resort's specialty. St. Moritz hosts a blizzard of special events. The **Gourmet Festival** draws top-tier chefs. Several uncommon sports competitions take place on snow, such as the annual polo and cricket matches, and the **White Turf** horse races.
February	**Hom Strom,** at Scuol in the Lower Engadine, observes the burning of Old Man Winter. On the second weekend in February, **dogsled races** run from Maloja to Sils. **Les Sommets Musicaux de Gstaad** presents two weeks of varied classical music with outstanding performers. **Fasnacht** is observed in different locales throughout Switzerland, but most festively in Basel, where it begins at 4 AM on the Monday after Ash Wednesday, with a costume parade. Luzern celebrates on the Thursday before Ash Wednesday, with a traditional **Fritschi** procession. On the same day Schwyz celebrates **Blätzli** with a mummers' procession of harlequins. Lugano and other towns in the Ticino celebrate Carnevale with risotto and sausages served in the streets.

Zürich

Zürich's Old Town

WORD OF MOUTH

"Zürich's Old Town is surprisingly charming, with a beautiful lake-front. I had a delicious lunch at the Zeughauskeller—William Tell's crossbow is mounted on the wall. Certainly the best-defended lunch I have ever eaten!" —Biz

"There is not much to see/do in Zürich? That is s-o-o-o not true! Zürich is very rich in architecture, in history, in museums, and day excursions. Just the city itself can keep you busy for days if you take the trouble to look and ask." —WallyKringen

WELCOME TO ZÜRICH

TOP REASONS TO GO

★ **A dip in the Middle Ages:** Museum-perfect in their leaded-glass and Gothic-wood details, a dozen medieval guildhalls have been transformed into time-burnished restaurants.

★ **Extreme Shopping:** Luxury-encrusted with noted shops, the Bahnhofstrasse is also lined with banks to refill your empty wallets.

★ **Amazing architecture:** The Old Town and the Left Bank's Oberdorf and Niederdorf have barely changed since the 18th century—savor their pedestrian-only cobblestone streets, and medieval churches.

★ **The Great Church:** The Grossmünster lords it over the city, both architecturally and psychically, for here Ulrich Zwingli taught the city to buckle down, fear the Lord, and hail the Protestant work ethic in the 15th century.

★ **Masterpieces Theater:** Set in nearby Winterthur, the Sammlung Oskar Reinhart is virtually wallpapered with legendary old master paintings.

1 The Altstadt. Zürich's Old Town is the main reason you're here, thanks to Gothic treasures like the Fraumünster, more shops than you could shake a tiara at, an amazing collection of restaurants, and it's all right on the lake.

2 Niederdorf & Oberdorf. Less dignified, more lively, Zürich's east bank is noted for its cultural goodies, including the velvet-and-cherub splendor of the star-studded opera house and the Kunsthaus Museum of Art.

3 The Zürichsee. It's a bit too narrow for decent waterskiing, but every other activity is on offer on this beautiful lake, from swimming to people-watching (every café with even one square foot of sidewalk space puts their tables outside). This may be the only major city in the world where you can actually swim in the heart of downtown—as hundreds do on hot summer days.

Street café on Hechtplatz

4 Zürich West. For something completely different, head here to check out the latest modern architecture–since the 1990s, the area has undergone an extreme makeover and old factories have made room for trendy lofts and hip clubs.

5 Winterthur. Zürich proper is surprisingly small, given its international cachet, but today the towns surrounding it have become city "suburbs," especially this museum-rich town famed for its art collections.

GETTING ORIENTED

Visitors are often surprised by the beauty of Zürich, perhaps imagining it one vast high-tech banking hall, all chrome and computers. But the city's location—straddling the Limmat River and flanked by two mini-mountains, the Zürichberg and the Ćetliberg—would tempt any landscape painter. Zürich may be small—it can be crossed in a mere 20 minutes by foot—but it has international cachet.

Christmas market in Zürich.

ZÜRICH PLANNER

How to Get Here

Zürich may not be the geographic center of the country, but in many ways it is the heart. You can get here from anywhere, by car or train, boat or bus.

The Swiss Federal Railways (SBB, 0900/300300, www.sbb.ch) manages everything—check them out when planning your trip.

Trains arrive hourly from Geneva (77 SF one-way), Bern (45 SF one-way), Luzern (22 SF one-way), Lugano (22 SF one-way). St. Gallen (27 SF one-way) and Basel (30 SF one-way).

There are also connections from Paris (with or without the TGV), Munich, Frankfurt, and Milan several times a day.

Switzerland's highway system also networks through Zürich: The A1 (from St. Gallen to Geneva and Bern), the A3 (from Chur to Basel), the A4 (from Luzern), and the A2 (from Lugano connecting through Luzern).

Winterthur is a mere 20 minutes to ½ hour away, depending on the type of transportation. By car, take the A1 in the direction of St. Gallen.

By train, take any one of the two to five trains leaving from the Hauptbahnhof or the Bahnhof Stadelhofen every hour (9.80 SF one-way).

New in 2006 is a special "Museumsbus Am Römerholz" that leaves from Winterthur's train station (Sektor G) and goes to the famous Oskar Reinhart art collection.

Not Everyone's a Millionaire

If restaurant prices are setting your credit card on fire, the local Migros or Coop are a great place to load up on picnic food, and take-out stands (mainly called "take-away"s after the British model) can be found all over the city center.

Something's Always Going On

If you see an elephant wandering around the streets of Zürich, don't worry: it just means the circus is in town. In the winter months, a series of circuses—with acrobats, fire-eaters, and lion tamers—travels throughout the country in red-and-white caravans, each stopping along the way in Zürich. In addition to the usual opera, theater, and concert seasons, the city holds a variety of events throughout the year.

One of Zürich's most important festivals is Sächsilüüte, a kind of Groundhog Day in which descendents of medieval guild members circle a burning snowman until its head blows off (how long this takes determines whether spring will come early or late). The annual debate has become almost as interesting as the event itself, as the male-only guilds refuse to let women participate.

When spring finally arrives, so does Jazznojazz, with jazz musicians playing at venues all over town. Summer is time for Christopher Street Day, a huge celebration of gay pride. Even if you don't speak German, you should still attend the Theater Spektakel, a two-week outdoor theater festival, for the excellent food. Sensuous dancing marks the nine days of Tangowoche, while techno music is the sound track for the lovefest called Street Parade.

Fall arrives with the Lange Nacht der Museen, when museums leave their doors open all night. Knabenschiessen, a country fair held on the outskirts of the city, lets youngsters test their aim at shooting competitions. Toward the end of the year is Expovina, a wine exhibition held on boats moored at Bürkliplatz, and then there's that elephant again.

Getting Around

Once you're here, it's a good idea to park the car if you have one, since those streets that aren't pedestrian zones are liable to be one-way—you'll get fewer headaches on foot and the city's public transit system (ZVV, 0840/988988, www.zvv.ch) is excellent, thanks to its trams and trains (buses only go to the suburbs).

The Zürich Card (15 SF) gets you 24 hours of municipal public transportation in the greater Zürich area, plus free entry into more than 40 museums (Tourist Information, Hauptbahnhof; 044/2154000, www.zuerich.com). A network of water taxis services the upper Limmat and the lake (044/7777777).

How's the Weather?

The temperate climate has four distinct seasons. Spring can be a mad mix of brilliant sun and rain, which means colorful blossoms abound. Summers are humid and have been quite hot in the last years, rivaling some Asian nations; evening thunderstorms are frequent.

Fall becomes crisp around the end of October and winter brings a low fog ceiling (this is when locals head for any nearby peak over 5,000 feet) or light-to-slushy snow that tends to melt after a week or so.

Careful!

If Swiss drivers have a reputation throughout Europe as being unnecessarily impolite in their lead-footedness, Zürich must be where they're all hatched and trained. With a good number of streets in town marked one-way, pedestrian-only, or with a speed limit of only 30 kph (18 mph), many drivers take out their frustrations on their fellow man. Pedestrian crossings seem to be a great place to line up as a target, and God forbid you should hesitate a nanosecond after the light has turned green before flooring it—the red-faced guy behind you in the Alfa will immediately inspire you to move along. The rate of road rage is unnervingly high in Zürich, although it's still not L.A.—most favor going after the object of their ire with their bare fists or a knife instead of a gun. Reassuring, isn't it? We should mention here that public transit is excellent throughout the city.

Finding a Place to Stay

Spending the night in Zürich is as expensive as eating out, though the options are no more outlandishly priced than those in the prestigious ski resorts. Deluxe hotels—the five-star landmarks—average between 450 SF and 600 SF per night for a double, and you'll be lucky to get a shower and toilet in your room for less than 140 SF.

Yet a full (if top-heavy) range of choices is available in the city center, so even if you're flying into Zürich on your way to a mountain retreat, don't shy away from a stopover of a day or two.

Luckily, almost all the hotels that cater to businesspeople during the week offer significantly cheaper weekend rates. Happily, there are enough hotels in town that you'll always find a bed, but if you have a certain style in mind, book early—high season covers July, August, and December.

The tourist office in the main train station helps with bookings (044/2154000, www.zuerich.com), but most hotels have their own up-to-date Web sites for booking ahead.

If you're on a skiing holiday, consider staying in a hotel at the mountain—don't commute from a Zürich homebase. Yes, resorts that are only one to two hours away may sound good on paper but you haven't experienced the horrendous traffic that entails.

And now imagine driving in that after a day on the slopes. Right.

Updated by
Katrin Gygax

WHEN THE POUND STERLING sagged in the 1960s, the wounded English blamed "the gnomes of Zürich," a term that evoked images of elfin Swiss bankers slyly manipulating world currencies behind closed doors. What the English failed to fathom was that the Zürichers' drive comes not from the mists of folkloric forests, but from the pulpit of the Grossmünster, and the fiery sermons of Reformation leader Ulrich Zwingli blasting the evils of idle hands and the devil's playthings. The resulting ironclad work ethic is what made Zürich one of the world's leading financial centers. One of Zwingli's lessons stressed the transient nature of wealth, and Zürichers show native caution in enjoying their fabulous gains. Nor have they turned their backs on the humble signposts of their heritage: the city's graceful, shuttered Gothic buildings still outnumber the newer chrome-and-glass towers.

Zürich, which sits astride the Limmat River at the point where it emerges from the Zürichsee (Zürich Lake) is, in fact, a very beautiful city. Its charming *Altstadt* (Old Town), which makes up a substantial part of the city center, is full of beautifully restored historic buildings. In the distance, snowy mountains overlook the lake, whose shores are dominated by century-old mansions. Few high-rise buildings disturb the skyline, and even their heights are modest by U.S. standards. In keeping with Zürich's solid bourgeois character, there are no dominating castles to haunt the Züricher with memories of imperialism.

The earliest known Zürichers, circa 4500 BC, lived by the lakeside in small houses perched on stilts. Underwater archaeologists have discovered a wealth of prehistoric artifacts dating back thousands of years, from Stone Age pottery to Bronze Age necklaces, and many such relics are on display at the Schweizerisches Landesmuseum (Swiss National Museum) near the main train station. At last count, the remains of 34 Stone Age and Bronze Age settlements are thought to be scattered around the lake.

In the 1st century BC the Romans, attracted by the city's central location, built a customhouse on a hill overlooking the Limmat River. In time the customhouse became a fortress, remnants of which can be seen on the Lindenhof, a square in the city center. The Romans were also accommodating enough to provide Zürich with its patron saints. Legend has it that the Roman governor beheaded a Christian brother and sister, Felix and Regula, on a small island in the river; the martyred siblings then picked up their heads, waded through the water, and walked up a hill before collapsing where the Grossmünster now stands.

After the Germanic Alemanni, ancestors of the present-day Zürichers, expelled the Romans in the 5th century, the region declined in importance until, four centuries later, the Carolingians built an imperial palace on the Limmat. Louis the German, grandson of Charlemagne, then founded an abbey here, appointing as the first abbess his own daughter. The abbey was built on the site of what is now the Fraumünster, near Bahnhofstrasse.

By the 12th century Zürich was already renowned as a center for commerce; many of its diligent merchants had made fortunes dealing in silk, wool, linen, and leather goods. By 1336, this privileged class had become too powerful in the view of the newly emerging band of tradesmen and laborers who, allied with a charismatic aristocrat named Rudolf Brun, overthrew the merchants' town council and established Zürich's famous trade guilds. Those 13 original guilds never lost power until the French Revolution—and have yet to lose their prestige. Every year, Zürich's leading businessmen dress up in medieval costumes for the guilds' traditional march through the streets, heading for the magnificent guildhalls.

If the guilds defined Zürich's commerce, the Reformation defined its soul. From his pulpit in the Grossmünster, Zwingli galvanized the region, and he ingrained in Zürichers a devotion to thrift and industriousness—so successfully that it ultimately led them into temptation: the temptation to achieve global influence and tremendous wealth. Today, the Zürich stock exchange is the fourth-largest in the world, after those of New York, London, and Tokyo.

Nevertheless, Zürich is not your typical cold-hearted business center. In 1916, a group of artists and writers rebelling against the restraints of traditional artistic expression—among them Tristan Tzara, Jean Arp and Hugo Ball—founded the avant-garde Dadaist movement here. The fertile atmosphere also attracted Irish author James Joyce, who spent years here while re-creating his native Dublin in his *Ulysses* and *A Portrait of the Artist as a Young Man.* Today the city's extraordinary museums and galleries and luxurious shops along Bahnhofstrasse, Zürich's 5th Avenue, attest to its position as Switzerland's cultural—if not political—capital.

The latest addition to the city's profile is Zürich West, an industrial neighborhood that is rapidly being reinvented, with former factories being turned into spaces for restaurants, bars, art galleries, and dance clubs. This scene of construction and restoration will most likely be ongoing well into 2008.

EXPLORING ZÜRICH

From the northern tip of the Zürichsee, the Limmat River starts its brief journey to the Aare and, ultimately, to the Rhine—and it neatly bisects Zürich at the starting gate. The city is crisscrossed by lovely, low bridges. On the left bank are the Altstadt, the grander, genteel pedestrian zone of the old medieval center; the Hauptbahnhof, the main train station; and Bahnhofplatz, a major urban crossroads and the beginning of the world-famous luxury shopping street, Bahnhofstrasse. The right bank constitutes the livelier old section, divided into the Oberdorf (Upper Village) toward Bellevue, and the Niederdorf (Lower Village), from Marktgasse to Central and along Niederdorfstrasse, which fairly throbs on weekends. Most streets between Central and Bellevue are pedestrian-only zones, as is the Limmatquai from Rudolf-Brun-Brücke to Münsterbrücke.

Scattered throughout the town are 13 medieval guildhalls, or *Zunfthäuser,* which once formed the backbone of Zürich's commercial society. Today most of these house atmospheric restaurants where high ceilings, leaded-glass windows, and coats of arms evoke the mood of merchants at their trade. Often these restaurants are one floor above street level because in the days before flood control the river would rise and inundate the ground floors.

Zürich is officially divided into a dozen numbered *Kreis* (districts), which spiral out clockwise from the center of the city. Kreis 1, covering the historic core, includes the Altstadt, Oberdorf, and Niederdorf. Zürich West is part of Kreis 5. Most areas in the city are commonly known by their Kreis, and a Kreis number is generally the most helpful in giving directions.

Numbers in the text correspond to numbers in the margin and on the Zürich map.

Bahnhofstrasse & the Altstadt

The Altstadt (Old Town) is home to several of Zürich's most important landmarks—the Lindenhof, St. Peters, the Fraumünster, and the Stadthaus—as well as the shop-lined Bahnhofstrasse.

Sights to See

Alfred Escher. Leave it to Zürich to have a statue that honors not a saint, not a poet or artist, but rather the financial wizard who single-handedly dragged Zürich into the modern age back in the mid-19th century. Escher (1819–82) established the city as a major banking center, championed the development of the federal railways and the city's university, and pushed through the construction of the tunnel under the St. Gotthard Pass. ⊠ *In the middle of Bahnhofpl., Kreis 1.*

Bahnhofstrasse. Reputedly "the most expensive street in the world"— thanks to all its extravagantly priced jewelry shops—Zürich's principal boulevard offers luxury shopping and hulking department stores, whereas much shifting and hoarding of the world's wealth takes place discreetly behind the banks' upstairs windows. You can enjoy your window shopping here in relative peace: the only vehicular traffic allowed are the municipal trams. The long-standing story of a treasure trove hidden below Bahnhofstrasse has been quashed, however—the subterranean vaults that once stored great piles of gold and silver now lie empty. In 1998 a local journalist was allowed access to the vaults; at the end of the dark labyrinths the scribe found nothing but empty rooms, the precious metals having been moved to a site near the airport several years earlier. ⊠ *Runs north–southwest of Limmat River, Kreis 1.*

★ ❻ **Fraumünster** (Church of Our Lady). Of the church spires that are Zürich's signature, the Fraumünster's is the most delicate, a graceful sweep to a narrow spire. It was added to the Gothic structure in 1732; the remains of Louis the German's original 9th-century abbey are below. Its Romanesque choir is a perfect spot for meditation beneath the ocher, sapphire, and ruby glow of the 1970 stained-glass windows by the Russian-born Marc Chagall, who loved Zürich. The Graubünden sculptor Alberto Giacometti's cousin, Augusto Giacometti, executed the fine painted window, made in 1930, in the north transept. ⊠ *Stadthausquai, Kreis 1* ☉ *Daily 10–4.*

A GOOD WALK

Begin at the **Hauptbahnhof** ❶ ▶, a massive 19th-century edifice. Directly behind the Hauptbahnhof is the **Schweizerisches Landesmuseum** ❷, housed in an enormous 19th-century neo-Gothic mansion; behind that is a shady green park. Walk northward to the tip of the park, cross on the left-hand side of the bridge, turn north a bit along Sihlquai, and head up Ausstellungsstrasse to the **Museum für Gestaltung** ❸, which holds an impressive collection of 20th-century graphic art. Back at the train station, look across Bahnhofplatz, and you'll see traffic careening around a statue of Alfred Escher, the man who brought Zürich into the modern age.

Cross the square to Bahnhofstrasse, Zürich's principal business and shopping boulevard. A quarter of the way up the street—about five blocks—veer left into Rennweg and left again on Fortunagasse, an atmospheric medieval street well removed from the contemporary elegance of Bahnhofstrasse. Climb up to the **Lindenhof** ❹, a quiet, gravel square with a view across the river to the Niederdorf. From here a maze of medieval alleys leads off to your right. Nestled among them is **St. Peters Kirche** ❺, whose tower has the largest clock face in Europe.

From St. Peters Kirche bear right on Schlüsselgasse and duck into a narrow alley, Thermengasse, which leads left; you'll walk directly over excavated ruins of Roman baths. At Weinplatz, turn right on Storchengasse, where some of the most elite boutiques are concentrated, and head toward the delicate spires of the

Fraumünster ❻. In the same square, you'll see two of Zürich's finest guildhalls, the **Zunfthaus zur Waag** ❼ and **Zunfthaus zur Meisen** ❽.

Wind left up Waaggasse past the Hotel Savoy to **Paradeplatz** ❾. From here you can take a quick side trip to the art collection at **Haus Konstruktiv** ❿ by going up Talackerstrasse to Sihlstrasse, turning left onto Selnaustrasse. Back at Paradeplatz, continue south on Bahnhofstrasse, which, as it nears the lake, opens onto a vista of boats, wide waters, and (on a clear day) distant peaks. At Bürkliplatz, look to your right: those manicured parks are the front lawn of the Hotel Baur au Lac, the aristocrat of Swiss hotels. Beyond, you'll see the modern structure of the Kongresshaus and the Tonhalle, where the Zürich Tonhalle Orchestra resides. Across General-Guisan-Quai is one of the local swans' favorite hangouts: the boat dock, which is the base for trips around the Zürichsee.

Here you can take General-Guisan-Quai west to Seestrasse to the **Museum Rietberg** (about a 25-minute walk) or turn left and cross the Quaibrücke (Quay Bridge) for one of the finest views in town, especially at night, when the floodlit spires are mirrored in the inky river, whose surface is disturbed only by drifting, sleeping swans. ⏲ **TIMING TIPS➡ The area is surprisingly compact; half a day is enough time for a cursory visit. If you're planning on museum hopping, the Schweizerisches Landesmuseum and Museum Rietberg merit at least two hours apiece.**

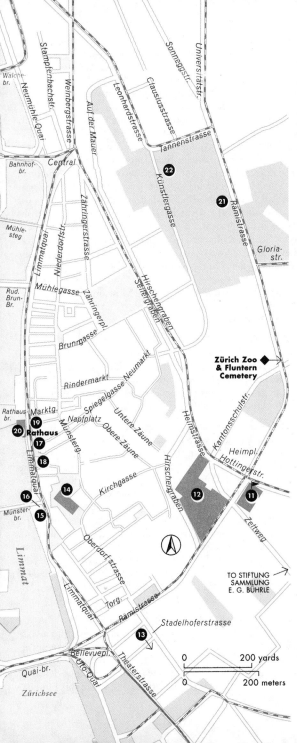

**OFF THE
BEATEN
PATH**

MUSEUM RIETBERG – Dancing Indian Shivas, contemplative Tibetan thangkas, late-18th-century literary paintings from China, and royal Benin bronzes from Nigeria: these are just a few of the treasures on view in the prodigious gathering of non-European art on view here. This is the only museum of its kind in Switzerland, with the main focus on Asia, Africa, and Ancient America, and thereby hangs a tale. Back in the 1920s, inspired by the new fashion and status of "exotic" Primitive Art (just like another person, who happened to be named Picasso), Baron Eduard von der Heydt began traveling to the four corners of the globe. He amassed a vast collection at bargain-basement prices (today, of course, many of these objects would break auction records). The crème de la crème is now on view at the Villa Wesendonck, the famous Neoclassical jewel that was once a fabled home to Richard Wagner (it was for the lady of the house that he wrote his *Wesendonck Songs*); other objects are on view in an adjacent museum, the Park-Villa Rieter. You will find Cambodian Khmer sculptures, jade Chinese tomb art, Japanese Noh masks, and even ancient Swiss masks—over the years other collections have donated quirky items to the baron's main holdings. From the city center follow Seestrasse south about 1¾ km (1 mi) until you see signs for the museum; or take Tram 7 to the Rietberg Museum stop. ⊠ *Gablerstr. 15, Kreis 2* ☎ *044/2063131* ⊕ *www.rietberg.ch* 🎫 *6 SF* ☉ *Tues.–Sun. 10–5; open until 8 on Wed., Apr.–Oct.*

▶ ❶ **Hauptbahnhof** (Main Railway Station). From the bustling main concourse of this immaculate 19th-century edifice you can watch crowds rushing to their famously on-time trains. Beneath lies a shopping mall, open daily from 8 to 8 (an exception to the closed-on-Sunday rule), with everything from grocery stores to clothing boutiques and bookshops. ⊠ *Between Museumstr. and Bahnhofpl., Kreis 1.*

❿ **Haus Konstruktiv** (Museum of Constructive Art). Housed in a former electrical substation set by the River Sihl—an impressive 1930s Modernist architectural statement in its own right—this collection traces the history of Constructive Art, which became one of the vogues of the 1930s–40s and had a big following in Switzerland (especially among its trailblazing graphic-art designers). The showpiece is the Rockefeller Dining Room, a 1963 salon designed by Swiss artist Fritz Glarner and looking very much like a pop-up Mondrian painting. Over the years, the collection has broadened to include minimal art, concept art, and neo geo work (a style based on Japanese animation). Featured artists include Sophie Taeuber-Arp, Paul Klee, and Max Bill. During the year there are several temporary shows. ⊠ *Selnaustr. 25, Kreis 1* ☎ *044/ 2177080* ⊕ *www.hauskonstruktiv.ch* 🎫 *14 SF* ☉ *Tues., Thurs., and Fri. noon–6, Wed. noon–8, weekends 11–6.*

❹ **Lindenhof** (Linden Court). On the site of this quiet square, overlooking both sides of the river, a Roman customhouse and fortress and a Carolingian palace once stood. The fountain was erected in 1912, commemorating the day in 1292 when Zürich's women saved the city from the Habsburgs. As the story goes, the town was on the brink of defeat as the Habsburg aggressors moved in. Determined to avoid this humiliation, the town's women donned armor and marched to the Lindenhof. On seeing them, the enemy thought they were faced with another army and promptly beat a strategic retreat. Today, the scene could hardly be less martial, as locals play boccie and chess under the trees. ⊠ *Bordered by Fortunag. to the west and intersected by Lindenhofstr., Kreis 1.*

❸ **Museum für Gestaltung** (Design Museum). Envisioned as an academy devoted to design and applied arts, this imposing structure—it was de-

---

TOUT SWEET

Zürich's top confiserie, Sprüngli (Paradeplatz., Kreis 1, 044/2244711), the landmark chocolatier and café for wealthy Bahnhofstrasse habitués, concocts heavenly truffles and *Luxembourgli,* small cream-filled cookies that require immediate eating. Good, plain hot lunches and salads are also served. There are also branches on Hauptbahnhof and Löwenplatz.

---

signed by Adolf Steger and Karl Egender as a Functionalist manifesto— is today the main repository of Switzerland's important legacy in graphic design, posters, and applied arts. Innovative temporary exhibitions focus on architecture, poster art, graphic design, and photography, and recent shows included such subjects as "Cheese, Please," "Gay Chic," and "The Most Beautiful Books in Switzerland." ⊠ *Ausstellungstr. 60, Kreis 5* ☎ *044/4466767* ⊕ *www.museum-gestaltung.ch* ⊠ *9 SF* ☉ *Tues. and Wed. 10–7, Thurs. 10–8, Fri.–Sun. 10–7.*

❾ **Paradeplatz** (Parade Square). The hub of Bahnhofstrasse and a tram junction, this square is a great place to observe a microcosm of the local upper crust—furrowed-brow bankers striding to work while their fur-trimmed wives struggle with half a dozen bags and the dilemma of where to shop next. While you're at it, spoil your taste buds with incredible chocolate from the Sprüngli café. ⊠ *Intersection of Bahnhofstr. and Poststr., Kreis 1.*

★ ❺ **St. Peters Kirche.** Dating from the early 13th century, Zürich's oldest parish church has the largest clock face in Europe. A church has been on this site since the 9th century. The existing building has been considerably expanded over the years: styles range from a Romanesque choir to a Baroque nave. The tower, for example, was extended in 1534, when the clock was added. Keep an eye out for inexpensive or even free classical concerts. ⊠ *St. Peterhofstatt, Kreis 1* ☎ *No phone* ☉ *Weekdays 8–6, Sat. 9–4, Sun. noon–7.*

★ ❷ **Schweizerisches Landesmuseum** (Swiss National Museum). Housed in a gargantuan neo-Gothic building dating from 1889, the Swiss National Museum owns an enormous collection of objects dating from the Stone Age to modern times. There are costumes, furniture, early watches, and a great deal of military history, including thousands of toy soldiers reenacting famous battles. In the hall of arms there's a splendid mural, painted by the late-19th-century Bernese artist Ferdinand Hodler, called *The Retreat of the Swiss Confederates at Marignano.* The work depicts a defeat in 1515 by the French. ⊠ *Museumstr. 2, Kreis 5* ☎ *044/ 2186511* ⊕ *www.musee-suisse.ch* ⊠ *5 SF* ☉ *Tues.–Sun. 10–5.*

❽ Zunfthaus zur Meisen. Set on the bank of the Limmat across the river from the towering Fraumünster is Zürich's most beautiful guildhall, comprising a magnificent suite of reception salons, several of which are topped by extravagant Baroque stucco ceilings. Erected for the city's wine merchants in the 18th century, the Zunfthaus today is a fitting showplace for the Swiss National Museum's ceramics collection. The Kilchberg-Schooren porcelain works flourished in Zürich during 1763–90 and their masterwork—a 300-piece dining service created for the Monastery of Einsiedeln in 1775—takes center stage, along with exquisite figurines and table decor. Also on view are Nyon porcelains, Swiss pottery, and faiencework. Enter on the Fraumünster side. ✉ *Münsterhof 20, Kreis 1* ☏ *044/2212807* ⊕ *www.musee-suisse.com/e/index2.html* 🎫 *3 SF* ☉ *Tues.–Sun. 10:30–5.*

❼ Zunfthaus zur Waag (Scales Guildhall). Renaissance in style—note the broad Tuscan columns and decorative strapwork on the grand facade—this circa-1637 guildhall was the meeting place for linen weavers and hat makers. Today it houses a restaurant of the same name, offering Zürich specialties and "small deliciousnesses." The main salon is staidly Biedermeier in style, so try to snag a seat in the walnut-lined Zunft-Zaal guildhall, lined with stained-glass windows. Even better are the tables right in front of the building, while an adjacent time-stained, medieval cloister is the evocative setting for a drink. ✉ *Münsterhof 8, Kreis 1* ⊕ *www.zunfthaus-zur-waag.ch.*

Niederdorf & Oberdorf

As soon as you step off the Quai Bridge on the right bank of the Limmat River, you'll notice a difference: the atmosphere is more casual. The area is also the center of Zürich's nightlife—both upscale and down, with the city's opera house and its historic theater, as well as plenty of bars and clubs. As you explore the area along Münstergasse to Marktgasse, parallel to the river, you'll notice a less Calvinistic bent. Each of the narrow streets and alleys that shoot east off Marktgasse (which quickly becomes Niederdorfstrasse) offers its own brand of entertainment. Niederdorfstrasse eventually empties onto the Central tram intersection, across the river from the main train station; from there it's easy to catch a tram along Bahnhofstrasse or the Limmatquai.

Sights to See

㉑ Graphische Sammlung (Graphics Collection). The impressive collection of the Federal Institute of Technology includes a vast library of woodcuts, etchings, and engravings by such European masters as Dürer, Rembrandt, Goya, and Picasso. Pieces from the permanent collection are often arranged in thematic exhibitions. Take Tram 6 or 10 from the Bahnhofplatz or Central stops or Tram 9 from Bellevue to the ETH/Universitätsspital stop. ✉ *Rämistr. 101, Kreis 1* ☏ *044/6324046* ⊕ *www.gs.ethz.ch* 🎫 *Free* ☉ *Mon., Tues., Thurs., and Fri. 10–5, Wed. 10–7.*

⓮ Grossmünster (Great Church). This impressive cathedral is affectionately known to English speakers as the "Gross Monster." Executed on the plump twin towers (circa 1781) are classical caricatures of Gothic forms bordering on the comical. The core of the structure was built in the 12th

FodorśChoice
★

A GOOD WALK

Start at the Quai Bridge and head up Rämistrasse to Heimplatz, where you'll find the **Schauspielhaus Pfauenbühne** ⑪ ▶. Across Heimplatz is the **Kunsthaus** ⑫, indispensable for art lovers. Head back down Rämistrasse to Bellevue—where you can catch a tram to the magnificently impressive private art collection of the **Stiftung Sammlung E. G. Bührle** ⑬—and follow Limmatquai downstream to the gaunt, imposing **Grossmünster** ⑭, with its distinctive stout twin towers.

Head back down the steps to the banks of the Limmat, where you'll find the 18th-century **Helmhaus** ⑮. Now an art museum, the Helmhaus is attached to the late-15th-century **Wasserkirche** ⑯, one of Switzerland's most delicate late-Gothic structures. Along the Limmatquai a series of former guildhalls houses popular restaurants, the 13th-century **Zunfthaus zum Rüden** ⑰, **Zunfthaus zur Zimmerleuten** ⑱, and the **Zunfthaus zur Saffran** ⑲ among them. Across the Limmatquai, the striking Baroque **Rathaus** ⑳ seems to rise up from the river.

Head back across the Limmatquai and up into the Niederdorf streets, which meander past tiny houses, art galleries, antiques shops, and neo-punk boutiques. Follow Marktgasse to **Rindermarkt,** which joins the picturesque Neumarkt and Spiegelgasse streets at a tiny medieval square where you'll see a fine early Gothic tower, the Grimmenturm. There's another Gothic tower farther down Spiegelgasse at Napfplatz, used during the 14th century by Zürich bankers. From Napfplatz take Obere Zäune up to the broad medieval **Kirchgasse,** packed with antiques shops, galleries, and bookstores. From here you can either return to the Grossmünster or venture north to see the **Graphische Sammlung** ㉑, with its woodcuts, etchings, and engravings; or head to the **Zoologisches Museum** ㉒.

🕙 TIMING TIPS→ A quick overview of the Niederdorf and Oberdorf won't take more than a half day, but it's the kind of area where there's always something new to discover, no matter how often you come back. Leave yourself extra time if you'd like to window-shop or invest a couple of hours in one of the galleries or museums, especially the Kunsthaus.

century on the site of a Carolingian church dedicated to the memory of martyrs Felix and Regula, who allegedly carried their severed heads to the spot. Charlemagne is said to have founded the church after his horse stumbled over their burial site. On the side of the south tower an enormous stone Charlemagne sits enthroned; the original statue, carved in the late 15th century, is protected in the crypt. In keeping with what the 16th-century reformer Zwingli preached from the Grossmünster's pulpit, the interior is spare, even forbidding, with all luxurious ornamentation long since stripped away. The only artistic touches are modern: stained-glass windows by Augusto Giacometti, and ornate bronze doors in the north and south portals, dating from the late 1940s.

⊠ *Zwinglipl., Kreis 1* ☎ *044/2525949* ⊙ *Daily 9–6; tower weekdays 9:15–5; cloister weekdays 9–6.*

⑮ Helmhaus. The open court of this museum once served as a linen market. Inside, there are changing exhibitions of contemporary, often experimental, art by Zürich-based artists. In spring the museum hosts an exhibition of works from the city's annual competition for young artists. ⊠ *Limmatquai 31, Kreis 1* ☎ *044/2516177* ☜ *Free* ⊙ *Tues., Wed., and Fri.–Sun. 10–6, Thurs. 10–8.*

Kirchgasse. Antiques, art, and book enthusiasts will delight in the shops on this street. No. 13 was Zwingli's last home before he was killed in battle (1531) while defending the Reformation.

DADA DADDY'S CURE-ALL

Several artistic and political figures made their homes on narrow Spiegelgasse—Lenin lived at No. 14, just before the Russian Revolution, and at No. 12 the exiled revolutionary German playwright Georg Büchner (1813–37) wrote *Woyzeck* before dying of typhoid. At the foot of the street a plaque marks the site of the Cabaret Voltaire, where the Dadaist movement took shape, conceived in Zürich by French exile Hans Arp, who in the 1920s proclaimed the new movement one that could "heal mankind from the madness of the age."

---

⑫ Kunsthaus (Museum of Art). With a varied and high-quality permanent
FodorsChoice collection of paintings—medieval, Dutch and Italian Baroque, and Im-
★ pressionist—the Kunsthaus is possibly Zürich's best art museum. The collection of Swiss art includes some fascinating works; others might be an acquired taste. Besides works by Ferdinand Hodler, with their mix of realism and stylization, there's a superb room full of Johann Heinrich Füssli paintings, which hover between the darkly ethereal and the grotesque. And then there's Picasso, Klee, Degas, Matisse, Kandinsky, Chagall, and Munch, all satisfyingly represented. ⊠ *Heimpl. 1, Kreis 1* ☎ *044/2538484* ⊕ *www.kunsthaus.ch* ☜ *Varies with exhibition* ⊙ *Tues.–Thurs. 10–9, Fri.–Sun. 10–5.*

★ ⑳ Rathaus (Town Hall). Zürich's striking Baroque government building dates 1694–98. Its interior remains as well preserved as its facade: there's a richly decorated stucco ceiling in the banquet hall and a fine ceramic stove in the council room. ⊠ *Limmatquai 55, Kreis 1* ☎ *043/2596801* ☜ *Free* ⊙ *By appointment only.*

Rindermarkt. Fans of Gottfried Keller, commonly considered Switzerland's national poet and novelist, will want to visit this street. The 19th-century writer's former home, at No. 9, became famous thanks to his novel *Der Grüne Heinrich* (*Green Henry*). Opposite is the restaurant, Zur Oepfelchammer, where Keller ate regularly. ⊠ *Street between Marktg. and Neumarkt, Kreis 1.*

▶ ⑪ Schauspielhaus Pfauenbühne (Peacock Theater). During World War II this was the only German-language theater in Europe that wasn't muzzled by the Nazis, and it attracted some of the Continent's bravest and best artists. It has been presenting plays ever since it was built in 1884; today its productions aren't always so risky, but they are stunningly

Ulrich Zwingli, Freedom Fighter

VISITORS TO ZÜRICH SOON HEAR about Ulrich Zwingli, the no-nonsense (and, one suspects, humor-free) religious reformer who taught the city to buckle down, work hard, and fear the Lord. But who was this much revered man of the cloth, and why is he depicted holding a huge sword in the statue that stands in front of the Wasserkirche?

In 1484 Zwingli was born in the tiny village of Wildhaus in the canton of St. Gallen. He entered the priesthood, eventually rising to the head position at the Grossmünster in the city of Zürich. He had no problem declaring publicly where he differed with the teachings of the Catholic Church. His first quarrel, around 1512, was over the evils of the Swiss mercenary service propagated by the Pope. A few years later, around 1519, he joined the fight against the church's growing practice of exacting payment for the forgiving of sins.

Taking a closer look at the New Testament, Zwingli came up with his own very simple theology: if it's not in the Bible, it doesn't apply. This focus on both the Old and New Testaments soon spread throughout the Christian world, affecting Protestant congregations all the way to the English colonies in America. While Martin Luther's form of protest was largely peaceful, Zwingli was not above getting into the fray. As people took up arms over their right to worship as they saw fit, Zwingli suited up and went to battle. He died in 1531, along with 500 of his compatriots, clutching that very big sword at the Battle of Kappel am Albis in the canton of Zürich.

---

mounted and performed, in German of course. There are no tours, so to see the interior you must see a show. ☒ *Rämistr. 34, Kreis 1* ☎ *044/ 2587777* ⊕ *www.schauspielhaus.ch.*

🚇 **Stiftung Sammlung E. G. Bührle.** A stunning array of Cézannes, Manets, Monets, and Degases make this eyeknocking collection one of the best art museums in Europe. Amazingly, it was all put together in the space of a single decade. During the 1950s, Zürich industrialist E.G. Bührle purchased the finest offerings from the world's most prestigious art dealers, winding up with a collection studded with legendary Impressionist and Post-Impressionist works, including Cézanne's *Self Portrait with Palette*, Renoir's *Little Irene*, and Degas's *Little Dancer*. The museum also encompasses religious sculptures (with great holdings of medieval Pietà wooden sculptures) as well as Spanish and Italian paintings from the 16th to 18th centuries and gorgeous landscapes by Dutch masters like Meindert Hobbema and Salomon van Ruysdael. But the core of the collection

FodorsChoice ★

FAR-SIGHTED VIEWING

When Emil-George Bührle toured visitors around his famed collection, he would ping-pong from Renoir to Rembrandt to Degas, and back again. "That is the way one ought to go around museums," he would say. "It gives you a new angle of vision."

remains French 19th-century and all the great names are here, from Courbet and Manet to Picasso, with forays into the Nabis, Fauve, and Cubist schools. Housed in an 1886 villa, there is little period splendor on view but nothing could outshine these masterpieces. Take Tram 11 from Bellevue, then Bus 77 from Hegibachplatz to the Altenhofstrasse stop. ⊠ *Zollikerstr. 172, Kreis 8* ☎ *044/4220086* ⊕ *www.buehrle.ch* ⊠ *9 SF* ☉ *Tues., Wed., Fri., and Sun. 2–5.*

🔟 **Wasserkirche** (Water Church). One of Switzerland's most delicate late-Gothic structures, this church displays stained glass by Augusto Giacometti. Both the church and the Helmhaus once stood on the island on which martyrs Felix and Regula supposedly lost their heads. ⊠ *Limmatquai 31, Kreis 1* ☉ *Wed. 2–5, Sat. noon–5.*

🔵 🔢 **Zoologisches Museum.** Engaging and high-tech, the Zoological Museum allows you a close look in its accessible displays on Swiss insects, birds, and amphibians. You can examine butterflies and living water creatures through microscopes and listen to birdcalls as you compare avian markings. ⊠ *Karl Schmid-Str. 4, Kreis 1* ☎ *044/6343838* ⊕ *www.unizh.ch/ zoolmus* ⊠ *Free* ☉ *Tues.–Fri. 9–5, weekends 10–4.*

🔟 **Zunfthaus zum Rüden.** Now housing one of Zürich's finest restaurants, this 13th-century structure was the noblemen's guildhall. Peek inside at the barrel-vaulted ceiling and 30-foot beams; or better yet, stop for a meal. ⊠ *Limmatquai 42, Kreis 1.*

🔟 **Zunfthaus zur Saffran.** Portions of this guildhall for haberdashers date from as early as 1389. The modern restaurant downstairs has outdoor seating underneath medieval arches facing the river. ⊠ *Limmatquai 54, Kreis 1.*

🔟 **Zunfthaus zur Zimmerleuten.** Dating from 1708, this was the carpenters' guild. Its main restaurant draws business groups to a number of lovely dark-wood halls; its former storage cave houses a cozy restaurant of the same name. ⊠ *Limmatquai 40, Kreis 1.*

Zürich Environs: Zürich West to Winterthur

Switzerland's grandest collection of old master paintings, Zürich's famous Zoo, the city's snazziest contemporary Kunsthalle, and James Joyce's grave are some of the striking attractions located not far from the city center's borders. They may require a pleasant tram ride or train excursion but they are all worth the trip.

Zürich's West sector is one of the city's most happening districts. Although banking is an important part of Zürich's economy, it's not the only one; starting around 1860, the city was a major center for the machine industry, supplying transportation companies with ball bearings, cables, and the like. With this industry in a decline since the early 1990s there has been a shift toward information technology and the service industry, leaving a great swath of land downstream from the city center with empty warehouses. Today these cavernous spaces are being snatched up by young entrepreneurs. The result, these days anyway, is part construction chaos, part swinging cultural center. Bars, restaurants, and dance clubs sprout up almost daily. The area is loosely bordered by Hardstrasse, Hardturmstrasse, and Pfingstweidstrasse; to get there by public transportation, take Tram 4 or 13 to Escher Wyss Platz. It's roughly a 10-minute trip from the Hauptbahnhof. The character of this area is developing—stay tuned.

Sights to See

Fodor'sChoice ★ **Am Römerholz—Die Sammlung Oskar Reinhart** (Oskar Reinhart Collection at Schloss Am Römerholz). Lucas Cranach's *Portrait of Johannes Cuspinian*, Pieter Breughel the Elder's *Adoration of the Magi in the Snow*, Peter Paul Rubens' *Decius Mus*, Edouard Manet's *Au Café*, Toulouse-Lautrec's *Clownesse Cha-U-Kao*—you get the picture. This is one of the greatest private art collections in Switzerland, perhaps only rivaled by the Sammlung Emil-George Bührle in Zürich. The jewel in the crown of Winterthur's art museums, Am Römerholz is virtually wallpapered with legendary paintings. Located 20 km (12 mi) northeast of Zürich, Winterthur made its fortune through the textile industry and it blossomed thanks to prosperous merchants who developed a love of art. They bequeathed the town some notable art museums, including the Villa Flora/Sammlung Hahnloser (www.villaflora.ch)—a Sezession-style villa with works by van Gogh, Redon, Vuillard, and Matisse—and the Museum Oskart Reinhart am Stadtgarten (www.museumoskarreinhart.ch), which focuses on "lesser-known" painters that Reinhart hunted down, such as Caspar David Friedrich and Arnold Böcklin. Reinhart's most magnificent treasures wound up at the villa "Am Römerholz," built in 1915 on the hill overlooking town. The collection ranges five centuries, with pride of place going to German and Early Netherlandish paintings of the 16th century, 17th-century French and Flemish painting, and Impressionist masterworks. Works by Gerard David, Poussin, Daumier, van Gogh, and nearly 200 other artists stagger the eye, tribute to the extremely cultured upbringing Reinhart (1885–1965) received. Winterthur is a half hour from Zürich by train, on the main rail route to St. Gallen; trains depart about every 15 minutes. From the train station's Sektor G, take the "Museumsbus" (5 SF), which travels the 15-minute route (from station: 9:45, 10:45 . . . until 4:45; from museum: 10, 11 . . . until 5). By car, follow the autobahn signs for Winterthur–St. Gallen. Take the Winterthur-Ohringen exit onto Schaffhauserstrasse into town, then left on Rychenbergstrasse to Haldenstrasse. ✉ *Haldenstr. 95, Winterthur* ☏ *052/2692740* ⊕ *www.roemerholz. ch* 🎫 *10 SF* ☉ *Tues.–Sun. 10–5, open until 8 on Wed.*

James Joyce's Grave. The inimitable Irish author not only lived and wrote in Zürich, but died here as well. The city's most famous literary resident is buried in the Friedhof Fluntern (Fluntern Cemetery); atop his grave sits a contemplative statue of the writer, complete with cigar. A few steps away is the grave of another renowned author, Nobel prize winner Elias Canetti. The cemetery is adjacent to the Tram 6 terminus. ☉ *Mar., Apr., Sept., and Oct., daily 7–7; May–Aug., daily 7 AM–8 PM; Nov.–Feb., daily 8–5.*

Kunsthalle (Center of Contemporary Art). Set in West Zürich, this Kunsthalle is one of two major art venues on the top floors of a former brewery. It presents new local and international artists in huge, stark, white rooms. A survey of Richard Prince's paintings and Keith Tyson's installations mixing objects, paintings, and photography have drawn large crowds of modern art lovers in the past few years. Works are always cutting edge: you can say you saw it here first. There are four smaller galleries and a well-stocked art bookstore in the same building. ⊠ *Limmatstr. 270, Kreis 5* ☎ *044/2721515* ⊕ *www.kunsthallezurich.ch* ⌨ *8 SF* ☉ *Tues., Wed., and Fri. noon–6, Thurs. noon–8, weekends 11–5.*

Migros Museum für Gegenwartskunst (Migros Museum of Contemporary Art). One floor below the Kunsthalle, this airy, white loft has the same focus—up-and-coming contemporary artists—but is privately funded by Switzerland's largest department store chain, Migros. Shows of recent work are interspersed with exhibitions from the extensive Migros collection, which includes works by Andy Warhol. The museum sponsors regular discussions with the artists, often in English. ⊠ *Limmatstr. 270, Kreis 5* ☎ *044/2772050* ⊕ *www.migrosmuseum.ch* ⌨ *8 SF* ☉ *Tues., Wed., and Fri. noon–6, Thurs. noon–8, weekends 11–5.*

Zürich Zoo. This is one of Europe's outstanding zoos, with more than 1,500 animals, including Asian elephants, black rhinos, seals, and big cats. One of the more unusual attractions is a huge dome stocked with flora and fauna you might encounter in a jungle in Madagascar. Set in a tree-filled park, the zoo is just east of the city center and easily reached by Trams 5 and 6. ⊠ *Zürichbergstr. 221, Kreis 6* ☎ *044/2542505* ⊕ *www.zoo.ch* ⌨ *22 SF* ☉ *Mar.–Oct., daily 9–6; Nov.–Feb., daily 9–5.*

WHERE TO EAT

$$$–$$$$ ✕**Casa Ferlin.** Crimson velvet wallhangings, a baronial fireplace, and 19th-century, brocade-covered banquettes add up to one of Zürich's most sumptuous interiors. Happily, the food is even more impressive, and the quality of what may be Zürich's best homemade pasta keeps regulars coming back. This family-run establishment, in business for almost a century, offers excellent traditional Italian dishes such as beef ravioli, veal fillet in lemon-sage sauce and zabaglione marsala. The lunch crowd is mostly financial bigwigs, while evenings attract entire local families. ⊠ *Stampfenbachstr. 38, Kreis 1* ☎ *044/3623509* ⊕ *www.casaferlin.ch/* ⌨ *Reservations essential* ☰ *AE, DC, MC, V* ☉ *Closed weekends and mid-July–mid-Aug.*

★ **$$$–$$$$** ✕**Haus zum Rüden.** The most culinarily ambitious of Zürich's many Zunfthaus (historic guildhall) dining places, this fine restaurant is also the most architecturally spectacular, combining a wooden barrel-vaulted ceiling and 30-foot beams. Slick modern improvements—including a glassed-

EATING WELL IN ZÜRICH

Since the mid-1990s, Zürich's restaurant trade has boomed. The new establishments, both Swiss and international, tend to favor lighter, leaner meals served in bright spaces that are often open to the street. The traditional cuisine, no longer ubiquitous but still easily found, is called *nach Zürcher Art*, meaning "cooked in the style of Zürich." Think meat, mushrooms, potatoes, butter, cream—an extremely rich cuisine, perfectly suited to the leaded-glass and burnished-oak guildhalls.

In exploring Zürich's core, you will want to enter at least one of these famous medieval union clubhouses scattered along the riverfront neighborhoods; the best way is to dine in one, as all but the Zunfthaus zur Meisen have been converted into restaurants. Having polished off a traditionally meat-heavy meal, ask if you can have a peek into their other dining rooms—they are, for the most part, museum-perfect in their leaded-glass and Gothic-wood detail.

Zürich's signature dish, which you'll encounter throughout both French and German Switzerland, is

geschnetzeltes Kalbfleisch, or in French *émincé de veau*: bite-size slices of milky veal (and sometimes veal kidneys) sautéed in butter and swimming in a rich brown sauce thick with cream, white wine, shallots, and mushrooms. Its closest cousin is *Geschnetzeltes Kalbsleber* (calves' liver), served much the same way. You may also find *Spätzli*, flour-egg dough fingers, either pressed through a sieve or snipped, gnocchi-style, and served in butter.

Another culinary must is Zürich's favorite portable food, sausage and *Bürli* (a crunchy roll), eaten separately, two-fisted style. The best are to be had at Bellevue at the Hintere Sterne, an outdoor stand run by gruff men who are a tradition in themselves. *Kalbsbratwurst* (veal) is mild, the smaller *Cervelat* (pork) saltier. Join the locals and munch away while waiting for a tram.

Zürichers also have a definite sweet tooth: refined cafés draw crowds for afternoon pastries, and chocolate shops vie for the unofficial honor of making the best chocolate truffles in town.

in elevator—manage to blend intelligently with the ancient decor and old-world chandeliers. Innovative entrées might include cream of parsley soup with snails, or duck breast in honey ginger sauce. The river views are especially impressive at night; ask for a window table. ⊠ *Limmatquai 42, Kreis 1* ☎ *044/2619566* ▤ *AE, DC, MC, V.*

$$$–$$$$ ✗ **Petermann's Kunststuben.** Serious and clubby-chic, this is one of Switzerland's gastronomic meccas. Listed as one of Forbes's most expensive
Fodor'sChoice restaurants in the world, and set in an 1879 house with rooms replete
★ with aubergine-hued walls, gigantic bouquets, Venetian glass lanterns, and modern paintings ("Kunststuben" means art studio), Petermann's is 9 km (5 mi) south of Zürich in Küsnacht, a village near Rapperswil. Though it's south of the city center, sitting on the lake's eastern shore,

this formal restaurant is more than worth the investment of time and effort to get here. Chef Horst Petermann never rests on his laurels: the ever-changing International French menu may include scrambled eggs with truffles and foie gras, lobster in anise sauce, salmon with caviar crème, or Tuscan dove with pine nuts and herbs. The presentation here is fantastic, with ingredients so strikingly arranged on the plate you feel you should hang the main course on the wall, not eat it. On the small side, the restaurant nearly doubles in summer when you can book a table on the flower-fragant outdoor terrace. ⊠ *Seestr. 160, Küssnacht* ☎ *044/9100715* ⊕ *www. kunststuben.com* ⌕ *Reservations essential* ☐ *AE, DC, MC, V* ⊘ *Closed Sun. and Mon., 2 wks in Feb., and 3 wks in late summer.*

$$-$$$$ ✕ **Seerose.** As soon as it even vaguely looks like it'll be warm enough, the hip deck-shoe crowd drives, runs, cycles, or powerboats to one of the best places on the lake. It not only has its own dock, it *is* its own dock, jutting far out and offering fabulous views. The food isn't bad either: seasonal ingredients make the difference for dishes such as oxtail ragout or lemon sole with basmati rice. Sunglasses required. ⊠ *Seestr. 493, Kreis 2* ☎ *044/4816383* ☐ *AE, DC, MC, V.*

★ $$$ ✕ **Veltliner Keller.** Though its rich, carved-wood decor borrows from Graubündner Alpine culture, this dining spot is no tourist trap. The house, built in 1325 and functioning as a restaurant since 1551, has always stored Italian-Swiss Valtellina wines, which were carried over the Alps to Zürich. There is a definite emphasis on the heavy and the meaty, but the kitchen is flexible and reasonably deft with more modern favorites as well: veal steak with Gorgonzola, grilled salmon, and dessert mousses. ⊠ *Schlüsselg. 8, Kreis 1* ☎ *044/2254040* ☐ *AE, DC, MC, V* ⊘ *Closed weekends.*

$$-$$$ ✕ **Baur au Lac Rive Gauche.** Its nondescript entrance off a noisy streetcorner belies the light, beige cubist decor inside, which attracts crowds of young business executives and expense-account padders. The cuisine is light, trendy and all off the grill—from upscale surf and turf to deer with applesauce and raisins. The wine list taps Hotel Baur au Lac's impressive cave. ⊠ *Talstr. 1, Kreis 1* ☎ *044/2205060* ⌕ *Reservations essential* ☐ *AE, DC, MC, V.*

$$-$$$ ✕ **Kindli.** In compliance with the kitchen's ban on the use of packaged foods, the meals served at this warm, inviting restaurant are prepared with seasonal ingredients. The results are such innovative dishes as fried pasta with courgettes, leeks and pumpkin, or beef fillet with onion mustard sauce. There is also a five-course meal accompanied by a glass

1

or two of wine preselected for each course. ⊠ *Pfalzg. 1, Kreis 1* ☎ *043/8887678* 🍴 *AE, DC, MC, V.*

$$–$$$ ✕ **La Salle.** This is a favorite haunt of theatergoers heading for the Schauspielhaus Schiffbauhalle—it conveniently shares the same building. The glass, steel, and concrete interior mixes well with the brick elements left from the original factory building. Beneath an enormous Murano glass chandelier, elegantly dressed patrons enjoy delicate dishes such as chicken with sauerkraut or wolffish with arugula and zucchini. The hefty wine list can be sampled at the apricot-color bar, where a smaller version of the menu is available. ⊠ *Schiffbaustr. 4, Kreis 5* ☎ *044/2587071* 🍴 *AE, DC, MC, V.*

$$–$$$ ✕ **Zunfthaus zur Schmiden.** The sense of history should be strong here, as this was the guild house of blacksmiths and barbers, founded in 1412. While there are time-burnished allurements—wood paneling, leaded glass, and tile stoves—the historic vibe of the main room is counteracted by the modern white ceiling and casements. To really channel history, take a peek at the Zunftsaal, a 19th-century banqueting room extravaganza. At your table, Zürich's meat classics (Geschnetzeltes, liver or steak with Rösti) come garnished with seasonal vegetables, and there's a considerable selection of alternatives, fish among them. The guild's own house-label wine is fine. ⊠ *Marktg. 20, Kreis 1* ☎ *044/2505848* ⊕ *www.zunfthausschmiden.ch* 🍴 *AE, DC, MC, V.*

$$–$$$ ✕ **Zunfthaus zur Waag.** With its magnificent Renaissance-inspired facade, this airy guildhall, with whitewashed woodwork and leaded-glass windows looking out to the Fraumünster, remains a lovely dining spot. The Zunft-Saal (guildhall) is a pine-wood showpiece, which greatly outshines the the main restaurant—a rather dull Biedermeier room. The kitchen offers light, seasonal dishes such as vegetable taglioni with spinach, or lamb with white beans, tomatoes and polenta. To drink in the impressive architecture, opt for outside tables on the edge of the cobblestone square in warm weather. ⊠ *Münsterhof 8, Kreis 1* ☎ *044/2169966* ⊕ *www.zunfthaus-zur-waag.ch* 🍴 *AE, DC, MC, V.*

★ $$–$$$ ✕ **Zunfthaus zur Zimmerleuten/Küferstube.** Although the pricier Zunfthaus upstairs is often overwhelmed with large banquets, at substreet level a cozy, candlelit haven called the *Küferstube* (Coopers' Pub) serves atmospheric meals in a dark-beamed Old Zürich setting. Sumptuous traditional standards include dishes using almost all parts of the animal, such as liver with sage and sweetbreads in Riesling butter. ⊠ *Limmatquai 40, Kreis 1* ☎ *044/2505361* ⊕ *www.kramergastronomie.ch* 🍴 *AE, DC, MC, V.*

$–$$$ ✕ **Angkor.** A bit of Siem Reap in the middle of Zürich West: the lavish interior is full of stone carvings and wood latticework that seem right out of Ta Prohm, but minus the jungle. The menu is huge and heaped with green curry, oyster sauce, and ginger. The lunch specials are a good deal for those on a budget. Tables double in number with outside summer seating on the square. ⊠ *Giessereistr. 18, Kreis 5* ☎ *043/2052888* 🍴 *AE, DC, MC, V.*

$–$$$ ✕ **Bodega Española.** The coats of arms of old Spanish provinces and garlands of onions and garlic encircle the dark-paneled interior of this upstairs Niederdorf restaurant. It specializes in big steaks, seafood, omelets,

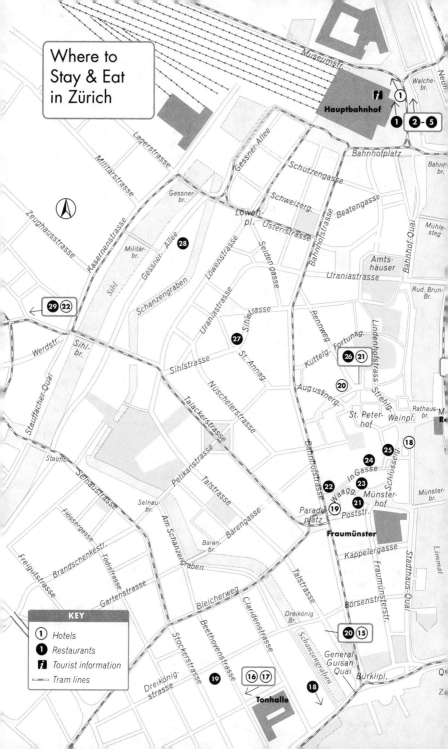

Where to Stay & Eat in Zürich

KEY

- ① Hotels
- ● Restaurants
- 𝒊 Tourist information
- ▭▭ Tram lines

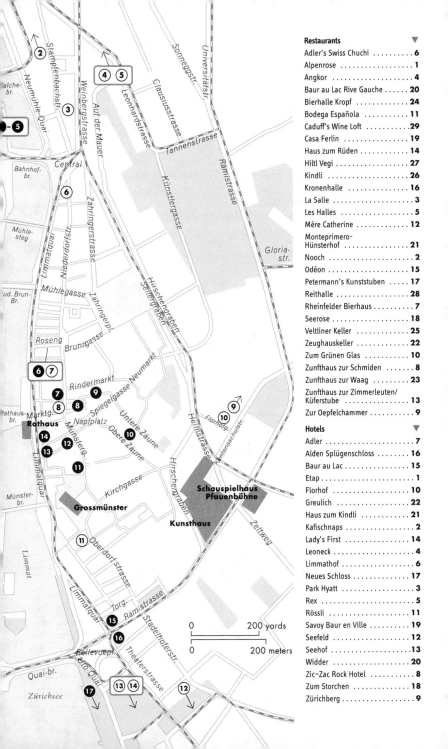

and paella. Be sure to sample the excellent house rioja (a Spanish wine specialty shop adjoins, so the choice is extensive) and crown your meal with a Cuban cigar. Downstairs is a smoky bar that serves amazing tapas. ⊠ *Münsterg. 15, Kreis 1* ☎ *044/2512310* 🗐 *AE, DC, MC, V.*

★ **$–$$$** ✕ **Caduff's Wine Loft.** In a 19th-century whitewashed former warehouse, industrial lighting, parquet floors, and the occasional strategically placed cactus set the minimalist tone for the kitchen's delicious, simple cuisine. The market determines the menu, which could be anything from lentil tartare with cottage cheese to veal shoulder in mustard sauce with truffle polenta. If you can't decide on a wine, you're welcome to browse downstairs in the candlelit cellar—there are only about 1,000 bottles to choose from. ⊠ *Kanzleistr. 126, Kreis 4* ☎ *044/2402255* 🗐 *AE, DC, MC, V.*

$–$$$ ✕ **Kronenhalle.** From Stravinsky, Brecht, and Joyce to Nureyev, Deneuve, **Fodor's**Choice and Saint-Laurent, this beloved landmark has always drawn a stellar ★ crowd. The vast dining salon is a former 1845 beer hall but now has a Sezession vibe. The interior goes way beyond Art Nouveau, though, as the eye is drawn to medieval heraldic crests painted high up on the walls and, hanging just below them, an astonishing collection of 20th-century art. Every panel of gleaming wood wainscoting frames works by Picasso, Braque, Miró, Chagall, or Matisse, collected by patroness-hostess Hulda Zumsteg (her riches come from the family's legendary couture textiles firm), who owned the restaurant from 1921 until her death in 1985. The tradition is carried on by the family trust, and robust cooking is still served in hefty portions: fish in sage butter, veal steak in morel sauce, duck *à l'orange* with red cabbage, and Spätzli. There's no shame in ordering the sausage and Rösti just to take in the animated and genial scene. ⊠ *Rämistr. 4, Kreis 1* ☎ *044/2516669* ⊕ *www.kronenhalle. com* ⌕ *Reservations essential* 🗐 *AE, DC, MC, V.*

$–$$$ ✕ **Monteprimero–Münsterhof.** Upstairs, the understated elegance of its simple furnishings and medieval walls exposed and scrubbed bare don't distract from what's on your plate: seasonal side dishes complement grilled meats and local fish. If you've come just for the wide variety of tapas, the ground floor is more casual. ⊠ *Münsterhof 6, Kreis 1* ☎ *044/ 2114340* 🗐 *AE, DC, MC, V.*

★ **$–$$$** ✕ **Zum Grünen Glas.** This French-inclined restaurant in a quiet corner of the Niederdorf is part of the trend toward lighter food and portions that don't overflow your plate. You might try angler fish in white wine sauce or *osso buco* with potato *gnocchi,* then finish with a lemon sorbet. Wainscoting, parquet floors, and crisp white tablecloths make for a comfortable dining room; an outside courtyard is open in summer. ⊠ *Untere Zäune 15, Kreis 1* ☎ *044/ 2516504* 🗐 *AE, DC, MC, V.*

★ **$–$$$** ✕ **Zur Oepfelchammer.** Dating from 1801, this was once the haunt of Zürich's beloved writer Gottfried Keller. One section is a dark and heavily graffitied bar, with sagging timbers and slanting floors; there are also two welcoming little din-

ONE SWINGING PLACE

The historic decor at Zur Oepfelchammer is suprisingly "interactive." Any guest who succeeds in swinging around the room's famous wooden rafters three times wins free wine for their table. You'd be amazed at the amount of diners who make the attempt.

ing rooms with coffered ceilings and plenty of carved oak and damask—opt for the cozy, charming Gaststübe (not the more staid Stübli). Traditional meat dishes—calves' liver, Geschnetzeltes Kalbfleisch—are lightened up with fresh seasonal veggies. The place is always packed, and service can be slow, so stake out a table and plan to spend the evening. ⊠ *Rindermarkt 12, Kreis 1* ☎ *044/2512336* ⊕ *www.oepfelchammer. ch/* ⊟ *MC, V* ☯ *Closed Sun. and Mon.*

$$ ✕ **Alpenrose.** It doesn't get more Swiss than this: the ingredients, the recipes, the wines, and the decor are all Helvetian. (The cook is German, but never mind.) This former local greasy spoon has been buffed to an elegant shine, keeping the wainscotting and etched glass windows, adding linen tablecloths, a stuffed chamois head, and paintings of the Matterhorn and other well-known landmarks. Enjoy *engadiner pizokel* (flour dumplings) with ham, or duck breast with dried plum sauce and mashed potatoes. ⊠ *Fabrikstr. 12, Kreis 5* ☎ *044/2713919* ⊕ *www.restaurant-alpenrose.ch/* ⊟ *MC, V* ☯ *Closed Mon. and mid-July–mid-Aug.*

★ **$–$$** ✕ **Adler's Swiss Chuchi.** Right on the Niederdorf's main square, Hirschenplatz, this squeaky-clean Swiss-kitsch restaurant has an airy, modern decor, with Alpine-rustic chairs, and Big Boy–style plastic menus. It serves good home-cooked national specialties; the fondue, usually a winter dish, is served year-round. Excellent lunch menus are rock-bottom cheap and served double quick. ⊠ *Roseng. 10, Kreis 1* ☎ *044/2669666* ⊟ *AE, DC, MC, V.*

$–$$ ✕ **Bierhalle Kropf.** Under the mounted boar's head and restored century-

Fodor's Choice old murals depicting gallivanting cherubs, businesspeople, workers, and

★ shoppers share crowded tables to feast on generous hot dishes and a great selection of sausages. The *Leberknödli* (liver dumplings) are tasty, the potato croquettes are filled with farmer's cheese and garnished with a generous fresh salad, and the *Apfelküechli* (fried apple slices) are tender and sweet. The bustle and clatter provide a lively, sociable experience, and you'll more than likely get to know your neighbor. ⊠ *In Gassen 16, Kreis 1* ☎ *044/2211805* ⊟ *AE, DC, MC, V* ☯ *Closed Sun.*

$–$$ ✕ **Hiltl Vegi.** Founded in 1898, when vegetarians were regarded as "grass eaters," this restaurant has more than proved its staying power. It was taken over in 1904 by Bavarian Ambrosius Hiltl, who married the cook; the current patron, Rolf Hiltl, is their great-grandson. The enormous buffet offers everything from curried chick peas to stuffed jalapenos, from breaded cheese dumplings to ratatouile with rice. ⊠ *Sihlstr. 28, Kreis 1* ☎ *044/2277000* ⊟ *AE, DC, MC, V.*

$–$$ ✕ **Mère Catherine.** This popular bistro with a Provençal veneer presents blackboard specials, with the chef turning out onion soup, venison carpaccio, seafood, and a few meat dishes, such as lamb saddle in an herb crust. The young, bohemian clientele also enjoys the restaurant's small, hipster-packed Philosophe bar next door. On warm evenings, opt for courtyard seating. ⊠ *Nägelihof 3, Kreis 1* ☎ *044/2505940* ⊟ *AE, MC, V.*

★ **$–$$** ✕ **Reithalle.** In a downtown theater complex behind Bahnhofstrasse, this old military riding stable now does its duty as a noisy and popular restaurant. Its past is plain to see, as candles are perched on the mangers and beams. Young locals share long tables arranged mess-hall-style to sample French and Italian specialties, many of them vegetarian, as well as an excellent international list of open wines listed on the blackboard. In summer the courtyard is lined with communal tables. ⊠ *Gessnerallee 8, Kreis 1* ☎ *044/2120766* ⊟ *AE, MC, V.*

$–$$ ✕ **Rheinfelder Bierhaus.** Locals know this dark, smoky Niederdorf institution by its unsettling nickname, Bluetig Tuume or the Bloody Thumb. It is famous locally for its *entrecôte café de Paris* (steak with herb butter), sausage standbys, and the pride of the Spanish/Romansch owners: a freshly homemade paella, which must be ordered in advance. ⊠ *Marktg. 19, Kreis 1* ☎ *044/2512991* ⊟ *No credit cards.*

★ **$–$$** ✕ **Zeughauskeller.** Built as an arsenal in 1487, this enormous stone-and-beam hall offers hearty meat platters and a variety of beers and wines in comfortable Germanic chaos. The waitstaff is harried and brisk, especially at lunchtime, when crowds are thick. Unlike the shabbier beer halls in Niederdorf, this one is clean and bourgeois, reflecting its Paradeplatz location. They're not unaccustomed to tourists—menus are posted in English, Japanese, and at least 10 other languages—but locals consider this their home away from home. ⊠ *Bahnhofstr. 28, at Paradepl., Kreis 1* ☎ *044/2112690* ⊟ *AE, DC, MC, V.*

¢–$$ ✕ **Les Halles.** This old warehouse space in Zürich West has not so much been renovated as cleaned up and then highlighted with an eclectic mix of antiques and '50s collectibles, all of which are for sale. The fare is health conscious—made from organic ingredients sold in the attached health food store—and includes couscous with vegetables, chicken with peppers, and tomatoes and eggplant. It's famous for mussels during the season. In summer, snag a table on the multitiered veranda out back. ⊠ *Pfingstweidstr. 6, Kreis 5* ☎ *044/2731125* ⊟ *AE, DC, MC, V.*

$ ✕ **Nooch.** Zürich's first Japanese noodle bar is spacious and uncluttered, and tables are large enough for sharing without cramping your style or compromising your privacy. Hearty but health-conscious soups made with ramen, soba, and udon noodles are the specialty. The kitchen's pledge is to use fresh seasonal ingredients without preservatives, MSG, cream, or butter, and to add as little animal fat as possible. The restaurant also has what may be the city's largest gastronomic smoke-free zone: only 4 tables out of 26 have been set aside for smokers. ⊠ *Heinrichstr. 267, Kreis 5* ☎ *043/3668535* ⊟ *AE, DC, MC, V.*

★ **¢–$** ✕ **Odéon.** This historic café–restaurant was once frequented by the pre-Revolution Lenin, who nursed a coffee while he read the daily papers. These days, an air of countercultural chic mixes with the cigarette smoke. You can nurse a coffee, too, or choose from a menu of burgers, BLTs, and pasta. ⊠ *Limmatquai 2, Kreis 1* ☎ *044/2511650* ⊟ *AE, DC, MC, V.*

WHERE TO STAY

$$$$ ▣ **Alden Splügenschloss.** Constructed at the turn of the 20th century as luxury apartments, this Relais & Châteaux property consists entirely of suites, all done in beige with chocolate leather accents and filled with such amenities as flat-screen televisions. Each sleek marble bath has its own whirlpool. The lobby retains some alluring fin-de-siècle accents.

1

The location—in a spare banking district—may be a little out of the way for sightseeing, but if you're looking for peace and quiet, this hotel is worth the effort. ⊠ *Splügenstr. 2, Kreis 1, CH-8002* ☎ *044/2899999* 🖷 *044/2899998* ⊕ *www.alden.ch* ↪ *22 suites* ⚘ *2 restaurants, in-room broadband, in-room data ports, bar* ⊟ *AE, DC, MC, V* ⦿ *BP.*

★ **$$$$** 🖼 **Baur au Lac.** Austria's Empress Elisabeth paved the way (spending an entire summer here with a retinue of 60 people). The Russian Tsarina and German Emperor Wilhelm II followed; Richard Wagner arrived and premiered the first act of his *Die Walküre* here, accompanied on the piano by his father-in-law, Franz Liszt. Kings and queens, empresses and dukes took turns visiting (but let's not forget Arthur Rubinstein, Marc Chagall, Henry Moore, and Placido Domingo), making this hotel a truly upper-crust establishment ever since it opened its doors in 1844. The perfume of days gone by has, alas, largely dissipated, and there is nary an empress, duchess, or maharajah in sight these days. This is still one highbrow patrician—it even goes so far as to turn its broad back to the commercial center; its front rooms overlook the lake, the canal, and the manicured lawns of its own private park. Le Hall, the vast lobby, has a Jugenstil flavor and is just the place to apertif the late afternoon away. Upstairs, the signature classic room decor gleams with rich fabrics, Empire mirrors, and such ultramodern comforts as triple-glazed windows and CD players. In summer, meals (including breakfast) are served in the glassed-in pavilion along the canal; in winter, in the glowing Restaurant Français. ⊠ *Talstr. 1, Kreis 1, CH-8022* ☎ *044/2205020* 🖷 *044/ 2205044* ⊕ *www.bauraulac.ch* ↪ *84 rooms, 42 suites* ⚘ *2 restaurants, café, in-room safes, minibars, in-room data ports, Wi-Fi, gym, hair salon, bar, dance club, meeting rooms* ⊟ *AE, DC, MC, V.*

★ **$$$$** 🖼 **Park Hyatt.** Just a few blocks from the lake, the wide open spaces of the city's first American-style luxury hotel are accented in black marble, rich maple, and lots of gleaming glass. Rooms have parquet floors with soft carpets, burgundy and beige fabrics on the furnishings, and floor-to-ceiling windows. Locals frequent the restaurant, which uses only local seasonal ingredients for dishes such as caramelized halibut with pine nuts and beef tenderloin with white-truffle risotto. ⊠ *Beethovenstr. 21, Kreis 1, CH-8002* ☎ *043/8831234* 🖷 *043/8831235* ⊕ *www. hyatt.ch* ↪ *142 rooms, 12 suites* ⚘ *Restaurant, café, room service, in-room safes, minibars, in-room DVD, in-room broadband, in-room data ports, Wi-Fi, health club, sauna, bar, lounge, babysitting, dry cleaning, laundry service, Internet, airport shuttle, no-smoking rooms* ⊟ *AE, DC, MC, V.*

★ **$$$$** 🖼 **Romantik Hotel Florhof.** Replete with a general away-from-it-all atmosphere, this is a pretty-as-a-picture, protected 17th-century merchant's mansion. In a dreamily quiet residential area by the Kunsthaus (yet just a few tram stops away from the main rail station), this Romantik property is an anti-urban hotel, a gentle antidote to the bustle of downtown commerce. Once a bargain option, today the Florhof pampers guests with its polished wood, blue-willow fabric, and wisteria-sheltered garden. The restaurant serves light, seasonal menus, and meals on the terrace on a summer's night near the Neptune fountain are positively rhapsodical. ⊠ *Florhofg. 4, Kreis 1, CH-8001* ☎ *044/2502626* 🖷 *044/*

2502627 ⊕ *www.florhof.ch* ⇨ *33 rooms, 2 suites* ⚠ *Restaurant, in-room safes, minibars, in-room broadband; no a/c in some rooms* ⊟ *AE, DC, MC, V* ⦿ *BP.*

$$$$ 🏨 **Savoy Baur en Ville.** Directly on the Paradeplatz, at the hub of the banking, shopping, and sightseeing districts, this is one of Zürich's 19th-century landmarks. Despite its venerable age, the hotel perennially improves itself, regularly sprucing up its rooms and amenities to maintain its conservative sleekness. The rooms, with gray-stone bathrooms, walk-in closets, and period furniture, typify what the hotel calls its "past-modern" decor. There are two fine restaurants—one French, one Italian—as well as a slick café–bar. ⊠ *Am Paradepl., Poststr. 12, Kreis 1, CH-8022* ☎ *044/2152525* 🖷 *044/2152500* ⊕ *www.savoy-baurenville.ch* ⇨ *112 rooms, 8 suites* ⚠ *2 restaurants, in-room broadband, in-room data ports, Wi-Fi, bar, meeting rooms; no a/c* ⊟ *AE, DC, MC, V* ⦿ *BP.*

$$$$ 🏨 **Widder.** Zürich's most captivating hotel was created when 10 adja-
Fodor'sChoice cent medieval houses were gutted and combined—now steel fuses with
★ ancient stone and timeworn wood. Behind every door is a fascinating mix of old and new; a guest room could mix restored 17th-century frescoes and stone floors with a leather bedspread and halogen bell jars. Probably the most spectacular is Room 210 in the Haus zum Pferch, built circa 1300, which got a Baroque make-over in the 17th century. Modernists will cotton to Room 509 in the Haus zum Bankknecht, a bi-level aerie of glass panels and modern daubs that was once occupied by the city's butcher guild in centuries gone by. Set in the heart of Zürich's historic quarter, many of the houses look out into a communal courtyard, while others flaunt views of the Rennweg or the Augustinerkirche church. Four suites have private roof terraces; in the basement you can mosey into the wine cellar to sample and discuss the vintages. ⊠ *Rennweg 7, Kreis 1, CH-8001* ☎ *044/2242526* 🖷 *044/2242424* ⊕ *www.widderhotel.ch* ⇨ *42 rooms, 7 suites* ⚠ *2 restaurants, in-room fax, in-room safes, minibars, in-room broadband, in-room data ports, Wi-Fi, bar, library, meeting rooms* ⊟ *AE, DC, MC, V.*

$$$$ 🏨 **Zum Storchen.** The central location of this airy 600-year-old structure—
Fodor'sChoice tucked between the Fraumünster and St. Peters Kirche on the gull-stud-
★ ded bank of the Limmat River—is stunning. Rebuilt in 1939 and since renovated, the modern hotel is impeccable and intimately scaled. It has warmly appointed rooms, some with French windows that open over the water. Deluxe corner rooms, with views toward both river and lake, are worth fighting for, as are seats at the terrace café, where dessert is the panaromantic vista of the Altstadt. ⊠ *Weinpl. 2, Kreis 1, CH-8001* ☎ *044/2272727* 🖷 *044/2272700* ⊕ *www.storchen.ch* ⇨ *75 rooms* ⚠ *Restaurant, café, in-room fax, in-room safes, minibars, refrigerators, in-room broadband, in-room data ports, bar, business services, no-smoking rooms* ⊟ *AE, DC, MC, V* ⦿ *BP.*

$$$–$$$$ 🏨 **Haus zum Kindli.** This charming little bijou hotel could pass for a 3-D Laura Ashley catalog, with every cushion and bibelot as artfully styled as a magazine ad. The result is welcoming, intimate, and less contrived than many hotels' cookie-cutter decors. Even the restaurant downstairs is filled with English bookcases and floral prints. Guests earn 10% off menu prices, though they must vie with crowds of locals for a seat near the cabaret stage. ⊠ *Pfalzg. 1, Kreis 1, CH-8001* ☎ *043/*

8887676 ⌖ 043/8887677 ⊕ www.kindli.ch ⤳ 16 rooms ⌂ Restaurant, minibars, Wi-Fi, Internet room; no a/c ⊟ AE, DC, MC, V ⫟⃝⫠ BP.

$$$–$$$$ ⊡ **Seefeld.** In the heart of the lakeside district—close to restaurants, the opera, and movie theaters—this friendly, no-nonsense hotel is a real find. The guest rooms are comfortable, with hardwood floors, sleek furnishings, and sparkling bathrooms. Thanks to double-glazed windows, they are also quite quiet. The king-size beds are a treat not usually found in this country. ⊠ Seefeldstr. 63, Kreis 8, CH-8008 ☎ 044/3874141 ⌖ 044/3874151 ⊕ www.hotel-seefeld.ch ⤳ 64 rooms ⌂ In-room fax, in-room safes, minibars, in-room data ports, gym, bar, dry cleaning, laundry service, Internet room, no-smoking rooms; no a/c ⊟ AE, DC, MC, V ⫟⃝⫠ BP.

$$–$$$$ ⊡ **Neues Schloss.** Managed by the Arabella-Sheraton chain, this intimate hotel in the business district, just a few minutes' walk from Paradeplatz, offers a warm welcome, good service, and classic decor. Its Le Jardin restaurant (closed Sunday) is popular with theatergoers for its preperformance menu. ⊠ Stockerstr. 17, Kreis 1, CH-8022 ☎ 044/2869400 ⌖ 044/2869445 ⤳ 58 rooms ⌂ Restaurant, in-room fax, in-room safes, minibars, in-room data ports, Wi-Fi ⊟ AE, DC, MC, V.

$$$ ⊡ **Greulich.** The uncluttered rooms at this out-of-the-way designer hotel underscore the quietness of the neighborhood. Bathrooms are sunny and separated from the rooms by milky glass, making both spaces seem larger. The hotel wraps around a birch tree–filled courtyard, which in summer acts as the ground floor restaurant's main dining room. The kitchen offers Spanish-Swiss specialties, taking its mandate from the slow-food movement. ⊠ Herman-Greunlichstr. 56, Kreis 4 CH-8004 ☎ 043/2434243 ⌖ 043/2434200 ⊕ www.greulich.ch ⤳ 10 rooms, 8 suites ⌂ Restaurant, in-room broadband, in-room data ports, Internet room; no a/c ⊟ AE, DC, MC, V.

★ $$$ ⊡ **Rössli.** Ultrasmall but friendly, this hotel is in the heart of Oberdorf. The chic white-on-white decor mixes stone and wood textures with bold textiles and mosaic tiles. Extras include safes and bathrobes—unusual in this price range. Some singles are tiny, but all have double beds. The suite on the top floor has a roof terrace with a marvelous view of the Limmat and the Altstadt. ⊠ Rösslig. 7, Kreis 1, CH-8001 ☎ 044/2567050 ⌖ 044/2567051 ⊕ www.hotelroessli.ch ⤳ 16 rooms, 1 suite ⌂ In-room safes, minibars, in-room data ports, Wi-Fi, bar; no a/c ⊟ AE, DC, MC, V ⫟⃝⫠ BP.

$$$ ⊡ **Seehof.** Offering the best of both worlds, this lodging is in a quiet neighborhood, yet is conveniently close to the opera, movie theaters, and the lake. It's a favorite of hip business executives and travelers looking for seclusion. The interior's leitmotif is modern, minimal; the bright rooms' parquet floors and white walls and furnishings give them a fresh, crisp look. The bar downstairs has a good selection of wines; in summer a garden terrace adds to the charm. ⊠ Seehofstr. 11, Kreis 1, CH-8008 ☎ 044/2545757 ⌖ 044/2545758 ⊕ www.hotelseehof.ch ⤳ 19 rooms ⌂ In-room safes, minibars, in-room data ports, Wi-Fi, bar; no a/c ⊟ AE, DC, MC, V ⫟⃝⫠ BP.

$$–$$$ ⊡ **Lady's First.** Once a rooming house for country girls attending school in the big city, this boutique hotel has two floors that cater exclusively to women—a first in Switzerland. A stylish palette and steel furnishings join the original 1900 parquet floors and high stuccoed ceilings. The extensive wellness center offers saunas, massages, and various treatments, and the use of the facilities is included in the room rate. (Nonguests can also book spa time.) ⊠ *Mainaustr. 24, Kreis 8, CH-8008* ☎ *044/ 3808010* 🖷 *044/3808020* ⊕ *www.ladysfirst.ch* ⤴ *28 rooms* ⌂ *In-room broadband, in-room data ports, sauna, spa, steam room; no a/c* ☰ *AE, DC, MC, V* ⦿| *BP.*

$$-$$$ 🏨 **Zürichberg.** You may do a double-take when you walk into the lobby of the Schneckenhaus (Snail House) annex here and discover a miniversion of New York City's Guggenheim Museum's white ramp. Starkly and colorfully modern, this hotel—set about 3 mi outside the city center—is a change-of-pace place. The view from atop the prestigious hill that gives its name to both the neighborhood and the hotel is a big draw here; locals flock to the excellent Kiebitz restaurant to gaze down at the city from the outdoor terrace. But no one will cough at the crisply minimalistic rooms, all with parquet floors and many hued in deep orangey reds. Tram 6 heads straight to the hotel from the Hauptbahnhof. ⊠ *Orellistr. 21, Kreis 7, CH-8044* ☎ *044/2683535* 🖷 *044/2683545* ⊕ *www. zuerichberg.ch* ⤴ *66 rooms* ⌂ *2 restaurants, café, in-room fax, in-room safes, minibars, in-room data ports, dry cleaning, laundry service, Internet room, meeting rooms; no a/c* ☰ *AE, DC, MC, V* ⦿| *BP.*

$$ 🏨 **Adler.** Smack in the middle of Niederdorf, this is a smart, state-of-the-art hotel. From the gleaming lobby to the sleek, modular rooms, the ash-and-granite decor makes the most of tight spaces. Hand-painted murals of city landmarks remind you you're in Zürich. The hotel does not add a surcharge to phone calls made from the rooms. The restaurant off the lobby, Adler's Swiss Chuchi, is known locally as a great year-round place for fondue. ⊠ *Roseng. 10, Kreis 1, CH-8001* ☎ *044/ 2669696* 🖷 *044/2669669* ⊕ *www.hotel-adler.ch* ⤴ *52 rooms* ⌂ *Restaurant, in-room safes, minibars, in-room data ports, Wi-Fi; no a/c* ☰ *AE, DC, MC, V* ⦿| *BP.*

$-$$ 🏨 **Leoneck.** From the cowhide-covered front desk to the edelweiss-print curtains, this budget hotel wallows in its Swiss roots but balances this indulgence with no-nonsense conveniences such as built-in pine furniture and tile baths (albeit with cow-print shower curtains). There isn't much space to stretch out, though, and the furnishings sometimes show their age. The adjoining restaurant, Crazy Cow, slings out its own Swiss kitsch (Rösti-burgers) in an over-the-top decor of milk cans, miniature Matterhorns, and the ubiquitous black-and-white bovines. ⊠ *Leonhardstr. 1, Kreis 1, CH-8001* ☎ *044/2542222* 🖷 *044/2542200* ⊕ *www. leoneck.ch* ⤴ *78 rooms* ⌂ *Restaurant, in-room fax, in-room data ports, Wi-Fi, Internet room, no-smoking rooms; no a/c* ☰ *AE, DC, MC, V* ⦿| *BP.*

$-$$ 🏨 **Rex.** Its parking-garage architecture brightened up with assertive colors and jazz posters, this foursquare property has some businesspeople's necessities (computer connections, desks big enough to spread out your papers), without the depth of service offered by more expensive hotels. Its restaurant, the Blauer Apfel, draws a loyal, young professional lunch clientele to its cool, blue-halogen-lighted tables. It's three stops from Central heading north on Tram 7 or 15. ⊠ *Weinbergstr. 92, Kreis 6, CH-8006* ☎ *044/3602525* 🖷 *044/3602552* ⤴ *37 rooms* ⌂ *Restaurant,* *in-room safes, minibars, in-room data ports, Wi-Fi; no a/c* ▤ *AE, DC, MC, V* ◉❘ *BP.*

$ ⊞ **Limmathof.** This spare but welcoming hotel inhabits a handsome, historic building and is ideally placed on the Limmatquai, minutes from the Hauptbahnhof and steps from the Limmatquai and Central tram stops. All rooms have tile bathrooms and plump down comforters. There's an old-fashioned wood-paneled Weinstube (wine bar) and a bright vegetarian restaurant that doubles as the breakfast room. ⊠ *Limmatquai 142, Kreis 1, CH-8023* ☎ *044/2676040* ≞ *044/2620217* ⊕ *www. limmathof.com* ⇴ *62 rooms* ♿ *Restaurant, in-room data ports, Weinstube; no a/c* ▤ *AE, DC, MC, V* ◉❘ *BP.*

$ ⊞ **Zic-Zac Rock Hotel.** Perfectly set in the lively Niederdorf, this hotel lets you indulge your inner groupie. All rooms are named after rock personalities, from Lenny Kravitz to U2, and decorated accordingly. Framed albums, portraits, and gold records hang on the pastel yellow walls. Furnishings are no-frills but comfortable; most rooms share showers and toilets. The American restaurant and bar downstairs draw plenty of nonguests and on weekends the hotel fairly throbs with bass. ⊠ *Marketg. 17, Kreis 1, CH-8001* ☎ *044/2612181* ≞ *044/2612175* ⊕ *www. ziczac.ch* ⇴ *49 rooms, 7 with bath, 2 suites* ♿ *2 restaurants, bar, airport shuttle; no a/c* ▤ *AE, DC, MC, V.*

¢–$ ⊞ **Kafischnaps.** Away from the throb of downtown but still only a 15-minute walk back, this is the best deal in town for those on a budget. Rooms are spartan but beautifully designed, each with its own color scheme. Beds are very comfy, with down quilts and soft pillows. The smoky café downstairs doubles as the reception area and breakfast room. Reservations can only be made online. ⊠ *Kornhausstr. 57, Kreis 6, CH-8037* ☎ *043/5388116* ⊕ *www.kafischnaps.ch* ⇴ *5 rooms* ♿ *Café, Wi-Fi; no a/c, no phones, no TV in some rooms* ▤ *AE, DC, MC, V* ◉❘ *BP.*

¢ ⊞ **Etap.** Working on the principle that cheap should only mean inexpensive, this chain hotel is a dependable pick. Every room around the world is exactly the same: violet-and-gray walls and carpeting, one double bed, a single bunk set above it, and shower and toilet in separate, immaculate fiberglass modules. The rate for two is always the same. The location gives this branch an edge—it's in the hip, industrial Zürich West neighborhood. Take Tram 4 or 13 from the Hauptbahnhof to Escher Wyss Platz; the Etap is within easy walking distance from there. ⊠ *Technoparkstr. 2, Kreis 5, CH-8005* ☎ *044/2762000* ≞ *044/2762001* ⊕ *www.etaphotel.com* ⇴ *160 rooms* ♿ *No a/c, no room phones* ▤ *AE, MC, V.*

NIGHTLIFE & THE ARTS

Nightlife

Of all the Swiss cities, Zürich has the liveliest nightlife. The Niederdorf is Zürich's nightlife district, with cut-rate hotels, strip joints, and bars crowding along Marktgasse, which becomes Niederdorfstrasse. On Thursday and weekend nights, the streets flow with a rowdy crowd of club and bar hoppers. In Zürich West, the locales are all a shade hipper. In winter things wind down between midnight and 2 AM, but come summer most places stay open until 4 AM.

Bars

DOWNTOWN A welcoming bar that tips a wink to Spain's most famous film director, **Almodobar** (✉ Bleicherweg 68, Kreis 1 ☎ 043/8444488) is as eclectic as its clientele. Sitting on the zebra-skin stools in the bar you'll probably spy young designers in leather pants and faux-fur jackets. **Barfüsser** (✉ Spitalg. 14, Kreis 1 ☎ 044/2514064), established in 1956, claims to be one of the oldest gay bars in Europe. It has comfortable lounge chairs and space to mix and mingle. There's also excellent sushi. **Barrique** (✉ Marktg. 17, Kreis 1 ☎ 044/2525941) is a vinotheque featuring a world-renowned wine list. **Café Central Bar** (✉ Central 1, Kreis 1 ☎ 044/2515555), in the Hotel Central, is a popular neo–Art Deco café by day and a piano bar by night.

> ### YOU SAY YOU WANT A REVOLUTION?
>
> Serving a young, arty crowd until 4 AM, Odéon (Limmatquai 2, Kreis 1, 044/2511650) is a cultural icon, a place where Mata Hari danced, Lenin and Trotsky plotted the revolution, and James Joyce scrounged drinks. It gets gayer as the evening wears on, but everyone goes because the place is so chic.

Cranberry (✉ Metzgerg. 3, Kreis 1 ☎ 044/2612772) stocks broad selections of rum and port; it also has an upstairs cigar room. The **James Joyce Pub** (✉ Pelikanstr. 8, off Bahnhofstr., Kreis 1 ☎ 044/2211828) is a beautifully paneled Irish pub where the wood is as dark as the Guinness. The **Jules Verne Panorama Bar** (✉ Uraniastr. 9, Kreis 1 ☎ 043/8886666) is a wine bar with a wraparound view of downtown. The narrow bar at the **Kronenhalle** (✉ Rämistr. 4, Kreis 1 ☎ 044/2511597) draws mobs of well-heeled locals and internationals for its prize-winning cocktails. At **Purpur** (✉ Seefeldstr. 9, Kreis 2 ☎ 044/4192066), a Moroccan-style lounge, you can take your drinks lying down on a heap of throw pillows while DJs mix ambient sound.

ZÜRICH WEST At **Basilica** (✉ Heinrichstr. 237, Kreis 5 ☎ 043/3669383), hipsters lounge in an Italianate setting of red velvet and marble statues. Once you get past the name, you'll find that **Hard One** (✉ Heinrichstr. 269, Kreis 5 ☎ 044/4441000) has great views of Zürich West and a good choice of champagnes.

Not just for intellectuals, **I.Q.** (✉ Hardstr. 316, Kreis 5 ☎ 044/4407440) has a fully stocked whiskey bar. **Spheres** (✉ Hardturmstr. 66, Kreis 5 ☎ 044/4406622) is a bar and bookstore with a great selection of international magazines.

Dancing

The medieval-theme **Adagio** (✉ Gotthardstr. 5, Kreis 1 ☎ 044/2063666) books classic rock, jazz, and tango musicians for well-dressed thirtysomethings. Zürich's exclusive set meets at **Indochine** (✉ Limmatstr. 275, Kreis 5 ☎ 044/4481111), whose gorgeous interior evokes Southeast Asia. The music floats between pop, disco, house, and techno. **Kaufleuten** (⊠ Pelikanstr. 18, Kreis 1 ☎ 044/2253333) is a local landmark that draws a well-dressed, upwardly mobile crowd. It's a popular performance space for established artists such as Prince and Nina Hagen who are looking for an intimate venue. The Rolling Stones once showed up unannounced for an impromptu concert.

Mascotte (⊠ Theaterstr. 10, Kreis 1 ☎ 044/2524481), blasting everything from funk and soul to house and techno, is popular with all ages. A legendary techno club, **Oxa Dance Hall** (⊠ Andreastr. 70, Oerlikon, Kreis 1 ☎ 044/3116033) draws thousands of casual young Swiss who dance all night (and often well into the next day). Take Tram 14 from the Hauptbahnhof to the Oerlikon terminus.

Jazz Clubs

Casa Bar (⊠ Münsterg. 30, Kreis 1 ☎ 044/2612002 ⊕ www.casabar. ch), long the sole bastion of jazz here, now has excellent competition. **Moods** (⊠ Schiffbaustr. 6, Kreis 5 ☎ 044/2768000) hosts international and local acts in the hip Zürich West district. The popular **Widder Bar** (⊠ Widderg. 6, Kreis 1 ☎ 044/2242411), in the Widder Hotel, attracts local celebrities with its 800-count "library of spirits" and top-name acts.

The Arts

Despite its small population, Zürich is a big city when it comes to the arts; it supports a top-rank orchestra, an opera company, and a theater. Check *Zürich News,* published weekly in English and German, or "Züri-tipp," a German-language supplement to the Friday edition of the daily newspaper *Tages Anzeiger.* The city's annual **Züricher Festspiele**— a celebration of opera, ballet, concerts, theater, and art exhibitions— runs from late June through mid-July. You'll need to book well ahead for this—details are available from the tourist office or **Info- und Ticketoffice** (⊠ Postfach, CH-8023 ☎ 044/2063434). Tickets to opera, concert, and theater events can also be bought from the tourist office. Tickets for almost any event can be purchased in advance by telephone from **Ticketcorner** (☎ 0900/800800). Depending on the event, **Musik Hug** (⊠ Limmatquai 28–30, Kreis 1 ☎ 044/2694100) makes reservations. The music store **Jecklin** (⊠ Rämistr. 30, Kreis 1 ☎ 044/2537676) promotes and sells tickets for various music events.

Film

Movies in Zürich are serious business, with films presented in the original language. Check newspapers and the ubiquitous posters, and watch for the initials *E/d/f,* which means an English-language version with German (Deutsch) and French subtitles. **Metropole** (⊠ Badenerstr. 16, Kreis 4 ☎ 0900/556789) has a great sound system and the largest screen in Zürich. The **Zurich Film Festival** takes place every year in early October (⊕ www.zurichfilmfestival.org).

Music

The Zürich Tonhalle Orchestra, named for its concert hall, the **Tonhalle** (⊠ Claridenstr. 7, Kreis 1 ☎ 044/2063434), which was inaugurated by Brahms in 1895, enjoys international acclaim. There are also solo recitals and chamber programs here. The season runs from September through July; tickets sell out quickly, so book through the Tonhalle.

Opera

The permanent company at the **Opernhaus** (✉ Theaterpl., Kreis 1 ☎ 044/2686666) is widely recognized and difficult to drop in on if you haven't booked well ahead, but single seats can sometimes be secured at the last minute. Performances are held from September through July.

Theater

The venerable **Schauspielhaus Pfauenbühne** (✉ Rämistr. 34, Kreis 7 ☎ 044/2587777) has a long history of cutting-edge performances with a strong inventive streak; during World War II this was the only German-language theater in Europe that remained independent. Nowadays its main stage presents finely tuned productions (in German), while experimental works are given in the Keller (cellar). Its sister stage, the **Schauspielhaus Schiffbauhalle** (✉ Schiffbaustr. 4, Kreis 1 ☎ 044/2587777), is home to large-scale productions, also in German.

During late August and early September the **Theaterspektakel** takes place, with circus tents housing avant-garde theater and experimental performances on the lawns by the lake at Mythenquai.

SHOPPING

Many of Zürich's designer boutiques lie hidden along the narrow streets between Bahnhofstrasse and the Limmat River. Quirky bookstores and antiques shops lurk in the sloping cobblestone alleyways leading off Niedorfstrasse and Oberdorfstrasse. The fabled Bahnhofstrasse—famous because it's reputedly the most expensive street in the world—is dominated by large department stores and extravagantly priced jewelry shops.

The store-lined **Bahnhofstrasse** concentrates much of Zürich's most expensive (from elegant to gaudy) goods at the Paradeplatz end. There's another pocket of good stores around **Löwenstrasse,** southwest of the Hauptbahnhof. The **Niederdorf** offers less expensive, younger fashions, as well as antiques and antiquarian bookshops. The west bank's Altstadt, along **Storchengasse** near the Münsterhof, is a focal point for high-end designer stores.

> ## AN "A" FOR PACKAGING
>
> It's hard to fight constant cravings for decadent chocolates when you're walking around Zürich thanks to the many chocolate confiseries, especially the branches of Teuscher (Storcheng. 9, 044/2115153; Bahnhofstr. 46, 044/2111390; Jelmoli, Bahnhofstr. at Seidengasse, 044/2204387; Café Schober, Napfg. 4, 1 044/2518060). Not only do these serve up elaborate ice cream sundaes and cakes, the shops blaze with boxes of pralines and champagne truffles all wrapped up in stunning fabrics, silk roses, and troll figurines. The beautiful boxes make a fine keepsake.

Many city-center stores are open weekdays 9–8, Saturday 8–4. Most close on Sunday, with the exception of the shops at the Hauptbahnhof and the Stadelhofen train station. Many smaller shops, particularly in the Niederdorf area, open later in the morning or the early afternoon and are closed entirely on Monday.

Department Stores

COOP (⊠ Bellevuepl., Kreis 1 ☎ 043/2688700) is cheap and cheerful. **Globus** (⊠ Bahnhofstr. and Löwenpl., Kreis 1 ☎ 044/2266060) sells men's and women's designer clothes and housewares. There is also a pricey but irresistible delicatessen in the basement. **Jelmoli** (⊠ Bahnhofstr. and Seideng., Kreis 1 ☎ 044/2204411) has top-notch brand-name merchandise and swarms of staffers. **Manor** (⊠ Bahnhofstr. 75, Kreis 1 ☎ 044/2295699) is dependable and affordable.

Markets

At **Bürkliplatz** (⊠ Lake end of Bahnhofstr., Kreis 1), there's a flea market from 6 to 3:30 every Saturday from May to October. There's a curio market on the **Rosenhof** (⊠ Niederdorfstr. and Marktg., Kreis 1) every Thursday from 10 to 9 and Saturday from 10 to 4 between April and Christmas. A **Christmas market** is held in the main train station and along Niederdorfstrasse starting in early December.

Specialty Items

Books

The antiquarian bookshops in the upper streets of the Niederdorf area are rich with discoveries—and most have selections of books in English. **Biblion** (⊠ Kirchg. 40, Kreis 1 ☎ 044/2613830) specializes in antique books and binding. The **EOS Buchantiquariat Benz** (⊠ Kirchg. 17 and 22, Kreis 1 ☎ 044/2615750) is a superb general bookshop spread over two storefronts. Both sell secondhand books as well as antiquarian tomes. The eclectic **medieval art & vie** (⊠ Spiegelg. 29, Kreis 1 ☎ 044/2524720), sells books, music, and replicas of medieval artifacts, including reproduction medieval shoes, jewelry, and water bottles.

Collectibles

In the center of town virtually every street has some kind of antiques or collectibles shop. Especially intriguing are "modern antiques" shops, which carry odds and ends from recent decades. **1000-Objekte** (⊠ Schoffelg. 3, Kreis 1 ☎ 079/6605788) has modern and antique glass and collectibles. **Eselstein** (⊠ Stadelhoferstr. 42, Kreis 1 ☎ 044/2611056) stocks items from the 1950s through the 1970s ranging from lamp shades to standing ashtrays, plus such finds as Russian samovars. **Hannibal** (⊠ St. Jakobstr. 39, Kreis 4 ☎ 044/2426044) is a delightful lumber room of postwar vases, chairs, pedal-operated trash bins, and rotary-dial telephones (remember them?).

Food

Inhale tempting smells from around the world at **H. Schwarzenbach** (⊠ Münsterg. 19, Kreis 1 ☎ 044/2611315), an old-style, open-bin shop with oak shelves lined with coffee, dried fruits, nuts, and grains. Whet your palate at **Scot & Scotch** (✉ Wohllebg. 7, Kreis 1 ☎ 044/2119060) with any one of 400 whiskeys from around the globe (nosings and tastings on request). **Teuscher** (✉ Storcheng. 9, Kreis 1 ☎ 044/2115153 ✉ Bahnhofstr. 46, Kreis 1 ☎ 044/2111390 ✉ Jelmoli, Bahnhofstr. at Seidengasse, Kreis 1 ☎ 044/2204387 ✉ Cafe Schober, Napfg. 4, Kreis 1 ☎ 044/2518060) specializes in elaborate ice-cream sundaes and cakes.

Men's Clothes

Zürich's most elegant department store, **Grieder** (✉ Bahnhofstr. 30, Kreis 1 ☎ 044/2243636), carries designs by Armani and Zegna, among others. **Trois Pommes** (✉ Storcheng. 6, Kreis 1 ☎ 044/2124710) is the central boutique of a series of designer shops scattered through the Storchengasse area; the racks are heavily stacked with such high-profile international designers as Jil Sander, Versace, Donna Karan, and Dolce & Gabbana.

Toys

AHA (✉ Spiegelg. 14, Kreis 1 ☎ 044/2510560) sells hypnotic optical-illusion gifts in styles and sizes to suit all ages. **Pastorini Spielzeug** (✉ Weinpl. 3, Kreis 1 ☎ 044/2287070) is a four-story mother lode of original and creative playthings, many hand-carved.

Women's Clothes

Beatrice Dreher Presents (✉ Gassen 14, Kreis 1 ☎ 044/2115548) carries Chloë and Krizia. You can snag some of last season's fashions at deep discounts at Trois Pommes' bargain-basement **Check Out** (✉ Tödistr. 44, Kreis 1 ☎ 044/2027226), where DKNY, Calvin Klein, and Dolce & Gabbana are jumbled on the racks. **En Soie** (✉ Strehlg. 26, Kreis 1 ☎ 044/2115902) stocks gleaming, sometimes raw-textured silks, but although the fabrics are sophisticated, there's still an element of whimsy. At **Sonja Rieser** (✉ Froschaug. 2, Kreis 1 ☎ 044/2513847) the selection of gorgeous handmade hats runs from elegant to wild. For the absolute latest, go to the main **Trois Pommes** (✉ Storcheng. 6, Kreis 1 ☎ 044/2110621) for Jil Sander, Alaïa, and Comme des Garçons.

ZÜRICH ESSENTIALS

Transportation

BY AIR

Unique Zürich Airport is Switzerland's most important airport and the 10th-busiest in the world. It's 11 km (7 mi) north of the city.

🖪 Airport Information **Unique Zürich Airport** ☎ 0900/300313.

AIRPORT TRANSFERS It's easy to take a Swiss Federal Railways feeder train directly from the airport to Zürich's Hauptbahnhof (main station). Tickets cost 5.80 SF one way, and trains run every 10–15 minutes, arriving in 10 minutes. Taxis cost dearly in Zürich. A ride into the center costs 50 to 60 SF and takes around 20 minutes. Most larger hotels have their own shuttles to and from the airport.

🖪 Train Information **Hauptbahnhof** ☎ 0900/300300 ⊕ www.rail.ch.

CARRIERS Some 60 airlines, including American, United, and, of course, Swiss Air Lines, known as Swiss, serve the Unique Zürich Airport. You can also catch domestic and European flights out of Unique on Swiss.
🔝 Airlines & Contacts **Swiss** ☎ 0848/852000.

BY CAR

The A2 expressway from Basel to Zürich leads directly into the city. A1 continues east to St. Gallen. Approaching from the south and the St. Gotthard route, take A14 from Luzern (Lucerne); after a brief break of highway (E41) it feeds into A3 and approaches the city along the lake's western shore. You can take A3 all the way up from Chur in Graubünden.

BY TAXI

Taxis are very expensive, with an 8 SF minimum but no charge for additional passengers. An available taxi is indicated by an illuminated rooftop light. You can order a cab by calling Züri Taxi or Alpha Taxi.
🔝 Taxi Companies **Alpha Taxi** ☎ 044/7777777. **Züri Taxi** ☎ 044/2222222.

BY TRAIN

There are straightforward connections and several express routes leading directly into Zürich from Basel, Geneva, Bern, and Lugano. All roads lead to the Hauptbahnhof in the city center.
🔝 Train Information **Hauptbahnhof** ☎ 0900/300300 ⊕ www.rail.ch.

BY TRAM

ZVV, the tram service in Zürich, is swift and timely. It runs from 5:30 AM to midnight, every 6 minutes at peak hours, every 12 minutes at other times. All-day passes cost 7.20 SF and can be purchased from the same vending machines at the stops that post maps and sell one-ride tickets; you must buy your ticket before you board. Free route plans are available from VBZ Züri-Linie (Zürich Public Transport) offices, located at major crossroads (Paradepl., Bellevue, Central, Limmatpl.). Stops are clearly signposted. The **Zurich Card** (15 SF) gets you 24 hours of travel in the greater Zürich area on all trams, buses, trains, boats, cable cars and cog-wheel trains, plus free entry into over 40 museums. It's available from **Tourist information** (⊠ Hauptbahnhof, Kreis 1, CH-8023 ☎ 044/2154000).
🔝 **ZVV** ☎ 0848/988988 ⊕ www.zvv.ch.

Contacts & Resources

EMERGENCIES

Dial ☎ 117 for the police in case of an emergency, or ☎ 144 for an ambulance. Doctors and dentists can be referred in case of emergency by the English-speaking operators who staff the *Notfalldienst* (Emergency Service) phones. In Kreis 1, the pharmacy Bellevue Apotheke is open 24 hours.
🔝 **Bellevue Apotheke** ⊠ Theaterstr. 14, Kreis 1 ☎ 044/2525600. **SOS Aerzte** (Emergency House Calls) ☎ 044/3604444. **Zürich Universitätsspital** ⊠ Schmelzbergstr. 8, Kreis 1 ☎ 044/2551111.

ENGLISH-LANGUAGE MEDIA
Orell Füssli's the Bookshop has a wide selection of new books in English.
🗐 Bookstores **Orell Füssli, The Bookshop** ✉ Bahnhofstr. 70, Kreis 1 ☎ 044/2110444.

INTERNET & MAIL
🗐 Internet & Mail Information A network of Wi-Fi **Hotspots** is rapidly growing throughout Switzerland ⊕ www.hotspots.ch ⊕ www.swisshotspots.ch; here are two of the best in Zürich: **e-café urania** ✉ Uraniastr. 3, Kreis 1, Zürich ☎ 044/2103311; **Quanta** ✉ Limmatquai 94, entrance on Niederdorfstr. Kreis 1 ☎ 044/2607266. **Die Post, Fraumünster post office** ✉ Kappelerg. 1, Kreis 1. **Die Post, maintrain station post office** ✉ Bahnhofpl. 15, Kreis 1.

TOUR OPTIONS
BICYCLE TOURS From May to September, Friday through Sunday at 10:30 AM, you can take a 2½-hour bike tour from the opera house for 25 SF. The tour is given in German and English; bikes are supplied. Reservations are necessary only for four or more people. **Zurich by Bike** (☎ 076/3087016 ⊕ www.zurichbybike.ch).

BUS TOURS Three introductory bus tours with English commentary are offered by the tourist office. Cityrama's daily tour covers the main city sights and then goes on to Rapperswil to see the rose gardens and castle. The trip lasts three hours, leaving at 11 AM; it costs 45 SF. The Zürich Trolley Experience (32 SF) gives a good general idea of the city in two hours; it leaves at 9:45 AM, noon, and 2 PM. The Combo Tour goes farther and includes a train trip to the top of the nearby Üetliberg. This is also a daily tour, given at 9:45 AM, noon, and 2 PM; it takes four hours and costs 40 SF. All tours start from the Hauptbahnhof. **Tourist information** (✉ Hauptbahnhof, Kreis 1, CH-8023 ☎ 044/2154000).

The tourist bureau also offers day trips by coach to Luzern, up the Rigi, Titlis, or Pilatus mountains, and the Jungfrau.

WALKING TOURS Daily from June to October, the tourist office offers two-hour walking tours (20 SF) that start at the Hauptbahnhof. You can join a group with English-language commentary, but the times vary, so call ahead. **Tourist information** (✉ Hauptbahnhof, Kreis 1, CH-8023 ☎ 044/2154000).

VISITOR INFORMATION
🗐 Tourist Information **Hotel reservations** ✉ Hauptbahnhof, Kreis 1, CH-8023 ☎ 044/2154040 🖶 044/2154044. **Tourist information** ✉ Hauptbahnhof, Kreis 1, CH-8023 ☎ 044/2154000.

Eastern Switzerland & Liechtenstein

APPENZELL, SCHAFFHAUSEN, ST. GALLEN

Snowboarding in Heidiland. Ascent to Mt. Gonzen with snowshoes.

WORD OF MOUTH

"Stein-am-Rhein is amazing. The buildings in the old town are covered with paintings from the 16th century—absolutely beautiful"

—bettyk

"In the spring, EVERYPLACE in Switzerland (even in the middle of some of the cities) has cows on rolling green hills! However, the most typical "Heidi" place is in and around Appenzell, with its late spring/early summer processions of cows wearing flowers and bells. In Switzerland, if you want cows, you got 'em!"   —LynnneUS

WELCOME TO EASTERN SWITZERLAND & LIECHTENSTEIN

TOP REASONS TO GO

★ **A Bibliophile's Paradise:** Pretend you live in the Rococo richness of the library at the Abbey of St. Gallen, with all the time in the world to read its 100,000 priceless books.

★ **The Cows Finally Come Home:** Take part in an Appenzell Alpfahrt festival, when cows are herded up into the nearby mountain slopes (in spring) or back down (in fall) by locals in their embroidered finery.

★ **Fast Forward to the 1400s:** Open a new window in Schaffhausen—the *City of Oriel Windows*—then discover the medieval magic of the preserved old town of Stein-am-Rhein.

★ **The Rhine Maidens:** See Europe's 3rd-largest river in its adolescent phase as it snakes its way to Germany. Take a lunch-boat ride, cycle along the river's grassy banks, or visit storybook castles.

★ **Lofty Liechtenstein:** Yes, it's fun to go to a tiny country for a day and get your passport stamped but keep in mind it's mostly about high-finance banking here.

1 **Schaffhausen & the Rhine.** A trip from the Rhine falls through **Schaffhausen** and up-river to **Stein-am-Rhein** transports you back to medieval and Renaissance times. The house facades, alive with colorful frescoes and oriel windows, attract tourists by the busload.

2 **Bodensee to St. Gallen.** Vast and windy, **Bodensee**—the famous Lake Constance—offers a resort-town mellowness compared to the nearby city of **St. Gallen**, whose biggest draw is the manuscript-stuffed Abbey library (as well as a decent 18th-century cathedral, a picturesque old town full of hearty restaurants, and its own symphony orchestra). Head south to **Appenzell**, whose idyllic rural appeal is literally milked to the fullest, with museums devoted to cheese-making, cow herding, and the crafts of local dairy farmers.

GERMANY
Schaffhausen
Neuhausen am Rheinfall
Untersee
Stein-am-Rhein
A7
A1
Winterthur
Wil

Schaffhausen, town of bridges

Taking a break near the Rhine

3 Liechtenstein & the Walensee. If you don't brake quickly enough for tiny **Liechtenstein**, you may wind up in Austria. But you'll want to slow down for this fairy-tale realm lorded over by a princely castle (which may be viewed inside only by its princely family), a bevy of banks, and a post office famed for its unique stamps. Head back into Switzerland to see the spectacular Walensee lake.

GETTING ORIENTED

Quiet cousins to fast-paced, international Zürich, the eastern cantons often play the wallflower to more spectacular touristic regions, but are mistakenly overlooked: lush and hilly, with orchards and gardens, its north dominated by the romantic Rhine, towered over by Mt. Säntis (8,200 feet), and dotted with lovely hidden lakes—as well as the enormous Bodensee (Lake Constance)—the region is as varied as it is beautiful.

Konstanz
Gottliben Kreuzlingen
Bodensee
Roamanshorn
Frauenfeld
Amriswil
Rorschach
A1
Gossau   St. Gallen   A13
2
Appenzell   Rankweil   *Rhein River*
Wattwil   **AUSTRIA**
ALPSTEIN
Nesslau   Haag
CHURFIRSTEN **3** Buchs **LIECHTENSTEIN**
A3   Sargans   Vaduz
Walensee
Näfels *FLUMSER BERGE* Triesenberg
A3 A13 Malbun
Sargans
Landquart

0   10 mi
0   10 km

The main street in Appenzell

EASTERN SWITZERLAND PLANNER

How's the Weather?

The four seasons are clearly defined here: nicely balanced periods of sun and rain bring springtime blossoms and flowers with a vengeance, thanks to the many orchards and fields.

Summer temperatures zoom upward to between 70 and 90 degrees, depending if it's a dry or wet one (although in recent years dry summers seem to be prevailing).

The abundance of deciduous trees in this region means splashes of color in a crisp-aired, windy fall.

Winter dumps lots of snow and brings temperatures hovering around -5 Celsius in town, down to -25 on some mountaintops.

Summers in eastern Switzerland provide the best weather and activities but also the greatest traffic, both on roads and in towns; spring and fall are good alternatives.

Though most places in this region are not too terribly crowded even in summer, Stein-am-Rhein is an exception.

It receives enough coach tours to virtually paralyze the village with pedestrians during high season; if you go, arrive earlier in the day or come on a weekday when crowds are a bit thinner.

Happily, the region is among Switzerland's most rural and quiet country roads beckon in all seasons.

Making the Most of Your Stay

This is the lazy part of Switzerland; a great place to enjoy the scenery while toodeling down back roads or gazing out the train window at the greenery on the way to the next quiet town. Take along a stack of books to read on the hotel balcony or a picnic lunch for your stop in a meadow en route.

In winter, pick a ski resort or a large town such as Schaffhausen or St. Gallen as your home base—unless you're looking for complete, peaceful seclusion, in other words, inescapable boredom.

In summer, think of the many swimming opportunities offered by the Rhine and the Bodensee, pack at least one bathing suit, and take a leisurely lunch-boat ride. St. Gallen is the best place from which to take day trips to the region's highlights if you have a car.

Go "Flea"-ing

Some of the least developed land is in Eastern Switzerland, which means plenty of old houses stuffed with plenty of old furnishings, art pieces, and gewgaws.

This being Switzerland, commerce has responded: outdoor/indoor flea markets abound, as do secondhand thrift shops, called Bröckenhäuser (Brockenhaus in the singular)—every town has at least one.

Antiques dealers regularly troll the area, but it's still possible to find a bargain here and there, especially in out-of-the-way villages. Let the hunt begin!

Getting Around

Although Eastern Switzerland is topographically the country's lowest region, it's still fairly rugged. It won't take long to see the major sights, but they are spread throughout the region, so leave time each day to be in transit. Train travel here is more complicated than in neighboring areas, requiring more intercity changes, so plan your itinerary accordingly. If you're planning to visit all the locations mentioned in this chapter as part of a circular tour, the easiest way to see the sights is with a car. The towns are all well-connected by a network of roads—from expressways to narrow local routes meandering through the countryside—but because many regions are separated from one another by mountains or steep hills, public transportation is circuitous from one town to the other. Zürich is the public transportation hub for the four regions hereabouts: Schaffhausen/Stein-am-Rhein; St. Gallen/Appenzell; the Toggenburg Valley; and Liechtenstein. Schaffhausen gets you the quickest to Stein-am-Rhein, the Rhine Falls, Arenenberg, Gottlieben, and Kreuzlingen/Konstanz; St. Gallen is also close to Arenenberg, Gottlieben and Kreuzlingen/Konstanz, as well as being central to Rorschach and the Appenzell region.

Hanging in the 'Hood

While the rest of the world hikes through the Berner Oberland in summer, many locals, especially from nearby Zürich, head for Mt. Säntis and its neighboring hills in Eastern Switzerland.

The area offers something for all levels, whether you're panting to hike the 4½ hours all the way up to the top of the 1,500-foot peak, take an hour-long stroll around the cow pastures of the nearby hills, or drive directly to one of the many country restaurants for an outdoor pint, a meal and a look at the skyhigh views, it's all quickly reachable, some of it in less than an hour.

Finding a Place to Stay

During the summer high season, Stein-am-Rhein and Gottlieben are chock full because there's no town around to catch the overflow—book early. St. Gallen has a large convention center; you should make your reservation in advance here, too, because you never know who may be in town. Prices also tend to escalate during conventions. Other destinations will usually still have a room or two on short notice. For romantic getaways, consider the castellated Drachenburg and Waaghuus in Gottlieben, a teeny-tiny village on the misty bank of the Rhine, or the secluded Park-Hotel Sonnenhof with a magnificent view in Liechtenstein, vacation home to local celebrities, international jet-setters, and affluent businesspeople.

More and more hotels in this region are throwing away their Formica and commissioning hand-painted furniture to complement the beams they've so carefully exposed. However, bargain renovations tend toward the crisp if anonymous look of light tongue-in-groove pine paneling and earth-tone ceramic baths. The prices are somewhat lower on average here, with only slight variations from high to low season. Half board is rarely included.

WHAT IT COSTS In Swiss francs

	$$$$	$$$	$$	$	¢
Restaurants	over 60 SF	40 SF–60 SF	25 SF–40 SF	15 SF–25 SF	under 15 SF
Hotels	over 350 SF	250 SF–350 SF	175 SF–250 SF	100 SF–175 SF	under 100 SF

Restaurant prices are per person for a main course at dinner. Hotel prices are for two people in a standard double room in high season, including tax and service.

Updated by
Katrin Gygax

DESPITE ITS PROXIMITY TO ZÜRICH, this Germanic region, with Germany to the north and Austria to the east, maintains a personality apart—a personality that often plays the wallflower when upstaged by more spectacular touristy regions. Happily, the truth is that the region does not lack for a satisfying variety: its north dominated by the romantic Rhine, the region is lush with orchards and gardens, a generous share of mountains (including Mt. Säntis, at roughly 8,200 feet), and lovely hidden lakes, as well as the enormous Bodensee (Lake Constance). Because the east draws fewer crowds, those who do venture in find a pleasant surprise: this is Switzerland sans kitsch, sans the hard sell, where the people live out a natural, graceful combination of past and present. And although it's a prosperous region, with its famous textiles and fruit industry, its inns and restaurants cost noticeably less than those in adjoining areas.

The region covers a broad sociological spectrum, from the thriving city of St. Gallen, with its magnificent Baroque cathedral, to the plateau valley of Appenzell, where women were prohibited from voting in cantonal elections until the federal court intervened on their behalf in 1991 (federal law had granted women the national vote in 1971). On the last Sunday in April in Appenzell city, you still can witness the *Landsgemeinde,* an open-air election for cantonal issues counted by a show of hands.

Architecture along the Rhine resembles that of old Germany and Austria, frequent features being half-timbers and rippling red-tile roofs. In cities like Schaffhausen, masterpieces of medieval frescoes decorate town houses, many of which have ornate first-floor bay windows called oriels. In the country, farmhouses are often covered with fine, feathery wooden shingles as narrow as Popsicle sticks, which weathering has turned to chinchilla gray. Appenzell has its own famous architecture: tidy, narrow boxes painted cream, with repeated rows of windows and matching wood panels. The very countryside itself—conical green hills, fruit trees, belled cows, neat yellow cottages—resembles the naive art it inspires.

Exploring Eastern Switzerland

The cantons of Glarus, Schaffhausen, Thurgau, St. Gallen, and Appenzell harbor some of Switzerland's oldest traditions. Although the cities have plenty of energy, the countryside in these parts changes little over the years. In the northern part of the region are the old Rhine city of Schaffhausen, the dramatic Rheinfall, and the preserved medieval town of Stein-am-Rhein. The Bodensee occupies the northeastern corner of Switzerland, just below Germany. Farther south are the textile center of St. Gallen, the hilly Appenzell region, and the resort area of the Toggenburg Valley. The tiny principality of Liechtenstein lies just across the eastern border, within easy driving distance.

SCHAFFHAUSEN & THE RHINE

Known to many Swiss as Rheinfallstadt (Rhine Falls City), Schaffhausen is the seat of the country's northernmost canton, which also shares its name. To gaze upon the grand mist-sprayed Rheinfall, arguably the most famous waterfall in Europe, is to look straight into the romantic past of Switzerland. Goethe and Wordsworth were just two of the world's best-known wordsmiths to immortalize the falls' powerful grandeur.

Schaffhausen

▶ ★ **To & From:** *From/to Zurich, the fastest connection is the once-hourly S16 commuter train, which takes 58 minutes and costs 17.60 SF each way. There are two trains every hour to and from St. Gallen that connect through Winterthur (travel time 86 min.; 27 SF each way). The S3 commuter does a scenic milk run up the Rhine to the Bodensee and St. Gallen every hour, stopping at almost every town along the way. Another favorite method of travel is by boat up the Rhine to the Bodensee. There are three to four (on Sun.) boats daily: the first leaves Schaffhausen at 9:10, the last returns from Kreuzlingen at 3 PM, or at 5 PM going only as far as Stein-am-Rhein (30 SF for an all-day pass; the boats also offer lunch; Schweizerische Schifffahrtsgesellschaft Untersee und Rhein, 052/6340888, www.urh.ch). The Schweizerische Bodensee-Schiffahrtsgesellschaft (071/ 4667888, www.sbsag.ch) line also caters to guests traveling the Bodensee (Lake Constance). For departure times and prices for trains and buses for most destinations in this chapter, check with www.sbb.ch—the main Swiss public transportation Web site—or call 0900/300300 (1,19 SF per minute). Remember, if you have a Swiss Pass or another rail-discounting card, it also applies to the buses. Schaffhausen is 48 km (29 mi) northeast of Zürich, 20 km (12 mi) west of Stein-am-Rhein.*

A city of about 74,000, Schaffhausen was, from the early Middle Ages on, an important depot for river cargoes, which—because of the rapids and waterfall farther along—had to be unloaded there. The name *Schaffhausen* is probably derived from the skiff houses along the riverbank. The city has a small but beautiful *Altstadt* (Old Town), whose charm lies in its extraordinary preservation; examples of late Gothic, Baroque, and Rococo architecture line the streets. It doesn't feel like a museum, though; these buildings are very much in use, often as shops or restaurants, and lively crowds of shoppers and strollers throng the streets. Many streets (including Vorstadt, Fronwagplatz, Vordergasse, and Unterstadt) are pedestrian-only.

Sights to See

❸ **Fronwagplatz.** Lined with shops and cafés, this square is a favorite place for young people to stroll, especially in the evening. A large 16th-century fountain-statue of a prosperous burgher, the **Metzgerbrunnen,** watches over the market-

---

THE REDS ARE COMING!

Back in the 19th century, England's William Cox wrote, with characteristic British modesty, that the local cleaniness, behavior, and dress in Schaffhausen made him feel as if "I could think for a moment that I am in England." Others attribute the un-Swiss nature of the natives to the fact that they do not live surrounded by mountains, which are said to make most Alp dwellers introspective. Another reason may be the fine red wines produced by the region!

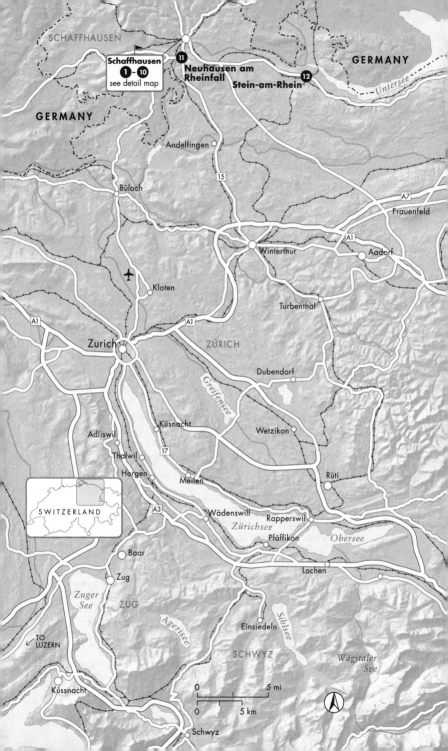

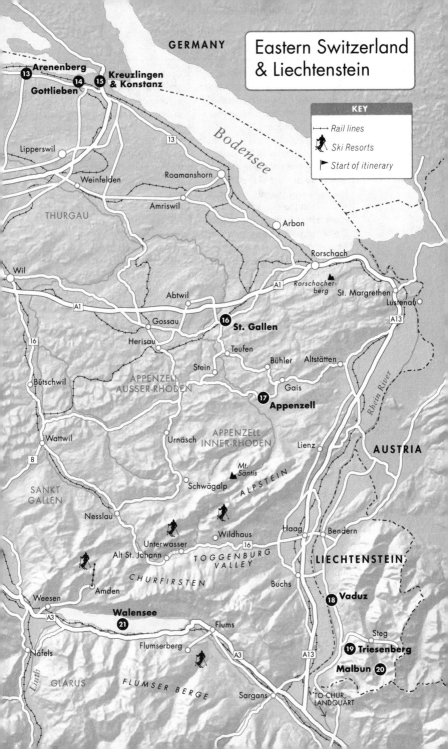

A GOOD WALK

Upon entering the Old Town, it becomes obvious why Schaffhausen is also known as the *Erkerstadt*–the City of Oriel Windows. Begin your walk at the north end of the Old Town at the **Schwabentorturm ❶ ▶**, where one of the two remaining defense towers houses one of the gates to the town. Continue along Vorstadt, glancing at the oriel windows, many dating from the 17th century. If you cast your gaze up above the houses every now and then, you can see the other tower peek out above the rooftops. The brilliantly painted facade of **Zum Goldenen Ochsen ❷** will be on your right–its oriel window is striking. Vorstadt then leads into **Fronwagplatz ❸**, with its clock tower and the Mohrenbrunnen and Metzgerbrunnen fountains at its north and south ends.

Continue east along the Vordergasse, where on your right you'll find the fine mansion **Haus zum Ritter ❹**, followed by the **Schmiedstube ❺**, the Smiths' Guild House. Farther up the street to your left is the imposing St. Johannkirche. To the right of the church lies the Haus zum Sittich, a bright yellow structure with Renaissance oriel windows and relief sculpture. Take a left at the fork in the road up ahead to see the duplex **zur Wasserquelle** and **zur Zieglerburg ❻**. Across from the duplex stands the Tellenbrunnen fountain.

Double back to the fork in the road and stroll down the tail end of Vordergasse. As you wait at the pedestrian crossing at Bachstrasse, the gray-and-white **Gerberstube ❼** welcomes you to this quieter part of town. Farther along the Unterstadt looking north is a group of odd houses with crooked and sharp angles. This is the entrance to the **Munot ❽**. The meandering steps that lead to the tower are flanked by vineyards. After taking in the view from the tower, double back to the pedestrian crossing at Bachstrasse. Cross the street and take the first left. You will come upon a cluster of large buildings that house the city library and the **Münster zu Allerheiligen ❾**. Head west on Münsterplatz. This leads you straight to the entrances of the Münster and the **Museum zu Allerheiligen ❿**. After visiting there, head up the hill to the government buildings on your left. The Altes Zeughaus (Old Armory), built by Johannes Jacob Meyer, is regarded as a good example of Swiss Renaissance architecture.

⊙ TIMING TIPS→ **The entire walk takes about two hours, including the hike up to the Munot. You may want to linger at the Munot if the weather is clear and the view particularly good. A visit to the Museum zu Allerheiligen will add another hour. Keep in mind that the museum is closed on Monday and has a late-morning opening.**

place. The **clock tower** once held the market scales; its astronomical clock (1564) records not only the time but also solar eclipses, seasons, and the course of the moon through the zodiac. Across the square, a reproduction of the 1535 **Mohrenbrunnen** (Moor's Fountain) represents Kaspar of the Three Kings. The original fountain is stored in the Museum zu Allerheiligen.

7 Gerberstube (Tanners' Guild House). A pair of lions frames the doorway of the remarkable Baroque building. A two-handled tanner's knife used to stretch between the lions, but unfortunately the vibrations of nearby roadworks in the neighborhood caused it to collapse. A restaurant now occupies the building. ⊠ *Bachstr. 8.*

4 Haus zum Ritter (Knight's House). The city's finest mansion dates from 1492. Its fresco facade was commissioned by the resident knight, Hans von Waldkirch. Tobias Stimmer covered all three stories with paintings on classical themes, which are now displayed in the Museum zu Allerheiligen; the reproduction of the original was made in the 1930s. ⊠ *Vorderg. 65.*

NEED A BREAK? Snag an outdoor table at **Santa Lucia** (⊠ Schwertstr. 1 ☎ 052/6252255) for one of many spaghetti dishes offered, from the classic garlic and olive oil to jumbo shrimp and tomatoes. Located smack-dab in the middle of the old town, it is perfect for people-watching.

8 Munot. Built between 1564 and 1585 in full circle form based on an idea by Albrecht Dürer, the massive stone ramparts served as a fortress allowing the defense of the city from all sides. From its top are splendid Schaffhausen and Rhine Valley views. ⊠ *Munotstieg* 🎫 *Free* ☉ *May–Sept., daily 8–8; Oct.–Apr., daily 9–5.*

9 Münster zu Allerheiligen (All Saints Cathedral). This beautiful cathedral, along with its cloister and grounds, dominates the lower city. Founded in 1049, the original cathedral was dedicated in 1064, and the larger one that stands today was built in 1103. Its interior has been restored to Romanesque austerity with a modern aesthetic (hanging architect's lamps, Scandinavian-style pews). The **cloister,** begun in 1050, combines Romanesque and later Gothic elements. Memorial plates on the inside wall honor noblemen and civic leaders buried in the cloister's central garden. You'll also pass through the aromatic **herb garden;** it is recreated so effectively that you may feel you've stepped into a tapestry. ⊠ *Klosterpl. 1* 🎫 *Free* ☉ *Tues.–Fri. 8–5, weekends 8–8.*

10 Museum zu Allerheiligen (All Saints Museum). This museum, on the cathedral grounds, houses an exten-

THE DING-DONG TOLLS

Centerpiece of the main courtyard, the cathedral's enormous Schiller Bell was cast in 1486; it hung in the tower of the cathedral until 1895. Its inscription, VIVOS–VOCO/MORTUOS–PLANGO/FULGURA–FRANGO ("I call the living, mourn the dead, stop the lightning"), allegedly inspired the German poet Friedrich von Schiller to write his "Lied von der Glocke" ("Song of the Bell").

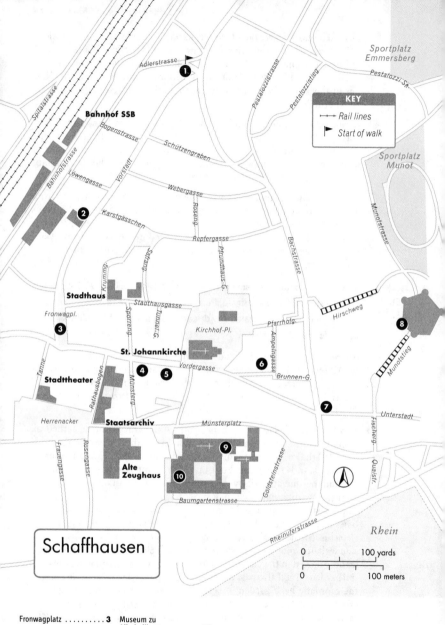

Schaffhausen

KEY

---- Rail lines

▶ Start of walk

sive collection of ancient and medieval historical artifacts, as well as displays on Schaffhausen industry. The period rooms are definitely worth a look; they cover 15th- to 19th-century interiors. The best of these is the 15th-century refectory, which was rented out and all but forgotten until its rediscovery, in 1924. Temporary exhibitions on various themes reach international caliber. Museum literature is available only in French or German. ✉ *Klosterpl. 1* ☎ *052/6330777* ⊕ *www.allerheiligen.ch* ⛟ *9 SF* ☯ *Tues.–Sun. 11–5.*

❺ Schmiedstube (Smiths' Guild House). With its spectacular Renaissance portico and oriel dating from 1653, this building is an embodiment of Schaffhausen's state of suspended animation. Framed over the door are the symbols of the tongs and hammer for the smiths, and that of a snake for doctors, who depended on the smiths for their tools and thus belonged to the guild. ✉ *Vorderg. 61.*

▶ **❶ Schwabentorturm** (Swabian Gate Tower). Once a part of the city wall, the tower dates from 1370. Inside the arch on the keystone is a relief from 1933 that bears a wise caution for anyone crossing the street: LAPPI TUE D'AUGE UF ("Open your eyes, you idiot!"). The tower's counterpart, the **Obertorturm,** lies just off the Fronwagplatz.

❷ Zum Goldenen Ochsen (At the Golden Ox). This late-Gothic building had a Renaissance-style portico and oriel window added to it in 1609. Flanking the windows are three floors of exterior frescoes depicting historic and mythological figures, most from the Trojan War. ✉ *Vorstadt 17.*

❻ Zur Wasserquelle and Zur Zieglerburg (At the Spring and At the Brick Castle). This Rococo duplex dates from 1738; since they are now private residences, you can see them only from the outside. Across the street are the **Tellenbrunnen,** a fountain-statue of Wilhelm Tell copied from the 1522 original, and, farther up Vordergasse, the **St. Johannkirche** (St. John's Church), whose Gothic exterior dates from 1248. ✉ *Vorderg. 26/28.*

Where to Stay & Eat

$–$$$ ✕ **Beckenburg.** Locals flock here to sample innovative twists on Mediterranean staples, such as chicken breast stuffed with shrimp in lemongrass-Pernod sauce. The tables are set apart far enough to give you lots of privacy, and the staff is attentive without being intrusive. Beechwood and metal tables and chairs complement the 300-year-old wood accents and the imposing Venetian chandelier that hangs over the room. ✉ *Neustadt 1* ☎ *052/6252820* 🖃 *AE, DC, MC, V* ☯ *Closed Sun.*

$–$$ ✕ **Restaurant Falken.** This busy restaurant caters to crowds with a palate for simple local fare—Rösti, breaded fish, and *Geschnetzeltes* (sliced veal in cream sauce). The *Tagesteller* (daily special) is an especially good deal at lunchtime. Though plain and cafeteria-like, it's an excellent choice for families; it even houses a small bowling alley. ✉ *Vorstadt 5* ☎ *052/6253221* 🖃 *AE, DC, MC, V.*

$–$$ ✕ **Wirtschaft zum Frieden.** Dating back to 1789, this local favorite offers three delightful settings: a small stübli full of waxed and weathered wood, a graceful tile-stove dining room with antiques, and a private garden thick with wisteria and luxuriant trees. The stübli serves up a wide variety of salads and soups, such as creamed curry soup with dates, while things get more elaborate in the upstairs dining room, with multicourse meals including lamb fillet, *Rösti* potatoes, and green beans tossed with bacon. ⊠ *Herrenacker 23* ☎ *052/6254767* ≡ *AE, DC, MC, V* ⊘ *Closed Tues.*

★ $$$–$$$$ ✕☷ **Rheinhotel Fischerzunft.** Following a complete renovation in the 1990s, this Relais & Châteaux property has a modern sheen that's welcoming but may seem out of place in this medieval city on the Rhine. Of the 10 guest rooms—some in fussy florals, others in sleek, jewel-tone solids—seven overlook the river. Every guest, however, shares the lovely Rhine view at breakfast. The restaurant's mixed nautical and Asian decor reflects the chef's Franco-Chinese leanings: he trained in Hong Kong and has created a brilliant, eclectic menu with such dishes as skate piccata with cabbage, chanterelle mushrooms, black beans, and ginger. ⊠ *Rheinquai 8, CH-8200* ☎ *052/6320505* ⊟ *052/6320513* ⊕ *www.fischerzunft. ch* ⇨ *6 rooms, 4 suites* ⚬ *Restaurant, IDD phones, in-room safes, in-room broadband, minibars; no a/c* ≡ *AE, DC, MC, V* ⦶⊙ *BP.*

$$ ☷ **Kronenhof.** This fine, quiet city hotel in the heart of Schaffhausen's Old Town has a traditional shutter- and flower-trimmed facade. Inside, however, all is modern, with tidy well-constructed rooms cheered by birch furniture, cherry-stained paneling, and abstract prints. The American cafeteria look in the main restaurant seems at odds with the excellent, refined versions of local dishes, including fresh fish and homemade pasta. ⊠ *Kirchhofpl. 7, CH-8200* ☎ *052/6357575* ⊟ *052/6357565* ⊕ *www.kronenhof.ch* ⇨ *38 rooms, 2 suites* ⚬ *Restaurant, café, in-room safes, minibars, in-room data ports, bar, Wi-Fi, Internet room; no a/c* ≡ *AE, DC, MC, V* ⦶⊙ *BP.*

$–$$ ☷ **Park-Villa.** Except for the no-nonsense elevator tacked onto the exterior, this Belle-Epoque mansion has been transformed into a small hotel with little disruption to its grand but familial style. Many of the original furnishings—inlaid pieces, chandeliers, Persian rugs—remain. The upper floors are modern but retain their eccentric shapes, and some have Rhine or fortress views. The fine old garden room is luxurious and a steal (the toilet is down the hall); all the other rooms have full baths. The hotel sits slightly apart, and uphill, from the Old Town. ⊠ *Parkstr. 18, CH-8200* ☎ *052/6356060* ⊟ *052/6356070* ⊕ *www.parkvilla. ch* ⇨ *21 rooms, 4 suites* ⚬ *Restaurant, tennis court, bar, Wi-Fi; no a/c* ≡ *AE, DC, MC, V* ⦶⊙ *BP.*

Sports & the Outdoors

Bicycles are a popular mode of transportation. They can be rented at the **train station** (☎ 051/2234217) in Schaffhausen.

Neuhausen am Rheinfall

⓫ To & From: *The nicest way to get to the Rhein falls is to walk (30 min.)*
Fodor'sChoice *the Rheinuferweg (Rhine bank trail) from Schaffhausen's old town:*
★ *follow the yellow hiking trail signs. The S33 commuter train (0900/ 300300, www.sbb.ch) leaves every half hour, takes 5 minutes and costs 2.80 SF each way. Neuhausen is 3 km (1¾ mi) south of Schaffhausen.*

Fist Food

St. Gallen is almost as famous for its *Olma Bratwurst* as for the textiles it used to manufacture for shipment throughout the world. But while the textile industry is in decline, there's no chance the cream-color sausage with its sides crisply browned to perfection will be disappearing from the region anytime soon. Locals get theirs from **Gemperli** (Schmidg. 34), the butcher, who makes them from a recipe that dates back to 1438. You'll be offered mustard or even ketchup, but aficionados eat theirs plain—there's more than enough taste, thanks to the many spices mixed in with the ground veal. If sweets are more your thing, try a *St. Galler Biber*—a gingerbread patty with almond paste filling—from **Konfiserie Scherrer** (Marktg. 28). One Biber can replace a whole meal; they are so rich you may find yourself living on lettuce and water for the next 24 hours.

Adjacent to Neuhausen, on the north bank of the Rhine, a series of magnificent waterfalls powers the city's industry (arms, railroad cars, aluminum). The **Rheinfall** is 492 feet wide, drops some 82 feet in a series of three dramatic leaps, and is split at the center by a bushy crag straight out of a 19th-century landscape painting. The effect—mists, roaring water, jutting rocks—is positively Wagnerian; Goethe saw in the falls the "ocean's source," although today's jaded globetrotter's have been known to find them "cute." There's a footpath, Rheinuferweg, that leads from Schaffhausen's Old Town along the river to the falls (a 25- to 35-minute walk). It is marked with the standard yellow hiking-trail signs. From Neuhausen there's a good view toward **Schloss Laufen,** a 12th-century castle that overlooks the Rheinfall.

Stein-am-Rhein

⑫ **To & From:** *The least complicated route is from/to Schaffhausen via* **Fodor's**Choice *the train (0900/300300, www.rail.ch) that departs every half hour (25* ★ *min.); tickets cost 7.20 SF each way. Stein-am-Rhein is 20 km (13 mi) east of Schaffhausen.*

Stein-am-Rhein, a nearly perfectly preserved medieval village and one of Switzerland's loveliest towns, lies at the point where the Rhine leaves the Bodensee. Crossing the bridge over the river, you see the village spread along the waterfront, its foundations and docks rising directly out of the water. Here, restaurants, hotels, and shops occupy 16th- and 17th-century buildings, and the Rhine is calm and lazy—nothing like the sprawling industrial trade route it becomes farther downstream.

The **Rathausplatz** (Town Hall Square) and main street, Unterstadt, are flanked by tight rows of shingled, half-timber town houses, each rivaling the next for the ornateness of its oriels, the flamboyance of its frescoes. The elaborate decor usually illustrates the name of the house: Sonne (Sun), Ochsen (Ox), Weisser Adler (White Eagle), and so on. Most of the artwork dates from the 16th century. The **Rathaus** (Town Hall) itself was built between

1539 and 1542, with the half-timber upper floors added in 1745; look for its fantastical dragon waterspouts, typical of the region.

The Benedictine **Kloster St. Georgen** (Monastery of St. George), a half-timber structure built in 1007, houses a cloister and a small museum devoted to examples of woodwork and local paintings. ✉ *Edge of Old Town, just upstream from the last bridge over the Rhine before the Bodensee* ☎ *052/7412142* 💵 *3 SF* ⏲ *Museum: Apr.–Oct., Tues.–Sun. 10–5.*

Directly above the town, atop vineyards and woods, stands the 12th-century hilltop castle of **Hohenklingen,** which offers broad views of the Rhine Valley and the lake beyond. Extensive restorations are scheduled to be completed in September 2007.

Where to Stay & Eat

★ **$$–$$$** ✕ **Sonne.** Upstairs, you'll find a formal dining room (ceiling beams, damask, and Biedermeier) where chef Philippe Combe's inventive, contemporary dishes—calf cheeks with mashed potatoes—command top prices. Downstairs in the bistro, he offers salads, regional sausages, and selections from the fine wine list, dished up in a spare, chic, gentrified pub: more beams, stone, stucco, and parquet. ✉ *Rathauspl.* ☎ *052/7412128* 💳 *AE, DC, MC, V* ⏲ *Closed Tues. and Wed.*

¢–$ ✕ **Weinstube zum Roten Ochsen.** A beautiful frescoed facade invites passersby into this warm little Weinstube, where dark antiques surround a *Kachelofen* (tile stove) and candles glow on the tables. The menu mixes Mediterranean staples with Asian flavors—you'll find lamb tandoori alongside osso buco with polenta and Spanish tapas. If you're tired of meat, there's a broad vegetarian selection as well. ✉ *Rathauspl. 129* ☎ *052/7412328* 💳 *No credit cards.*

★ **$$** 🏨 **Adler.** With one of the most elaborately frescoed 15th-century facades on the Rathausplatz, this hotel has a split personality: flamboyant on the outside, no-nonsense inside. The decor is airy, slick, and immaculate, with gray industrial carpet, white stucco, and blond wood throughout. Double-glaze windows cut the noise from the square. A local family runs the hotel, so family groups will fit right in. The cheerful restaurant serves excellent regional cooking, along with some French dishes. ✉ *Rathauspl. 15, CH-8260* ☎ *052/7426161* 📠 *052/7414440* 🌐 *www.adlersteinamrhein.ch* 🛏 *25 rooms* 🛎 *Restaurant; no a/c* 💳 *AE, DC, MC, V* ⏲ *Closed Jan. and Feb.* 🍽 *BP.*

★ **$$** 🏨 **Rheinfels.** Even some of the bathrooms have ceiling beams in this fine old waterfront landmark, which was built between 1508 and 1517. The public spaces have creaking pine-plank floors and suits of armor on display, and every room—modernized in beige and rose tones—has a Rhine view. The hotel's suite is in essence an apartment; it has its own separate entrance, a one-car garage, and a boat jetty. The restaurant specializes in top-quality freshwater fish. Both the hotel and the restaurant are closed on Wednesday, except in July and August. ✉ *Rhig. 8, CH-8260* ☎ *052/7412144* 🌐 *www.rheinfels.ch* 📠 *052/7412522* 🛏 *16 rooms, 1 suite* 🛎 *Restaurant, minibars, meeting rooms; no a/c* 💳 *MC, V* ⏲ *Closed Jan. and Feb.* 🍽 *BP.*

$ 🏨 **Zur Rheingerbe.** Right on the busy waterfront promenade, this small inn has wood-panel ceilings and big furniture reminiscent of Sears (sculptured carpet, spindle beds). Some rooms overlook the Rhine. The excellent first-floor restaurant has a full-length bay window along the riverfront. The hotel and restaurant are closed on Wednesday. ⊠ *Schifflände 5, CH-8260* ☎ *052/7412991* 🖷 *052/7412166* ⊕ *www.rheingerbe. ch* ⇨ *7 rooms* ♿ *Restaurant* ☰ *AE, DC, MC, V.*

Arenenberg

⓭ *20 km (12 mi) east of Stein-am-Rhein, 40 km (25 mi) east of Schaffhausen.*

Fodor'sChoice ★

East of Stein-am-Rhein, the Rhine opens up into the Untersee, the lower branch of the Bodensee. In its center lies the German island of Reichenau. Charles the Fat, great-grandson of Charlemagne, was buried here. The villages on either side of the Untersee are dominated by castles. On the Swiss side, behind the village of Mannenbach (nearly opposite Reichenau), the **Arenenberg Napoleonmuseum** is housed in a magnificent castle given to the municipality by Empress Eugénie of France in homage to her husband, Napoléon III, who grew up here with his mother, Hortense, sister-in-law of Napoléon I. Today the schloss serves as a museum and lovers of decorative arts with prize its ravishing

> ### MISSING LINKS
>
> Lovers of Napoleonic esoterica should want to visit two nearby châteaux with distant links to Bonaparte's glory. The Duchess of Dino, a companion of Hortense de Beauharnais (the de Beauharnais were the famous family the emperor married into) and mistress to the Duke of Talleyrand, went to live in Salenstein in 1817. Eugensberg Castle was built four years later by Eugène de Beauharnais, the son of Empress Joséphine. Inquire for directions at the Arenenberg museum.

period rooms dating from the Second Empire. Outside is a glorious park, studded with ancestral statues. ⊠ *Behind Mannenbach* ☎ *071/6643260* ⊕ *www.napoleonmuseum.tg.ch* 🎟 *10 SF* ⊗ *Mid-Apr.–mid-Oct., Tues.–Sun. 10–5, Mon. 1–8; mid-Oct.–mid-Apr., Tues.–Sun. 10–5.*

Gottlieben

⓮ *5 km (3 mi) east of Arenenberg, 45 km (28 mi) east of Schaffhausen.*

The village of Gottlieben has a Dominican monastery-castle, where the Protestant reformers Jan Hus and Jerome of Prague were imprisoned in the 15th century by order of Emperor Sigismund and antipope John XXIII, who was himself confined in the same castle a few years later. Today, though the castle can be viewed only from the outside, Gottlieben offers a romantic, half-timber waterfront promenade—and two fine old hotels—before you reach the urban complex of Kreuzlingen and Germany's Konstanz.

Where to Stay

$$–$$$ **Fodor'sChoice** ★

🏨 **Drachenburg und Waaghaus.** On the misty banks of the Rhine between the Bodensee and the Zellersee this half-timbered apparition of onion domes, shutters, and gilt gargoyles was first built in 1702 and retains its historic air despite modern expansion and ranks of Mercedes in the parking lot. The original early-18th-century Drachenburg lies across the way from the second building, the Waaghaus. A third house catches the overflow. Every effort has been made inside to live up to the exterior's promise, though the original Drachenburg is the most atmospheric by far: It has gleaming old staircases, four-poster beds, brocade, chaise longues, and crystal sconces scattered throughout the labyrinths of rooms and parlors. The scale is grand but cozy, and Rhine-view rooms are furnished like honeymoon suites. Its restaurants vary in ambience; the most sophisticated is the one in the original house. ⊠ *Am Schlosspark, CH-8274* ☎ *071/6667474* 🖷 *071/6691709* ⊕ *www.drachenburg. ch* 🛏 *58 rooms, 2 suites* ♨ *2 restaurants, in-room safes, minibars, bar; no a/c* ⊟ *AE, DC, MC, V* ☉ *Closed Dec. 24–Jan. 5* ¶◎¶ *BP.*

BODENSEE TO ST. GALLEN

Along the shores of the Bodensee, orchards stripe rolling hills that slowly rise to meet the foothills of the Alps around St. Gallen. About 2,000 years ago this region lay on the northeastern border of the Roman Empire, Arbon (Arbor Felix) being the first stop on the trade route for goods coming into the empire from points east. Today the region is mostly rural, with clusters of farmhouses dotting the grassy slopes. In summer the lake teems with vacationers, but in other seasons it remains a distinctly tranquil area.

Bodensee

Known in English as Lake Constance, the Bodensee is about 65 km (40 mi) long and 15 km (9 mi) wide, making it second in size in Switzerland only to Lac Léman (Lake Geneva). The strong German flavor of the towns on its Swiss edge is seasoned with a resort-village mellowness; palm trees fringe the waterfront. This isn't the Mediterranean, though; as the lake is not protected by mountains, it is turbulent in stormy weather and even on fine days is exposed to the wind. Nonetheless, it draws European vacationers in summer for swimming, windsurfing, and fishing. Many Swiss have built tidy homes along the lakefront.

Sports & the Outdoors

HIKING As a summer resort destination, the area around the Bodensee is usually thronged with hikers. For timed hiking itineraries, topographical maps, and suggestions on the areas best suited to your style of wandering, consult the Tourismusverband Ostschweiz (Tourist Association of Eastern Switzerland; www.ostschweiz-i.ch).

SWIMMING People do swim in the Bodensee; there are several public beaches, usually more grass than sand. Most have changing rooms and concession stands. **Arbon** (☎071/4461333) has a gravel beach—getting into the water can be a little rough on tender feet. **Kreuzlingen** (☎ 071/6881858) has some sand at the water's edge, though you'll be spreading your towel on the grass. **Romanshorn** (☎ 071/4631147) is also mostly grass.

Kreuzlingen & Konstanz

⑮ *7 km (4 mi) east of Gottlieben, 46 km (28 mi) east of Schaffhausen.*

The German city of Konstanz, with its Swiss-side twin of Kreuzlingen, dominates the straits that open into the Bodensee. Though Kreuzlingen itself offers little of interest to travelers, Konstanz has a lovely, concentrated *Altstadt* (Old Town) area. It's easily accessible from the Swiss side, though your passport may be checked even if you pass on foot. Konstanz belonged to Switzerland until 1805; today the two border towns share the dominant German influence.

EN ROUTE About halfway between Kreuzlingen and Rorschach (follow Highway 13 east along the Bodensee), you'll come to the small town of **Romanshorn.** An industrial town and an important ferry port for Friedrichshafen in Germany, this is also a surprisingly enjoyable resort with fine views of the Swiss and Austrian mountains.

Between Romanshorn and Rorschach on Highway 13, **Arbon** (known to the Romans as Arbor Felix) lies on a little promontory jutting out into the Bodensee, surrounded by lovely meadows and orchards. It was a Celtic town before the Romans came in 60 BC and built military fortifications. Evidence of the Romans can be found in an interesting collection of relics in the late-Gothic St. Martinskirche.

St. Gallen

⑯ **To & From:** *There are two trains (0900/300300, www.sbb.ch) each hour from/to Zurich, clocking in at just over an hour each; The fare is 27 SF each way. Trains also arrive from and leave to Appenzell every half hour, costing 10.40 SF each way. St. Gallen is 14 km (9 mi) southwest of Rorschach, 94 km (59 mi) southeast of Schaffhausen.*

Switzerland's largest eastern city, bustling St. Gallen is dominated by students during the school year. The narrow streets of the *Altstadt* (Old Town) are flanked by a wonderful variety of boutiques and antiques shops. The city has been known for centuries as both an intellectual center and the source of some of the world's finest textiles. St. Gallus, an Irish missionary, came to the region in 612 to live in a hermit's cell in the Steinach Valley. In 719 an abbey was founded on the site where he died. Soon a major cultural focus in medieval Europe, the abbey built a library of awesome proportions.

> ### A-STITCHING WE WILL GO
>
> St. Gallen's history as a textile capital dates from the Middle Ages, when convent workers wove linen toile of such exceptional quality that it was exported throughout Europe. The industry expanded into cotton and embroidery, before collapsing in 1918. Today, St. Gallen dominates the small luxury market for fine handmade textiles and magnificently historic finery is on view at the Textilmuseum (Textile Museum; Vadianstrasse. 2, 071/2221744, www.textilmuseum.ch, 5 SF, open Mon.-Sat. 10-noon and 2-5, Sun. 10-5, 1st Wed. of each month 10-5).

Fodor'sChoice   The abbey was largely destroyed in the Reformation and was closed down
★   in 1805, but its magnificent Rococo **Stiftsbibliothek** (Abbey Library), built
between 1758 and 1767, still holds a collection of more than 100,000
books and manuscripts. The library hall itself is one of Switzerland's
treasures. You enter behind the cathedral and change into the provided
large, gray carpet slippers to protect the magnificently inlaid wood
flooring. The hall is a gorgeous explosion of gilt, frescoes, and undulating balconies, but the most striking aspect by far is the burnished woodwork, all luminous walnut and cherry. Its contents, including incunabula
and illuminated manuscripts that are more than 1,200 years old, con-
stitute one of the world's oldest and finest scholarly collections. Also
on display, incongruously, is an Egyptian mummy dating from 700 BC.
⊠ *Klosterhof 6c* ☎ *071/2273416* ⊕ *www.stiftsbibliothek.ch* 🎫 *7 SF*
☉ *Mon.–Sat. 10–5, Sun. 10–4. Closed mid-Nov.–early Dec.*

★   The **Kathedrale** (Cathedral) is an impressive sight. Begun in 1755 and
completed in 1766, it is the antithesis of the library, though the nave
and rotunda are the work of the same architect, Peter Thumb. The scale
is outsize and the decor light, bright, and open despite spectacular excesses of wedding-cake trim. ⊠ *Klosterhof* ☎ *071/2273381* ☉ *Daily
9–6, except during services.*

**NEED A
BREAK?**   **Café Seeger** (⊠ Oberer Graben 2 ☎ 071/2229790) is a relaxing Viennese-style
café and restaurant. The sidewalk seating area is a great place to watch the
stylish young patrons go by.

The grounds of the abbey and the cathedral border the **Old Town,** which
demonstrates a healthy symbiosis between scrupulously preserved Renaissance and Baroque architecture and a thriving modern shopping scene.
The best examples of oriel windows, half-timbering, and frescoes can be
seen along Gallusstrasse, Schmiedgasse, Marktgasse, and Spisergasse, all
pedestrian streets. For a good picnic spot, head to the **Mühleggbahn,** a self-
service funicular that runs up the hillside to a lovely view of St. Gallen
and the Bodensee. Once up top, take two immediate right turns to the
wooden stairs leading to a paved path with park benches. ⊠ *Off the abbey
end of the Old Town* ☎ *071/2439595* 🎫 *2 SF* ☉ *Daily 6 AM–11:30 PM.*

Where to Stay & Eat

$$$ ✕ **Am Gallusplatz.** Rubbing shoulders with the town cathedral, this
noted St. Gallen landmark entices with a castlelated exterior, turreted
and hued in pink. Inside, things get more stolid, with most of the ac-
tion taking place in the main Rôtissie room—a large chamber replete
with cross-vaulted ceilings and heavy chandeliers. The menu is based
on market-fresh ingredients and may include such favorites as *Tafelspitz*
(beef stew) with fresh vegetables and potatoes but can also get nouvelle,
as witness the Scotch lamb Provençal. There's also an enormous wine
list. ⊠ *Gallusstr. 24* ☎ *071/2233330* ⊕ *www.gallusplatz.ch/* ⊟ *AE, MC,
V* ☉ *Closed Mon.*

$–$$$ ✕ **Concerto.** The glassed-in terrace of the Tonhalle concert hall provides
a year-round spring setting and a beautiful view of its park. The all-day

2

kitchen serves up inventive twists on local standards—fish wrapped in bacon with tomato sauce, for example—and has dishes for all appetites and pocketbooks. ✉ *Museumstr. 25* ☎ *071/2420777* ▭ *AE, MC, V.*

$–$$$ ✕ **David 38.** On a quiet street outside the bustle of the Old Town (and a favorite of local businesspeople), this hip, sleek eatery serves both Asian-flavored inventions—rock lobster in piri-piri sauce with lemongrass risotto—and the traditionally Mediterranean—ravioli *piemontese* in sage butter is a winner. ✉ *Davidstr. 38* ☎ *071/2302838* ⊕ *www. david.38.ch* ▭ *AE, MC, V* ⊘ *Closed Sun.*

$–$$$ ✕ **Netts Schützengarten.** In the corner of the local brewery, this bistro polishes a 19th-century industrial look, with copper pipes, exposed brick, and hardwood floors. Owner Köbi Nett's travels have resulted in a far-reaching menu: Spanish tapas, Indonesian shrimp curry, Olma Bratwurst. The beer is tapped directly from the vats next door. ✉ *St. Jakobstr. 35* ☎ *071/2426677* ▭ *AE, MC, V* ⊘ *Closed Sun.*

★ $–$$$ ✕ **Schlössli.** Tidy, bright, and modern despite its setting in a historic building, this first-floor (second-floor to Americans) landmark has a less woody atmosphere than peers like the Schäfli, but better cooking. Look for inventive dishes such as poached mixed seafood in saffron sauce. The café draws casual family groups and locals at lunch; businesspeople choose the slightly more formal dining room that adjoins it. ✉ *Am Spisertor, Zeughausg. 17* ☎ *071/2221256* ▭ *AE, DC, MC, V* ⊘ *Closed weekends.*

$–$$$ ✕ **Zum Goldenen Schäfli.** Of the first-floor (second-floor to Americans) restaurants that are St. Gallen's trademark, this is the most popular, and its slanting floors groan under crowds of locals and tourists. The low ceiling and walls are all aged wood and it's easy to imagine coach-and-four passengers lifting a pewter stein in centuries gone by. The menu offers regional standards lightened up for modern tastes. Lemon risotto with jumbo shrimp, for example, is a favorite. ✉ *Metzgerg. 5* ☎ *071/ 2233737* ▭ *AE, DC, MC, V* ⊘ *Closed Sun. No lunch Sat.*

$$$–$$$$ ▦ **Einstein.** Tucked back into a slope at the edge of the Old Town, this former embroidery factory is now an upscale business-class hotel, with sleek Hiltonesque interiors (polished cabinetry, subdued floral fabrics), a uniformed staff, and a five-star attitude. The generous breakfast buffet, laid out in the skylighted top-floor loft, is not included in the room price. The bar is dark, leathery, and American-business, appropriate to the clientele. An annex housing a business center, a gym, and two pools is due to be completed in 2009. ✉ *Berneggstr. 2, CH-9001* ☎ *071/ 2275555* 🖷 *071/2275577* ⊕ *www.einstein.ch* ⇌ *62 rooms, 3 suites* ♨ *Restaurant, in-room fax, minibars, in-room data ports, Wi-Fi, bar, meeting rooms; no a/c* ▭ *AE, DC, MC, V.*

$$ ▦ **Weissenstein.** With as quiet a location as you can get in the heart of the city, this hotel is all about relaxation. Comfy Swedish feather duvets cover large double beds; a rarity in a region where "double" usually means two singles pushed together. Bathrooms are small but up-to-date. In summer you can take your breakfast on the shady terrace. ✉ *Davidstr. 22, CH-9000* ☎ *071/2280628* 🖷 *071/2260630* ⊕ *www.cityweissenstein.ch* ⇌ *20 rooms* ♨ *Restaurant, in-room safes, minibars, in-room data ports, Wi-Fi, Internet* ▭ *AE, DC, MC, V* ⊚ *BP.*

$–$$ 🏠 **Vadian.** A narrow town house tucked behind half-timber landmarks in the Old Town, this is a discreet and tidy little place with an alcohol-free policy. Most of its tiny rooms have beige stucco walls, knotty pine furniture, and modern tile baths. Rooms without bath are a better bargain. ✉ *Gallusstr. 36, CH-9000* ☎ *071/2281878* 📠 *071/2281879* ⊕ *www.hotel-vadian.com* 🛏 *13 rooms, 6 with bath* ♿ *No a/c* ▭ *AE, DC, MC, V* ⦿ *BP.*

Sports & the Outdoors

🌀 **Säntispark.** Just outside St. Gallen lies this year-round, family-friendly sports and spa park. There is something to please (and exhaust) everyone—racquet sports, bowling, miniature golf, or billiards. Children can dive into the wave pool at the water park and enjoy the rides and playgrounds. For relaxing, the solarium, sauna, and massage center are available at an additional charge. Sports equipment can be rented. ✉ *From main train station in St. Gallen, 15 min by Bus 7 (Abtwil), or by car along Hwy. A1, exit Winkeln* ☎ *071/3131515* ⊕ *www.saentispark. ch* 🛏 *18 SF for 1.5 hrs, each additional hr 1.50 SF* ☉ *Weekdays 9 AM–10 PM, weekends 8 AM–10 PM.*

Shopping

ANTIQUE PRINTS　An outstanding assortment of antique prints of Swiss landscapes and costumes is sold at a broad range of prices at **Osvald Oliver** (✉ Marktg. 26 ☎ 071/2235016). The pictures are cataloged alphabetically by canton for easy browsing.

TEXTILES &　Although the region's textile industry has now shrunk down to a few
EMBROIDERY　local specialists, it's still world renowned for its quality. You'll find some fine examples at **Rocco Textil** (✉ Spiserg. 41 ☎ 071/2222407), which has a small but wonderful selection of embroidery, linens, and lace. The shop is an especially good source for custom work. **Sturzenegger** (✉ Oberergraben 46 ☎ 071/2224576), the better-known embroidery firm, established in 1883, sells its own line of linens and lingerie, designed and manufactured in the local factory.

Appenzell

🏅 **To & From:** *Every half hour there is a direct train (0900/300300, www.*
Fodor'sChoice　*sbb.ch) from/to St. Gallen that takes 48 minutes. If you want a change*
★　*of scenery, an alternate route goes via Herisau. 10.40 SF each way for both routes. Appenzell is 20 km (12 mi) south of St. Gallen, 98 km (60 mi) southeast of Schaffhausen.*

Isolated from St. Gallen by a ridge of green hills, Appenzell is one of Switzerland's quieter regions. Fellow Swiss think of its people as hillbillies, citing their quirky sense of humor and old-fashioned costumes. The city of St. Gallen melts away into undulating hills spotted with doe-eyed cows, a steep-pastured, isolated verdure reminiscent of the Ozarks. Prim, symmetrical cottages inevitably show rows of windows facing the valley. Named Appenzell after the Latin *abbatis cella* (abbey cell), the region served as a sort of colony to the St. Gallen abbey, and its tradition of fine embroidery dates from those early days. The perfect chance to see this embroidery is during a local festival, such as the Alpfahrten, when cows are herded up or down the mountains. Women's hair is coiffed in tulle, and their dresses have intricate embroidery and lace, often with an edelweiss motif; men wear embroidered red vests and suspenders decorated with edelweiss or cow figures. These traditional costumes are taken very seriously; they can cost thousands of francs, but in this case, pride supersedes economy. A small highway (No. 3) leads into the hills through Teufen; the quaint Appenzell–Teufen–Gais rail line also serves the region.

The town of Appenzell blends some of the best and worst of the region, offering tourists a concentrated and somewhat self-conscious sampling of the culture. Its streets lined with bright-painted homes, bakeries full of *Birnebrot* (pear bread) and souvenir *Biber* (almond and honey cakes), and shops full of machine-made embroidery, Appenzell seems to watch the tourists warily and get on with its life while profiting from the attention. Its **Landsgemeindeplatz** in the town center is the site of the famous open-air elections (until 1991, for men only), which take place the last Sunday in April. Embroidery is big business here, but it's rare to find handmade examples of the local art; though women still do fine work at home, it's generally reserved for gifts or heirlooms. Instead, large factories have sprung up in Appenzell country, and famous fine-cotton handkerchiefs sold in specialty shops around the world are made by machine here at the Dörig, Alba, and Lehner plants.

> **WHAT'S IN A NAME?**
>
> True, the demanding embroidery technique for which the name Appenzell became famous can no longer be found in the town of its birth. Though this makes for a somewhat faux souvenir, the imports do a fine job of capturing the intricacies of Appenzell embroidery. In a sign-of-the-times switcheroo, Margreiter (Hauptg. 29, 071/7873313) carries a large stock of handkerchiefs turned out in the local factories. Very popular are ones embroidered with motifs of edelweiss. Trachtenstobe (Hauptg. 23, 071/7871606) offers high-quality lace, embroidery, and crafts.

The **Museum Appenzell** showcases handicrafts and local traditions, regional history, and an international embroidery collection—it's a good general overview of the area's history and culture. The building itself dates from 1560. An English-language guide is available. ✉ *Hauptg. 4* ☎ *071/7889631* ⊕ *www.museum.ai.ch* 💷 *7 SF* ⊙ *Apr.–Oct., daily 10–noon and 2–5; Nov.–Mar., Tues.–Sun. 2–5.*

Where to Stay & Eat

$–$$ ✕ **Traube.** The traditional interior here may be understated, but in summer the place to sit is on the outside terrace or in the quiet garden hidden from major streets. The menu leans to pork and potatoes; fondue and Appenzeller *Chäshörnli* (cheese and macaroni) round out the mostly heavy offerings. The daily lunch special is usually around 20 SF. ✉ *Marktg. 7* ☎ *071/7871407* ⊟ *MC, V* ⊙ *Closed Mon.*

★ **$–$$$** ✕📷 **Hof.** One of Appenzell's most popular restaurants serves hearty regional meats and cheese specialties, such as *Käseschnitte* (cheese toast) and *Käsespätzli* (Spätzli with cheese), to locals and tourists who crowd elbow to elbow along shared tables and talk over the clatter from the bar. The rustic-wood decor, ladder-back chairs, and the display of sports trophies add to the local atmosphere. If you can still move after all that cheese, play skittles at the in-house lanes after dinner. The furnishings, walls, and floors of the rooms upstairs are all blond wood, making them resemble saunas. ✉ *Engelg. 4, CH-9050* ☎ *071/7874030* 🖨 *071/7875883* ⊕ *www.gasthaus-hof.ch* 🛏 *17 rooms* ⚲ *Restaurant; no a/c* 🖃 *AE, DC, MC, V* ◯| *BP.*

★ **$$** ✕🖭 **Appenzell.** Although only built in 1983, this comfortable lodging has all the gabled Gemütlichkeit of its neighbors, with a view over the Landsgemeindeplatz. Homey rooms, warmed with polished wood, owe their airiness to the traditional rows of windows. The fine woodwork and antiques in the breakfast room are remnants of the previous house on the property. With stained glass, new carved wood, and laminated menus, the popular restaurant downstairs has the look of an upscale American pancake house, but the cooking is right on the regional target, with mostbröckli, *Pastetli* (miniature puff pastry shells filled with chicken and mushrooms), Siedfleischteller (pot au feu), and a *Hauptgass* (an Appenzeller cheese gratin with pork, prosciutto, and tomato). ✉ *Landsgemeindepl., CH-9050* ☎ *071/7881515* 🖨 *071/7881551* ⊕ *www.hotel-appenzell.ch* 🛏 *16 rooms* ⚲ *Restaurant, café, patisserie, in-room broadband, Internet room, no-smoking rooms; no a/c* 🖃 *AE, DC, MC, V* ◯| *BP.*

$$$ 🖭 **Säntis.** A member of the Romantik hotel group, this prestigious hotel has a crisp and formal ambience, though the earliest wing has been a hotel-restaurant since 1835. Old-style touches—inlaid wood furnishings, painted beams—mix comfortably with the jewel-tone rooms and gleaming walnut cabinetry; some rooms have four-poster or canopy beds. The first-floor restaurant serves regional specialties in either of two wood-lined dining rooms, one Biedermeier, the other a folksy Appenzeller style. Guests can borrow bikes for free. ✉ *Landsgemeindepl., CH-9050* ☎ *071/7881111* 🖨 *071/7881110* ⊕ *www.romantikhotels.com/Appenzell* 🛏 *31 rooms, 6 suites* ⚲ *Restaurant, in-room safes, minibars, Wi-Fi, sauna, bar, no-smoking rooms; no a/c* 🖃 *AE, DC, MC, V* ⊙ *Closed early Jan.–early Feb.* ◯| *BP.*

$ 🖭 **Freudenberg.** This is a cookie-cutter modern chalet, but its setting on a velvety green hillside overlooking town is the most scenic and tranquil hotel you'll find in the area. Built in 1969, it has guest rooms that are bright and airy, with Appenzeller murals and modern, white-tile bathrooms. Four rooms have balconies, and the broad, shaded café—festive in the evening with strings of yellow lights—shares the picture-pretty views. Ten minutes from the city center on foot, it is also easily accessible by car. ✉ *Riedstr. 57, CH-9050* ☎ *071/7871240* 🖨 *071/7878642* ⊕ *www.hotel-freudenberg.ch* 🛏 *7 rooms* ⚲ *Restaurant, café; no a/c* 🖃 *AE* ◯| *BP.*

Shopping

CHEESES   Picnickers can sample the different grades of Appenzeller cheese and its unsung mountain rivals at **Mösler** (✉ Hauptg. 13 ☎ 071/7871317). **Sutter** (✉ Marktstr. 8 ☎ 071/7871333) has a good selection of locally made cheeses.

CLOSE UP

The Best Offense?

There is an article in Liechtenstein's constitution that states that every able-bodied man up to 60 years old must be prepared to defend his country at a moment's notice, but there hasn't been an official army since 1868. It wasn't always so: Liechtenstein was treaty-bound in the 18th century to contribute five men to the army of the Holy Roman Empire, as well as to cover the expenses of "half a cavalryman." This was increased to 80 men when Liechtenstein joined the German Confederation in 1814, but the expense of keeping an armed force was so steep that it was disbanded after the Austro-Prussian War came to a close. Since then, the only peacekeepers in the country have been the police force, which is augmented whenever necessary by a contingent of auxiliary service members. When all else fails, Switzerland has been known to offer its troops for civil service, such as helping to combat floods or mountain slides.

LIQUEURS Butchers, bakers, and liquor shops up and down the streets offer souvenir bottles of Appenzeller Bitter (Alpenbitter), a very sweet aperitif made in town. A well-balanced eau-de-vie called Appenzeller Kräuter, made of blended herbs, is another specialty.

LIECHTENSTEIN & THE WALENSEE

When you cross the border from Switzerland into the principality of Liechtenstein, you will see license plates marked FL: this stands for Fürstentum Liechtenstein (Principality of Liechtenstein). You are leaving the world's oldest democracy and entering a monarchy that is the last remnant of the Holy Roman Empire—all 160 square km (59 square mi) of it. If you don't put the brakes on, you'll wind up quickly in Austria.

This postage-stamp principality was created at the end of the 17th century, when a wealthy Austrian prince, Johann Adam von Liechtenstein, bought out two bankrupt counts in the Rhine Valley and united their lands. In 1719 he obtained an imperial deed from Emperor Karl VI, creating the principality of Liechtenstein. The noble family poured generations of wealth into the new country, improving its standard of living, and in 1862 an heir, Prince Johann the Good, helped Liechtenstein introduce its first constitution as a "democratic monarchy" in which the people and the prince share power equally. Today the principality's 32,000 citizens enjoy one of the world's highest per-capita incomes—prosperous (though discreet) local industries range from making jam to molding false teeth—and pay virtually no taxes. Back in Switzerland, the Walensee and Flumserberg region is sparsely populated, with a long lake flanked on both sides by steep mountains with beginner to intermediate ski areas. In summer the action moves downhill, where swimmers enjoy the cool water at several beaches along the lake.

Vaduz (Liechtenstein)

⑱ To & From: *There are no direct trains to Vaduz, Liechtenstein's capital city; you have to stop on the Swiss side of the Rhine and take a bus across the river. From/to St. Gallen via Buchs, by train (0900/ 300300, www.sbb.ch) and bus, the trip takes 79 minutes and costs 22.80 SF each way. If you're traveling from/to Zurich, take the 2-hour fast train to Sargans, where the connecting bus takes you to Vaduz. Travel time: 150 min.; cost: 34.80 SF each way. Vaduz is 31 km (18 mi) southeast of Appenzell, 159 km (98 mi) southeast of Schaffhausen.*

THE PHILATOPHILE SMILE

Liechtenstein is sometimes called the unofficial, per capita world champion of stamp collecting. To buy some of its famous stamps, whether to send a postcard to a philatelist friend or to invest in limited-issue commemorative sheets, you must line up with the tour-bus crowds at the popular post office on the Städtle.

Arriving in downtown Vaduz (there are exits from the A13 expressway from both the north and the south), a visitor could make the mistake of thinking Liechtenstein's only attraction is its miniature scale. Liechtenstein's small **Postmuseum** demonstrates the principality's history as a maker of beautifully designed, limited-edition postage stamps. Have your passport stamped for 2 SF at the **Fremdenverkehrszentrale** (tourist office) in the same building, or at the information booth at the bus terminal in summer. ⊠ *Städtle 37* ☎ *423/2366105* 🎫 *Free* ☾ *Daily 10–noon and 1:30–5.*

The **Kunstmuseum Liechtenstein** (Liechtenstein Museum of Art) offers ever-changing exhibitions, showing at any time only a fraction of the country's extraordinary art collection, amassed by countless princes of Liechtenstein. Most of their treasures are now on view in the family's Palais Liechtenstein in Vienna—so spectacular a showcase it is worth a trip in itself to the city—but there are enough holdings to present exhibitions here, ranging from Roman mythological art to old masters. ⊠ *Städtle 32* ☎ *423/2350300* ⊕ *www.kunstmuseum.li* 🎫 *8 SF* ☾ *Tues., Thurs., and Fri.–Sun., 10–5, Wed. 10–8.*

The **Liechtensteinisches Landesmuseum** (National Museum), in a former tavern and customhouse with a modern annex built into the cliff, covers the geology, history, and folklore of the principality. ⊠ *Städtle 43* ☎ *423/2396820* ⊕ *www.landesmuseum.li* 🎫 *8 SF* ☾ *Tues., Wed., and Fri.–Sun., 10–5, Thurs. 10–8.*

The **Ski Museum Vaduz** is a small shrine to the region's preferred pastime. Here you'll find numerous variations on the Alpine theme, including skis, sleds, ski fashion, and literature. ⊠ *Fabrikweg 5* ☎ *423/2321502* ⊕ *www. skimuseum.li* 🎫 *6 SF* ☾ *Weekdays 2–6, or by appointment.*

At the top of a well-marked hill road (you can climb the forest footpath behind the Engel hotel) stands **Vaduz Castle**. Here, His Serene Highness Hans–Adam II, reigning prince of Liechtenstein, duke of Troppau and

Jaegerndorf, reigns in a gratifyingly romantic fortress-home with red and white medieval shutters, massive ramparts, and a broad perspective over the Rhine Valley. Originally built in the 12th century, the castle was burned down by troops of the Swiss Confederation in the Swabian Wars of 1499 and partly rebuilt during the following centuries, until a complete overhaul that started in 1905 gave it its present form. It is not open to the public, as Hans-Adam II enjoys his privacy. He is the son of the late, beloved Franz Josef II, who died in November 1989 after more than a 50-year reign. Franz Josef's birthday, August 15, is still celebrated as the Liechtenstein national holiday.

> **THE MOVEABLE FEAST**
>
> Ironically, prosperity has built the lower reaches of Liechtenstein into a modern community, full of big, new cream-color bungalows that hardly seem picturesque to tourists seeking traces of the Holy Roman Empire. In fact, most of the great art of the reigning family has been packed off to Vienna's newly renovated Palais Liechtenstein. Since they've now reopened this splendid 18th-century gallery to the public, no one can begrudge the fact that their family Schloss Vaduz is still private.

Hans-Adam II has been known to join the crowds below to watch the fireworks while wearing jeans; his two photogenic teenagers often make the party pages in Vienna.

Where to Stay & Eat

★ $ ✕ **Wirtschaft zum Löwen.** Though there's plenty of French, Swiss, and Austrian influence, Liechtenstein has a cuisine of its own, and this is the place to try it. In a wood-shingle landmark farmhouse on the Austrian border, the friendly Biedermann family serves tender homemade *Schwartenmagen* (the pressed-pork mold unfortunately known as headcheese in English), pungent *Sauerkäse* (sour cheese), and Käseknöpfli, plus lovely meats and the local crusty, chewy bread. Be sure to try the region's distinctive wines. When driving here on Route 16, keep an eye out for Schellenberg, posted to the left; if you zip past it, you'll end up in Austria. ⊠ *FL-9488 Schellenberg, 10 km (6 mi) north of Vaduz off Rte. 16* ☎ *423/3731162* ⊕ *www.loewen.li* ⊟ *AE, MC, V* ⊘ *Closed Wed. and Thurs.*

$$$$ ✕🖼 **Park-Hotel Sonnenhof.** With a superb view over the valley and mountains beyond, this hillside retreat offers understated luxury minutes from downtown Vaduz. The clean, comfortable rooms are decorated in bright colors. The public areas are full of antiques, rugs, woodwork, and familial touches. The restaurant serves excellent, unstodgy French food and local fish such as pike-perch with pine nuts, carrots, and rice. ⊠ *Mareestr. 29, FL-9490* ☎ *423/2390202* 🖷 *423/2390203* ⊕ *www. sonnenhof.li* ⌦ *17 rooms, 12 suites* ⌂ *Restaurant, in-room safes, minibars, Wi-Fi, pool, sauna, meeting rooms; no a/c* ⊟ *AE, DC, MC, V* ⊘ *Closed late Dec.–early Jan.* ⍾ *BP.*

★ $$–$$$ ✕🖼 **Real.** Here you'll find rich, old-style Austrian-French cuisine in all its buttery glory prepared by Martin Real, son of the unpretentious former chef, Felix Real (who still presides over the 20,000-bottle wine cellar). There's an abundance of game in season, richly sauced seafood, and soufflés. The ambience is old school and even the salads are prepared at your table. Downstairs, the more casual Stübli atmosphere is just right for *Geschnetzeltes mit Rösti* (veal in cream sauce with hash brown potatoes). Upstairs in this Relais & Châteaux establishment, the guest rooms are small but airily decorated. ⊠ *Städtle 21, FL-9490* ☎ *423/2322222* 🖷 *423/2320891* ⊕ *www.hotel-real.li* 🔄 *11 rooms, 2 suites* ♤ *Restaurant, Stübli, in-room safes, minibars; no a/c* ⊟ *AE, DC, MC, V* 🍴 *BP.*

$–$$ ✕🖾 **Engel.** This elegant, centrally located hotel-restaurant has a comfortable local ambience despite the tour-bus crowds. The restaurant downstairs dishes up home cooking, and there's a *Biergarten* (beer garden) where Liechtensteiners meet. Upstairs, the more formal restaurant serves Chinese cuisine. The guest rooms are in fresh colors, with tile bathrooms. ⊠ *Städtle 13, FL-9490* ☎ *423/2361717* 🖷 *423/2331159* 🔄 *20 rooms* ♤ *Restaurant, in-room safes, minibars, Internet room, pub; no a/c* ⊟ *AE, DC, MC, V.*

$$$ 🖾 **Residence.** Rice paper screens and down duvets mingle in a simple Japanese-European style. The smack-dab central location is a draw whether you're here on vacation or business, and both bath and conference rooms have state-of-the-art features. The restaurant serves market-fresh local fare and offers take-out if you're in the mood for a picnic. ⊠ *Städtle 23, FL-9490* ☎ *423/2392020* 🖷 *423/2392022* ⊕ *www. residence.li* 🔄 *24 rooms, 5 suites* ♤ *Restaurant, in-room safes, minibars, in-room broadband, bar; no a/c in some rooms* ⊟ *AE, DC, MC, V* 🍴 *BP.*

Sports & the Outdoors

BICYCLES & MOTORCYCLES   In Triesen (4 km [2½ mi] south of Vaduz), bikes can be rented from **Bike Garage** (⊠ Landstr. 256 ☎ 423/3900390).

Shopping

POTTERY   Though shops on the main street of Vaduz carry samples of the local dark-glaze pottery, painted with folksy flowers and figures, the central source is 8 km (5 mi) north of Vaduz at **Schaedler Keramik** (⊠ Rte. 16, Nendeln ☎ 423/3731414). Simpler household pottery is available for sale as well as the traditional and often ornate hand-painted pieces. Pottery making is demonstrated daily. The shop is open weekdays 8–5.

Triesenberg (Liechtenstein)

⑲ *3 km (2 mi) southeast of Vaduz, 162 km (100 mi) southeast of Schaffhausen.*

This cluster of pretty chalets clings to the mountainside, with panoramic views over the Rhine Valley. Triesenberg was settled in the 13th century by immigrants from the Valais in southwestern Switzerland. The **Walser Heimatmuseum** (Valais Heritage Museum) traces the culture of these immigrants. Furnishings and tools from farmers and craftsmen are displayed, and an entertaining 20-minute slide show (in English) illustrates their Alpine roots. ⊠ *Dorfenzentrum* ☎ *423/2621926* ⊕ *www.triesenberg. li* 🖾 *2 SF* ☉ *Sept.–May, Tues.–Fri. 1:30–5:30, Sat. 1:30–5; June–Aug., Tues.–Fri. 1:30–5:30, Sat. 1:30–5, Sun. 2–5.*

Malbun (Liechtenstein)

⑳ *5 km (3 mi) southeast of Triesenberg, 167 km (103 mi) southeast of Schaffhausen.*

In winter this 5,250-foot-high mountain resort near the Austrian border draws crowds of local families who come for the varied slopes, many of which are well suited to beginners. England's Prince Charles and Princess Anne learned to ski here while visiting the Liechtenstein royal family in Vaduz. In summer Malbun becomes a quiet, unpretentious resort with reasonable prices.

Skiing

Malbun is a sunny, natural bowl with low, easy slopes and a couple of difficult runs; you can ride a chairlift to the top of the Sareiserjoch and experience the novelty of skiing from the Austrian border back into Liechtenstein. Facilities are concentrated at the center, including hotels and cafés overlooking the slopes. The resort also has a **ski school** (☎ 423/2639770). One-day lift tickets cost 41 SF; five-day passes cost 152 SF.

> ### STOP AND SMELL THE ROSES
>
> Between the Walensee and Zürich, about 36 km (22 mi) northwest of Weesen, Rapperswil is a small town on Zürichsee (Lake Zürich) with pleasant views, summertime waterfront strolls, and no less than three rose gardens, which is why it is known as the "Swiss City of Roses." If rainy, go instead to the forbidding 13th-century Schloss Rapperswil (055/2101862), which looks like it's ripped from the pages of a Gothic novel. Inside is a museum on the history of Polish immigrants to Switzerland. It's open weekends from 1 to 5 in November, December, and March, and daily from 1 to 5 from April to October; admission is 4 SF.

Where to Stay

$–$$$ 🏨 **Alpenhotel.** The Vögeli family's welcoming smiles and good food have made this remodeled chalet a Liechtenstein institution. The old rooms are small, with creaky pine trim; the higher-priced rooms are modern stucco. ✉ *Malbun, FL-9490* ☎ *423/2631181* 🖷 *423/2639646* ⊕ *www.alpenhotel.li* 🛏 *21 rooms* ♨ *Restaurant, café, minibars, pool* 🚭 *AE, DC, MC, V.*

Sports & the Outdoors

Liechtenstein has a 162-km (100-mi) network of Alpine hiking trails, and another 243 km (150 mi) of valley hiking. Malbun and Steg are ideal starting points for mountain hikes. You can get trail maps at the tourist office or at magazine kiosks.

Walensee

㉑ *38 km (23 mi) northwest of Malbun, 65 km (36 mi) southeast of Zürich, 127 km (78 mi) southeast of Schaffhausen.*

Between Liechtenstein and Zürich, the spectacular, mirrorlike lake called the Walensee is a deep emerald gash that stretches 16 km (10 mi) through the mountains, reflecting the jagged Churfirsten peaks. At the western end of the Walensee, **Weesen** is a quiet, shady resort noted for its mild climate and lovely lakeside walkway. Six kilometers (4 mi) north of Weesen on a winding mountain road lies **Amden,** perched 3,116 feet above the Walensee in the relatively undiscovered region south of the Churfirsten Mountains.

Skiing

Despite its small size, **Amden** is a major winter sports center, offering modest skiing in a ruggedly beautiful setting. Easy and medium slopes with unspectacular drops and quick, short-lift runs provide good weekend getaways for crowds of local Swiss families. The highest trails start at 5,576 feet; there are two chairlifts, three T-bars, one children's lift, 25 km (16 mi) of downhill runs, and 8 km (5 mi) of cross-country trails. You can also take advantage of the **ski school** (☎ 055/6111115), a natural ice rink, and walking paths. One-day lift tickets cost 33 SF; six-day passes cost 150 SF.

Sports & the Outdoors

For sports enthusiasts, **Amden** also has a public **open-air skating rink,** the heated indoor pool **Hallenbad Amden** (☎ 055/6111588), and an **outdoor tennis court** (☎ 055/6111292). There are also many **public beaches** that dot the southern shore of the Walensee.

EASTERN SWITZERLAND ESSENTIALS

Transportation

BY AIR

Unique Zürich Airport, just north of Zürich, is about 48 km (30 mi) south of Schaffhausen, about 75 km (46 mi) west of St. Gallen, and 130 km (81 mi) northwest of Liechtenstein.

🚹 Airport Information **Unique Zürich Airport** ☎ 0900/300313.

BY BOAT & FERRY

Swiss Federal Railways provides regular year-round service on the Bodensee through Schweizer Bodensee Schiffahrtsgesellschaft (Swiss Bodensee Cruiseline Co., ⊕www.sbsag.ch), though fewer boats run in winter. The Schweizerisches Schiffahrtsgesellschaft Untersee und Rhein ship company (⊕ www.urh.ch) offers a winning combination of a boat ride on the Rhine with romantic views of storybook castles, citadels, and monasteries. Boats run regularly up- and downstream, docking at Schaffhausen, Stein-am-Rhein, Gottlieben, Konstanz, and Kreuzlingen. Prices vary according to the distance traveled; a day pass costs 30 SF. A one-way trip from Schaffhausen to Kreuzlingen takes about 4½ hours. On both boat lines, you'll travel free if you have a Swiss Pass.

🚹 Boat & Ferry Information **Schweizer Bodensee Schiffahrtsgesellschaft** ☎ 071/4667888. **Schweizerisches Schiffahrtsgesellschaft Untersee und Rhein** ✉ Freïerpl. 8, CH-8202 Schaffhausen ☎ 052/6340888.

BY BUS

The famous line of yellow Swiss Post postbuses are integrated into the national train and boat network, and provide much of the public transport in areas not served by trains, particularly to smaller towns and Liechtenstein, which has no rail service. The bus schedules are usually posted outside the town post office, but you can also obtain information from any train station. The smallest towns have one bus in the morning and one in the evening. In larger towns, buses run several times a day. (☎ 0900/300300 ⊕ www.sbbl.ch).

BY CAR

The A1 expressway from Zürich heads for St. Gallen through Winterthur. To reach Schaffhausen from Zürich, take A1 to Winterthur, then head north on the cantonal highway E41/15. You also can leave Zürich by way of the A4 expressway past Unique Zürich Airport, crossing through Germany briefly and entering Schaffhausen through Neuhausen am Rheinfall. From the south, the A13 expressway, shared with Austria, leads you from Chur along Liechtenstein to the east end of the Bodensee; from there, you take A1 into St. Gallen. Liechtenstein is best reached by car; from Zürich, take the A1 expressway to Sargans, then change to the A13 heading north and take the Vaduz exit. From St. Gallen, follow the A1 northeast to the Bodensee, where it changes into the A13. Follow this south approximately 50 km (31 mi) to the Vaduz exit.

Driving in eastern Switzerland allows you to see the best of this region; Highway 13 goes along the south shores of the Untersee and Bodensee and continues up through the hills to Appenzell. Neither St. Gallen nor Schaffhausen is a big enough city to warrant all-out panic, although you'll find it easiest to head directly for the center and abandon the car for the duration of your visit. Try to get into a parking lot, as finding a spot on the street can be difficult. In Schaffhausen, there's underground parking at the Stadttheater underneath Herrenacker. In St. Gallen, the Old Town is surrounded by underground parking lots. You'll find entrances on Burggraben, Oberergraben, and, most conveniently, on St. Georgenstrasse, right by the abbey.

BY TRAIN

A connection by train from the Zürich Hauptbahnhof into the SBB Bahnhof Schaffhausen takes about 40 minutes; into SBB Bahnhof St. Gallen or Sargans, about an hour. Connections from the south (Graubünden) are more difficult, as both Austria and the Alps intervene.

Rail connections are somewhat complicated in this area, especially if you want to visit more of Appenzell than its major towns. Schaffhausen and St. Gallen are the main hubs from which regional trains head into the countryside and along the Bodensee. The only railroads into the canton are the narrow-gauge line between St. Gallen and the town of Appenzell, which passes Teufen and Gais, and the Gossau–Appenzell–Wasserauen line. To see more of the territory, you may return to St. Gallen on this same line by way of Herisau.

Although there is no regional rail pass available for eastern Switzerland, the general Swiss Pass rail pass (available from Switzerland Tourism and from travel agents outside Switzerland) includes St. Gallen and Schaffhausen city transit as well as overall rail privileges. You cannot enter Liechtenstein by rail; the international express train that passes between Switzerland and Austria doesn't bother to stop in Liechtenstein. From the train stations at Buchs or Sargans, you can catch a postbus into Vaduz.

🚆 Train Information ☎ 0900 300 300 ⊕ www.rail.ch.

Contacts & Resources

EMERGENCIES

🚆 **Police** ☎ 117. **Ambulance** ☎ 144. **Doctor, dentist, late-night pharmacies** ☎ 1811. **Medical assistance** ☎ 071/4941111 St. Gallen.

INTERNET & MAIL

In smaller towns, ask your hotel concierge if there are any Internet cafés nearby.

🚆 Internet & Mail Information A network of Wi-Fi hotspots is rapidly growing throughout Switzerland. For information: ⊕ www.hotspots.ch ⊕ www.swisshotspots.ch. **Go East** ✉ Hechtacherstrasse 12, St. Gallen ☎ 071/2745121.**Kiosk Charregass** ✉ Oberstadt 16, Steni-am-Rhein ☎ 052/7412728. **Die Post main post office** ✉ Bahnhofstr. 34, Schaffhausen. **Die Post main post office** ✉ Bahnhofpl. 5, St. Gallen.

TOUR OPTIONS

The Schaffhausen tourist office gives daily guided walking tours with English commentary of the Old Town, the monastery, and the Munot. For a unique take on the city, try one of the nighttime guided walks, which focus on murders, pestilence, public hangings, and other dark events, available in English on request.

🚆 Tours **Schaffhausen tourist office** ✉ Herrenacker 15, CH-8201 ☎ 052/6324020 ⊕ www. schaffhausen-tourismus.ch.

VISITOR INFORMATION

The tourist office for all of eastern Switzerland is based in St. Gallen. There are small regional visitor information offices throughout eastern Switzerland. Liechtenstein's office is in its capital.

🚆 Main Tourist Offices **Tourismusverband Ostschweiz** (Tourist Association of Eastern Switzerland) ✉ Bahnhofpl. 1a, St. Gallen CH-9001 ☎ 071/2273737 🖷 071/2273767 ⊕ www.ostschweiz-i.ch. **Liechtenstein** ✉ Städtle 37, FL-9490 Vaduz ☎ 423/2396300 🖷 423/2396301 ⊕ www.tourismus.li.

🚆 Regional Tourist Offices **Appenzellerland** ✉ Hauptg. 4, CH-9050 Appenzell ☎ 071/ 7889641 ⊕ www.appenzell.ch. **Schaffhausen** ✉ Herrenacker 15, CH-8201 ☎ 052/ 6324020 ⊕ www.schaffhausen-tourismus.ch. **Stein-am-Rhein** ✉ Oberstadt 3, CH-8260 ☎ 052/7422090 ⊕ www.stein-am-rhein.ch. **Thurgau** ✉ Arbonerstr. 2, CH-8580 Amriswil ☎ 071/4141144 ⊕ www.thurgau-tourismus.ch.

Graubünden

AROSA, DAVOS, ST. MORITZ

Davos

WORD OF MOUTH

"The St. Moritz/Pontresina area offers great skiing, a lovely valley with cross-country walks (and polo on the frozen lake), St. Moritz's shops and restaurants, and the chance to take the Bernina Express."
—Cicerone125

"While the mountain scenery of the Engadine might not appear as gorgeous as in the Bernese Oberland, at first sight, it is still very impressive. Once you get deeper in the valleys and up to the viewing points (hiking, cable cars) you will be stunned." —Ingo

WELCOME TO GRAUBÜNDEN

TOP REASONS TO GO

★ **Chic, Chicer, Chicest:** From Arosa to Zuoz, every skiing resort is a place to be "scene" by the elite of four continents. Sparkling St. Moritz, Davos, and Klosters are perfect for chilling out, but don't forget your Gucci sunglasses.

★ **Heidi's Hideaway:** Shirley Temple immortalized the just-too-cute orphan but find out just how much her 1937 film differed from Joanna Spyri's beloved book with a visit to Maienfeld's Heidi Village.

★ **Beautiful Sgraffiti:** The Lower Inn Valley is home to some picture-perfect villages, famous for their folkloric dwellings graced with sgraffiti wall decorations. For the best close-ups, head to Guarda—so beautiful it is under federal protection.

★ **Keeping Body and Soul Together:** Palatial spa hotels and a landscape that inspired great painters and philosophers means Graubünden offers top-of-the-line rest and recuperation, "made in Switzerland."

1 **Heidi Country.** Everybody's favorite little Swiss miss lived here and, today, the village of Maienfeld pays homage to the legendary character with a Heidi Village, Heidi-Path, and Heidihof hotel. To the south lies Chur, the capital of Graubünden—largely modern, it has, in fact, nearly 11,000 years of history exhibited in the local museums, churches, even the streets. Then strike southeast for Arosa, a high-altitude village perfect for those who find the winter elegance of St. Moritz just a trifle overbearing.

Heidiland, the home of Heidi.

2 **The Upper Engadine & St. Moritz.** Take New York luxury, then Paris fashion, a bit of London and Milan as well, a drop of Munich, a handful of Rome, large swaths of premium ski slopes and crystalline lakes, add the bubbling "champagne climate" of dry air and sun, mix well and pour onto a few acres in a gorgeous high-altitude valley. How can anything compare to **St. Moritz?**

3 The Lower Engadine.
Bustling **Scuol** has maintained its ancient feel despite modern amenities. Nature lovers will have all wishes fulfilled in the famed Swiss National park, while art lovers will adore flower-boxed **Guarda** and the magnificent fortress at **Tarasp**, which seems lifted from the pages of a medieval illuminated manuscript.

GETTING ORIENTED

Covering about 2,800 square miles, Graubünden is the largest canton in Switzerland, occupying more than one-sixth of the country. With high mountains nestling chic resorts like St. Moritz, Davos, and Klosters, the Grisons (to use the French name) offers as much attitude as altitude. Cross any of the passes south to the Engandine Valley for quaint sgraffito-covered villages and more fresh air than you've ever dreamed of.

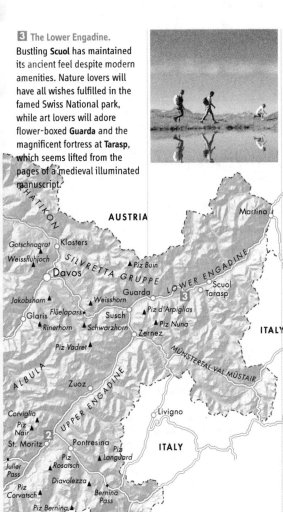

AUSTRIA

RHÄTIKON

Gotschnagrat   Klosters
Weissfluhjoch
Davos
SILVRETTA GRUPPE
Piz Buin
Jakobshorn   Weisshorn
Glaris   Flüelapass   Susch
Rinerhorn   Schwarzhorn
Piz Vadret
LOWER ENGADINE
Martina
Scuol
Tarasp
Guarda
Piz d'Arpiglias
Piz Nuna
Zernez
ITALY
MÜNSTERTAL VAL MÜSTAIR
ALBULA
Zuoz
UPPER ENGADINE
Livigno
Corviglia
Piz Nair
St. Moritz
Pontresina   Piz Languard
ITALY
Julier Pass
Piz Rosatsch
Piz Corvatsch   Diavolezza
Piz Bernina   Bernina Pass
Poschiavo

0   10 mi
0   10 km

Davos

3

GRAUBÜNDEN PLANNER

How's the Weather?

Graubünden has essentially two climatic regions. In the lower Rhine Valley (Chur, Heidi-Land, etc), there are normally four distinct and equal seasons.

Up in the Engadine, there are four seasons as well, but their distribution is heavily skewed toward winter.

Snow can remain until May, and after a brief spring and summer you may experience flurries or frozen dew in August.

So even if traveling in summer, pack some warm clothing, like a sweater and a windbreaker.

The fall colors are well worth a trip—perhaps not as spectacular as New England, but very inspiring.

Graubünden rivals the Bernese Oberland as Switzerland's winter wonderland, so December remains high season for such chic resorts as St. Moritz, Davos, and Klosters.

Finding a Place to Stay

Hoteliers in Graubünden invest fortunes in preserving Alpine coziness on both the outside and inside of their lodgings, which is not always the case in other parts of Switzerland. Wood is commonly used to soften interiors, and the source is often Arvenholz, the prized Swiss stone pine that grows here. Its wood is thick with knots and rich in natural color, which deepens over the years.

Prices in this popular region are comparatively high. Even higher prices can be charged for the winter holiday period and in February; during the rest of winter you may find special lower-priced packages that include ski tickets. Summer rates are also generally lower. Many hotels close between seasons, from April to mid-June and from mid-October to mid-December, but the dates and months vary each year, so be sure to check. In a few winter resorts there are hotels that stay closed all summer; we have not included these in our listings.

Hotels publish tariffs in various ways; double-check to see whether you're paying per person or per room, as well as whether you have demipension (half board). If you plan to stay in one place for more than a day or two, half board can cut costs. You may also want to ask about GästeKarte (guest cards), small booklets given by hotels that provide various deals on local transit or attractions. These are distributed in some resort towns, including Klosters, Davos, and Flims/Laax.

The quality of the skiing and outdoor life, plus the allurements of the social life means that many places are packed between Christmas and about January 15th—so make reservations well in advance for this time. If you are only interested in sports, you may wish to budget less for hotels by staying in more out-of-the-way villages and commute to such posheries as St. Moritz and Pontresina. After all, once you are in the Engadine, there are no great distances (Scuol to Sils Maria, for example, is about two hours by train and bus). Watch out if traveling between mid-October and November, or between Easter and beginning of June: Many hotels close for renovations and repairs.

Land of Plenty

Tourism is one of the economic mainstays of Graubünden and therefore restaurants tend to stay open throughout the day for the hungry visitor. The way to be sure is to look for a sign that bears the word *durchgehend*, meaning without a stop. Some places, however, will serve only snacks—or close entirely—between around 2:30 and 5:30. If traveling in the low season (November or April), you may encounter quite a few closed doors. If you're on the move, you may want to avoid restaurants altogether and simply opt for a visit to the butcher, the cheese shop, and the baker to pick up some regional specialties to enjoy as a picnic. Finally, the rugged and remote mountainscape is deceiving. Hikers and skiers will frequently encounter a cozy *Bergbeizli*, literally a mountain inn, where fine locally grown food is served up in a most congenial atmosphere.

Getting Around

Unless you intend to explore every nook and cranny of Graubünden or some of the more remote valleys, you will not really need a car. In fact, a car might cost more time and irritation than simply using public transportation. Virtually every village and major cable car, funicular or ski area is connected either by regular train service of the Rhätibahn (Rhätische Bahn or RhB, for short) trains or Swiss Post buses. On occasion, hotels often have pick-up service. Note that if you intend to use public transportation (recommended) a fair amount, you should consider purchasing a Swiss Pass or one of the many other options. For example, an 8-day Swiss Pass (giving you unlimited transportation on trains, buses, and ships; 50% discounts on many funiculars or cable cars; plus entrance to museums and many other perks) costs 362 SF. Compare this to the basic cost for a car rental: about 680 SF for 7 days—and you haven't tanked up yet or paid for parking.

Going Loco

Thanks to the Swiss Railways (SBB/CFF/FFS) and the affiliated narrow-gauge Rhätische Bahn (the Rhaeteian Railways, commonly referred to as the "Rhätibahn"), most destinations mentioned in the chapter are reachable by train; happily, Swiss Post buses stop in places where there is no train service.

Trains generally run from around 6 AM to 10:30 PM (schedules sometimes change between October and Easter).

With its signature picturesque red wagons, the Rhätibahn (or RhB) network of trains that traverse Graubünden, is tailor-made for sightseeing thanks to its "panorama" cars (with big windows) that allows travelers to truly enjoy some of Switzerland's most spectacular scenery along 400 km (248 mi) of narrow-gauge tracks.

Special short trips for rail enthusiasts include excursions on three remaining steam locomotives and trips in open carriages over the Bernina Pass.

The legendary Glacier Express from St. Moritz to Zermatt and other trains traverse spectacular terrain, the bright-red cars crossing bridges built unbelievably high over gorges.

WHAT IT COSTS In Swiss francs

	$$$$	$$$	$$	$	¢
Restaurants	over 60 SF	40 SF–60 SF	25 SF–40 SF	15 SF–25 SF	under 15 SF
Hotels	over 350 SF	250 SF–350 SF	175 SF–250 SF	100 SF–175 SF	under 100 SF

Restaurant prices are per person for a main course at dinner. Hotel prices are for two people in a standard double room in high season, including tax and service.

Updated by
Marton Radkai

THOUGH THE NAMES OF ITS RESORTS—St. Moritz, Davos, Klosters, Arosa—register almost automatic recognition, the region wrapped around them remains surprisingly unsung, untouched by the fur-clad celebs who make stage sets out of its sports centers, aloof to the glamour trends—quirky, resilient, and decidedly apart. Nowhere in Switzerland will you find sharper contrasts than those between the bronze seven-day citizens who jet into St. Moritz and the stalwart native farmers who nurse archaic dialects and gather their crops by hand as their Roman-Etruscan forebearers did. Resort life in winter contrasts sharply with the everyday existence of the native mountain farmers.

As it straddles the continental divide, its rains pour off northward into the Rhine, eastward with the Inn to the Danube and Black Sea, and south to the River Po, the landscape here is thus riddled with bluff-lined valleys. The southern half basks in crystalline light and, except for the Italian-speaking Ticino, receives the most sunshine in the country. Its 150 valleys and 615 lakes are flanked by 937 peaks, among them Piz Buin (10,867 feet) in the north and Piz Bernina (13,307 feet), the canton's highest mountain, in the south.Like many Swiss Cantons, Graubünden is culturally diverse. To the north it borders Austria and Liechtenstein, and in the east and south it abuts Italy. Swiss-German and Italian are widely spoken. The ancient Romansh language (literally, "Roman") is still predominant in the Lower Engadine and Surselva; it is estimated that 30% of Graubünden residents can speak it. The language dates back to the 1st century BC, when the area was conquered by the Romans and became a province called Rhaetia Prima. An alternative view on this point says the tongue predates the Romans and originated as long ago as 600 BC, when an Etruscan prince named Rhaetus invaded the region.

Anyone versed in a Latin language can follow Romansh's simpler signs (*abitaziun da vacanzas,* for example, is a vacation apartment), but Romansh is no easy matter to pick it up by ear. Nor do the Graubünders smooth the way: Rhaetian Romantisch is fragmented into five dialects, which developed separately in formerly isolated valleys, so that depending on where you are, the word for *house* can be seen written on the facades of homes as *casa, chasa, chesa, tga/tgesa, or tgea.* Even the name *Graubünden* itself comes in a variety of forms: Grisons (French), Grigioni (Italian), and Grischun (Romansh). It originates from the "Gray Confederation," one of three leagues that joined together in 1471 to resist the feudal Habsburg rulers. After a period as a "free state," Graubünden became a Swiss canton in 1803. With these dialects and their derivatives cutting one valley culture neatly off from another, it's no wonder the back roads of the region seem as removed from the modern mainstream as the once-a-century world of Brigadoon.

Exploring Graubünden

A spine of 9,800-foot peaks fairly neatly bisects the region into two very different sections, which are connected by the Julier, Albula, and Flüela passes. In the north is the region's capital, Chur; to the west lies Sur-

SKIING: SPORTY TO SNOBBISH

With Davos, site of the world's first ski lift, St. Moritz, arguably the world's ritziest resort, and a host of other hot spots within its confines, Graubünden has earned its reputation as an ultimate winter destination. You'll find downhill skiing and snowboarding for all skill levels, as well as miles of *Langlauf* (cross-country skiing) trails prepared for both the classic and skating techniques.

Sports shops can outfit you with the necessary equipment; in Davos and Flims-Laax you can even rent ski clothing. If you plan to spend a few days in one resort, check with local tourist offices for special packages. If you want to spend a day in a different resort within Graubünden, buy the lift ticket with your train ticket and the return fare will be nicely reduced. Remember that it was in Klosters that a fatal accident occured in the entourage of England's Prince Charles, whose group was skiing off-piste–an unhappy reminder to always avoid unmarked zones.

selva; and farther east are the famous ski resorts of Arosa, Klosters, and Davos. The southern part of the canton includes the Engadine, with its lakes, sophisticated resorts, and the National Park. The canton extends east to Austria and south toward Italy from the valleys of Bergell, Müstair, and Puschlav.

HEIDI COUNTRY

The Maienfeld region, with its hills and craggy peaks sloping down to sheltered vineyards, is the gateway from the north into Graubünden, but its claim to fame is that the legendary Heidi lived here. To the west in Surselva, the villages of Flims, Laax, and Falera together form the Alpine Arena, Graubünden's largest connected ski area. Arosa, to the east in the Schanfigg valley, is a quieter resort village that lies at the end of a spectacular, steep, winding road. The transportation hub of the region is Chur, the district capitol.

Chur

▶ ❶ **To & From:** *The Swiss Federal Railway trains that enter Graubünden only travel as far as Chur. From here the local Rhätische Bahn (RhB) takes over. Frequent trains arrive in Chur from Zürich (38 SF, 1 ¼ hr), Klosters (30 SF, 1 hr), Davos (30 SF, 1 hr), and Liechtenstein (10 SF, ½-hr). For departure times and prices for trains and buses for most destinations in this chapter, check with www.sbb.ch—the main Swiss public transportation Web site—or www.rhb.ch, or call 0900/300300 (1,19 SF per minute). Remember, if you have a Swiss Pass or another rail-discounting card, it also applies to the buses. Chur is 119 km (75 mi) southeast of Zürich, 77 km (48 mi) south of Appenzell.*

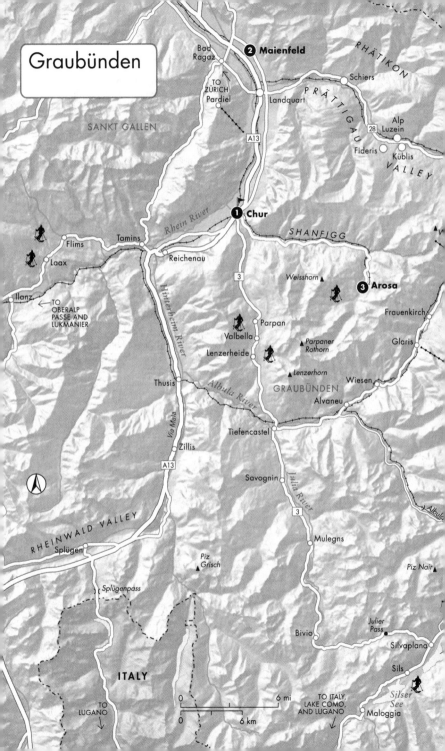

A small city (and cantonal capital) of 35,000, with a modern downtown and a busy rail crossroads, Chur is actually the oldest continuously settled site north of the Alps. Recent discoveries of Stone Age tools place Chur's origins back to roughly 11,000 BC. The Romans founded Curia Raetorium on the rocky terrace south of the river; from here, they protected the Alpine routes that led to the Bodensee. By AD 284 the town served as the capital of a flourishing Roman colony, Rhaetia Prima. Its heyday was during the Middle Ages, when it was ruled by bishops and bishop-princes. Narrow streets, cobblestone alleys, hidden courtyards, and ancient shuttered buildings still abound. The southern *fohn* wind that blows up through the Rhein Valley accounts in great part for the wine grapes that grows along the steep slopes around the town.

The **Rathaus** (Town Hall) originated as two structures in 1464, which were connected in 1540. At ground level, under the arches, is the old marketplace. In the open hall on the second floor is a model of the Old Town, which can help you plan a tour of the city. The Grosser Ratsaal (Council Chamber) has a timber ceiling dating from 1493; the Bürgerratskammer (Citizens' Council Chamber) has wall panels from the Renaissance. Both chambers have old ceramic stoves, the one in the Ratsaal depicting the various deadly sins, the group of human behaviors Christian theology warns against. Embedded in the wall beside the door opening onto Reichsgasse is a rod of iron about a foot long—the standard measure of a foot or shoe before the metric system was introduced. Although both chambers are generally closed to the public, very small groups can contact the tourist office to arrange a visit. ✉ *Poststr.*

The **Kirche St. Martin** (St. Martin's Church) was built in 1491 after a fire destroyed the original dating from the 8th century. Since 1526 it has been Protestant. On your right as you enter are three stained-glass windows created in 1919 by Augusto Giacometti, the father of the Graubünden sculptor Alberto Giacometti. The steeple dates from 1917; with permission from the sacristan, you can climb to the top to see the bells. Of note, too, is the 1716 fountain beside the church whose basin features the signs of the zodiac (with the exception of the figure on top, it is the original work). ✉ *Evangel. Kirchgemeinde, Kirchg. 12* ☏ *081/2522292* ⊙ *Weekdays 8:30–11:30 and 2–5.*

★ The **Rätisches Museum** provides a thorough, evocative overview of the canton's development. Displayed in a 1675 mansion, the collection includes not only furnishings and goods from the period, but also archaeological finds from the region, both Roman and prehistoric. There are also exhibitions of special interest on display most of the time. ✉ *Hofstr. 1* ☏ *081/2572889* ⊕ *www.raetischesmuseum.gr.ch* ▣ *5 SF* ⊙ *Tues.–Sun. 10–5.*

Opposite the Rätisches Museum, a stone archway under the **Hof-Torturm** (Citadel Gate Tower) leads into the court of the strong bishop-princes of Chur, once hosts to Holy Roman emperors passing through on their way to Italy or Germany—sometimes with whole armies in tow. The bishops were repaid for their hospitality by imperial donations to the people. The thick fortifications of the residence reflect the disputed powers of the bishops; by the 15th century, irate inhabitants who re-

EATING WELL IN GRAUBÜNDEN

Graubünden, with its myriad dialects and potent blend of Latin and German blood, has a cuisine as novel and unexpected as its culture. The Graubünden idea of fast food is a *salsiz* (a kind of small, rectangular-shape salami of deer, liver, or beef) and a piece of bread. Besides regional specialties like the ubiquitous *Bündnerfleisch* (air-dried beef pressed into rectangular loaves and shaved into translucent slices), *Gerstensuppe* (barley soup), and *Nusstorte* (shortbread with a chewy walnut-and-caramel filling), you will find a broad range of international cooking, notably in the larger resorts. Italian influence is strong and the Germanic *Spätzli* (tiny flour dumplings) coexist with gnocchi, risotto, and polenta.

You may feel you've stepped back into the Middle Ages when you sit down to *pizzoccheri neri* (buckwheat noodles with greens and potatoes, swimming in garlic butter and melted cheese) or to *maluns* (grated potatoes stirred in pools of butter until they form crisp balls). *Capuns* or *chrutcapuns* are bundles of Swiss chard smothered in butter and cheese and flavored with dried meat. These down-to-earth treats are making a comeback in either traditional or more modern interpretations. Year-round, but especially in fall, many menus feature wild game: the centuries-old hunting tradition is especially strong in this canton. Look for *Reh* or *Hirsch* (roe or red deer) and *Gems* (chamois), usually served with red cabbage, fruits, and chestnuts or in a *Pfeffer* (strongly flavored, peppery stew).

Most restaurants' wine lists include a selection of the red pinot noir and white Riesling Sylvaner from the Bündnerherrschaft region around Maienfeld, Jenins, and Malans as well as the hearty red Nebbiolo of the Veltlin. The latter is actually grown over the southern border in Valtellina, which was ceded to Italy in 1815, but some quantities have always been brought in bulk into the canton for bottling and can be considered, at least in spirit, to be Swiss. As an alternative to wine, try one of the regional mineral waters: Valser, Passugger, or Rhäzünzer.

Many restaurants in resort towns close from the end of April to mid-June and October to December; there are variations and exceptions, of course, so if you plan a visit in the off-season, check in advance.

peatedly rebelled were rebuffed and punished with excommunication. By 1526 the Reformation had broken the domination of the Church, although the city remains a Catholic bishopric today. The Hofkellerei Stübli is now at the base of the tower. Head up to the second floor and you can have a drink in the paneled room, dating from 1522, once used for church meetings. ⊠ *Hof 1.*

The **Kathedrale St. Maria Himmelfahrt** (Cathedral of the Assumption) was built between 1151 and 1272, drawing on stylistic influences from all across Europe. The structure on this site in prehistoric times was subsequently supplanted by a Roman castle, a bishop's house in the 5th century, and a Carolingian cathedral in the 8th century. The capitals of the columns are carved with fantastical beasts; at their bases are clustered less-threatening animals, such as sheep and marmots. In the choir is a magnificent 15th-century altar of gilded wood featuring nearly 150 carved figures. This late-15th century work comes from the workshop of Jakob Russ in Ravensburg, Germany. The cathedral is undergoing extensive renovations at press time but until its completion the reliquaries, altar pieces, paintings, and other treasures can be viewed at the Rätisches Museum. ⊠ *Hof* ☎ *081/2529250* ⊘ *Daily 8–7.*

Obere Gasse, once the main street through Chur and a major route between Germany and Italy, is now lined with small shops and cafés. At the end stands the 16th-century Obertor (Upper Gate), guarding the bridge across the Plessur River. ⊠ *Old Town, between the Obertor and Arcaspl.*

Collections at Graubünden's art museum, the **Bündner Kunstmuseum,** include works by well-known artists who lived or worked in the canton, including Angelika Kauffmann, Giovanni Segantini, Giovanni and Alberto Giacometti, and Ernst Kirchner. The building itself is a majestic neoclassical structure erected in 1875 as a private residence. ⊠ *Postpl.* ☎ *081/2572868* ⊕ *buendner-kunstmuseum.ch* 🗔 *7 SF* ⊘ *Tues., Wed., and Fri.–Sun. 10–noon, 2–5, Thurs. 10–noon, 2–8.*

OFF THE BEATEN PATH

VIA MALA – Heading toward the San Bernardino pass on the A13, turn off at Thusis and follow the sign for the Via Mala (the "bad road"), which was used by the Romans and traders over centuries. It runs about 6 km (3½ mi) alongside the narrow Hinterrhein gorge. Shortly after the start of the gorge, you can climb down 321 steps (for a fee of 5 SF) to view the river, rock formations, a mid-18th-century bridge, and old road itself. Continue to **Zillis** to see the church's renowned 12th-century painted wood ceiling, whose 153 panels mostly depict stories from the Bible. It is one of the world's oldest original artistic works from the Romanesque era.

Where to Stay & Eat

$–$$ ✕ **Calanda.** Young and old people meet here in this friendly, trendy place with a great big mural featuring the restaurant's specialty: chicken. You can enjoy a simple charcoal-roasted free-roaming bird on a bed of salad in exotic mango sauce, or a few helpings of wings, or curried chicken breast in a glass. Tuesday and Thursday are no smoking days. ⊠ *Postplatz* ☎ *081/2530880* ▭ *AE, V.*

$$–$$$ ✕▦ **Stern.** Like many of the good vintages on its wine list, this historic
Fodor'sChoice inn, built in 1677, just keeps getting better, especially under the loving
★ care of Adrian Müller. The restaurant serves local wines and focuses boldly on regional dishes such as *capuns, maluns,* or the filling *Ratsherrenplatte,* which combines vegetables, Pizokel, and a beef fillet. The family-owned and -run hotel neighbors the town's main church, but don't worry about lost sleep; its bells are silent at night. Rooms are modern and wood-clad; you can relax on a rooftop terrace or in the fireplace lounge. Note that the elevator goes only to the third floor. ⊠ *Reichg. 11, CH-7000* ☎ *081/2585757* 🖶 *081/2585758* ⊕ *www.stern-chur.ch* 🗗 *58 rooms*

      🔥 *Restaurant, cable TV, Internet room; no a/c* 🖃 *AE, DC, MC, V*
🍽 *BP.*

$$ 🖥 **Hotel ABC.** This *garni* (without a restaurant) business hotel is just yards
from the train station. (Note that the town's train and bus stations are
being renovated—estimated completion: Jan 2008. So for now you'll
have to step around a bevy of cranes; happily, there are no night trains
to keep you awake.) It occupies five floors of a corporate metal-and-
glass box; the entry is hidden between shops. Amenities and rooms are
state-of-the-art. 🖃 *Bahnhofpl., CH-7000* 🕿 *081/2526033* 🖷 *081/
2525524* ⊕ *www.hotelabc.ch* 📠 *40 rooms* 🔥 *Cable TV, sauna, busi-
ness services, meeting rooms, Internet room, no-smoking floor; no a/c*
🖃 *AE, DC, MC, V* 🍽 *BP.*

Nightlife
The futuristic **Giger Bar** (🖃 Comercialstr. 23 🕿 081/2537506) is a
strange space created by Academy Award winner H. R. Giger, a Chur
native who designed the sets for the famous film *Alien.*

Maienfeld

❷ **To & From:** *Trains connect Chur and Maienfeld between 9 AM and 9
PM twice every half hour (at 22 past and 5 minutes to the hour); between
6 PM and 9 AM trains leave three times per hour (the additional train is
at 13 past). The journey lasts no more than 14 minutes. Maienfeld is
17 km (11 mi) north of Chur.*

Above this graceful little village full of
fountains, vineyards, and old stucco
houses, the Zürich author Johanna
Spyri set *Heidi*, the much-loved chil-
dren's story of an orphan growing up
with her grandfather on an isolated
Alpine farm. Taken away to accom-
pany the invalid Clara in murky
Frankfurt, she languishes until return-
ing to her mountain home. Nursing
her fatally ill son, Spyri spent time in
Maienfeld and liked the mountains

> ### SWEETEST STORY
> ### EVER TOLD
>
> For the ultimate immersion in
> Heidi lore and folklore, check out
> "Heidi: Das Musical" (081/
> 7202099, www.heidimusical.ch),
> performed on an impressive lake-
> side stage during August in nearby
> Walenstadt.

behind, but it's questionable whether actual people inspired her tale.
Nonetheless you can hike from Maienfeld along the **Heidi-Weg** (Heidi
Path), either on the short circular route or continuing across steep open
meadows and through thick forest to what have now been designated
Peter the Goatherd's Hut and the Alm-Uncle's Hut. Here you might meet
today's version of that character, who enjoys a chat and can answer Heidi-
related questions in English. Along the way you'll take in awe-inspir-
ing Rhine Valley views from flowered meadows that would have suited
😊 Heidi beautifully. On both routes, you pass through **Heididorf** (Heidi Vil-
lage), in reality the hamlet of Oberrofels. Here you can find the house
that was used as a model for the illustrations in the original *Heidi*
books. It now houses Heidi-appropriate furnishings and life-size mod-
els of Heidi, Grandfather, and Peter. 🕿 *081/3301912* ⊕ *www.heidi-swiss.
ch* 📠 *5 SF* 🕐 *Mid-Mar.–mid-Nov., daily 10–5.*

As an alternative to walking the route, you can take a two-hour tour in a **horse-drawn carriage** (☎ 081/3301912). The cost is 30 SF per person. At the kitsch-happy **Heidihof Hotel** (☎ 081/3004747), an extended farmhouse, have a snack and take in the view or spend the night. For a more genuine "Heidi experience" you can sleep in straw at a nearby farm (inquire at the tourist office).

In Maienfeld, visit a few of the two dozen local wine merchants or enjoy a meal in the Knight's Hall of **Schloss Brandis**, a castle whose earliest portions date from the 10th century. ☎ *081/3022423* ⊘ *Closed mid-July–mid-Aug.*

Across the river (and cantonal border), just three minutes by train, you can visit the famous spa center at **Bad Ragaz** with its indoor-outdoor warm pools. ☎ *081/3032741* ⊠ *17 SF* ⊘ *Daily 7:30 AM–9 PM.*

Arosa

★ ❸ **To & From:** *The Rhätische Bahn (RhB) has departures from Arosa at least once an hour between 5:26 AM and 10:55 PM. The 9 AM train has open carriages in summer for an excellent sightseeing experience. Within town, you can ride the municipal buses for free if you have the Arosa Card. Arosa is 29 km (18 mi) southeast of Chur.*

Thanks to its high altitude, Arosa (5,900 feet) is a well-known winter and summer sports center offering brisk hiking, paragliding, and other activities in summer, and a long skiing or snowboarding season with a guarantee of snow. Its modest size, isolated location, quiet atmosphere, and natural beauty set it apart. There is little of the rush of Davos or the pretension of St. Moritz: this is a friendly, family-oriented spot staffed by upbeat, down-to-earth people. Even the well-heeled rarely dress for dinner. On a winter walk, you are more likely to be overtaken by sleds and horse-drawn carriages than by cars.

> **WORD OF MOUTH**
>
> "Arosa is a small skiing town, with limited activities for non-skiers (but if they are happy to sit with a book and take walks and admire the scenery . .). Arosa is only 30 minutes by train from Chur, which has a lovely old town. You could also take the Bernina Express train, one of the best scenic excursion trains in Switzerland. I have only skied Arosa as a ski-over from Davos, but thought it was good."
> –Cicerone

"I spent weeks up there," wrote author Hermann Hesse in 1934, "and I found a level of vigor and youth I would never have thought possible." Arosa lies at the end of a beautiful, winding 30-km (19-mi) road with grades of more than 12% and more than 360 turns. Taking the train from Chur is a lot less nerve-wracking than driving.

The town has two sections: Inner-Arosa, where the Walsers ("immigrants" from the Valais) built their wooden chalets in the 14th century, is at the end of the valley; Ausser-Arosa is near the train station and the Obersee (Upper Lake). Between the two is the impossible-to-miss casino, with its mosaic facade of screaming colors (it has now been converted into a theater/cinema). A convenient free bus shuttles through the town, and traffic is forbidden between midnight and 6 AM. After you deliver your luggage to your hotel, you probably won't be using your car again while in town.

Don't miss the light, water, and music show on the lake at 9:50 PM every Saturday from mid-June to mid-October (except in the event of heavy rain or wind). Drop into the *Eggahus,* one of the oldest and best kept buildings from Arosa's past. It was first mentioned in a 1550 document and now houses the **Schanfigger Heimatmuseum.** Besides the tools of the mountain farmer's difficult trade, this little museum has put together a slide show on local history. The museum building itself, a mid-16th-century wooden farmhouse, is a sight to behold. ⊠ *Poststr., Inner-Arosa* 📞 *No phone* 💶 *3 SF* ☉ *Late Dec.–early Apr., Tues. and Fri. 2:30–4:30; mid-June–mid-Oct., Mon., Wed., and Fri. 2:30–4:30.*

Skiing

Arosa's ski area is small compared with those of the Upper Engadine, Davos-Klosters, and the Alpine Arena (Flims-Laax). Closely screened in by mountains, the 5,900-foot-high resort has runs suitable for every level of skier. Its 15 lifts serve 70 km (43 mi) of trails. The slopes can be accessed directly from the valley at three points: the top of the village; behind the train station; and Prätschli, a "feeder" lift to the main ski area. The black piste on the **Weisshorn** (8,700 feet) is challenging, but most of the runs there, as well as on **Hörnli** (8,200 feet), are easy to intermediate. You can get snow-sports instruction at the official **Swiss Ski School** (📞 081/3771150). Another option for ski lessons is the **ABC Snowsport School** (📞 081/3565660). For snowboarding lessons, try **Swiss Ski and Snowboard School** (📞 081/3787500 and 081/3787505). Cross-country skiers or Nordic walkers will find instruction, guided tours, equipment, and information at the **Langlauf- und Schneeschuhzentrum Maran,** the Cross-country and Snow Shoe Center of Maran (📞 081/3772215). All schools have English-speaking instructors. A one-day lift ticket costs 55 SF; a six-day pass costs 256 SF. For cross-country skiing or snowshoeing, the Maran and Isla trails have 30 km (18 mi) of groomed trails. There are three official sled runs: Tschuggen, Prätschli, and Untersee. You can rent sleds at the train station or at **Stivetta Sport** (⊠ Innere Poststr. 📞 081/3772181).

Where to Stay & Eat

$$–$$$ ✕ **Le Bistro.** The decor fits the name, with tile floor, old French posters, and newspaper cuttings on the walls. The menu also leans toward French cuisine, with truffles and fried duck liver with apple and celery puree, for example, and several ponderous venison dishes. For lighter fare, try the fish creations such as salmon lasagna. ⊠ *Hotel Cristallo, Poststr.* 📞 *081/3786868* 🟰 *AE, MC, V* ☉ *Closed mid-Apr.–late June and mid-Oct.–early Dec.*

$–$$ ✕ **Hold.** This busy family restaurant sits literally at the foot of the slopes. The menu is mostly traditional fare, including a range of *Spätzli* (little dumplings) specialties—in curry sauce, or with Graubünden air-dried meat, for example—that will put an end to the greatest hunger pangs. Several advantages make it an especially good place to bring kids: there are children's meals for under 10 SF; it's adjacent to the children's ski school; and it has a small playroom. ✉ *Poststr.* ☎ *081/3771408* 💳 *AE, DC, MC, V* ⏲ *Closed after Easter–mid-June and mid-Oct.–early Dec.*

$$$–$$$$ ✕🏨 **Arve Central.** There are flowers in the window boxes here year-round—in winter, wooden blooms replace the real thing. The flower theme is carried throughout the whole hotel, from the deep-pile carpet to the room key rings and the staff's uniforms. There are good views on the south side; the rooms in back have neither balcony nor view. The wood-clad Arvenstube restaurant offers some of the best food in town with eclectic, changing menus. Herbs gathered from the kitchen's garden appear in dishes that range from risottos to steaks and rack of lamb. The restaurant is closed on Monday and Tuesday in May. ✉ *Off Poststr., CH-7050* ☎ *081/3785252* 📠 *081/3785250* 🌐 *www.arve-central.ch* 🛏 *45 rooms, 2 suites, 1 apartment* 👍 *Restaurant, pool, hot tub, sauna, bar; no a/c* 💳 *AE, DC, MC, V* 🍽 *MAP.*

$$$ ✕🏨 **Waldhotel National.** Hallowed as the hotel where Thomas Mann wrote part of his famous *Magic Mountain*—back in the early 1900s this was a "cure-hotel" for ailing patients—this large, chalet-inspired retreat is set in its own wooded grounds above Arosa. Peace is everywhere, intoxicatingly enjoyed as you ski or sled your way home in winter. North-facing rooms look over the forest, and south-facing ones look over the village and the mountains. All are tastefully decorated and have touches of golden pine. The Kachelofa-Stübli serves local and French specialties. Hotel residents enjoy their meals in the airy and very popular Thomas Mann Restaurant (reservations essential). ✉ *CH-7050* ☎ *081/3785555* 📠 *081/3785599* 🌐 *www.waldhotel.ch* 🛏 *79 rooms, 14 junior suites, 1 apartment* 👍 *2 restaurants, Stübli, in-room safes, minibars, cable TV, pool, hair salon, massage, sauna, piano bar* 💳 *AE, DC, MC, V* ⏲ *Closed mid-Apr.–mid-June and mid-Sept.–early Dec.* 🍽 *BP.*

★ **$$$$** 🏨 **Kulm.** Twenty-eight cowbells hanging above the reception desk are all that recall the hotel's past as a 19th-century wooden chalet. The current modern structure is a sporty luxury hotel, with a large foyer warmed by a modern fireplace and enlivened by a bar. Its position on the farthest edge of town, at the base of the slopes, is its biggest draw; from its wraparound windows you can take in acres of green hills or snowy slopes (south-facing rooms have balconies). Rooms have soft prints and neutral tones; bathrooms are tile and stone. In winter an Italian trattoria and a Thai restaurant join the main restaurants (jacket requested). The AlpinSpa wellness center is one of the best in the region, with everything from saunas to a "sound and aroma" grotto. ✉ *CH-7050* ☎ *081/3788888* 📠 *081/3788889* 🌐 *www.arosakulm.ch* 🛏 *122 rooms, 15 suites* 👍 *5 restaurants, in-room safes, minibars, cable TV, putting green, 2 tennis courts, pool, health club, spa, bowling, bar, piano bar, babysitting, parking (fee)* 💳 *AE, DC, MC, V* ⏲ *Closed late Sept.–early Dec. and mid-Apr.–mid-June* 🍽 *BP.*

$$–$$$$ 🏨 **Alpensonne.** Family-owned and run, this hotel is only about 200 yards from the ski lifts of Inner-Arosa. The public spaces are light and bright. Guest rooms are in soft colors with lots of wood. Some have showers only, and some of these are not yet tiled, so be sure to specify. Several family rooms are available, with multiple beds. Rooms facing south have great views. The café-Stübli serves meat and cheese fondues daily. Half board is available for an additional 25 SF per person. ⊠ *Poststr., CH-7050* ☎ *081/3771547* 📠 *081/3773470* ⊕ *www.hotelalpensonne. ch* 🛏 *35 rooms, 3 apartments* ⚒ *Restaurant, café, Stübli, minibars, cable TV, sauna, steam room, bar, recreation room; no a/c* ⊟ *AE, DC, MC, V* ⊙ *Closed late Apr.–late June and mid-Oct.–early Dec.* ⊺⊙⊦ *BP.*

★ **$–$$** 🏨 **Sonnenhalde.** The sensor-touch heavy pine door that welcomes you to this chalet hotel garni is your first sign of the prevailing happy marriage of charm and modern comfort. The sizable rooms are bright, with wall-to-wall wood and rustic decor. Some rooms easily accommodate extra beds (for an additional fee). Bathrooms have showers instead of tubs; the lowest-price rooms have only sinks and share the other facilities. ⊠*CH-7050* ☎*081/3771531* 📠*081/3774455* ⊕*www.sonnenhalde-arosa.ch* 🛏 *21 rooms, 14 with bath* ⚒ *Cable TV, sauna, steam room; no a/c* ⊟ *AE, DC, MC, V* ⊙ *Closed late Apr.–late June and mid-Oct.–early Dec.* ⊺⊙⊦ *BP.*

Nightlife & the Arts

BARS At the Hotel Eden, the **Kitchen Club** (⊠ Jory-Jenny-Str. ☎ 081/3787106) is a disco inside a kitchen dating back to 1907. A young crowd dances among old pots and pans while the DJ perches above antique refrigerators. The après-ski crowd here is chic—you should change out of your ski bibs first. In the casino, **Nuts** (⊠ Poststr. ☎ 081/3773940) plays the latest tunes for young people. For a more discolike experience, the **Gada Dancing** in the Hotel Carmenna plays tunes from the '70s and '80s in a refurbished stable (☎ 081/3771766).

MUSIC From Christmas to mid-April and in summer, concerts are given at 5 PM on Tuesday on the hand-painted organ in Arosa's 500-year-old, wooden-roof **Bergkirchli** (mountain chapel). A yodeling festival takes place in July, and music courses are given from June through October; get the program from **Kulturkreis Arosa** (☎ 081/3538747 📠 081/3538750).

Sports & the Outdoors

GOLF Europe's highest tee (6,209 feet) is on the eighth hole of Arosa's 18-hole course at **Maran** (☎ 081/3774242).

HIKING & BIKING The **Arosa tourist office** (☎ 081/378–7020) can arrange four-day walking or biking trips from Davos to Arosa.

SKATING & CURLING Arosa has several skating rinks. At the indoor **Eissporthalle** (☎ 081/3771745) you can watch ice hockey as well as take skating or curling lessons; there's an open-air rink alongside. Another option is the **InnerArosa rink** (☎ 081/3772930), which is open from Christmas to mid-February.

PRÄTTIGAU & DAVOS

The name "Prättigau" means "meadow valley," and it's just that—a lush landscape of alternating orchards, pastures, and pine-covered mountains (though the main highway is a very busy route). The predominant language is German, introduced by "immigrants" from the Valais in the 13th century, though most villages still have Romansch names. Prättigau's most renowned ski resort is Klosters. Its equally famous neighbor and ski-region partner, Davos, lies in the Landwasser Valley, over the Wolfgang Pass. If you prefer an urban experience, head to Davos; for a quieter village experience, look to Klosters.

Klosters

❹ **To & From:** *The Rhätische Bahn (RhB), or a combination of Swiss railways and the RhB, cover the distance in around one hour from Chur for 20 SF one-way. Klosters is 49 km (29 mi) east of Chur..*

At one time simply a group of hamlets, Klosters has become a small but chic resort, made up mostly of weathered-wood and white-stucco chalets. Author Peter Viertel and his wife, film luminary Deborah Kerr, made this their home base for decades. The village has two districts: Platz, which is older and busier, and Dorf, which lies on the main road toward Landquart. Klosters is famed for its skiing—British royal family members are faithful visitors—and makes the most of its access to the slopes of the Parsenn, above Davos. In Klosters Platz, the church of **St. Jacob**, dating from 1492, is the only remnant of the medieval monastery from which the village took its name. Its windows were painted by Augusto Giacometti.

A brief visit to the folk museum **Nutli-Hüschi** shows the resort's evolution from its mountain roots. This pretty wood-and-stone farmhouse with a stable was built in 1565. It shows how people lived and worked in the Prättigau in centuries past through exhibits of kitchen utensils, handcrafts, tools, and the spare regional furniture, including a child's bed that could be expanded as the child grew. ✉ *Monbielerstr. at Talstr.* ☎ *081/4102020* 💷 *2 SF* ☉ *Dec.–mid-Apr. and late June–mid-Oct., Wed. and Fri. 3–5.*

UP, DOWN & AROUND

In Graubünden, you'll find downhill skiing and snowboarding for all skill levels, as well as miles of *Langlauf* (cross-country skiing) trails prepared for both the classic and skating techniques. You can participate in moonlight or torchlight skiing at almost all of the resorts, usually followed by a get-together with fellow travelers. Sports shops can outfit you with the necessary equipment; in Davos and Flims-Laax you can even rent ski clothing. If you want to spend a day in a different resort within Graubünden, buy the lift ticket with your train ticket and the return fare will be just 1 SF.

Skiing

Klosters is known for its vast range of downhill runs, which, together with those of Davos, total 320 km (200 mi). These are divided almost equally among easy, moderate, and difficult pistes. From the Gotschnagrat (7,494 feet), skiers can connect to the Parsenn slopes, and try, for example, the famous Weissflüh run down to the village of Küblis. The sunny Madrisa slopes above Klosters Dorf offer relatively easy skiing and snowboarding. For instruction or to go on a snowshoe trek, contact the **Swiss Ski & Snowboard School** (☎ 081/4102828), which has a branch in both Platz and Dorf. The **Swiss Ski & Snowboard School Saas** (☎ 081/4226660), located near the train station in Klosters Platz, also offers the standard instruction plus special courses in carving, slalom skiing, and more; it has branches in both Platz and Dorf. There are 35 km (22 mi) of cross-country tracks and you can get lessons at the **Nordic Ski School** (☎ 081/4221040). Lift tickets to the combined Davos/Klosters area cost 65 SF for one day and up to 282 SF for six days, depending on how many and in which areas you want to ski. Bar code cards and KeyCards are used; you can activate them online (⊕ www.davosklosters. ch). Train or bus transport back to Klosters from other villages within the ski area is included in the price of the regional ski ticket.

Where to Stay & Eat

$$–$$$ ✕ **Alte Post.** In this warm local favorite (set in the Aeuja section of Klosters), pleasantly cluttered with ceramics and game trophies, choose from a menu with a wide variety of interesting dishes, from fish fondue and tripe Neuchatel (in white wine and caraway sauce), to beef marsala and risottos. Look for seasonal dishes, such as venison and, in winter, *tête de veau* (veal head) vinaigrette. If you like salmon, a special menu features the fish in every course but the sorbet (they smoke their own Norwegian salmon). ⊠ *Doggilochstr. 136, Klosters-Aeuja* ☎ *081/ 4221716* ▤ *DC, MC, V* ⊗ *Closed Mon. and Tues. and May and Nov.*

$–$$ ✕ **Höhwald.** This is a friendly, touristy restaurant up the hill from Klosters in Monbiel, with a large, open terrace that takes in valley and mountain views. Try their Graubünden specialties, for example Capuns, Prättigauer *Knödlis* (dumplings), and *Chäs-Gatschäder* (a mixture of bread, milk, and cheese). ⊠ *Klosters-Monbiel* ☎ *081/4223045* ▤ *AE, MC, V* ⊗ *Closed Tues. and mid-Apr.–May and late Oct.–Dec.*

★ **$$$–$$$$** ✕▤ **Walserhof.** The most sophisticated establishment in Klosters, Walserhof was built in 1981 with the weathered boards from an old farmhouse. The only drawback is its location on the main road through town; the best views take in either the street or fairly well-developed fields behind. Its restaurant and café are paneled with ancient carved wood; stone, stucco, and quarry tile are used elsewhere. The superb restaurant serves regional dishes, such as trout in cider and lamb stew with polenta. ⊠ *Landstr., CH-7250 Klosters-Platz* ☎ *081/4102929* 🖷 *081/4102939* ⊕ *www. walserhof.ch* ⇜ *11 rooms, 3 suites* ⚏ *Restaurant, café, minibars, cable TV, gym, sauna; no a/c* ▤ *AE, DC, MC, V* ⊗ *Closed Easter–late June and mid-Oct.–early Dec.* ▮○▮ *BP.*

$$–$$$$ ✕▤ **Rustico.** Good things come in small packages here—guest rooms are on a petite scale but are very attractive, with parquet floors, country cottons, and white-tile showers. The lounge area has a fireplace and leads out to a summer terrace dominated by a Buddha. The restaurant's white walls are interrupted with meditative art works (a water sculpture, for example). It serves Euro-Asian dishes created in-house, such as a monkfish saltimbocca on lobster risotto with summer vegetables and red wine butter foam. After dinner cigars, Havanas, are also on offer. The restaurant is closed on Wednesday in summer. ⊠ *Landstr. 194, CH-7250 Klosters-Platz* ☎ *081/4102288* 🖶 *081/4102280* ⊕ *www.rusticohotel. com* ⇨ *10 rooms, 2 suites* ⚑ *Restaurant, in-room safes, minibars, cable TV, sauna, billiards, bar; no a/c* ▭ *DC, MC, V* ☉ *Closed June and Nov.* ⦿ *BP.*

$–$$$$ 🏨 **Chesa Grischuna.** Located directly in the town center, this 1938 house built on the remains of a farmhouse, is one of the region's most popular places to stay. Whether you bowl in the vaulted cellar, play cards, or dance to the piano music at happy hour, you'll be surrounded by the coveted social mix of Klosters regulars. Every room, including those in the nearby chalet annex, is full of old carved wood, and some have balconies. There are antiques throughout, and plenty of public spaces, as this is a sociable place. The restaurant offers a mix of salads, snacks, and full-fledged meals at affordable prices. ⊠ *Bahnhofstr., CH-7250 Klosters-Platz* ☎ *081/4222222* 🖶 *081/4222225* ⊕ *www.chesagrischuna. ch* ⇨ *25 rooms, 19 with bath* ⚑ *Restaurant, cable TV, in-room data ports, Internet, bowling, bar; no a/c* ▭ *AE, MC, V* ☉ *Closed after Easter–early July and mid-Oct.–mid-Dec.* ⦿ *BP.*

$$–$$$ 🏨 **Sunstar Albeina.** This large and luxurious chalet-style hotel has easy access to the Madrisa slopes. In summer you can join special tennis or horseback-riding weeks. Rooms are tastefully decorated, with floral details. Rooms for a lower rate are available in summer or early December; they're on the north side of the building or in the Chesa Albeina guesthouse. The popular Dörfji Bar draws regulars. ⊠ *CH-7252 Klosters-Dorf* ☎ *081/4232100* 🖶 *081/4232121* ⊕ *www.sunstar.ch* ⇨ *59 rooms* ⚑ *Restaurant, minibars, cable TV, pool, massage, sauna, steam room, billiards, bar, playground; no a/c* ▭ *AE, DC, MC, V* ☉ *Closed mid-Apr.–mid-June and mid-Oct.–mid-Dec.* ⦿ *BP.*

$$ 🏨 **Silvapina.** This delightful hotel in an old chalet-style building, is fam-
Fodor'sChoice ily-run and family-welcoming. It is right by the station (trains don't run
★ at night) and a few minutes' walk from the slopes. Rooms are done either all in wood or in white with touches of pine. Bathrooms have showers instead of tubs; south-facing rooms have balconies. Half board is offered in winter for an additional 25 SF. ⊠ *CH-7252 Klosters-Dorf* ☎ *081/4221468* 🖶 *081/4224078* ⊕ *www.silvapina.ch* ⇨ *15 rooms, 3 apartments* ⚑ *Restaurant, Stübli, cable TV, sauna, billiards, Ping-Pong, bar; no a/c* ▭ *AE, MC, V* ☉ *Closed May and Nov.* ⦿ *BP.*

Nightlife

Revelers dance late into the night at the **Casa Antica** (⊠ Landstr. 176 ☎ 081/4221621), in a 300-year-old converted barn. A popular after-dinner spot, **Chesa Bar** (⊠ Bahnhofstr. 12 ☎ 081/4222222) has piano music and several intimate bar areas. In the Silvretta Parkhotel there's the **Kir Royal** (⊠ Landstr. 190 ☎ 081/4233435) disco and a piano bar.

Sports & the Outdoors

BIKING & HIKING The Klosters area has plenty of trails for exploring the countryside. The 250 km (155 mi) of summer hiking routes are reduced to 30 km (19 mi) of prepared paths in winter. There are 120 km (74½ mi) of mountain-biking routes. To rent mountain bikes, try the **Hew Bike Shop** (⊠ Klosters-Dorf ☎ 081/4223942). Another source for mountain bikes is **Andrist Sport** (⊠ Klosters-Platz ☎ 081/4102080).

GOLF   Not to be outdone by its neighbors, Klosters has also added a relatively tough 9-hole **Golf Klosters** (☎ 081/4221133, ⊕ www.golf-klosters.ch) with a unique feature: the caddy is included in the greens fee. The seventh hole provides the additional handicap of a jaw-dropping view of Klosters.

SKATING   Klosters's **Sportszentrum** (✉ Doggilochstr. 11, Klosters-Platz ☎ 081/4102131) has rinks for skating, hockey, curling, and ice bowling in season. Skate rentals are available.

SLEDDING   Klosters is big on sledding. The area has three sled runs: the 3.5-km (2-mi) Rinerhorn run is also illuminated at night. A day card costs SF 47, while a sled can be rented for SF 7 at the cable-car valley station with a 50-franc deposit. Evening runs on the lighted slope are 7–11 PM from January to March. They cost SF 18 for an evening. Day cards at Madrisa mountain cost SF 33. The run here is 8.5 km long (5 mi) and ends in Saas, where you can return by bus to Klosters (buses leave every hour or so until 7:24 PM). Sled rentals at the Madrisa cable-car station are SF 8. The third sled run begins at the midway station of the Gotschna cable car. Day passes cost SF 33; sled rentals at the station cost SF 10. Sleds are available for rental at **Andrist Sport** (✉ Klosters-Platz ☎ 081/4102080). **Sport Gotschna** (✉ Klosters-Platz ☎ 081/4221197) also rents sleds.

SWIMMING   The town's heated **outdoor swimming pool** (✉ Doggilochstr. ☎ 081/4221524) is open all summer. The indoor pool of the **Hotel Pardenn** (☎ 081/4232020) is open to the public. The indoor pool at the **Hotel Sport** (☎ 081/4233030) has a wall of windows. The 14 meter indoor pool at the **Silvretta Parkhotel** (☎ 081/4233435) is open to the public as well.

Davos

❺ **To & From:** *To go to Chur or Zürich (52 SF, 2 ½ hrs), change trains at Landquart. For St. Moritz, take the train from Davos Platz and transfer at Filisur. If heading to Scuol, train it from Davos Dorf and transfer in Klosters. The Vereina tunnel provides year-round train service from Klosters to Sagliains, near Susch–Lavin. Car-carrying trains leave from just above Klosters—road signs indicate a train carrying cars and the name Vereina—at 20 past and 10 to the hour beginning between 7 AM and 10 PM. The first passenger train is at 5:20 AM. Prices vary according to season. A passenger car costs 27 SF in summer, 35 SF in winter, and 40 SF during the peak winter season from mid-December to mid-March during daylight hours. Davos is 11 km (7 mi) southwest of Klosters.*

At 5,116 feet, this highest "city" in Europe is good for cold-weather sports even in the soggiest of winters. It's famous for its ice sports and skiing and almost more celebrated for hosting the annual World Economic Forum every January. The town and its lake lie in the Landwasser Valley, which runs parallel to the Upper Engadine, though they're separated by the vast Albula chain, reaching to more than 9,840 feet. On the opposite side of the valley stands the Strela chain, dominated by the Weissfluh.

Take note: this is a capital for action-oriented sports enthusiasts and not necessarily for anyone seeking a peaceful, rustic mountain retreat

Inspiring Graubünden

NIETZSCHE'S FAMOUS philosophical work *Thus Spoke Zarathustra* opens its second part with Zarathustra returning to the mountains "to seek the solitude of his cave." While the author's thinking may have been abstract, the cave and the mountains were probably quite real. For it was in Sils Maria, near St. Moritz, in the summer of 1883, that Nietzsche began writing this lengthy treatise on man and superman. His fundamental concept of recurrence came to him during a walk around nearby Silverplaner Lake.

For those seeking inspiration, Graubünden has always been a natural high. Countless artistic personalities have come to the canton for rest and relaxation and left with some great work of literature or art in their bags (or at least their heads, waiting to be created). Something in the clarity of the air and proximity to the sky seems to dispel all the cares and worries of the daily grind and set creative juices flowing. For some, like Marcel Proust, it was the "bracing air, the aroma of hay and the sound of the brooks." For others, such as Hermann Hesse, the "powerful, severe beauty" of the mountains around Arosa provided the vim and vigor to edit his novel about religion and salvation, *Narcissus and Goldmund*. (He had been immobilized by a skiing accident, making it easier to devote himself to his work.) Nietzsche, for his part, felt he had arrived in the "Promised Land" on his first trip to the Engadin in 1879.

The gentle meadows and mysterious, aromatic forests of pine embraced by rugged snow-tipped mountains have all done their part to enthrall visitors.

Goethe, Germany's greatest poet and writer, traveled through the hair-raising Via Mala gorge on his way back from Italy and had to stop for a while to draw some sketches of the almost eerie sights. Decades later he recalled the trip: "The road over the Splügen mountains is indescribably beautiful, the Via Mala is the most frightening rocky pass in all of Switzerland."

Perhaps a similar thrill was felt by Robert Louis Stevenson when he came to vacation in Davos during the winter season of 1881–82. What the foggy and damp landscape of his native Scotland failed to do, Graubünden accomplished, enabling him to finish *Treasure Island*.

Davos also sparked the imagination of novelist Thomas Mann. In June 1912, he accompanied his wife Katja on a cure in the comfortable, belle-epoque rooms of the Schatzalp sanatorium. There he saw the first outlines of his novel *The Magic Mountain*, symbolizing Europe and its political and social choices: either to bask in illness and submit to death, or to choose life and social commitment. Needless to say, his depiction of such an indolent society living in a morbid expectation of death—"flirting and taking their temperature"—did not please the people of Davos, whose community had made a name for itself as a serious spa for curing, or at least alleviating, tuberculosis. The fame of *The Magic Mountain*, however, has long made up for any acrimony, and now healthy and positive-minded guests can stay at the Schatzalp, which has become a fine hotel.

(especially at the end of December when there's an invasion of ice-hockey fans for the international Spengler Cup). Davos is divided into the Platz and the Dorf (village), which together are one noisier-than-average urban strip, though Dorf is calmer. The town's first visitors came to take cures for lung diseases in the bracing mountain air. Now, except for a few token historic structures and brightly painted buildings, the town is modern and architecturally undistinguished, and the center of town can be filled with the exhaust of city traffic. But no matter how densely populated and fast-paced the town becomes, the slopes are still spectacular and the regulars return.

Davos was once famous as a retreat for people suffering from respiratory problems, such as tuberculosis. It was the inspiration for Thomas Mann's novel *The Magic Mountain*. Recalling the days when the streets were lined with spittoons is the **Museum of Medicine,** which exhibits old-fashioned medical equipment. ☒ *Platzstr. 1, Davos-Platz* ☎ *081/4135210* ☞ *3 SF* ☉ *Thurs. 5–7, and by appointment.*

Among the town's few architectural highlights, the late-Gothic **Kirche St. Johann** (Church of St. John the Baptist) stands out by virtue of its windows by Augusto Giacometti. Nearby is the 17th-century Rathaus (Town Hall). ☒ *Rathausstutz 2.*

The **Kirchner Museum** boasts the world's largest collection of works by the German artist Ernst Ludwig Kirchner, whose off-kilter lines and unnerving compositions inspired the Expressionist movement. He traveled to Davos in 1917 for health reasons and stayed until his death in 1938. ☒ *Promenade 82, Davos-Platz* ☎ *081/4132202* ⊕ *www.kirchnermuseum.ch* ☞ *10 SF* ☉ *Easter–mid-July and Oct.–Christmas, Tues.–Sun. 2–6; mid-July–Sept. and Christmas–Easter, Tues.–Sun. 10–6.*

The **Wintersportmuseum** has a collection of equipment from sleds to ski bindings. ☒ *Promenade 43, Davos-Platz* ☎ *081/4132484* ☞ *5 SF* ☉ *Late June–mid-Oct., Tues. and Thurs. 4:30–6:30; Dec.–Apr., Tues., Thurs., and Sat. 4:30–6:30.*

Skiing

Davos can accommodate some 24,000 visitors on 325 km (202 mi) of runs. The steepish slopes of the **Parsenn-Gotschna** are accessed from town by the Schatzalp or Parsenn funiculars. When lines for the Parsenn are long, try the **Rinerhorn,** a 15-minute ride by bus or train. Here the slopes lead to the hamlet of **Glaris,** 7 km (4½ mi) from Davos. A must for the skilled skier is the descent from **Weissfluhgipfel** (9,330 feet) to **Küblis,** in the Prättigau. This magnificent, 13-km (8-mi) piste has a vertical drop of 6,560 feet and is classified as difficult at the top but moderate for most of its length. A real challenge for experts is the three-hour tour across the mountains to Arosa—which requires a guide and good weather conditions. An easy 2-km (1-mi) run is number 11, the Meierhofer Tälli, which Davosers renamed the Hillary Clinton run, as it's her favorite here. **Jakobshorn,** a ski and snowboard area on the west-facing side, is reached by cable car and lift from Davos-Platz. The **Pischa** ski area, on the Flüela Pass road, and the **Bünda** slope, in Davos-Dorf, are especially suitable for children and families.

Lift tickets to the combined Davos–Klosters area cost 65 SF for one day, 282 SF for six days and include transport between the ski areas. The **Snowsports School Davos** (✉ Promenade 157, Davos-Dorf ☎ 081/4162454) gives skiing, cross-country, snowboard, and telemark lessons. If you need to get outfitted for skiing, including clothing, go to **PaarSenn** (✉ Promenade 159, Davos-Dorf ☎ 081/4101013). For the expert skier (freestyle, off-piste, and the like) the place to go is **New Trend Skischool** (✉ Brämabüelstr. 11, Davos-Platz ☎ 081/4132040).

There are more than 75 km (47 mi) of prepared cross-country ski trails, for which there is no charge. The **cross-country ski school** (☎ 081/4162454) is in Davos-Platz.

Where to Stay & Eat

$–$$ ✕ **Bistro Angelo.** If you have had enough Bündner specialties, try this restaurant, which doubles as a shop selling wines and spirits, pasta and honey. The menu changes every few days depending on what produce is available. Fresh- and saltwater fish are the specialty here, as are affordable prices. ✉ *Promenade 119, Davos-Platz* ☎ *081/4165979* ▤ *AE, DC, MC, V* ☉ *Closed Sun. in summer.*

★ $–$$ ✕▥ **Hubli's Landhaus.** Though it's on the busy mountain highway between Davos and Klosters, this country inn is quiet as well as comfortable and attractive with its rustic decor. The strong point by far is the food. Chef Felix Hubli prepares sophisticated fare (goose liver pâté served on creamed onions, Scottish salmon in a balsamic vinaigrette) and serves it in two lovely dining rooms: one for visitors, one for demipension guests, who—considering the à la carte prices—get a terrific deal. The guest rooms are modestly priced, especially the ones with a sink and shared bathroom down the hall. ✉ *Kantonstr., CH-7265 Davos-Wolfgang* ☎ *081/4171010* 🖷 *081/4171011* ⊕ *www.hublis.ch* 🛏 *20 rooms* ♦ *2 restaurants, minibars, cable TV, sauna, bar; no a/c* ▤ *AE, DC, MC, V* ☉ *Closed Mon. and late Apr.–early June and mid-Oct.–mid-Dec.* ¶ *BP.*

$$$–$$$$ ▥ **Schatzalp.** About 950 feet above town on a quiet, car-free slope, this expansive hotel will transport you back to the grand spa days of Davos. It served once as a sanatorium, and is described in Mann's *Magic Mountain.* The rooms, lobby, foyer, and dining room are all decorated in elegant belle epoque style. Spend summer afternoons enjoying the breeze on the long veranda, or visiting the hotel's botanical garden featuring high-altitude plants from five continents. The hotel is only accessible by its own funicular, the Schatzalp-Bahn, in Davos-Platz near the Hotel Europe. ✉ *Mattastr., CH-7270 Davos-Platz* ☎ *081/4155151* 🖷 *081/4155252* ⊕ *www.schatzalp.ch* 🛏 *94 rooms* ♦ *Restaurant, minibars, cable TV, Internet, pool, sauna, piano bar; no a/c* ▤ *AE, DC, MC, V* ¶ *MAP* ☉ *Closed May, Oct. and Nov.*

$$$–$$$$ ▥ **Steigenberger Belvedere.** With its Neoclassical stone fireplace, wedding-cake white plaster, and period details, this is a grand hotel in every sense of the word. The enormous gray building with south-facing balconies is just above the main street. Rooms are decorated in woods ranging from rustic Arvenholz to classic mahogany. If it's cold outside, the murals of tropical birds and plants around the pool provide a comforting illusion. ✉ *Promenade 89, CH-7270 Davos-Platz* ☎ *081/4156000*

⌂ *081/4156001* ⊕ *www.davos.steigenberger.ch* ⌐ *131 rooms, 27 suites* ⌂ *3 restaurants, minibars, cable TV, Internet room, pool, hair salon, massage, sauna, steam room, bar; no a/c* ⊟ *AE, DC, MC, V* ⊙ *Closed late Apr.–late June and Nov.* ⎮⊙⎮ *BP.*

$$–$$$ ⊞ **ArtHausHotel Quisisana.** This old symmetrical and sober building, hued in a striking red, seems to exude a mysterious pull. Inside, the walls are brightened by lively abstract paintings. The artist, Diego do Clavadetscher—who goes by the *nom d'artiste* Diegodo—is, in fact, the owner and manager (he also painted the facade). Here and there, you'll find little minimalist touches—an ensemble of stones in an alcove, for example. Creative, freewheeling, relaxing, the hotel's guest rooms are fully functional, yet little works of art unto themselves. ⊠ *Platzstr. 5, CH-7270 Davos-Platz* ☎ *081/4100510* ⎙ *081/4137773* ⊕ *www.arthaushotel.ch* ⌐ *19 rooms* ⌂ *Restaurant, bar, cable TV; no a/c* ⊟ *AE, DC, MC, V.*

$$–$$$ ⊞ **Bünda.** This hotel, though not a very pretty building, is perfectly located right by the beginners' ski slope, the children's slope, and a ski school branch, as well as on the cross-country ski track. The Parsenn cable car is only a few minutes' walk. Rooms in the main building are small, some with showers instead of a tub and two share a bathroom. Larger, more expensive rooms are in an annex, connected to the hotel by an underground passage. ⊠ *Museumstr., CH-7260 Davos-Dorf* ☎ *081/4171819* ⎙ *081/4171820* ⊕ *www.buenda.ch* ⌐ *40 rooms* ⌂ *Restaurant, minibars, cable TV, in-room data ports, gym, sauna, steam room; no a/c* ⊟ *AE, DC, MC, V* ⊙ *Closed mid-Apr.–early June* ⎮⊙⎮ *BP.*

Nightlife & the Arts

BARS In the Hotel Europe, the **Ex Bar** (⊠ Promenade 63, Davos-Platz ☎ 081/4154141) is where hipsters gather to listen to live music.

CASINO The bright, glassed-in **Casino** (⊠ Hotel Europe, Promenade 63, Davos-Platz ☎ 081/4154141) is one of the meeting places for *le tout Davos,* as it were. It opens at 2 PM daily and does not require formal dress.

DANCING The **Cabanna Club** (⊠ Promenade 63, Davos-Platz ☎ 081/4154141) lures an energetic crowd with techno music—"scene-iors" usually head to the "Cava" (located under the Cabanna) to find more appropriate acoustic fare. The **Pöstli Club** (⊠ Promenade 42, Davos-Dorf ☎ 081/4154500) is a winter-only institution with a dance floor and music ranging from rock to folk and pop. In the Hotel Davoserhof, the **Rotliechtli Music Club** (⊠ Berglistutz 15, Davos-Dorf ☎ 081/4156666) attracts a young—or at least young at heart—crowd with somewhat traditional tastes in music.

MUSIC The annual Young Artists in Concert festival is held from mid-July to early August. Young musicians from all over the world practice and perform in churches and in the Congress Center.

Sports & the Outdoors

HIKING & BIKING Davos is threaded with more than 450 km (280 mi) of well-marked trails perfect for hiking or biking in winter and summer. Mountain bikes can be rented at the train station or at **Ettinger Sport** (⊠ Talstr. 6, Davos-Dorf ☎ 081/4135410 ⊠ Promenade 61, Davos-Platz ☎ 081/4106161).

Sailing and windsurfing are popular on Davos Lake. To rent boats or take a lesson with a sailing school, call **Segelschule Davosersee** (☎ 081/4165583). **Hans Heierling** (☎ 081/4165918) offers lessons and rents boats as well.

Davos has a long reputation as an important ice-sports center, with its enormous **Sports Center Davos** (✉ Talstr. 41 ☎ 081/4153600) and speed-skating rink, the biggest natural ice track in Europe. The Ice Stadium maintains one indoor and two outdoor rinks; rental skates are available.

THE LOWER ENGADINE

Like Dorothy landing in Oz, you may find your sudden arrival in this, the most picturesque and novel of Graübunden's many valleys, something of a shock. You'll hear people talk of *Schellenursli* (a legendary munchkin of a little boy with a bell), and there's even a sort of Scarecrow—for *Hom Strom* in February the children of Scuol make a figure out of hay to burn the winter away. Festivals and folklore abound, as do dense, fairy-tale forests and quaint village settings. "Allegra!" is the proper greeting on the street, reflecting the Romansh language and Latinate culture that have developed without obstruction here. The Roman roots of the region are also demonstrated in the houses—typically squat stucco bungalows with deep Etruscan-arch doors, thick Mediterranean walls, and sunken windows. Houses are large, with thick walls to keep the warmth in and the cold out. Windows are small, but the frames taper outward to let in as much light as possible. The outer walls are decorated using *sgrafitto* technique—a signature of the Engadine (produced by whitewashing a layer of dark stucco, with symbols scraped in the paint—usually, the name of the original builder appears with a quote or a poem and the extent and quality of the sgraffiti suggests the wealth and station of the owner). The Lower Engadine—more enclosed than its upper counterpart—shares the region's dry, crisp "champagne" climate.

Guarda

❻
Fodor's Choice
★

37 km (23 mi) east of Davos.

The former main road through the Inn valley (Engadine) was higher up on the slopes than today's road. It passed through Guarda, one of a pleasant chain of small villages that include Ardez and Ftan. Each has fine sgraffitied homes, but Guarda, where the architecture is government-protected, is particularly well suited for a leisurely exploration along its ancient, cobbled streets. The dark-on-light etchings on the facades (contrasting sharply with the bright flowers on the windowsills) draw pedestrians from one photo op to the next. As its name implies, Guarda ("watch") sits high on a hillside looking out over the valley and the peaks to the south, which reach up to 9,840 feet.

Where to Stay & Eat

★ **$-$$$** ✕☷ **Meisser.** This picturesque, family-owned hotel, made up of three ancient farmhouses, has sgraffiti and flower boxes on the outside, antiques and honey-color pine inside. The former hay barn and woodshed are now a luxurious restaurant serving tasty dishes such as chamois with a

CLOSE UP

The Bells of Chalandamarz

OLD MAN WINTER is an especially tough customer in Graubünden, but the locals, going back to Roman days, have a one-day festival to spook him out of his snowshoes and send him packing. On March 1, the youngest schoolchildren (six- to eight-year-olds) gather in the village squares of the Engadin and many other towns and villages in other valleys to celebate Chalandamarz. The name derives from the Latin *calendae martius*, literally the March calendar. Dressed in traditional costumes, the girls with a riot of silk and paper flowers in their hair, the children march through the villages ringing bells of all sizes (known as *talocs*) and singing songs. In the old days, they would stop at houses to collect food or other gifts that would be brought home to the families. Now cash is the preferred gift, used to fund the evening Chalandamarz dances.

The Chalandamarz procession in Guarda is special for two reasons. First, it takes place on the last day of February and only boys participate. Secondly, the town is the setting for the story "Schellenursli" ("A Bell for Ursli"), written by Selina Chönz with wonderful illustrations by Alois Carigiet. It tells of a young and poor goatherd named Ursli who, after many trials and tribulations, acquires the largest bell in town and is allowed to lead the procession. Within Switzerland, Schellenursli is as well known as Heidi. Graubünden has several Schellenursli trails. The one in St. Moritz, oddly, leads up to the "Heidihütte" where the 1970s TV series was shot.

walnut crust and elderberry sauce or *Lamm auf Alpenheu* (lamb simmered in aromatic local Alpine grasses). Rooms are simple and modern, though you can have a splendid carved-pine room if you pay a bit more. An adjacent, renovated 17th-century farmhouse has a half-dozen suites. ✉ CH-7545 ☎ 081/8622132 📠 081/8622480 ⊕ *www.hotel-meisser.ch* ➽ *21 rooms, 6 suites* ⟡ *2 restaurants, minibars, in-room data ports, bar, playground; no TV in some rooms* ☰ *AE, DC, MC, V* ☉ *Closed mid-Apr.–late June and early Nov.–late Dec.* ⟊ *BP.*

Scuol

❼ *13 km (8 mi) east of Guarda.*

The villages of Scuol and Tarasp-Vulpera effectively form one big resort. The area owes its popularity to the 20 mineral springs (traditionally used for liver cures), the beautiful surroundings (mountains and dense forests), and the proximity of the Parc Naziunal Svizzer. Previously popular only in summer, the villages now fill up in winter, thanks to skiing on the south-facing slopes of Motta Naluns.

A small town, Scuol has a petite but exemplary old town, with five fountains from which you can do a taste-test comparison of normal tap water against spring water. For the inside-and-out spa experience, head for the

★ **Bogn Engiadina Scuol,** one of Europe's most modern spas. It stands in the middle of town tucked against the mountainside—an elevator and a staircase in a silolike modern construction lead down to the entrance (unless you prefer coming up from the center of the old village). The calming blue interior, fantastic aquatic murals, and shifting reflections from backlighted pools start relaxing you before your toes even touch the water. Six pools, both indoor and outdoor, range in temperature from 60°F to 90°F. There are also saunas, solariums, steam rooms, and a massage area. A special Roman-Irish ritual treatment alternates between moist and dry heat, massage, and mineral baths. A therapy center offers mud baths, gymnastics, thalassotherapy, and electrotherapy (if you have a doctor's prescription). In addition to steeping in mineral water, you can drink it from four different sources near the entrance: wait for someone to serve you. Reservations must be made at least 24 hours ahead. ⊠ *Town center* ☎ *081/8612002* 🖅 *25 SF for bathing area with sauna for 2; 66 SF with Roman-Irish baths* ⊘ *June–Apr., daily 9 AM–10 PM.*

NEED A BREAK?

For a delicious ice cream of organic milk, a good coffee, or a quick e-mail check, stop in at the **Glatscharia Balnot** (⊠ Stradun 402, near the tourist office and bus station ☎ 081/8641643). The building is a riot of colorful, complex sgraffito ornamentation.

The other two villages lie on the opposite side of the river from Scuol. **Vulpera,** whose permanent residents number just five, has an 1876 Trinkhalle with its spring pumping out water rich in minerals said to be good for the digestive tract. From Vulpera you can take a 15-minute bus ride up to **Tarasp,** a cluster of houses, inns, and farms around a tiny lake. The Vulpera golf course straddles the road, so if you are traveling by car, you may want to close your windows! The village is dominated

Fodor's Choice by the magnificently picturesque stronghold **Schloss Tarasp**, perched 500
★ feet above. Looking like illustrator Howard Pyle's model for the Castle Drachenhausen in his beloved children's classic *Otto of the Silver Hand,* Tarasp lords over the valley with a impressive main tower, dating from the 11th century when the castle was built by the leading family of Tarasp. Tarasp became part of Austria in 1464; the imperial eagle still can be seen on the castle walls. In the early 1800s, Napoléon gave Tarasp to the canton Graubünden, newly part of the Swiss federation. The castle went through several owners and subsequent neglect before passing into private hands in the early 20th century. You must join a tour to see the interiors, which range from the Romanesque chapel to the opulent "baronial" 19th-century reception rooms; the schedule varies quite a bit, so call ahead for tour times. Special midnight tours are conducted during the full moon. The bus from Vulpera departs roughly every hour. It's a 1½ hour walk from Scuol, following a well marked path that goes over the Punt'Ota (high bridge). ☎ 081/8649368 ⊕ *www.schloss-tarasp.ch* 🖅 *10 SF* ⊘ *June–Oct., daily, times vary; Christmas–Easter, Tues. and Thurs., times vary.*

Skiing & Snowboarding

The region's ski area centers around 14 gondolas and lifts going up Scuol's **Motta Naluns,** at elevations between 4,100 and 9,184 feet. The 80 km (50 mi) of trails include the 12-km (7½-mi) Traumpiste (Dream Run), a good run of medium difficulty, with a few tough areas. There is a wide range of ski passes available for an equally wide range of prices on a sliding scale beginning at 50 SF for a day pass. Some passes even include use of the Bogn Engiadina Scuol spa. Tarasp has one short ski lift for beginners. Bus transport between Scuol/Sent and Scuol/Tarasp-Vulpera is free of charge if you have a ski pass.

Snowboarding is extremely popular on these broad, sunny slopes. Scuol's snowboard school, **The School** (☎ 081/8641723), is the oldest in Europe. You could also sign up with **Schweizer Schneesportschule Scuol** (☎ 081/8641723) for instruction in Alpine and cross-country skiing. There are 60 km (37 mi) of prepared cross-country tracks around Scuol. Rental equipment is available at sports shops in Scuol and next to the Motta Naluns cable-car station. As for children, they will find snowy excitement at the **Kinderland Nalunsin** (☎ 081/8612000) plus a daycare center for 7 SF per hour or 35 SF per day.

Where to Stay & Eat

$$$$
Fodor's Choice
★

×🏠 **Schlosshotel Chastè.** While many Swiss hoteliers are proud to claim a second generation of family ownership, this hidden treasure claims 500 years under the Pazeller family care. Now a Relais & Châteaux treasure, it started as a farm, then supplied provisions to builders of Tarasp Castle, which looms above. The family has preserved the bulging, sgraffitied stucco exterior, and behind the magnificently carved arvenholz wood door, extraordinary effort has been made to match and modernize. Each room varies a bit from the others: a canopy bed here, an antique trunk there. Rudolf Pazeller himself is the chef and offers a small but sophisticated menu; his fish dishes, such as the "Marriage of perch and char in white tomato sauce on southern vegetables and gnocchi," are outstanding. ✉ CH-7553 Tarasp ☎ 081/8613060 📠 081/8613061 ⊕ www.schlosshoteltarasp.ch 🛏 20 rooms ♨ Restaurant, Stübli, minibars, cable TV, hot tub, massage, sauna, steam room, bar; no a/c ☰ AE, DC, MC, V ⊙ Closed early Apr.–early June and mid-Oct.–mid-Dec. ⍨ BP.

> **SOME LIKE IT COLD**
>
> An alternative to the usual pine-wood guest room: an igloo perched on Motta Naluns. The "rooms" here at Igloo Village Scuol (CH-7550, phone 081/8622211, fax 081/8622210, www.element-scuol.ch), which are decorated by Inuit artist Angus Cockney, are ready at the beginning of January. Depending on the weather, the 47 spots (in 17 igloos) are habitable until mid-April. The price (140 SF) includes extra-thick sleeping bags; an evening meal of soup, fondue, and goulash; and a hot breakfast in the morning. One thing's for sure: you'll beat everyone else to the slopes.

★ **$$–$$$** 🏠 **Hotel Villa Post.** Landmarked by its distinctive turret, this former post office provides simply and tastefully decorated guest rooms and a familial atmosphere ideal for those seeking a peaceful home away from home. Guests are welcomed with a drink in the hotel's own museum, which displays vintage tableware from the grand days of tourism in the early 20th century. And for a full blast of yesteryear, simply go to the sumptuously wood-paneled Arvenstube restaurant, an opulent pine setting for local specialties made from market-fresh ingredients. A nightcap in front of the fireplace on winter evenings rounds off a most restful experience. The familial atmosphere is ideal for those seeking a peaceful home away from home. ⊠ *CH-7552 Vulpera* ☎ *081/8641112* 🖶 *081/8649585* ⊕ *www.villa-post.ch* 🛏 *25 rooms* ⌂ *Restaurant, minibars, cable TV; no a/c* ⊟ *AE, MC, V* ⊙ *Closed May and Nov.* ⌶◎⌶ *MAP.*

$–$$ 🏨 **Villa Engiadina.** This folly of towers and gables standing guard over Vulpera was built in 1902 and was transformed into a hotel in the late 1990s. Owing to the architecture, each room has a different shape and has been individually furnished. The rooms in the towers are especially attractive, offering a sprawling view of the valley. No. 107 has an antique bathroom, for example; No. 304 was once the house chapel. A no-smoking restaurant offers (among other things) fresh vegetables from the hotel's own garden. The homemade cakes have earned a reputation throughout the valley. A surcharge of 40 SF gives you half-board privileges. ⊠ *CH-7552 Vulpera* ☎ *081/8612244* 🖶 *081/8612266* ⊕ *www.villa-engiadina.ch* 🛏 *19 rooms* ⌂ *Restaurant, minibars, cable TV; no a/c* ⊟ *DC, MC, V* ⊙ *Closed Apr. and Nov.* ⌶◎⌶ *BP.*

Sports & the Outdoors

BIKING   Rental bicycles are available at sports shops and the Motta Naluns cable-car station. For the adventurous, bikes can be taken on the cable car; once on the mountain, you can explore on your own or join a guided tour. Contact the tourist office for details.

ICE SPORTS   Open-air ice rinks for hockey, curling, and skating are available in Scuol from early December to early March at **Sportanlage Trü** (☎ 081/8612006). **Eishalle Gurlaina** (☎ 081/8640272), in Scuol, has indoor skating facilities. There are three main sled runs, between 2½ and 7 km (1½ and 4½ mi) long. You can rent a sled at the Motta Naluns mountain station or from **Sport Conradin** (☎ 081/8641410). **Sport Heinrich** (☎☎ 081/8641956) rents sleds in Scuol.

Zernez

❽ *27 km (17 mi) southwest of Scuol.*

This friendly little crossroads is the last town before the higher valley of the Inn and lies along the route over the Ofen Pass to the Val Müstair and Italy. Serious hikers sporting loden hats, knickers, and sturdy boots come to stock up on picnic goods and topographical maps before setting off for the Parc Naziunal Svizzer. In winter there are cross-country trails. The alpine skiing areas of the Lower and Upper Engadine are accessible by public transport.

Where to Stay

$ 🏨 **Chasa Veglia.** "The old house" with its converted barn is down a quiet side street. The owner's wood-carving skills are on display at every turn, from the doors and chairs to ceilings and fretwork panels over the lighting fixtures. Rugs on parquet floors and a display of old farm and kitchen implements add to the atmosphere. One room is an exception, painted pink and decorated in an ultramodern style. Rooms are small; those without a bathtub have a shower, except for two rooms with only a toilet and sink. ⊠ CH-7530 ☎ 081/2844868 ⊕ *www.chasa-veglia. ch* ➽ *11 rooms, 9 with bath* ♨ *Cable TV; no a/c* ⊟ *No credit cards* ☉ *Closed early May–mid-June and early Nov.–late Dec.* †○| *BP.*

Parc Naziunal Svizzer

▶ ❾ *Access roads from Zernez, Scuol, S-Chanf, and the Ofen Pass.*

Fodor'sChoice
★
The Swiss National Park is a magnificent federal preserve of virtually virgin wilderness. Established in 1914, it covers 173 square km (107 square mi), including the Macun lakes near Lavin. Minute compared with a U.S. or Canadian national park, it has none of the developments that typically hint of "accessibility" and "attraction": no campgrounds, no picnic sites, no residents, few rangers. This is genuine wilderness, every leaf protected from all but nature itself. Dead wood is left to rot and insects to multiply. Rangers see that rules are obeyed—no fires, dogs, bikes, skis, or tents are allowed, and picking plants is forbidden. Although the last bear was shot in the Lower Engadine in 1904, the park is home to large herds of ibex (the heraldic animal on the Graubünden flag), chamois, red and roe deer, and marmots. Don't forget binoculars; without them you might not see much fauna—the animals give a wide berth to the 80 km (50 mi) of marked paths.

Remember these are wild animals and not likely to line up for Twinkies by the road. If big game make no appearance, you can just enjoy the scenery and watch out for a bearded vulture overhead. Before heading into the park, visit the brand new **Nationalpark-Haus** in Zernez, where you can watch a video in English, stock up on maps, and enjoy the natural history exhibit, which includes a "marmot underground experience." Guided walks in English are available on Tuesday and Thursday; reserve one to two days in advance to join a group (10 SF for adults) or book a private guided walk.

> ### CREATURES GREAT & SMALL
>
> This is no African big-game preserve. Sighting a group of ibex on a distant hill or great herds of male red deer, their antlers silhouetted above a snowy ridge, you may feel more privileged than when petting a dozen Yellowstone bison. If the big game makes no appearance, search your greedy soul and try to follow the park's advice: "Appreciate a butterfly or an ant as much as a herd of chamois."

Trails start out from parking lots off the park's only highway (visitors are encouraged to take buses back to their starting point)—a series of wild, rough, and often steep paths. Visitors are restricted to the trails except at designated resting places. The Il Fuorn–Stabelchod–Val dal Botsch trail marks botanical and natural phenomena with multilingual information boards and leads to a spectacular barren ridge at 7,672 feet; the round-trip journey takes about four hours. A three-hour route from picturesque S-chanf (pronounced sss-*chanff*) takes you into a deep glacial valley where ibex and chamois often gather; the return, by a riverside trail, passes a snack bar—just across the park border and thus permitted. ⊠ *Nationalpark-Haus, CH-7530 Zernez, leaving the village toward Ofen Pass* ☎ *081/8561378* 🖶 *081/8561740* ⊕ *www. nationalpark.ch* 🎫 *Free* ⊙ *June–Oct., Wed.–Mon. 8:30–6, Tues. 8:30 AM–10 PM.*

Where to Stay

$–$$ 🏨 **Il Fuorn.** This century-old mountain inn in the Swiss National Park is on the highway and makes an ideal base for hikers. Choose from either old-style rooms without bath or pine-and-stucco rooms with bath. Multibed rooms are available for groups or individuals for 37 SF with breakfast and 19 SF without. The plain Swiss cooking is augmented by some game specialties. Near the hotel is one of the medieval iron-smelting ovens that gave Ofen Pass its name. ⊠ *CH-7530* ☎ *081/8561226* 🖶 *081/8561801* ⊕ *www.ilfuorn.ch* ➷ *32 rooms, 12 with bath* ☖ *Restaurant, Stübli; no a/c, no TV in some rooms* ▱ *AE, DC, MC, V* ⊙ *Closed late Oct.–mid-May* ⑪ *BP.*

THE UPPER ENGADINE

Stretching from Brail to Maloja and with a gate to the Swiss National Park at S-chanf, this is one of the country's highest regions—the highest settlement is at 6,710 feet—and one of its most dazzling. From mountain peaks, such as Piz Corvatsch or Piz Nair, you can swoosh down world-class slopes or simply take in the dizzying view over the lakes and mountains. Besides summer and winter sports, both seasons are packed tight with cultural programs and events. Summer is also when the lowland farmers send their cows up to the high Alpine pastures so they can have a relaxing mountain holiday, too.

Pontresina

★ ⑩ **To & From:** *Trains connecting with Pontresina by and large follow the same schedule as those to and from St. Moritz, with a change in Samedan. Pontresina to Chur trains leave at 2 minutes past the hour, a two-hour journey for 37 SF with the change at Samedan. The same trains go to Scuol, departing from Samedan. The Scuol–St. Moritz trains also take you to Pontresina, with a transfer at Samedan. Pontresina is 38 km (24 mi) southwest of Zernez.*

On a south-facing shelf along the Flaz Valley, Pontresina is an exceptionally picturesque resort. It grew by converting its farmhouses to pensions and hotels for use by summer tourists. Today its climbing school is making a name for itself, and the village has become a popular hiking center. From here you can see clear across to the Roseg Valley, once filled with a glacier that has retreated to the base of Piz Roseg itself. The river Flaz winds through the valley from the Morteratsch glacier, which oozes down from Piz Bernina. Although the main street is built up with restaurants and shops, the resort still has a relaxed atmosphere. Every second Thursday in July and August, there's a street market in the lower part of the village, with locals selling fresh produce and handmade crafts. The altitude of Pontresina (6,000 feet) ensures wintry weather, and its access to skiing on the slopes of Diavolezza (9,751 feet) is convenient. In the off-seasons between Easter and mid-June and mid-October through Christmas, many hotels are closed.

The **Museum Alpin** gives some local history and documents the region's lifestyle over the centuries. It also exhibits the local flora, fauna, and mineral world; be sure to check out the room full of birds whose recorded songs can be heard at the push of a button. There's also an exhibit on mining in the Engadine. ⊠ *Via Maistra* ☎ *081/8427273* ⊕ *www.pontresina.com/museumalpin* ⊡ *5 SF* ☺ *Mid-June–mid-Oct. and late Dec.–mid-Apr., Mon.–Sat. 4–6.*

Skiing

There's a small beginners' slope in the village at San Spiert. The compact ski areas of Diavolezza (9,768 feet) and, on the other side of the road, Lagalb (9,705 feet), on the Bernina pass, complement the much more extensive ones of St. Moritz. All three are about 20 minutes away by bus. Lift tickets cost 69 SF for one day, 332 SF for a six-day regional ticket. Rides on the Engadin bus service are included in the price of a regional ski ticket. Newcomers can learn the basics at the **Ski and Snowboard School** (☎ 081/8388383). Below the village, on the Engadine Marathon Trail, is the **Tolais Cross-Country Ski Center** (☎ 081/8426844).

Where to Stay & Eat

$–$$$ ✕ **Steinbock.** Owned by the Walther family, proprietors of the neighboring Hotel Walther, this 17th-century house has been modernized in keeping with Engadine style—lots of wood and warm colors. The Colani Stübli serves regional and seasonal specialties, such as polenta *cun gorgonzola*, a filling cornmeal dish. The game dishes served in autumn are exceptional, especially the *Gemspfeffer* (chamois ragout cooked in wine) with hazelnut Spätzli and red cabbage. For dessert you might try *Nusskrapfen* (puff pastry with a sticky nut filling). ⊠ *Via Maistra* ☎ *081/8393626* ⊟ *AE, DC, MC, V.*

★ $ ✕ **Café Puntschella.** Either way you look here, you can't go wrong: your chair will face either the Roseg Valley or the spread of fresh-made pastries. The menu can satisfy all kinds of cravings, from bowls of breakfast muesli to plates of *Rösti* (pan-fried potatoes). A nice salad buffet will take care of diners looking for lighter foods. Locals know to ask for the beignetlike *Quarkinis* with vanilla sauce—as well as a seat on the terrace. ⊠ *Via Mulin* ☎ *081/ 8388030* ⊟ *V* ☺ *Closed Mon. and Tues. in May.*

$$$$ ✕⊡ **Grand Hotel Kronenhof.** This breathtaking building was completed in 1898, and the exterior has changed little since. The lobby and dining rooms, with elaborate

Fodor'sChoice
★

> **THE NEIGHS HAVE IT**
>
> Horse-drawn carriages and sleighs in Pontresina can be booked through M. Kaiser (081/8426274); V. Rietberger (081/8428353) is another vendor offering sleigh and carriage rides. The Roseg Valley "horse omnibus" is run by L. Costa (081/8426057) as a scheduled service in summer and winter—this trip is very popular, so be sure to make a reservation.

moldings, pink cherubs, and heavy chandeliers, are dazzling. The guest rooms are tastefully done with Biedermeier furniture. The lawn that sprawls out toward the Roseg Valley is a social center in summer and winter, with tennis courts doubling as an ice rink. The Rococo gold-and-gilt Grand restaurant serves international cuisine, including specialties such as roast lamb with an olive crust. The wood-burnished Kronen-stübli offers simpler regional fare: alpine macaronis with fried duck breast and liver, for example. ⊠ CH-7504 ☎ 081/8303030 🖷 081/8303031 ⊕ www.kronenhof.com 🛏 93 rooms ⚐ 2 restaurants, café, minibars, cable TV, 2 tennis courts, pool, hair salon, massage, sauna, steam room, bowling, ice-skating, bar; no a/c ⊟ AE, DC, MC, V ☉ Closed mid-Apr.–mid-June and mid-Sept.–mid-Dec. ⍟ BP.

$ ⚐ **Bahnhof.** Next to the entrance to the Roseg Valley, the cross-country skiing center, and the train station, the hotel offers dependable, low-key accommodations. Rooms have sinks with bathrooms down the hall; one room in an adjoining house has a shower. The restaurant, with its pink linen and flowers, offers simple fare at reasonable prices. ⊠ CH-7504 ☎ 081/8388000 🖷 081/8388009 ⊕ www.hotel-bahnhof.ch 🛏 21 rooms, 1 with bath ⚐ Restaurant, café; no a/c, no room TVs ⊟ AE, DC, MC, V ⍟ BP.

> ## WORD OF MOUTH
>
> "At Punt Muragl (081/8428232), off the highway between Samedan and Pontresina, you'll find the funicular for Muottas Muragl at 8,055 feet. Walk the gorgeous Philosophers' Path, dotted with quotations from famous minds such as Socrates and Descartes. Two lifts give access to easy skiing, or head back down on the 4-km (2½-mi) sled run. The funicular fare is 26 SF. At the top (incredible photos!), visit the Berghotel Muottas Muragl (closed mid-Apr.–late May and mid-Oct.–mid-Dec.) for a meal with a truly spectacular view."
>
> –MikeDall

Nightlife & the Arts

BARS & LOUNGES **Bar Pitschna Scena** (⊠ Hotel Saratz ☎ 081/8394000) has live music Thursday nights in summer and winter seasons. **Piano-Bar** (⊠ Sporthotel ☎ 081/8389400) is a cozy, blond-wood bar. The **Pöstlikeller** (⊠ Hotel Post, Via Maistra ☎ 081/8389300) features live music occasionally.

MUSIC The **Kurorchester Pontresina** plays chamber concerts daily between mid-June and mid-September at 11 AM in the Tais forest. Check with the tourist office for more information.

Sports & the Outdoors

BICYCLING Touring and mountain bikes can be rented at the **Fähndrich Sport** (☎ 081/8427155). **Bollinger Bike Shop** (☎ 081/8426262) rents all kinds of bikes and can suggest scenic routes. To take on steep mountain descents like Lagalb–Poschiavo, contact **Engadin Ferien** (☎ 081/8300001).

HIKING Pontresina and the top of the Alp Languard chairlift (open only in summer) are good starting points for hikers. The Diavolezza and Lagalb cable cars, which run in summer, also bring you to good hiking trails. For information on a variety of guided excursions, including mushroom hunting and glacier hiking, contact the tourist office. If you're staying overnight in Pontresina, the tours are free; day visitors pay a small fee.

ICE SPORTS There's a large **natural ice-skating rink** (☎ 081/8427341) off the main street; rental skates and instruction are available. From December through March, 10 curling rinks with instructors are available at **Sport-pavilion Roseg** (✉ Via Maistra ☎ 081/8426346 or 081/8426349).

MOUNTAIN **Bergsteigerschule Pontresina** (✉ Via Maistra ☎ 081/8388333), the biggest
CLIMBING mountain climbing school in Switzerland, offers instruction in rock and ice climbing for people of all skill levels. The company also leads guided tours in English.

St. Moritz

★ ⓫ To & From: *From Chur, trains leave all day (37 SF, 2 hrs) at 2 minutes to the hour until 9:58 at night. To Chur from St. Moritz, trains leave at 2 minutes past the hour, otherwise everything is the same. The trains going to St. Moritz also go to Pontresina, same timing and same price (37 SF, 2 hrs), although you must change at Samedan. St. Moritz-Scuol (25 SF, 1:17 hrs) follows the same schedule: at 2 past the hour, with change at Samedan. The trains from Scuol depart at 34 minutes past the hour. St. Moritz is 5 km (3 mi) west of Pontresina, 85 km (53 mi) southeast of Chur.*

Who put the *ritz* in St. Moritz? The approach to this celebrated city may surprise newcomers who, having heard the almost magical name dropped in the same breath as Paris and Rome, expect either a supremely cosmopolitan Old World capital or a resort whose spectacular natural setting puts other resorts to shame. It is neither. What makes St. Moritz's reputation is the people who go there and who have been going there, generation by generation, since 1864, when hotelier Johannes Badrutt dared a group of English resorters—already summer regulars—to brave the Alpine winter as his guests. They loved it, delighted in the novelty of snowy mountain beauty—until then considered something to be avoided—and told their friends. By the turn of the century, St. Moritz, Switzerland, and snow were all the rage. Not that St. Moritz had been a stranger to tourism before that. Since 1500 BC, when Druidic Celts first passed through, people have made the pilgrimage here to take healing waters from its mineral springs.

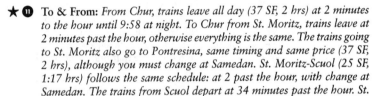

GOOD FOR WHAT AILS YOU

It is said that in the late 17th century the duke of Parma led a retinue of 25 followers over the mountain passes to taste St. Moritz's waters, and an 18th-century visitor from Germany described the coveted experience: "It puckers lips and tongue like the sharpest vinegar, goes to the head, and is like champagne in the nose."

St. Moritz catches social fire around the winter holidays—some New Year's Eve events have guest lists closed a year in advance—but the glitter fades by spring. Very ordinary people fill the streets come summer—the same hikers you might meet in any resort—and hotel prices plummet.

Then visitors see St. Moritz for what it really is: a busy, built-up old resort city sprawled across a hillside above an aquamarine lake, the St. Moritz See, surrounded by forested hills and by graceful, though not the region's most dramatic, peaks. Piz Rosatsch, with its glacier, dominates the view, with Piz Languard (10,699 feet) on the east and Piz Güglia (7,492 feet) on the west. St. Moritz-Dorf is the most like a downtown, with busy traffic and competitive parking in the shopping district. St. Moritz-Bad, the original spa-resort at the base of the lake, now bristles with brutish modern housing worthy of a Costa Moritza. At the top of the Dorf is St. Moritz's answer to Pisa—a leaning tower, all that's left of a 13th-century church. Other than that, don't expect a picturesque village that might appear on the lid of a chocolate box. St. Moritz has its fair share of unattractive buildings and, in winter, traffic snarls. But the latter have improved quite a bit since the creation of a pedestrian-only zone in the village. The town shows its best face from a distance, especially at dusk: from the *See* promenade—the popular walk around the lake—modern edges soften and the lake reflects the darkening mountains, warm hotel lights, and the grace that first made St. Moritz a star.

Even a hundred years of hype have not exaggerated its attractions as a winter sports center. The place that twice hosted the Olympic games (1928 and 1948)—and trademarked the shining sun as its logo—is still a sports marketing mecca, with excellent facilities for ice-skating, bobsledding, ski jumping, riding, and even winter golf, polo, and horse racing. But it does not have a corner on fine skiing: it shares a broad complex of trails and facilities with Sils, Silvaplana, Celerina, and Pontresina; only the slopes of Corviglia, Marguns, and Piz Nair are directly accessible from town.

The resort's events calendar is especially impressive. This is the place to see winter sports that were, or still are, found only here, such as polo and cricket played on snow, bobsledding on natural ice, and horse racing on snow, which includes *skikjöring* (skiers pulled by riderless horses). The frozen lake acts as the "white arena" for some events and provides the backdrop for others. A tent village complete with grandstands, palm trees, restaurants, bars, and art exhibitions is installed on the lake from late January through February. Watch for the annual winter Gourmet Festival in St. Moritz, when world-renowned chefs serve their specialties in local restaurants and hotels. The Grand Gourmet Finale is a gargantuan feast prepared by about 25 chefs and their assistants, usually presented on the frozen lake.

Besides challenging sports, the town offers relaxation at the **St. Moritz Bad** (spa complex). The local mineral springs have been known for more than 3,000 years; in 1535 the physician and alchemist Paracelsus praised the water, which is the richest in iron and carbonic acid in Europe. Massages and most treatments are done in individual cabins with private baths. Peat baths and packs need a doctor's prescription, but you can take a mineral bath anytime; try one with natural aromas such as pine or rosemary (35 SF). ☎ *081/8333062* ☉ *Weekdays 8–7, Sat. 8–noon.*

One of the few reminders that contemporary St. Mortitz was once an Engadine village is the **Engadine Museum,** a reproduction of the traditional sgraffitoed home. In a building dating from 1906, the museum has displays of furniture, tools, and pottery in rooms decorated in styles from different periods. ⊠ *Via dal Bagn 39* ☎ *081/8334333* 💷 *5 SF* ☉ *June–Oct., weekdays 9:30–noon, 2–5, Sun. 10–noon; Dec.–Apr., weekdays 10–noon, 2–5, Sun. 10–noon.*

The somewhat forbidding stone structure that houses the **Segantini Museum** showcases the work of Italian artist Giovanni Segantini (1858–99). His huge triptych *La Vita, La Natura, La Morte* hangs in the domed upper floor. Take a seat on the bench to absorb the meditations on life, nature, and death of this fine Impressionist artist. ⊠ *Via Somplaz* ☎ *081/8334454* ⊕ *www.segantini-museum.ch* 💷 *10 SF* ☉ *June–mid-Oct. and early Dec.–late Apr., Tues.–Sun. 10–noon, 3–6.*

Skiing

Don't let the whirlwind of activities at St. Moritz make you forget that its raison d'être is skiing. You can reach the **Corviglia–Piz Nair, Suvretta,** and **Marguns** slopes, immediately above St. Moritz, from the Chantarella–Corviglia funicular in Dorf, the Signal cableway in Bad, the Suvretta chairlift, and the Marguns gondolas in Celerina. There are 80 km (50 mi) of difficult, intermediate, and easy runs and a half pipe for snowboarders. The Upper Engadine ski region offers 350 km (217 mi) of prepared trails. The views from Corviglia, Piz Nair, and the Suvretta Paradise run are magnificent.

Descents behind Piz Nair (10,026 feet) eventually lead down to Marguns; they are often in shadow in early winter but have the best snow up to the end of the season. With the help of snowmaking equipment, conditions usually remain excellent until late April. The sunny Suvretta slopes are usually less crowded but do not benefit from snowmaking equipment. For instruction there are a number of choices, including the **Suvretta Snowsports School** (☎ 081/8363600). The **St. Moritz Ski School** (☎ 081/8300101 in town, 081/8335553 on Corviglia) is the oldest in Switzerland. You can join a group and go with an instructor on a free "ski safari," offered by any ski school, which begins in Sils and ends in St. Moritz Bad. Rental equipment is available at **Ski Service Corvatsch** (☎ 081/8387788) at the Corviglia valley and mountain stations. One-day tickets for St. Moritz are between 49 SF and 64 SF; for the whole Upper Engadine region a one-day pass costs between 56 SF and 69 SF. Six-day regional passes run between 262 SF and 332 SF. Prices include transportation between ski stations on the Engadin bus service and free entry to the public swimming pools in St. Moritz and Pontresina. For reports on daily snow conditions, call the **hotline** (☎ 0844/844944); the English-language version comes last.

Cross-country skiing has its base in St. Moritz Bad, where the **Langlauf school** (⊠ Parkhotel Kurhaus ☎ 081/8336233) offers lessons and excursions. You can try out the close-by Engadine Marathon track or the many side valleys. Near the school is a lighted circular trail of 3 km (2 mi) open from 5 PM to 9:30 PM.

Where to Stay & Eat

★ $$$$ ✕ **Chesa Veglia.** When Stavros Niarchos, the Princess of Baroda, and Elizabeth Taylor used to visit St. Moritz, this was their legendary watering hole. There are still princesses to be seen but if you "don't belong," you may be shown a far-off table in Siberia. Still if you want to enter the snobbism sweepstakes, this is a great place to begin. A 17th-century *Bauernhof* (farmhouse), it retains its raw beams and native carvings within a theme restaurant so self-consciously restored you may think you're in an American mall—an effect enhanced by the restaurant's fragmentation into three theme rooms (an upscale grill, a Stübli, and a pizzeria). Despite the rustic-luxe setting, the main menu aspires to international cuisine; you can order *côte de boeuf à la moelle et aux truffes* (beef with marrow and truffles), carpaccio, and terrine *de lièvre* (hare pâté) at prices that are St. Moritz–high. There are good fruit tarts at teatime, when the atmosphere is at its most convincing; later, you'll find dinner and dancing with live entertainment and piano music in the grill. ⊠ *Via Veglia 2* ☎ *081/8372800* ⊟ *AE, DC, MC, V.*

$$$–$$$$ ✕ **Jöhri's Talvò.** Roland Jöhri's restaurant, in a 17th-century Engadine house, marries the best of Graubünden tradition with classic French elegance. Both the cooking and decor reflect this philosophy, from the delicate linens softening weathered woodwork to the luxurious touches that curb the heaviness of local dishes, like *capuns sursilvan* (a local specialty from the Sursilvan area, capuns is a kind of tiny cheese lasagne wrapped in a collard leaf) with chanterelles. A popular fish menu could include a house-style bouillabaisse or Arctic char from Sils lake with summer vegetables. The desserts are elaborate works of art. But be prepared to spend as much on a meal as on a hotel room. ⊠ *Champfèr, 3 km (2 mi) southwest of St. Moritz, about 330 feet from the postbus stop* ☎ *081/8334455* ⌕ *Reservations essential* ⊟ *AE, DC, MC, V* ☺ *Closed mid-Apr.–mid-June and mid-Oct.–mid-Dec.*

$–$$$ ✕ **Engiadina.** With its plain linoleum and pine trim, this could pass for a St. Moritz diner, though its raison d'être is fondue; champagne fondue is the house specialty. Other favorites are *steak-frites* (steak with french fries) and escargots. It's a popular oddity in this ritzy resort. ⊠ *Schulhauspl.* ☎ *081/8333265* ⊟ *AE, DC, MC, V.*

★ $–$$ ✕ **Meierei.** On a winding, private forest road partway around the lake, this *Landgasthof* (country inn) is a rural mirage, an incongruity in the city but spiritually allied to the mountains and lake. It started in the 17th century as a farm where the bishop stopped over when traveling; later, it became a dairy restaurant and—about 150 years ago—a hotel. Today it's sought out for its restaurant, which serves light meals and such modern combinations as pumpkin gnocchi with lobster. Its sun terrace is also a popular meeting spot for day hikers, walkers, cross-country skiers, and horseback riders. (If you're not a guest, you'll have to walk in, as only guests may drive in.) The rustic themes of the dining areas are loosely translated into guest-room decor, with most rooms combining brown tones and wood with green-tone carpet. Some have newer, all-tile baths. If you don't want a full meal, you can have just coffee and *Apfelstrudel* or Bündnerfleisch and a glass of wine. ⊠ *Via Dim Lej* ☎ *081/8333242* ⊕ *www.hotel-meierei.ch* ⊟ *AE, DC, MC, V* ☺ *Closed late Mar.–mid-June and mid-Oct.–mid-Dec.*

★ **$$$$**   ✕🏨 **Badrutt's Palace.** With its pseudo-Gothic stone and mismatched sprawl of architectural excess, the Palace is pure Hollywood, all glitz and conspicuous consumption. Back in the 1950s and 1960s when it was run by master hotelier Cappy Badrutt, this spot was the most important mecca for world high society during December and early January; today, the celeb count is lower but winter is still its prime time: flagrant and showy, with Rolls-Royces and Lear jets discharging guests willing to pay more per night than for a transatlantic flight, it is crammed with beautiful people and wealthy wannabes who made token appearances on the slopes before checking in at the hairdresser. This place definitely has its standards—jacket and tie for public rooms, for example. Nowhere in Switzerland will you find more facilities—the hotel even has its own ski school and a private cinema, and now flaunts the Daniela Steiner spa, a disco, a driving range, a summer barbecue, to name a few goodies. The restaurant is as vast as a mess hall, beswagged and chandeliered; the Grill-Room is a celadon jewel box and enjoys a culinary reputation beyond the guest list. Rooms are surprisingly discreet and rather like a lot of other hotel rooms at a third the price—but it's not the drapes you're paying for. ⊠ *Via Serlas, CH-7500* ☎ *081/8371000* 🖷 *081/8372999* ⊕ *www.badruttspalace.com* 🛏 *170 rooms, 39 suites* ⅃ *3 restaurants, minibars, room TVs with video games, in-room data ports, driving range, 3 tennis courts, pool, gym, hair salon, spa, ice-skating, 3 bars, nightclub, business center; no a/c* ▭ *AE, DC, MC, V* ⊘ *Closed mid-Apr.–late June and early Sept.–mid-Dec.* |◎| *BP.*

$$$–$$$$ ✕🏨 **Schweizerhof.** This big-city hotel in the center of town was built in 1896 and is still grand. Public areas are heavy with carved wood and moldings, and the Victorian splendor is almost oppressive. A lighter touch is the painted ceiling of the guests' dining room, with its glittering birch forest. Guest rooms leave romantic fantasy behind—they're slick postmodern with burled-wood cabinets and contemporary color schemes. The informal Acla restaurant serves up solid meals such as chateaubriand and Wiener schnitzel. An outdoor restaurant opens in summer, and the hotel has its own mountain hut on the Suvretta slope. The rooftop wellness center offers saunas, steam baths, massages, and superb views over the lake. ⊠ *Via dal Bagn, CH-7500* ☎ *081/8370707* 🖷 *081/8370700* ⊕*www.schweizerhofstmoritz.ch* 🛏*73 rooms, 10 junior suites* ⅃*2 restaurants, in-room safes, minibars, cable TV, health club, massage, 4 bars; no a/c* ▭ *AE, DC, MC, V* |◎| *BP.*

$–$$$ ✕🏨 **Corvatsch.** This family-run hotel in the middle of St. Moritz-Bad will make you feel right at home, even if the views from the windows are not the best in town. Friendly service and a drink by the crackling fire in the cosy "living room" is often all one needs at the end of a long day hiking or skiing. The large and airy restaurant has a great deal to choose from, including seasonal dishes featuring lots of venison and pastas. Guests needing a sauna can visit the neighboring Laudinella. ⊠ *Via Tegiatscha, 7500 St. Moritz-Bad* ☎ *081/8375757* 🖷 *081/8375758* ⊕*www.hotel-corvatsch.ch/* 🛏*27 rooms, 1 suite* ⅃*Restaurant, bar, cable TV; no a/c* ▭ *MC, V.*

$–$$$ ✕🏨 **Veltlinerkeller.** This bright, genial restaurant has nothing swanky about it—just lots of wood, ancient moldings in the form of grapes, a few outsize game trophies, and a welcoming wood fire where the meat is roasted while you watch. The owner mans the grill, and his touch with Italian-Romansh cooking is light and straightforward. In addition to grilled meats and whole trout, there are good and varied homemade pastas served family style from crockery bowls. The nine double rooms upstairs are finished in slick quarry tile and stucco, with cotton floral prints and all-tile baths. ⊠ *Via dal Bagn* ☎ *081/8221777* 🖷 *081/8221789* ➷ *9 rooms* ⌂ *Restaurant, cable TV; no a/c* ▤ *AE, DC, MC, V* ⏃⃝❙ *BP.*

$ ✕▣ **Bellaval.** This affordable hotel at the train station provides its guests with simple rooms at good value. And for those traveling without a car, it's perfect. Train lovers might consider the rooms facing the rails (the trains do not run at night). The other sides of the house face either the town, the lake, or both. The unpretentious restaurant, serving a wide range of fondues and other Swiss specialties, including many vegetarian dishes, draws many locals. The favorite sitting place, of course, is the section in the old Rhätibahn railcar, part of which turns into a popular bar at night, the RhBar. ⊠ *Via Grevas 55, CH–7500 St. Moritz-Dorf* ☎ *081/8333245* 🖷 *081/8366060* ⊕ *www.bellaval-stmoritz.ch* ➷ *23 rooms* ⌂ *Restaurant, bar, cable TV, Internet corner; no a/c* ▤ *AE, MC, V, DC.*

$$$$ ▣ **Kulm.** This luxury hotel can claim its share of St. Moritz superlatives: it was the first hotel here (1856) *and* the first house to have electricity in all of Switzerland (1878). Modern comfort has come a long way since: for instance, the Panorama Healthclub, with a saltwater grotto and top-notch fitness gym. Elsewhere, the hotel's discreetly done in slightly old-fashioned good taste—cream, gold, and scarlet. The facilities are top quality, the breakfast room is pure Wedgwood, and the à la carte restaurant—Rôtisserie de Chevaliers—is a romantic vaulted space, serving (predictably enough) old-style haute cuisine. In the Rôtisserie (open only in winter) and the main dining room, jacket and tie are a must, but more casual dining options are also available. Half board is included in the price over the winter holidays, with a 30 SF refund if the meal is not taken. ⊠ *Via Maistra, CH-7500* ☎ *081/8368000* 🖷 *081/8368001* ⊕ *www.kulmhotel-stmoritz.ch* ➷ *139 rooms, 41 suites* ⌂ *4 restaurants, minibars, cable TV, in-room data ports, putting green, 3 tennis courts, health club, hair salon, ice-skating, 2 bars; no a/c* ▤ *AE, DC, MC, V* ⊙ *Closed early Apr.–late June and mid-Sept.–mid-Dec.* ⏃⃝❙ *MAP.*

★ $$$$ ▣ **Suvretta House.** The hotel has many assets: a unique location outside the village with stupendous views of Piz Corvatsch and the Silvaplana Lake, a private ski school, and access to the Corvilgia slopes just outside the front door. In the health complex you can soak in an outdoor hot tub (even in winter) or dream under the sauna's night sky reproduced with tiny lights. Jacket and tie are requested after 7 PM in the lobby and main dining room, but a casual downstairs area reserved for guests has English-style lounges, an informal restaurant, and even a children's restaurant. ⊠ *Via Chasellas 1, CH-7500 St. Moritz-Suvretta* ☎ *081/8363636* 🖷 *081/8363737* ⊕ *www.suvrettahouse.ch* ➷ *170 rooms, 10 junior suites* ⌂ *4 restaurants, in-room safes, cable TV, in-room data ports, driving range, 3 tennis courts, pool, health club, hair salon, massage, ice-skating, 2 bars, shops; no a/c* ▤ *AE, DC, MC, V* ⊙ *Closed mid-Apr.–late June and early Sept.–mid-Dec.* ⏃⃝❙ *BP.*

$$–$$$$ 🏨 **Languard.** Set in the town center, this delightful little hotel stands between the Eden and the Kulm, sharing their lovely mountain views. Details like sgraffiti, carved ceilings, and fine darkened pine in some rooms preserve the best from its earlier days. The big corner rooms deserve their higher price; back rooms are small, but all have tile baths. Front rooms have mountain and lake views. In the small sitting area, check out the collection of skiing trophies won by the owner's father, who used to run St. Moritz's ski school. ⊠ *Via Veglia (off Via Maistra), CH-7500* 🕿 *081/8333137* 🖷 *081/8334546* ⊕ *www.languard-stmoritz.ch* 🛏 *22 rooms* ⚐ *In-room safes, minibars, cable TV; no a/c* 🚭 *AE, DC, MC, V* ⊗ *Closed late Apr.–early June and mid-Oct.–early Dec.* �𝍫 *BP.*

$$–$$$$
Fodor'sChoice
★
🏨 **Waldhaus am See.** This is another world, a good hotel perched on a peninsula overlooking the lake and mountains with a merely peripheral view of St. Moritz's urban turmoil (well filtered through double glass) across the highway. With a big, sunny balcony, dining rooms with views, and a clientele ranging from family clans to senior citizens, it's a vacation lodge geared to leisurely one- to two-week stays. The reasonably priced restaurant stocks more than 1,500 wines, and owner-entrepreneur Claudio Bernasconi has introduced Switzerland's most extensive whiskey bar (as well as his handpicked selection of ties for sale); according to the *Guinness Book of World Records,* the Devil's Place bar holds the record for the world's largest selection of whiskies. Guest rooms are plain, with pine trim and some dated plumbing, though many modern baths have been added in recent years. Sunny corner doubles have tiny bays over the lake. In winter and summer half board is included in the price; in May and November prices include breakfast only. ⊠ *Via Dim Lej, CH-7500* 🕿 *081/8366000* 🖷 *081/8366060* ⊕ *www.waldhaus-am-see.ch* 🛏 *51 rooms, 2 apartments* ⚐ *Restaurant, Stübli, cable TV, gym, sauna, bar; no a/c* 🚭 *AE, DC, MC, V* �𝍫 *BP.*

Nightlife & the Arts

To find out what's happening, check the English-language section in the weekly *Engadin Information* brochure, available at the tourist office, hotels, and shops.

BARS & LOUNGES The après-ski clique favors the Steffani Hotel's **Cava** (⊠ Via Traunter Plazzas 🕿 081/8369696). Choose from the world's largest selection of whiskies at the **Devil's Place** (⊠ Via Dim Lej 🕿 081/8366000). This bar in the Waldhaus am See is mentioned in the *Guinness Book of World Records.* For elegant but informal surroundings try the **Grischuna** (⊠ Schulhauspl. 🕿 081/8370404). Hotel Hauser's open-air **Roo** (⊠ Via Traunter Plazzas 🕿 081/8334402) attracts those who've spent the day on the slopes.

CASINOS The **Casino St. Moritz** (⊠ Via Mezdi 29 🕿 081/8375454) is located in the Kempinski Grand Hôtel des Bains in St. Moritz-Bad and offers roulette, poker, black jack, and slot machines with a "fantasy jackpot." It's open Sunday through Thursday until 3 AM, Friday and Saturday until 4 AM. It closes in May and November.

DANCING **Anton's Bar** (⊠ Via Chasellas 1 🕿 081/8363636), a winter-season spot at the Suvretta House, is jacket-and-tie formal. **Diamond** (⊠ Via Maistra 33 ☎ 081/8349735), as a club, lounge, and restaurant, is a place with wide appeal to the young and chic. In Badrutt's Palace, the **King's Club** (✉ Via Serlas ☎ 081/8371000), has a Moorish decor. Open only in winter, it has a steep cover charge on weekends. For more formal dancing to live music, try the winter-only **Sunny Bar** (✉ Via Maistra ☎ 081/8368000). This old-style dance hall is in the Kulm. In the basement of the Steffani Hotel is **Vivai** (✉ Via Traunter Plazzas ☎ 081/8336939), which opens for both the winter and summer seasons.

MUSIC The musical highlight in St. Moritz is the **Snow & Symphony Music Festival** (☎ 081/8344646), which takes place over 10 days in early spring. Prize-winning classical and jazz musicians, chamber orchestras, and a symphony orchestra give roughly 20 concerts. The performances are held in hotels and on mountaintops. The **Engadine Concert Weeks** (☎ 081/8426573) take place from mid-July to late August, with smaller-scale performances throughout the Upper Engadine. The **St. Moritz Chamber Orchestra** gives free daily concerts in summer at 10:30 AM in the spa center's hall or park. Contact the tourist office for more information.

Sports & the Outdoors

BOBSLEDDING In 1890 and 1891, the first bobsled races were held on the road between St. Moritz and Celerina. The present-day run, built each year from natural ice, follows roughly the same course; it's the only one of its kind in the world. You can watch the **Olympia Bob Run** (☎ 081/8300200) races for around 5 SF. Or you can tear along the run yourself by riding behind an experienced pilot. The ride costs 210 SF; book well in advance. The run is open from late December through early March.

GOLF Samedan's 18-hole **Engadine Golf Course,** the oldest on the continent, (☎ 081/8510466) is about 10 minutes by car from St. Moritz. It's open from late May to early October. The **St. Moritz Golf Club** (☎ 081/8368236) has a 9-hole course in the Kulm Park.

HIKING There are dozens of hiking and walking routes around St. Moritz, all well signposted. Maps are available at the tourist office. Most cable cars, funiculars, and some chairlifts run in summer, providing access to higher trails, including the magnificent Via Engiadina path along the mountainside at roughly 6,560 feet to the beginning of the valley. The full walk takes about six hours, but you can descend to valley level earlier if you are tuckered out.

ICE-SKATING & CURLING The lakeside outdoor **Ludains Skating Rink** (✉ St. Moritz-Bad ☎ 081/8335030) is open from mid-July to late April. Skate rentals are avail-

---

NO STANDING HERE

On the world's one and only Cresta Run, riders on skeletons (a metal toboggan) rush headfirst down a winding ice channel from St. Moritz to Celerina, accelerating to about 90 mph. You can watch the runs every morning from the path or the roof of the Junction Hut. If you'd like to try the run, contact the St. Moritz Tobogganing Club (081/8333117). It's a private club, but they do allow temporary memberships (for 450 SF) that will give you 5 runs. The Cresta is open from late December to the last day of February. Note that the run is not open to women.

able. The skating and curling rinks at the **Kulm** (☎ 081/8368000) hotel are open to the public in winter; rental skates and curling lessons are available.

GRAUBÜNDEN ESSENTIALS

Transportation

BY AIR

Engadin Airport is used mainly by private planes. At 5,600 feet, it's the highest airport in Europe. The closest international airports are Zürich (about 2 hours from Chur) and Lugano (about 2½ hours from St. Moritz). 🛈 Airport Information **Engadin Airport** ✉ Samedan, 5 km [3 mi] from St. Moritz ☎ 081/ 8525433.

BY BUS

You can take the Swiss postbus (postauto) system's *Palm Express* from Lugano in the Ticino to St. Moritz. The 3¾-hour trip passes through a corner of Italy and over the Maloja Pass. The bus runs twice daily from mid-June through mid-October; reservations are essential. Owners of a Swiss Pass will need to purchase the additional Alpine Ticket for 15 SF.

Postautos are a good way to wind your way up Alpine switchbacks over the region's great passes—that is, if you're not inclined to motion sickness. You can also use them to make circle tours with some careful study of the schedule. Information is available at all post offices. The main ski resorts have "sport bus" shuttles, which connect the villages and mountain stations. The service is usually included in the price of your lift ticket or on presentation of a "guest card" (check to see if your hotel offers these discount booklets).
🛈 Bus Information *Palm Express* ☎ 081/8376764 or 091/8078520 ⊕ www.swisspost. com. Note that the timetable and itinerary search is the same as Swiss Railways, so you will receive schedules for both bus and trains.

BY CAR

Graubünden is mountainous with few major highways. Drivers can enter either by way of the San Bernardino Pass from the south or from the north on A13, the region's only expressway. Coming from Austria and Munich, the A27 leads into the Lower Engadine; roads over the Ofen and Bernina passes lead into the Engadine from the South Tyrol and Veltline areas of Italy respectively, and the approach to the Upper Engadine from Italy is over the Maloja Pass. The Oberalp and Lukmanier passes lead from Uri and Ticino respectively to the Surselva region to join A13.

The A13 expressway cuts a swift north–south route through Graubünden. A car is definitely necessary if you want to explore deeper into the countryside. Fine valley roads connect the rest of the area, though to move from one resort to another you may have to crawl over a mountain pass. If you're traveling in winter, make sure to check the status of the passes beforehand. The San Bernardino old road and the Oberalp, Albula, and Flüela passes usually close, but the San Bernardino Tunnel and the Maloja, Bernina, Julier, and Ofen passes are usually open to traffic. Local road condition information is generally broadcast in German, French, and Italian, but you could also ask for the latest reports at the tourist offices. The Lukmanier is the only pass in the region that can stay open in winter. Trains through the Vereina tunnel shuttle cars between Klosters and Sagliains (Susch–Lavin). The tunnel has made the Lower Engadine quickly accessible during the winter, when the Flüela pass is seldom open. Tickets are between 27 SF in summer and 40 SF in winter. Cars can also be taken by rail from Thusis to Samedan via the Albula tunnel; the service is limited and reservations are essential. The cost per car is 145 SF.

🚗 Car Transport/Rail Reservation ☎ 081/6511113.

BY TRAIN

Thanks to an extensive rail network with trains running at a good frequency, a trip to Graubünden can be done without even a car–unless you insist on traveling up every tiny valley. A Swiss Pass gives you access to all trains and buses (supplemented at times by the Apline Pass). A Flexi-Pass can be used if you intend to use the trains only on certain days. The Swiss Federal Railway trains that enter Graubünden only travel as far as Chur. From there the fine local Rhätische Bahn (RhB) takes over—from its brand new train and bus station. The *Bernina Express* runs from Chur to St. Moritz via the Albula route and on to Italy past the spectacular Bernina peaks, lakes, and glaciers. The *Engadine Star,* which began service in 2000, makes its way from Klosters to St. Moritz in a couple of hours. The glamorous *Glacier Express,* billed as "the slowest express in the world," connects St. Moritz with Zermatt via the Oberalp Pass, crossing 291 bridges during its 7½-hour journey. The train includes an antique burnished-wood dining car; you can book a table through Passaggio Rail. Reservations for these trains are mandatory and can be made at almost any European rail station. As on the federal railways, a variety of reduced-price passes are available. For information on the local train network, contact Rhätische Bahn or the regional tourism office, Graubünden Holidays.

🚆 Train Information **Passaggio Rail** ✉ CH-7000 Chur ☎ 081/2521425. **Rhätische Bahn** ☎ 081/2549100 ⊕ www.rhb.ch. **Swiss Federal Railway (SBB/CFF/FFS)** ☎ 0900/300300 ⊕ www.rail.ch.

Contacts & Resources

EMERGENCIES

There are national lines and many local lines for emergencies in Graubünden. For the general line for the criminal **police,** dial ☎ 117. The general number for an **emergency doctor or ambulance** is ☎ 144. Klinik Gut in St. Moritz specializes in urgent care. **Doctors, dentists, and emergency pharmacies** are listed in resort tourist periodicals or can be requested by calling information at ☎ 111.

🏥 Doctors **Arosa** ☎ 081/3772728. **Chur** ☎ 081/2523636. **Klosters** ☎ 081/3080808. **Pontresina** ☎ 081/8427766 or 081/8426268. **St. Moritz** ☎ 081/8330033. **Zernez** ☎ 081/8561215 or 081/8561616.

🏥 Local Ambulances **Chur** ☎ 081/3533535. **Davos** ☎ 081/4101111. **Klosters** ☎ 081/4221713. **Upper Engadine** ☎ 081/8518888.

🏥 Local Hospitals **Chur** ☎ 081/2566111. **Davos** ☎ 081/4148888. **Klinik Gut, St. Moritz** ☎ 081/8334141. **Upper Engadine/Samedan** ☎ 081/8518111. **Scuol** ☎ 081/8611000.
🚓 Local Police **Arosa** ☎ 081/3771938. **Chur** ☎ 081/2544341. **Davos** ☎ 081/4137622. **Flims** ☎ 081/9111164. **Klosters** ☎ 081/4221236. **Pontresina** ☎ 081/8426271. **St. Moritz** ☎ 081/8322727. **Scuol** ☎ 081/8641414. **Zernez** ☎ 081/8561212.

INTERNET & MAIL

Most hotels have a Wi-Fi hot spot, known in German as WLAN. Some offer connection for free, other connections must be paid for by scratch card or credit card online. Cost is usually 5 SF for 30 minutes, 19 SF for 2 hours (note that once the clock is ticking, it will not stop). Many hotels have some form of public Internet access in the lobbies (Internet corners) for those traveling without a laptop. If you need a more private connection, ask your hotel concierge if there are any Internet cafés nearby. Not all post offices have public Internet access. The Swiss post office has one general toll-free phone number: 0848/888888.

📧 Internet & Mail Information **Business center St. Moritz** ✉ Via dal Bagn 52 (Gallaria C. Badrutt), St. Moritz ☎ 081/8344555. **Espresso Bar** ✉ Poststr. (in the Casino), Arosa ☎ 081/3787062 🕐 Closed Sun. **Street Café** ✉ Grabenstr. 47, Chur ☎ 081/2537914. **Expert RoRo** ✉ Promenade 123, Davos ☎ 081/4201111. **Post office Chur** ✉ Gürtelstr. 14, Bellinzona. **Post Office Davos** ✉ Bahnhofstr. 3–9, Davos. **Post Office St. Moritz** ✉ Via Serlas 23, St. Moritz Dorf.

SPORTS & THE OUTDOORS

HIKING Arosa, Davos, and Lenzerheide-Valbella offer special hiking packages. You can walk from Davos to Arosa one day and from Arosa to Lenzerheide the next. No need to worry about booking a hotel or transporting your luggage, as it's all taken care of. A seven-day program lets you spend more time in each resort. Contact local tourist offices or the regional tourist office, Graubünden Holidays. Similar arrangements can be made in the Engadine; call Engadin Ferien for information.
📧 **Engadin Ferien** ☎ 081/8300001 ⊕ www.engadinferien.ch.

WALKING The Arosa tourist office offers guided tours and nature walks daily from June through October; you can visit a cheese maker, a regional museum, and a 15th-century chapel. The Davos and Klosters tourist offices arrange guided walks at least once a week from July to September. The Chur tourist office arranges guided tours from April to October every Wednesday at 2:30. To explore on your own, pick up a map from the tourist office and follow the green and red footprints on the pavement. The Pontresina tourist office offers guided walking tours of its Old Town from mid-June to mid-October. It also offers guided botanical excursions, glacier treks, and hiking trips to the Swiss National Park, plus mushroom-picking outings in season (usually August and September). If you are staying in Pontresina, these trips are free; day visitors pay a small fee. Guides for all of the above tours speak English.

VISITOR INFORMATION

The canton's tourist information center is Graubünden Holidays. Although a few of the local tourism Web sites do not have English translations yet, all tourist offices have English-speaking staff and plenty of printed information in English.

▉ Local Tourist Offices Arosa ✉ CH-7050 ☎ 081/3787020 ⊕ www.arosa.ch. **Bündner Herrschaft/Maienfeld** ✉ CH-7304 Maienfeld ☎ 081/3301912 or 081/3025858 ⊕ www.buendnerherrschaft.ch. **Chur** ✉ Grabenstr. 5, CH-7002 ☎ 081/2521818 🖷 081/2529076 ⊕ www.churtourismus.ch. **Davos** ✉ Promenade 67, CH-7270 ☎ 081/4152121 ⊕ www.davos.ch. **Flims-Laax** ✉ Alpenarena, CH-7032 ☎ 081/9209200 🖷 081/9209201 ⊕ www.alpenarena.ch. **Klosters** ✉ Alte Bahnhofstr. 6, CH-7250 ☎ 081/4102020 ⊕ www.klosters.ch. **Pontresina** ✉ Rondo Center, CH-7504 ☎ 081/8388300 ⊕ www.pontresina.ch. **St. Moritz** ✉ Via Maistra, CH-7500 ☎ 081/8373333 ⊕ www.stmoritz.ch. **Scuol & Tarasp-Vulpera** ✉ CH-7550 ☎ 081/8612222 ⊕ www.scuol.ch. **Zernez** ✉ CH-7530 ☎ 081/8561300 ⊕ www.zernez.ch.

▉ Regional Tourist Office Graubünden Holidays ✉ Alexanderstr. 24, CH-7001 Chur ☎ 081/2542424 🖷 081/2542400 ⊕ www.graubuenden.ch.

The Ticino

BELLINZONA, LOCARNO, LUGANO

4

Lago di Dentro Cadlimo Piz Tanelin

WORD OF MOUTH

"If you are regretting missing Italy, consider the Ticino, Switzerland's Italian region. I call it Italy Lite; all the wonders of Italy (food, wine, enthusiastic people, language) and none of the inconveniences."
—Catbert

"Please don't miss taking a boat ride to Gandria . . . it's gorgeous! No cars. We ate at a little Italian restaurant overlooking the water on a flower-filled porch—heavenly!"
—LLindaC

WELCOME TO THE TICINO

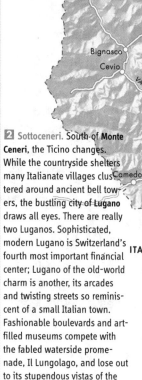

TOP REASONS TO GO

★ **Luscious Lugano:** Nowhere in the Ticino does Italian chic and Swiss quality mingle so perfectly. But there is more going on here than people-watching and ice-cream tasting: Churches, museums and the restored Old Town also demand attention.

★ **Land o' Lakes:** Gaze at the verdant mountains, cozy villages, and palm-fronted shores from the vantage point of the elegant old ferry boats that ply the waters of the Lago Maggiore and Lago di Lugano.

★ **Castle-topped Bellinzona:** Old cobble-stone streets, shady arcades, and the three fortresses that once upon a time held the line between Italy and the wild Swiss take the visitor back to an age when this region belonged to Milan.

★ **Get a View:** Monte Bré (near Lugano) can be climbed on foot or by funicular, which is faster and far less tiring. Either way: the view from the top is one that will literally take your breath away.

Saturday market in Bellinzona.

1 Soraceneri. Capital of the Ticino, **Bellinzona** has always been a famous crossroads thanks to three passes—St. Gothard, the Lukmanier, and the San Bernardino—from the north. The town's great castles—Castelgrande, Montebello, and Sasso Corbaro—prove that Bellinzona was always in the firing line. To the west along Lago Maggiore lies **Locarno**, Switzerland's sunniest town, with its bevy of Baroque and Renaissance churches (including the clifftop Santuario della Madonna del Sasso). Just beyond are the lakeside promenades of **Ascona**, so beloved by painters, and the **Brissago Islands**, Switzerland's most beautiful botanical garden.

2 Sottoceneri. South of **Monte Ceneri**, the Ticino changes. While the countryside shelters many Italianate villages clustered around ancient bell towers, the bustling city of **Lugano** draws all eyes. There are really two Luganos. Sophisticated, modern Lugano is Switzerland's fourth most important financial center; Lugano of the old-world charm is another, its arcades and twisting streets so reminiscent of a small Italian town. Fashionable boulevards and art-filled museums compete with the fabled waterside promenade, Il Lungolago, and lose out to its stupendous vistas of the blue lake and bluer peaks. On Lago di Lugano's southern shores lies a gaggle of gorgeous villages: **Gandria**, **Campione**, and **Morcote**.

GETTING ORIENTED

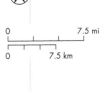

Even in Switzerland, this Italian-cultured canton is something of a step-daughter to the other cantons. It does have everything to make it Swiss: high mountains, gorgeous lakes with clean waters, and excellent service. And yet the air has that unmistakable redolence of the Mediterranean. A little inaccessible—wedged into Italy, it hides "behind" a virtual curtain of snow-capped peaks—the Ticino is a happy harbor for Switzerland's Italian-speaking minority.

View from Lake Lugano

```
0          7.5 mi
|----|----|----|
0          7.5 km
```

THE TICINO PLANNER

Finding a Place to Stay

The hotel industry of this Mediterranean region of Switzerland capitalizes on its natural assets, with lakeside views of Lago Maggiore and Lago di Lugano, and swimming pools and terraces that pay homage to the omnipresent sun.

As the Ticino is at its best in spring and fall, and packed with sunseekers in summer, many hotels close down for the winter.

Tourist offices often publish lists of those remaining open, so if you're planning to come in low season—and even in January the lake resorts can be balmy—check carefully. Keep in mind that most hotels are not air-conditioned, in spite of hot spells in July and August.

Vacation resorts don't depend on the demipension (half board) system as much as their mountain counterparts, but arrangements can be made.

And remember, there are several festivals in all towns in summer, notably Locarno and Lugano—expect full hotels. Crowds arrive for the region's Good Friday folk processions, for Carnevale (February), and Locarno's International Film Festival in August

Otherwise, the Ticino is moderately well visited throughout most of the year, except in late fall and after the Christmas/New Year period.

How's the Weather?

No one complains about the weather in the Ticino. Palm trees, magnolia, century plants, and full-bodied wines suggest why so many "northerners" come to the canton for their vacation: the weather is milder than elsewhere in Switzerland in winter, while stark summer temperatures are moderated by the lakes and the mountains.

There can be some surprises, though, since you are in the Alps. Sudden storms and drops in temperature are a possibility. So make sure you have a few warm clothes along and something waterproof.

If you intend to trek up the valleys or up to the summit of a mountain, you will definitely need something warm along besides robust hiking boots and sunglasses. Winters are cold up in the mountains, but around the lakes several degrees warmer than elsewhere in Switzerland.

Lush and Mediterranean, the Ticino is gorgeous in springtime; the season starts as early as mid-March here, making the region a popular late-winter escape.

In summertime, lakeside activity surges, and the weather can at times be hot. Warm summer nights are incredibly romantic, particularly on the Lago di Lugano.

Crowds fill the promenades at Lugano and Locarno throughout the summer, but neither waterfront becomes unpleasantly jammed—although the road from Bellinzona to Locarno and Lugano is usually packed.

Great Grotti Grits

The best place to sample Ticino's down-to-earth delicacies is in one of the numerous *Grotti*, stone buildings sometimes isolated in the woods, sometimes carved deep in the adjoining rock, where they serve simple meals and bring wine in a *boccalino* (small jug).

Some are set deep in the mountains and forests, others can be reached only by boat and have little more than a few picnic tables and a string of festive lights. Some serve only cold meats, but a few offer one or two hot dishes each day.

To experience an authentic grotto, avoid the ones with ristorante in their names; the categories of eating establishments are carefully regulated, so these will always be pricier—and not the real thing.

Getting Around

As with most of Switzerland, bus lines and railroad tracks crisscross the area. Good thing, as parking in towns is difficult, making a car more a liability than a pleasure.

Add to that the fact that the Ticinese are not completely considerate drivers, which causes much additional chaos on the roads, especially during rush hours.

Happily, Lugano, Locarno, and Bellinzona are very well connected by train, and all the main sights within the towns can be seen on foot.

There is regular bus service to Ascona from Locarno, or up the Verzasca and Maggia valleys. Lugano to Morcote, and so on, can be easily done by bus as well.

Two alternatives, of course, are the boats for sights along the Lake Lugano's shore, or alternatively renting bicycles (do one way by bike and returning either by bus or by ferry).

Making the Most of Your Stay

The important parts of the Ticino are all fairly close to one another but, depending on the amount of time you have, you might want to choose one or two home-base locations. Locarno or Ascona will allow you easy and quick access to the Verzasca and Maggia Valleys and to all the sites and sights along the Lago Maggiore.

Lugano gives you fast access to the Lago di Lugano and the gems of Gandria, Morcote, and Campione. From Bellinzona, you will have good access to all sights in the chapter.

There's lots to do if you want to. If not, you can enjoy long meditative walks in the mountains or along the lakes. Shopping in Lugano, touring the lakes by ferry, or hopping a funicular up a mountain and just enjoying the air, followed by a simple meal in a "grotto," will give you classic Ticinese moments.

On the other hand, more active types will have lots of sports options available, from skiing and snowboarding in winter, to swimming, climbing, paragliding, rafting, or golf during the warm months. If in need of a big and bustling city, remember that Milan is 1–1½ hours away by train from Lugano.

WHAT IT COSTS In Swiss francs

	$$$$	$$$	$$	$	¢
Restaurants	over 60 SF	40 SF–60 SF	25 SF–40 SF	15 SF–25 SF	under 15 SF
Hotels	over 350 SF	250 SF–350 SF	175 SF–250 SF	100 SF–175 SF	under 100 SF

Restaurant prices are per person for a main course at dinner. Hotel prices are for two people in a standard double room in high season, including tax and service.

Updated by
Marton Radkai

VISITORS A BIT WEAK ON THEIR GEOGRAPHY might hear the names Lugano, Ascona, Locarno, and Bellinzona and assume—quite naturally—that they're in Italy. Color photographs of the region might not even set them straight: nearly every publicity shot shows palm trees and mimosas, azure waters and indigo skies. Surely this is the Italian Mediterranean or the coast of the Adriatic. But behind the waving date palms are telltale signs: fresh paint, manicured gardens, punctual trains. There's no mistake about it: it's a little bit of Italy, but the canton Ticino is decidedly Swiss.

For the German Swiss, it's a little bit of paradise. They can cross over the St. Gotthard or San Bernardino passes and emerge into balmy sunshine, fill up on gnocchi and polenta in shaded *grotti* (rustic outdoor restaurants), drink merlot from ceramic bowls, gaze at the waters of Lago Maggiore (Lake Maggiore)—and still know their lodging will be strictly controlled by the Swiss Hotel Association. Plus, they never even have to change currency. The combination is irresistible, and so in spring, summer, and fall they pour over the Alps to revel in low-risk Latin delights.

And the Ticinese welcome them like rich, distant cousins, to be served and coddled and—perhaps just a bit—tolerated. For the Italian-speaking natives of the Ticino—a lonely 8% of the Swiss population—are a minority in their own land, dominated politically by the German-speaking Swiss, from whom they are set apart by language as well as culture. Their blood and politics are as Mediterranean as their climate: in a battle over obligatory seat belts, the Ticinese consistently voted to reject the federal intrusion. They were voted down by their Germanic neighbors—a 70% majority—and when they protested, it was brought to vote again, and again they were defeated. Nowadays the Ticinese defy the federal law—and the local policemen, Ticinese themselves, of course, turn a blind and supportive eye.

Their Italian leanings make perfect sense: an enormous mountain chain blocks them from the north, pushing them inexorably toward their lingual roots. Most of the territory of the Ticino belonged to the pre-Italian city-states of Milan and Como until 1512, when the Swiss Confederation took it over by force. It remained a Swiss conquest—oppressed under the then-tyrannical rule of Uri, Schwyz, and Unterwalden, the very cantons now revered for forming the honorable Confederation of Switzerland—until 1798, when from the confusion of Napoléon's campaigns it emerged a free canton, and in 1803 it joined the confederation for good.

It remains a canton apart nonetheless, graceful, open, laissez-faire. Here you'll instantly notice differences in manner and body language among Ticinese engaged in conversation; you'll also notice fewer English-speaking Swiss. The climate, too, is different: there's an extraordinary amount of sunshine here, more than in central Switzerland and even more than in sunny Italy, immediately across the border. Mountain-sports meccas aside, this is the most glamorous of Swiss regions: the waterfront promenades of Lugano, Locarno, and Ascona, lined with pollards, rhododendrons, and bobbing yachts, blend a rich social mix of jet-set resorters. A drive of a few miles brings the canton's impoverished past into view:

foothill and mountain villages still scattered with low-roof stone cabins, although nowadays those cabins often prove to have been gentrified into chic vacation homes.

Although they're prosperous, with Lugano standing third in banking, after Zürich and Geneva, the Ticinese hold on to their past, a mountain-people culture that draws them to hike, hunt, and celebrate with great pots of risotto stirred over open outdoor fires. It's that contrast—contemporary glamour combined with an earthy past—that grants travelers a visit that's as balanced and satisfying as a good merlot.

Exploring the Ticino

The canton is geographically divided into two regions by the small mountain range (1,817 feet) called Monte Ceneri, which rises up south of the valley below Bellinzona. Extending northeast and northwest of Monte Ceneri in the windswept Sopraceneri region are several mountainous valleys, including Valle di Blenio, Valle Maggia, Valle Verzasca, and Valle Leventina. Included in this region north of or, literally, above Monte Ceneri are Locarno and Ascona, which share a peninsula bulging into Lago Maggiore. The more developed southern region, Sottoceneri ("below Ceneri"), is home to business and resort towns, notably Lugano.

SOPRACENERI

The mountainous valleys of Valle di Blenio, Valle Maggia, Valle Verzasca, and Valle Leventina reach, like the fingers of a hand, south from the Alps into the basin of Lago Maggiore and Monte Ceneri, in the Sopraceneri. At the tips are the sun-kissed resorts of Locarno and Ascona, both on the northern edge of Lago Maggiore. Here the true spirit of the canton is still evident in the numerous small valley communities, each of which is politically autonomous although some have fewer than 100 inhabitants. The Sopraceneri reveals a slightly slower-paced, homier side of the Ticino, leaving the flashier offerings to Lugano in the south.

Bellinzona

❶ **To & From:** *Transportation gateway to the Ticino, Bellinzona is not only* **Fodor'sChoice** *on the Zürich–Milan route but has frequent trains running nearly every* **★** *half-hour to and from Locarno (30 min.; 8 SF) and Lugano (45 min.; 11 SF). Note that the Swiss Federal Railway is here called the Ferrovie Federali Svizzere (FFS). Buses to smaller villages leave from the bus depot at the train station. For schedules for destinations in this chapter, check either the Swiss railway's Website, www.sbb.ch, or call 0900/300300 (1,19 SF per min.). Remember, if you have a Swiss Pass or another rail-discounting card, it also applies to the buses. Bellinzona is 141 km (88 mi) south of Luzern, 150 km (93 mi) south of St. Moritz.*

All roads lead to Bellinzona, the fortified valley city that guards the important European crossroads of the St. Gotthard and San Bernardino routes. As the capital of the Ticino, its importance through the ages is evident in the three massive fortified castles that rise over its ancient center. As the only example of late medieval military architecture preserved

along the Alpine range, the castles and fortifications have been named a World Heritage site by UNESCO. They were built by the Sforza and Visconti families, the dukes of Milan who ruled northern Italy and its environs for centuries. In the 15th century, many of the surrounding valleys began falling into the hands of the expanding Swiss confederation. Bellinzona, however, remained Italian until Milan itself—and Bellinzona—was occupied by the French in 1503. Bellinzona decided to cast its lot with the Swiss Confederation. Ironically, the names of the castles built in part to keep the Swiss at bay were then changed to Schwyz, Uri, and Unterwalden—the three core cantons of the Swiss Confederation. Eventually the names were changed again, and the fortresses are known today as Castelgrande, Castello di Montebello, and Castello di Sasso Corbaro.

> ## WORD OF MOUTH
>
> "The three castles in Bellinzona are most interesting. They do live opera in the summer at the largest (and lowest); the view from the smallest (and highest) castle is wonderful and you can do a pleasant hike down from the top back into town (take a taxi to the top)."
> —BTilke
>
> "In Bellinzona, we had a great lunch on the square and walked to the three castles. They don't have furnished rooms (as at Gruyères or Chillon)—still, the views are great. I remember seeing a post bus stop at one castle, so it's probably easy to get from one to the other."
> —LLindaC

The three castles have been exceptionally well restored, and each merits a visit (a walk along the ramparts at night is particularly appealing), but the city itself should not be overlooked: it's a classic Lombard town, with graceful architecture, red cobblestones, and an easy, authentically Italian ambience. It's relatively free of tourists and thus reveals the Ticino way of life, complete with a lively produce market on Saturday featuring boar salami, wild mushrooms, and local cheeses.

The **centro storico** (Old Town), with its heavy-column arcades, wrought-iron balconies, and shuttered facades, exhibits the direct influence of medieval Lombardy. The small area is distinguished by red cobblestones.

The **Palazzo Civico,** located in the Old Town on the Piazza Nosetto, is a splendid Renaissance structure that was rebuilt in the 1920s. Its courtyard is framed by two stacked rows of delicate vaulted arcades decorated with sgrafittos depicting Bellinzona in the 19th century. The top floor consists of an airy loggia. The **Castelgrande** was first mentioned in a document from the 6th century. The current structure, however, dates from the 1200s. The massive exterior is dominated by two heavy, unmatched towers and the remaining portion of a crenellated wall that once stretched all the way to the river. Modern renovations have added an elaborate complex of restaurants and museums, including historical and archaeological exhibitions. The 14th-century ceiling murals, created to embellish the wooden ceiling of a local villa (now demolished), offer a peek at privately commissioned decorative art. A dramatic audiovisual history of Bellinzona and the Ticino Valley is shown in one room.

EATING WELL IN THE TICINO

Of all the Swiss regions, Ticino can be the most pleasurable in which to eat, as the stylish and simple cuisine of Italy has been adopted virtually intact. Because the Ticinese were once a poor mountain people, their everyday cooking shares the earthy delights of another once-poor mountain people, the Piedmontese, whose steaming polenta and rib-sticking gnocchi break bread with game and meaty porcini mushrooms. *Manzo brasato* (savory braised beef with vegetables), *busecca* (vegetable soup with tripe), and osso buco are standards, as are any number of variations on risotto. Game offerings usually include *coniglio* (rabbit), *lepre* (hare), and *capretto* (roast kid). Wherever you eat, *il piatto del giorno* (the daily special) can help you economize.

As in the rest of Switzerland, local cold meats come in a broad variety, from myriad salamis to prosciutto *crudo*, the pearly pink cured raw ham made famous in Parma. Any food product made locally is called *nostrano*, and the prosciutto crudo nostrano is worth asking for, as you won't find a match for its forthright, gamey flavor back home. Eat it with bread and sweet butter to balance the salt. Most cooks import Italian cheeses—Parmigiano-Reggiano, sharp pecorino—though there are good, hard, white mountain varieties (Piora, Gesero) in most shops. Tiny *formaggini*—little molds of ultrafresh goat cheese—taste best with coarsely ground black pepper and olive oil. Or try the *zincarlin*, a fresh cheese mixed with parsley, garlic, and pepper.

The local wine is merlot; a warm, generous wine counted as one of the top Swiss reds. The wine is poured into an individual *boccalino*, a traditional ceramic pitcher, or a small ceramic bowl, to be drunk from like a cup. Instead of beer to quench locals' thirsts, a mix of *gazosa* (lemon-lime soda) and *vino nostrano* (the house red wine) is de rigueur. If you want a real Italian-style espresso, one-finger deep and frothing with golden foam, ask for *un liscio*. Otherwise they'll serve it with cream, Swiss style, and might even charge you extra. If you want a shot of grappa (grape brandy) thrown in, ask for it *corretto*—literally, "correct." Or finish off your meal with a shot of *Nocino*, a traditional walnut liqueur also known as *Ratafiá* (from *rata fiat*, meaning "it's done"). Walnuts picked before San Giovanni's day (June 25) are soaked in grappa and mixed with a secret combination of herbs and spices. Most Nocino is produced privately from closely guarded recipes—no two taste alike.

✉ *Monte San Michele* ☎ *091/8258145* 🎫 *4 SF, 8 SF combination ticket for Castelgrande, Castello di Montebello, and Castello di Sasso Corbaro* ⊘ *Daily 10–6.*

The sober late-Renaissance facade of the **Chiesa Collegiata di San Pietro e San Stefano** (Church of St. Peter and St. Stephen), begun in the 16th century, stands across from the Castelgrande. Its Baroque interior is richly decorated with frescoes and stucco work by a host of Ticino artists. Of

Ticino's Fossil Trove

Rooted firmly on the southern shores of Lago di Lugano, the 3,595-foot Monte San Giorgio has been an irresistible draw for paleontologists since the mid-19th century. Scientific excavations in its five successive strata have regularly churned out extremely well-preserved fossils, allowing scientists to study the evolution of various groups of marine creatures of the geological era known as the Middle Triassic (245–230 million years ago). Thousands of the reptiles, fish, and invertebrates found here—some of them unique specimens—have made their way into museums of paleontology in Zürich, Lugano, and Milan.

No wonder, then, that UNESCO added the entire region—an area measuring 2,098 acres and extending across the communities of Meride, Riva San Vitale, and Brusino Arsizio—to the list of World Heritage natural sites in July 2003. This designation for Monte San Giorgio is Switzerland's second such honor, coming two years after that for the glaciers spanning the Jungfrau, Aletsch, and Bietschhorn summits.

particular note is the late-18th century Crucifixion attributed to Simone Peterzano that serves as a central altar painting. ⊠ *Piazza Collegiata* ☎ *091/8252131.*

The most striking of Bellinzona's three castles is the **Castello di Monte-bello.** Its core, the oldest section located behind two drawbridges, dates from the 13th century; the palace and courtyard are from the 15th century, with spectacular walkways around the top of the encircling walls. The center structure houses an attractive, modern Museo Civico (Civic Museum) and the Museo Archeologico (Archeological Museum), with exhibits on local history and architecture, including an impressive collection of Gothic and Renaissance stone capitals. ⊠ *Salita ai Castelli* ☎ *091/8251342* ☎ *4 SF, 8 SF combination ticket for Castelgrande, Castello di Montebello, and Castello di Sasso Corbaro* ☉ *Mar.–Nov., daily 10–6.*

The **Castello di Sasso Corbaro** is a massive and forbidding fieldstone construction; the almost complete absence of curvature is typical of the Sforza style. It was designed by a Florentine military engineer and built in 1479 for the duke of Milan, who insisted the work be completed in six months, as indeed it was. Temporary art exhibitions are held in the Belvedere and in the Emma Paglia Room. Ambitious walkers can reach the castle in about 45 minutes by treading uphill from the Castello di Montebello along a switchback road through woods; if you're driving, follow the signs to Artore. ☎ *091/8255906* ☎ *4 SF, 8 SF combination ticket for Castelgrande, Castello di Montebello, and Castello di Sasso Corbaro* ☉ *Apr.–Oct., Tues.–Sun. 10–6.*

Chiesa San Biagio (Church of St. Biagio), one of Bellinzona's two Italianate churches, is a spare medieval treasure guarded on the exterior by an outsize fresco of a soldierly Christ. The 12th-century late-Romanesque structure suggests a transition into Gothic style. Alternating natural red brick and gray stone complement fragments of exquisitely colored 14th-century frescoes. ⊠ *Via San Biagio 13, Bellinzona-Ravecchia* ☏*091/8252131.*

Chiesa Santa Maria delle Grazie (Church of St. Mary of Grace) was first mentioned in the 15th century, when it was part of a Franciscan monastery, which has now been turned into a retirement home. The church's most remarkable feature is the huge fresco on a wall segmenting the main nave painted by an unknown Lombard artist some time around 1500. It depicts the Crucifixion in the center, surrounded by 15 vignettes from the life of Christ. The church fell victim to a fire in 1996, but was completely restored and reopened in 2006. ⊠ *Via Convento, Bellinzona-Ravecchia* ☏ *091/8252131.*

The city's art gallery, **Museo Villa dei Cedri,** sporadically dips into its coffers—made up of a donated private collection—to mount worthwhile exhibits. Behind the garden and grounds, the city maintains a tiny vineyard used to produce its very own merlot, available for sale inside. ⊠ *Piazza San Biagio 9* ☏ *091/8218520* ⊕ *www.villacedri.ch* ✍ *8 SF* ◷ *Tues.–Fri. 2–6, weekends 11–6.*

Where to Stay & Eat

★ **$$–$$$** ✕ **Castelgrande.** Now that the oldest of the city's castles has been renovated, its chic, modern restaurant merits a visit. Don't expect a quick cafeteria lunch served to shorts-clad tourists: this is a serious experience, with a daringly cool, post-Memphis decor and sophisticated efforts from the Italian chef, such as goose liver with blueberries or pigeon and pearl onions in sweet-and-sour sauce. The wine list flaunts more than 70 Ticino merlots. With a lighter atmosphere, the terrace is a great spot to soak up views and sunshine. ⊠ *Monte San Michele* ☏ *091/8262353* ⊕ *www.castelgrande.ch* ⊟ *AE, DC, MC, V* ◷ *Closed Mon.*

★ **$$–$$$** ✕ **Malakoff.** In this small family restaurant just up the hill from the town center, chef Rita Fuso prepares traditional Italian fare from impeccable high-quality ingredients. The pasta is homemade, and the vegetables and meats come from local farms; some of the herbs come from the Fusos' own garden. Try seasonal variations on standard regional fare, such as risotto with chanterelles and blueberries. The best bet (and a great value) is the daily two-course special, such as homemade rabbit terrine with salad followed by loin of lamb in morel sauce. The Fusos are so passionate about food that smokers are asked to abstain until after the meal so as not to ruin their palate. ⊠ *Carrale Bacilieri 10* ☏ *091/ 8254940* ⊟ *MC, V* ◷ *Closed Sun.*

$–$$ ✕ **Osteria Sasso Corbaro.** From the heights of the ancient Castello di Sasso Corbaro, this atmospheric restaurant serves meals inside a beautifully restored hall or outside, at wooden tables, in the shady, walled-in courtyard. The cooking is simple and regional, with cold and grilled meats, trout, and seasonal vegetables. Good local wines round out the experience. ⊠ *Castello Sasso Corbaro* ☏ *091/8255532* ⊟ *AE, DC, MC, V* ◷ *Closed Mon. and Nov.–Feb.*

¢–$ ✕▣ **Grotto Paudese.** Immaculate, friendly, and family-run, this grotto-cum-bed-and-breakfast perches high above the town in the tiny hamlet of Paudo. Its mere handful of rooms are tastefully simple, if a bit small; the owners squeeze in the occasional antique chest of drawers. There's an unsurpassed view of the twinkling valley and the Alps beyond. The adjoining grotto is warmly traditional, turning out a robust daily meal (homemade pasta, polenta, and the like). The inn is roughly a 15-minute drive up from Bellinzona. Going east into the Val Morobbia, follow signs for Pianezzo and then for Paudo. ⊠ *CH-6582 Paudo* 📠 *091/8571468* 🛏 *4 rooms* △ *Restaurant, bar; no a/c, no room phones, no room TVs* 🍽 *V* ⊘ *Closed mid-Dec.–Feb.* 🍴 *BP.*

$$ 🏨 **Locanda Brack.** The shady terrace, discriminating wine list, and excellent homemade pastas using mostly organic ingredients are what attract visitors and locals alike to this osteria perched on the hillside of Gudo, right between Bellinzona and Locarno. But Marco and Gesa Brack also run a very fine bed and breakfast in the converted farmhouse. Each room has either a balcony with a spectacular view of the Ticino valley, or a peaceful terrace nestled into the hillside. Furnishings are simple and tasteful. ⊠ *Via delle Vigne, CH-6515* 📞 *091/8591254* 📠 *091/8592098* 🛏 *7 rooms* △ *Restaurant, bar, Internet, pool; no a/c* 🍽 *V, MC* ⊘ *Dec.–Feb.* 🍴 *BP.*

Locarno

❷ **To & From:** *From Bellinzona, trains are a 20–30 minute ride for 7.80 SF. Trains from Bern are frequent; The trip lasts about 4 hours; trains pass through Luzern and the Gotthard and is 70 SF. There are two trains daily from Geneva, at 11:10 AM and 3:10 PM., that pass through Domodossola and the Centovalli on a trip that takes around 4 ½ hours. The Centovalli is all twists and turns, so if you suffer from motion sickness, you may wish to avoid this route. Locarno is 25 km (16 mi) west of Bellinzona, 45 km (28 mi) northwest of Lugano.*

Superbly placed on the sheltered curve of the northernmost tip of Lago Maggiore and surrounded on all sides by mountains, Locarno is Switzerland's sunniest town. Subtropical species of flora flourish here, with date palms and fig trees, bougainvillea and rhododendron, and even aloe vera burgeoning on the waterfront. Its two-legged fauna are no less colorful: every spring, summer, and fall the arcaded streets and cafés teem with exotic characters in fur coats and T-shirts, lamé, and leather. Don't forget your sunglasses—you don't show your face in Locarno without a stylish set of shades, especially during August, when the town makes worldwide news with its film festival, showcas-

THE MIGHT OF THE GARTER

Along the wisteria-lined waterfront, there are cafés where visitors mingle with the locals engaged in the time-honored mid-morning Italian habit of putting the world right. Back in 1925, four visitors had something else in mind, when Briand, Stresseman, Mussolini, and Chamberlain signed the Locarno Pact here. It might have been called something different, as the story goes that the meeting was to be held elsewhere but the French minister's mistress insisted on Locarno. If so, one admires her taste.

ing the latest cinema on an outdoor screen in the Piazza Grande; it also hosts international artists in concert.

Modern Locarno is actually made up of three communities so tiny and close together that you often don't notice you've moved from one to another: Locarno, Muralto, and Minusio. The town's raison d'être is its waterfront, which has a graceful promenade curving around the east flank of the bay, and a beach and public pool complex along the west. Its clear lake is often as still as glass, reflecting the Ticinese Alps across to the south. Locarno's Lombard-style arcades and historic landmarks continually draw visitors inland as well. There are a few pedestrians-only streets in the heart of the Old Town.

★ The **Piazza Grande** is the heart of the Old Town and its social center, too: from under the crowded arcades shoppers spill onto the square to lounge in cafés and watch each other drink, smoke, and pose. **Chiesa Nuova** (New Church ⊠ Via Cittadella) is an exuberantly decorated Baroque church (1630) with a disproportionately large statue of St. Christopher on the facade. Renovation work began in 2006. Down the street from the New Church, the **Casa dei Canonici** (House of the Canons ⊠ Via Cittadella) dates from the same period. Note the lovely interior courtyard; it's now a private house.

The harmonious, almost delicate **Chiesa di San Francesco** (Church of St. Francis ⊠ Via S. Francesco) and its convent stand cheek-by-jowl with the painfully bulky, modern building that houses the Department of Education, Culture, and Sports of the city of Locarno. The history of the parish goes back to the early 13th century, and was allegedly founded by Saint Anthony of Padua. The current church was begun in 1538, however, on the remains of earlier constructions. The most remarkable aspect of the interior, perhaps, is the series of frescoes, some of which are unfortunately in very poor shape. Note the fine marble carvings and paintings in the side altars. Concerts are performed every spring and fall in the church sanctuary; contact the tourist office for more information. The 17th-century **Chiesa di Sant'Antonio** (Church of St. Anthony ⊠ Piazza Sant'Antonio) stands on a small plaza in the midst of narrow streets lined with splendid old houses in both medieval and Baroque styles.

Immediately to the left of the Church of St. Anthony stands the **Casa Rusca,** an 18th-century residence that now serves as the city art gallery. Its permanent collections include the work of Jean Arp, and temporary exhibits highlight both Swiss and international artists. ⊠ *Piazza Sant'Antonio* ☎ *091/7563185* 🎫 *7 SF* ⏱ *Tues.–Sun. 10–5.*

Built in 1300 as a stronghold of the dukes of Milan, Castello Visconteo was soon virtually destroyed by the invading Swiss Confederates. Today it contains a **Museo Civico e Archeologico** (Municipal and Archaeological Museum), with Roman relics—including a major glass collection—and Romanesque sculpture. ⊠ *Piazza Castello 2* ☎ *091/7563461* 🎫 *7 SF* ⏱ *Apr.–Oct., Tues.–Sun. 10–noon, 2–5.*

★ Offering a God's View of Locarno and the lake, the **Santuario della Madonna del Sasso** (Sanctuary of the Madonna of the Rock) breathtakingly crowns the hilltop hamlet of Orselina—pilgrims make the steep hike but most opt for the short funicular that starts from close to the train station (round-trip costs 6.60 SF). Open to regular visitors by appointment only, the sprawling church complex stands where, in 1480, Brother Bartolomeo da Ivrea had a vision of the Virgin Mary; the sanctuary was completed seven years later and was gradually enlarged to include a monastery, a Way of the Cross, and a church. Within the sanctuary, you'll find several side chapels featuring statues depicting scenes from the New Testament, such as the Last Supper. Several halls are incongruously filled with modern votive candleholders. The church, which was given a neo-Renaissance facade in the late 19th century, is a lavishly decorated affair. Among its artistic treasures are Bramantino's 1520 *The Flight into Egypt* and Ascona-born Antonio Ciseri's *Christ Carried to the Sepulcher*, a dramatic, Caravaggesque procession scene painted in 1870. A small museum has been arranged showing the history of the Sanctuary. Admission rates depend on the number of visitors. ✉ *Via Santuario 2, Orselina 2* ☎ *091/7436265* 🚪 *By appointment only.*

OFF THE
BEATEN
PATH

CIMETTA – A winter-sports center with views of Monte Rosa, the Swiss Alps, and the Italian Apennines, Cimetta (5,482 feet) can be reached only by chairlift; first you must catch a hypermodern cable car designed by the Ticinese star architect Mario Botta from the district of Orselina (accessible using the funicular near the train station) to Cardada, then a chairlift to the resort. But don't be put off; the ride is part of the fun: as the lake falls away below, you'll sail over meadows and wooded hills. Cimetta is also a hiker's paradise. The round- trip costs 33 SF. ☎ *091/ 7353030* ⊙ *Apr.–Oct., daily 8–8; late Dec.–Mar., Mon.–Thurs. 9–6, Fri.–Sun. 8–8.*

Where to Stay & Eat

$$$
Fodor'sChoice
★

✕ **Centenario.** Across from the waterfront east of the town center, this gracious *ristorante* serves innovative Franco-Italian cuisine that's unashamedly nouvelle and absolutely top quality, from its moderately priced business lunch to the all-out *menu de dégustation* (sampling menu). Specialties include rack of lamb in mustard sauce with asparagus and roasted foie gras with celery root and apples. You can have an aperitif on the lakefront terrace before sitting down to a meal in an environment plush with Persian rugs, quarry tile, and gleaming silver. ✉ *Lungolago 13, Locarno-Muralto* ☎ *091/7438222* 🚪 *AE, MC, V* ⊙ *Closed Sun. and Mon., last 3 wks in July and first 3 wks in Feb.*

$-$$

✕ **Casa del Popolo.** The politics lean left at this popular restaurant, whose tables spill out onto "Corporation Square" (Piazza Corporazione), but the Italian favorites are done just right for all. Try the amazingly delicate *piccata alla Milanese* (veal cutlets pounded thin, coated in egg, and sautéed), the spicy *penne all'arrabbiata* (pasta with red pepper and tomato sauce), or any of the 20 varieties of pizza. Red-check tablecloths and occasional appearances by the local politico round it all out. ✉ *Piazza Corporazione* ☎ *091/7511208* 🚪 *No credit cards.*

$

✕🏠 **Cittadella.** This popular dining spot in the Old Town offers inexpensive regional food—pizzas, pastas, simply prepared fish—in its casual downstairs trattoria, and fancier fish dishes in the more formal restaurant upstairs. The preparation is light, the flavors subtle with oils and herbs. Upstairs are a handful of pleasing rooms, some up under the rafters, all with classic stone-tile floors in cream and red. They may be simple, but they're a great bargain. ⊠ *Via Cittadella 18, CH-6600* ☎ *091/ 7515885* 🖷 *091/7517759* ⤴ *11 rooms* ⚹ *2 restaurants; no a/c, no room phones* ▤ *AE, DC, MC, V* ⦿| *BP.*

¢–$ ✕⊞ **Hotel Navegna.** It may not look like much from the outside, but this
Fodor'sChoice is a true diamond in the rough, right on the lake farther up the shore
★ from the promenade. The rooms are simply furnished in bright florals, and there's a fireplace in the living room for damp days. But it's the inventive Ticinese cooking that earns raves for gregarious owner Enrico Ravelli, who supplies the kitchen with fresh poultry, eggs, vegetables, and herbs from his own farm in the hills. The phenomenally delicate homemade pastas shouldn't be missed. It's easiest to reach the hotel via the Minusio exit from the A13 highway. ⊠ *Via alla Riva 2, CH-6648 Locarno-Minusio* ☎ *091/7432222* 🖷 *091/7433150* ⊕ *www.navegna. ch* ⤴ *20 rooms* ⚹ *Restaurant, bicycles; no a/c* ▤ *MC, V* ⊙ *Closed late Dec.–Easter* ⦿| *BP.*

$$ ⊞ **Dell' Angelo.** What better place to start your day or experience the goings-on in Locarno than at the tip of Piazza Grande. The Dell' Angelo was based on a 1674 structure but rebuilt in 1976, with ground-floor arches and solid, iron-trimmed balconies. Inside is a somewhat staid interior design, with wrought-iron grills, fluffy bedspreads, and darkly stained furniture, but you can eat amid chintz and damask under the faded remains of frescoed vaulting in the upstairs restaurant. The restaurant on the ground floor features wood-oven pizzas and other delights. The breakfast terrace on the fourth floor provides a plunging view of the hustle and bustle on the Piazza Grande, or a front seat for any events held there. ⊠ *Piazza Grande, CH-6601* ☎ *091/7518175* 🖷 *091/ 7518256* ⊕ *www.hotel-dell-angelo.ch* ⤴ *55 rooms* ⚹ *Restaurant, minibars, in-room safes, parking* ▤ *AE, V, MC* ⦿| *BP.*

Nightlife & the Arts

BARS The **Bar Lungolago** (⊠ Via Bramantino 1, Locarno ☎091/7515246) draws a young and style-conscious crowd. **Simba Bar** (⊠ Lungolago Motta 3a ☎ 091/7523388) is very popular with young Swiss and Italians. A fun experience on a hot summer night is the little **Katjaboat** (⊠ Viale Verbano 25, Locarno ☎ 079/6863990), a bar docked opposite the Hotel Rosa-Seegarten; it occasionally sets off into the lake broadcasting jazzy sounds and crooners.

CASINO The **Casinò di Locarno** (⊠ Via Largo Zorzi 1, Piazza Grande ☎ 091/ 7511535) has 195 slot machines and *boule* (a type of roulette). It's open every day from noon to 3 AM, and until 4 AM on Friday and Saturday nights.

FILM The **Locarno International Film Festival** (⊠ Via B. Luini 3a ☎ 091/7562121 ⊕ www.pardo.ch), gaining ground on the prestige front because of the caliber of the films it premieres, takes place every August in the Piazza Grande.

MUSIC One of the latest events to be held on the Piazza Grande is **Moon and Stars** (⊠ Piazza Grande ☎ 0900/800800 in Switzerland only ⊕ www.moonandstarslocarno.ch), a series of evening concerts by international pop stars held during the second week of July.

THEATER The **Teatro di Locarno** (⊠ Palazzo Kursaal, Via Largo Zorzi 1 ☎ 091/7561093) hosts international theatrical companies from October through May. For tickets contact the Locarno tourist office.

Valle Maggia

❸ **To & From:** *Getting into Ticino's valleys usually requires buses, which have infrequent departures from the Locarno train station. The trip up the Valle Maggia, for example, costs 22.80 SF and lasts nearly 1 ½ hours to San Carlo. The Ferrovie Autolinee Regionali Ticinesi runs a train into the Valle Maggia up to Ponte Brolla (departures are more frequent in the earlier morning and later afternoon) where you must take a bus. Valle Maggia is 4 km (2 mi) northwest of Locarno, 30 km (19 mi) northwest of Lugano.*

A drive through this rugged agricultural valley that stretches northwest from Locarno will give you a sense of the tough living conditions endured for centuries by Ticinese farmers, whose descendants today quarry granite. The valley is cut so far into the earth in part that sunlight in winter never seems to reach bottom—a stark contrast to sunny Locarno, only a short distance south. Until the 1920s, many Valle Maggia natives immigrated to the United States; some returned, bringing with them several English phrases that still pepper the local dialect. As you pass through Gordevio, Maggia, Someo, and Cevio—the latter, the valley's main village—you feel as if you're in a time capsule. There's little commercialization, and the mostly 17th-century houses call to mind a movie set. Bignasco, just beyond Cevio, is the last village before the valley splits in two as you continue north.

> ### FAITH, HOPE & CLARITY
>
> Beyond Bignasco, to the east, lies the Val Lavizzara. At Peccia the road splits again, with Val Sambuco to the east. Nearly at the end of this valley, in tiny Mogno, stands a beautiful modern chapel built in 1994 by world-renowned Ticinese architect Mario Botta (who has designed headline-making structures, including the San Francisco Museum of Modern Art). Constructed in simple lines, the Minimalist chapel is built of granite ashlars in two colors, creating remarkable patterns.

Ascona

❹ **To & From:** *From Locarno, pick up the bus (2,80 SF, tickets are available at machines) on the lake end of the Piazza Grande. It leaves every 15 minutes. You can also take the ferry over for a more romantic, 30-minute ride (8 SF round-trip). No trains head to Ascona. Ascona is 3 km (1¾ mi) west of Locarno.*

Although it's only a few minutes from Locarno, tiny Ascona has a life of its own. Little more than a fishing village until the end of the 19th century, the town was adopted by a high-minded group of northerners who arrived to develop a utopian, vegetarian artists' colony on **Monte Verità**, the hillside park behind the waterfront center. Influenced by Eastern and Western religions as well as the new realms of psychology, its ideals attracted thousands of sojourners, including dancer Isadora Duncan and psychologist C. G. Jung. You can visit the group of Monte Verità buildings, including the unusual flat-roof, wooden Casa Anatta, and view papers and relics of the group's works. ☎ *091/7910327* 🎫 *6 SF* ☉ *Apr., May, and Sept., Tues.–Sun. 2:30–6:30; July and Aug., Tues.–Sun. 3–7.*

Monte Verità's influence spread and its reputation grew throughout the world. Today the still-small village of 5,000 attracts artists, art restorers, and traditional bookbinders to its ancient, narrow streets. On the waterfront, however, it's a sun-and-fun scene, with the pedestrians-only ★ **Piazza Motta** crowded with sidewalk cafés and the promenade on the water's edge swarming with boats. Behind Piazza Motta, a charming labyrinth of lanes leads uphill past art galleries (not all showing gallery-quality work) to **Via Borgo,** lined with contemporary shops and galleries.

OFF THE BEATEN PATH

ISOLE DI BRISSAGO – Alpine drama and subtropical colors are wed in Brissago, yet another flowery lakefront resort at the lowest elevation in Switzerland, which is an easy excursion by car or bus from Ascona. The main attraction, however, lies offshore: federally preserved as botanical gardens, the Brissago Islands are set like jewels in the lake and teem with more than 1,000 species of subtropical plants. Plaques identify the flora in Italian, German, and French; an English guide to the plants is for sale at the gate (8 SF). Have lunch or drinks at the restaurant, in a beautifully restored 1929 villa that now doubles as a seminar center. Boats bound for the islands depart regularly from Brissago, Porto Ronco, Ascona, and Locarno. You must leave with the last boat back to the mainland—usually around 6 PM—so check the schedule carefully when planning your excursion. Purchase your ticket at the entrance to the gardens or when you book your boat trip; Swiss Boat Pass discounts apply. ☎ *091/7516140 for boat, 091/7914361 for tour* 🚤 *Boat: 15 SF round-trip from Ascona, 24 SF round-trip from Locarno; gardens: 8 SF* ☉ *Daily 9–6.*

Where to Stay & Eat

$–$$$ ✕ **San Pietro.** Tucked away in a maze of tiny streets, this little gem offers creative Italian-influenced pasta and fish dishes. Sample its local fish fillet in lemon basil sauce, ravioli with vegetables and almonds, or any of the grilled specialties. The most romantic tables are in the intimate garden, slipped between the walls of neighboring houses. ✉ *Passagio S. Pietro 6* ☎ *091/7913976* 🖃 *AE, DC, MC, V* ☉ *Closed Mon. and Jan.*

$–$$ ✕ **Grotto du Rii.** On your way to or from Italy, this beautiful stone **Fodor'sChoice** grotto-house with lush flowers pouring out of its window boxes is ★ straight out of a fairy tale. The rooms inside cast their spell as they are cozily crammed with all manner of folkloric charm—carriage-wheel lamps, mounted animals, fireplace inglenooks. Before your meal, enjoy the rosemary-infused wine on the terrace at the foot of Intragna's vineyards. Mainstays such as osso buco with polenta may be followed with the more daring *dolcesorpresa* (surprise dessert). On Tuesday night, the four-course meal accompanied by Ticinese musicians is a good deal. The restaurant is a short walk from the Centovalli train station. Intragna, whose church tower is the tallest in the Ticino, is a good spot from which to begin a hike into the hills. ⊠ *Via Cantonale, Intragna* ☎ *091/7961861* ⊕ *www.grottodurii.ch* ⊘ *Closed Wed.*

$–$$ ✕ **Osteria Nostrana.** The tables of this bustling restaurant spread into the piazza overlooking the lake. Inside, rough wooden ceilings, marble-top tables, chandeliers, and a hodgepodge of photos and posters add to its charm. Look for the spaghetti Enzo (with porcini mushrooms, bacon, and cream) along with daily and seasonal specials. The wine list, with more than 100 Italian and Swiss vintages, deserves consideration. ⊠ *Piazza Motta* ☎ *091/7915158* ▭ *AE, DC, MC, V.*

$$$$ ✕▦ **Giardino.** The Great Gatsby would feel in his element here, in this
Fodor'sChoice Relais & Château property that's as glamorous and atmospheric as a
★ Mediterranean villa, despite its creation from thin air in 1986. It's a movie-set of a resort—indeed, it's been used as such by Swiss television—and every palm tree, statue, and sparkling fountain is in its picturesque place. Portuguese ceramics, Florentine floor tiles, Veronese marble, ceramic room-number plaques in della Robbia style, and even a Swiss-baroque, carved-wood conference chamber from Zürich's Bierhalle Kropf have been imported. The luxury borders on decadence: the sheets are pure linen, ground-floor rooms have small, private gardens, and there's a landscaped pool, not to mention a chauffeured Bentley, an antique-bus shuttle service, and pink bicycles for guest use. But there's gold behind the glitter. The restaurants are excellent: Aphrodite, with modern Italian and vegetarian cuisine, rates among the best in Switzerland. The Osteria runs close behind with its regional Italian specialties. Varied weekly programs include a sunrise mountaintop breakfast, lunch on the hotel's boat, simple hikes and bike-and-picnic excursions. On Sunday there's Teatro Giardino: dinner theater including ballet one week, singing waiters, jazz, or opera the next. The charming manager, Hans Leu, keeps things grounded—he'll even pick you up at the train station on his pink Harley, if you like. Prepare to be spoiled. ⊠ *Via Segnale 10, CH-6612* ☎ *091/7858888* 🖶 *091/7858899* ⊕ *www.giardino.ch* ⇝ *54 rooms, 18 suites, 5 apartments* ♨ *2 restaurants, café, in-room safes, minibars, pool, gym, hair salon, sauna, steam room, bicycles, piano bar, wine bar, babysitting* ▭ *AE, DC, MC, V* ⊘ *Closed mid-Nov.–mid-Mar.* ⦿ *MAP.*

★ **$$$–$$$$** 🏨 **Castello Seeschloss.** Dating from 1250, though completely rebuilt within, this Romantik property is a romantic enough hotel as is—not even taking into account its garden setting and position across from the waterfront. Its interior is rich with frescoes, beams, vaults, and heavy masonry, recently lightened with a contemporary touch. Each room is different: a wrought-iron bed in the back tower, a blue wooden canopy bed in room 203, or the lavishly redone front tower room with a loft. Most impressive are the lakeside rooms, which have original 16th- to 18th-century frescoes. There is a private courtyard for summer-night dining, along with an isolated pool. Honeymooners, take note: deluxe rooms in the towers start at prices not much higher than standard doubles. Ask for an air-conditioned room in summer. ⊠ *Piazza Motta, CH-6612* ☎ *091/7910161* 🖶 *091/7911804* ⊕ *www.castello-seeschloss.*

ch 🛏 *45 rooms* ♿ *3 restaurants, minibars, pool, bar; no a/c in some rooms* ⊟ *AE, DC, MC, V* ☉ *Closed Jan. and Feb.* ⦿ *BP.*

$$–$$$ ⬚ **Tamaro.** The shuttered windows of this 18th-century patrician house look out on the waterfront; inside, you can lounge in sitting rooms richly furnished with antiques, books, and even a grand piano. The rooms range from lavish corner doubles with lake views and reproduction antiques to tiny quarters overlooking the courtyard that are an excellent value. There's a private sun terrace high over the street with fine lake views. ✉ *Piazza G. Motta 35, CH-6612* ☎ *091/7854848* 🖷 *091/7912928* 🌐 *www.hotel-tamaro.ch* 🛏 *51 rooms* ♿ *3 restaurants, café, in-room safes, minibars, pool, bicycles, meeting rooms, no-smoking rooms; no a/c* ⊟ *AE, DC, MC, V* ☉ *Closed mid-Nov.–Feb.* ⦿ *BP.*

Nightlife & the Arts

The ideals that brought Isadora Duncan here still bring culture to Ascona: every year it hosts a series of world-class jazz and classical music concerts. The lakefront piazza serves as an open-air stage for almost daily summer entertainment, with mime, theater, and live pop bands. Locarno's August film festival is only a cab ride away across the peninsula.

BARS & DANCING   In Hotel Eden Roc, **La Brezza** (✉ Via Albarelle 16 ☎ 091/7857171 🌐 www.edenroc.ch) is the place to sip bellinis (peach liqueur with champagne) and listen to live music.

MUSIC   **JazzAscona New Orleans & Classics** (☎ 091/7910091 🌐 www.jazzascona. com) seeks out performers a cut above standard Dixieland and swing groups and brings an amazing international selection of them to its open-air bandstands in June and July. The **Settimane Musicali** (☎ 091/7910091 🌐 www.settimane-musicali.ch) bring in orchestras, chamber groups, and top-ranking soloists to Ascona and Locarno. Events run from late August to mid-October.

SOTTOCENERI

Although Monte Ceneri is no Everest, it marks the borderline between the Sopraceneri with its vastly different southern cousin "below" the Ceneri. The Sottoceneri is the Ticino with attitude, where culture and natural beauty join forces with business and commerce. The resort town of Lugano is an international glamour magnet, but even there the incredible scenery and traditional warmth haven't been completely upstaged.

Lugano

▶   **To & From:** *From Bellinzona, trains take about 30 minutes and cost 11.60 SF (unless you purchase a cheaper Zürich–Lugano direct ticket); trains leave several times per hour. Trains from Locarno run at least once an hour (with a change usually in Bellinzona or Giubiasco); the trip lasts nearly one hour and costs 16.20 SF. Lugano is 1–1 ½ hours away from Milan, with very frequent connections, 12.80 SF. Trains coming from Geneva pass either through Bern/Luzern, or Zürich for 5–6 hour journeys. Postal buses spider out from Lugano to hamlet and main towns*

A GOOD WALK

Begin at the **Piazza della Riforma** ❺ ▶, which is dominated by the **Palazzo Civico** ❻, or town hall. Look up to the gable above the clock to see the city's coat of arms. (The building also houses the tourist office, whose entrance is on the lake side.)

On the western side of the square the Piazza della Riforma bleeds into the **Piazza Rezzonico,** which contains a large fountain by Otto Maraini dating from 1895.

From the Piazza Cioccaro walk up the shop-lined staircase street of Via Cattedrale. The street curves left, ending at the **Cattedrale di San Lorenzo** ❼. Take a moment to enjoy the view from the church square.

Head back and then south along the waterfront promenade known as **Il Lungolago** ⓬, and at the Imbarcadero Centrale (Central Wharf) take the underpass to cross the road, coming back up at the Piazza della Riforma.

Leave the piazza at the northeast side through a portico onto the Via Canova. After crossing over the Via della Posta/Via Albrizzi, you come to the **Museo Cantonale d'Arte** ⓭, on your right.

Continue straight ahead to the 17th-century church of San Rocco, with its neo-Baroque facade. Turn left onto Via Carducci before you reach the church and you'll find a small orange-tile pedestrian entranceway into the **Quartiere Maghetti**—a town within a town. It's a tangle of streets full of porticoes, little squares, shops, and offices, a modern take on old forms, created in the early 1980s by the architects

Camazind, Brocchi, and Sennhauser.

Exit the Quartiere Maghetti onto Via Canova (you'll be behind the church now) and continue east, crossing Via Stauffacher.

On your left is the open **Piazza dell'Independenza.** Cross over the wide Corso Elvezia to enter the **Parco Civico** ⓮. Inside the grounds, in addition to the nearly 15 acres of greenery, you'll find the **Museo Civico di Belle Arti** ⓯ and **Museo Cantonale di Storia Naturale** ⓰.

From here you can opt to spend the afternoon at the **Lido** ⓱, the city's public beach and pool, just east of the park across the River Cassarate.

Or you can head back to town along the waterfront promenade, and take in the stunning mountain views: straight ahead, the rocky top of Monte Generoso (5,579 feet), and flanking the bay at right and left, respectively, Monte San Salvatore and Monte Brè.

🕑 TIMING TIPS→ **It's best to walk through the city in the morning, before it gets too hot. A quick overview, without much time in the museums or parks, takes a couple of hours. Or make a day of it, taking in the main sights in the morning, stopping for lunch, and then spending the afternoon in the museums or on the Lido. Remember that the museums are closed on Monday.**

Lugano

from the depot on Via Serafino Balestra. Lugano is 45 km (28 mi) south-east of Ascona, 39 km (24 mi) southeast of Locarno.

Strung around a sparkling bay like Venetian glass beads, with dark, conical mountains rising primordially out of its waters and icy peaks framing the scene, Lugano earns its nickname as the Rio of the Old World. Of the three world-class waterfront resorts, Lugano tops Ascona and Locarno for architectural style, sophistication, and natural beauty. Too bad it recently lost its main museum—the fabulous Old Master painting collection of Baron Hans-Heinrich Thyssen-Bornemieza has been packed off to Madrid and is no longer in state at Lugano's Villa Favorita. This isn't to say that it has avoided the pitfalls of a successful modern resort: there's thick traffic right up to the waterfront, much of it in manic Italian style, and it has more than its share of concrete waterfront high-rise hotels with balconies skewed to produce "a room with a view" regardless of aesthetic cost. Yet the sacred *passeggiata*—the afternoon stroll to see and be seen that winds down every Italian day—asserts the city's true personality as a graceful, sophisticated resort. It's not Swiss, not Italian. . . just Lugano. Note: Many phone numbers in Lugano have—an inexplainable oddity—a Locarno prefix.

Heading out of the Piazza della Riforma on the north side, onto the Via Luvini, you come to the **Piazza Dante,** which is dominated by a large department store and a bank. From here, if you pop over one street east to the busy Via Pretorio, you can get a look at Lugano's oldest building, the Pretorio (1425), at No. 7. Back at Piazza Dante, turn left down Via Pessina, which leads you into the **Piazza Cioccaro,** on your right. Here the funicular from the train station terminates and the typical *centro storico* (Old Town) begins, its narrow streets lined with chic clothing shops and small markets offering pungent local cheeses and porcini mushrooms.

What to See

❼ Cattedrale di San Lorenzo (Cathedral of St. Lawrence). Behind this church's early Renaissance facade is a Baroque interior (with frescoes that could use some restoring) and a baptismal font dating from 1430. The church has premedieval origins: it became a collegiate church in 1078. Eight centuries later it became a cathedral. ⊠ *Via Cattedrale, Old Town.*

★ ❾ Chiesa di Santa Maria degli Angioli (Church of St. Mary of the Angels). The simple facade doesn't prepare you for the riches within. Begun in the late 15th century, the church contains a magnificent fresco of the *Passion and Crucifixion,* as well as *The Last Supper* and *Madonna with the Infant Jesus,* all by Bernardino Luini (1475–1532). ⊠ *Piazza Luini, Old Town.*

❿ Giardino Belvedere (Belvedere Gardens). This lakefront sculpture garden frames a dozen modern works with palms, camellias, oleanders, and magnolias. At the far west end there's a public swimming area. ⊠ *On lake side of Quai Riva Antonio Caccia near Piazza Luini, Old Town* 🕬 *Free* ☉ *Daily 24 hrs.*

🄶 Lido. The city's public beach has two swimming pools and two restaurants. To reach it, you'll have to cross the Cassarate River. Heading east from the Parco Civico, cross Viale Castagnola and then turn toward the lake. The main swimming-area entrance is just ahead on the right. Everyone from families to scenesters comes here to cool off. ⊠ *Via Cassarate 6* ☎ *091/9714041* ⊛ *Beach 7 SF* ☉ *May and Sept., daily 9–7; June–Aug., daily 9–7:30.*

★ ⑫ **Il Lungolago** (lake promenade). This 2-km (1-mi) waterfront path lined with pollarded lime trees, funereal cypresses, and graceful palm trees stretches from the Lido all the way to the Paradiso neighborhood. Il Lungolago is the place to see and be seen—while taking in the views, of course. At night luminous fountains turn the lake near the Parco Civico into a special attraction.

⑪ **Museo d'Arte Moderna** (Museum of Modern Art). Consistently outstanding temporary exhibitions are the hallmark of this museum, whose permanent collection includes Chagall, Monet, Pissarro, Rousseau, and Futurist artist Umberto Boccioni. Brochures are available in English. ⊠ *Villa Malpensata, Riva Antonio Caccia 5, Lungolago* ☎ *058/8667201* ⊕ *www.museodartemoderna-lugano.ch* ⊛ *11 SF.*

⑬ **Museo Cantonale d'Arte** (Cantonal Art Museum). A group of three palaces dating from the 15th to the 19th centuries was adapted for this museum. Its exhibits include paintings, sculpture, and photography, including some important avant-garde works. The permanent collection holds works by Klee, Turner, Degas, Renoir, and Hodler as well as contemporary Ticinese artists. Descriptive material is available in English. ⊠ *Via Canova 10, Old Town* ☎ *091/9104780* ⊕ *www.museo-cantonale-arte.ch* ⊛ *Permanent collection 7 SF, plus 3 SF for temporary exhibits* ☉ *Tues. 2–5, Wed.–Sun. 10–5.*

⑯ **Museo Cantonale di Storia Naturale** (Cantonal Museum of Natural History). A museum since 1854, it contains exhibits on fossils, animals, and plants (there's a large section on local crystals that is especially interesting for people intending long hikes in the mountains), mostly those typical of the region. The museum is located in a high school. Note, too, that all labels are in Italian. ⊠ *Viale Cattaneo 4, Parco Civico* ☎ *091/9115380* ⊛ *Free* ☉ *Tues.–Sat. 9–noon, 2–5.*

⑮ **Museo Civico di Belle Arti** (Municipal Art Museum). The restored Villa Ciani, with its lofty vaulted ceilings and tile floors, displays hundreds of works by Swiss and European artists from the 15th to the 20th centuries. Especially noteworthy is the extensive collection of paintings by Futurist artist Umberto Boccioni, Cesare Tallone, and Impressionists Monet, Rousseau, and Matisse. English-language brochures are available. ⊠ *Villa Ciani, Parco Civico* ☎ *091/8007210* ⊛ *5 SF* ☉ *Tues.–Sun. 10–noon, 2–6.*

⑥ **Palazzo Civico** (Town Hall). This Neoclassical Lombard structure dates from 1844. Inside there's a large inner yard surrounded by a four-sided arcade, with a wide vestibule on the piazza side. It houses the town council and tourist office. ⊠ *Piazza della Riforma, Old Town.*

⑭ **Parco Civico** (City Park). A green oasis in the city center, the park has cacti, exotic shrubs, and more than 1,000 varieties of roses, as well as

VIEWTIFUL!

The serious view hound may want to reach the top of one of the three peaks that define the landscape around Lugano. Monte Brè (091/9713171, www.montebre.ch, funicular 20 SF round-trip, open daily 9:15–12:15 and 2–6:45) has a funicular that departs every 30 minutes from the east end of Lugano in Cassarate. At the top are several well-marked hiking trails, as well as an "art trail" in the summit village of Brè, a path studded with pieces of sculpture. Monte San Salvatore (091/9852828, www.montesansalvatore.ch, open mid-Sept.–mid-May, daily 9–6:30; mid-May–mid-June, daily 8:30–6:30;

mid-June–mid-Sept., daily 8:30–11 PM) can be reached via the funicular in Paradiso. At the top are a huge relief model of the entire Sottoceneri region and marked "nature itinerary" paths, which have signs pointing out flower and tree specimens. For yet more spectacular views take a boat from Lugano across to Capolago, where you can take the 40-minute cogwheel train up Monte Generoso (091/6305111 www.montegeneroso.ch, train 38 SF round-trip, open mid-Mar.–early Nov., trains run daily 10:15–3:15, with departures every hour); the top has a restaurant and lots of marked hiking trails.

an aviary, a tiny deer zoo, and a fine view of the bay from its peninsula. ⊠ *South of Viale Carlo Cattaneo, east of Piazza Castello.*

❽ Parco del Tassino (Tassino Park). On a plateau just behind and south of the train station, this park offers lovely bay views from its rose gardens. A small deer park and playground make it very child-friendly. ⊠ *Take Bus 2 east to San Domenico stop in Castagnola, or use funicular from Old Town to train station* ⌨ *Free.*

★ ❺ Piazza della Riforma (Reformation Square). In the early 19th century, several buildings were removed in order to enlarge the square—providing more room for the present-day café tables. Commonly referred to simply as "la Piazza," it's the social and cultural heart of the city and the site of markets and open-air music performances. ⊠ *Just north of the Imbarcadero Centrale, Old Town.*

Where to Stay & Eat

★ $$$–$$$$ ✕ **Al Portone.** Silver and lace dress up the stucco and stone here, but the ambience is strictly casual. Chef Roberto Galizzi pursues *nuova cucina* (contemporary Italian cuisine) with ambition and flair. You might choose duck liver with mango chutney and pears, lobster in squid-ink sauce, or lamb with eggplant and zucchini stew. Or you could *lascia fare a Roberto* (leave it to Robert)—as he calls his menu de dégustation. ⊠ *Viale Cassarate 3, Lugano/Cassarate* ☎ *091/9235511* ▭ *AE, DC, MC, V* ☉ *Closed Sun., Mon., and first 2 wks in Aug.*

★ $$$ ✕ **Santabbondio.** Ancient stone and terra-cotta blend with pristine pastels in this upgraded grotto, where subtle, imaginative, new Franco-Italian cuisine *du marché* (based on fresh produce) is served in intimate little dining rooms and on a shady terrace. Watch for perch with mango and sage or beef fillet with figs in balsamic vinegar to confirm the local opinion: chef Martin Dalsass is the canton's best. There's a good selection of open wines. You'll need a cab to get here, but it's worth the trip. ⊠ *Via Fomelino 10, Lugano/Sorengo* ☎ *091/9932388* ☱ *AE, DC, MC, V* ☉ *Closed Sun., Mon., first wk of Jan., and last wk of Feb.*

$–$$$ ✕ **Da Raffaele.** Having a meal in this family-run Italian restaurant feels like being let in on a neighborhood secret. Start with a pasta, like the marvelous homemade orecchiette (ear-shape pasta) or *mezzelune* (half moons) stuffed with ricotta and spinach, then try something from the grill, like *gamberoni alla griglia* (grilled shrimp). The staff doesn't speak English, but their warmth needs no translation. The restaurant is just outside the city in a residential neighborhood, but is easily reached by car or bus (take Bus 8 or 9 from the train station to the last stop, Viganello). ⊠ *Contrada dei Patrizi 8/Via Pazzalino, Viganello* ☎ *091/9716614* ☱ *AE, MC, V* ☉ *Closed Sun., last wk of July, first 2 wks of Aug. No lunch Sat.*

★ $–$$$ ✕ **Locanda del Boschetto.** Tucked away at the end of a cul-de-sac in a residential neighborhood (not far from the Lugano South exit on the autostrada), the grill is the first thing you see in this grotto-style ristorante, a specialist in pure and simple seafood *alla griglia* (grilled). The decor is a study in linen and rustic wood, and the service is helpful and down-to-earth. ⊠ *Via Boschetto 8, Paradiso* ☎ *091/9942493* ☱ *AE, DC, MC, V* ☉ *Closed Mon., Aug., and first 2 wks of Nov.*

$–$$$ ✕ **Orologio.** Snowy tablecloths and chairs stand out against dark hardwood floors in this open, minimalist restaurant. The attentive staff is quick to bring you modern Italian dishes such as thinly sliced octopus with olive oil, jumbo shrimp with saffron and fresh garlic, or lamb cutlets with caramelized spring onions and almond potatoes—but they retreat to let you linger over coffee. ⊠ *Via Nizzola 2, Old Town* ☎ *091/9232338* ☱ *AE, DC, MC, V* ☉ *Closed Sun. and 2 wks in Aug.*

★ ¢–$$ ✕ **La Tinera.** Tucked down an alley off Via Pessina, this cozy basement taverna squeezes loyal locals and tourists onto hard wooden chairs and benches for authentic regional specialties, hearty meats, and pastas. Local wines are served in traditional ceramic bowls. ⊠ *Via dei Gorini 2, Old Town* ☎ *091/9235219* ☱ *AE, DC, MC, V* ☉ *Closed Sun. and Aug.*

$ ✕ **Grotto Figini.** Absolutely authentic, this grotto pulls in a rowdy local crowd for a boccalino of good merlot and a satisfying, rib-sticking meal of polenta and grilled meats. Don't expect English or other tourists, and

---

HESSE'S HAVEN

In the tower of the Casa Camuzzi, a fabulous jumble of old houses on a hilltop in Montagnola, the Herman Hesse Museum (091/9933770, www.hessemontagnola.ch, 7.50 SF, open Mar.–Oct., Tues.–Sun. 10–6:30; Nov.–Feb., weekends 10–5:30) is tiny but impressive. The Nobel Prize–winning author lived here the last 43 years of his life, writing *Siddhartha* and *Steppenwolf*. His rooms have been meticulously preserved; you can see his papers, books, desk, glasses, even his straw hat. Take the postbus marked Agra-Montagnola from Lugano's train station.

don't take personally the stares you'll receive when you first walk in. It's in a short stretch of woods on a hill in Gentilino, above Lugano-Paradiso. After your meal you can stroll down the shady road to see old *grotti* hidden in the overgrown hillside. ✉ *Via ai Grotti, Gentilino* 🕾 *091/9946497* ▤ *V* ☉ *Closed Mon. and mid-Dec.–Feb.*

★ $$$$ ✕▦ **Ticino.** Set on a time-stained square and around the corner from picturesquely porticoed Via Nassa, this 500-year-old former monastery is fully protected as a historical monument. Shuttered windows look out from every room onto a glassed-in garden, while vaulted halls are lined with art and antiques. Guest rooms are unpretentious yet elegant, with pleasing details such as embroidered towels and special orthopedic mattresses. The formal restaurant is full of dark-wood wainscoting and leather banquettes. The menu blends Ticinese, Mediterranean, and French cuisine; it's famous for its fresh seafood and rack of lamb with herbs. The hotel is steps from the funicular to the train station. ✉ *Piazza Cioccaro 1, Old Town, CH-6901* 🕾 *091/9227772* 🖷 *091/9236278* ⊕ *www.romantikhotels.com/lugano* 🛏 *18 rooms, 2 suites* 🍴 *Restaurant, bar, library, no-smoking rooms; no a/c in some rooms* ▤ *AE, DC, MC, V* ☉ *Closed Jan. No lunch weekends* ⎮◎⎮ *BP.*

★ $$$$ ✕▦ **Villa Principe Leopoldo & Residence.** Spectacularly perched on the Collina d'Oro hillside high over Lake Lugano, this extravagant designed mansion offers a nonpareil location and old-world service. If only it had the splendor to match. Although the villa was built in 1868 on behalf of Prince Leopold of Hohenzollern, most of the public rooms and guest rooms are staidly modern in taste—gracefully lush but with little patina or fireworks. You may not care once you take a glance at the stunningly arranged pool-and-terrace complex encircled by a double staircase (a slightly baroque touch of Bel Air). Fabulous creations from chef Dario Ranza, such as pink grapefruit risotto with shrimp or sea bass baked in a salt crust, make dining here a notable experience. Too bad the snoozily traditional dining decor could use a little salt and pepper. ✉ *Via Montalbano 5, Collina d'Oro, CH-6900* 🕾 *091/9858855* 🖷 *091/9858825* ⊕ *www.leopoldohotel.com* 🛏 *67 rooms, 24 suites* 🍴 *2 restaurants, minibars, 2 tennis courts, 2 pools, health club, massage, 2 bars, Internet, meeting rooms, no-smoking rooms* ▤ *AE, DC, MC, V* ⎮◎⎮ *BP.*

$ ✕▦ **Pestalozzi.** This older hotel right in the middle of town and a few steps away from the lake offers excellent value. The newly restored rooms are simple, clean, and functionally furnished. The restaurant offers a new menu for each day featuring mostly Ticinese dishes, including several vegetarian selections. One peculiarity: traditionally, no alcohol is served, so for an exploration of local wines, you will have to find another place. ✉ *Piazza Indipendenza, CH-6901* 🕾 *091/9214646* 🖷 *091/9222045* ⊕ *www.attuale.com/pestalozzi.html* 🛏 *55 rooms* 🍴 *Internet room, no-smoking rooms; no a/c in some rooms* ▤ *AE, MC, V.*

$$$$ ▦ **Splendide Royale.** One of the last palace-style hotels in Ticino, this
FodorsChoice landmark villa was first converted into a hotel in 1887 and, gorgeously,
★ much of the Victorian luster of its public spaces—with their marble, pillars, terrazzo, chandeliers, and antiques—has been respectfully pre-

served. The management may not wish you to add your signature to those of Sophia Loren, Lauren Bacall, Gloria Swanson, Igor Stravinsky, and Tina Turner in their Livre d'Or but just entering the lobby will make you feel like a true V.I.P. Even the smallest room here is done up in stylish decor, while the historic suites here are showstoppers, replete with 19th-century frecoes and Venetian chandeliers. More modern types can opt for the 1983 wing, where discreetly modern rooms are decorated in beech, beige, and gold. All rooms have heated floors in the bathrooms; the balconies and terraces open onto lake or garden views—for the Cinerama version of Lake Lugano, head to the elegant La Veranda restaurant. ⊠ *Riva A. Caccia 7, CH-6900* ☏ *091/9857711* 🖷 *091/9857722* ⊕ *www.splendide.ch* 📠 *88 rooms, 8 suites* ♨ *Restaurant, in-room safes, minibars, pool, massage, sauna, piano bar, business services, meeting rooms* 🞕 *AE, DC, MC, V* ☌ *BP.*

> ### SYLVAN GLADES
>
> For an idyllic daytime excursion, take a short tram trip out of Lugano's city center to the fabled Castagnola parks, which surround the Villa Favorita (the famous Thyssen-Bornemieza estate now closed to the public). The Parco degli Ulivi (Olive Park) spreads over the lower slopes of Monte Brè and offers a romantic landscape of silvery olive trees mixed with wild rosemary; you enter it from the Sentiero di Gandria (Gandria Footpath). Parco San Michele (St. Michael Park), also on Monte Brè, has a public chapel and a broad terrace that overlooks the city, the lake, and the Alps.

$$$–$$$$ 🏨 **Du Lac.** This comfortable, bright hotel offers more lakefront luxury than many of the glossier hotels farther down the same beach. Owned by the same family since it was founded in 1920, this lodging has been regularly renovated. Huge, impressive needlework tapestry art reproductions, handmade by the owner's father, cover the walls of the generously sized lobby and restaurant. The rooms are all spacious and face the lake; those on the sixth floor are the quietest. There's a private swimming area on the lake. ⊠ *Riva Paradiso 3, Lugano-Paradiso, CH-6902* ☏ *091/9864747* 🖷 *091/9864748* ⊕ *www.dulac.ch* 📠 *52 rooms, 1 suite* ♨ *Restaurant, minibars, pool, health club, massage, beach, waterskiing, bar, Internet, meeting rooms, no-smoking rooms; no a/c* 🞕 *AE, DC, MC, V* ☺ *Closed Jan. and Feb.* ☌ *BP.*

$$ 🏨 **Park-Hotel Nizza.** Tucked into the dense tropical foliage of the lower slopes of Monte San Salvatore, this former villa mixes old and modern comforts. Most rooms are small, but all are quiet and comfortable; panoramic views of the lake below don't cost extra. The hotel has its own farm and vineyards on the hill behind—the source of the organic produce used by the kitchen. The restaurant makes its own wine, with some very original labels designed by the owner. Summer meals are served in the garden; there's a special farmer's breakfast on Tuesday and a cocktail party on Friday evening. ⊠ *Via Guidino 14, Lugano-Paradiso, CH-6902* ☏ *091/9941771* 🖷 *091/9941773* ⊕ *www.villanizza.com* 📠 *28 rooms* ♨ *Restaurant, in-room safes, minibars, pool, hot tub, bar,*

playground, Internet, no-smoking rooms; no a/c ⊟ *AE, MC, V* ☺ *Closed late Oct.–3 wks before Easter* †○| *BP.*

$ ⌂ **San Carlo.** Ideally located on the main shopping street, this friendly hotel is one of the best deals in town. It's near the funicular and a block from the waterfront. The rooms are tiny, but clever carpentry makes the most out of small spaces, creating niches for a mirror, a television, or a hideaway bed. The breakfast room is small, so breakfast in bed is encouraged. ⊠ *Via Nassa 28, Old Town, CH-6900* ☎ *091/9227107* 🖷 *091/9228022* ⬐*22 rooms* ⛄ *No-smoking rooms; no a/c* ⊟ *AE, DC, MC, V* †○| *BP.*

Nightlife & the Arts

BARS Just off the Piazza delle Riforma, **Bottegone del Vino** (⊠ Via Magatti 3, Old Town ☎ 091/9227689) has a great selection of wine accompanied by good local cheeses and tapas. It's closed on Sunday. **Hotel Eden** (⊠ Riva Paradiso 1, Old Town ☎ 091/9859200) has a popular piano bar. For a refined place to enjoy a cocktail, head to the palatial **Splendide Royale** (⊠ Riva A. Caccia 7, Lungolago ☎ 091/9857711).

CASINO In addition to slot machines and gaming tables, the three-floor **Casinò Lugano** (⊠ Via Stauffacher 1, Old Town ☎ 091/9737111) has a bar and restaurant.

DANCING On Friday and Saturday nights, **Dancing Morandi** (⊠ Via Trevano 56, Molino Nuovo ☎ 091/9712291) is a great place to dance to songs from the '70s and '80s. The lively **Disco Prince** (⊠ Via Stauffacher 1, Old Town ☎ 091/9233281) has a DJ and attracts a younger crowd. With three dance floors, **Titanic** (⊠ Via Cantonale, Pambio-Noranco ☎ 091/9856010) is the region's biggest disco.

MUSIC The free **Blues to Bop Festival** livens up the Piazza della Riforma at the end of August. In July, **Estival Jazz** brings jazz and world music to the Piazza della Riforma. From April to June, the city hosts its **Lugano Festival,** which draws world-class orchestras and conductors.

Shopping

Cute novelty shops and antiques stores line the staircase street of **Via Cattedrale.** All the top designers can be found in the shops lining the pedestrian-only **Via Nassa.** If it's Italian and international designer clothing bargains you're after, explore the factory outlet store called **Fox Town** (⊠ Via Angelo Maspoli, Mendrisio ☎ 091/6405020). It's open daily from 11 to 5.

Gandria

🔞 *7 km (4 mi) southeast of Lugano.*

Fodor's Choice
★ Although today its narrow waterfront streets are crowded with tourists, the tiny historic village of Gandria merits a visit, either by boat or by car. Gandria clings vertiginously to the steep hillside; a labyrinth of stairways and passageways lined with flower-filled balconies hangs directly over open water. Souvenir and crafts shops now fill its backstreet nooks, but the ambience of an ancient fishing village remains.

CLOSE UP

A Century of Wine

Roughly 6,000 tons of wine grapes—about 7% of Switzerland's total production—are grown each year in the rolling hills of the Ticino. Leading the way is the popular merlot grape, introduced in 1905. It wasn't a success solely because it grows well in this region. An epidemic of phylloxera was destroying the country's vineyards, and the merlot grape proved to be the most resistant.

Merlot now accounts for 80% of the region's wine production. Thanks to technological advances, the Ticino also produces white and blush varieties. A sampling of merlot in the region's grotti, restaurants, and vineyards will reveal a wide range of wines, including some very fine vintages with top-quality barrel maturation. If you want to learn more about the wines of the region, you might wish to follow *le strade del vino* (the wine roads), which map out 69 restaurants, 43 wine producers, and five *enotecas* of note. For information, contact **Ticinowine** (☎ 091/6901353 ⊕ www.ticinowine.ch).

Campione

⑲ *18 km (11 mi) south of Gandria, 12 km (7 mi) south of Lugano.*

In the heart of Swiss Italy lies Campione. Here, in this southernmost of regions, the police cars have Swiss license plates but the police officers inside are Italian; the inhabitants pay their taxes to Italy but do it in Swiss francs. Its narrow streets are saturated with history, and the surrounding landscape is a series of stunning views of Lago di Lugano and Monte San Salvatore.

In the 8th century, the lord of Campione gave the tiny scrap of land, less than a square kilometer (½ square mi) in area, to the monastery of St. Ambrosius of Milan. Despite all the wars that passed it by, Campione remained Italian until the end of the 18th century, when it was incorporated into the Cisalpine Republic. When Italy unified in 1861, Campione became part of the new Kingdom of Italy—and remained so. There are no frontiers between Campione and Switzerland, and it benefits from the comforts of Swiss currency, customs laws, and postal

EMPTY YOUR POCKETS

Somehow, there's a fascination about smuggling even if you've never brought so much as a single cigarette over your allowance through the green Nothing-to-Declare channel. The subject is brought to life at the Museo Doganale (091/9104811, free admission, open Palm Sun.–Oct., daily 1:30–5:30), set across Lago di Lugano from Gandria, almost in Italy. Known as the "Smuggler's Museum," it bristles with ingenious containers, weapons, and contraband exhibits, which explore the romantic history of clandestine trade between Italy and Switzerland. You can catch a boat from the jetty in Gandria.

TICINO EXCURSIONS: SOUTH TO ITALY

HEAD SOUTH OF THE TICINO'S GANDRIA, and you can be in Italy in a few minutes (just like the smugglers of Gandria's famous past). The road south runs from above this village. Alternatively, go by boat from Lugano to Porlezza at the Italian end of Lago di Lugano. Then by road to Menaggio, hardly any distance. Close at hand are the world famous, paradisical gardens of the Villa Monasterio and Villa Carlotta. Other visits to Italy are also easy, but remember your passport—to Como itself (frequent trains from Lugano) or to Cannobio (short journey on the lakeside road from Ascona or Locarno). Inquire locally about market days: they are always fun in Italy.

Heading out from Lugano itself, follow the Paradiso highway and take the broad Melide causeway across the upper and lower sections of Lago di Lugano. This joins the northern land mass to the Mendrisiotto region, the southernmost section of Switzerland. At the connecting village of Bissone, visit the Casa Tencalla (Place Borromini 11), a lovely arcaded Italian Renaissance building furnished in 17th-century Lombard style, with very local art of the period. Several painters—notably Tencalla (whose frescoes adorn the town's church of San Carpoforo)—hailed from this town but its most celebrated native son was Francesco Borromini, leading architect of the Baroque in Rome.

Heading south you'll arrive at Riva San Vitale, located 9 km (5½ mi) south of Campione and 13 km (8 mi) south of Lugano. It rivals Campione for its odd history: in 1798 its people

objected to new boundaries and declared themselves an independent republic. Their glory lasted 14 days before a small cantonal army marched in and persuaded them to rejoin Switzerland. A 5th-century Battistèro (baptistery) remains, still containing its original stone font—a remarkable and extremely rare relic.

About 4 km (2 mi) south of Riva San Vitale is colorful Mendrisio, cradle of the Ticinese wine industry. This region, known as the Mendrisiotto, shelters many Italianate villages clustered around ancient bell towers. Fall is particularly lovely here. Mendrisio has a reputation as the friendliest town in the Ticino, credible because of all that wine. But its past has frequently been troubled. It was caught up in the protracted medieval row between the Guelphs and the Ghibellines, respectively supporters of Pope and Emperor. The local ruling family were the Torriani, who were Guelphs who won in the end but only after great bloodshed.

Mendrisio has an enchanting atmosphere and is famous for its medieval religious processions, held on the Thursday and Friday before Easter. On Maundy Thursday, that depicting Christ's journey to Calvary is held, with knights on horseback, Roman soldiers, and Biblical characters, all passing under archways of 17th-century banners hung from windows and balconies. That on Good Friday is a particularly evocative torchlight parade recalling the events of the Crucifixtion. In town, there are historic monuments including the Chiesa di San Giovanni and the Palazzo Torriani-Fontana.

and telephone services. Despite its miniature scale, it has exercised disproportionate influence on the art world: in the Middle Ages, a school of stonemasons, sculptors, and architects from Campione and the surrounding region worked on the cathedrals of Milan, Verona, Cremona, Trento, and Modena—even the Hagia Sophia in Istanbul.

Nightlife & the Arts

Today, Campione is a magnet for gamblers thanks to its **Casino** (✉ Piazza Milano 1 ☎ 091/6401111) now housed in a brand new building designed by star architect Mario Botta, which looks like some huge brown UFO that has landed on the little town. When you're not playing the tables you can have dinner in the restaurant or enjoy a show. Men are required to wear a jacket, but they don't have to wear a tie in summer.

EN ROUTE If you wish to see all of Switzerland's monuments in a few hours, then stop in the town of **Melide** 8 km (5 mi) south of Lugano. The **Swissminiatur** (☎ 091/6401060 ⊕ www.swissminiatur.ch ☞ 15 SF ⊗ Mar. 15–Oct., daily 9–6) has all the sights and sites you could wish for at a 1:25 scale installed on a 3.5-acre plot. These include such diverse monuments as the Bern Minster, the Swiss national circus Knie, the railway station at Sion, or the autobahn pit stop at Würenlos. Nearly 3.5 km (2 mi) of miniature train tracks have been laid out and are busily used by passenger and freight stock.

Morcote

⓴
Fodor'sChoice
★

11 km (7 mi) northwest of Campione, 10 km (6 mi) south of Lugano. A half-hour bus ride connects you to Lugano.

At the southernmost tip of the glorious Ceresio Peninsula is the atmospheric village of Morcote, its clay-color houses and arcades looking directly over the waterfront. A steep and picturesque climb leads up to the **Chiesa di Madonna del Sasso** (Church of the Madonna of the Rock), with its well-preserved 16th-century frescoes; its elevated set-

★ ting affords wonderful views. The **Parco Scherrer** is a remarkable garden created over a period of decades by the Swiss businessman Arthur Scherrer (1881–1956). This folly rising from the lakeside brings together architectural samples from around the world—an Egyptian sun temple, a Siamese teahouse, and an Indian palace, for example—within the setting of a carefully landscaped garden. ⊕ *www.lugano-tourism.ch* ☞ *7 SF* ⊗ *Mar.–Oct., Wed.–Mon. 10–6; July and Aug., daily 10–6.*

Where to Stay & Eat

★ $$-$$$ ✕⌂ **Carina Carlton.** Somehow, this family-run hotel has managed to fit a host of pretty and spacious rooms, a restaurant, a generous terrace, and an outdoor pool into the narrow strip between the mountain and the lake. It's a wonderful place to enjoy the peace of the lake—interrupted only by the cars driven in the usual aggressive fashion along the shore road—a mere 20 minutes from Lugano. The restaurant awaits for lunch or dinner with a wide range of Swiss, Ticinese, and Italian dishes with odd creative Asian touches: chicken breast with vegetables and soy on noodles, for example. ✉ *Riva da Sant' Antoni, CH-6922 Morcote* ☎ *091/9961131* 🖷 *091/9961929* ⊕ *www.carina-morcote.ch* 🔊 *23 rooms ⌂ Restaurant, outdoor pool, minibar, no-smoking rooms; no a/c* ☰ *AE, DC, MC, V* ⍾⃝⃒ *BP* ⊗ *Nov.–Feb.*

$$–$$$
Fodor's Choice
★
✕⌂ **Dellago.** Combining a soothing atmosphere, personal service, and unpretentious savoir faire, this stylish refuge right on the lake spoils its guests. At dinnertime the casual lakeside terrace lures many locals, devotees of chef and co-owner Klaus Höckel, who whips up astounding entrées such as the gleaming buttermilk-port tower with smoked salmon cured in lemongrass, ginger, and honey or tiger prawns marinated in tamarind-garlic pesto and served on a sumptuous bed of leeks, shiitake mushrooms, and sprouts. Individually decorated rooms are equipped with a range of treats: ask for surround-sound stereo, a private rooftop hot tub, a DVD player, or a plasma TV. After a refreshing breakfast—replete with homemade jams, fine teas, and a selection of unusual breads—why not take the hotel paddle boat out for a spin? ✉ *Lago di Lugano, CH-6815 Melide* ☎ *091/6497041* 🖷 *091/6498915* ⊕ *www.hotel-dellago.ch* 🔊 *50 rooms ⌂ Restaurant, bar; no a/c in some rooms* ☰ *AE, DC, MC, V* ⍾⃝⃒ *BP.*

★ **$–$$**
✕⌂ **Bella Vista.** High above Lago di Lugano, surrounded by vineyards, lies this outstanding getaway. A handful of superb rooms occupy two restored 17th-century houses; the decor is a mix of antique and ultramodern. One sleek room has the original fireplace; the tower suite's bathroom is done in granite and glass. All have beautiful views. The restaurant is equally luxe. The menu includes several lobster dishes, homemade pastas, and a heavenly potato gratin. In fine weather you'll be served on the outdoor terrace, which has a truly spectacular view. Vico Morcote is about 2 km (1¼ mi) south of Melide; follow the sign from the main road. ✉ *Strada da Vigh 2, CH-6921 Vico Morcote* ☎ *091/9961143* 🖷 *091/9961288* 🔊 *9 rooms, 2 suites, 1 apartment ⌂ Restaurant, bar; no a/c* ☰ *AE, DC, MC, V* ⍾⃝⃒ *BP* ⊗ *Closed Jan.*

THE TICINO ESSENTIALS

Transportation

BY AIR

The nearest international airport is in Italy. Malpensa, near Milan, is one of the biggest hubs in southern Europe.

🛈 Airport Information **Aeroporto Lugano-Agno** ✉ 7 km [4½ mi] west of Lugano, Agno ☎ 091/6051226. **Linate** ✉ 10 km [6 mi] east of Milan ☎ 0039/274852200. **Malpensa** ✉ 50 km [31 mi] northwest of Milan ☎ 0039/274852200.

AIRPORT
TRANSFERS
To get to Lugano from Aeroporto Lugano-Agno, contact Fly Car Lugano. Bus Express Chiasso connects Milan's Malpensa Airport with Lugano.
🛈 Taxis & Shuttles **Bus Express Chiasso** ☎ 091/9948878. **Fly Car Lugano** ☎ 091/8078520.

Swiss International Air Lines, known as Swiss, Switzerland's domestic carrier, has direct connections to Lugano's airport, Aeroporto Lugano-

Agno, from Zürich Airport and Cointrin in Geneva, and other European destinations.

🛈 Airlines & Contacts **Swiss** ☎ 0848/852000.

BY BOAT & FERRY

Lago di Lugano and Lago Maggiore are plied by graceful steamers that carry passengers from one waterfront resort to another, offering excellent views of the mountains. Steamer travel on Lago di Lugano is included in the Swiss Pass; tickets can be purchased near the docks before departure. On Lago di Lugano, the Navigazione Lago di Lugano (Navigation Company of Lake Lugano) offers excursions around the bay to Gandria and toward the Villa Favorita.

Boats owned by Navigazione Lago Maggiore-Bacino Svizzero (Swiss Navigation Company of Lake Maggiore) cruise Lago Maggiore. Discounts are given for Swiss and Swiss Boat passes.

🛈 Boat & Ferry Information **Navigazione Lago di Lugano** ✉ Casella Postale 56, CH-6906 Lugano ☎ 091/9715223 ⊕ www.lakelugano.ch. **Navigazione Lago Maggiore-Bacino Svizzero** ✉ Lungolago Motta, CH-6600 Locarno ☎ 091/7511865 ⊕ www.navlaghi.it.

WORD OF MOUTH

"A great way to tie in with the Bernina Express rail route is to take the Palm Express Swiss postal bus, one of the finest of the fabled Swiss postal bus rides and so named because it links Lugano and the palm-fringed Swiss Riviera to St. Moritz. From Lugano it heads out along along the shores of idyllic Lake Lugano (passing ancient Gandria) and then enters Italy, going overland to Lake Como and stopping for a break at cute Menaggio, one the Lake Como's marquee resorts. Hugging the lake, it traverses a wide valley to Chiavenna, a lovely bustling regional town, and then re-enters Switzerland, plying the lush Bregaglia Valley via a series of incredibly sharp hairpin turns that the bus somehow barely navigates (during which the driver's hand is constantly on the loud oompah-like sounding horn to alert oncoming traffic). It finally corkscrews up the gorgeous Majola Pass, entering the Upper Engadine to arrive at St. Moritz."   —PalQ

BY BUS

The Palm Express scenic postbus route carries visitors from St. Moritz to Lugano via the Maloja Pass and Italy; reservations are strongly recommended. It takes about four hours and can be arranged at any train station or tourist office. You can also contact Railtour Suisse.

There's a convenient postbus sightseeing system here that you can use to get around the region, even into the backcountry. La Posta (post and telegraph office) publishes illustrated booklets with suggested itineraries and prices; you can get them through the Autopostale Ticino-Moesano or through local tourist and post offices. Postbus excursion prices are reduced with the Locarno or Lugano Holiday Passes and are free with the Swiss Pass.

🛈 Bus Information **Autopostale Ticino-Moesano** ✉ Via S. Balestra, CH-6900 Lugano ☎ 091/8078520 ⊕ www.post.ch. **Railtour Suisse** ☎ 031/3780000.

BY CAR

There are two major gateways into the Ticino: the St. Gotthard Pass, in the northwest, and the San Bernardino Pass, to the northeast. From the St. Gotthard Pass, the swift A2 expressway leads down the Valle Leventina to Bellinzona, where it joins with A13, which cuts south from the San Bernardino. A2 directs the mingled traffic flow southward past Lugano to Chiasso and the Italian border, where the expressway heads directly to Como and Milan. As an alternative, there's the St. Gotthard Tunnel—17 km (11 mi) of dense air and darkness speeding you through the Alps rather than over them. If traffic is light, it can cut an hour off your travel time, but if the passes are closed and it's holiday migration time, tunnel traffic can be nasty.

A car is a real asset here if you intend to see the mountain valleys—and a hindrance in the congested lakeside resorts. Lugano is particularly difficult to drive through, and the parking garages are usually packed. Traffic between Bellinzona and Locarno can move at a crawl during high season. There's a handful of main roads between towns, but secondary roads peter out. Wherever you are in the Ticino, the Italian (read: fast and risky) driving style dominates.

BY TRAIN

The St. Gotthard route connects south from Zürich, cuts through the pass tunnel, and heads into Bellinzona and Lugano. Side connections lead into Locarno from Brig, crossing the Simplon Pass and cutting through Italy. Swiss Pass travelers do not have to pay Italian rail fares to cross from Brig to Locarno via Domodossola. Trains connect out of Zürich's airport and take about three hours to Lugano, Locarno, and Ascona; from Geneva, catch the Milan express, changing at Domodossola, Locarno, and Bellinzona. Trains do not go directly into Ascona but stop at Locarno: you must connect by taxi or local bus. For train information from Lugano, call the Swiss Federal Railway, here called the Ferrovie Federali Svizzere (FFS).

Secondary rail connections here are minimal and can make all but the most mainstream rail sightseeing a complicated venture; most excursions will require some postbus connections. Nevertheless, there is a regional discount pass called the Holiday Pass FART. The pass is valid for the Lugano and Locarno areas and gives you unlimited free travel for three or seven consecutive days on local transit routes (bus and train) and a 30% to 50% discount on others. Passes are available from the train station or tourist office.

🚆 Train Information **Ferrovie Federali Svizzere (FFS)** ☎ 0900/300300 1.19 SF per minute.

Contacts & Resources

EMERGENCIES
🚔 **Police** ☎ 117. **Medical Assistance/Ambulance** ☎ 144. **Lugano Civic Hospital** ☎ 091/8116111. **Lugano Dental Clinic** ☎ 091/9350180.

INTERNET & MAIL

In smaller towns, ask your hotel concierge if there are any Internet cafés nearby.

🔢 Internet & Mail Information **Verbano Bar** ✉ Piazza Grande 5, Locarno ☎ 091/751-1764. **Post office Bellinzona** ✉ Viale Stazione 18, Bellinzona. **Post office Locarno** ✉ Piazza Grande 3, Locarno. **Post office Lugano** ✉ Via della Posta 7, Lugano.

TOUR OPTIONS

The *Wilhelm Tell Express* carries you by paddle steamer and rail from Luzern over the St. Gotthard Pass and into Locarno and Lugano with a guide and running commentary in English. Inquire at any rail station for details. The *Bernina Express,* Europe's highest Alp-crossing railway, takes you from Chur to St. Moritz in the *Glacier Express;* then you cross the Alps over the Bernina Pass into Italy (in summer it's even possible in an open-air train car) and continue into Lugano. Several variations are possible. Both offer discounts for Swiss Pass and Swiss Boat Pass holders. Inquire at any railway station for information and reservations.

Guided walks are available in all areas covering cultural, historical, architectural, and natural interests. English-language brochures with maps are available from local tourist offices for both guided and self-guided tours.

VISITOR INFORMATION

The principal tourist authority for the Ticino is Ticino Turismo.

🔢 Local Tourist Office **Bellinzona** ✉ Viale Stazione 18, CH-6500 ☎ 091/8252131. **Biasca** ✉ Contrada Cav. Pellanda 4, CH-6710 ☎ 091/8623327. **Lago Maggiore (Locarno, Ascona, and Brissago Islands)** ✉ Via Largo Zorzi 1, CH-6600 Locarno ☎ 091/7910091. **Lugano** ✉ Piazza della Riforma, CH-6900 ☎ 091/9133232. 🔢 Regional Tourist Offices **Ticino Turismo** ✉ Viale Stazione 18, CH-6501 Bellinzona ☎ 091/8252131 🖷 091/8254120 ⊕ www.ticino-tourism.ch.

Luzern & Central Switzerland

LUZERN, WEGGIS, RÜTLI MEADOW, WILLIAM TELL COUNTRY

Benedictine monastery in Einsiedeln, Canton Schwyz

WORD OF MOUTH

"Nothing prepared us for the views that we had when we came out of the Luzern train station. I took out my camera and armed it ready to shoot. However, I had a problem: where to shoot first! It was all so beautiful."   —gabrieltraian

"Visiting the legendary Rütli Meadow—the 'birthplace' of Switzerland—in the heart of Wilhelm Tell Country was an ascension-into-heaven moment."   —Cheyne2

WELCOME TO LUZERN & CENTRAL SWITZERLAND

TOP REASONS TO GO

★ **Luzern.** The must-see spot on the tour, it offers not only the things you've heard of —the Chapel Bridge, the Lion Monument—but other treasures like the Rosengart Picassos and that perfect table for two under the chestnut trees on the lakeside promenade.

★ **Mountain Majesty:** Thanks to cable cars and cog railways, hill thrills— and some of the most staggering panoramas—can be yours atop Mts. Pilatus, Titlis, and Rigi.

★ **William Tell Country:** As with all good legends, the story of the famous archer who shot an apple from his son's head with a crossbow may have little basis in fact but don't tell that to the crowds who visit his home turf in and around Altdorf.

★ **A Paddleboat Steamer Ride:** Smart white steamers, some of them beautifully kept and picturesque old paddle-steamers—ply Lake Luzern and offer a voyage back into time.

1 Luzern. The little big city, **Luzern** offers a full cultural palette: wander through the medieval solidity of the Old Town; shop your way through the many boutiques; take a boat cruise to a yodeling beat; and listen to divas sing in Jean Nouvel's architectural wonder, the Kultur- und Kongresszentrum.

2 Luzern Environs. Towering over **Luzern**, Mt. Pilatus is dramatic and impressive, with a restaurant teetering on its razor-sharp ridge at the top. Take the "golden round-trip," which includes a bus from Luzern, a cable car trip to the top, a cogwheel train back down the other side, and a boat ride back to Luzern. Head south to **Engelberg**—noted for its outdoor sports—where you can take the gondola up to the top of Mt. Titlis, gasping at the view, the loftiest in central Switzerland.

The Tell Chapel on Lake Uri

3 William Tell Country.

Hallowed by myths, the **Urnersee** is the southern—and by far most romantic—leg of Lake Luzern. Dramatic mountains run steeply into the lake as sharp peaks stab into the clouds, a landscape that has inspired many a master, from Rossini to Wagner, Schiller to Twain (bring along your sketchbook or journal). **Weggis** and **Vitznau** are the Riviera towns, sheltered by coves and addresses to the rich. Farther south, pay your respects to the historic **Rütli Meadow**; the picturesque Tell Chapel, just across the lake; and **Altdorf**, where Wilhelm Tell first became a legend.

GETTING ORIENTED

To enter Luzern is to approach the very heart of historic Switzerland, for the sharply indented shoreline of the Vierwaldstättersee (Lake Lucerne) was the cradle of the Swiss Confederation, forged here in the 13th century on the Rütli Meadow as the world's first democracy. Most-visited Luzern, with its Old Town, sits on one end of the lake; the quieter but equally historic Altdorf, "home" of Wilhelm Tell, on the other. In between is probably the most beautiful stretch of lakeshore in Switzerland.

5

Küssnacht
Rigi Kulm ▲ A4
Meggen
Weggis
Luzernersee Vitznau ▲ Rigi Scheidegg
▲ Bürgenstock Schwyz
A2 Ennetbürgen Gersau Brunnen
ths Beckenried Seelisberg
Vierwaldstättersee Rütli Meadow
Stanserhorn ▲ Klewenalp A2
Schwalmis ▲ Chaiserstock ▲
Srisen ▲ Urnersee 3
Grafenort Altdorf
Bürglen
Wissigstock ▲ ▲ Brunnistock
Windgällen ▲
Engelberg Erstfeld
ENGELBERGERTAL ▲ Schlossberg A2
Silenen
Mt Titlis ▲ Spannort ▲
Amsteg

0 ———— 5 mi
0 ———— 5 km

The Water Tower of Lucerne

LUZERN & CENTRAL SWITZERLAND PLANNER

Getting Around

When visiting this area, you must change modes of transit frequently to see it all; part of the region's interest is the variety of boats, trains, and other less common modes of transportation you'll take to reach the sights.

On any given day, you may walk through the lovely Old Town of Luzern, ascend Mt. Pilatus by cable car and descend by cogwheel train, take a lake steamer, or drive to the Rütli Meadow.

Many of the towns in this region are scattered around the unusually shaped Vierwaldstättersee, so sometimes a ferry will be faster than a freeway and a train often makes more sense than a car. That noted, the road network around the Vierwaldstättersee is excellent and many roads have spectacular views.

The Swiss Federal Railways (SBB, 0900/300300, www.sbb.ch), manages trains, boats, and buses.

Direct rail connections from Geneva, Zurich, and Basel run through Luzern, from which there is public transportation to every part of the region.

How's the Weather?

The geographic heart of Switzerland enjoys four distinct seasons, temperate in the valleys and more extreme in the mountains. Spring, summer, and fall are perfect for warm-weather outdoor activities. Fall becomes crisp around October and winter brings snow to the highlands. Keep in mind that snow can stay as late as May and come as early as August over 6,500 feet. Avoid walking in creek beds: a hidden rainstorm high in the mountains can turn a trickling brook into a rushing torrent in a matter of seconds and has swept away many a hiker or canyoner. If you're going up and down mountains, dress like an onion: the warmth of the valley, needless to say, can be quickly replaced by a cold breeze 5,000 feet higher.

Small Town, Big Style

In a town of less than 60,000 inhabitants, where a local philanthropist can afford to buy prime real estate to put her private art collection on display, where the lakeside is teeming with villas and the concert hall attracts international greatness in the form of Cecilia Bartoli and Renée Fleming, the Ugly Tourist can stick out like a sore thumb in Luzern. Although residents appreciate the value of comfortable clothes, this is definitely not the place to let it all hang out: huge droopy T-shirts, ill-fitting Bermuda shorts, and baseball caps will get you looks of distain, seated only in McDonald's, and denied entrance to most churches and museums. Of course we don't mean you in particular, it's those other guys. . . .

WHAT IT COSTS In Swiss francs

	$$$$	$$$	$$	$	¢
Restaurants	over 60 SF	40 SF–60 SF	25 SF–40 SF	15 SF–25 SF	under 15 SF
Hotels	over 350 SF	250 SF–350 SF	175 SF–250 SF	100 SF–175 SF	under 100 SF

Restaurant prices are per person for a main course at dinner. Hotel prices are for two people in a standard double room in high season, including tax and service.

Take the Slow Boat to . . .

One of the joys of traveling in this region is to tour Lake Luzern on one of its time-stained 19th-century paddleboat steamers. These are a slow but extremely scenic and therefore worthwhile mode of transportation; you'll find locals on day trips traveling along with you. Remember that this is a very unrushed part of the country, where people tend to enjoy the slow moments and avoid the hectic ones; impatience may get you ignored, so chill and enjoy.

The Vierwaldstättersee (to use the German name for Lake Luzern) has a very good network of steamers—only two are historic paddlesteamers, however—which connect virtually every community on the lakeside. The larger boats have full restaurant facilities and even the smaller ones offer refreshments. As elsewhere in Switzerland, they link, where practical, with both the train and postbus services. The round-trip/excursion tickets offer best value for the money. Services are frequent in the peak season with, for example, hourly departures from the lovely boat dock in Luzern, but in the off-peak season services are limited so check on availability when you arrive. Swiss Passes allow deep discounts.

Finding a Place to Stay

All budgets are covered in central Switzerland, from backpacker-type multibed rooms to luxurious suites with 1,000-thread-count silk sheets. In the mountains, high season means the winter ski season, in the valleys summer is more expensive. As the terrain and climate vary radically between balmy lakefronts and icy heights, check carefully for high and low seasons before booking ahead.

Resorts such as Weggis and Vitznau cut back service considerably in winter, just when Engelberg comes alive. Book early for ever-popular Luzern. Which, unlike most Swiss urban areas, has high and low seasons. Prices drop by as much as 25% in winter, approximately November through March.

Rates are often calculated on a per-person basis, so it's wise to confirm rates, particularly if you're traveling as anything other than a couple. Local tourist offices are a big help with in-person reservations, but most hotels have their own up-to-date Web sites for booking ahead.

Seven Days of Madness

Although Carnival (called Fasnacht in German) is celebrated throughout the country, the party aspect to the celebration is taken most seriously in Luzern.

On the first Thursday seven weeks before Easter each year, seven days of madness follow, alive with parades, confetti, dancing, singing, and, of course, the odd bit of drinking.

The parades begin with an orderly parade of Guggä—elaborately costumed brass and drums bands that can turn any pop tune into a festive event—that soon (d)evolves into a writhing, rowdy old-town festival as each group splinters off down an alley and plays more or less nonstop throughout the week.

Guests are encouraged, if not downright expected, to join in. Most locals take the week off—there's no getting any work done anyway.

To paraphrase Chuckles the Clown: a little song, a little dance, a little confetti down your pants.

Updated by
Katrin Gygax

WITH THE MIST RISING OFF THE WAVES and the mountains looming above the clouds, it's easy to understand how Wagner could have composed his *Siegfried Idyll* in his mansion beside the lake. This is inspiring terrain, romantic and evocative. When the waters roil up, you can hear the whistling chromatics and cymbal clashes of Gioacchino Rossini's thunderstorm from his 1829 opera, *Guillaume Tell*. It was on Lake Luzern, after all, that Wilhelm Tell—the beloved, if legendary, Swiss national hero—supposedly leaped from the tyrant Gessler's boat to freedom. And it was in a meadow nearby that three furtive rebels and their cohorts swore an oath by firelight and planted the seed of the Swiss Confederation.

The Rütli Meadow on the western shore of Lake Luzern is the very spot where the Confederates of Uri, Schwyz, and Unterwalden are said to have met on the night of November 7, 1307, to renew the 1291 Oath of Eternal Alliance—Switzerland's equivalent of the U.S. Declaration of Independence. With this oath, the world's oldest still-extant democracy was born, as the proud charter territories swore their commitment to self-rule in the face of the Habsburgs' Holy Roman Empire. Every August 1, the Swiss national holiday, citizens gather in the meadow in remembrance of the oath, and the sky glows with the light of hundreds of mountaintop bonfires.

Wilhelm Tell played an important role in that early rebellion, and his story, especially as told by German poet and playwright Friedrich von Schiller in his play *Wilhelm Tell* (1805), continues to stir those with a weakness for civil resistance. Here, around the villages of Altdork, Bürgen, and the stunningly picturesque lakeside Tell Chapel thousands come to honor the memory of the rebellious archer and, well, tell tales.

Yet for all its potential for drama, central Switzerland and the area surrounding Lake Luzern are tame enough turf: neat little towns, accessible mountains, smooth roads, resorts virtually glamour-free—and modest, graceful Luzern (Lucerne) astride the River Reuss much as it has been since the Middle Ages.

An eminently civilized region, Zentralschweiz (Central Switzerland) lacks the rustic unruliness of the Valais, the spectacular extremes of the Berner Oberland, and the eccentricity of Graubünden. It's also without the sophistication and snob appeal of jet-set resorts or the cosmopolitan mix of Geneva, Basel, and Zürich. Instead, villages here range neatly around their medieval centers; houses are tidy, pastel, picture-book cottages, deep-roofed and symmetrical, each rank of windows underscored with flowers. Luzern, the capital, hosts arts festivals and great shopping but little native industry. Serene and steady as the Reuss that laps at the piers of its ancient wooden bridges, it's an approachable city in an accessible region.

Central Switzerland's popularity with tourists has spawned an infrastructure of hotels, restaurants, museums, excursions, and transportation that makes it one of the easiest places in Switzerland to visit, either by car or by rail—and one of the most rewarding. As Wagner exclaimed, "I do not know of a more beautiful spot in this world!"

Exploring Luzern & Central Switzerland

Called variously the Vierwaldstättersee, the Urnersee, or the Luzernersee—it depends on which end you are standing—Lake Luzern and its environs take in not only the four cantons that abut the lake—Luzern, Uri, Schwyz, and Unterwalden—but the canton of Zug as well. Unterwalden itself is divided politically into two half-cantons: Obwalden (upper) and Nidwalden (lower). It was the canton of Schwyz that gave Switzerland its name.

The narrow, twisting lake flows from Flüelen, where the Reuss opens into the Urnersee, its southernmost leg. This is the wildest end of the lake, where much of the Tell story was set. The north end of the lake is flanked by the region's highest points, Mt. Pilatus (6,953 feet) and Mt. Rigi (5,894 feet). Luzern lies in a deep bay at the lake's northwest extreme and at the point where the rivers Reuss and Emme part ways. Zug stands apart, on the northern shore of its own Lake Zug, which is divided from Lake Luzern by the mass of Mt. Rigi.

Numbers in the text correspond to numbers in the margin and on the Central Switzerland and Luzern (Lucerne) maps.

LUZERN

▶ **To & From:** *Luzern's centrally located main station brings hourly trains in from Basel (30 SF one-way), Bern (30 SF one-way), and Zurich (22 SF one-way). Geneva trains arrive through Bern or Olten (70 SF one-way). Directly outside the station's entrance is the quay where lake boats that form part of the public transit system can take you to a variety of towns along the Vierwaldstättersee, including Weggis, Vitznau, Flüelen (with a bus connection to Altdorf), and Brunnen. For departure times and prices for trains and buses for most destinations in this chapter, check www.sbb.ch—the main Swiss public transportation Web site—or call 0900/300300 (1,19 SF per min). Remember, if you have a Swiss Pass or another rail-discounting card, it also applies to the buses. Central Switzerland has its own discount Tell Pass; for info, see Essentials at end of this chapter or log on to www.lakeluzern.com. Luzern is 57 km (36 mi) southwest of Zürich.*

Luzern city is a convenient home base for excursions all over central Switzerland. The countryside here is tame, and the vast Vierwaldstättersee offers a prime opportunity for a lake steamer cruise. Where the River Reuss flows out of Lake Luzern, Luzern's Old Town straddles the narrowed waters. There are a couple of discount passes available for museums and sights in the city. One is a museum pass that costs 30 SF and grants entry to all

GETTING AROUND

Parking is limited and the old town of Luzern is pedestrian only; it is best to park your car and walk. All destinations in this region mentioned here are small, reachable by train or boat, and can easily be traveled on foot once you get there.

Central Switzerland

KEY

- ᛍ Cable Carl Funicular
- ⊢ Rail lines
- ═══ Tunnel
- ⛴ Ferry
- 🎿 Ski Resorts
- ▲ Start of itinerary

SWITZERLAND

Luzern 1–16
see detail map

17 **Mt. Pilatus** ▲

18 **Stans**

19 **Engelberg**

20 **Bürgenstock**

21 **Weggis**

22 **Vitznau**

23 **Seelisberg**

24 **Altdorf**

25 **Bürglen**

26 **Rütli Meadow**

27 **Schwyz**

The Tellskapelle

Vierwaldstättersee

Urnersee

Zuger See

Lauerzer See

Luzernersee

Alpnacher See

Sarner See

Zugersee

LUZERN

OBWALDEN

NIDWALDEN

ENGELBERGERTAL

URI

SCHWYZ

GROSSCHLIERENTAL

Verkehrshaus

Goldau

Arth

Küssnacht

Meggen

Littau

Malters

Kriens

Hergiswil

Stansstad

Ennetmoos

Kerns

Alpnachstad

Sarnen

Giswil

Kaiserstuhl

Stöckalp

Melchtal

Ennetbürgen

Beckenried

Gersau

Brunnen

Seelisberg

Klewenalp

Grafenort

 Aa

Flüelen

Erstfeld

Silenen

Amsteg

TO ANDERMATT

Rigi Kulm ▲
Rigi Kaltbad ▲
Rigi Scheidegg

▲ Axen

▲ Chaiserstock

▲ Windgällen

▲ Braunistock

▲ Schlossberg

▲ Spannort

▲ Wissigstock

▲ Mt Titlis

▲ Sirsen

▲ Schwalmis

▲ Nünalphorn

▲ Hohmad

▲ Gräfimattstand

▲ Heilffistock

▲ Stanserhorn

▲ Mittaggüpfi

5 mi

5 km

A14

A2

A8

A4

A2

A2

A2

8

10

17

4

museums for one month. If you're staying in a hotel, you may also want to pick up a special visitor's card; once stamped by the hotel, it entitles you to discounts at most museums and other tourist-oriented businesses. Both passes are available at the tourist office.

Old Town & Beyond

Sights to See

❸ Altes Rathaus (Old Town Hall). In 1606 the Luzern town council held its first meeting in this late-Renaissance-style building, built between 1602 and 1606. It still meets here today. ⊠ *Rathausquai, facing the north end of Rathaus-Steg.*

❹ Am Rhyn-Haus. Also known as the Picasso Museum, this spot contrasts a beautiful, 17th-century building with its modern holdings. The collection consists of Picasso drawings from the 1950s onward as well as some of his most important sculptures, including *Femme au chapeau.* There are also more than 100 photographs of the artist. For a choice selection of Picasso paintings, head to the affiliated collection, the Sammlung Rosengart. ⊠ *Furreng. 21* ☎ *041/4103533* 💷 *8 SF, 18 SF for combination ticket to Sammlung Rosengart* ⊙ *Apr.–Oct., daily 10–6; Nov.–Mar., daily 11–1, 2–4.*

★ ⓭ Bourbaki-Panorama. The panorama was the IMAX theater of the 19th century; its sweeping, wraparound paintings brought to life scenes of epic proportions. The Bourbaki is one of only 30 remaining in the world. Painted by Édouard Castres between 1876 and 1878 (he was aided by many uncredited artists, including Ferdinand Hodler), it depicts the French Army of the East retreating into Switzerland at Verrières, a famous episode in the Franco-Prussian War. As you walk around the circle, the imagery seems to pop into three dimensions; in fact, with the help of a few strategically placed models, it does. There's a recorded commentary in English. Its conical wooden structure is surrounded by a modern glass cube filled with shops, movie theaters, and a restaurant. ⊠ *Löwenpl. 11* ☎ *041/4123030* ⊕ *www.bourbakipanorama.ch* 💷 *8 SF* ⊙ *Daily 9–6.*

❾ Franziskanerkirche (Franciscan Church). Since its construction in the 13th century, this church has been persistently remodeled. It still retains its 17th-century choir stalls and carved wooden pulpit. The barefoot Franciscans once held a prominent social and cultural position in Luzern, which took a firm stance against the Reformation and today remains approximately 70% Roman Catholic. ⊠ *Franziskanerpl., just off Münzg.*

⓯ Gletschergarten (Glacier Garden). This 19th-century tourist attraction was excavated between 1872 and 1875 and has been dramatically pocked and polished by Ice Age glaciers. A private museum on the site displays impressive relief maps of Switzerland. ⊠ *Denkmalstr. 4* ☎ *041/4104340* ⊕ *www.gletschergarten.ch* 💷 *12 SF* ⊙ *Apr.–Oct., daily 9–6; Nov.–Mar., daily 10–5.*

❽ Historisches Museum (Historical Museum). Housed in the late-Gothic armory dating from 1567, this stylish institution exhibits numerous city icons, including the original Gothic fountain that stood in the Weinmarkt.

A GOOD WALK

Start at the **Kultur- und Kongresszentrum** ❶ ▶, near the train station, which gives you a beautiful view of all the places you'll see in Luzern. Walk down Pilatusstrasse to see the city's latest addition to its cultural offerings, the **Sammlung Rosengart** ❷. Cut north to Bahnhofstrasse, taking a left to the modern bridge, the Rathaus-Steg, and head north to the **Altes Rathaus** ❸, across the bridge. This late-Renaissance building is on Rathausquai, the city's main avenue. Just to the right of the Rathaus is the **Am Rhyn-Haus** ❹, now a museum dedicated to Picasso. Turn left and climb the stairs past the ornately frescoed Zunfthaus zur Pfistern, a guildhall dating from the late 15th and early 16th centuries, to the Kornmarkt, where the grinding din of the grain market was once heard. Cut left to the **Weinmarkt** ❺, a fountain square.

Leave the square from its west end, turn right on Kramgasse, and head west across the Mühlenplatz to the **Spreuerbrücke** ❻, an unlikely exhibition space for dark paintings of the medieval plague epidemic. Crossing the bridge to the left bank, you'll find a pair of museums, the **Natur-Museum** ❼ and the **Historisches Museum** ❽. From the end of the Spreuerbrücke, cut back upriver along Pfistergasse, veer left on Bahnhofstrasse, and turn right into Münzgasse to the **Franziskanerkirche** ❾. Return to Bahnhofstrasse and head to the **Jesuitenkirche** ❿. Continuing east past the Rathaus-Steg Bridge, you'll see the **Kapellbrücke** ⓫, the oldest bridge of its kind in Europe.

After crossing the Kapellbrücke, break away from Old Town through thick pedestrian and bus traffic at Schwanenplatz to Schweizerhofquai.

Double back and take the first right, St. Leodegarstrasse, to the **Hofkirche** ⓬. Go back down the church steps, doubling back on St. Leodegarstrasse, turn right, and continue on to Löwenstrasse. Turn right and walk up to Löwenplatz and the **Bourbaki-Panorama** ⓭, which dominates the square with its mix of Victorian and modern architecture.

Beyond the plaza, up Denkmalstrasse, is the **Löwendenkmal** ⓮, called by Mark Twain "the most mournful and moving piece of stone in the world." Immediately adjoining the small park that shades the lion lies the **Gletschergarten** ⓯. Return down Denkmalstrasse and, at Löwenplatz, turn right on Museggstrasse, which cuts through an original city gate and runs parallel to the watchtowers and crenellated walls of Luzern, constructed around 1400. The fifth tower is **Zytturm** ⓰.

⏱ TIMING TIPS→ **The Old Town is easy to navigate and ideal for walking. You can take in the sights on this route in about three hours; to this add another hour each to see the Natur-Museum and Historisches Museum, and time to linger at the Kapellbrücke and the Löwendenkmal. Note that both the Natur-Museum and the Historisches Museum are closed Monday.**

Reconstructed rooms depict rural and urban life. ⊠ *Pfisterg. 24* ☎ *041/ 2285424* ⊕ *www.hmluzern.ch* ✉ *10 SF* ☉ *Tues.–Sun. and holidays 10–5.*

⑫ Hofkirche. This sanctuary of St. Leodegar was first part of a monastery founded in 750. Its Gothic structure was mostly destroyed by fire in 1633 and rebuilt in late-Renaissance style, so only the towers of its predecessor were preserved. The carved pulpit and choir stalls date from the 17th century, and the 80-rank organ (1650) is one of Switzerland's finest. Outside, Italianate loggias shelter a cemetery for patrician families of old Luzern. ⊠ *St. Leodegarstr. 6* ☎ *041/4182020* ☉ *Call for hrs.*

OFF THE
BEATEN
PATH

VERKEHRSHAUS – Easily reached by steamer, car, or Bus 8 or 6, the Swiss Transport Museum is almost a world's fair in itself, with a complex of buildings and exhibitions both indoors and out, including live demonstrations, dioramas, and a "Swissorama" (360-degree screen) film about Switzerland. Every mode of transit is discussed, from stagecoaches and bicycles to jumbo jets and space capsules. The museum also houses the country's first IMAX theater. If you're driving, head east on Haldenstrasse at the waterfront and make a right on Lidostrasse. Signs point the way. ⊠ *Lidostr. 5* ☎ *041/3704444* ⊕ *www.verkehrshaus.org* ✉ *24 SF* ☉ *Apr.–Oct., daily 10–6; Nov.–Mar., daily 10–5.*

⑩ Jesuitenkirche (Jesuit Church). Constructed in 1666–77, this Baroque church with a symmetrical entrance is flanked by two onion-dome towers, added in 1893. Inside, its vast interior, restored to its original splendor, is a rococo explosion of gilt, marble, and epic frescoes. Nearby is the Renaissance **Regierungsgebäude** (Government Building), seat of the cantonal government. ⊠ *Bahnhofstr., just west of Rathaus-Steg* ☎ *041/ 2100756* ⊕ *www.jesuitenkirche-luzern.ch* ☉ *Daily 6 AM–6:30 PM.*

FodorśChoice
★

⑪ Kapellbrücke (Chapel Bridge). The oldest wooden bridge in Europe snakes diagonally across the Reuss. When it was constructed in the early 14th century, the bridge served as a rampart in case of attacks from the lake. Its shingle roof and grand stone water tower are to Luzern what the Matterhorn is to Zermatt, but considerably more vulnerable, as a 1993 fire proved. Almost 80% of this fragile monument was destroyed, including many of the 17th-century paintings inside. However, a walk through this dark, creaky landmark will take you past polychrome copies of 110 gable panels, painted by Heinrich Wägmann in the 17th century and depicting Luzern and Swiss history, stories of St. Leodegar and St. Mauritius, Luzern's patron saints, and coats of arms of local patrician families. ⊠ *Between Seebrücke and Rathaus-Steg, connecting Rathausquai and Bahnhofstr.*

FodorśChoice
★

▶ ★ ① Kultur- und Kongresszentrum (Culture and Convention Center). Architect Jean Nouvel's stunning glass-and-steel building manages to both stand out from and fuse with its ancient milieu. The lakeside center's roof is an oversized, cantilevered, flat plane; shallow water channels thread inside, and immense glass plates mirror the surrounding views. The main draw is the concert hall, which opened in 1998. Although the lobbies are rich in blue, red, and stained wood, the hall itself is refreshingly pale, with acoustics so perfect you can hear the proverbial pin drop. Among the annual music events is the renowned International Music Festival.

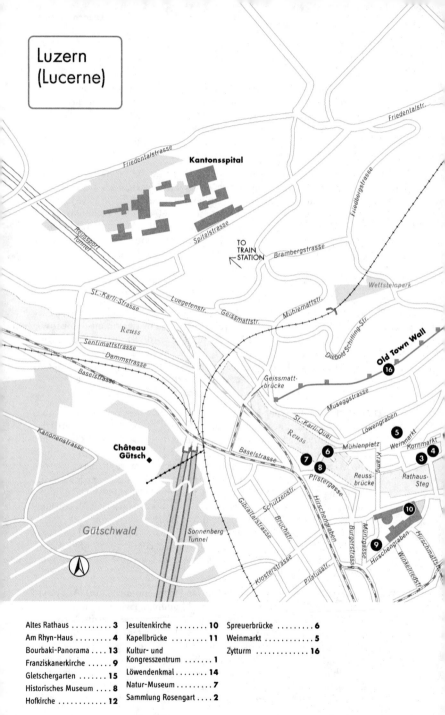

Luzern (Lucerne)

Kantonsspital

Friedentalstrasse

Friedentalstr.

Friedbergstrasse

Reussport Tunnel

Spitalstrasse

TO TRAIN STATION

Brambergstrasse

Wettsteinpark

St.-Karli-Strasse

Luegetenstr.

Geissmattstr.

Mühlemattstr.

Diebold-Schilling-Str.

Old Town Wall

Reuss

Sentimattstrasse

Dammstrasse

16

Baselstrasse

Geissmatt-brücke

Museggstrasse

Kanonenstrasse

Château Gütsch

Reuss

St.-Karli-Quai

Löwengraben

Weinmarkt

5

Kornmarkt

Baselstrasse

Mühlenplatz

6

Kramg.

3 4

7

8

Pfistergasse

Reuss-brücke

Rathaus-Steg

Gütschwald

Sonnenberg Tunnel

Schutzenstr.

Bruchstr.

Hirschengraben

Münzgasse

Burgerstrasse

10

9

Hirschengraben

Hirschmattstr.

Gibraltarstrasse

Klosterstrasse

Pilatusstr.

Winkelriedstr.

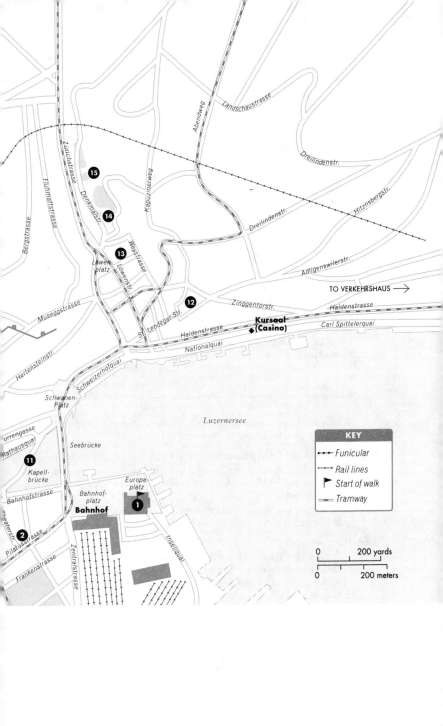

KEY

- Funicular
- Rail lines
- Start of walk
- Tramway

TO VERKEHRSHAUS →

Kursaal
(Casino)

Luzernersee

Bahnhof

Schwanen-Platz

Kapell-brücke

Löwen-platz

0   200 yards

0   200 meters

EATING WELL IN CENTRAL SWITZERLAND

Rooted in the German territory of Switzerland and the surrounding farmlands, central Switzerland's cuisine is down-home and hearty. In the mountains there are Alpine cheese specialties (*Aelpler Magrone*–pasta, butter, cheese, and fried onions); in the orchard country around Zug, there are such cherry specialties as *Zuger Kirschtorte*, a rich white cake soaked with cherry schnapps. Pears from the local orchards are dried, then spiced and poached in sweetened red *Dole* (wine).

Luzern takes pride in its *Kügelipaschtetli*, puff-pastry nests filled with tiny veal meatballs, chicken, or sweetbreads; mushrooms; cream sauce; and occasionally raisins.

But here the real *cuisine du marché*, based on fresh market ingredients, focuses on lake fish. Lake Luzern and its neighboring Zugersee (Lake Zug) produce an abundance of *Egli* (perch), *Hecht* (pike), *Forellen* (trout), and *Felchen* (whitefish); Zug produces its own exclusive *Röteln*, a red-bellied relative of the trout.

Restaurants—especially along waterfronts—trade heavily in these freshwater fish, whether they come from the region or not. Ask, and you may get an honest answer: the sources vary, but the style of preparation remains local. In Zug whole fish may be baked with sage, bay leaves, shallots, cloves, and plenty of white wine and butter; a Luzern tradition has them sautéed with tomatoes, mushrooms, and capers.

A museum focuses on rotating exhibits of new international artists. ⊠ *Europapl. 1* ☏ *041/2267070* ⊕ *www.kkl-luzern.ch.*

★ ⓮ **Löwendenkmal** (Lion Monument). The Swiss guards who died defending Louis XVI of France at the Tuileries in Paris in 1792 are commemorated here. Designed by Danish sculptor Berthel Thorwaldsen and carved out of a sheer sandstone face by Lucas Ahorn of Konstanz, this 19th-century wonder is a simple, stirring image of a dying lion. The Latin inscription translates, "To the bravery and fidelity of the Swiss." ⊠ *Denkmalstr.*

☾ ❼ **Natur-Museum** (Natural History Museum). Unusually modern display techniques bring nature lessons to life here. The museum focuses on local natural history, with panoramas of early Luzern settlers and live animals for children to meet. ⊠ *Kasernenpl. 6* ☏ *041/2285411* ⊕ *www. naturmuseum.ch* ⊠ *6 SF* ⊘ *Tues.–Sun. 10–5.*

❷ **Sammlung Rosengart** (Rosengart Collection). A father-and-daughter team amassed this amazing group of works by major late-19th- and 20th-century artists. Now housed in a former bank building, the collection, opened to the public in 2002, reveals their intensely personal approach; the Rosengarts acquired according to their own tastes instead of investment potential. Here you can see Miro's *Dancer,* Léger's *Contraste de formes,* and works by Cézanne, Monet, Matisse, Klee, and Chagall. There's an especially rich selection of Picassos; the artist painted the daughter, Angela Rosengart, five times. You can buy a combination ticket to see the Picasso drawings in the Am Rhyn-Haus. ⊠ *Pilatusstr. 10* ☎ *041/ 2201660* ⊕ *www.rosengart.ch* ✑ *15 SF, 18 SF for combination ticket to the Am Rhyn-Haus* ⊗ *Apr.–Oct., daily 10–6; Nov.–Mar., daily 11–5.*

❻ Spreuerbrücke (Chaff Bridge). This narrow covered bridge dates from 1408. The weathered wood structure's interior gables hold a series of eerie, well-preserved 17th-century paintings by Kaspar Meglinger of the *Dance of Death*. Medieval in style and inspiration, they chronicle the plague that devastated all of Europe in the 14th century. ⊠ *Between Geissmattbrücke and Reussbrücke, connecting Zeughaus Reuss-Steg and Mühlenpl.*

❺ Weinmarkt (Wine Market). What is now the loveliest of Luzern's several fountain squares drew visitors from all across Europe in the 15th to 17th centuries with its passion plays. Its Gothic central fountain depicts St. Mauritius (patron saint of warriors), and its surrounding buildings are flamboyantly frescoed in 16th-century style. ⊠ *Square just west of Kornmarkt, north of Metzgerainli.*

⓰ Zytturm (Time Tower). The clock in this fifth watchtower was made in Basel in 1385 and still keeps time. ⊠ *North of and parallel to Museggstr.*

Where to Stay & Eat

★ $$–$$$ ✕ **Galliker.** Step past the ancient facade and into a room roaring with local action. Brisk waitresses serve up the dishes *Mutti* (Mom) used to make: fresh *Kutteln* (tripe) in rich white wine sauce with cumin seeds; real *Kalbskopf* (chopped fresh veal head) served with heaps of green onions and warm vinaigrette; and authentic Luzerner Kügelipaschtetli. Occasional experiments in a modern mode—such as steak with wasabi sauce—prove that Peter Galliker's kitchen is no museum. Desserts may include raspberries with peppermint ice cream. ⊠ *Schützenstr. 1* ☎ *041/2401002* ⊟ *AE, DC, MC, V* ⊗ *Closed Sun., Mon., and mid-July–mid-Aug.*

$$–$$$ ✕ **Old Swiss House.** This popular establishment pleases crowds with its beautifully contrived collection of 17th-century antiques, its leaded glass, and an old-world style now pleasantly burnished by more than 130 years of service. The standing menu includes specialties from around the country: veal and *Rösti* (fried shredded potatoes), lake fish, and chocolate mousse. ⊠ *Löwenpl. 4* ☎ *041/4106171* ⊟ *AE, DC, MC, V* ⊗ *Closed Mon. and Feb.*

$–$$$ ✕ **Bodu.** A touch of Paris in the heart of Luzern. The darker, barlike entrance leads to the bright main room with a terrace overlooking the river. Advertising posters from the '20s and '30s look down on simple wooden tables and a green-and-yellow checkered floor. Sumptuous dishes like lake fish with eggplant and herb ravioli, or duck à l'orange, are based on fresh market ingredients. ⊠ *Kornmarkt 5* ☎ *041/4100177* ⊟ *AE, DC, MC, V.*

$–$$ ✕ **Pfistern.** One of the architectural focal points of the Old Town waterfront, this floridly decorated guild house—the guild's origins can be traced back to 1341—provides an authentic medieval setting in which to sample reasonably priced local fare. Lake fish and *pastetli* (meat pies with puff pastry) are worthy local options. Inside, it's woody and pub-like, if slightly down-at-the-heels, but in summer the small first-floor balcony or the riverside arcade may provide the best seat in town. ⊠ *Kornmarkt 4* ☎ *041/4103650* ▭ *AE, DC, MC, V.*

$–$$ ✕ **Rebstock/Hofstube.** Formerly a 16th-century tavern, this spot is now a meeting place for Luzern's art and media set. The lively brasserie hums with locals lunching by the bar, and the more formal old-style restaurant glows with wood and brass under a low-beamed parquetry ceiling. Fresh market ingredients are combined for modern, international fare, including rabbit and snails, as well as East Asian and vegetarian specialties. ⊠ *St. Leodegarpl. 3* ☎ *041/4103581* ▭ *AE, DC, MC, V.*

★ **$$$$**   ✕▣ **Palace Hotel.** This waterfront hotel drinks in the broadest possible lake views. Built in 1906, it has been brilliantly refurbished so that its classical look has a touch of postmodernism. Rooms are large enough for a game of badminton, and picture windows afford sweeping views of Mt. Pilatus. The hotel's elegance also seeps into its restaurant, Jasper ($$–$$$$). The contemporary cuisine—think veal with celery mousse and truffle sauce—is faultlessly prepared and formally presented. The bar has a clubby look—leather chairs, brass fixtures, and a long oak bar. ⊠ *Haldenstr. 10, CH-6002* ☎ *041/4161616* 🖷 *041/4161000* ⊕ *www.palace-luzern.com* ⇆ *178 rooms, 45 suites* ♻ *2 restaurants, in-room safes, in-room data ports, Wi-Fi, health club, massage, bar, laundry service, meeting rooms, parking (fee); no a/c* ▭ *AE, DC, MC, V.*

★ **$$$–$$$$**   ✕▣ **Des Balances.** Built in the 19th century on the site of two ancient guildhalls, this waterfront property is full of style. State-of-the-art tile baths, up-to-date pastel furnishings, and one of the best sites in the heart of the Old Town make this the slickest in its price class. Rotes Gatter ($$–$$$$), the hotel's chic restaurant, has a combination as desirable as it is rare: a soigné interior, shimmering river views, and a sophisticated menu including beef with seasonal local mushrooms and classics such as baby chicken with rosemary, risotto and green beans. The restaurant has a more casual, less expensive bistro area as well. ⊠ *Weinmarkt, CH-6000* ☎ *041/4182828* 🖷 *041/4182838* ⊕ *www.balances. ch* ⇆ *50 rooms, 7 suites* ♻ *Restaurant, in-room safes, minibars, meeting rooms; no a/c* ▭ *AE, DC, MC, V* ⦿ *BP.*

★ **$$$–$$$$**   ✕▣ **Wilden Mann.** The city's best-known hotel creates a gracious and authentic experience of old Luzern, with stone, beams, brass, and burnished wood everywhere. Even the street is atmospheric—across the way is a 16th-century pharmacy. The hotel's reputation extends to its restaurants: the Burgerstube ($–$$$$) is cozy with its dark beams and family crests, whereas vaulting and candlelight make the Liedertafel ($–$$$$) more formal. Both menus strike a fine balance between old-style local cooking and savvy French cuisine, with main dishes such as pike-perch with chanterelle mushroom ravioli and desserts like port wine cherries. ⊠ *Bahnhofstr. 30, CH-6003* ☎ *041/2101666* 🖷 *041/2101629* ⊕ *www. wilden-mann.ch* ⇆ *42 rooms, 8 suites* ♻ *2 restaurants, minibars, in-room data ports, Wi-Fi, library; no a/c* ▭ *AE, DC, MC, V* ⦿ *BP.*

$$$$ ▣ **National Hotel.** This monumental landmark, founded in 1870, was once home base to Cesar Ritz, the man who invented the world's first modern luxury hotel. The inner sanctums of this lodging trumpet a florid

---

splendor, down to the last cupola, crown molding, and Corinthian column. The hotel's mansarded facade stretches the length of two city blocks, dominating the lakeside promenade. The French provincial rooms have brass beds; the domed bar is decked with mahogany and aglitter with crystal; and the marble-columned breakfast hall may be the most splendid in Switzerland. ✉ *Haldenstr. 4, CH-6003* ☎ *041/4190909* 🖷 *041/4190910* ⊕ *www.national-luzern.ch* ⇘ *78 rooms, 10 suites* ⚲ *4 restaurants, café, in-room safes, minibars, in-room data ports, Wi-Fi, pool, health club, massage, piano bar, babysitting, parking (fee); no a/c* ☰ *AE, DC, MC, V.*

$$$$ 🏨 **Schweizerhof.** Built in the 1840s and expanded in the 1860s, this imposing structure has hosted Napoléon III, Leo Tolstoy, and Mark Twain—and Richard Wagner lived here while his lakefront home at Tribschen was being completed. The rooms all have sweeping views of the lake and mountains. Their period style has a modern twist: gilt mirrors, richly colored carpets, and marble-and-tile bathrooms cover the luxury bases, and Internet access and voice mail keep you connected. ✉ *Schweizerhofquai 3, CH-6002* ☎ *041/4100410* 🖷 *041/4102971* ⊕ *www.schweizerhof-luzern.ch* ⇘ *101 rooms, 6 suites* ⚲ *2 restaurants, café, in-room safes, minibars, in-room data ports, gym, bar, meeting rooms, free parking; no a/c* ☰ *AE, DC, MC, V.*

> **SNAPSHOT FROM HISTORY**
>
> The elegant promenade restaurant at the National Hotel is just steps away from where the Empress Elisabeth of Austria was stabbed to death in 1898.

$$$–$$$$ 🏨 **The Hotel.** Architect Jean Nouvel, who also designed Luzern's Kultur- und Kongresszentrum, focuses on ultrahip design; parquet floors are this lodging's only remaining old-world touch. Metal blocks act as cupboards, and mirrors, puffy chairs, and dark walls add to the look. But the highlight of each room is the enlarged movie still that covers the ceiling. Fellini, Wenders, and von Trier are represented, among others, and yes, the photograph is positioned so that you see it best while lying on your bed. An Asian/French fusion restaurant attracts locals as well as hotel guests. ✉ *Sempacherstr. 14, CH-6000* ☎ *041/2268686* 🖷 *041/2268690* ⊕ *www.the-hotel.ch* ⇘ *10 rooms, 15 suites* ⚲ *Restaurant, minibars, in-room data ports, Wi-Fi, bar* ☰ *AE, DC, MC, V.*

$$$–$$$$ 🏨 **Montana.** This 1910 palace glows with beeswaxed beauty, its luxurious original woodwork, parquet, and terrazzo are all in superb condition. The public rooms flank the ground floor's south side and on a clear day offer a magnificent view of the lake and the mountains. The guest rooms are made up in art deco style, with bold patterns and funky furniture. Those in back overlook a hillside, while the front doubles (slightly costlier) have balconies overlooking the city and lake. The building is perched on a slope above town, accessible by funicular from the lakeshore Haldenstrasse or by car. ✉ *Adligenswilerstr. 22, CH-6002* ☎ *041/4190000* 🖷 *041/4190001* ⊕ *www.hotel-montana.ch* ⇘ *55 rooms, 10 suites* ⚲ *Restaurant, in-room safes, minibars, bar, free parking; no a/c* ☰ *AE, DC, MC, V* ⑪ *BP.*

$$$ ⊞ **Hofgarten.** This gracious 12th-century house has been artfully modernized with an eclectic mix of colors and themes. One room contains a 5-foot-tall antique stove (still operable), and another resembles the interior of a clipper ship. The Hofgarten has one of Luzern's best vegetarian restaurants, with dishes that could satisfy even a meat lover. ⊠ *Stadthofdstr. 14, CH-6006* ☎ *041/4108888* ⊟ *041/4108333* ⊕ *www. hofgarten.ch* ⟿ *17 rooms, 1 suite* ⚐ *Restaurant, parking (fee); no a/c* ⊟ *AE, DC, MC, V* ⟲❘ *BP.*

$$$ ⊞ **Krone.** Spotless and modern, this hotel softens its edges with pastel linens and walls; look in the recessed niche of one of the interior walls for a stone shrine retained from the original structure. The rooms facing the Weinmarkt have high ceilings and tall windows that let in lots of light. Rooms to the back have no direct sun but are still bright and a little larger. The restaurant has a no-alcohol policy. ⊠ *Weinmarkt 12, CH-6004* ☎ *041/4194400* ⊟ *041/4194490* ⊕ *www.krone-luzern.ch* ⟿ *25 rooms* ⚐ *Restaurant, café, minibars; no a/c* ⊟ *AE, DC, MC, V* ⟲❘ *BP.*

$$ ⊞ **Zum Weissen Kreuz.** This completely modernized historic hotel in the bustling heart of the Old Town has a tongue-in-cheek combination of sleek modern lines with gilded frames and fat cherubs. The rooms are small but well-designed, with hardwood floors and retro '60s furnishings. The entire hotel, including the popular pizzeria with its wood-burning pizza oven, is no-smoking. ⊠ *Furrerg. 19, CH-6004* ☎ *041/4188220* ⊟ *041/4188230* ⊕ *www.hotel-wkreuz.ch* ⟿ *21 rooms, 1 suite* ⚐ *Restaurant, fans, minibars, in-room DVD, Wi-Fi, Internet room; no a/c, no smoking* ⊟ *AE, DC, MC, V.*

$–$$ ⊞ **Löwengraben.** For something completely different, spend a night in jail—which this hotel was until several years ago. Bright paint, comfortably simple beds, modular bathroom facilities, and the odd antique furnishing take the blues out of the jailhouse and replace it with funky charm. Although the rooms are small, the fun atmosphere that radiates from the bars and restaurants downstairs adds to the draw. ⊠ *Löwengraben 18, CH-6004* ☎ *041/4107830* ⊟ *041/4107832* ⊕ *www.jailhotel.ch* ⟿ *51 rooms, 4 suites* ⚐ *2 restaurants, 2 bars, nightclub, no-smoking rooms; no a/c, no room TVs* ⊟ *AE, MC, V* ⟲❘ *BP.*

$–$$ ⊞ **Schlüssel.** This spare, no-nonsense lodging on the Franziskanerplatz attracts young bargain hunters. It's a pleasant combination of tidy modern touches (quarry tile, white paint) and antiquity: you can have breakfast or a simple hot meal in a low, cross-vaulted "crypt" and admire the fine old beams in the lobby. Ask for a room on one of the two floors renovated in 2006. Two of the old rooms overlook the square's Franciscan church (be prepared for morning church bells). ⊠ *Franziskanerpl. 12, CH-6003* ☎ *041/2101061* ⊟ *041/2101021* ⊕ *www.luzern-schluessel. ch* ⟿ *10 rooms* ⚐ *Restaurant, WI-Fi; no a/c* ⊟ *MC, V.*

★ ¢–$ ⊞ **Tourist.** Despite its collegiate atmosphere, this cheery dormlike spot is anything but a backpackers' flophouse. It has a terrific setting on the Reuss around the corner from the Old Town. Its spare, modern architecture is brightened with fresh, trendy colors and framed prints, and rooms that don't have a river view face the quiet backyard instead. The staff is young and helpful, and the coed four-bed dorms (sex-segregated in high season) draw sociable travelers with their rock-bottom prices.

There are also seven private-bath doubles. Shared baths are well maintained. ⊠ *St. Karli Quai 12, CH-6004* ☎ *041/4102474* 🖷 *041/4108414* ⊕ *www.touristhotel.ch* ↪ *11 rooms, 1 suite* ⚓ *Bar, laundry facilities, Internet; no a/c, no room phones, no smoking* ⊟ *AE, DC, MC, V.*

Nightlife & the Arts

For information on goings-on around town, go to the tourist office for a copy of the German/English *Luzern City Guide,* published quarterly by the city. Get it stamped by your hotel for discounts on museums, public transit, and special events.

Nightlife

BARS & LOUNGES In the Hotel Montana, **Louis Bar** (⊠ Adligenwilerstr. 22 ☎ 041/4190000) offers live jazz in the style of Louis Armstrong. While you're there, sip one of the 80 Scotch whiskies behind the bar. The beautiful **Meridiani** bar (⊠ Klosterstr. 12 ☎ 041/2404344) pours everything from coffee to cognac. Students and young professionals mix and mingle at **Oops** (⊠ Zentralstr. 10 ☎ 041/2102255). If you need a jolt, choose from 60 different kinds of coffee.

Opus (⊠ Bahnhofstr. 16 ☎ 041/2264141) specializes in fine wines, many served by the glass. **P1** (⊠ Pilatusstr. 1 ☎ 041/2201315) is a drinks-and-dancing penthouse lounge with a fabulous view.

CASINO The most sophisticated nightlife in Luzern is found in the **Grand Casino Luzern** (⊠ Haldenstr. 6 ☎ 041/4185656 ⊕ www.grandcasinoluzern. ch), an early-20th-century building on the lake's northern shore near the grand hotels. You can play *boule* (a type of roulette) in the Gambling Room; dance in the Club; watch the cabaret in the Casineum; or have a meal in Olivio, a Mediterranean restaurant with views of the mountains and the lake.

The Arts

FILM Movie theaters, concentrated on the south bank along Pilatusstrasse and Bahnhofstrasse, usually screen films in their original language. You can also catch a show in the Bourbaki-Panorama development.

FOLKLORE The *Night Boat* (☎ 041/3194978) sails from the Landungsbrücke—a dock right on the Bahnhofplatz-Europlatz—every evening from May through September. This pleasant lake cruise has meals, drinks, and a folklore show. Performances at the **Stadtkeller** (⊠ Sternenpl. 3 ☎ 041/4104733) come with yodelers, dirndled dancers, and more.

MUSIC Luzern, the cultural hub of central Switzerland, hosts the annual **Lucerne Festival** (⊠ Hirschmattstr. 13 ☎ 041/2264480) from mid-August to mid-September in the Kultur- und Kongresszentrum. Outstanding performers come from all over the world; past guests have included mezzo-soprano Cecilia Bartoli and pianist András Schiff. Performing at the Kultur- und Kongresszentrum, the **Luzerner Symphonieorchester** (⊠ Europapl. ☎ 041/2103060 ⊕ www.lucernefestival.ch), the local orchestra in residence, has a season that runs from October through June.

THEATER The **Luzerner Theater** (⊠ Theaterstr. 2 ☎ 041/2281414 ⊕ www.luzerner-theater.ch), directly on the waterfront on the Bahnhof side of town, is home to Luzern's principal theater group, which stages plays in German and operas in their original language.

Sports & the Outdoors

Bicycling
The standard Swiss practice of renting bicycles from the **train station** (⊠ Bahnhofpl. ☎ 051/2273261) comes in handy here, as the lake-level terrain offers smooth riding.

Boating
Pedal-, motor-, and sailboats are available in Luzern through **Marina Charter** (⊠ Alpenquai 13 ☎ 041/3607944). **SNG Luzern** (⊠ Alpenquai 11 ☎ 041/3680808), open weekdays only, offers fair-weather boat rentals from April to October and year-round hour-long boat tours for 25 SF. **Werft Herzog AG** (⊠ Nationalquai ☎ 041/4104333) specializes in motorboats for up to 10 passengers.

Swimming
At the **Lido** (⊠ Lidostr. ☎ 041/3703806), past the casino and near the Verkehrshaus, you can swim in Lake Luzern from May to September, daily from 9 to 8.

Water Sports
Contact **Dobler und Ingold** (⊠ Alpenquai 13 ☎ 041/3608244) to rent windsurfing equipment. **Waterfun** (⊠ Alpenquai/Tribschen dock ☎ 079/4177676) offers wakeboarding and waterskiing.

Shopping

The best shopping in the region is concentrated in Luzern, which, although it no longer produces embroidery or lace, still offers a wide variety of Swiss handicrafts as well as the luxury goods appropriate to its high profile. The pedestrian zone along Hertensteinstrasse is packed with boutiques and department stores. In summer most shops stay open until 9 PM; on Sunday morning they open after 11 AM. On Thursday night year-round, shops stay open until 9.

Department Stores
The main department store in town is **Globus** (⊠ Pilatusstr. 4 ☎ 041/2270707); it's a good place to hunt for souvenirs. **Migros** (⊠ Hertensteinstr. 9 ☎ 041/4170740) specializes in groceries and inexpensive items.

Embroidery
The main producer of Swiss embroidery is **Sturzenegger** (⊠ Buobenmatt 2 ☎ 041/4101958) of St. Gallen, which sells its own machine-made lace and embroidered goods as well as Hanro and Calida underwear. The store also stocks a conservative line of women's dresses and blouses.

Handicrafts & Gifts
Aux Arts du Feu (⊠ Schweizerhofquai 2 ☎ 041/4101401) offers high-end china and crystal. **Bookbinders Design** (⊠ Hertensteinstr. 3 ☎ 041/4109506), an upscale stationer, stocks precision writing instruments and brightly colored, handmade, recycled-paper products. **Schmid-Linder**

(⊠ Denkmalstr. 9 ☎ 041/4104346) carries an extensive line of Swiss embroidery and linen as well as cuckoo clocks, cowbells, and a large stock of wood carvings from Brienz, in the Berner Oberland.

Markets
From May to October, a **Flohmärt,** or flea market, takes place every Saturday from 8 to 4 at Untere Burgerstrasse, not far from the Franziskanerkirche. For locally made crafts, there's a **Handwerksmarkt** on the Weinmarkt. It takes place on the first Saturday of every month from April through December.

Watches
Competition is fierce, and the two enormous patriarchs of the watch business advertise heavily and offer inexpensive souvenirs to lure shoppers into their luxurious showrooms. **Bucherer** (⊠ Schwanenpl. 5 ☎ 041/3697700) represents Piaget and Rolex. **Gübelin** (⊠ Schweizerhofquai 1 ☎ 041/4105142) is the exclusive source for Audemars Piguet, Patek Philippe, and its own house brand.

Women's Clothing
The czarina of women's fashion in Luzern is Christina De Boer, who runs a group of designer boutiques. **Christina De Boer** (⊠ Werchlaubeg. 14 ☎ 041/4106239) is an exclusive boutique with cashmere fashions and high-end labels such as Jil Sander and Rena Lange. **Rive Gauche** (⊠ Pilatusstr. 14 ☎ 041/2108916) has a wide variety of mid-range labels such as Gabriele Seba.

LUZERN ENVIRONS

Since Luzern doesn't have the sprawling suburbs associated with most cities, bucolic landscapes are just a short day trip away. Craggy mountaintops, lush hills dotted with grazing cows, and peaceful lakeside villages are easily reached by boat, train, or car.

Mt. Pilatus

⑰ **To & From:** *If you don't have time for the 4-hour hike, there are two ways to get to the top of Mt. Pilatus (www.pilatus.ch): from Luzern by bus to Krienz and from there to the summit by cable car (74 SF roundtrip) and back, or by returning down the other side by cogwheel train to Alpnachstad and getting on the boat back to Luzern (81.60 SF roundtrip). Mt. Pilatus is 10 km (6 mi) southwest of Luzern.*

Unlike Queen Victoria, who rode to the summit of this 6,953-foot mountain by mule in 1868, you can travel there and back by cable car for a hefty 74 SF from Luzern.

Take a bus from the train station in Luzern to the suburb of Kriens, where you catch a tiny, four-seat cable car that flies silently up to Fräkmüntegg (4,600 feet); then change to the 40-seat cable car that sails through open air up the rock cliff to the summit station (5,560 feet). From here a 10-minute walk takes you to the **Esel,** at the center of Pilatus's multiple peaks, where views unfold over the Alps and the sprawling, crooked Lake Luzern.

A pleasant variation for the return trip to Luzern from Mt. Pilatus involves riding a steep cogwheel train, often down gradients inclined nearly 48%, through four tunnels that pierce sheer rock, to Alpnachstad. From there take the train or the ferry, which leaves from the jetty across from the train station, back to Luzern, all for 81.60 SF. To go on to Engelberg, get off the Luzern-bound train at Hergiswil, where you can cross the track and climb aboard the small, private Stans-Engelberg train that heads up the Engelbergertal (Engelberg Valley).

BEHIND THE NAME
Mt. Pilatus was named either from the Latin *pileatus* (wearing a cap), to refer to its frequent cloud covering, or, more colorfully, for the ghost of Pontius Pilate, who supposedly haunts the summit. (His body, it was said, was brought here by the devil.) For centuries it was forbidden to climb the mountain and enrage the ghost, who was said to unleash deadly storms.

Stans

18 *10 km (6 mi) southeast of Mt. Pilatus, 10 km (6 mi) south of Luzern.*

In the heart of lush valley terrain and mossy meadows, Stans is an old village whose appealing Old Town center is dotted with the deep-roof houses typical of central Switzerland. This was the home of the beloved Heinrich Pestalozzi, the father of modern education. When the French army invaded the village in 1798, slaughtering nearly 2,000 citizens, it was Pestalozzi who gathered the orphaned children into a school, where he applied his progressive theories in the budding science of psychology to the practice of education. Instead of rote memorization and harsh discipline, Pestalozzi's teaching methods emphasized concrete examples (using plant specimens to teach botany, for example) and moral as well as intellectual development—quite a liberal education. He also championed the idea of fostering a child's individuality.

The bell tower of the **Pfarrkirche St. Peter und St. Paul** (Church of Sts. Peter and Paul) is in Italian Romanesque style with increasing numbers of arched windows as it rises. The incongruous steeple was added in the 16th century. ⊠ *Knirig. 1.*

On the town square stands a 19th-century **monument to Arnold von Winkelried,** a native of Stans who martyred himself to lead the Swiss Confederates to victory over the Austrians at the battle of Sempach in 1386. The Austrians, armed with long spears, formed a Roman square so that the Swiss, wielding axes and halberds, couldn't get in close enough to do any damage. Shouting, "Forward, confederates, I will open a path!" von Winkelried threw himself on the spears, clasping as many of them as he could to his breast—creating an opening for his comrades. ⊠ *Knirig., facing the Pfarrkirche St. Peter und St. Paul.*

EN ROUTE A two-part journey on a nostalgic 1893 funicular and an ultramodern cable car takes you to the **Stanserhorn** (6,200 feet), from whose peak you can see the Titlis, the highest point in central Switzerland. You can also

Watch Your Step!

CLOSE UP

Dozens of people are injured or even killed while hiking in the Alps, many of them travelers who misjudge the steep inclines and unsteady ground. Although all of the trails are regularly maintained and most high-level walkways have railings, there are hazards every hiker should keep in mind. For example, slippery conditions in the loose gravel or on patches of grass after it rains or snows can often lead to a fall.

The best way to ward off injury is to bring a good pair of hiking boots, a walking stick, and to maintain a slow and careful pace. Pay attention to weather conditions: summer storms can develop suddenly. These days locals take along a cell phone just in case; reception is good in almost every corner of the country.

5

see the Jungfrau. ⊠ *Stans* ☎ *041/6188040* ▣ *52 SF round-trip* ⊘ *Apr.–Nov., daily 8:30–4:30.*

Engelberg

19 **To & From:** *Besides by car, the only way to Engelberg is the train from Luzern that leaves every hour (16.20 SF one-way) and also stops in Stans. Engelberg is 19 km (12 mi) south of Stans, 34 km (21 mi) south of Luzern.*

At the top of the village of Obermatt, Engelberg (3,280 feet) is a popular resort for skiers from nearby Zürich, but its slopes are limited in comparison with those of St. Moritz, Wengen, and Zermatt. From Luzern, the resort is easily reached on an hourly train. Engelberg clusters at the foot of its Benedictine **Kloster** (monastery), founded in 1120; inside there's one of the largest organs in the country. Until the French invaded in 1798, massacring thousands, this monastery ruled the valley. The monastery grounds are open to the public daily and include a cheese shop, a small vegetable garden, and a florist. ☎ *041/6396161* ▣ *6 SF* ⊘ *Grounds daily, 8–8; guided tours of Kloster in German with English information sheet: Mid-Jan.–Apr. and July–mid-Oct., Wed.–Sat. 10 and 4.*

OFF THE
BEATEN
PATH

MOUNT TITLIS – This is perhaps the most impressive of the many rocky peaks that surround the Obermatt's long, wide bowl. Thanks to a sophisticated transportation system that benefits skiers, hikers, climbers, and sightseers alike, it's possible to ride a small cable car up to the tiny mountain lake (and famous ski area) called Trübsee (5,904 feet). From there change and ascend to Stand to catch the Rotair cable car, which rotates to give 360-degree panoramas on its way up to the summit station on the Titlis. There's an ice grotto (serving drinks from a solid-ice bar) and a restaurant whose views take in the Jura Mountains, the Graubünden and Bernese Alps, and what from this perspective looks like a puny Pilatus. ⊠ *Engelberg* ☎ *041/6395050* ▣ *79 SF round-trip.*

Skiing

At the base of the 9,906-foot-high Titlis, **Engelberg** has two funicular railways, seven cable cars, 13 lifts, 45 km (28 mi) of downhill runs, 34 km (21 mi) of cross-country trails, 3½ km (2 mi) of toboggan runs, and ice-skating. About half the runs are intermediate level, and there are plenty of easy slopes as well; advanced skiers will have relatively slim pickings. A **ski school** (☎ 041/6395454) and **snowboard school** (☎ 041/6395455) are in the **Tourist Center** (☎ 041/6397777).

Where to Stay & Eat

★ **$–$$** ✕ **Bierlialp.** The delicious pizzas that come from this trattoria's stone oven are 18-inch extravaganzas—and that's a single serving. The modern decor is softened by warm candlelight and an even warmer welcome. For a more elaborate entrée, try the black tagliatelle with St. Peter's fish, or homemade ravioli with porcini mushrooms. ⊠ *Dorfstr. 21* ☎ *041/ 6371717* ⊟ *AE, MC, V.*

★ **$–$$** ✕ **Engelberg.** Rosmarie and Robert Infanger serve haute cuisine at prices that are refreshingly sane; favorites include pork steak with mushrooms in red wine and chateaubriand. Linen tablecloths and candlelight mellow the traditional post-and-beam interior. ⊠ *Dorfstr. 14* ☎ *041/ 6397979* ⊕ *www.hotel-engelberg.ch* ⊟ *AE, MC, V.*

★ **$** ✕🏠 **Alpenclub.** This is the real McCoy: an old-fashioned chalet, built in 1856, with every square inch pine paneled and dark timbered. It's got all the requisites, such as down-quilted beds, a glowing fondue Stübli, and a sunny terrace looking out on snowy peaks. It's lively, casual, and, above all, cheap. It draws mobs of young skiers to its disco bar and pizzeria, and families to its firelit restaurant (all serve à la carte only). Though it stands slightly beyond the urbanized center, it's not for quiet retreats, at least in ski season. ⊠ *Dorfstr. 5, CH-6390* ☎ *041/6371243* 🖷 *041/ 6370337* ⊕ *www.alpenclub.ch* ⇢ *9 rooms* ♨ *Restaurant, pizzeria, Stübli, bar; no a/c* ⊟ *AE, DC, MC, V* ⊙ *Closed May and June.*

$–$$$ 🏠 **Schweizerhof.** Though the exterior suggests a once–grande dame, this lovely old fin de siècle structure has been attentively remodeled inside to combine a fresh, light, knotty-pine look with plush Edwardian comforts. Guest rooms are modern and airy. Bay-window corner doubles are worth asking for. Four family suites with separate bed- and living rooms make this a perfect option for families and small groups. ⊠ *Dorfstr. 42, CH-6390* ☎ *041/6371105* 🖷 *041/6374147* ⊕ *www. schweizerhof-engelberg.ch* ⇢ *30 rooms, 10 suites* ♨ *Restaurant, in-room safes, in-room data ports, Wi-Fi, gym, sauna, steam room; no a/c* ⊟ *AE, DC, MC, V* ¶⦿ *BP.*

Sports & the Outdoors

MOUNTAIN BIKING Mountain biking is very popular here; there's a well-traveled path from the Jochpass to the Trübsee. Free bike maps are available at the tourist office. You can rent bikes from **Bike 'n' Roll** (⊠ Dorfstr. 31 ☎ 041/ 6380255 ⊕ www.bikenroll.ch).

TENNIS The **Sporting Park Engelberg** (⊠ Engelbergstr. 11 ☎ 041/6396000 ⊕ www.sportingpark.ch) has two indoor courts and six outdoor courts; the shop also rents equipment.

WILLIAM TELL COUNTRY

Perhaps it was only destiny that Switzerland was born right here. Take one look at the spectacular mix of snowy peaks, sapphire lakes, and picturesque meadows surrounding the Urnersee—the southern leg of Lake Luzern—and you'll realize this very beauty may have inspired the pack signed in 1291 between the clans of Schwyz, Unterwalden, and Uri. This Oath of Eternal Alliance announced the creation of a new realm—the world's first democracy. Believe it or not, this is not the only iconic historical event in this region. Although now considered by some to be mere myth, this is also the hallowed ground where Wilhelm Tell was born and played out the legend that has thrilled millions to this day. Every year, thousands of Swiss make a pilgrimage here, taking a lake steamer from Luzern all the way down to the Urnersee (or driving the same route along the northern lakefront highway to Brunnen) to find their way to the Rütli Meadow—the birthplace of Switzerland—and to then trace the story of Tell in neighboring lakeside villages. If you want "go high," you can opt to ascend Rigi Kulm, the summit of Mt. Rigi, by train or cable car.

If you choose to take a lake cruise, depart at any convenient time (schedules are available at the ticket and tourist offices) from the main docks by the train station; the boat will be marked for Flüelen. First-class seats are on top; each level has a restaurant-café. The exterior seats are only slightly sheltered; if you want to sit inside, you may feel obligated to order a drink. Take advantage of the boat's many stops—you can get on and off at will.

Bürgenstock

⓴ To & From: *Trains depart from Luzern 10 times a day (45 min); you then transfer to a cog railway for a 5-minute ride up to Bürgenstock. Lake steamers, departing from Luzern, shorten the trip to 30 minutes. Bürgenstock is 20 km (13 mi) southeast of Luzern.*

The rich have always headed to Lake Luzern, thanks, in good part, to the famous Bürgenstock hotel resort. This haute monde hideaway, perched atop its own Alp, lured many celebs to these parts—Audrey Hepburn, Sophia Loren, Sean Connery, and Shirley MacLaine once colonized the chalets around here. Now partly under renovation, the hotel takes a back seat to the area's wonderful hiking. Most Flüelen-bound boats go to the base of the Bürgenstock, where visitors can take a funicular to the isolated resort at the top of a ridge. Though the plateau isn't terribly high—only 1,500 feet—it rises dramatically above the water and offers striking views over the region. Bürgenstock also can be approached by car, up a steep, sometimes dangerous road, from Stansstad, on the road between Luzern and Stansand—but watch out: it was designed with so many switchbacks to prevent playboys speeding their Ferraris.

Where to Stay

$$$–$$$$
Fodor's Choice
★

Bürgenstock Hotels & Resort. Where only an eagle's nest should be, a quartet of hotels—dating from 1873, 1904, 1991, and 2007—take luxury to new heights, literally. Perched 1,600 feet over Lake Luzern, this

Babylonian complex was masterminded by the famous Frey family. Now comes news that a large part of the complex will be closed until 2009 for renovation. Hopefully, they will not touch the fin de siècle splendor: 19th-century frescoes, Art Nouveau wickerwork chairs, stained-glass windows, and the 14th-century late-Gothic chapel. And few can complain about the latest and greatest in facilities—they blasted out hillsides to accommodate pools and a stunning golf course. Long host to kings, queens, and celebs like Walt Disney and Charlie Chaplin, the hotel still welcomes V.I.P.s (who often arrive on the heli-pad). Guest rooms range from small to spacious; all are understated, but many will be getting a new face-lift in the years ahead. The full-service health club, with such spa services as aromatherapy and massage, is a great place to get pampered. Bring along your hiking boots, as the hotel has a restaurant perched on top of the nearby Hammetschwand Peak, along with one down by the lake. The food is nouvelle and slimming but, of course, you'll need chubby wallets. ⊠ *Bürgenstock, CH-6363* ☎ *041/6129010* 🖷 *041/6129011* ⊕ *www.buergenstock-hotels.ch* ➟ *200 rooms, 75 suites* 🖧 *5 restaurants, in-room safes, minibars, in-room data ports, 9-hole golf course, tennis courts, 2 pools (1 indoor), lake, fitness classes, gym, hair salon, massage, bicycles, 2 bars, shop, laundry service, Internet, business services, convention center, meeting rooms, helipad; no a/c* ▭ *AE, DC, MC, V* ⫶◎⫶ *BP.*

Weggis

★ ❷ **To & From:** *Boats come from Luzern and Flüelen every 1 to 1 ½ hours during daylight hours. A bus between the two towns goes every hour, a boat every 1 to 1 ½ hours during daylight hours (5 SF one-way). Weggis has a cable car up to the top of the Rigi (www.rigi.ch), while Vitznau has a cog-wheel train (each ca. once per hour, 35 SF one-way). Weggis is 25 km (15 mi) northeast and across the lake from Bürgenstock, 20 km (12 mi) northeast of Luzern.*

With a pretty waterfront park and promenade, Weggis is a summer resort town known for its mild, almost subtropical climate. It's far from the highway and accessible only by the secondary road, so you get a pleasant sense of isolation. The famed **Mt. Rigi** (1,798 meters [5,900 feet]) is just a cable-car ride away from Weggis: follow signs for the Rigibahn, a station high above the resort (a 15-minute walk). From here you can ride a large cable car to **Rigi-Kaltbad**, a small resort on a spectacular plateau; walk across to the electric rack-and-pinion railway station and ride the steep tracks of the Vitznau–Rigi line to the summit of the mountain. Take an elevator to the **Rigi-Kulm** hotel to enjoy the views indoors or walk to the crest (45 minutes) to see as far as the Black Forest in one direction and Mt. Säntis in the other. Or consider climbing to the top, staying in the hotel, and getting up early to see the sun rise over the Alps—a view that astounded both Victor Hugo and Mark Twain. With Lake Luzern on one side and Lake Zug on the other, Mt. Rigi can seem like an island.

You have the option of returning to Luzern from Weggis by taking a different railway down, from Rigi to Arth-Goldau; the two lines were built by competing companies in the 1870s in a race to reach the top and capture the lion's share of the tourist business. The line rising out of the lakefront resort of Vitznau won, but the Arth-Goldau line gets plenty of business, as its base terminal lies on the mainstream St. Gotthard route. The round-trip fare from Vitznau or Arth-Goldau to Rigi-Kulm is 58 SF.

Skiing
Mt. Rigi, at 5,900 feet, has two funicular railways, three cable cars, seven lifts, 30 km (19 mi) of downhill runs, 14 km (9 mi) of cross-country trails, 14 km (9 mi) of ski-hiking trails, and curling.

Where to Stay & Eat

$$–$$$ ✕ **Renggli's.** This very popular restaurant is ideally located on the waterfront, with its own private dock and a terrace overlooking the lake. The focus is on local lake fish specialties and seafood, accompanied by market-fresh side dishes. If you're a meat eater, the schnitzel or tournedos are also excellent. ⊠ *Seestr. 21* ☎ *041/3900170* ▭ *AE, DC, MC, V* ☉ *Closed Wed. in July and Aug.*

$$$–$$$$ 🏨 **Albana.** This lush Jugendstil hotel has fabulous lake and mountain views. The grand public areas are its best features, with 15-foot ceilings—one painted with cherubs and clouds and trimmed in gold leaf. A pair of antique Venetian chandeliers glistens over the restored period furniture. The dusty-pink-and-white rooms, however, have modern furniture; the white-tile bathrooms have spacious tubs. Eight rooms have the original parquet floors—these are the ones to ask for. The restaurant's menu is imaginative; try the scallop carpaccio, or beef fillet with horseradish root in a nest of potatoes. ⊠ *Luzernerstr. 26, CH-6353* ☎ *041/3902141* 🖨 *041/3902959* ⊕ *www.albana-weggis.ch* ⇗ *57 rooms* ⚹ *Restaurant, in-room safes, sauna, steam room, bar, meeting rooms; no a/c* ▭ *AE, DC, MC, V* ⅼⓄⅼ *BP.*

★ **$$$–$$$$** 🏨 **Beau-Rivage.** Built in 1908 but much modernized, this attractive business-class resort concentrates its comforts on a small but luxurious waterfront site, with a restaurant above the manicured lawn, a small swimming pool with mountain views, and lounge chairs at the lake's edge. Its rooms glow with rosy wood, brass, and pastel fabrics. It's at the center of town, near the boat landing. ⊠ *Gotthardstr. 6, CH-6353* ☎ *041/3927900* 🖨 *041/3901981* ⊕ *www.beaurivage-weggis.ch* ⇗ *40 rooms* ⚹ *Restaurant, in-room safes, minibars, Wi-Fi, pool, hot tub, steam room, bar, meeting rooms; no a/c* ▭ *AE, DC, MC, V* ☉ *Closed Nov.–Mar.* ⅼⓄⅼ *BP.*

$–$$ 🏨 **Rigi-Kulm.** This high-altitude hotel is perfect for mountaintop stopovers; built in 1950 and rather generic, it still has the air of a rugged but genteel lodge. Southern rooms have rustic decor and great views. (Be warned, however: if it's raining during your stay, the views disappear.) A short walk from the summit, at 5,900 feet, it's accessible by cable car from Weggis to Rigi-Kaltbad, then by cogwheel rail; or by cogwheel from Vitznau or Arth-Goldau. Or you can climb up from Weggis, allowing either three hours

BICYCLING & TENNIS

The tourist office (☎ 041/3901155) at Weggis rents bicycles and has information about public tennis courts.

or, as Mark Twain required, three days, depending on your penchant for resting. ⊠ *Rigi Kulm CH-6410* ☎ *041/8550303* 🖷 *041/8550055* ⊕ *www.rigikulm.ch* 🗗 *40 rooms* ⚴ *Restaurant, café; no a/c, no room TVs* ☱ *AE, DC, MC, V* |O| *BP.*

Vitznau

🔞 *4 km (2½ mi) southeast of Weggis, 26 km (16 mi) east of Luzern.*

For a quintessentially scenic, quiet spot, stop over in Vitznau, a tiny waterfront resort that competes with Weggis in balmy weather. Small as this village may be, it looms large on the tourist radar. Not only is Vitznau address to the magnificently palatial Park Hotel (opened 1902), it is home to Switzerland's first-ever cog-railway (opened May 21, 1871); the Mühlefluh fortress (the first artillery fortress in the country); the shipyards where Lake Luzern's fabled paddleboat steamers were initially built; and is today the best place to see the world's largest Swiss flag, proudly displayed on a face of Mt. Rigi overlooking Vitznau.

Where to Stay

★ $$$$ 🏨 **Park Hotel.** Set in a fairy-tale lakefront palace, this isolated but lavish retreat dominates the tiny lakefront village of Vitznau. Constructed in 1902 and enlarged in 1985, it's a vaulted and beamed Edwardian dream in impeccable modern form. Even the corridors are grand, with massive oak triple doors and Persian runners stretching over quarry tile. Rooms are decorated in timeless pastels, and lakefront rooms command dreamy Alpine views. The back rooms overlook the slopes of the Rigi, dotted with grazing cows. With the hotel's restaurants—the Panorama is a white-on-white chandeliered extravaganza—and all the activities available, you could easily find yourself not wanting to budge. ⊠ *Kantonstr., CH-6354* ☎ *041/3996060* 🖷 *041/3996070* ⊕ *www.parkhotel-vitznau. ch* 🗗 *71 rooms, 32 suites* ⚴ *2 restaurants, café, in-room safes, Wi-Fi, 2 tennis courts, indoor-outdoor pool, health club, sauna, steam room, solarium, beach, dock, waterskiing, bicycles, bar, playground, Internet room, meeting rooms; no a/c* ☱ *AE, DC, MC, V* ☉ *Closed Nov.–mid-Apr.* |O| *BP.*

$–$$ 🏨 **Rigi.** Less than a third of the price of the grandiose Park Hotel, this solid lodging has modernized interiors and a welcoming atmosphere in its public areas. A dozen rooms have balconies with lake views; four have small kitchenettes. The hotel is one block from the boat landing and close to the Rigibahn (which means there's some traffic noise during the day). Both the restaurant and the Stübli serve good, simple fish dishes, and there's a pleasant garden terrace. ⊠ *Seestr., CH-6354* ☎ *041/ 3972121* 🖷 *041/3971825* ⊕ *www.rigi-vitznau.ch* 🗗 *36 rooms* ⚴ *Restaurant, Stübli, some kitchenettes, some minibars; no a/c* ☱ *AE, DC, MC, V* |O| *BP.*

Sports & the Outdoors

SWIMMING   Because of a quirk of climate, Vitznau's bay is naturally warmer than Luzern's Lido, making this a great place to swim.

TENNIS   The closest tennis courts are in nearby Weggis, where the **tourist office** (☎ 041/3901155) manages the public courts.

From Vitznau a boat tour will take you across Lake Luzern to **Becken-ried**, from which a cable car leads up to Klewenalp (5,250 feet), a small resort overlooking the lake. The area is excellent for hiking, with breath-takingly panoramic views of the lake and mountains on clear days. If you're driving, you could also follow the north shore to Gersau, a tiny lake resort that was an independent republic—the world's smallest—from 1332 to 1798. From Gersau the boat snakes around the magnif-icently beautiful peninsula of the Seelisberg; the 1980 completion of a 9¼-km (6-mi) tunnel through the peninsula, south of the lake, opened the way for even swifter north–south travel between Luzern and points north and the St. Gotthard route and points south.

Rütli Meadow

23 14 km (8 mi) southeast of Vitznau, 15 km (10 mi) northwest of Altdorf
Fodor'sChoice on Urnersee, 35 km (22 mi) southeast of Luzern. The lake steamers from
★ Luzern make frequent stops here.

At the south end of Lake Luzern, past the gorgeously scenic Seelisberg Peninsula, the narrow, majestic Urnersee nestles some of the most his-toric—or, at least, romantic—landmarks in the region. The Schillerstein, on the right as you cruise past the peninsula, is a spectacular natural rock obelisk extending nearly 85 feet up out of the lake onto which has been carved a gigantic dedication: *to the author of wilhelm tell, friedrich von schiller. 1859.* About 10 minutes beyond the rock, the lake steamer pulls up at the quaint, 19th-century landing dock for perhaps the most historically significant site in central Switzerland: the Rütli Meadow, where the confederates of Schwyz, Unterwalden, and Uri are said to have met in 1307 to renew the 1291 Oath of Eternal Alliance. You head up the hillside for a five-minute walk to emerge on a grassy plateau where you'll find a rock and flagpole to honor the sacred spot. Nearby is a medieval rock bench nestled by towering trees—the per-fect spot to think about another monumental event that took place here centuries later: amid threats of a 1940 German invasion, General Guisan, Swiss army commander in chief, summoned hundreds of offi-cers to the meadow to reaffirm their commitment to the Swiss Con-federation in a secret, stirring ceremony. Afterwards, head back down the hill to study the small video presentation (perhaps also take a photo of a costumed historical interpreter) and be sure to stop in the time-burnished, 19th-century chalet snackshop, with its lovely stained-glass salons and picturesque wood verandas.

Altdorf

24 20 km (12 mi) south of Rütli Meadow, 35 km (22 mi) southeast of Luzern.

Schiller's play *Wilhelm Tell* sums up the tale for the Swiss, who perform his play religiously in venues all over the country—including the town of Altdorf, just up the road from the Rütli Meadow. Leave the steamer at Flüelen, the farthest point of the boat ride around the lake, and connect by postbus to Altdorf, the capital of the canton Uri and, by popular if not scholarly consensus, the setting for Tell's famous apple-shooting scene.

Was Wilhelm Tell Norwegian?

ACCORDING TO an 18th-century story by Gilg Tschudi, Wilhelm Tell performed his heroic deeds in 1307. But that puts him several centuries behind two 11th-century Norwegians named Eindridi and Hemingr. To force Eindridi to accept Christianity, King Olaf is said to have ordered him to shoot a "writing plate" from his son's head. Eindridi's wife persuaded the king to drop the matter. Hemingr was not so lucky. After the hunter won several athletic challenges, an irate King Harald ordered him to shoot not a mere apple, but a hazelnut from his son's head. Hemingr made the shot and, like Tell, took his revenge on the ruler.

A century later, a tippler named Toko bragged about his skill with a bow. The Dane was forced by a king to shoot an apple off his son's head. As Tell would later do, Toko kept an arrow destined for the king should he fail. Toko was then forced to ski down a cliff into the North Sea, a feat he miraculously survived.

A 17th-century English ballad tells of Adam Bell, Clim of the Clough, and William of Cloudesley—outlaws who live off the king's deer, Robin Hood style. In the ballad, William of Cloudesley is the man with the bow:

"An apple upon his head he set,

And then his bowe he bent;

Syxe score paces they were outmet,

And therefore Cloudesley went . . .

Toko's story was in a book that includes the tale of Amleth, a Danish prince, which Shakespeare used for his play *Hamlet*. If Shakespeare had chosen Toko's story, who knows what form Tell's legend might have taken?

Though there are no valid records of Wilhelm Tell's existence, and versions of the legend conflict with historical fact, no one denies the reality of his times, when central Switzerland—then a feudal dependent of Austria but by its own independent will not yet absorbed into the Holy Roman Empire—suffered brutal pressures and indignities under its local rulers. The mythical Gessler was one of those rulers, and his legendary edict—that the proud Swiss should bow before his hat suspended from a pole in the village square at Altdorf—symbolizes much crueler oppressions of the time. Schiller's Tell was a consummate hero: brisk, decisive, a highly skilled helmsman as well as marksman, and not one for diplomatic negotiations. He refused to kneel and provoked his famous punishment: to shoot an apple off his young son's head before a crowd of fellow townsmen. If he refused, both would be killed. Tell quietly tucked an arrow in his shirt bosom, loaded another into his crossbow, and shot the apple clean through. When Gessler asked what the second arrow was for, Tell replied that if the first arrow had struck his child, the second arrow would have been for Gessler and would not have missed.

For this impolitic remark, Tell was sentenced to prison. While deporting him across Lake Luzern, the Austrians (including the ruthless Gessler) were caught in a violent storm (remember your Rossini) and turned to Tell, the only man on board who knew the waters, to take the helm.

Unmanacled, he steered the boat to a rocky ridge, leapt free, and pushed the boat back into the storm. Later he lay in wait in the woods near Küssnacht and shot Gessler in the heart. This act of justified violence inspired the people to overthrow their oppressors and swear the Oath of Eternal Alliance around a roaring bonfire, laying the groundwork for the Swiss Confederation.

There's an often-reproduced **Tell monument** in the village center, showing a proud father with crossbow on one shoulder, the other hand grasping his son's hand; it was sculpted by Richard Kissling in 1895.

Sports & the Outdoors

BIKING You can rent bikes at the **train station** (☎ 051/2214532) in Flüelen. Mountain bikes and motorbikes can be rented and serviced in Altdorf through **Zweirad Affentranger** (⊠ Gotthardstr. 53 ☎ 041/8701315).

Bürglen

🞕 *3 km (1¼ mi) southeast of Altdorf, 40 km (25 mi) southeast of Luzern.*

Tell was supposedly from the tiny, turreted town of Bürglen, just up the road from Altdorf. The **Tell-Museum** devoted to him displays documents and art related to the legend. ⊠ *Postpl.* ☎ *041/8704155* ⊕ *www.tellmuseum.ch* 🏷 *5 SF* 🕙 *Mid-May–June and Sept.–late Oct., daily 10–11:30, 1:30–5; July and Aug., daily 9:30–5:30.*

The Tellskapelle

🞖 *14 km (9 mi) north of Altdorf, 41 km (26 mi) southeast of Luzern.*

Fodor'sChoice ★

Have your Nikons ready for this magnificently picturesque lakeside chapel set at the foot of the Axen mountain. A shrine to Wilhelm Tell, it is adjacent to the **Tellsplatte**, which was the rocky ledge onto which Tell, the rebellious archer, leaped to escape from Gessler's boat, pushing the boat back into the stormy waves as he jumped. Built in 1500, it was restored in high Victorian fashion in 1881. It contains four frescoes of the Tell legend (painted at the time of restoration), showing the taking of the oath on the Rütli Meadow, Tell shooting the apple's on his son's head, Tell's escape, and Gessler's death. This is but one of the many scenic highlights that line the shore of the Urnersee, some of which are incorporated into "The Swiss Way" (Der Weg der Schweiz; www.weg-der-schweiz.ch/). Since Switzerland's septicentennial, central Switzerland has marked and developed this historic foot trail, which covers 35 km (21½ mi) of lakefront lore in 26 sections, each honoring one of Switzerland's cantons. You'll trace the mythical steps of Wilhelm Tell and the genuine steps of medieval forerunners, climb through steep forests and isolated villages, and visit the holiday resort of Brunnen. Complete information and maps can be requested through Zentralschweiz Tourismus (Central Switzerland Tourism). This trail weaves in and out of the famous Axenstrasse, a road carved in the 19th century out of the living rock (in certain stretches), offering spectacular vistas and lakeside perches.

Schwyz

㉗ *12 km (7 mi) north of the Tellskapelle, 44 km (27 mi) east of Luzern.*

This historic town is the capital of the canton Schwyz, root of the name Switzerland, and source of the nation's flag. Switzerland's most precious archives are stored here as well. Traces of an independent settlement at Schwyz have been found from as far back as the Bronze Age (2500 BC–800 BC), but it was its inhabitants' aid in the 1291 Oath of Allegiance that put Schwyz on the map. You can see the beautifully scripted and sealed original document as well as battle flags and paintings of the period in Schwyz's **Bundesbriefmuseum** (Federal Charters Museum). ⊠ *Bahnhofstr. 20* ☎ *041/8192064* ⊕ *www.bundesbriefmuseum.ch* 🎟 *4 SF* ⊗ *May–Oct., Tues.–Fri. 9–11:30, 1:30–5, weekends 9–5; Nov.–Apr., Tues.–Fri. 9–11:30, 1:30–5, weekends 1:30–5.*

Fodor's Choice
★

Schwyz has several notable Baroque churches and a large number of fine old patrician homes dating from the 17th and 18th centuries, not least of which is the **Ital-Redinghaus** with its magnificent interior, antique stoves, and fine stained glass. A visit to this grand house includes a peek inside the neighboring **Bethlehemhaus,** the oldest wooden house in Switzerland, dating from 1287. There is no parking on the grounds; park on the nearby town square and walk 50 yards to the entrance off Reichsstrasse. ⊠ *Rickenbachstr. 24* ☎ *041/8114505* ⊕ *www.irh.ch* 🎟 *4 SF* ⊗ *May–Oct., Tues.–Fri. 2–5, weekends 10–noon and 2–5.*

Curiously, many of Schwyz's splendid houses owe their origin to the battlefield. The men of Schwyz had a reputation as fine soldiers and were in demand in other countries as mercenaries during the 16th and 17th centuries. They built many of the houses you can see today with their military pay. Schwyz's most famous landmark is the **Rathaus** (Town Hall); its richly frescoed exterior (1891) depicts the Battle of Morgarten, where the Austrian army was defeated by the Swiss. The building is still used as the Town Hall. ⊠ *Hauptpl. 1.*

LUZERN & CENTRAL SWITZERLAND ESSENTIALS

Transportation

BY AIR

AIR LINES   Swiss Air Lines, known as Swiss, flies in most often from the United States and the United Kingdom.
🛈 Airlines & Contacts **Swiss** ☎ 877/359-7947 in U.S., 0845/601-0956 in U.K.

AIRPORTS   The nearest airport to Luzern is Unique Zürich Airport, which is approximately 54 km (33 mi) northeast of Luzern.
🛈 Airport Information **Unique Zürich Airport** ☎ 0900/300313.

BY BOAT & FERRY

It would be a shame to see this historic region only from the shore; some of its most impressive landscapes are framed along the waterfront, as seen from the decks of one of the cruise ships that ply the lake. Rides on these are included in a Swiss Pass or a Swiss Boat Pass. Individual tickets can be purchased at Luzern's departure docks; the fee is based on the length of your ride. You can arrange any combination of transportation, such as a leisurely cruise from Luzern to Flüelen at the lake's southernmost point, lasting about 3½ hours and costing 45 SF for second class, 69 SF for first class. A return train trip, via the Arth-Goldau railroad line, takes little more than an hour. The discount Tell Pass gives you free boat rides.

🚢 **Schiffahrtsgesellschaft des Vierwaldstättersees** ⊠ Quay in front of train station ☎ 041/3676767 ⊕ www.lakeluzern.ch. Swiss Federal Railways also covers boat information ☎ 0900/300300 ⊕ www.rail.ch.

BY BUS

The postbus network carries travelers faithfully, if slowly, to the farthest corners of the region. It also climbs the St. Gotthard and the Furka passes (remember, these are closed in winter). For schedules and prices, call Swiss Federal Railways. If you're staying in a Luzern hotel, you'll be eligible for the special Guest-Ticket, offering unlimited rides for three days for 14 SF. The Tell Pass (regional train pass, for more information see "By Train" below) includes free postbus travel.

🚌 **Swiss Federal Railways** ☎ 0900/300300 ⊕ www.rail.ch.

BY CAR

It's easy to reach Luzern from Zürich by road, approaching from national expressway A3 south, connecting to A4 via the secondary E41 in the direction of Zug, and continuing on A4, which turns into the A14, to the city. A convenient all-expressway connection between the two cities is due to open in 2010. From Basel in the northwest, it's a clean sweep by the A2 to Luzern. Approaching from the south, take the A2 to Altdorf, where a tunnel sweeps you through to the shores of the lake. If you're heading for resorts on the north shore, leave the expressway at Flüelen and follow the scenic secondary route.

Although Mt. Rigi and Mt. Pilatus aren't accessible by car, nearly everything else in this region is. The descent from Andermatt past the Devil's Bridge, which once carried medieval pilgrims from the St. Gotthard Pass and drew thrill seekers during the 19th century, now exemplifies awe-inspiring Swiss mountain engineering: from Göschenen, at 3,627 feet, to the waterfront, it's a four-lane expressway.

BY TRAIN

Luzern functions as a rail crossroads, with express trains connecting hourly from Zürich, a 49-minute trip, and every two hours from Geneva, a 3½- to 4-hour trip changing at Bern. Trains enter from the south via the St. Gotthard Pass from the Ticino and via the Furka Pass from the Valais. For rail information, call the Bahnhof.

Swiss National Railways is enhanced here by a few private lines (to Engelberg, Pilatus, the Rigi Kulm) that make it possible to get to most sights. If you don't have a Swiss Pass, there's a central Switzerland regional discount pass, called the Tell Pass, on sale from April to October. The 15-day pass grants you five days of unlimited free travel on main routes, 10 days at half fare. The seven-day pass gives you two days free, five at half fare. (Besides the national lines, most private rail lines will also accept the pass.) The ticket can be bought at rail or boat ticket offices, on cruise boats, from travel agencies, or from tourist offices. The 15-day pass costs 188 SF second class, 220 SF first class; the seven-day pass costs 140 SF second class, 160 SF first class. Plan your itinerary carefully to take full advantage of all discount rates; before you buy a regional pass, add up your excursions à la carte. Remember that many routes always charge half price. All boat trips and the private excursions to Rigi and Pilatus are free to holders of regional passes—but getting to the starting point may cost you half the ususal price. If you plan to cover a lot of ground, however, you may save considerably. Choose your free days in advance: you must confirm them *all* with the first inspector who checks your pass.

🚉 **Bahnhof** ⊠ Bahnhofpl. ☎ 0900/300300 ⊕ www.sbb.ch.

Contacts & Resources

EMERGENCIES

For medical emergencies or to contact the police, refer to the phone numbers listed below. If your car breaks down, contact the Swiss Automobile Club or the Touring Club of Switzerland.

🚉 **Medical Emergencies** ☎ 144. **Police** ☎ 117. **Swiss Automobile Club** ☎ 031/3283111. **Touring Club of Switzerland** ☎ 022/4172727.

INTERNET & MAIL

A network of Wi-Fi Hotspots is rapidly growing throughout Switzerland. In Luzern, Café Parterre also offers Internet access. In smaller towns, ask your hotel concierge if there are any Internet cafés nearby.

🚉 Internet Information **Hotspots** ⊕ www.swisshotspots.ch. **Café Parterre** ⊠ Mythenstr. 7, Luzern ☎ 041/2202043.

🚉 Post Office Information Engelberg: **Salomon Station** ⊠ Talstation Titlis-Rotair, Engelberg ☎ 041/6380002. Luzern: **Die Post (main post office)** ⊠ Bahnhofpl. 4, Luzern.

TOUR OPTIONS

The Luzern tourist office offers English-language walking tours of the city daily from May to October and Wednesday and Saturday from November to April. Tours take about two hours and cost 18 SF. Schiffahrtsgesellschaft des Vierwaldstättersees offers historic and Alpine theme cruises with English commentary daily from May to October.

🚉 Tour Operator Recommendations **Schiffahrtsgesellschaft des Vierwaldstättersees** ⊠ Werftestr. 5, CH-6002 Luzern ☎ 041/3676767.

VISITOR INFORMATION

The principal tourist office for the whole of central Switzerland, including the lake region, is Zentralschweiz Tourismus (Central Switzerland Tourism; www.lakeluzern.ch). The main tourist office for the city of Luzern is in the Bahnhof, off Track 3. There are also local tourist offices and an accommodations service in many of the region's towns, often near the train station.

🛈 Local Tourist Information **Altdorf** ✉ Schützeng. 11, CH-6460 ☎ 041/8720450. **Engelberg** ✉ Klosterstr. 3, CH-6390 ☎ 041/6397777 ⊕ www.engelberg.ch. **Luzern** ✉ Bahnhof: Zentralstr. 5, CH-6002 ☎ 041/2271717 ⊕ www.luzern.com. **Schwyz** ✉ Obersteisteg 14, CH-6430 ☎ 041/8555950 ⊕ www.schwyz-tourismus.ch. **Stans** ✉ Bahnhofpl. 4, CH-6370 ☎ 041/6108833 ⊕ www.stans.ch. **Vitznau** ✉ Seestr., CH-6354 ☎ 041/3980035 ⊕ www.vitznau.ch. **Weggis** ✉ Seestr. 5, CH-6353 ☎ 041/3901155 ⊕ www.weggis.ch.

BASEL THROUGH THE AGES

IT ALL BEGAN ABOUT 2,000 YEARS AGO. The Celts first built a small settlement on the hill where the Münster, Basel's cathedral, now stands. In 44 BC the Romans planned to establish a town at the site of the present city of Augst, 12 km (7 mi) east of Basel. The murder of Julius Caesar delayed the project until AD 15 but on its completion it was called Colonia Augusta Raurica. By the third century AD the Romans had moved their town to the site of the Münster, the better to defend themselves against attack by German tribes. In 401, however, the Romans abandoned Basilia, driven away by the increasingly aggressive Germans. Despite the growing spread of Christianity, it was not until Henry II incorporated the city into the Holy Roman Empire that stabilty returned in the 11th century. In 1006 the bishop of Basel was made ruler of the town, and throughout the Middle Ages these prince-bishops ruled the roost.

All the while, the city's traders and merchants profited from Basel's strategic site on the Rhine, but more than trade flowed up and down the Rhine. As Basel became rich in commerce, so she also became rich in ideas. Geography had long since made the city a natural meeting point, for thinkers and politicians as much as for merchants. And in 1431 this status was officially recognized, so to speak, when the Council of Basel, an ecumenical conference on church reform, was convened in the city. During it, Basel consolidated her role as an intellectual and political center. Among those attending the conference was Enea Silvio Piccolomini. It was he who, as Pope Pius II, gave permission for the university to be built. With it, Basel's leading role as an intellectual center was assured.

Union with the Swiss Confederation in 1501 and the adoption of the teachings of the Reformation some 30 years later further strengthened the city: the armies of the Confederation had more than demonstrated their superiority over the Holy Roman Empire and newly Protestant Basel welcomed a flood of Protestant refugees who brought with them the silk-weaving skills that made Basel a prosperous textile center.

The Thirty Years War in the 17th century—a cataclysmic religious struggle that devastated vast areas of Germany—was turned to shrewd advantage by Switzerland. Having managed to avoid being sucked into the war, the Swiss were nonetheless invited to the peace negotiations by the victorious French, whose armies had been greatly assisted by Swiss mercenaries. Johann Rodolf Wettstein, Basel's Lord Mayor, managed to obtain from both the Habsburgs and the French formal recognition of Swiss neutrality. He argued that Switzerland's central location in Europe and consequent control of numerous strategic rivers and Alpine passes made her guaranteed neutrality vital. Basel's happy path to greater prosperity continued largely unchecked from the 18th century to today, since Basel's intellectual tradition has played a great part in establishing the many chemical and pharmaceutical industries which are the foundation stones of the city's wealth.

Basel

Couple on the Rhine shore of Lesser Basel with a view of the Mittlere Bruecke and the Cathedral.

WORD OF MOUTH

"I was only in Basel for a day but I just have to chime in and say that I loved it! It has a 'medieval university town' flavor to me, and we did do quite a lot of walking. Many of the side streets are absolutely charming with the various colors used in the shutters and trim and the flowerboxes and all. Don't forget to take a pastry and hot chocolate break!"

–Amy1

WELCOME TO BASEL

TOP REASONS TO GO

★ **Three Corners:** Not many cities offer a more cosmopolitan mix. Here Switzerland merges with Germany and France, and Basel is home to some 150 nationalities.

★ **Art Attack:** This city of the arts has galleries full of Old Master paintings and some pictures so contemporary the paint is still drying—over 30 museums cater to every taste.

★ **Fasnacht:** Each spring during its three-day Lenten celebration the city streets are filled with spectacularly costumed revelers, bands, and pipers.

★ **Münster Madness:** Not only is this cathedral an amazing piece of architecture it offers fabulous views of the city and the river Rhine.

★ **Noble Dust:** A short boat ride from Basel, the Colonia Augusta Raurica is the oldest Roman settlement on the Rhine, complete with a restored 1st-century BC theater.

1 A Bridge Too Far. Having the first bridge across the Rhine, built 1225, brought wealth to Basel. Its position now where the Mittlere Rheinbrücke stands offers fine views of the city. The three kings on the facade of Hotel Les Trois Rois were a traditional decoration for a thoroughfare of magnitude. Overlooking the waters, the beloved Lällekönig gargoyle is also worth a glance.

2 **Kunstmuseum:** The Museum of Fine Arts and its younger sister, the Museum of Contemporary Art, are fine establishments in which to meet up with Old Masters and modern upstarts.

Beyeler Foundation

GETTING ORIENTED

Shouldering the Swiss Jura Mountains, the German Black Forest, and the French Vosges, Basel is Switzerland's third largest city and the central conurbation for the northwest of the country. Bordering both banks of the Rhine, Basel is 730 feet above sea level—the lowest altitude of any Swiss city north of the Alps. From here the river turns 90 degrees north and widens into a majestic waterway.

6

Mittlere Rheinbrücke

3 **Medieval District:** The Altstadt (Old Town) borders the marketplace, which lies in front of the majestic red Town Hall, and is host to a thriving consumables market. Winding alleyways lead off to maze of shopping possibilities.

BASEL PLANNER

How's the Weather?

Basel is located in the Rhine Valley, which affords it an agreeably mild climate. Warm Mediterranean air also wafts this way from the Rhone Valley. On average the sun is supposed to shine for 1,680 hours; the average temperature in January, the coldest month, is 1 Celsius (34 F), in July, the warmest, 19 Celsius (66 F). Fog is rare unlike in other Swiss regions and the average rainfall is the lowest north of the Rhône.

Tour Options

Basel Tourismus organizes a daily two-hour walking tour of the city. This starts from the tourist information office in the Stadtcasino and caters to German, French, and English speakers. Tours take place from May to mid-October, Monday through Saturday at 2:30. From mid-October to April the walking tours are held every Saturday at 2:30. The cost is 15 SF.

Priceless

Yes, Basel can be pricey but its vistas and views are priceless. Just sit on the steps of the Rhine on the Kleinbasel side of the Mittlere Rheinbrücke on a sunny afternoon and drink in its great view of the Old Town and the Münster—a great chance to people-watch and absorb the character of the city.

Coming & Going

Basel is a transportation hub, with French, German, and Swiss train stations. Be sure to get off at the Swiss station Schweizerische Bundesbahnen (SBB) on Centralbahnstrasse; many a weary traveler has walked an hour from the German side of town. Klein-Basel (Small Basel), east of the Rhine in German territory, is an industrial center (with some new sights); the more affluent Grossbasel (Greater Basel) on the western side contains most of the sights and the Altstadt (Old Town). To reach the Altstadt from the SBB, head north (left) on Heuwaage-Viadukt, turn right on Steinenvorstadt and continue until you reach the central square, Barfüsserplatz. To reach outlying areas, take the tram. Indeed, the best way to see Basel is by foot or by tram, as the landmarks, museums, and even the zoo radiate from the old town center on the Rhine, and the network of rails covers the territory thoroughly. Taxis are costly, less efficient, and less available than the ubiquitous tram.

Penny Pinchers

Hotel guests in Basel receive a complimentary Basel Mobility Ticket, which allows free use of all public transportation within the city during their stay. Many museums offer free entry between 4 PM and 5 PM on selected weekdays as well as on the first Sunday of each month.

Most Baslers eat their main meal at lunch time, so look out for the "Tagesmenu" (Daily Menu) at restaurants as this will offer a reasonably priced couple of courses. Most students find refuge from expensive restaurants at the self-service joints in Migros Market (Unt. Regbgasse 11, near Clarapl.) or the ever-present Coop grocery stores. On Markplatz, a big daily market sells fruit, veggies, bread, cheese sandwiches, and even egg rolls. Here, too, is Basel's oldest tearoom (open since 1870—but closed Sunday and Monday), the Schiesser Café. You can buy beautiful chocolates downstairs, then down coffee and a scumptuous pastry or cold lunch with a polite local crowd upstairs.

Making the Most of Your Time

If you are in town for just a day, your best bet is to take a stroll through Basel's Old Town, making sure to see the Münster and the sweeping views from the terrace overlooking the Rhine.

Art enthusiasts could decide to circle from here directly to the Kunstmuseum, and shoppers may want to head down one of the winding alleyways into the Freie Strasse or the Marktplatz.

A leisurely late-afternoon walk across the Mittlere Rheinbrücke and upstream along the sunny Kleinbasel riverside promenade (Oberer Rheinweg) is a good way to see the town in its best light.

If you are sticking around for longer, then take in some of the city's smaller museums, perhaps in the picturesque St. Alban quarter. From here take a ferryboat across the river and head east to the Museum Tinguely.

Or organize your day around a trip to Riehen; the Fondation Beyeler's stunningly well-rounded (and beautifully presented) collection of 20th-century art can be reached in a mere 20 minutes by tram.

In summer you could opt to take a boat trip to the Roman ruins of Augusta Raurica, east of Basel. Or take a driving tour of, or catch a local train to, some of the small villages scattered south of the city, such as Balsthal, Holderbank, Oberer Hauenstein, Langenbruck, and Liestal to experience the more rural delights of the area.

Cool off in very hot weather like the locals by taking a dip in the Rhine; swimmers can often be seen from the Mittlere Rheinbrücke and there are a number of popular bathing spots along the banks.

Feeling Festive

From three days of Carnival craziness during Fasnacht at the beginning of the year to the bejeweled streets and Christmas market that mark the end of it, Basel hosts events for all tastes all year round.

Fasnacht is spectacularly celebrated with fifes, drums, and fabulous oversize masks. You'll spot the stock characters year-round: Ueli the clown; the Vogl Gryff (griffin); and the Lällekönig,who sticks out a mechanical tongue.

There are daily happenings, such as the Marktplatz market, weekly ones like the Barfüssermarkt on Barfüsserplatz every Thursday, 7 AM to 8 PM, which features stalls selling clothes, jewelry, crafts from around the world, basket work, shoes, and much more.

The biggest, most glamorous blowout is Art Basel. Every June, one of the world's leading contemporary art shows (its new sister show, Art Basel Miami Beach, held in December, is its only rival for sheer star power) takes over the town.

Basel even has its own marathon, run every September since 2005, and let us not forget that it is home to the Davidoff Swiss Indoors each October, the world's third-largest indoor tennis tournament.

A new addition to the calendar is the Basel Tattoo in July, featuring top-class professional bands with a total of more than 1,000 participants from Switzerland and abroad. Plus there is the Herbstmesse (Autumn Fair) in October–November with its funfairs and wine convention.

Updated by
Sharon-Anne
Wilcox

THOUGH IT LACKS THE GILT AND GLITTER of Zürich and the Latin grace of Geneva, in many ways Basel (Bâle in French) is more sophisticated than either. Situated at the frontier between two of Europe's most assertive personalities—France and Germany—and tapped directly into the artery of the Rhein (Rhine), the city has grown remarkably urbane, cosmopolitan, and worldly wise, yet is delightfully eccentric as well. Its imagination has been fed by centuries of intellectual input: Basel has been host to Switzerland's oldest university (1460) and patron to some of the country's—and the world's—finest minds. As a northern center of humanist thought and art, it nurtured the painters Konrad Witz and Hans Holbein the Younger, as well as the great Dutch scholar Erasmus. And it was Basel's visionary lord mayor Johann Rudolf Wettstein who, at the end of the Thirty Years' War, negotiated Switzerland's groundbreaking—and lasting—neutrality.

Each day, more than 30,000 French and German commuters cross into Basel. Banking activity here is surpassed only by that of Zürich and Geneva, and every month representatives of the world's leading central banks meet at the Bank for International Settlements in the city center. Enormous international pharmaceutical firms—among them Novartis and Roche—crowd the riverbanks. Yet Basel's population remains modest, hovering around 188,000; its urban center lies gracefully along the Rhine, with no building so tall as to block another building's view of the cathedral's twin spires. Two blocks from the heart of the thriving shopping district you can walk along medieval residential streets cloaked in perfect, otherworldly silence to Minster Mount, where the Romanesque-Gothic cathedral offers superb views over the Old Town and the Rhine all the way to the surrounding mountains.

The high number of museums per capita is a reflection of Basel's priorities: the city has more than 30, including the world-class Kunstmuseum, the Museum Tinguely, and the Fondation Beyeler. As high culture breeds good taste, Basel has some of the most varied, even quirky, shopping in Switzerland, all within walking distance. But you can still get a beer and a bratwurst here: Baslers almost exclusively speak German or their own local version of *Schwyzerdütsch,* called *Baseldütsch.* On the Marktplatz, hungry shoppers stand in front of a mobile kitchen, holding bare *Wienerli* (hot dogs) and dipping the pink tips into thick golden mustard. They also indulge in *Kaffe und Kuchen*—the late-afternoon coffee break the neighboring Germans live for—but Baslers have their own version: instead of a large slice of creamed cake, they select tiny sweet gems—two or three to a saucer, but petite nonetheless—and may opt for a delicate Chinese tea instead of a Kaffe.

The Celts were the first to settle here, around 500 BC, on the site of the Münsterhügel (cathedral mount). During the 1st century BC the Romans established a town at Augst, then called Colonia Augusta Raurica; the ruins and the theater, 10 km (6 mi) outside town, can be visited today. By the 3rd century, the Romans had taken the present cathedral site in Basel proper, naming the town Basilia (royal stronghold). Germanic invaders banished them around 450, and it wasn't until the Holy Roman emperor Henry II took Basel under his wing in the 11th century that stability returned. His image and that of his wife, Kunegunde, adorn the cathedral and the Rathaus (Town Hall). Henry built the original cathedral—on the site of a church destroyed in 916 by a raiding band of Hungarian horsemen—and established Basel as one of the centers of his court. In 1006 the bishop of Basel was made ruler of the town, and throughout the Middle Ages these prince-bishops gained and exerted enormous temporal and spiritual powers. Though prince-bishops are no more, Basel still uses one of their symbols in its coat of arms—a striking black staff.

Yet Basel is first and foremost a Renaissance city in the broadest sense of the word: a city of intellectual and artistic rebirth. In 1431 the Council of Basel, an ecumenical conference whose chief objective was church reform, was convened here, bringing in—over a period of 17 years—the great sacred and secular princes of the age. One of them, who later became Pope Pius II, granted permission for the founding of the university and established Basel as the cultural capital it remains today.

> **GETTING AROUND**
>
> The best way to see Basel is on foot or by tram, as the landmarks, museums, and even the zoo radiate from the Old Town center on the Rhine, and the network of rails covers the territory thoroughly. Taxis are costly, less efficient, and less available than the ubiquitous tram. Parking in the city center is competitive and in some areas nonexistent. If you've driven in by car, you'll save time and hassle by heading straight for an all-day garage, such as the Parkhaus Elisabethen, on Heuwaage near the SBB train station. Expect to pay around 25 SF per day. For details, see the Essentials section.

Art and academia over the ages haven't made Basel a stuffy place, however. The Baslers' Lenten celebration of Fasnacht (related to Mardi Gras, or Carnival) turns the usual workings of the city on its ear. The streets are filled with grotesquely costumed revelers bearing huge homemade lanterns scrawled with comments and caricatures relating to local current events. Although the festivities last only three days, you'll see masks displayed and sold everywhere all year long, and you'll hear strains of fife-and-drum marches wafting from the guild houses' upper windows in rehearsal for the celebration. Like confetti lodged between the cobblestones, there always seems to be a hint of Fasnacht, age-old and unpredictable, even in Basel's most sedate and cultivated corners.

EXPLORING BASEL

The Rhine divides the city into two distinct sections: on the southwestern bank lies Grossbasel (Greater Basel), the commercial, cultural, and academic center. Directly upriver from Grossbasel wind the quiet medieval streets of St. Alban, where you can stroll along the Rhine, peek into antiques shops, then dine in a cozy bistro. The opposite bank, to the northeast, is Kleinbasel (Little Basel), a Swiss enclave on the "German" side of the Rhine that is the industrial quarter of the city. Here is the convention center, chain stores galore, and hotels with terraces that afford glorious views of the Münster (cathedral).

Numbers in the text correspond to numbers in the margin and on the Basel map.

Old Town

If you stand in the middle of the Marktplatz, or even just watch river traffic from the Mittlere Rheinbrücke, it's easy to envision the Basel of centuries ago. On a bend of the Rhine, Basel's Old Town is full of majestic Gothic spires and side streets that are largely unchanged since the 1600s. Still, woven through the delicately preserved architecture of the Old Town are impressive state-of-the-art museums and miles of shop-lined pedestrian zones.

Sights to See

Basler Papiermühle/Schweizer Papiermuseum und Museum für Schrift und Druck (Basel Paper Mill/Swiss Museum for Paper, Writing and Printing). Though its name sounds esoteric, this museum, in a beautifully restored medieval waterfront mill with a still functioning waterwheel, is surprisingly accessible. Demonstrations of papermaking, typesetting, and bookbinding reveal much about the ancient craft. You can participate in a 12-step papermaking process, beginning with the pulpy raw material simmering in the "visitors' vat." Kids can try out quills and ink or spell out their names in pieces of type for printing. Most descriptions have an English translation, but some special exhibits are described in German text only. ⊠ *St. Alban-Tal 35, St. Alban* ☎ *061/ 2729652* ⊕ *www.papiermuseum.ch* 🎫 *12 SF* ☉ *Tues.–Sun. 2–5.*

> ### YOU GOTTA HAVE ART
>
> With a renowned collector's hand-picked paintings (the Fondation Beyeler), an homage to unique mechanized art (the Museum Tinguely), and one of the world's oldest public art collections (the Kunstmuseum), Basel easily earns a high rank in the art world, especially each June when it hosts one of the world's most glamorous modern art fairs, Art Basel (www. artbasel.com). The BaselCard is a must, offering unlimited admission to participating museums for one, two, or three days. It can be purchased for 20 SF, 27 SF, or 35 SF (for one, two, or three days) at Basel Tourismus and at most hotels.

Blaues und Weisses Haus (Blue House and White House). Built between 1762 and 1768 for two of the city's most successful silk merchants, these were the residences of the brothers Lukas and Jakob Sarasin. In 1777 the emperor Joseph II of Austria was a guest in the Blue House, and the roster of subsequent visitors' names—including Czar Alexander of Russia, Emperor Francis of Austria, and King Friedrich Wilhelm III of Prussia, who met for dinner here in 1814—brings this historical site's guest book over the top. The restored houses are both white with blue trim, but they're distinguished by their gates: the one at the Blue House is made of intricate iron, and the White House is composed of stately wood. ⊠ *Martinsg., Grossbasel.*

Fasnacht-Brunnen (Carnival Fountain). Created by the Swiss artist Jean Tinguely, known for his work in mechanized media, this witty, animated construction was commissioned by the city in 1977. Its whimsically styled

Fasnacht

Dating from the Middle Ages, Fasnacht, Switzerland's best-known festival, draws people from all over the world. Beginning at 4 AM on the Monday following Ash Wednesday, all lights are turned off and the city is illuminated by the lanterns of the *Cliques* (carnival associations). The event features a blast of fifes and drums, boisterous *Guggemusik* (played by enthusiastic, rather than talented, marching bands), and a covering of confetti. The streets are absolutely packed with zillions of onlookers who have fortified themselves against the cold morning with a bowl of the traditional *Mehlsuppe* (flour soup). A colorful masked procession traverses the Old Town until dawn, and continues for the next two days. Nearby Liestal stages its own spectacular ceremony during which burning stacks of wood are paraded through the town and finally heaped together. While other Fasnacht celebrations in Switzerland are usually held on or around February 27 and 28, Basel holds its festival a week later—check with the tourist board Web site for all the spectacular details.

metal figures busily churn, lash, and spray with unending energy. It is especially impressive in winter when the jets of water freeze, creating unique airborne sculptures. ⊠ *Theaterpl., Grossbasel.*

㉓ Fischmarkt (Fish Market). Fishmongers once kept their catches market-fresh here on this square, whose fountain basin served as a sort of communal cooler. The fountain itself dates from 1390 and holds figures of the Virgin Mary, St. Peter, and John the Baptist. ⊠ *Northwest of Marktpl., Grossbasel.*

㉖ Fondation Beyeler (Beyeler Foundation). For decades, the most prestigious art collectors and world-famous billionaires would make a pilgrimage to Basel to worship at the feet of one of modern art's greatest gallery owners, Ernst Beyeler. Magnificent Monets, legendary Toulouse-Lautrecs, and the finest Giacometti sculptures were the Swiss "souvenirs" these power-players came home with—that is, if Herr Beyeler approved of you. At the end of his phenomenal career, he wound up deeding his own incomparable collection to the public and, in the Basel suburb of Riehen, commissioned noted architect Renzo Piano to build a public museum to house it. Today, the holdings of Ernst and Hildy Beyeler present an astonishingly well-rounded collection of 20th-century and contemporary art and Piano's simple, introverted lines direct attention to the 200 paintings and objects. Rightly so, as the collection's catalogue reads like a who's who of modern artists—Cézanne, Matisse, Lichtenstein, and Rauschenberg.

FodorsChoice ★

In this limpid setting of natural light and openness, Giacometti's wiry sculptures stretch toward the ceiling and Monet's water lilies seem to spill from the canvas into an outdoor reflecting pool. Indigenous carved figures from New Guinea and Nigeria stare into faces on canvases by Klee and Dubuffet. A stellar selection of Picassos is juxtaposed with pane-

A GOOD WALK

Six bridges link the two halves of the city; the most historic and picturesque is the **Mittlere Rheinbrücke** ① ▸. On the corner at Schifflände, you can see a facsimile (now leering above the restaurant on the first floor) of the infamous **Lällekönig** ②, a 17th-century gargoyle once mechanized to stick out his tongue and roll his eyes at his rivals across the river.

Walking across the bridge, you'll see Basel's peculiar, gondola-like ferryboats, attached to a high wire and angling silently from shore to shore, powered only by the swift current of the river (you can ride one for 1.20 SF). Across the Rhine, gaze at the seated **statue of Helvetia,** one of Basel's many tongue-in-cheek sculptures.

Back across the Mittlere Rheinbrücke in Grossbasel, turn left up a steep alley called the **Rheinsprung,** banked with 15th- and 16th-century houses. Turn right at Archivgässlein, and you'll come to the **Martinskirche** ③, the city's oldest parish church, dating from 1288.

Continue along Martinsgasse to the elegant neighboring courtyards of the **Blaues und Weisses Haus** ④, meeting place of kings. Just beyond, turn left and head toward the fountain adorned by a mythical green basilisk into the Augustinergasse. At No. 2 is the entrance to the **Naturhistorisches Museum** ⑤ and the **Museum der Kulturen Basel** ⑥. Under this one roof you'll find one of the world's foremost natural history and prehistory collections.

Augustinergasse leads into the Münsterplatz, dominated by the

striking red-sandstone 12th-century **Münster** ⑦, burial place of Erasmus and Queen Anna of Habsburg. Walk around to the church's river side to a terrace called the Pfalz, which affords wide views of the river, the Old Town and, on a clear day, the Black Forest.

From the Münsterplatz, head down Rittergasse and go past its elegant villas and courtyards to the first busy cross-street. Ahead of you is St. Alban-Vorstadt, which leads to the **St. Alban-Tor** ⑧, one of the original 13th-century city gates. St. Alban-Tal leads from St. Alban-Vorstadt down to St. Alban-Rheinweg on the Rhine to the **Basler Papiermühle/Schweizer Papiermuseum und Museum für Schrift und Druck** ⑨ and the **Museum für Gegenwartskunst** ⑩. Leave the museums by way of the St. Alban-Rheinweg along the riverside, ascend the Wettstein Bridge stairways, and head left onto St. Alban-Graben. Here is the imposing **Kunstmuseum** ⑪, home of one of Europe's oldest public collections.

Continue down St. Alban-Graben to the intersection of Steinenberg. A few blocks straight ahead into Elisabethenstrasse will take you to the **Haus zum Kirschgarten** ⑫, a showcase of 18th- and 19th-century decorative arts. To circle back into the Old Town, however, veer right on Steinenberg, which goes by the **Kunsthalle** ⑬. Just beyond the art gallery, the whimsical Tinguely-Brunnen, or **Fasnacht-Brunnen,** puts on a show on the Theaterplatz. (A Richard Serra sculpture, usually covered in graffiti, also punctuates the square.) Zoo enthusiasts may want to take advantage of the tram service along Steinentorstrasse to reach the **Zoologischer Garten** ⑭, west of the SBB train station.

Continue on Steinenberg until it opens out onto the bustling Barfüsserplatz. Here the **Puppenhaus Museum** ⑮ displays toys from the 18th and 19th centuries, and the **Historisches Museum** ⑯ exhibits annals and objects from Basel's proud past in the mid-14th-century Franciscan Barfüsserkirche, or Church of the Shoeless Friars.

Behind the tram concourse on Barfüsserplatz, follow the pedestrian zone to Leonhardsberg, which leads left up the stairs to the late-Gothic **Leonhardskirche** ⑰. Continue along the church walk into Heuberg street, the spine of one of the loveliest sections of old Basel.

A network of small streets threads through the quarter, lined with graceful old houses from many periods: Gothic, Renaissance, Baroque, Biedermeier.

Heuberg feeds into Spalenvorstadt, which will take you ahead two blocks to the **Holbeinbrunnen,** styled from a drawing by Hans Holbein.

The Spalenvorstadt stretches on to the impressive 14th-century **Spalentor** ⑱, another of Basel's medieval city gates. Spalengraben curves north from here past the buildings of the Universität, one of the six oldest universities in German-speaking Europe. Nearby Petersplatz is the site of the 13th-century **Peterskirche** ⑲.

Petersgasse, behind the Peterskirche, presents an exemplary row of

houses, some only a single window wide. Several small streets scale downhill from here, among them the Totengässlein, which leads past the **Pharmazie-Historisches Museum** ⑳. The steep stairs wind on in the direction of the **Marktplatz** ㉑, the historic and modern heart of Basel, with its towering **Rathaus** ㉒.

Leading off the south end of the Marktplatz, main shopping streets Freie Strasse and Gerbergasse are lined with international shops and department stores.

The north end heads toward **Fischmarkt** ㉓. Marktgasse leads to the historic **Les Trois Rois Hotel** ㉔. If you're feeling energetic, walk to the **Museum Tinguely** ㉕ by crossing over the Mittlere Rheinbrücke and heading east toward Solitude Park on Kleinbasel's sunny waterfront promenade Oberer Rheinweg.

Or take a 20-minute tram ride (No. 6 from Barfüsserplatz, Marktplatz, or Schifflände) to the **Fondation Beyeler** ㉖, with its legendary collection of modern art masterpieces and a green park.

⏱ TIMING TIPS➜ Moving at a rapid clip you can see the major sights, as well as a cross-section of the cultural and artistic collections, in four to six hours. A more leisurely itinerary, including strolling around the Old Town shops and visiting museums on the Kleinbasel side, will while away at least a full day, if not two. If you're looking to save a few francs, many museums are free the first Sunday of the month and from Tuesday to Saturday between 4 and 5 PM. Most museums are closed Monday.

6

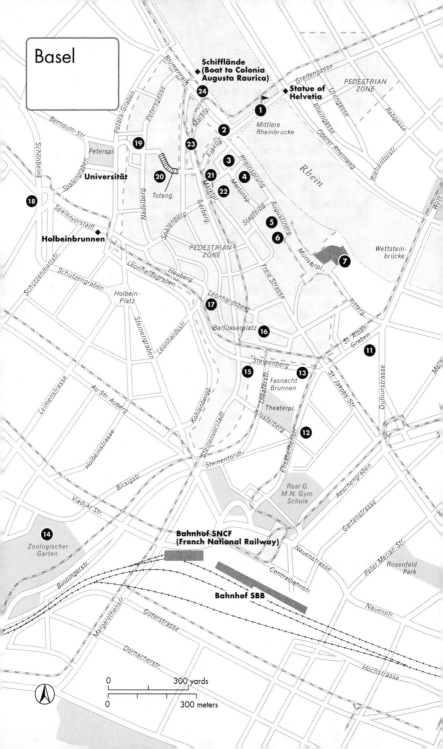

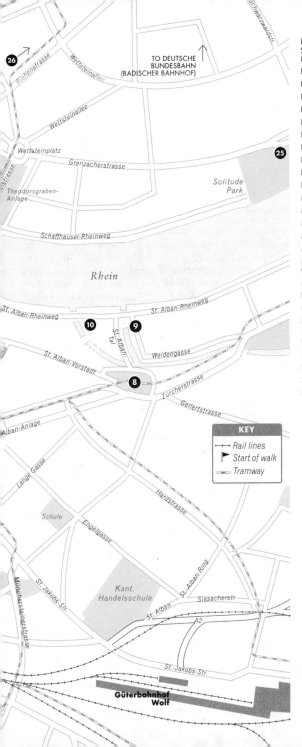

glass views of blue skies and neighboring fields. The harmony of the collection notwithstanding, personal preference is a perceivable theme. The tram trip from Schifflände takes about 20 minutes. Public tours in English are often offered on Sunday, or private tours can be arranged. ✉ *Baselstr. 101, Riehen* ☎ *061/6459700* ⊕ *www.beyeler.com* 🏷 *21 SF* ⊗ *Thurs.–Tues. 10–6, Wed. 10–8.*

⑫ **Haus zum Kirschgarten** (Kirschgarten House). This 18th-century home was built as a palace for a young silk-ribbon manufacturer. Nowadays it contains the 18th- and 19th-century collections of the city's Historical Museum, displayed as furnishings in period rooms. The timepieces, porcelain, and faience are especially outstanding. ✉ *Elisabethenstr. 27–29, Grossbasel* ☎ *061/2058678* ⊕ *www.hmb.ch* 🏷 *7 SF (1st Sun. of month free; Tues.–Sat. 4–5 free)* ⊗ *Tues.–Fri., Sun. 10–5, Sat. 1–5.*

★ ⑯ **Historisches Museum** (Historical Museum). Housed within the **Barfüsserkirche** (Church of the Shoeless Friars), which was founded by the barefoot Franciscans in 1250 and rebuilt during the mid-14th century, the museum has an extensive collection of tapestries, wooden sculptures, coins, armor, and other vestiges of Basel's past. An underground gallery displays fully reconstructed **medieval and Renaissance guild rooms**, complete with stained glass, ceramic stoves, and richly carved wood. Downstairs, in the back of the church, the **Münster Treasury** contains priceless reliquaries in gold. Despite its status as one of the finest examples of Franciscan architecture north of the Alps, the church was deconsecrated in the 19th century and turned into a warehouse until it was rescued in 1894 and converted to its present-day use as a museum. Most descriptions are in German only. ✉ *Barfüsserpl., Grossbasel* ☎ *061/ 2058600* ⊕ *www.hmb.ch* 🏷 *7 SF (1st Sun. of month free; Mon., Wed.–Sat. 4–5 free)* ⊗ *Wed.–Mon. 10–5.*

★ ⑬ **Kunsthalle** (Basel Art Gallery). A must-do for lovers of contemporary art, managed through Basel's community of artists, the Basler Kunstverein, this museum has hosted landmark, precedent-setting exhibits of contemporary art since 1872. In addition to showing the work of several modern masters from an early stage of their careers (Klee and Picasso), the gallery was the first in Europe to display works by American Abstract Expressionists. It is renowned as one of the world's most active institutions dedicated to the presentation of modern art. The building was renovated in 2004 and features an on-site theater that hosts video installations, performances, and local and foreign films. ✉ *Steinenberg 7, Grossbasel* ☎ *061/2069900* ⊕ *www.kunsthallebasel.ch* 🏷 *10 SF includes admission to Architektur museum* ⊗ *Tues., Wed., Fri. 11–6, Thurs. 11–8:30, weekends 11–5.*

⑪ **Kunstmuseum** (Museum of Fine Arts). In a city known for its museums,
FodorśChoice the Kunstmuseum is Basel's heirloom jewel. It was built between 1932
★ and 1936 to house one of the oldest public art collections in Europe, owned by the city since 1661; the imposing facade gives way to an inner courtyard studded with statues. Inside is the world's largest assemblage of paintings by members of the Holbein family, an exceptional group of works by Konrad Witz, and, in fact, such a thorough gathering of the works of their contemporaries that the development of painting in

the Upper Rhine is strikingly documented. Other Swiss artists are well represented: from Basel's own Arnold Böcklin to Klimt-like Ferdinand Hodler. The museum's other forte is its international 20th-century collection, from Georges Braque to Jasper Johns. ⊠ *St. Alban-Graben 16, Grossbasel* ☎ *061/2066262* ⊕ *www.kunstmuseumbasel.ch* 🎟 *15 SF, includes admission to Museum für Gegenwartskunst* ☉ *Tues., Thurs.–Sun. 10–5, Wed. 10–7.*

★ ❷ **Lällekönig.** When a famous gate tower on the Grossbasel side was destroyed, lost along with it was the notorious Lällekönig, a 15th-century gargoyle of a king whose mechanized clockwork caused the apparatus to stick out his tongue and roll his eyes at the "lesser" citizens across the river. Kleinbasel residents seek symbolic revenge even today, though. Every year during the Vogel Gryff festival, a birdlike figure dances to the midpoint of the bridge, gives the Lällekönig a flash of his backside, and takes the party back to Kleinbasel. You can see a facsimile of the Lällekönig on the corner of what is now a chain restaurant at Schifflände while the original still ticks and taunts away in the nether regions of the Historical Museum. ⊠ *Schifflände, Grossbasel.*

⑰ **Leonhardskirche** (St. Leonard's Church). Like virtually all of Basel's churches, this one was destroyed in the 1356 earthquake before being rebuilt in the Gothic style, although its original Romanesque crypt remains. Its High Gothic wooden pulpit is distinctive. Free organ concerts are often held on Friday evenings. ⊠ *Leonardskirchpl., Grossbasel* ☉ *Daily 9–5.*

㉔ **Les Trois Rois Hotel** (Three Kings Hotel). The statues on the facade depict the biblical three wise men and are thought to date from 1754. The young general Napoléon Bonaparte stayed here in 1797 (an opulently decorated suite is still named after him), followed by other stellar guests, including Princess Victoria, Charles Dickens, and Picasso. In

PHOTO-OP

Set in the heart of the prettiest area of old Basel, the fanciful Holbeinbrunnen fountain found its inspiration in several other art works. Created by an unknown 16th-century stonemason, it depicts a group of dancing farmers, copied from a drawing by Hans Holbein; above stands a bagpiper, copied from a Dürer engraving. The fountain itself is a replica, the original having been moved to the Historical Museum, and can be found on Spalenvorstadt, 2 blocks up the tram tracks toward Spalentor.

1887 the great Hungarian-born Jewish writer Theodor Herzl stayed here during the first Zionist Congress, which laid the groundwork for the founding of the state of Israel. ⊠ *Blumenrain 8, Grossbasel.*

㉑ **Marktplatz** (Marketplace). Flowers, fruits, and vegetables are sold most mornings from open stands in this central square, Basel's historic and modern heart. In fall and winter passersby purchase bags of hot roasted chestnuts, the savory scent of which wafts through the square. ⊠ *Tram crossroads at foot of Rathaus, south of Marktg.* ☉ *Market: Mon.–Sat. 6 AM–1:30 PM.*

❸ **Martinskirche** (St. Martin's Church). The excellent acoustics make this church popular for concerts, although it's rarely used for services. The lower portions of the tower date from 1288, making it the oldest parish church in town; the upper part was rebuilt after the earthquake of 1356. The fountain outside, with the statue of a warrior in battle dress, dates from the 16th century. ⊠ *Martinsg., Grossbasel.*

☞ ★ ❶ **Mittlere Rheinbrücke** (Middle Rhine Bridge). Basel's most historic bridge is a good metaphor for the city's successful mix of custom and commerce. It is used as a catwalk for many of Basel's centuries-old celebrations, while beneath its span processions of barges continually glide through its low-slung arches. First built around 1225, the bridge made possible the development of an autonomous Kleinbasel and the consequent rivalry that grew between the two half towns. A stone bridge replaced the wooden one at the turn of the 20th century. ⊠ *Schifflände, Grossbasel.*

★ ❼ **Münster** (Cathedral). Basel's cathedral evolved into its current form through a combination of the shifts of nature and the changing whims of architects. The site started as a 9th-century Carolingian church, then became a cathedral, which was consecrated by Henry II in 1019. Additions, alterations, and reconstructions in late Romanesque–early Gothic style continued through the 12th and 13th centuries. When Basel's devastating earthquake destroyed much of the building in 1356, subsequent reconstruction, which lasted about a century, adhered to the newly dominant Gothic style. The facade of the north transept, the **Galluspforte** (St. Gall's Door), is a surviving remnant of the original Romanesque structure. It's one of the oldest carved portals in German-speaking Europe—and one of the loveliest. Slender, fine-tooled columns and rich high-relief and freestanding sculptures frame the door. Each of the evangelists is represented by his symbol: an angel for Matthew, an ox for Luke, a lion for Mark, and a bulbous-chested eagle for John. Above, around the window, a wheel of fortune flings little men off to their fates.

Inside on the left, following a series of tombs of medieval noblemen whose effigies recline with their feet resting on their loyal dogs, stands the strikingly simple **tomb of Erasmus.** Below the choir, you can see the delicately rendered death portraits on the double **tomb of Queen Anna of Habsburg** and her young son, Charles, from around 1285. The vaulted **crypt** was part of the original structure and still bears fragments of murals from 1202.

The Münsterplatz square itself is one of the most satisfying architectural ensembles in Europe, its fine town houses set well back from the cathedral, the center filled with pollarded trees. ⊠ *Münsterpl., Grossbasel* ⊕ *www.baslermuenster.ch* ☉ *Easter–mid-Oct., weekdays 10–5, Sat. 10–4, Sun. noon–5; mid-Oct.–Easter, Mon.–Sat. 11–4, Sun. noon–4.*

NEED A BREAK?
It's hard to beat the plaza tables of **Zum Isaak** (⊠ Münsterpl. 16, Grossbasel ☎ 061/2614712 ⊕ www.zum-isaak.ch) for scenic value; it has a direct view of the cathedral's towers. It's open for lunch, dinner, or just a piece of Madame Iselin's *Schoggikuchen* (chocolate cake) and coffee.

6 **Museum der Kulturen Basel** (Basel Museum of Cultures). You'll experience a moment of extreme cultural contrast here—walk in from the cobblestone street, and you'll suddenly find yourself at a woven-palm "culthouse" from Papua, New Guinea. This is one of the world's foremost ethnographic collections, with 32,000 pieces gathered from the far corners of the globe. The extensive ground-floor exhibits on Oceania and Melanesia include standing pole figures, dance staffs, and bristling headdresses. The museum shares its space with the Natural History Museum. Key parts of the collection have English-language information sheets. ✉ *Augustinerg. 2, Grossbasel* ☎ *061/2665600* ⊕ *www.mkb.ch* 🎫 *7 SF (1st Sun. of month free; Tues.–Sat. 4–5 free)* ⊙ *Tues.–Sun. 10–5.*

10 **Museum für Gegenwartskunst** (Museum of Contemporary Art). Bringing Basel's art collections up to the present, this museum focuses on works from the 1960s forward. The fittingly modern building looks as though it has shouldered its way in between the street's half-timber houses. The exhibitions change frequently, so pick up a brochure from a tourist office to see which artists' works will be on view at the time you visit. The language of the exhibition materials typically corresponds to the nationality of the artists. ✉ *St. Alban-Rheinweg 60, Grossbasel* ☎ *061/2728183* ⊕ *www.kunstmuseumbasel.ch/* 🎫 *18 SF, Tues.–Sat. 4–5 free, includes admission to Kunstmuseum* ⊙ *Tues.–Sun. 11–5.*

6

★ ☾ **25** **Museum Tinguely.** Stay alert and be ready to get involved—the fascinating mechanized artworks of 20th-century master Jean Tinguely invite close inspection and interaction. As you circle the installations, some a story high, you may wonder: how do they work? what do they mean? and where did he find this stuff? Born in Fribourg, Tinguely is best known for his whimsical *métamécaniques* (mechanical sculptures), which transform machinery, appliances, and items straight from the taxidermy shop into ironic and often macabre statements. For instance, *Le Ballet des Pauvres*, from 1961, suspends a hinged leg with a moth-eaten sock, a horse tail and fox pelt, a cafeteria tray, and a blood-soaked nightgown, all of which dangle and dance on command. The wing projecting over the Rhine has a splendid river view of Basel. Many of the museum's "sculptures" are activated at preset times, typically every 5–15 minutes, and it pays to wait and see them in action. Schedules are listed on each work's nameplate, and information sheets are available in English. ✉ *Paul Sacher-Anlager 1, Kleinbasel* ☎ *061/6819320* ⊕ *www.tinguely.ch* 🎫 *10 SF* ⊙ *Tues.–Sun. 11–7.*

☾ **5** **Naturhistorisches Museum** (Natural History Museum). Under the same monumental roof as the Museum der Kulturen Basel, this museum outlines the earth's biological history from prehistoric to modern times, including some impressive examples of mammals, reptiles, and invertebrates. There's also a focus on local fossil finds and indigenous minerals from the Alps and Jura regions. Most descriptive materials are in German only. ✉ *Augustinerg. 2, Grossbasel* ☎ *061/2665500* ⊕ *www.nmb.bs.ch* 🎫 *7SF (1st Sun. of month free, Tues.–Sat. 4–5 free)* ⊙ *Tues.–Sun. 10–5.*

19 **Peterskirche** (St. Peter's Church). Evidence of Basel's late-Gothic heyday, the 13th-century St. Peter's Church sits across from **Petersplatz,** a lovely park next to the **Universität** (University). In the rose-lighted chapel are some interesting 14th-century frescoes. Call for information about services. ⊠ *Across Peters-Graben from Peterspl., Grossbasel* ☎ 061/2618724.

⑳ Pharmazie-Historisches Museum (Museum of Pharmaceutical History). Although pharmaceuticals as the topic of an entire museum may seem like too much of a necessary thing, this collection showcases Basel's roots in the industry that dominates the banks of the Rhine today. There are original and re-created pharmacy counters and all kinds of beakers, flacons, and ceramic measures. The old remedies on display now seem like ingredients for a witches' brew: insects, adders, even poisonous plants. The museum is housed in Zum Vorderen Sessel, a home once frequented by Erasmus. You can request an English-language information sheet. ⊠ *Totengässlein 3, Grossbasel* ☎ *061/2649111* ⊕ *www.pharmaziemuseum.ch* ⊠ *5 SF* ☉ *Tues.–Fri. 10–6, Sat. 10–5.*

☾ ⑮ Puppenhaus Museum (Doll House Museum). Bordering on the Barfüsserplatz, this museum has several floors filled with 18th- and 19th-century toys (including a cast of 2,000 Teddy bears) and classic miniature furnishings, displayed in highly detailed settings and landscapes. ⊠ *Steinenvorstadt 1, Grossbasel* ☎ *061/2259595* ⊕ *www.puppenhausmuseum.ch* ⊠ *7 SF* ☉ *Daily 10–6.*

★ ㉒ Rathaus (Town Hall). This bright red late-Gothic edifice, built to honor the city's entry into the Swiss Confederation in 1501, towers over the Marktplatz. Only the middle portion actually dates from the 16th century; pseudo-Gothic work was added in 1900. A massive clock with figures of the Madonna, the emperor Henry II, and his wife, Kunegunde, adorns the center of the facade; all around it is a series of colorful frescoes, painted in 1608. Step into the courtyard, where the frescoes continue. ⊠ *Marktpl., Grossbasel.*

NEED A BREAK? Choose a few jewel-like pastries and order leaf-brewed tea in the carved-wood environs of the clubby upstairs tearoom of the Confiserie Schiesser (⊠ *Marktpl. 19, Grossbasel* ☎ *061/2616077* ⊕ *www.confiserie-schiesser.ch*), steeping since 1870 in its prime location opposite the Town Hall.

Rheinsprung. A row of 15th- and 16th-century houses line this steep little alley in Grossbasel. Number 11 housed Basel's university when it was founded in 1460. ⊠ *Grossbasel, parallel to and south of Rhine, between Eiseng. and Stapfelbg.*

❽ St. Alban-Tor (St. Alban's Gate). This original medieval city gate is set amid a lovely garden near remnants of the town's ramparts. Parts of the gate date from the 13th century. ⊠ *St. Alban-Berg, St. Alban.*

WORD OF MOUTH

"The best atmosphere in Basel is definitely during Art Basel, the annual cutting-edge art exposition which usually takes place mid-June. A lot of trendy people around (but no hotel rooms!). During those some ten days, you think you are in a different town. If ever possible, I never miss that event."–Ursula12

A GOOD WALK

A scenic 1 hour, 55 minute boat ride will take you to Kaiseraugst, known for its thermal spas. From there walk uphill, following the signs to the ruins of **Augusta Raurica**, a 2,000-year-old Roman settlement that has been almost entirely rebuilt. Stop in for a map and a peek at the excavated treasures in the **Römermuseum**. Boats (Basler Personenschiffahrts-Gesellschaft ☎ 061/6399500 ⊕ www.bpg.ch) to

Augst depart from the Shifflände twice a day in high season. For a round-trip fare of 45 SF, you'll cruise slowly up the Rhine, passing the Old Town and the Münster.

🕙 TIMING TIPS➜ **Augst merits at least a half day, slightly more if you go by boat. Drinks and cold snacks are available on all cruises, hot meals on some. The last boat returning to Basel each day leaves Augst around 4:30 PM.**

⓲ **Spalentor** (Spalen Gate). Like the St. Alban-Tor, the Spalentor served as one of Basel's medieval city gates. More imposing than graceful, the 14th-century structure has a toothy wooden portcullis; note Basel's coat of arms atop the gate. ⊠ *Spalenvorstadt, Grossbasel.*

Statue of Helvetia. What would the woman pictured on most Swiss coins do if freed from the confines of currency? With spear and shield set aside (and with a packed suitcase in hand), this humanistic interpretation shows her seemingly contemplating the possibilities from a perch not far from the border of her homeland and the wide world beyond. ⊠ *Kleinbasel, northeastern bank of Rhine, near Mittlere Rheinbrücke, Kleinbasel.*

🐾 ⓮ **Zoologischer Garten** (Zoological Garden). Referred to by Baslers as *Zolli,* and famed for its armored rhinoceroses as well as its gorillas, pygmy hippopotamuses, and Javanese monkeys, this is no ordinary zoo. It is very child-friendly, and the enormous restaurant-pavilion in the center serves kid-size meals. ⊠ *Binningerstr. 40, Grossbasel* ☎ *061/2953535* ⊕ *www. zoobasel.ch* 🎟 *16 SF* 🕙 *Jan. and Feb., Nov. and Dec., daily 8–5:30; Mar. and Apr., Sept. and Oct., daily 8–6; May–Aug., daily 8–6:30.*

Colonia Augusta Raurica (Augst)

Founded in 44–43 BC, Augst is the oldest Roman settlement on the Rhine and today has been largely reconstructed as a noted museum of ancient Roman antiquities (one suspects the Swiss might have done the same with Rome's Colosseum if they had gotten their hands on it). The site is reachable by car from Basel in 10 minutes or in summer via a leisurely boat trip up the river. From the SBB Bahnhof take train S1 to Kaiseraugst, or bus 70 from Basel-Aeschenvorstadt to Augst; thereafter it takes approximately 10 minutes from both these stops to walk to the Roman Museum. To view the restoration areas scattered around the almost suburban neighborhood, be prepared for a fair bit of walking.

Sights to See

★ **Augusta Raurica.** The remains of this 2,000-year-old Roman settlement have been extensively rebuilt, with substantial portions of the ancient town walls and gates, streets, water pipes, and heating systems all in evidence. Restoration of the 1st-century BC theater is expected to be completed by July 2007.

Römermuseum (Roman Museum). Roman daily life is vividly depicted in this rebuilt ocher-hue home. Everything from the thermal baths to the ancient board games in the sitting rooms has been completely re-created. The museum also exhibits a treasure trove of Roman-era coins and silver unearthed in 1962. The objects, dating mostly from the 4th century, are believed to have been buried by the Romans in 350 to protect them from the ravages of the Alemanni, the German tribes who drove the Romans out of Switzerland. Trilingual (English/French/German) brochures are available. ⊠ *Giebenacherstr. 17, Augst* ☎ *061/8162222* ⊕ *www.augusta-raurica.ch* ☜ *7 SF* ⊙ *Mar.–Oct., Mon. 1–5, Tues.–Sun. 10–5; Nov.–Feb., daily 10–noon, 1:30–5.*

WHERE TO EAT

Of course Basel can't help but show the sophistication of generations of cosmopolitan influence, so the city boasts a wide variety of innovative eateries, many of them world-class (and priced accordingly). In fact, dining in Basel tends to be a pricey venture, whether your sausage is stuffed with lobster and truffles or mere pork. To keep expenses down, look out for lunch specials (*Tagesmenu*).

★ **$$$–$$$$** ✕ **Bruderholz.** Chef Patrick Zimmermann continues in the vein of the late master chef Hans Stucki at what is still one of Basel's best spots. Classics include frog's legs with black truffles, and chestnut honey duck with Sicilian blood oranges. The service at this restaurant, in the residential neighborhood of Bruderholz, is formal. Take tram 15 from Marktplatz, direction Bruderholz to Radio Studio Basel. ⊠ *Bruderholzallee 42, Bruderholz* ☎ *061/3618222* ⊕ *www.stucki-bruderholz.ch* ⌕ *Reservations essential* ▤ *AE, DC, MC, V* ⊙ *Closed Sun. and Mon.*

$$$–$$$$ ✕ **Chez Donati.** Now under the wing of Les Trois Rois hotel, this much-loved establishment still serves up a selection of Italian standards and is famous for its antipasti. Other specialties include osso buco and braised beef. The traditional, gilt-framed Venetian paintings are supplemented with modern art (the Art Basel crowd has long convened here, including once-regulars Andy Warhol and jean Tinguely), but you can still get a view of the Rhine from your white-draped table. ⊠ *St. Johanns-Vorstadt 48, Grossbasel* ☎ *061/3220919* ⊕ *www.lestroisrois.com* ▤ *AE, DC, MC, V* ⊙ *Closed Sun. and Mon.*

$$–$$$$
Fodor'sChoice
★ ✕ **Teufelhof.** Monica and Dominique Thommy have transformed a grand old Heuberg mansion into a cultural center boasting two restaurants, a trendy bar, and even medieval ruins in the basement. The formal Bel Étage showcases Michael Baader's masterly culinary inventions, including reindeer fillets in rose-hip sauce and St. Pierre fillet with tarragon risotto and lobster sauce. Sip wines by the glass, then buy the bottle in the house wineshop. The casual, high-tech *Weinstube* serves 10 dishes

that change daily, plus a three-course menu. ✉ *Leonhardsgraben 49, Grossbasel* ☎ *061/2611010* ⊕ *www.teufelhof.com* ⊟ *AE, DC, MC, V* ⊙ *Bel Étage closed Sun. and Mon. No lunch Sat.*

★ **$–$$$$** ✕ **Schlüsselzunft.** A favorite of many, but closed at this writing for a massive renovation (reopening date is expected to be in late 2007), this historic guildhall holds an elegant little restaurant with a ceramic stove, as well as an inexpensive courtyard brasserie and café called the Schlüsselhöfli. The restaurant, which in the past drew a business-lunch crowd, was noted for its well-bred seasonal cuisine such as *Bâloise,* meaning liver with onions, and a Basel-style salmon dish. The brasserie served a cheaper menu that changed daily. ✉ *Freie Str. 25, Grossbasel* ☎ *061/2612046* ⚐ *Reservations essential* ⊟ *AE, MC, V* ⊙ *Closed Sun.*

$$$ ✕ **Zum Goldenen Sternen.** Dating from 1506, this *Gasthof* claims to be the oldest restaurant in Switzerland, though the building has been moved from the center to its current Rhine-side site. The impeccable restoration retains the antique beams, stenciled ceilings, and unvarnished planks, yet without seeming contrived (in summer you can also opt for *al fresco* eating on the river terrace out front or in the garden out back). Though it could easily play a secondary role, the food almost lives up to the setting: game and fish are strong suits—one favorite is the *Fisch Harmonie,* a sampling of six kinds of fish with saffron sauce. There's also a seven-course tasting menu that changes monthly. The management does its best to discourage smoking and the use of cell phones. ✉ *St. Alban-Rheinweg 70, St. Alban* ☎ *061/2721666* ⊕ *www.sternen-basel. ch* ⚐ *Reservations essential* ⊟ *AE, DC, MC, V.*

Fodor'sChoice ★

$$–$$$ ✕ **Löwenzorn.** This is a classic, comfortable gathering place serving typical Swiss food. The menu features everything from *cordon bleu* (bread-stuffed veal) to vegetarian offerings. Regulars come for a beer, a full plate, and some laughs with the friendly staff. With stained-glass lamps, ceramic stoves, and nice woodwork, it's a nice mix of bistro and beer hall. ✉ *Gemsberg 2–4, Grossbasel* ☎ *061/2614213* ⊕ *www.loewenzorn.ch* ⊟ *AE, DC, MC, V.*

$$–$$$ ✕ **St. Alban-Eck.** This bistro, a five-minute walk behind the Kunstmuseum, is a well-known landmark in the Old Town. In a half-timber historic home, it's a real *petit coin sympa* (friendly little place), with plank wainscoting in natural wood, framed historic prints, and net curtains. The cuisine gracefully mixes Swiss and French favorites: sole, salmon, grilled entrecôte, and beef medallions in duck-liver sauce with market vegetables. ✉ *St. Alban-Vorstadt 60, St. Alban* ☎ *061/2710320* ⊕ *www. st-alban-eck.ch* ⚐ *Reservations essential* ⊟ *AE, DC, MC, V* ⊙ *Closed Sun. No lunch Sat.*

$$–$$$ ✕ **Zur Harmonie.** Local business people pack this *Jugendstil* (art nouveau) marvel, with its parquet floors and etched mirrors. Choose from a selection of delicious French and Swiss favorites, such as mussels, Wiener schnitzel, or the popular sausage salad with french fries. ✉ *Petersgraben 71, Grossbasel* ☎ *061/2610718* ⊕ *www.harmonie-basel.ch* ⚐ *Reservations essential* ⊟ *AE, DC, MC, V* ⊙ *Closed Sun.*

$$ ✕ **Susu's.** Chef Sven Tweer fuses Asian and Mediterranean influences to create classic dishes with a twist. In the first floor restaurant, suavely decorated in contemporary fashion, choose from dishes such as lamb

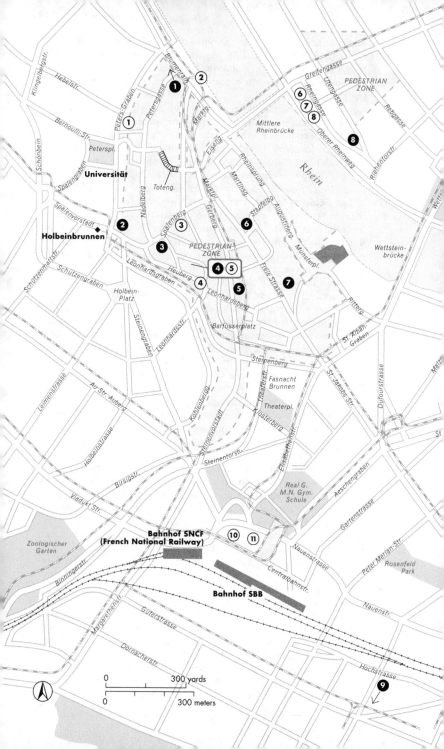

EATING WELL IN BASEL

WHEN THE GERMANIC HORDES arrived here to rout the Romans, they brought their favorite foods along with them. When Baslers enjoy a home-cooked meal, it's inevitably sausage, schnitzel, and *Spätzli* (tiny flour dumplings) washed down with beer.

The city's restaurants also pay more than a little homage to the cooking of the city's French neighbors. And being very cosmopolitan, there's an ever-changing—depending on what's in fashion—array of other cuisines available. Other than top-drawer places, Basel is full of comfortable haunts lined with

carved wood and thick with the mingled odors of cooking meat and cigar smoke.

The proximity of the Rhine means that most restaurants serve a variety of freshwater fish. If Basel could claim a regional specialty, it would be salmon. (These days much of it is shipped in from elsewhere, but the Rhine variety is making a comeback.) The meaty fish is best served *nach Basler-Art* (Basel-style), meaning in a white-wine marinade with fried onions on top. Try it with a bottle of the fruity local Riesling-Sylvaner.

with a pecan crust, Szechuan chicken, Zander Italian-style, or their trademarked Wok Your Way. Downstairs is a soup bar offering five different varieties daily and a confiserie with coffee and tea lounge, which becomes a bar after 6 PM. ✉ *Gerber. 73/ Falknerstr. 52* ☎ *061/ 2616780* ⊕ *www.susus.ch* ▤ *AE, MC, V* ✆ *Closed Sun.*

★ **$–$$** ✕ **Restaurant/Café Papiermühle.** With the plashing of the paper mill's waterwheel in the background, this is a restful spot for lunch or an afternoon snack (it's only open until 6 PM except on Friday). The hand-scrawled chalkboard usually includes two set meals, brunch favorites (quiches and *Birchermüsli*, the original, creamy, fruity version of muesli), salads, soups, and pasta dishes. Hand signals, however, are all you'll need to point out one of the homemade cakes. Every Friday night from 7 PM until midnight there is an Italian antipasti buffet. ✉ *St. Alban-Tal 37, St. Alban* ☎ *061/2724848* ⊕ *www.papiermuseum.ch* ▤ *No credit cards* ✆ *Closed Mon.*

★ **¢–$$** ✕ **Brauerei Fischerstube.** If you're serious about sampling the local color, stop in here for a cold one. The Fischerstube brews its own lagers and ales in the deep, frothing copper tanks at the end of the room. The house label, Ueli Bier, named for a Fasnacht clown, comes in a 5-liter tower served at your table or a 15-liter keg you can take home. Pretzels hang on racks on the sanded wooden tables, and the menu includes such local dishes as fillet steak and grilled *Würstli* (sausages). There's a beer garden out back. ✉ *Rheing. 45, Kleinbasel* ☎ *061/6926635* ⊕ *www. uelibier.ch* ✑ *Reservations essential* ▤ *AE, DC, MC, V.*

¢–$ ✕ **Café Pfalz.** This bookish little self-service café, down a narrow street near the cathedral, dishes out lunchtime veggie plates, sausages, and quiche in a trim beechwood-and-black contemporary setting. The impressive salad bar usually holds 25 different types of preparations. There is also a juice bar and at least one hot daily special. ☒ *Münsterberg 11, Gross-basel* ☏ *061/2726511* ⊕ *www.salat-laden.ch* ☱ *No credit cards* ☉ *Closed weekends. No dinner.*

WHERE TO STAY

With its industry, its banking, and its busy convention center offering a different trade fair most months, Basel is a city that prides itself on being a business center. The drawback, however, is that hotel prices tend to be steep, bargains in short supply, and amenities—minibars, data ports, meeting rooms—more important than atmosphere in the all-out competition for expense-account travelers. When there's a trade fair in town, prices shoot through the roof and every bed for miles can be filled, so book well ahead.

$$$$
Fodor\'sChoice
★
🏨 Les Trois Rois. Voltaire, Napoléon, Kaiser Wilhelm II . . . and now you? Basel's leading rendezvous for the rich and famous ever since three 11th-century kings (Conrad II, Henry III, and Rudolf III) once convened here, the Drei Könige—to use its German name—has long been an integral part of Basel history. Once a small inn on the banks of the Rhine, then a coach stop, it was given a regal makeover in 1835. Today, the furnishings have regained their 19th-century grandeur, with ravishing colors of cream, gilt, and powder blue; ornate woodwork, paintings and tapestries nudge the opulence factor ever higher. The lobby is a symphony of beiges, walnuts, and Sezession-style armchairs; the bar, a resplendent statement in rouge-reds and sunny oranges. There is a feast here for the stomach as well as the eyes: the formal Cheval Blanc restaurant serves up French *cuisine classique* on the broad, awning-shaded Rhine terrace (well heated into fall); the Brasserie proffers a stunning glass wall overlooking the river; while Chez Donati pays its respects to Piedmontese Italian food and hot modern art. All in all, while expanded, restored (by the Counts des Boisrouvray), and a virtual tourist attraction (those three statues of kings on the facade), this hotel remains surprisingly intimate and understated in the best Swiss way. Note: Riverside rooms get higher rates but you can be sure the Rolling Stones and opera star Montserrat Caballé splurged on them. ☒ *Blumenrain 8, Grossbasel, CH-4001* ☏ *061/2605050* 🖷 *061/2605060* ⊕ *www.lestroisrois.com* ⌨ *83 rooms, 18 suites* ♨ *3 restaurants, room service, in-room safes, in-room DVD, Wi-Fi, gym, sauna, bar, dry cleaning, laundry services, business services, parking (fee), no-smoking floors* ☱ *AE, DC, MC, V* ⦿ *EP.*

$$–$$$$
🏨 Basel. This all-modern hotel has become part of the Old Town neighborhood, its bars and restaurants filling with locals after work. The wood-panel rooms are accented with contemporary leather furniture and chrome; polished marble adds luster to the baths. The clientele during the week is almost exclusively business executives, which means there's plenty of room on the weekends. ☒ *Münzg. 12, Grossbasel, CH-4001* ☏ *061/2646800* 🖷 *061/2646811* ⊕ *www.hotel-basel.ch* ⌨ *69 rooms, 3 suites* ♨ *2 restaurants, in-room safes, minibars, Wi-Fi, bar, dry cleaning, laundry services, parking (fee), meeting rooms, no-smoking floors* ☱ *AE, DC, MC, V* ⦿ *BP.*

★ $$$ **Euler.** An archetypal old-world hotel, this landmark attracts a loyal business clientele that mingles over a *Cüpli* (glass of champagne) in the famous leather-and-red-velvet bar. Duvets billow over the bed frames in some of the cushier rooms and suites; standard rooms are furnished classically with reproduction antique furnishings and have glazed windows to cut out tram-traffic noise, unavoidable because of its city center location. ✉ *Centralbahnpl. 14, Grossbasel, CH-4002* ☎ *061/2758000* 📠 *061/2758050* 🌐 *www.hoteleuler.ch* *55 rooms, 9 suites* *Restaurant, room service, in-room safes, minibars, Wi-Fi, piano bar, babysitting, meeting rooms, parking (fee), no-smoking rooms; no a/c in some rooms* 💳 *AE, MC, V* 🍽 *EP.*

★ $$$ **Teufelhof.** This bastion of style and cuisine has an Art Hotel whose nine rooms are works of art in their own right: each has been redecorated by a different Swiss artist. They range from motifs of anamorphic flowers to felt installations to a commentary on the Bible—all should bring joy to readers of *Artforum.* By contrast, the serenely simple rooms of the adjoining Gallery Hotel function collectively as a canvas for one particular artist to show off work from one of his periods (in ever-changing shows); in addition, modernist furniture by Achille Castiglioni and other masters provide striking accents. An in-house theater puts on various shows in German from mid-September to early May. In-room TVs are available upon request. ✉ *Leonhardsgraben 49, Grossbasel, CH-4051* ☎ *061/2611010* 📠 *061/2611004* 🌐 *www.teufelhof.com* *29 rooms, 4 suites* *2 restaurants, café, room service, in-room safes, Wi-Fi, bar, wineshop, theater; no a/c, no room TVs* 💳 *AE, DC, MC, V* 🍽 *BP.*

$$–$$$ Fodor's Choice ★ **Krafft.** Smack on the waterfront sits this elegant mansion with mosaic-tile entrance hall, glittering chandeliers, and a sinuous atrium stairwell. Renovated throughout, the Krafft has an airy and elegant feel about it; the wooden flooring has been restored and rooms are simply furnished with Swiss designer furniture. A snazzy tea and drinking water station is a refreshing addition to each floor. The traditional dining room and ever-popular waterfront terrace offer spectacular views of the Old Town, while the downstairs Zem Schnooggeloch (Mosquito's Den) is welcoming on colder days. ✉ *Rheing. 12, Kleinbasel, CH-4058* ☎ *061/6909130* 📠 *061/6909131* 🌐 *www.hotelkrafft.ch* *45 rooms* *Restaurant, Wi-Fi, meeting rooms; no a/c, no smoking* 💳 *AE, DC, MC, V* 🍽 *CP.*

$$–$$$ **Merian am Rhein.** With top rooms overlooking the Rhine, this hotel has a modern, airy look accented with touches of gray wood, russet leather, and Le Corbusier chairs. The hotel is most famed for its Café Spitz, which has been a meeting place since the early 13th century, but you wouldn't guess it to look at it; now it's done in postmodern beeches, linens, and halogen lamps. Fish dominate the decor as well as the menu. In summer, opt for the lovely restaurant terrace over the water. ✉ *Rheing. 2, Kleinbasel, CH-4058* ☎ *061/6851111* 📠 *061/6851112* 🌐 *www.hotelmerianbasel.ch* *65 rooms* *Restaurant, café, room service, in-room safes, minibars, cable TV, Wi-Fi, meeting rooms, parking (fee), no-smoking floor; no a/c* 💳 *AE, DC, MC, V* 🍽 *CP.*

$$ **Rochat.** Location is this modest but roomy property's main asset; it's across from the university. The main building, a brownstone dating from 1898, has a dormlike feel, while the whitewashed annex, with its twisting hallways, comes across as a scaled-down inn. The restaurant does

not serve alcohol. ✉ *Petersgraben 23, Grossbasel, CH-4051* ☎ *061/ 2618140* 🖷 *061/2616492* ⊕ *www. hotelrochat.ch* 🛏 *50 rooms* ⛾ *Restaurant, café, in-room safes, minibars, Wi-Fi, meeting rooms, parking (fee), no-smoking rooms; no a/c in some rooms* ⊟ *AE, DC, MC, V* ⦿ *BP.*

★ **$–$$** 🏨 **Central.** This establishment is under the same management as the nearby Euler, where, in fact, you head to pick up your key. Rooms

can be on the small side but are tasteful and cheerful; dashes of vivid color include tangerine bedspreads. The hotel is reached via a newly constructed corridor from its parent hotel, with which it shares a fine level of service. ✉ *Kücheng. 7, Grossbasel, CH-4002* ☎ *061/2758000* 🖷 *061/ 2758050* ⊕ *www.hoteleuler.ch* 🛏 *23 rooms* ⛾ *Wi-Fi, parking (fee); no a/c* ⊟ *AE, MC, V* ⦿ *EP.*

★ **$–$$** 🏨 **Hotel Brasserie Au Violon.** The former residents here—priests and prisoners—never had it so good. Housed in a 12th-century building that served as a cloister and then a prison, the hotel now captivates its clientele with subdued elegance, a peaceful location, and a terrific restaurant. There are some reminders of the building's austere past—rooms overlooking the courtyard still conform to cell-block arrangements, with uniformly tight square footage. Rooms facing the town offer more space. The brasserie, with its mirrored bar, art deco fixtures, and iron-leg tables, serves French classics. ✉ *Im Lohnhof 4, Grossbasel, CH-4051* ☎ *061/2698711* 🖷 *061/2698712* ⊕ *www.au-violon.com* 🛏 *20 rooms* ⛾ *Restaurant, TV in some rooms; no a/c, no smoking* ⊟ *AE, MC, V* ⦿ *EP* ⊘ *Closed between Christmas and New Year.*

★ **$** 🏨 **Hecht am Rhein.** Situated between two more expensive hotels, this budget lodging offers faded comfort and a friendly staff. The rooms here seem bigger than in the neighboring establishments and are simply furnished with aged leather chairs, wood-backed beds, and an astonishing selection of art prints. Each floor has a large seating area and clean, bright, and inviting showers. There is a welcoming breakfast room on the top floor. The popular terrace restaurant serves pizza in summer. ✉ *Rheing. 8, Kleinbasel, CH-4058* ☎ *061/6901515* 🖷 *061/6810788* 🛏 *30 rooms* ⛾ *Restaurant; no a/c, no room TVs* ⊟ *DC, MC, V* ⦿ *BP.*

¢–**$** 🏨 **EasyHotel.** Located in Kleinbasel, the first EasyHotel in Switzerland opened in 2005. Rooms are compact, minimalist, and contemporarily decorated with orange detail; some come without windows (these have air-conditioning and are bargains in price). The lobby has vending machines, but the restaurant next door is open early until late. Rooms can only be booked via the Internet site. ✉ *Riehenring 109, Kleinbasel, CH-4058* ☎ *0900327927 (1.50 SF/min)* ⊕ *www.easyhotel.com* 🛏 *24 rooms* ⛾ *Pay TV, Wi-Fi (fee); no a/c in some rooms, no room phones, no smoking* ⊟ *AE, MC, V* ⦿ *EP.*

6

NIGHTLIFE & THE ARTS

For a complete listing of events, pick up a copy of *Basel Live,* a booklet published every two weeks. It's written partially in English. *Basel Events,* another listings publication, comes out monthly and is fully bilingual (German-English). Both are available at the tourist office and usually at hotel desks. If you'd like to play it by ear, the Steinenvorstadt is crowded with cinemas, bars, and young people, and on the Kleinbasel side, there are late-night bars along the Oberer Rheinweg.

Nightlife

Bars & Lounges

The extremely popular **Bar des Arts** (⊠ Barfüsserpl. 6, Grossbasel ☎ 061/2735737), a bistro/pub/lounge, pulls in an interesting mix of patrons. It began as an arty experiment, but the crimson interior of **Bar Rouge** (⊠ Level 31 Messeturm, Am Messepl., Kleinbasel ☎ 061/3613031) has caught on. The bar is on the top floor of the trade-fair tower. The landmark **Brauner Mutz** (⊠ Barfüsserpl. 10, Grossbasel ☎ 061/2613369) is a big beer hall with long wooden tables and a stein in every fist.

Campari Bar (⊠ Steinenberg 7, Grossbasel ☎ 061/2728383), behind the Kunsthalle and Tinguely Fountain, pulls in an artsy crowd with its pop-art interior and tree-canopied terrace. Inside the Hotel Euler, the **Euler Bar** (⊠ Centralbahnpl. 14, Grossbasel ☎ 061/2758000) draws a conservative crowd after work. A pianist plays from 6 PM until midnight, on the patio when the weather is warm. **Sperber** (⊠ Münzg. 12, Grossbasel ☎ 061/2646800) has the feel of an English pub; there's live music some evenings.

Dancing & Nightclubs

A wood-trimmed and mirrored club that offers garage, electro, funk, and jazz, **The Annex** (⊠ Binningerstr. 14, Grossbasel ☎ 061/2830070) is open Friday, Saturday, and Monday. **Atlantis** (⊠ Klosterberg 13, Grossbasel ☎ 061/2289696) offers live music, club nights, and a restaurant with a summer roof terrace. You have to be 25-plus to enjoy the three floors of music at **Disco-Bar Club 59** (⊠ Steinenvorstadt 33, Grossbasel ☎ 061/2815950) where the DJ rages through disco to rock and reggae.

The Arts

Advance bookings for many live performances can be made inside Bider & Tanner at **au Concert** (⊠ Aeschenvorstadt 2, Grossbasel ☎ 061/2722229). You can also purchase tickets at **TICKETCORNER** (⊠ On 5th floor inside Manor department store, Greifeng. 22, Kleinbasel ☎ 061/6854619).

Film

Movies in Basel are usually shown in the original language with subtitles. Most theaters are along Steinenvorstadt in the Old Town, and the titles and times are prominently posted. In summer there are open-air cinemas located in various locations, such as on the Münsterplatz.

Music

The **Musik-Akademie der Stadt Basel** (⊠ Leonhardsstr. 6, Grossbasel ☎ 061/2645757) is an important music academy drawing top-drawer international performers. The **Stadtcasino** (⊠ Steinenberg 14, Grossbasel ☎ 061/2737373) hosts the Basel Symphony Orchestra, the Basel Chamber Orchestra, and a wide range of visiting performers.

Theater

The **Musical Theater** (⊠ Feldbergstr. 151, Kleinbasel ☎ 061/6998899) is the venue for touring companies. **Theater Basel** (⊠ Theaterstr. 7, Grossbasel ☎ 061/2951133) hosts opera, operetta, and dance performances, as well as drama (usually in German); it is closed from the end of June to mid-August.

SHOPPING

The major downtown shopping district stretches along **Freie Strasse** and **Gerbergasse,** where you can find many one-of-a-kind boutiques. More reasonably priced shops along **Steinenvorstadt** cater to a younger crowd.

Department Stores

Coop City (⊠ Gerberg. 4, Grossbasel ☎ 061/2699250) carries a wide selection of clothing and household goods, as well as groceries in the basement. **Globus** (⊠ Marktpl. 2, Grossbasel ☎ 061/2684545) is an upscale department store, with gourmet edibles and sleek clothes. Whether you're in need of socks, toothpaste, or chocolate on the cheap, head to **Manor** (⊠ Greifeng. 22, Grossbasel ☎ 061/6854699). In the main train station, the supermarket **Migros** (⊠ Centralbahnpl., Grossbasel ☎ 061/ 2799745) stays open until 10 PM, seven days a week.

Specialty Stores

Antique Books

Among many fine competitors, **Erasmushaus** (⊠ Bäumleing. 18, Grossbasel ☎ 061/2289933) has one of the city's largest collections of fine antique manuscripts, books, and autographs, mostly in German but including some multilingual art publications. If they can not help you in the search for a particular tome, they will be happy to supply the names of the other specialist shops in the Basel area.

Calligraphy

Abraxas (⊠ Rheinsprung 6, Grossbasel ☎ 061/2616070) is a great source for fine writing instruments and paraphernalia, from thick paper and delicate fountain pens to luxurious sealing waxes and reproductions of antique silver seals. **Scriptorium am Rheinsprung** (⊠ Rheinsprung 2, Grossbasel ☎ 061/2613900) mixes its own ink and undertakes commissions on demand.

Crafts & Gifts

Though primarily specializing in home furnishings, **Atelier Baumgartner** (⊠ Spalenberg 8, Grossbasel ☎ 061/2610843) also stocks Swiss and Eu-

CLOSE UP

Mad About Soccer

Founded in 1893, Fussball Club Basel (www.fcbasel.ch) is one thing that can encourage the city's normally reserved residents to wave their arms, stomp their feet, and scream at the top of their lungs. Although the soccer team enjoyed many successful seasons in the 1960s and 1970s, its luck then seemed to run out. This didn't squash the support of its loyal fans, however. With most of the city backing the team, and whole families turning out to watch the matches, tickets are hard to come by. Surprising really, when you realize that their home stadium, St. Jakob-Park, is one of Switzerland's largest arenas. But when there's a game against their rivals from Zürich, the 30,000 seats are filled. Such devotion has helped FC Basel to become, once again, one of the most successful clubs in Switzerland. In recent years the team has topped the internal league more than once. In 2008 the opening game and the semifinals of the European Soccer Championships will be held at St. Jakob Park.

ropean handicrafts, including music boxes and nutcrackers from the Erzgebirge region of Germany. **Heimatwerk** (✉ Schneiderg. 2, Grossbasel ☎ 061/2619178) sells a selection of exquisite Swiss crafts. **Zem Baselstab** (✉ Schnabelg. 8, Grossbasel ☎ 061/2611016) has Fasnacht figurines and other Basel paraphernalia.

English-Language Media
Bider & Tanner (✉ Aeschenvorstadt 2, Grossbasel ☎ 061/2069999). **Thalia Bücher** (✉ Freie Str. 32, Grossbasel ☎ 061/2642626).

Food Specialties
Bachmann & Co. (✉ Gerberg. 51, Grossbasel ☎ 061/2613583 ✉ Blumenrain 1, Grossbasel ☎ 061/2614152 ✉ Centralbahnpl. 7, Grossbasel ☎ 061/2712627) carries a Basel specialty called *Leckerli,* a chewy cookie made of almonds, honey, dried fruit, and kirsch. **Glausi's** (✉ Spalenberg 12, Grossbasel ☎ 061/2618008) has a fine selection of Swiss cheeses and even ages its own. The famous **Läckerli-Huus** (✉ Gerberg. 57, Grossbasel ☎ 061/2642323) sells a variety of sweets, including wonderful Leckerli. A large selection of gift canisters and a shipping service make getting gifts home a cinch. **Schiesser** (✉ Marktpl. 19, Grossbasel ☎ 061/2616077), a convivial tearoom that opened in 1870, sells carefully crafted (and costly) confections in its downstairs shop.

Linens
Caraco (✉ Gerberg. 77, Falknerstr. entrance, Grossbasel ☎ 061/2613577) sells handmade Swiss lace and embroidered goods. **Langenthal** (✉ Gerberg. 26, Grossbasel ☎ 061/2610900) offers mostly Swiss products: tea towels, tablecloths, and folk-style aprons. **Sturzenegger** (✉ Theaterstr. 4, Grossbasel ☎ 061/2616867) specializes in household items, including lace from St. Gallen among other things.

Lingerie

Beldona (⌧ Freie Str. 103, Grossbasel ☎061/2731170) stocks classy Swiss lingerie. **Fogal** (⌧ Freie Str. 4, Grossbasel ☎ 061/2611220) sells Swiss hosiery; look out for its tray of clearance goods. **Sturzenegger** (⌧Theaterstr. 4, Grossbasel ☎061/2616867) carries an extensive line of undergarments with labels such as Hanro.

Men's Clothes

Classic Herrenmode (⌧ Fischmarkt 5, Grossbasel ☎061/2610755) car-ries formal and casual shirts, cash-

mere pullovers, and underwear. Serving gentlemen for over 100 years, **Fein-kalle & Co.** (⌧ Gerberg. 48, Grossbasel ☎ 061/2611233) has an im-peccable selection of designer wear from Armani to Brioni and Isaia.

> **THAT TIME OF YEAR ALL YEAR**
>
> Highly specialized handiwork comes from Johann Wanner (Spalenberg 14, Grossbasel, 061/2614826), which sells Christmas goods year-round, including handblown, hand-painted, and hand-molded ornaments, tin Vic-torian miniatures, Tartan ribbons, Advent cards and calendars, and Christmas cards.

Shoes

Müki (⌧ Münsterberg 14, Grossbasel ☎ 061/2712436) focuses on func-tional yet stylish European-made kids' shoes, plus designer minis from Dolce & Gabbana and Moschino. **Rive Gauche** (⌧ Schneiderg. 1, Gross-basel ☎ 061/2611080) carries high-end designer shoes. This is the place to satisfy that Prada, Mui Mui, or Marc Jacobs craving.

Toys

Bercher & Sternlicht (⌧ Spalenberg 45, Grossbasel ☎ 061/2612550) has miniature trains and accessories. **Spielegge** (⌧ Rümelinspl. 7, Grossbasel ☎ 061/2614488) places an emphasis on wood, with chisel-carved pup-pets and whimsical watercolor puzzles of fairy-tale scenes. **Spielhuus** (⌧ Eiseng. 8, Grossbasel ☎ 061/2649898) is a good source for board games and reasonably priced children's toys, as well as fanciful Fasnacht costumes.

Women's Clothes

Le Mouton à Cinq Pattes (⌧ Eiseng. 6, Grossbasel ☎ 061/2620007) sounds the siren call of a bargain; you'll find mostly cut-rate French and Italian styles. **Trois Pommes** (⌧ Freie Str. 74, Grossbasel ☎ 061/2729255) dominates the high end of fashion, with Jil Sander, Prada, Gucci, and Dolce & Gabbana.

BASEL ESSENTIALS

Transportation

BY AIR

CARRIERS There are connecting flights from Zürich into EuroAirport on Swiss.
✈ Airlines & Contacts **Swiss** ☎ 061/3253525 for reservations, 0848/852000 within Switzerland.

AIRPORTS Basel uses EuroAirport (just across the border in France), which is shared by Mulhouse in France and Freiburg in Germany. Direct flights link Basel to most major European cities. The nearest intercontinental airport is Unique Zürich Airport, which is approximately 80 km (50 mi) southeast of Basel.

✈Airport Information **EuroAirport** ☎061/3252511 ⊕www.euroairport.com. **Unique** Zurich Airport (Flughafen Zürich AG) ☎ 0900/300313 ⊕ www.unique.ch.

AIRPORT Regular bus service runs between EuroAirport and the SBB train sta-
TRANSFERS tion in the center of Basel. The trip takes about 15 minutes and costs 3.80 SF per person.

One-way taxi fare from the airport to the Basel center is approximately 45 SF; it takes about 15 minutes in light traffic and up to 30 minutes at rush hours (around 7:30 AM to 8:30 AM, noon to 2 PM, and 5 PM to 7 PM). There are normally cabs at the taxi stand, but if you need to call one from the airport, make sure you leave the building on the Swiss side.

✈ Taxis & Shuttles **33er Taxi** ☎ 061/3333333. **Mini Cab** ☎ 061/7777777. **Taxi-Zentrale** ☎ 061/2222222.

BY CAR

The German Autobahn A5 enters Basel from the north and leads directly to the Rhine and the center of the city. From France, the auto route A35 (E9) peters out at the frontier, and secondary urban roads lead to the center. The A2 Autobahn leads off to the rest of Switzerland. Since most of the city's sights are within walking distance of downtown, it's advisable to park your car for the duration of your visit.

BY TRAIN

There are two main rail stations in Basel. The Schweizerische Bundesbahnen (locally known as the SBB Bahnhof) in Grossbasel connects to destinations in Switzerland, France, and with the Intercity to Germany. The Deutsche Bundesbahn (known as the Badischer Bahnhof) in Kleinbasel runs services to Germany.

✈Train Information **Deutsche Bundesbahn** ✉Schwarzwalderstr. and Riehenstr., Kleinbasel ☎ 061/6901215. **Schweizerische Bundesbahnen** ✉ Centralbahnstr., Grossbasel ☎ 0900/300300.

BY TRAM

Most Basel trams run every 6–8 minutes all day, and every 15 minutes in the late evening. Tickets must be bought at the automatic machines at every stop (which give change). Stops are marked with green-and-white signs; generally the trams run from 5:30 or 6 in the morning until midnight or shortly thereafter. *Mehrfahrtenkarten* (multijourney cards) allow you 12 trips for the price of 10 and can be purchased from the ticket office at Barfüsserplatz. *Tageskarten* (day cards), from the ticket machines at the tram stops, allow unlimited travel all day within the central zone for 8 SF. Guests at hotels in Basel receive a complimentary Basel Mobility Ticket for free use of all public transportation for the duration of their stay. Holders of the Swiss Pass travel free on all Basel public transport systems.

Contacts & Resources

EMERGENCIES

For medical emergencies (including late-night pharmacy referrals) or to contact the police, refer to the phone numbers listed below.

🚹 **Hospital (Unispital)** ☎ 061/2652525. **Medical Emergencies** ☎ 061/2611515. **Police** ☎ 117.

INTERNET & MAIL

🚹 **Internet Cafés Computerstudio Mausklick** ✉ Klingentalstr. 7, Kleinbasel ☎ 061/6834182 ⊕ www.mausklickbasel.ch. **Thalia Bücher AG** ✉ Freie Str. 32, Grossbasel ☎ 061/2642626 ⊕ www.thalia.ch.

🚹 **Post Offices Die Schweizerische Post Basel (main post office)** ✉ Rüdeng. 1, Grossbasel ☎ 061/2661616. **Die Schweizerische Post (next to SBB Bahnhof)** ✉ Postpassage 9, Grossbasel ☎ 061/2785435.

TOUR OPTIONS

Basel Tourismus organizes a daily two-hour walking tour of the city. This starts from the tourist information office in the Stadtcasino and caters to German, French, and English speakers. Tours take place from May to mid-October, Monday through Saturday at 2:30. From mid-October to April the walking tours are held every Saturday at 2:30. The cost is 15 SF.

VISITOR INFORMATION

The main tourist information desk in Basel is in the Stadtcasino at Barfüsserplatz and is open weekdays 8:30–6:30, Saturday 10–5, Sunday and holidays 10–4. The Basel tourism branch at the SBB train station can also help you with hotel reservations and museum information.

🚹 **Tourist Information Basel Tourismus** (Basel Tourism) ✉ Stadt-Casino, Steinenberg 14, Grossbasel ☎ 061/2686868 🖷 061/2686870 ⊕ www.baseltourismus.ch. **Basel Tourismus** ✉ Bahnhof, SBB, Grossbasel ☎ 061/2686868.

CHEESE: FRIBOURG'S CALLING CARD

A TRAVELER CRUISING SWITZERLAND'S EMERALD HILLS and villages far from industrial turf can't help but notice the damp, fresh, earthy ephemera of the dairy that hangs in the air—a mild, musky tang that scents the cream, thickens the chocolate, and alchemizes the cheese. And no where else will you smell this as strongly as in the region of Fribourg—this is the region that gave birth to the most famous cheese that goes into fondue, Gruyère, and its sits shoulder-to-shoulder with two other areas that gave us great cheeses: Emmentaler (near Bern) and Tête de Moine from the Jura mountains. Today, as always, Swiss cheese is most delightfully experienced in that most satisfying of all Swiss dishes, fondue, which first became fashionable in America during the 1950s ski craze. Those who have not acquire the habit feel uncomfortably replete after only a few mouthfuls. Halfway through the repast a halt is called, presumably to draw breath, and the pause is mellowed by a small glass of Kirsch—the perfect digestif (guests are warned never to drink water or beer after fondue but only white wine, Kirsch, tea, or coffee).

The word fondue comes from the French *fondre* ("to melt"). With its pungent crushed garlic and sting of kirsch stirred through the creamy molten mass, its flavors are relatively complex. Different regions press the subtlety further by demanding specific blends of local chees to create the only true fondue: Proportions of aged Gruyère and milder Emmental vary, and in Fribourg, it's also made with a creamy Vacherin. No matter which province you try it in, it is comforting to know that the convival system of sharing fondue around a table dates back to the ancient peasant tradition of circling around a common pot for the family meal. For that matter, cheese is available around the clock. A good Swiss breakfast won't be served without a fan of brown-skinned slices of Gruyère, Emmental (the one with the holes that gave "Swiss cheese" its name), or Appenzeller. Cubed cheese may show up in your lunch salad of *Käsesalt*. And after a French-style meal, there's always the cheese course.

The great commercial cheese factories of Gruyères and Emmental still stir their cheese in vast copper cauldrons, and their fires are still fueled by wood. Holding vast amount of cheeses aging for months to years, the storage racks of the biggest producers—the stacks, as it were—could rival those of the Library of Congress. But head into the hills of Fribourg and you'll see that if the cheese industry has one foot in the factory it has the other on the farm. In old copper pots over wood fires, each family of cheesemakers stirs its own daily milk, gathers up the thick curd in broad cheesecloth, squeezes out excess whey with a wooden press, and molds the cheese into a round wheel. Each cheese is stamped with the family brand and carried down into the village, where a modern cooperative *affineur* carefully supervises its aging—with each cheese washed and turned according to a schedule well tested over the centuries—until the farmer reclaims the finished product to sell or keep as he likes.

Fribourg & Neuchâtel

7

WORD OF MOUTH

"There's just something about the entire character of the place that makes it what I would call 'real hometown Swiss'—its so non-touristy, so serene, and so much like what Switzerland probably is like without all the visitors."

–Wayne4

"The medieval town of Gruyères—where the cheese comes from— is pretty, there's a nice little castle, and you can have great fondue and raclette (surprise!)."

–Andre

WELCOME TO FRIBOURG & NEUCHÂTEL

TOP REASONS TO GO

★ **Stir the Melting Pot:** Fondue—officially known as fondue fribourgeoise—was invented here partly to honor the region's famous, fabulous Gruyère cheese.

★ **Switzerland's Largest Lake:** Lac Neuchâtel is a great place for a boat trip, to try out wakeboarding, or to savor the fine fish served on its shores.

★ **You say Schloss:** And I say Chateau. In either language, this area has some of Switzerland's most impressive castles, from Grandson to Gruyères.

★ **Home-Grown Talent:** Whether it's the clockwork extravaganzas of Tinguely or the disturbing alienlike creations of Giger, these two sculptors are true eye-knockers.

★ **Gorgeous Gruyères:** Step into a postcard in this perfect specimen of a medieval stronghold, its single main street cozy within the ramparts.

1 Fribourg. One of Switzerland's best-kept secrets, Fribourg's medieval Old Town features steep, cobbled streets and bridges in all styles from wooden to suspension. Get enlightened with the cathedral's noted Art Nouveau stained glass.

Wakeboarding on Lake Neuchâtel.

2 Gruyères. Be sure to visit a modern and traditional demonstration dairy, both making the famous Gruyère cheese, then tour this car-free village, picture-box perfect with its castle and geranium-clad houses.

3 Murten. This bilingual lakeside resort with its boat-lined waterfront seems far too peaceful to have been home to a fierce battle—but back in 1476 the Swiss Confederates trounced the Burgundians here.

Fribourg

FRANCE

VAL DE TRAVERS

Fleurier

A5

Yverdon

Vallorbe

A1
A9

A1

Lausanne

Lac Léman

Gruyères castle

Tramelan

FRANCHES MONTAGNES

Biel

Le Chaux
De Fonds

*Bieler
See*   Lyss

A5

Aarberg

Neuchâtel   **4**

Ins

Kerzers

Boudry

*Lac de
Morat*   Murten   **3**

A1

Bern

Lac Neuchâtel

Neuenegg

*Schiffenen
See*

A12

Düdingen

1   Payerne

Fribourg

1

Moudon

*Lac de la
Gruyère*

▲ *Vounetse*

Bulle

A12   Gruyères   **2**

Châtel-
St-Denis

HAUTE GRUYÈRE

A9

*Dent
de Lys* ▲

▲ *Vanil
Noir*

0   5 mi

Vevey

0   5 km

A9

GETTING
ORIENTED

This area is roughly organized like a hand. At the wrist are the Alpine foothills of Fribourg; these curve gently down to the palm of flatter Neuchâtel, with the long ellipse of Lac Neuchâtel. Beyond lie the Jura's rugged fingers, which form valleys in the Jura Mountains and finally come to rest on the plateaus.

7

4 Neuchâtel. Flanked by vineyards, this French-accented city celebrates the grape each fall with a weekend of parades and feasting. Enjoy its architecture—Romanesque to Rococo—and discover the Bronze Age lifestyle of stilt-house people at Latènium.

Murten

FRIBOURG & NEUCHÂTEL PLANNER

The Good Table

Both Fribourg and Neuchâtel have a plethora of top-quality, French-influenced, *gastronomique* (ultragourmet) restaurants. They offer far cheaper lunch menus (three or more courses) or at least an *assiette du jour* (daily special) for less than 20 SF.

No one here lays down strict dress codes. Ever sensible, the Swiss expect common sense from their customers: the fancier the restaurant, the fancier the attire, but you won't be thrown out for not wearing a tie.

Restaurants open about 6 in the evening, though diners tend to arrive closer to 7:30, and kitchens wind down between 9:30 and 10.

Lunch is usually served from 11:30 to 2, but you can often get simple fare even after that.

Try a crêperie for a quick, cheap meal that still has local flavor. The closer you are to France, the more of these you'll find.

Finding a Place to Stay

As they become more tourist-oriented, Fribourg and Neuchâtel are developing a better hotel infrastructure. Fribourg is the best equipped, though there's still only a handful of choices in the Old Town.

In Neuchâtel most lodgings are along the lake. Don't expect air-conditioning either; assume hotels don't have it unless it's specified. Many hotels offer more than one meal plan, so even if BP (breakfast plan) is specified in a review, it doesn't hurt to ask if another plan is available.

How's the Weather?

Spring and fall are beautiful times to visit anywhere in this region.

During the summer temperatures reach an average of 18-20° C (65-68°F), which is comfortable, but crowds tend to pick up, especially in Gruyres.

During a heatwave it's not unusual for temperatures to soar to 30° C (86°F). In winter, the average temperature is 0-3° C (32-38°F). In the pre-Alps region, there can be long periods of snowfall.

January is great for winter sports. You can't be sure of snow in December, and in February, some canton or other (not to mention the Germans, English, Dutch, and Italians) will invariably have school vacations, so slopes get pretty crowded. When the snow lasts, March is also ideal for skiing.

Making the Most of Your Time

Though the major sights themselves don't require too much time to visit, they are scattered throughout the region so it takes a while to get to them. You can easily explore much of this area by train or bus, while renting a car allows you to combine locations more efficiently. If you have only one or two days, try to take in one or more of the cities. Neuchâtel and Fribourg have very different characters and a day can easily be spent walking around the city centers, visiting a few of their museums, and sampling their restaurants. If you cut out the museums, then each of these could be combined with a trip to one of the smaller towns we mention nearby. Check the distances in the chapter and, if traveling by public transport, ask the local tourist office in advance about what is possible.

More time allows you to tour the area and take in its subtle differences. If you start at Fribourg, cut south to the castle at Gruyères, and from there circle northwest through the ancient town of Murten on your way to Neuchâtel. From Neuchâtel head south along the Route du Vignoble (Vineyard Road) to the château town of Grandson and onto Yverdon-les-Bains. Or spend some time pursuing the many sporting opportunities that the different seasons and towns have on offer. Alternatively the summer is the perfect time to take a long trip on the Lake of Neuchâtel or to enjoy a hike.

Throughout the year you'll encounter lighter tourist traffic here than in any other region. Summer is a lovely time, when forest glades become ripe with the smells of the woods but crowds tend to pick up, especially in Gruyères. Spring and fall are beautiful times to visit anywhere in this region. January is great for winter sports. You can't be sure of snow in December, and in February, some canton or other (not to mention the Germans, English, Dutch, and Italians) will invariably have school vacations, so slopes get pretty crowded. When the snow lasts, March is also ideal.

Feeling Festive

When the Alpine grass thins out in the fall, the cows of Haute Gruyères are led down to the village with huge bells around their necks and flowers and pine branches attached to their horns. Not to be outdone by their beasts, the cowherds wear their Sunday best: a dark blue jacket with embroidered edelweiss motifs and puffy short sleeves that optically double the width of the wearer's shoulders. To avoid two weeks of continual congestion on the roads, the foothill villages of Charmey (last Saturday in September) and Albeuve (first Saturday in October) have the herds descend together, making a folk festival of it—La Dèsalpe. Decorated cows, heifers, sheep, goats, and even pigs are paraded through the streets from 9 AM until about 3 PM. The partying goes on all day, with flag throwing, marching bands, alpenhorn playing, and stalls selling Bénichon (Kilbi in Swiss German) specialties. This harvest feast fetes not only the return of the cattle from the high pastures to the plains but also the season's final yield: chimney-smoked ham, served hot with *moutarde de Bénichon* (sweet mustard); mutton stew with plump raisins and potato puree; and tart *poires-à-Botzi* (pears poached in liquor and lightly caramelized). Don't worry if you miss La Dèsalpe itself, the restaurants across the region serve versions of Bénichon all fall.

WHAT IT COSTS In Swiss francs

	$$$$	$$$	$$	$	¢
Restaurants	over 60 SF	40 SF–60 SF	25 SF–40 SF	15 SF–25 SF	under 15 SF
Hotels	over 350 SF	250 SF–350 SF	175 SF–250 SF	100 SF–175 SF	under 100 SF

Restaurant prices are per person for a main course at dinner. Hotel prices are for two people in a standard double room in high season, including tax and service.

Updated by
Sharon-Anne
Wilcox

SHOULDERED BY THE MORE PROMINENT CANTONS of Bern and Vaud, the cantons of Fribourg and Neuchâtel are easily overlooked by hurried visitors. If they do stop, it is usually for a quick dip into Fribourg and Gruyères. That leaves the rest of this largely untouched area to the Swiss, who enjoy its relatively unspoiled nature and relaxed approach to life.

Although the strict cantonal borders are a messy reflection of historic power struggles, the regional boundaries are unmistakable, even to an outsider. Fribourg starts in the pre-Alpine foothills above Charmey and rolls down across green hills, tidy farms, and ancient towns until it reaches the silty shores of the Murten, Neuchâtel, and Biel lakes. The region of Neuchâtel begins in these silt-rich fields (which grow everything from lettuce to tobacco), sweeps across Lac Neuchâtel to its chateaux- and vineyard-lined western shore, and rises up to the Jura Mountains.

The Röstigraben (or Hash-Brown Trench, so called because Swiss Germans eat lots of *Rösti*) is the tongue-in-cheek name for the linguistic border where French meets German. It runs through Fribourg and butts up against the northern borders of Neuchâtel. In some towns you can walk into a *boulangerie* (bread bakery) selling dark *Vollkornbrot* (whole-grain bread) or find a family named Neuenschwand who hasn't spoken German for generations.

FRIBOURG

With its landscape of green hills against the craggy peaks of the pre-Alps, Fribourg is one of Switzerland's most rural cantons. Its famous Fribourgeois cows—the Holsteins (black and white, the colors of the cantonal coat of arms)—provide the canton with its main income, although light industry is replacing the cows. Fondue was invented here, as was Gruyère cheese and Switzerland's famous *crème-double* (double cream).

Fribourg

 To & From: *Direct trains from Fribourg to major Swiss cities: Geneva, two per hour (1 hr 25 min, 37 SF); Lausanne, two per hour (45–50 min, 22 SF); Bern, two per hour (22–35 min, 12.40 SF); Basel via Bern, no direct link (1 hr 30 min, 45 SF); Zurich, one per hour (1 hr 24 min, 51 SF). Buses leave from behind Fribourg's train station for villages in the surrounding canton. For departure times and prices for trains and buses for most destinations in this chapter, check with www.sbb.ch—the main Swiss public transportation Web site—or call 0900/300300 (1,19 SF per min). If your knowledge of French or German are good, then Fribourg and Neuchâtel offer Web sites with information on regional services: www.tpf.ch and www.trn.ch. Remember, if you have a Swiss Pass or another rail-discounting card, it also applies to the buses. Fribourg is 34 km (21 mi) southwest of Bern.*

Between the rich pasturelands of the Swiss plateau and the Alpine foothills, the Sarine River (called the Saane by German speakers) twists in an S-curve, its sandstone cliffs joined by webs of arching bridges. In one of the curves of the river is the medieval city of Fribourg. The city

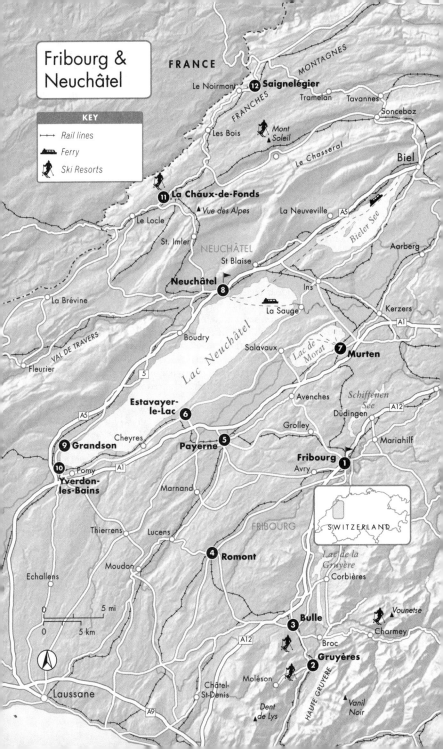

grew in overlapping layers; it's an astonishing place of hills and cobblestones, ramparts and Gothic fountains, ancient passageways and worn wooden stairs, red-orange rooftops and sudden views. Only on foot can you discover its secret charm as one of the finer ensembles of medieval architecture in Europe.

Fribourg is a stronghold of Catholicism; it remained staunchly Catholic even during the Reformation. The evidence is everywhere, from the numerous chapels and religious orders to the brown-robed novitiates walking the sidewalks. Fribourg University, founded in 1889, remains the only Catholic university in Switzerland. It is also the only bilingual institution of its kind and reflects the region's peculiar linguistic agility. Two-thirds of the people of Canton Fribourg are native French speakers, one-third are native German speakers, and many switch easily between the two. In the Basse-Ville neighborhood, old-timers still speak a unique mixture of the two languages called Boltz. The city is officially bilingual, although French predominates.

> ## AROUND THE WHIRL
>
> Bicycling is popular here, and itineraries are dazzling. Swiss Federal Railways (CFF/SBB) offers reasonably priced rentals at many train stations. Bicycles must be reserved at least one day in advance; in summer you should call at least three days in advance. In addition, tourist offices in Fribourg run a unique program for the Broye region called Bike Broye. They've charted 20 different biking itineraries (a vineyard or abbey tour, for example), each of which can be paired with an overnight package. Contact the Avenches tourist office two months in advance.

At its very core, and a good place to start a walk, is the **Basse-Ville** (Lower City), tucked into a crook of the river. Here you'll find the 11th- through 16th-century homes of the original village as well as a lively café and cellar-theater scene. The oldest bridge in this city of bridges is the **Pont de Berne** (Bern Bridge), to the north of the Basse-Ville. Once the only access to the territory of Bern, it's made entirely of wood.

As the town expanded from the Basse-Ville, it crossed the river over the Pont du Milieu (Middle Bridge) to a narrow bank, the Planche-Inférieure, with its picturesque terraced houses. As the town prospered, it spread to the more stately 16th- and 17th-century **Planche-Supérieure,** a large, sloping, open triangular *place* (square) that was once the busy livestock market. It is now lined with several upscale restaurants and cafés. From here you can walk up to the **Chapelle de Lorette** (Loreto Chapel), once a favored pilgrimage site, for the best view of Fribourg. When the Pont St-Jean was built in the 17th century, making the northern bank of the river readily accessible, the merchant houses and walled cloisters of the **Neuve-Ville** (New Town) popped up.

From the steep, partially cobbled rue Grand-Fontaine (best avoided at night unless you like red-light districts), you can spy narrow passageways and hidden courtyards, or you can take the funicular up and walk down the Rue des Alpes to the **Hôtel de Ville,** or Rathaus (Town Hall). This is the seat of the cantonal parliament, built on the foundations of the château of Berthold IV of Zähringen, who founded the town of Fribourg in 1157. The symmetrical stairways were added in the 17th century, as were the clockworks in the 16th-century clock tower.

From the place de Tilleul, the shop-lined rue de Lausanne and rue des Alpes climb upward, their tightly spaced 18th-century buildings hiding terraced gardens of surprising size. The 19th- and 20th-century section of the city begins at the top of rue de Lausanne; nearby are the main buildings of the university. The 21st century has arrived in the form of the Fribourg Center shopping mall, close to the station.

A block away from the Hôtel de Ville, the Gothic **Cathédrale St-Nicolas** (St. Nicholas Cathedral) rears up from the surrounding gray 18th-century buildings. Its massive tower was completed in the 15th century, two centuries after construction of the cathedral was begun in 1283. Above the main portal, a beautifully restored tympanum of the Last Judgment shows the blessed being gently herded left toward Peter, who holds the key to the heavenly gates; those not so fortunate head right, led by pig-face demons, into the jaws and cauldrons of hell. Inside you can see the famous 18th-century organ as well as the rare, restored 1657 organ. The exceptional stained-glass windows, installed between 1873 and 1983, are executed in a number of styles, including Pre-Raphaelite and Art Nouveau. In the **Chapelle du St-Sépulcre** (Chapel of St. Sepulchre) a group of 13 figures dating from 1433 portrays the entombment of Christ. If you can handle the 365 steps, climb up the tower for a panoramic view. (During services, you won't be allowed in.) ⊠ *rue St-Nicolas* ⌕ *Free, tower 3.50 SF* ☉ *To tourists: Mon.–Wed. and Fri. 9–6, Thurs. 9–2.30, 4–6, Sat. 9–5, Sun. 2–6; tower Mar.–Nov., Mon., Fri., and Sat. 10–noon, 2–5, Sun. 2–5.*

From the cathedral slip through the rue des Épouses to the Grand-rue, lined with 18th-century patrician homes. At the end of this street is the **Pont de Zaehringen** (Zähringen Bridge), with views over the Pont de Berne, the Pont de Gottéron, and the wooden remains of the ancient towers that once guarded the entrance to the city. You're now in the area where Duke Berthold IV first established his residence and founded the city in 1157.

NEED A BREAK? The terrace of **Le Café du Belvédère** (⊠ 36 Grand-rue ☎ 026/3234407) has a fabulous view up the river to the Planche-Supérieure. Inside it's a *café littéraire* by day and a lively bar and meeting spot at night. An eclectic mix of '70s plastic furniture and a huge, rounded plastic bar contrast wonderfully with the wood-beamed, old cottagey feel of the building. The friendly staff serves a selection of teas, coffees, and homemade syrups as well as alcohol, and you can get Asian snacks from the excellent Thai restaurant upstairs.

The 13th-century **Église des Cordeliers** (Church of the Franciscan Friars), north of the cathedral, is attached to a Franciscan friary. The lightness of its white walls and the rose-, gray-, and alabaster-color ceiling contrast with the Gothic darkness of the cathedral. A 16th-century polyptych by the anonymous Nelkenmeister, or Maîtres à l'Oeillet (who signed their works only with red and white carnations), hangs over the high altar. A carved wood triptych, believed to be Alsatian, and a 15th-century retable of the temptation of St. Anthony by the Fribourg artist Hans Fries, adorn the side walls. At the entrance to the

> **GO FOR THE VIEWS!**
>
> Climb the 365 steps of the tower of Cathédrale St-Nicolas for a stunning panoramic view.

cloister leading to the friary is a 13th-century five-panel fresco depicting the birth of the Virgin Mary. ⊠ *6 rue de Morat* ☎ *026/3471160* 🎫 *Free* ☉ *Mon.–Sat. 9–6, Sun. noon–6.*

Near the Église des Cordeliers, the **Musée d'Art et d'Histoire de Fribourg** (Fribourg Museum of Art and History) is housed in the Renaissance Ratzé mansion and, incongruously, an old slaughterhouse connected by an underground passage. The mansion displays 12th- to 19th-century art and history, including several works by Hans Fries. The 19th-century slaughterhouse, a stark stone structure modernized with steel-and-glass blocks, provides the setting for a provocative mix of sacred sculptures and the kinetic, scrap-iron whimsies of native son Jean Tinguely (1925–91). The attic gallery displays 19th- and 20th-century paintings from Swiss artists as well as from Delacroix, Courbet, and others. Take a breather in the quiet sculpture garden overlooking the river. Limited descriptive material in English is available upon request, and guided tours in English can be booked in advance. ⊠ *12 rue de Morat* ☎ *026/3055140* ⊕ *www.fr.ch/mahf* 🎫 *6–8 SF* ☉ *Tues., Wed., and Fri.–Sun. 11–6, Thurs. 11–8.*

☺ Once the city's tram terminal, the **Espace Jean Tinguely–Niki de Saint Phalle** now houses a selection of whirring, tapping, spinning metal sculptures by Jean Tinguely and a wall full of the voluptuous, colorful work of his wife, Niki de Saint Phalle. Her works are titled in English, while his need no explanation. Kids (16 and under free) are often fascinated by Tinguely's work. Something is happening somewhere all the time: skis are walking, a potted plant is turning, a toy rabbit is being hit on the head. ⊠ *2 rue de Morat* ☎ *026/3055140* 🎫 *4–6 SF* ☉ *Wed. and Fri.–Sun. 11–6, Thurs. 11–8.*

The **Musée Suisse de la Machine à Coudre** (Swiss Sewing Machine Museum) displays an example of almost every sewing machine ever built (more than 250). There's also a collection of contraptions created to ease the life of handworkers and housewives before the age of electricity, including useful household firsts such as vacuum cleaners and washing machines. A side room is packed with curiosities from bygone days, such as chestnut-hulling boots. Owner Edouard Wassmer will charm you with anecdotes and history. ⊠ *58 Grand-rue* ☎ *026/4752433* ⊕ *www.museewassmer.com* 🎫 *Free* ☉ *By appointment only.*

Where to Stay & Eat

$$–$$$ ✕ **Auberge de Zaehringen.** The oldest private house in Fribourg, now a brasserie, has been owned by only three families during its 700 years. The warmly lighted restaurant offers gracious service in a no-smoking environment, with traditional dishes on its menu such as beef fillet in a green

EATING WELL IN FRIBOURG & NEUCHÂTEL

The cuisines of these two regions all use robust, seasonal food: perch from the lakes, game and mushrooms from the forested highlands, and, of course, the dairy products of Fribourg and Gruyères. In the lake towns, menus are thick with *perche* (perch), *sandre* (a large cousin of the perch), *bondelle* (a pearly fleshed trout found exclusively in Lac Neuchâtel), or *silure* (catfish). Mushrooms are another strong suit, from the delicate *Schwämli* (*chanterelles* in French) to the robust *Steinpilz* (*bolets* in French), fat, fleshy mushrooms with a meaty texture and taste. These are particularly wonderful when sautéed and served with slices of dark bread or with local rabbit or venison, along with a glass of Neuchâtel pinot noir.

Many regions of Switzerland are known for fondue, but Fribourg is the source of *fondue fribourgeoise*, the combination of the canton's two greatest cheeses—Gruyère and Vacherin Fribourgeois—into a creamy *moitié-moitié* (half-and-half) blend. The Vacherin can be melted alone for an even creamier fondue, and potatoes can be dipped instead of bread.

Those familiar cows dotting the green landscape of the Fribourg countryside yield more than cheese, however. An additional debt of gratitude is owed them for producing crème-double, a Gruyères specialty that rivals Devonshire cream. A rich, extra-thick, high-fat cream that—without whipping—almost supports a standing spoon, it is served in tiny carved-wood *baquets* (vats), to be spooned over a bowl of berries and meringues.

7

pepper sauce. There are more exotic choices, too, like grilled salmon with mango and eggplant. ⊠ *13 rue de Zaehringen* ☎ *026/3224236.*

$$–$$$ ✕ **Des Trois Tours.** If you have a penchant for innovative, excellent food

Fodor'sChoice that is superbly presented, try this restaurant gastronomique just out-
★ side town. You can eat in the sunny, plant-filled bistro; in the more discreet ocher-and-blue dining room; or on the shady terrace in summer. Fast beforehand because a *menu du marché* (market menu) costs 110 SF to 135 SF, and you'll want to relish it all. Perhaps you'll eat your way from the lasagna of crêpes and wild mushrooms to the mosaic of fruits and sorbets via a mouthwatering series of mains and a groaning cheese trolley, but then again, perhaps not. The menu changes every month. ⊠ *15 rte. de Bourguillon, Bourguillon* ☎ *026/3223069* ⌂ *Reservations essential* ▤ *AE, DC, MC, V* ☺ *Closed Sun. and Mon. plus late July–early Aug. and late Dec.–early Jan.*

$–$$$ ✕ **Auberge de la Cigogne.** In the Basse-Ville, a friendly husband-and-wife team have created a flower-filled cozy restaurant (seating 35 to 40) from a former blacksmith shop. Opposite the wooden bridge, the building dates from 1771 and its fresco is the last one in Rococo-style in Fribourg. The menu is daring and changes five times a year, featuring dishes like caramelized veal with ginger and lemon, served with spiced basmati rice;

or turbot grilled on the bone with homemade orange butter and pureed potatoes flavored with virgin olive oil. For vegetarians there is a polenta cake, which once cut into oozes buffalo mozzarella; or ask for the seasonal house dish. ✉ *24 rue d'Or* ☎ *026/3226834* 💳 *AE, DC, MC, V* ⏲ *Closed Sun. and Mon.; late Feb.–early Mar.; first 2 wks Sept.*

GETTING THERE

To reach restaurant Des Trois Tours, take the 127 bus from Fribourg train station to Bourguillon; it leaves every hour until early evening (10-15 min. journey; 3.20 SF). There is also a night bus. Taxis take around the same amount of time and cost 20-30 SF.

$$ ✕ **L'Epée.** It's a good idea to make reservations at this popular brasserie in the Basse-Ville. The food is delicious and reasonably priced, the staff is friendly, and the view up to the cathedral and the Neuve-Ville is a real draw—from inside or the terrace, by day or night. Options include ricotta-filled ravioli in an onion and mushroom sauce, an oh-so-tender rack of lamb with basil, and meringues with *vin cuit* (cooked wine) and Gruyère cream. ✉ *39 Planche-Supérieure* ☎ *026/3223407* 💳 *MC, V* ⏲ *Closed Sun. and late July–late Aug. No dinner Mon.*

¢ ✕ **Xpresso Café.** On the fourth floor of the Fribourg Center, this café–crêperie does waffles and crêpes—both savory and sweet. You can also choose from a wide selection of teas and coffees. ✉ *10 av. de la Gare* ☎ *026/3417808* 💳 *No credit cards* ⏲ *Closed Sun. No dinner.*

★ **$$** ✕🏨 **Au Sauvage.** The Sauvage began in the 1600s as a cloister, became an inn during the cattle-market days in the 18th and 19th centuries, and is now a sophisticated auberge with a striking blend of minimalism and medieval details. In the guest rooms, thick, whitewashed stone walls hide TVs, while sleek bathrooms include elegant vanities. The small dining room ($$–$$$), under the original vaulted ceiling, serves French-influenced cuisine, such as beef in a pesto-and-cheese crust and fish served with exotic fruit and green curry. One room (and bathroom) is wheelchair accessible. ✉ *12 Planche-Supérieure, CH-1700* ☎ *026/3473060* 📠 *026/3473061* 🌐 *www.hotel-sauvage.ch* 🛏 *17 rooms* 👍 *Restaurant, in-room safes, minibars, cable TV, Wi-Fi, bar, meeting room, free parking, some pets allowed (fee); no smoking* 💳 *AE, MC, V* ⏲ *Restaurant closed Sun., Mon., and July* 🍽 *BP.*

$$ 🏨 **Hôtel de la Rose.** In a typical 17th-century sandstone house, this hotel is within walking distance of museums, churches, the cathedral, and the Old Town. The hotel is friendly and familial, all rooms have been recently renovated and offer tea/coffee making facilities. Ask for a quiet room away from the main street. ✉ *1 rue de Morat, CH-1702* ☎ *026/3510101* 📠 *026/3510100* 🌐 *www.hotelrose.com* 🛏 *40 rooms* 👍 *Restaurant, coffee shop, in-room safes, minibars, cable TV with movies, Wi-Fi, bar, laundry service, business services, meeting room, some pets allowed (fee), parking (fee), no-smoking rooms* 💳 *AE, DC, MC, V* 🍽 *BP.*

$–$$ 🏨 **Auberge aux 4 Vents.** This small hotel with its fabulous gardens and
Fodor's Choice ★ themed rooms is very popular so book early, especially for Babylone with its red-and-white tiled interior and raised bed, or Bleue where a cast-iron bath takes center stage. Grandfey is a turn-off because it's close to the northern *autoroute* (expressway) exit. The hotel can be reached by

bus from Fribourg (Bus No.1 direction Portes de Fribourg/St. Leonard. Get off at Poya [fare 2.20 SF] and then it's a charming 10-minute walk up the rue de Grandfey). ⊠ *124 Grandfey, CH-1702* ☎ *026/3473600* 🖷 *026/3473610* ⊕ *www.auberge.aux4vents.ch* ⇥ *8 rooms* ⌂ *Restaurant, in-room safes, Wi-Fi, outdoor pool, meeting room, free parking, some pets allowed (fee); no TV in some rooms* ⊟ *MC, V* ⊘ *Closed first 3 wks of Jan.* ¶⊙∣ *BP.*

¢ 🖭 **Ibis.** Near the northern *autoroute* (expressway) exit, this modern budget hotel (opened May 2004) appeals to those traveling by car. At the edge of town, it's close to the casino and the convention center (Le Forum). Rooms are simple, appointed in turquoise and ocher; triple-glazed windows keep out most of the noise from the main road. Some rooms have pull-out beds so children under 12 can stay for free. Two rooms are accessible and fully equipped for people in wheelchairs. The hotel has air-conditioning. ⊠ *21 rte. du Lac, CH-1763 Granges-Paccot* ☎ *026/ 4697900* 🖷 *026/4697910* ⊕ *www.accorhotels.com* ⇥ *82 rooms* ⌂ *Snack bar, Wi-Fi, bar, laundry service, free parking, some pets allowed (fee), no-smoking floors* ⊟ *AE, DC, MC, V.*

Nightlife

BARS To get a feel for Fribourg's nightlife, try one of the cellar bars scattered throughout the Old Town, such as **La Cave de la Rose** (⊠ 1 rue de Morat ☎ 026/3510101), which stays open into the wee hours of the morning. **Elvis et Moi** (⊠ 13 rue de Morat ☎ 026/3220755) offers live music and DJs in a kitsch Elvis-inspired interior. It's open every night except Sunday from 5. An 18th-century inn, seemingly in the middle of nowhere, has been turned into **Planet Edelweiss** (⊠ 1 Mariahilf, Düdingen ☎ 026/ 4920505), a lively *restaurant de nuit* and disco. Its diverse crowd (ranging from bankers to farmers) doesn't get going until after 10, and the bar stays open until 2 AM Sunday–Thursday, 4 AM Friday and Saturday. The 12-minute taxi ride from town runs about 25 SF.

CASINO Near the northern autoroute exit, the **Casino de Fribourg** (⊠ 11 rte. du Lac, Granges-Paccot ☎ 026/4677000) opened in 2003. In addition to roulette, blackjack, poker, and 100 poker machines, the casino has a restaurant and offers regular shows. A five-minute taxi ride from town costs around 12 SF.

▌ EN ROUTE On the way from Fribourg or Charmey to Gruyères, chocoholics should consider stopping at the tantalizing **Nestlé chocolaterie** (chocolate factory), in the otherwise unassuming town of Broc. Founded by Alexandre Cailler in 1889 and bought by Nestlé in 1929, it offers a 40-minute tour and video, followed by a chocolate tasting. Look for chocolate-brown signs marking the way. ⊠ *Broc* ☎ *026/9215151* 🎫 *Free* ⊙ *May–Oct., weekdays 9:30–4.*

Gruyères

❷ **To & From:** *To connect with Gruyères via public transport, buses from* **Fodor'sChoice** *Fribourg (1 hr, 20 SF) are your best bet. You can also opt to take one* ★ *of the hourly trains to Bulle from Fribourg (1 hr, 18 SF) and transfer to a bus (6 times daily, 10 min, 3.50 SF) to Gruyères's train station, set a*

15-minute walk outside the village center. If training from Lausanne or Zürich, transfer to a local train at Palézieux—this rail journey takes about five hours. Gruyères is 35 km (21 mi) south of Fribourg.

Rising above the plain on a rocky crag and set against a backdrop of Alpine foothills, the castle village of Gruyères seduces from afar. This perfect specimen of a medieval stronghold comes complete with a cobbled main street, stone fountains, and well-preserved houses whose occupants try to outdo each other with picturesque facades and geranium displays in summer. The town was once the capital of the Alpine estates of the Burgundian counts of Gruyères, and its traditional crest bears a stylized crane (*grue*). Gruyères is car-free, so you'll have to park in one of three lots outside town and either walk up or catch the tourist train from the Maison du Gruyère. You can also take one of many buses from outside the train station at Fribourg to Bulle, and then change to a bus to Gruyères (an hour-long trip costing about 18 SF).

> ## LOCAL SPECIALTIES
>
> Gruyères is known for its blue-and-white or dark-red-and-white pottery decorated with the *grue*, as well as for creamy, nutty cheeses (Vacherin and Gruyère, spelled without the town's *s*), and the 48%-butterfat crème-double, which is served with a bowl of berries or crumbly, sweet meringues.

Between 1080 and 1554, 19 counts held political power over this region, and they built and expanded the **château**. Little is known about them except for the last, Michel. A lover of luxury and a big spender, he expanded the estates and then fled his creditors in 1555. In 1849 a wealthy Geneva family bought the castle and encouraged painter friends to decorate a room now known as Corot's room as it features four of his landscapes. Also worth seeing is the Knights' Room with its impressive 19th-century fresco cycle depicting local legends, and the aptly named Fantastic Art Room for contemporary work. ☎ *026/9212102* ⊕ *www.chateau-gruyeres.ch* 🖃 *6.50 SF* ⊙ *Apr.–Oct., daily 9–6; Nov.–Mar., daily 10–4:30.*

Most people will get enough of an idea about the enormously talented but equally tormented H. R. Giger just by sitting in the Giger Bar, opposite the **Giger Museum**. Here you can admire ceiling buttresses that look like elongated backbones with ribs, and his ingenious trademark chairs: yet more spines and ribs, with pelvises for headrests. Giger won an Academy Award for his set design for the horror film *Alien;* he's not likely to win any prizes for his cheerful, healthy outlook on life (or women). That said, a few of his sculpture/furniture pieces are very good. Just avoid looking at the walls if you want to enjoy lunch afterward. ⊠ *Château St. Germain* ☎ *026/9212200* ⊕ *www.hrgigermuseum.com* 🖃 *12 SF* ⊙ *Apr.–Oct., daily 10–6; Nov.–Mar., Tues.–Fri. 11–5, weekends 10–6.*

Before going up to town, you can visit the very touristy **Maison du Gruyère**, a demonstration *fromagerie* (cheese dairy) where the famous cheese is produced with fully modernized equipment. Demonstrations are given three to four times a day depending on the season. ⊠ *Pringy-Gruyères* ☎ *026/9218400* ⊕ *www.lamaisondugruyere.ch* ⊠ *5 SF* ☉ *June–Sept., daily 9–7; Oct.–May, daily 9–6.*

Where to Stay & Eat

$–$$ ✕ **Auberge de la Halle.** The unfussy interior of this medieval house, with its massive raftered ceiling and smooth stone floor, feels like a 16th-century burgher's home. Choose the front rooms for people-watching or the back terrace for admiring the town ramparts while you savor traditional Gruyères dishes, such as fondue with potatoes. ⊠ *Main St.* ☎ *026/9212178* ⊟ *AE, DC, MC, V.*

★ **$$–$$$**   ✕⊞ **De Ville.** This welcoming hotel has large, airy rooms, tastefully renovated in 2000, that mix bright Tuscan colors with traditional pine furniture. Back rooms overlook the valley, front rooms the village. The restaurant ($–$$$) serves steaming fondue, raclette, and other Swiss dishes. ⊠ *Main street, CH-1663* ☎ *026/9212424* 🖷 *026/9213628* ⇋ *8 rooms* ⚐ *Restaurant, cable TV; no smoking* ⊟ *AE, DC, MC, V* ⏐◯⏐ *BP.*

$$ ✕⊞ **Hostellerie St-Georges.** The management of this well-situated hotel changed in 2003, and it has since upgraded its restaurant to gastronomique status ($–$$$); the daily menus are a treat. The four double rooms are spacious and cheerful, and have traditional wood decor and white, edelweiss-embroidered bed linen, plus breathtaking mountain views. Ten single rooms are also available. A massive fireplace anchors the evening dining area; during lunch, enjoy the stunning views from the large, light-filled winter garden. ⊠ *Main street, CH-1663* ☎ *026/9218300* 🖷 *026/9218339* ⊕ *www.st-georges-gruyeres.ch* ⇋ *4 rooms* ⚐ *Restaurant, in-room safes, minibars, cable TV, some pets allowed (fee)* ⊟ *AE, DC, MC, V* ☉ *Closed over winter* ⏐◯⏐ *BP.*

★ **$–$$**   ⊞ **Hostellerie des Chevaliers.** This traditional, family-friendly hotel is also well-equipped for business conferences. Standing outside the main gates of Gruyères, it has the same views overlooking the valley and the castle as in-town lodgings, without the noise. Room decor mixes regional antiques, handsome woodwork, and ceramic stoves with contrasting color schemes. Though the hotel no longer has a restaurant, breakfast is served in the dining room, and additional meal plans are offered using the restaurant of the Hostellerie St-Georges. ⊠ *CH-1663* ☎ *026/9211933* 🖷 *026/9212552* ⊕ *www.gruyeres-hotels.ch* ⇋ *34 rooms* ⚐ *Dining room, in-room safes, minibars, cable TV, meeting rooms, free parking, some pets allowed (fee), no-smoking rooms* ⊟ *AE, DC, MC, V* ☉ *Closed Jan. and Feb.* ⏐◯⏐ *BP.*

$ ⊞ **Fleur de Lys.** From its vaulted, stenciled reception area to its pine-and-beam restaurant, this is a welcoming little hotel. Plain rooms contain '50s-style wooden furniture, and a large rear terrace and garden have a wonderful view of the mountains and castle. ⊠ *CH-1663* ☎ *026/9218282* 🖷 *026/9213605* ⇋ *10 rooms* ⚐ *Restaurant, café, cable TV, bar, Wi-Fi, some pets allowed (fee)* ⊟ *AE, DC, MC, V* ☉ *Closed Feb.* ⏐◯⏐ *BP.*

OFF THE
BEATEN
PATH

FROMAGERIE D'ALPAGE – For a more authentic, historical perspective on cheese making than the Maison du Gruyère provides, visit the Magnin family's cheese-making operation on the edge of Moléson village. Watch the true Gruyère cheese, called *Gruyère d'alpage,* being made in a cauldron over an open fire in the low-roofed chalet, as it has been made since the 17th century. There is also a 15-minute video, subtitled in English, describing the process of cheese making. A small restaurant serves traditional local dishes. ⊠ *Moléson-sur-Gruyères* ☎ *026/9211044* ⊕ *www. fromagerie-alpage.ch* ✆ *3 SF* ⊙ *Mid-May–late Sept., daily 9:30–6; demonstrations 10 and 2.30.*

Skiing

At 3,609 feet, **Moléson**, Gruyères's "house mountain," offers skiing up to 6,568 feet and wraparound views of the pre-Alps and on to Lac Léman (Lake Geneva). The area has three cable cars, four lifts, 20 km (12 mi) of downhill ski runs, and 8 km (5 mi) of cross-country trails.

Bulle

❸ To & From: *Trains from Fribourg to Bulle, one per hour, change in Romont (45 min, 16.80 SF) or direct bus service from Fribourg station, one per hour (32 min, 14.20 SF). Bulle is 5 km (3 mi) northwest of Gruyères, 31 km (19 mi) southwest of Fribourg.*

With 16,000 inhabitants, the town of Bulle has many attractions worthy of a larger destination: a castle (not open to the public), three-storied patrician houses lining the cobblestone main street, and a scenic backdrop so perfect you might think it has been painted. You can learn about Gruyères traditions at the **Musée Gruérien**, which contains displays of folk costumes, handicrafts, and farm tools—it even has a full reproduction of a flagstone farmhouse kitchen and dining room. ⊠ *25 rue de la Condémine* ☎ *026/9127260* ✆ *5 SF* ⊙ *Tues.–Sat. 10–noon, 2–5, Sun. 2–5.*

Romont

❹ To & From: *Trains from Fribourg to Romont, two direct per hour (30 min, 9.20 SF). Ramont is 15 km (9 mi) northwest of Bulle, 49 km (30 mi) southwest of Fribourg.*

The best way to approach this 13th-century town of two broad streets is to leave the highway and drive up to its castle terrace. The fortress's 13th-century ramparts surround the town, forming a belvedere from which you can see the Alps—from Mont Blanc to the Berner Oberland. You'll also find a 12th-century Cistercian convent, the 17th-century Capuchin monastery, and the lovely 13th-century Collégiale, one of the purest examples of a Gothic church in Switzerland, with period (and modern) windows, sculptures, choir stalls, a screen, and an altarpiece.

Inside the castle, the **Musée du Vitrail** (Stained-Glass Museum) shimmers with crisscrossing shafts of colored light from its glass panels, both ancient and contemporary. A slide presentation traces the development of the craft, and a workshop area demonstrates current techniques. The museum now includes a donated collection of reverse painting on glass. ⊠ *Château* ☎ *026/6521095* ⊕ *www.romont.ch* ✆ *7 SF* ⊙ *Tues.–Sun. 10–1, 2–6.*

Payerne

❺ To & From: *Trains from Fribourg to Payerne, one direct per hour (30 min, 7.80 SF); from Neuchâtel to Payerne, two per hour, change at Murten or Yverdon (47–52 min, 17–21 SF). Payerne is 15 km (9 mi) north of Romont, 18 km (11 mi) west of Fribourg.*

The meandering streets in this market town are filled with pastel-painted 18th-century buildings, now shops and restaurants. Above them stands a magnificent 11th-century **église abbatiale** (abbey church), one of the finest examples of Romanesque art in Switzerland. You can visit its restored austere abbey, including a grand barrel-vaulted sanctuary and primitive capital carvings on the pillars. The church often hosts painting exhibitions and organ concerts. ☎ 026/6626704 ⬛3 SF if no exhibition ☉ Summer: Tues.–Sun. 10–noon, 2–6; winter: Tues.–Sun. 10–noon, 2–5.

Estavayer-le-Lac

❻ To & From: *Trains from Fribourg to Estavayer-le-Lac, one direct per hour (35 min, 11.40 SF); from Neuchâtel to Estavayer-le-Lac, one per hour, change at Yverdon (41 min, 18.20 SF). Estavayer-le-Lac is 7 km (4 mi) northwest of Payerne, 51 km (32 mi) southwest of Neuchâtel.*

Modest Estavayer-le-Lac, on the shore of Lac Neuchâtel, can still be navigated using a map drawn in 1599. It has retained much of its medieval architecture, from the arcades of the town center to the gracious, multi-towered medieval **Château de Chenaux,** which now houses city government offices.

For something completely different, visit the quirky **Musée de Grenouilles** (Frog Museum). Here are displays of 108 embalmed frogs posed like people in scenes of daily life from the 19th century. Other exhibits include an authentic 17th-century kitchen, various military and household artifacts dredged from Lac Neuchâtel, and more than 200 Swiss railroad lanterns. ✉ 13 rue des Musées ☎ 026/6632448 ⊕ www.museedesgrenouilles.ch ⬛5 SF ☉ Mar.–June, Sept., and Oct., Tues.–Sun. 10–noon, 2–5; July and Aug., daily 10–noon, 2–5; Nov.–Feb., weekends 2–5.

Where to Stay

$ 🏨 **Hotel du Lac.** Although this blocky, semi-modern hotel is short on old-world charm, it's the only lodging in town with a lakeside location. The harbor and grassy park are completely relaxing; you can watch the swans nesting from the terrace in spring. Rooms are unpretentious and in need of renovation. ✉ 1 pl. du Pont, CH-1410 ☎ 026/6635220 🖷 026/6635343 ⊕ www.hotel-restaurant-du-lac.ch ⬛ 36 rooms ⬥ Restaurant, café, cable TV, in-room data ports, meeting room, some pets allowed ▭ AE, DC, MC, V ⦿ BP.

Murten

★ ❼ To & From: *Trains from Fribourg to Murten, one per hour (25 min, 10.40 SF); from Neuchâtel to Murten, one direct per hour (24 min, 11.40 SF).*

Murten is 19 km (12 mi) northeast of Estavayer-le-Lac, 17 km (11 mi) north of Fribourg.

The ancient town of Murten, known in French as Morat, is a popular resort on the Murtensee/Lac de Morat (Lake Murten). The bilingual town has a boat-lined waterfront, Windsurfer rentals, a lakeside public pool complex, grassy picnic areas, and a promenade as well as a superbly preserved medieval center. Leave your car in the parking area in front of the 13th-century gates and stroll the fountain-studded cobblestone streets. Climb up the worn wooden steps to the town ramparts for a view of the lake over a chaos of red roofs and stone chimneys.

The town's most memorable moment came on June 22, 1476, when the Swiss Confederates—already a fearsomely efficient military machine—attacked with surprising ferocity and won a significant victory over the Burgundians, who were threatening Fribourg under the leadership of Duke Charles the Bold. Begun as a siege 12 days earlier, the battle cost the Swiss 410 men, the Burgundians 12,000. The defeat at Murten prevented the establishment of a large Lothringian kingdom and left Switzerland's autonomy unchallenged for decades. Legend has it that a Swiss runner, carrying a linden branch, ran from Murten to Fribourg to carry the news of victory. He expired by the town hall, and a linden tree grew from the branch he carried. Today, to commemorate his dramatic sacrifice, some 15,000 runners participate annually on the first Sunday in October in a 17-km (11-mi) race up the steep hill from Murten to Fribourg. As for the linden tree, it flourished in Fribourg for some 500 years, until 1983, when it was ingloriously felled by a drunk driver. It has been replaced with a steel sculpture.

The **Musée de Morat** (Murten Museum) is in the town's old mill, complete with two water-powered mill wheels. On view are prehistoric finds from the lake area, military items, and trophies from the Burgundian Wars. ⊠ *Lausannestr., southern end of historic center* ☎ *026/ 6703100* ⊕ *www.museummurten.ch* ⊠ *6 SF* ☉ *Apr.–Oct., Tues.–Sat. 2–5, Sun. 10–5.*

Where to Stay & Eat

\$–\$\$\$ ✕ **Ringmauer.** Whether in the simpler brasserie or the dining section, this rustic restaurant in the city wall offers good value for the money. Try the confit *de canard* (duck leg in a garlic and parsley sauce) or the regional pan-fried perch fillets. You can enjoy the terrace in summer and take your predinner drinks by the fire in winter. (There are even some hotel rooms but these could be closed for renovation.) ⊠ *Deutsche Kirchg. 2,* ☎ *026/6701101* ⊟ *MC, V* ☉ *Closed Sun. and Mon.*

★ **\$\$\$\$**   ✕▦ **Le Vieux Manoir au Lac.** A manicured park spreads around this stately, turreted mansion just 1 km (½ mi) south of Murten on Lac de Morat. Most of the rooms have lake views and have been individually decorated. The restaurant's (\$\$\$) seasonal sampling menus have a French-Continental bent. Options might include chateaubriand with spring onions and béarnaise sauce or fried fillet of pike-perch and a pan-fried Norwegian lobster served with a fennel and cardamom puree. ⊠ *18 rue de Lausanne, CH-3280 Murten-Meyriez* ☎ *026/6786161* ☎ *026/*

6786162 ⊕ *www.vieuxmanoir.ch* ⤵ *34 rooms* ⚑ *Restaurant, in-room safes, minibars, cable TV, Wi-Fi, massage, kayaks, bicycles, business services, meeting rooms, free parking, some pets allowed (fee)* ▤ *AE, DC, MC, V* �‖�‖ *BP.*

★ **$–$$$** ✕⊞ **Weisses Kreuz.** Owned by the same family since 1921, this hotel has two buildings: one with lake views and the other across the street with Old Town views. The latter has rooms extraordinarily furnished with complete antique bedroom sets—Biedermeier, Art Nouveau, Louis XVI, Empire. Simpler rooms, in pine or high-tech style, cost less. The lovely formal dining room ($$–$$$), open May to September, specializes in fish—perch with pine nuts and tomato, roasted pike with wild fennel and a mix of shrimp, and a variety of fish crisply fried. ⊠ *Rathausg. 3, CH-3280* ☏ *026/6702641* 📠 *026/6702866* ⊕ *www.weisses-kreuz. ch* ⤵ *27 rooms* ⚑ *Restaurant, cable TV, business services, convention center* ▤ *AE, DC, MC, V* ⊘ *Closed Dec. and Jan.* �‖�‖ *BP.*

$–$$ ✕⊞ **Schiff am See.** The Schiff nabbed an ideal setting; its sheltered terrace gives onto a shady park and the waterfront promenade. Inside you'll find an eclectic collection of heavy wood furniture and antiques. The gourmet restaurant, Lord Nelson ($–$$$), has lake views and wraps around the garden. Specialties include local fish and inventive combination meat dishes such as beef tournedos and giant shrimp. The Schiff is a "velo-hotel"; bicycles are welcome, and the staff can help you rent one in town. ⊠ *53 Ryf, CH-3280* ☏ *026/6702701* 📠 *026/6703531* ⊕ *www.hotel-schiff.ch* ⤵ *15 rooms* ⚑ *Restaurant, minibars, cable TV, lake, bar, meeting room, some pets allowed (fee)* ▤ *AE, DC, MC, V* �‖�‖ *BP.*

LAC NEUCHÂTEL

The region of Neuchâtel belonged to Prussia from 1707 to 1857, with a brief interruption caused by Napoléon and a period of dual loyalty to Prussia and the Swiss Confederation between 1815 and 1857. Yet its French heritage remains untouched by Germanic language, diet, or culture. Some boast that the inhabitants speak "the best French in Switzerland," which is partly why so many summer language courses are taught here.

Neuchâtel

★ ⚑ **8** **To & From:** *Direct trains from Neuchâtel to major Swiss cities: Geneva, one per hour (1 hr 10 min, 37 SF); Lausanne, one per hour (41 min, 24 SF); Bern, two per hour (40–50 min, 17.60 SF); Basel, one per hour (1 ½ hrs, 34 SF); Zürich, one per hour (1 hr 35 mins, 49 SF). Trains from Fribourg to Neuchâtel, one direct per hour (53 min, 19 SF). Take Bus No. 7 to Place Pury to get Littoral Neuchâtel buses (ww.tnneuchatel. ch; 1.85 to 3 SF) to countryside villages. Neuchâtel is 28 km (17 mi) northwest of Murten, 48 km (30 mi) northwest of Fribourg.*

At the foot of the Jura Mountains, flanked by vineyards, and facing southeast, the city of Neuchâtel enjoys panoramic views of Lac Neuchâtel and the range of the middle Alps, including the majestic mass of Mont Blanc and the Bernese Oberland. Lac Neuchâtel, at 38 km (24 mi) long and

8 km (5 mi) wide, is the largest lake located entirely within Switzerland. (The much larger lakes of Geneva and Constance are shared with France and Germany, respectively.) A prosperous city, Neuchâtel has a reputation for precision work, beginning with watchmaking in the early 18th century. Broad avenues in the lower part of town border-

ing the lake are lined with neo-Romanesque yellow-sandstone buildings, which inspired author Alexandre Dumas to call Neuchâtel "a city with the appearance of an immense *joujou* [toy] dressed in butter." The cathedral and the 12th-century castle, which today houses the cantonal government, sit gracefully above the city's bustling old marketplace. You can stroll (or cycle or rollerblade) along the lakeside promenade as far as Hauterive, the next village to the north. Neuchâtel's biggest annual festival is the winemakers' three-day celebration of the grape harvest, the *fête des vendanges.* It's celebrated the last weekend of September with parades and fanfare throughout the city.

The extent of French influence in Neuchâtel is revealed in its monuments and architecture, most notably at the **Église Collégiale** (Collegiate Church). The handsome Romanesque and Burgundian Gothic structure dates from the 12th century, with a colorful tile roof. The church contains a strikingly realistic and well-preserved grouping of life-size painted figures called *le cénotaphe,* or monument, to the counts of Neuchâtel. Dating from the 14th and 15th centuries, this is considered one of Europe's finest examples of medieval art. Anyone not wanting to climb steep streets can reach the church from the Promenade Noire off the place des Halles by an inconspicuous elevator—*ascenseur publique.* ⊠ *12 rue de la Collégiale* ☎ *032/8896000* 🖾 *Free* ⊗ *Weekdays 8–noon, 1:30–5.*

The **Tour des Prisons** (Prison Tower), which adjoins the Collegiate Church, has panoramic views from its turret. On your way up, stop in one of the original wooden prison cells. ⊠ *rue Jehanne-de-Hochberg* ☎ *No phone* 🖾 *1 SF* ⊗ *Apr.–Sept., daily 8–6.*

The architecture of the **Old Town** demonstrates a full range of French styles. Along rue des Moulins are two perfect specimens of the Louis XIII period, and—at its opposite end—a fine Louis XIV house anchors the place des Halles (market square), also notable for its turreted 16th-century **Maison des Halles.** The Hôtel de Ville (Town Hall ⊠ rue de l'Hôtel de Ville) opened in 1790 east of the Old Town. It was designed by Pierre-Adrien Paris, Louis XVI's architect. There are also several fine patrician houses, such as the magnificent **Hôtel DuPeyrou** (⊠ 1 av. DuPeyrou), home of the friend, protector, and publisher of Jean-Jacques Rousseau, who studied botany in the nearby Val-de-Travers. Most of the Old Town is a pedestrians-only zone, though public buses do run through it.

Behind the Hôtel DuPeyrou, the new **Galeries de l'Histoire** (History Gallery) houses models of Neuchâtel from the year 1000 to 2000. ⊠ *7 av. DuPeyrou* ☎ *032/7177920* ⊕ *www.mahn.ch* 🖾 *Free* ⊗ *Wed.–Sun. 1–5.*

★ Thanks to a remarkably unprovincial curator, the **Musée d'Art et d'Histoire** (Museum of Art and History) displays a striking collection of paintings gathered under broad themes—nature, civilization—and mounted in a radical, evocative way. Fifteenth-century allegories, early Impressionism, and contemporary abstractions pack the walls from floor to ceiling: interacting, conflicting, demanding comparison. You may climb a platform (itself plastered with paintings) to view the higher works. This aggressive series of displays is framed by the architectural decorations of Neuchâtel resident Clement Heaton, whose murals and stained glass make the building itself a work of art.

This novel museum also has the honor of hosting three of this watch-making capital's most exceptional guests: the **automates Jaquet-Droz,** three astounding little androids, created between 1768 and 1774, which once toured the courts of Europe like young mechanical Mozarts. Pierre Jaquet-Droz and his son Henri-Louis created them, and they are moving manifestations of the stellar degree to which watch making had evolved by the 18th century. Le Dessinateur (the Draughtsman) is an automated dandy in satin knee pants who draws graphite images of a dog, the god Eros in a chariot pulled by a butterfly, and a profile of Louis XV. La Musicienne (the Musician) is a young woman playing the organ. She moves and breathes subtly with the music and actually strikes the keys that produce the organ notes. L'Écrivain (the Writer) dips a real feather in real ink and writes 40 different letters. Like a primitive computer, he can be programmed to write any message simply by changing a steel disk. The automatons come alive only on the first Sunday of the month, at 2, 3, or 4 (or by appointment), but the audiovisual show re-creates the thrill. ✉ *1 Esplanade Léopold-Robert* ☎ *032/ 7177925* ⊕ *www.mahn.ch* 🎟 *8 SF, free Wed.* ☽ *Tues.–Sun. 11–6.*

Named after the Swiss writer and artist Friedrich Dürrenmatt, the **Centre Dürrenmatt,** perched high above Neuchâtel, houses an exhibition area devoted to modern literature and visual arts. Architect Mario Botta designed a curving, skylit underground space connected to Dürrenmatt's former home (now a private library and offices). Many of Dürrenmatt's paintings are disturbing, reflecting a bleak worldview that tends to be softened by the humor, albeit acerbic, in his writing. Letters and excerpts of his books are also on display, and each artwork is accompanied by a quote. Group tours can be booked in advance. ✉ *74 chemin du Pertuis-du-Sault* ☎ *032/202060* ⊕ *www.cdn.ch* 🎟 *8 SF* ☽ *Wed.–Sun. 11–5.*

★ ☾ The **Laténium,** an interactive archaeological museum, displays artifacts discovered in and around the lake and explains (in French and German) how they were recovered. The lifestyles of the *la Tène* Celts and Bronze Age lake dwellers are skillfully depicted. A sculpted menhir from Bevaix, a village southwest of Neuchâtel, resembles a man. Inside the museum you can see the remains of a 60-foot-long Gallo-Roman barge; outside in the park, its reconstruction is moored near a full-scale wooden Bronze Age house on stilts. There is a pamphlet in English, and guided tours in English can be booked in advance. ✉ *Espace Paul Vouga, 2068 Hauterive* ☎ *032/8896917* ⊕ *www.latenium.ch* 🎟 *9 SF* ☽ *Tues.–Sun. 10–5.*

**OFF THE
BEATEN
PATH**

From Neuchâtel take the road to La Chaux-des-Fonds for 15 km (9½ mi) to the pass **COL DE LA VUE DES ALPES** – where the parking area on this high ridge affords, on a clear day, spectacular views of the Alps, including the Eiger, Mönch, Jungfrau, and Mont Blanc.

Where to Stay & Eat

$$-$$$ ✕ **Au Boccalino.** Just north of Neuchâtel, this restaurant gastronomique has a tiny winter-garden brasserie and a main dining room discreetly decorated in pale gray and muted blue. Despite its proximity to the lake, there's neither terrace nor view, and charming owner-chef Claude Frôté wants it that way. Customers should come for his innovative regional food (an evening menu will cost between 110 SF and 180 SF) and, above all, his wine. He keeps 25,000 bottles in stock, and connoisseurs can reserve a predinner *apéro* in the cellar (for up to 12 people). Try traditional tripe, pork tongue, foie gras of duck with passion fruit, or veal poached with vanilla and mint. ⊠ *11 av. Bachelin, St-Blaise* ☎ *032/7533680* ⌂ *Reservations essential* ☰ *AE, DC, MC, V* ☉ *Closed Sun. and Mon.; mid-July–mid-Aug.; and late Dec.–early Jan.*

$$-$$$ ✕ **Le Cardinal Brasserie.** Stop and have a perfect café crème (coffee with cream) or a light meal along with the Neuchâteloise at one of the most authentic cafés in the Old Town. The interior has some striking Art Nouveau elements; the molded ceiling, etched windows, and blue-and-green decorative tile all date from 1905. Fish is the specialty, and large platters of *fruits de mer* (shellfish) in season are a delicious treat. ⊠ *9 rue du Seyon* ☎ *032/7251286* ☰ *AE, DC, MC, V.*

$-$$$ ✕ **Du Banneret.** The chef often emerges to greet diners in the brasserie portion of this popular restaurant, housed in a late-Renaissance building at the foot of the rue du Château. Dishes are mostly regional fare, such as homemade pasta with fresh wild mushrooms and lake trout. In the upstairs dining room, the food takes a strong Italian twist. ⊠ *1 rue Fleury* ☎ *032/7252861* ☰ *AE, DC, MC, V* ☉ *Closed Sun. and Mon.*

¢ ✕ **Bach & Buck.** Simply furnished and seating 70, this crêperie opposite the Jardin Anglais is an ideal spot to grab a cheap but tasty meal. The 130 types of crêpes include savory, vegetarian, sweet, and with liqueurs. The Provençale (tomatoes, cheese, herbes de Provence, plus your choice of other ingredients) is a lunchtime favorite. ⊠ *22 av. du 1er-Mars* ☎ *032/7256353* ☰ *No credit cards* ☉ *No lunch Sun. July and Aug.*

$$-$$$ ✕⌂ **La Maison du Prussien.** In the gorge of Vauseyon, 10 minutes from Neuchâtel, this restored 18th-century brewery nestles alongside a roaring woodland stream. Polished beams, yellow-sandstone highlights, and lush views are undeniably atmospheric. Every room is different, and three have fireplaces. The winter-garden restaurant ($$$–$$$$) offers innovative seasonal cuisine; or you can enjoy a simpler lunch on the terrace overlooking the stream. Take the tunnels under Neuchâtel toward La Chaux-de-Fonds, exit toward Pontarlier-Vauseyon, and watch for the hotel's signs. ⊠ *Au*

GETTING THERE
Auberge de l'Aubier is in Montézillon, which is linked by hourly train service to Neuchâtel. The trip takes 16 minutes and costs 5.40 SF. The hotel is about five minutes from the train station.

Gor du Vauseyon, 11 rue des Tunnels, CH-2000 ☎ *032/7305454* 📠 *032/7302143* ⊕ *www.hotel-prussien.ch* 🛏 *6 rooms, 4 suites* ⚹ *Restaurant, café, minibars, in-room DVD, bar, meeting room, some pets allowed (fee)* ☐ *AE, DC, MC, V* ⊘ *Closed mid-July–mid-Aug. and late Dec.–early Jan.*

$ ✕🖽 **Du Marché.** Opening directly onto the place des Halles, this is a delightful place for a hearty plat du jour or a carafe of local wine. Inside, pass through the lively bar–café to the steamy, old-wood brasserie for a bowl of tripe in Neuchâtel wine or salt pork with lentils. Upstairs, a pretty little dining room ($–$$$; closed Sunday) serves more sophisticated fare. Plain, functional rooms with tidy tile bathrooms down the hall are good value. Double-glazed windows keep out the noise. ⊠ *4 pl. des Halles, CH-2000* ☎ *032/7232330* 📠 *032/7232333* ⊕ *www. hoteldumarche.com* 🛏 *10 rooms* ⚹ *Restaurant, café, cable TV* ☐ *AE, DC, MC, V* ◉❙ *BP.*

★ **$$$$** 🖽 **Beau-Rivage.** This thoroughly elegant, restored 19th-century hotel sits gracefully on the lakeshore; on a clear day there's a splendid view of the Alps. The warmly lighted interior, with high ceilings and wild-cherry wood, exudes calm. Two-thirds of the spacious rooms have lake views. The sophisticated dining room, done in pale green, offers a fine selection of wines, after-dinner cigars, and brandies. The hotel has air-conditioning. ⊠ *1 esplanade du Mont Blanc, CH-2001* ☎ *032/7231515* 📠 *032/ 7231616* ⊕ *www.beau-rivage-hotel.ch* 🛏 *56 rooms* ⚹ *Restaurant, in-room safes, minibars, cable TV, Wi-Fi, bar, babysitting, business services, some free parking, some pets allowed (fee)* ☐ *AE, DC, MC, V.*

★ **$–$$** 🖽 **Le Café-Hôtel de L'Aubier.** In the pedestrian zone at the foot of the château, this delightful hotel offers light, modern, spacious rooms whose warm color schemes are inspired by the spice they are named after. Cheaper rooms have their own sink but share a bathroom. The central location sometimes makes it noisy on weekends. The café (closed Monday breakfast and Sunday) and terrace offer inexpensive but good fare: breakfasts, salads, and desserts (try the chocolate tart), with a selection of teas and coffees. ⊠ *1 rue du Château, CH-2000* ☎ *032/7101858* 📠 *032/ 7101859* ⊕ *www.aubier.ch* 🛏 *9 rooms, 3 with bath* ⚹ *Café, some pets allowed, no-smoking floors; no TV in some rooms* ☐ *MC, V.*

Sports & the Outdoors

SWIMMING There are **public beaches** at many villages and resorts on the lake. A **municipal complex** (⊠ Nid du Crô, 30 rte. des Falaises ☎ 032/7226222) has outdoor and indoor pools.

Nightlife

Neuchâtel has an ever-changing selection of restaurants de nuit and *bars musicaux,* establishments that pulse with disco music until the wee hours of the morning and sometimes serve food—along the lines of steak *frites* (steak and fries)—to keep you going. **Café Trio** (⊠ 3 rue des Moulins ☎ 032/7242224) is open until 2 on Friday and Saturday. Also open on Friday and Saturday (from 10:30 PM to 4 AM), at **Casino de la Rotonde** (⊠ 14 Faubourg du Lac ☎ 032/7244848) are the **Discothèque Golden Eyes** and **Latino Labodega,** both offering music.

┌──
│ EN
│ ROUTE

To the west of Neuchâtel lie some of Switzerland's best vineyards, their grapes producing chiefly white and rosé wines that are light and slightly sparkling. The wines are bottled before the second fermentation, so they have a rather high carbonic acid content. **Château Boudry** offers wine tasting by appointment and houses the **Musée Cantonale de la vigne et du vin** (Cantonal Museum of Vines and Wines). ⊠ *Château Boudry, Boudry* 🕾 *032/8421098* ✉ *Museum 5 SF* ☉ *Museum Wed.–Sun. 2–6.*

Grandson

❾ *29 km (18 mi) southwest of Neuchâtel.*

This lakeside village in Canton Vaud has a long history. It is said that in 1066 a member of the Grandson family accompanied William of Normandy (better known as the Conqueror) to England, where he founded the English barony of Grandson. Otto I of Grandson took part in the Crusades. When the Burgundian Wars broke out in the late 15th century, the **Château de Grandson** (Grandson Castle), built in the 11th century and much rebuilt during the 13th and 15th centuries, was in the hands of Charles the Bold of Burgundy. In 1475 the Swiss won it by siege, but early the next year their garrison was surprised by Charles, and 418 of their men were captured and hanged from the apple trees in the castle orchard. A few days later the Swiss returned to Grandson and, after crushing the Burgundians, retaliated by stringing their prisoners from the same apple trees. After being used for three centuries as a residence by the Bernese bailiffs, the castle was bought in 1875 by the de Blonay family, who restored it to its current impressive state, with high, massive walls and five cone turrets. Inside, you can see reproductions of Charles the Bold's Burgundian war tent and two jousting knights astride their horses—in full armor. There are also *oubliettes* (dungeon pits for prisoners held *in perpetua*), torture chambers, and a model of the Battle of Grandson, complete with 20-minute slide show (in English if you get in quickly enough to push the right button). Cassette-guided tours of the town are available from a desk at the Tourist Office (Maison des Terroirs). The dungeons now house an extensive vintage car museum, with motorbikes and even a Penny Farthing bicycle. 🕾 *024/ 4452926* ⊕ *www.grandson.ch* ✉ *12 SF* ☉ *Apr.–Oct., daily 8:30–6; Nov.–Mar., Mon.–Sat. 8:30–noon, 2–5, Sun. 8:30–5.*

Yverdon-les-Bains

❿ **To & From:** *Trains from Fribourg to Yverdon-les-Bains, one direct per hour (54 min, 16.80 SF); from Neuchâtel to Yverdon-les-Bains, two direct per hour (18 min, 13.40 SF). Yverdon-les-Bains is 6 km (2½ mi) southwest of Grandson, 38 km (24 mi) southwest of Neuchâtel.*

This pastel-color lakefront town at the southernmost tip of Lac Neuchâtel has been appreciated for its thermal waters and sandy, willow-lined shoreline since the Romans first invaded and set up thermal baths here. In the 18th century its fame spread across Europe. Today the **Thermal Center** is completely up-to-date, with indoor and outdoor pools, whirlpools, and massage jets. Swim caps are mandatory. ⊠ *22 av. des Bains* 🕾 *024/ 4230232* ✉ *17 SF* ☉ *Mon.–Sat. 8 AM–10 PM, Sun. 8–8.*

In the center of the Old Town sits the turreted, mid-13th-century **Château de Yverdon-les-Bains.** Most of the castle is now a museum, with exhibits on locally found prehistoric and Roman artifacts, Egyptian art, natural history, and of course, local history. A special room is dedicated to the famous Swiss educator Johann Heinrich Pestalozzi (1746–1827), who spent 20 years here. His influential ideas on education led to school reforms at home and in Germany and England. ☎ *024/4259310* 🎫 *8 SF* ⊘ *June–Sept., Tues.–Sun. 11–5; Oct.–May, Tues.–Sun. 2–5.*

In front of Yverdon's **Hôtel de Ville** (Town Hall)—an 18th-century building notable for its French-inspired neo-classical facade—stands a bronze monument of Pestalozzi, grouped with two children. The charming, bustling town center is closed to traffic. Along the waterfront you'll find parks, promenades, a shady campground, and a 2-km (1¼-mi) stretch of little beaches.

EXCURSION INTO THE JURA

Straddling the French frontier from Geneva to Basel is a range of low-riding mountains (few peaks exceed 4,920 feet), which fall steeply down to the mysterious River Doubs, Lac des Brenets, and Doubs Falls to the north and to Lac Neuchâtel and the Lac de Bienne to the south. The secret of this region, known as the Jura, is the sunny plateau atop the mountains, with lush pastures and gentle woods just made for excellent hiking, biking, horseback riding, and cross-country-skiing opportunities. Jura is the youngest Swiss canton. In 2004, it celebrated the 25th anniversary of its independence.

La Chaux-de-Fonds

⓫ *22 km (14 mi) north of Neuchâtel.*

Actually part of Canton Neuchâtel, La Chaux-de-Fonds (called "Tschaux" by locals) sits high on the Jura plateau. In the early 18th century, watchmaking was introduced as a cottage industry to create income for an area otherwise completely dependent on farming. Over the years the town became the watchmaking capital of Switzerland. Destroyed by fire at the end of the 18th century, the city was rebuilt on a grid plan around the central, broad, tree-lined avenue Léopold-Robert. It is a city of incongruities: pastel-painted town houses and stone villas, working-class cafés and cultural institutions.

Famed architect Charles-Édouard Jeanneret, otherwise known as Le Corbusier, was born here. His birthplace can be seen, although not toured, along with the École d'Art, where he taught, and several villas he worked on between 1906 and 1917. Only one of his buildings is open to the public: the **Villa Turque,** north of the main avenue. It has a glowing terra-cotta-brick facade, rounded wings, and curved edges. A 20-minute video about Le Corbusier is available in English. The tourist office has a brochure outlining a walk that passes by his buildings. ✉ *147 rue du Doubs* ☎ *032/9123123* 🎫 *Free* ⊘ *1st and 3rd Sat. of month 10–4 or by appointment; call weekdays 9–11, 2–5.*

The **Musée des Beaux-Arts** (Museum of Fine Arts), a striking neoclassical structure, was designed by Le Corbusier's teacher, L'Éplattenier. It contains works by the noted Swiss artists, such as Léopold Robert, as well as three of Le Corbusier's works: a furniture set, an oil painting (*Femme au Peignoir*), and a tapestry (*Les Musiciennes*). Perhaps the most famous artist in the collection is, rightly, Swiss: Ferdinand Hodler (1853–1918), who was born in Bern but spent most of his career in Geneva. His most beautiful works are his Swiss landscapes, touched as they are with accents of Symbolism and Art Nouveau. The museum also usually has a temporary exhibit. ⊠ *33 rue des Musées* ☎ *032/9130444* ⊡ *8 SF, Sun. 10–noon free* ☉ *Tues.–Sun. 10–5.*

★ The **Musée International d'Horlogerie** (International Timepiece Museum) displays a fascinating collection of clocks and watches that traces the development of timekeeping and the expansion of watchmaking as an art form. You can see audiovisual presentations on the history and science of the craft, observe current repairs on pieces from the collection in an open work area, and browse the gift shop, which sells replicas as well as the latest timepieces by stellar local watchmaking firms (Corum, Girard-Perregaux, Ebel, and so on). Some explanatory material is in English, and group tours in English can be arranged. ⊠ *29 rue des Musées* ☎ *032/9676861* ⊕ *www.mih.ch* ⊡ *12 SF* ☉ *Tues.–Sun. 10–5.*

Where to Stay & Eat

★ $–$$ ✕ **Auberge de Mont-Cornu.** Just southeast of town, this converted farmhouse has an idyllic setting. Friendly staff serve everything from simple sandwiches to traditional regional dishes; the fondue with cream is renowned. Rooms are wood-paneled and chock-full of authentic extras: a grandfather clock, a gramophone with record, and a huge glazed-tile oven. In summer sit outside in the flower-filled garden and take in the view of wooded hills and the sound of distant cowbells. ⊠ *116 Mont-Cornu* ☎ *032/9687600* ⌳ *Reservations essential* ⊟ *AE, MC, V* ☉ *Closed Mon. and Tues. and Dec.–Feb.*

$$$ ✕⌂ **Grand Hôtel les Endroits.** Set in a tranquil green suburb above town, this modern, family-run hotel offers just about everything. Rooms are spacious and light, with discrete pastels and warm wood set off by touches of black. Many have balconies or open onto a grassy area. Eat in the no-smoking restaurant ($–$$$), in the brasserie (¢–$$), or on the large terrace. ⊠ *94–96 bd. des Endroits, CH-2300* ☎ *032/9250250* ⊞ *032/ 9250350* ⊕ *www.hotel-les-endroits.ch* ⇄ *42 rooms, 4 suites* ⌂ *Restaurant, café, minibars, cable TV, sauna, bicycles, Internet, business services, some pets allowed (fee), no-smoking rooms* ⊟ *AE, DC, MC, V* ⎮⊙⎮ *BP.*

Saignelégier

⓬ *26 km (16 mi) northeast of La Chaux-de-Fonds.*

A small, fairly modern town, Saignelégier is known mostly for its lush surroundings, horseback riding, and cross-country skiing. The Marché-Concours National de Chevaux (National Horse Fair), held since 1897, takes place on the second Sunday in August and draws crowds from throughout Switzerland and France, as does the Fête des Montgolfières (Hot-Air Balloon Festival) the second weekend of October.

Where to Stay & Eat

$$$–$$$$ ✕ **Hôtel-Restaurant Georges Wenger.** One of Switzerland's top gourmet
Fodor'sChoice restaurants is just 6 km (4 mi) from Saignelégier. Chef Georges Wenger
★ creates elegant, savory dishes with both a regional and seasonal bent and has a flair for unusual combinations, such as langoustines with a subtle, gingery almond-milk and rhubarb sauce. An excellent selection of cheeses and a fine wine cellar round out the experience. If you feel you can't tear yourself away, you can spend the night; upstairs are a handful of luxurious, individually decorated rooms. ⊠ *2 rue de la Gare, Le Noirmont* ☎ *032/9576633* 🖶 *032/9576634* ⊕ *www.georgeswenger. grandestables.ch* 🖃 *AE, DC, MC, V* ☉ *Closed late July–early Aug., late Dec.–late Jan., and Mon. and Tues.*

FRIBOURG & NEUCHÂTEL ESSENTIALS

Transportation

BY AIR

Frequent flights from the United States and the United Kingdom arrive on Swiss and other international carriers, either at Geneva's Cointrin or Unique Zürich airports.

AIRPORTS Fribourg lies between Geneva's Cointrin Airport (138 km [86 mi] to the southwest) and Unique Zürich Airport (180 km [112 mi] to the northeast). Train connections to both are good. The Bern-Belp Airport is a small international airport 34 km (21 mi) northeast of Fribourg, near Bern.

🔢 Airport Information **Bern-Belp Airport** ☎ 031/9602111. **Cointrin Airport** ☎ 022/7177111, 0900/571500 for arrivals and departures. **Unique Zürich Airport** ☎ 0900/300313.

BY BOAT & FERRY

There are frequent boat trips on the lakes of Neuchâtel and Murten (Morat) in summer and usually a host of themed evening trips. Contact La Navigation Lacs de Neuchâtel et Morat for more information.

🔢 Boat & Ferry Information **Navigation Lacs de Neuchâtel et Morat** ☎ 032/7299600 ⊕ www.navig.ch.

BY BUS

Postbus connections, except in the principal urban areas, can be few and far between; plan excursions carefully using the bus schedules available at the train station, or phone the local tourist office for advice.

BY CAR

An important and scenic trans-Swiss artery, the A12 expressway cuts from Bern to Lausanne, passing directly above Fribourg. A parallel route to the northwest extends the A1 between Zürich and Bern, connecting Bern to Murten, Payerne, and Lausanne. There is an expressway, the A5, between Neuchâtel and Yverdon but as this runs through a lot of tunnels, if you have the time take the national road for a scenic view of the lake coast.

The charms of this varied region can be experienced easily by car, and there are scenic secondary highways throughout. Keep in mind that some towns, like Gruyères, are car-free or have pedestrians-only centers; in these cases, parking lots are easy to find.

BY TRAIN

The main train route connecting Basel, Zürich, and Geneva passes through the Fribourg station between Bern and Lausanne. Neuchâtel has hourly connections to main Swiss cities. Regional train services to smaller destinations leave from the larger towns of Fribourg and Neuchâtel, though buses may be a more direct route. Ask the local tourist office for information.

🗈 ☎ 0900/300300 [1.19 SF per min].

Contacts & Resources

EMERGENCIES

In case of any emergency, dial ☎ 117. For an ambulance and/or doctor, dial ☎ 144.

🗈 Emergency Contacts **Fribourg police** ☎ 117 or 026/3051818. **Neuchâtel police** ☎ 117 or 032/8889000.

🗈 Medical Contacts **Dental referrals** ☎ 026/3223343 in Fribourg, 032/7222222 in Neuchâtel. **Medical referrals** ☎ 144.

INTERNET & MAIL

Internet cafés are rare in this region. Try asking your hotel concierge if there are any public Internet terminals nearby. Some hotels may have a computer with Internet access hidden away, which they allow guests to use upon request, often for a small fee.

🗈 Post Office Information **Main post office** ✉ av. de Tivoli 3 CH-1700 Fribourg ☎ 0848/888888. **Main post office** ✉ pl. de la Gare 2 CH-1663 Gruyères ☎ 0848/888888. **Main post office** ✉ Bahnhofstr. 10 CH-3280 Murten ☎ 0848/888888. **Main post office** ✉ 2 Espace de l'Europe CH-2000 Neuchâtel ☎ 0848/888888. **Main post office** ✉ 6 av. de la Gare CH-1400 Yverdon-les-Bains ☎ 0848/888888.

VISITOR INFORMATION

🗈 Local Tourist Offices **Estavayer-le-Lac** ✉ 11 rue de L'Hôtel de Ville, CH-1470 ☎ 026/6631237 ⊕ www.estavayer-le-lac.ch. **Fribourg** ✉ 1 av. de la Gare, CH-1701 ☎ 026/3501111 🖶 026/3501112 ⊕ www.fribourgtourism.ch. **Gruyères** ✉ CH-1663 ☎ 026/9211030 ⊕ www.gruyeres.ch. **Murten** ✉ 6 Franz-Kirchg., CH-3280 ☎ 026/6705112 ⊕ www.murten. ch. **Payerne** ✉ 10 pl. du Marché, CH-1530 ☎ 026/6606161 ⊕ www.payerne.ch. **Yverdon-les-Bains** ✉ 2 av. de la Gare, CH-1401 ☎ 024/4236101 ⊕ www.yverdon-les-bains. ch/tourisme.

🗈 Regional Tourist Offices **Fribourg** ✉ 107 rue de la Glâne, CH-1700 ☎ 026/4025644 🖶 026/4023119 ⊕ www.pays-de-fribourg.ch. **Neuchâtel** ✉ Hôtel des Postes, CH-2002 ☎ 032/8896890 🖶 032/8896291 ⊕ www.neuchateltourisme.ch.

Bern

8

WORD OF MOUTH

"Apparently, I am easily amused. . . . We spent four nights in Bern
and loved it. We walked up to the Rose Garden for a wonderful
roof-top view of the city and toured the Clock Tower, Einstein's house,
the Klee Museum, and the Swiss Parliament. Very, very interesting."

–Jean464

"The only thing I didn't like about Bern—the shops' prices."

–FainaAgain

WELCOME TO BERN

TOP REASONS TO GO

★ **Lived-in History:** UN-ESCO only made Bern a World Heritage Site in 1983 but the city's cobblestone arcades and clock towers have been beautifully preserved since the 1400s.

★ **Feats of Klee:** The spectacular Zentrum named for Paul Klee—the whimsical painter artist who hopscotched across art—is a tour de force of vibrant creativity.

★ **Undercover Shopping:** Bern's got it all—from couture fashion to artisan chocolatiers—and, thanks to those famous arcaded streets, you can even enjoy window shopping in rainy weather.

★ **The Ziebelemärit:** Think of an object—a train car, an alarm clock, a teddy bear—and you will likely see it rendered in onion at November's city-wide celebration of the humble veg.

★ **Those Sunbathing Swiss:** Warm summer days lure swimmers to the Marzili's sweeping lawns and swift, icy stretch of river below the Federal parliament building.

1 Old Town. Watch the clock turn back to 1191, when the Zytglogge marked Bern's outer edges and the city sloped gently down to the river by the Untertorbrücke. Today, the historic Rathaus, Münster, painted fountains, and 18th-century guildhalls rub shoulders with arcades and cellars full of restaurants and quirky boutiques.

2 City Center. The swath of land between the Zytglogge and the Hauptbahnhof is Bern's most commercially vibrant, a dense warren of narrow streets and pedestrian passageways studded with shops, hidden alleys, grand architecture, and the Swiss Federal Government complex.

GETTING ORIENTED

Few capital cities are as charming and compact as Bern, Switzerland's political nerve center. Alluring medieval streets, frolicsome fountains, and palpable history coexist so easily with outdoor markets and traditional cheese-and-potatoes that it's easy to forget this is actually a fully wired, surprisingly young 21st-century urban center.

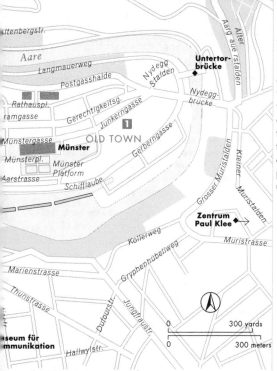

Map labels:
Ittenbergstr.
Aare
Langmauerweg
Postgasshalde
Rathauspl.
ramgasse
Gerechtigkeitsg.
Junkerngasse
Münstergasse
OLD TOWN
Münster
Münsterpl.
Aarstrasse
Münster Platform
Schifflaube
Nydegg Stalden
Untertorbrücke
Nydeggbrücke
Gerberngasse
Grosser Muristalden
Kleiner Muristalden
Muristalden
Alter Aargauerstalden
Zentrum Paul Klee
Kollerweg
Gryphenhübeliweg
Muristrasse
Marienstrasse
Thunstrasse
Dufourstr.
Jungfraustr.
seum für mmunikation
Hallwylstr.

0 — 300 yards
0 — 300 meters

8

3 Museum District. The Kirchenfeld neighborhood is a masterpiece of late 19th-century urban planning, where a top array of Bern's museums are grouped together in a tight, easy-to-visit cluster on the south bank of the river Aare.

The Zentrum Paul Klee.

BERN PLANNER

Getting Around

The most efficient, flexible, cheap, and enjoyable way to navigate Bern's cobblestones is on foot. Cars that attempt to enter the downtown area are steered right back out again and parking is scarce unless you opt for a (modern, well-lit) municipal parking garage; taxis suffer the same fate and fares reflect the torturous routing.

Public transport, which means buses and trams, is both plentiful and easy to use. Bern is easy to navigate: count 10 minutes to walk at a steady clip from the Hauptbahnhof to the Bärengraben; about five to take the bus.

From the station, the main shopping street, Spitalgasse, leads straight through Bärenplatz; this square and the adjacent Bundesplatz mark the center of town. Most sights are on or near Spitalgasse, which becomes Marktgasse, Karngasse, and Gerechtigkeitsgasse. Trams and buses are handy for getting outside the Altstadt.

Bern's Best Photo-Ops

As Albert Einstein discovered to his delight in 1902, the weather has been bested in Bern.

"Both sides of the road are completely lined by old arcades so that one can stroll from one end of the city to the other in the worst downpour without getting noticeably wet," he wrote to his fiancé in 1902.

Sturdy 15th-century pillars support the low vaulted roofs of these picturesque Lauben (arcades), which extend to the edge of the sidewalk along 6 km (4 mi) of Altstadt streets and shelter stores of every description.

Steeply angled cellar doors at street level lead down to additional underground eateries and businesses, while brilliantly colored and carved Brunnen (fountains), historically the city's water sources and congregation points, punctuate the main thoroughfares.

Ten of the most prominent fountains are the work of Hans Gieng, who created them between 1542 and 1549.

Finding a Place to Stay

In any other city Bern's visiting population—a strangely comfortable mix of diplomats, bankers, conventioneers, businesspeople, art lovers, backpackers, and tourists—would inspire hotels to compete with each other about how best to pamper their guests. Not here.

Switzerland's Federal capital has only one (stellar) palace hotel and even it does not make extravagant luxury a selling point. What you'll find instead is high standards across the rates: clean, modern facilities, thoughtful amenities, and friendly, attentive service.

If you are content to seek atmosphere in the city rather than your hotel room, it's not a bad deal.

To Market, To Market

Bern has been a market town since the Middle Ages, and seasonal outdoor markets are still an integral part of daily life. The most elaborate is the Zibelemärit (Onion Market), a Fasnacht-tinged remnant of a 15th-century Autumn Market that lasted two weeks; 19th-century farmers' wives, notably from Fribourg, developed the habit of coming to Bern on the first day of the market to sell their excess produce, in particular onions, and today half of the 700 stalls that line the City Center on the fourth Monday in November display a vast assortment of items made with onions—everything from wreaths to alarm clocks to soup. The Weihnachtsmarkt (Christmas Market) fills the air throughout December with the scent of evergreens and holiday excitement; window boxes burst into bloom following the one-day Geranienmarkt (Geranium Market) in mid-May.

The Bernese also descend on daily, weekly, and monthly markets, their wicker baskets and wheeled carts in tow. The often organic fruits and vegetables that await them form swaths of color on wooden tables with computerized pan scales; men and women in smocks or aprons hover behind them. It's courteous to ask for assistance rather than serve yourself, but hesitate and they will move on to weigh a handful of apricots or a wedge of cheese for the next customer. Butchers and fishmongers display locally raised meat and fish in mobile cooling trailers; fresh herbs may be had in season; and a tangle of shoppers and carts spill out from coffee bars lining the squares. Note that the socializing happens largely along the perimeter—market shopping demands your full attention.

How's the Weather?

Architecture can be a big tip-off: covered stone arcades, dark underground cellars, small windows, and thick stone walls were all medieval coping tactics in the face of bad weather. Bern can be cold and wet and miserable in winter, its indoor spaces warmed with fires and packed with people. But it is mild and sunny from spring through autumn, when every restaurant that can sets up camp in the street, windows are thrown open, and people take to the river by the Marzili with unrestrained glee. Summer is warm and July through mid-August is vacation season—note that many restaurants close up shop for a few weeks.

Making the Most of Your Time

The Bernese do not scurry around their city, and neither should you—its considerable charms are best discovered at a slow, steady pace with a plan to get from A to B but no fixed idea how.

It is technically possible to see the major sights in a day, but you'd miss seeing the sun set over medieval rooftops, you wouldn't be able to linger in restaurants, and this is a city that comes out at night.

Do pace yourself as you wander the streets, do visit the museums at a steady clip, and do get a running start on the narrow curved steps up the Münster steeple.

Indulge any urges to explore Marzili or Matte, to pursue your curiosity at the markets, to take a sudden chocolate break, to feed the bears, or to admire the fountains—although it is indeed strange to find the latter sitting in the middle of main-street traffic.

8

Updated
by Jennifer
McDermott

THOUGH BERN IS THE FEDERAL CAPITAL, you won't find much cosmopolitan nonsense here: The *cuisine du marché*, based on the freshest ingredients available in the local market, features fatback and sauerkraut: the annual fair fêtes the humble onion; and the president of the Swiss Confederation has been known to take the tram to work. Warm, friendly, down-to-earth, the Bernese are notoriously slow-spoken; ask a question, and then pull up a chair while they formulate a judicious response. Their mascot is a common bear; they keep some as pets in the center of town. Walking down broad medieval streets past squares crowded with farmers' markets, past cafés full of shirt-sleeved politicos, you might forget that Bern is the geographic and politcal hub of a sophisticated, modern, and prosperous nation.

In fact, at first glance, you might take the city (Berne in French) for a thriving country town rather than a major European capital. Arriving in the city center, either by car or by train, most visitors see only its old town and miss altogether the modern sprawl of banking and industry that surrounds it. Although Bern is full of patrician houses and palatial hotels, there is no official presidential residence: the seven members of the coalition government, each of whom serves a year as president, have to find their own places to live when in Bern.

Bern wasn't always so effacing. It earned its pivotal position through a history of power and influence that dates from the 12th century, when Berchtold V, Duke of Zähringen, expanded his fortress at the tip of a sharp meander in the River Aare. He chose the site for its impregnable location and its proximity to the great kingdom of Burgundy, which spread across France and much of present-day French-speaking Switzerland. Then he named his new city for the first animal he killed in the local woods (an unlucky but immortal brown bear).

By the 14th century Bern had grown into a strong urban republic. When the last Zähringens died, the people of Bern defeated their would-be replacements and, in 1353, became the eighth canton to join the rapidly growing Swiss Confederation. It was an unlikely union: aristocratic, urban Bern allied with the strongly democratic farming communities of central Switzerland. But it gave the Bernese security against the Habsburg Holy Roman Empire and cleared the way for westward expansion.

Setbacks did occur—the wooden city was gutted by fire in 1405—but by the late 15th century three decisive victories over the Duke of Burgundy had made Bern the most powerful city-state north of the Alps, with a territorial reach that soon extended southwest to Geneva and municipal coffers full of gold, silver, and precious textiles. The Reformation reached Bern in 1528; by the mid-16th century the city had assumed the leading role in Switzerland and Swiss affairs.

Bern stayed on top. The 17th and 18th centuries saw a boom in development fueled not so much by commerce as by the export of troops and military know-how—the ruling aristocracy saw its raison d'être in politics, foreign policy, the acquisition of additional territory, and the forging of alliances. The landed gentry, meanwhile, grew fat on the fruits of the city's rich agricultural lands. Napoléon seized those lands briefly

THE GRAND TOUR

IF YOU HAVE 1 OR 2 DAYS

Bern is best explored the old-fashioned way—on foot—so start your visit with a morning wander through the arcades and plazas east of the Hauptbahnhof. Pause to watch the mechanical figures strike noon atop the Zytglogge, then descend to the cellar of the Kornhaus for lunch. All 344 stairs up the Münster steeple could be necessary to recover from your Bernerplatte, but don't under any circumstances miss the view. The Bundeshaus is closed for renovations, but plenty of 16th-century fountains remain and the bears await their carrots in the Bärengraben. Hop on a bus from there to the Zentrum Paul Klee, then head back into town for a lighter, Italian, meal; the Bar Toulouse-Lautrec deserves a peek on your way home. Spend your second day museum-hopping from Alpine relief models (Schweizerisches Alpines Museum) to postage stamps (Museum für Kommunikation) to cutting edge art (Kunsthalle Bern), then round out the day with a climb to the Rosengarten for a sunset view of the Altstadt.

IF YOU HAVE 3 TO 5 DAYS

Additional days will allow you to go at a more Bernese pace. Spend a morning at the market on Waisenhausplatz and peruse the shops along Münstergasse. Head down to Marzili or Matte, take a dip in the Aare, and ride the Marzilibahn back up the hill, or take the tram out to Wabern and climb the Gurten for breathtaking Alpine views. When the sun goes down, head in the other direction for an evening at Marians Jazzroom. Visit Einstein's living quarters the next day, stop for fondue around the corner, and take in a temporary exhibit at the Kunstmuseum.

from 1798 until his defeat in 1815, and the 1814 Congress of Vienna forced Bern to part with its western and eastern territories, forming the Cantons of Vaud and Aargau, but by the 1830s the Bernese were back in charge. When the Swiss Confederation took its contemporary, federal form in 1848, Bern was a natural choice for its capital.

Yet today it's not the massive Bundeshaus (Federation Building) that dominates the city but instead its perfectly preserved arcades, fountains, and thick, sturdy towers—all remnants of its heyday as a medieval power. Bern owes its architectural unity to a major fire that swept through town in 1405, destroying most of the houses, then mainly of wood. It was rebuilt in sandstone, and its arcades stretch on for some 6 kilometers (4 mi). They're the reason UNESCO granted Bern World Landmark status, with the pyramids and the Taj Mahal.

EXPLORING BERN

From the time it was built on a high, narrow peninsula above the rushing Aare, Bern's streets have followed the river's flow. The original town began by what is now the Nydegg bridge—it controlled the ferry crossing there—and spread westward, uphill to the *Zeitglockenturm* (known locally as the *Zytglogge,*), a clock tower constructed in 1191 to mark Bern's first significant western gate. Further expansion in 1256 stretched the city to where the Käfigturm now stands; one last Medieval growth spurt, hot on the heels of a resounding victory over the Burgundians in 1339, moved the city walls west yet again to the present-day train station, the *Hauptbahnhof.*

The bustling, commercial City Center radiates out from that train station. To get to the *Altstadt* (Old Town), follow the trams across Bärenplatz and through the Käfigturm. Marzili and Matte, former working-class and still flood-prone neighborhoods, lie together along the riverbed of the Aare. All of these areas are easily explored on foot, but in Marzili and Matte, you may want to take your cue from the locals: walk down, ride up. The cluster of museums in Kirchenfeld, on the south side of the river, is a short (spectacular) walk or tram ride away.

Numbers in the text correspond to numbers in the margin and on the Bern map.

Old Town & City Center

Fire destroyed the original, predominantly wooden structures that comprised the Altstadt, the historical heart of the city that perches above the Aare. The Bernese rebuilt using local sandstone and today's arcaded, cobblestone streets radiate Medieval appeal. Eclectic upscale boutiques inhabit some of the oldest buildings, downhill from the Zytglogge; Marktgasse and Spitalgasse favor chain and department stores.

What to See

★ ☾ ❽ **Bärengraben** (Bear Pits). Bern almost certainly gets its name from the local contraction of the German *Bären,* due to Berchtold V's supposed first kill in the area, and the image of a bear is never far away, from the official coat of arms to chocolate morsels. The city has kept live bears since 1513, when victorious Bernese soldiers brought one back from the Battle of Novara and installed it in a hut on what is now Bärenplatz; the current neo-Gothic castle structure and wooded location date from 1857. Keeper-approved treats are sold between the two pits on the river side; plaques and pamphlets in English describe the bears and their lifestyle. ⊠ *Grosser Muristalden 6, Bärengraben* ☎ *031/3281212* 🎟 *Free* ☉ *Apr.–Oct., daily 9:30–5; Nov.–Mar., daily 9:30–4:30.*

❿ **Bundeshaus** (Houses of Parliament). Conceived as a national monument and the beating heart of the Swiss Confederation (the seven-member Federal Government, the 46-member Council of States, and the 200-member National Council all meet here), this massive, majestic domed complex built between 1852 and 1902 takes its symbolism seriously. Twenty-six fountains out front represent the Swiss Cantons; solemn statues inside depict the swearing of the oath on which the Union is founded; and two huge murals, one in each Chamber, represent the Vierwaldstättersee (Lake Lucerne) and a Landsgemeinde (outdoor cantonal assembly) scene, respectively the place where Swiss democracy was founded and the means by which it flourished. The entire complex is closed for

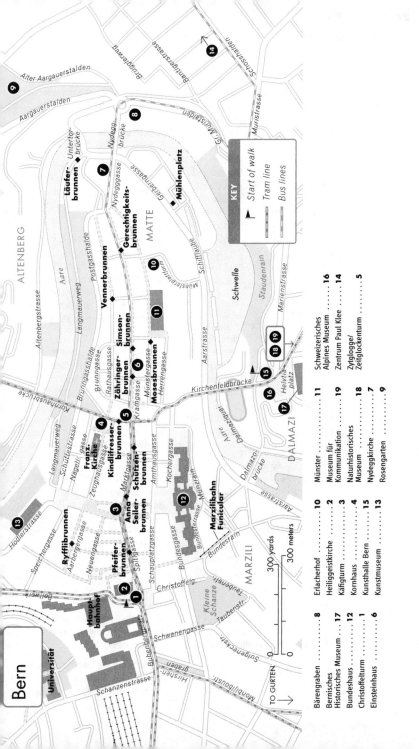

Bern

KEY

▲ Start of walk

▭ Tram line

▭ Bus lines

A GOOD WALK

Begin in the main hall of the Hauptbahnhof, facing the arrivals and departures board, then turn 180 degrees and head through the main bank of escalators into the Christoffel-unterführung (Christoffel underpass). The somewhat patchy black linoleum tiles in the floor will lead you to the remnants of the city's third gate, the **Christoffelturm ❶** ▶, and a 15th-century bridge. Take a moment to examine the images of the tower prior to its 1865 demolition, then ride the escalator up to the Loeb department store.

To your left, on the far side of Spitalgasse, is the **Heiliggeistkirche ❷**, named for a Medieval monastic order and consecrated in 1729. Duck inside for a peek at its colorful Baroque ceiling, then follow the trams left past the cheerful Pfeiferbrunnen (Bagpiper Fountain) to the first intersection, Bärenplatz. Here you may or may not find a market spread out on both sides of the square.

Keep following the trams (carefully) through the **Käfigturm ❸**, a 17th-century prison tower built on the site of the city's 13th-century main gate, and continue down the street (now called Marktgasse) to admire the Anna Seilerbrunnen (Anna Seiler Fountain), an allegory on moderation named for the woman who founded Bern's main hospital in 1354.

The Schützenbrunnen (Musketeer Fountain), originally positioned to face the home of a 16th-century rifle society, is a little farther along, past the stately Kaiserhaus (a department store until 1972), on your right.

At the next intersection, the end of Marktgasse, follow the trams to the left to the Kindlifresserbrunnen, atop which an ogre (most likely a Fasnacht character) sits munching on several small children.

The imposing 18th-century **Kornhaus ❹**, behind the fountain, is home to two restaurants and the 21st-century Kornhausforum (Media and Design Center).

Walk through the former market hall between the restaurants and head down Zeughausgasse to the front of the Französische Kirche (French Church), built for the Dominicans in the late 13th century and used by French-speaking Protestants since 1623.

Nip inside for a look at the elegant 13th-century rood screen and wall paintings that range from intricate ivy to the Last Judgment, then loop around the other side of the church along Nägeligasse back to the Kornhausplatz. On your left is the neo-Baroque Stadttheater, Bern's Opera House.

Cross the street before the bridge and examine the dramatic 1849 equestrian monument to Rudolf von Erlach, the Bernese victor over the Burgundians in the 1339 Battle of Laupen, then head inland again to the intersection where the trams turn.

On your left, dominating the town center, is the mighty **Zytglogge ❺**, Bern's original western gate and communal horological reference point since 1530.

Walk through the tower past the standard measurements on the left wall and turn around to view the actual clock face. If the minute hand is approaching the hour, you'll be treated to a show.

From the Zytglogge continue down Kramgasse, Bern's medieval main street. The painted figures and insignia above some houses indicate their connections to specific guilds; others date from the city's 18th-century height of prosperity.

The Zähringerbrunnen (Zähringer Fountain), commemorates Bern's founder, Berchtold V (though he's depicted as a bear); the Simsonbrunnen (originally called the Butcher's Fountain) presents the biblical hero Samson in mid-fight with a young lion.

A different but no less epic victory occurred at No. 49, the **Einsteinhaus** ⑥, where a young man named Albert struggled to make his name in physics.

Detour briefly to the left into the alley-like Kreuzgasse, just past the only fountain so far that does *not* have any painted figures, and have a look at the Rathaus, Bern's 15th-century Town Hall and current seat of the Cantonal government.

The heavily armed standard-bearer guarding it from atop the Vennerbrunnen (Ensign Fountain), to the right, personifies Bern's renowned military prowess.

To the left of the Rathaus is the Catholic Church of Saint Peter and Paul, a mini-cathedral with turn-of-the-century stained glass and Alpine flower motifs.

Retrace your steps back to Kramgasse (called Gerechtigkeitsgasse from this point on) and continue down the hill.

The Gerechtigkeitsbrunnen (Justice Fountain), considered the crown jewel of Bern's fountains, presents the emperor, the pope, the sultan, and the Mayor of Bern in the service of an impartial Justice wearing what passed for classical garb in the Renaissance.

As you pass the Hotel zum Goldenen Adler, the 18th-century successor to the city's oldest guesthouse, head for the middle of the street and look down.

The Stadtbach, a stream channeled from the Hauptbahnhof down the city's main thoroughfare since 1249, was restored to view in 2005 and now flows uphill for a distance of 10 feet (3 meters).

Veer left where the main street becomes Nydeggasse and aim downhill into Nydeggstalden.

The **Nydeggkirche** ⑦, set back from the road on your right, occupies the site of Duke Berchtold's original fortress and thus represents the oldest part of the city.

From the church courtyard either return to the road and curve steeply downhill to the river or head for the far end of the church and take the covered Burgtreppe stairs down to Mattenenge, turning left then right when you get to the bottom.

Both routes will leave you facing Bern's oldest river crossing, the Untertorbrücke, or Lower Gate Bridge, with the Läuferbrunnen (Messenger Fountain) and its bear-human duo sheltering under a tree to your left.

Cross the swift, blue-green Aare and either veer uphill to the right through the parking lot then turn

8

left at the traffic circle or, for a steeper, more peaceful climb, head left past the Landhaus to the paved footpath marked "Rosengarten" and zigzag to the right on Lerberstrasse.

In both cases, when you reach Aargauerstalden you will be rewarded with a view of the Altstadt that gets better and better as you follow the wide, tree-lined cobblestone boulevard up the hill.

From here either head back down the hill to the traffic circle and cut directly across it to watch the city's mascots flirt with onlookers in the **Bärengraben** ⑧ or, if legs and lungs and time permit, continue up Aargauerstalden to the traffic light, cross the street, and follow Laubeggstrasse to the second gate on the right.

Walk straight through the carefully tended **Rosengarten** ⑨ to see the best view of all—the city's bridges, rooftops, and, on clear days, the Gurten, Bern's local hill. Meander through the flowerbeds and take the cobblestone footpath below the restaurant back down to Alter Aargauerstalden, the traffic circle, and the Bärengraben.

The Altes Tramdepot (Old Tram Depot), behind the pits, sheltered city trams from 1890 to 1901 and now houses a restaurant, a brewery, and a tourist information center with a multimedia history of Bern.

Cross back to the Altstadt by way of the Nydeggbrücke and veer left into Junkerngasse, a street named for its 17th-century upper crust inhabitants.

The facade of Friedrich Traffelet's house, No. 22, represents the major life stages in lacy silhouette; the

trompe l'oeil images adorning No. 51 date from 1897 and depict the Zeerleder family tree from 1335 to 1806.

In between these houses, at No. 47, the graceful wrought-iron gates of the **Erlacherhof** ⑩ enclose a mosaiclike cobblestone courtyard and the current seat of Bern's municipal government.

At the top of Junkerngasse sits the pride of the city: the magnificent, Gothic **Münster** ⑪. Turn left before the cathedral, however, and walk out onto the Münsterplattform (a medieval graveyard turned Reformation-era art dump turned pleasure garden) for a look at the grand front facades of the houses you just passed.

Below their terraces, kitchen gardens, and one-time vineyards lies the Matte neighborhood, accessible from the graffiti-coated Mattetreppe or the exposed steel elevator visible on your right.

The front of the Münsterplattform overlooks the Matteschwelle weir and the Kirchenfeldbrücke. Exit the park by the small gate leading to the Münsterplatz and turn right for the entrance to the cathedral.

When you've had your fill of religious iconography and bird's-eye city views, head right past the solemn Mosesbrunnen toward the arcades along Münstergasse.

The enclosed 1895 balcony connecting two 16th-century houses at No. 62, the Oberes May-Haus, is noteworthy for its stone tracery and the muscled fool holding it up.

Turn left at the end of Münstergasse, head past the Kultur-Casino (home to Bern's

Symphony Orchestra), and cross the street before the bridge.

The pedestrian Bundesterrasse will lead you past sparkling river views and underneath the Hotel Bellevue Palace terrace to a glass plaque explaining that the portico of the **Bundeshaus** ⑫, along with the rest of the parliament building complex, is closed to the public until 2008.

Linger along the open portion of the Bundesterrasse if the weather is clear and you can see the distant peaks of the snow-capped Berner Oberland; head down the hill before the hotel underpass to explore the bohemian Marzili neighborhood or go swimming in the Aare (the bright red Marzilibahn, a cable railway, will transport you from the intersection of Münzrain and Bundesrain back up to the other side of the closed portico); or turn right at the glass plaque and head uphill past parked cars to Kochergasse.

The scaffolded front of the Bundeshaus and the Swiss National Bank loom over the Bundesplatz, to your left (to your right if coming from the Marzilibahn); there may also be a market between you and the 26 water jets springing 13 feet (4 meters) up from the pavement between March and November.

Take Schauplatzgasse from here back to Bubenbergplatz and the Hauptbahnhof, where the walk began.

Return to the main hall of the Hauptbahnhof for a separate outing focused on art. Head right from the arrivals and departures board this time, take the escalator up to Neuengasse, and turn left into Genfergasse.

The **Kunstmuseum** ⑬, at the end of the street, presents a multicentury

span of fine art and major temporary exhibits.

Turn left when you exit the building and right at the police headquarters (once the city's orphanage) into Waisenhausplatz, then meander back to the train station through shopping passages and alleyways linking Aarbergergasse and Neuengasse.

The Ryfflibrunnen (Crossbowman Fountain), named for a soldier who played a pivotal role in the 1339 Battle of Laupen, is positioned halfway along Aarbergergasse.

The Hauptbahnhof is also your point of departure for a day spent exploring the worlds of art, music, and creativity at the **Zentrum Paul Klee** ⑭, a spectacular wavelike structure built into the hillside outside town in Schöngrün.

Head up the main escalators to the tram and bus stops on Bubenbergplatz and ride the Number 12 bus for 10 minutes to the end of the line.

TIMING
Bern's downtown is not large but it can be steep and there's a lot to absorb. Shops in the arcades often represent worlds to be discovered, you will never be far from a café, and the operative word throughout the city is "slow"—the Bernese way of life is to make time and enjoy it.

8

renovation until 2008 but the Web site has photos and a virtual tour. ⊠ *Bundespl. 3, City Center* ☎ *031/3228522* ⊕ *www.parlament.ch* ☒ *Free* ⊙ *No tours until 2008.*

➤ ❶ **Christoffelturm** (Christoffel Tower). Timelines (in English), 14th-century maps, 19th-century photographs, and St. Christopher's huge limewood head give context to the thick stone foundations of Bern's third city gate. The tower was built between 1344 and 1366 and destroyed in 1865 after a tight vote in favor of the train station. ⊠ *Christoffel-unterführung, City Center.*

★ ❻ **Einsteinhaus** (Einstein's House). The sofa comes from Princeton, but the rest of this genteel apartment has been lovingly re-created to evoke the world of 1905, the Miracle Year in which then-tenant Albert Einstein, a badly paid, newly married young clerk in Bern's Patent Office, developed and published his *Special Theory of Relativity.* All signage is in English. ⊠ *Kramg. 49, Altstadt* ☎ *031/3120091* ⊕ *www. einstein-bern.ch* ☒ *6 SF* ⊙ *Oct.–Mar., Tues.–Fri. 10–5, Sat. 10–4; Apr.–Sept., daily 10–5.*

> **DID YOU KNOW?**
>
> Albert Einstein wrote and published his *Special Theory of Relativity* in Bern, in 1905.

❿ **Erlacherhof** (Erlach House). Mayor Hieronymus von Erlach did not live to see the elegant mansion he commissioned in 1746, but it remains the only private edifice in Bern with a formal courtyard and a garden terrace (visible from the Münsterplattform). Commandeered by the French in 1798, it was purchased by the city in 1832 and served as the Swiss Federal parliament building from 1848–58. Ask at the reception for access to the ceremonial banquet room. ⊠ *Junkerng. 47, Altstadt* ☎ *031/ 2216201.*

❷ **Heiliggeistkirche** (Church of the Holy Ghost). Built in the shadow of the huge Christoffelturm on the site of a disused monastery hospital, this Baroque church, laid out like a Huguenot Temple, turned out to be a survivor as town walls, houses, gates, and fountains crashed down around it to create today's busy transport hub. Serenity does still reign within, where natural light floods the green sandstone supporting a magnificent vaulted stucco ceiling. ⊠ *Spitalg. 44, City Center* ☎ *031/3707171* ⊕ *www.heiliggeistkirche.ch* ☒ *Free* ⊙ *Tues.–Fri. 11–6:30.*

❸ **Käfigturm** (Prison Tower). The current tower, completed in 1643, served as the city's prison until 1897. Reconfigured as the Confederation's Political Forum in 1999, it now hosts political events and exhibitions. ⊠ *Marktg. 67, City Center* ☎ *031/3227007* ⊕ *www.kaefigturm.admin. ch* ☒ *Free* ⊙ *Weekdays 8–6.*

❹ **Kornhaus** (Granary). Wine stocked the cellar and grain filled the top three floors of this granary for 100 years during Bern's Golden Age. Then the 1814 Vienna Congress separated the city from its territories and this monumental Baroque storage depot lost its function overnight. The cellar was renovated in 1893 and painted four years later; today it houses a restaurant where waiters scurry past images of Bernese women in traditional costume, Renaissance musicians, and a who's who of folkloric characters. The **Kornhausforum** (Media and Design Center) organizes contemporary design, architecture, video, photography, and applied art exhibits upstairs. ⊠ *Kornhauspl. 18, Altstadt* ☎ *031/3129110* ⊕ *www.kornhausforum.ch* 🕮 *9–12 SF, varies by exhibit* ☉ *Tues.–Fri. 10–7, weekends 10–5.*

NEED A BREAK?

Outdoor tables, a sunny central location, light meals, homemade pastries, 10 kinds of coffee, and open doors from 8 AM 'til midnight give the **Kornhaus Café** (⊠ Kornhauspl. 18, Altstadt ☎ 031/3277270) a constant, marketlike buzz.

★ ⓭ **Kunstmuseum** (Museum of Fine Arts). The permanent collection, one of the largest and most diverse in Switzerland, begins with the Italian Trecento (notably Duccio and Fra Angelico) then follows Swiss art from Niklaus Manuel in the 15th century through Albert Anker and Ferdinand Hodler in the 19th and on to Giovanni Giacometti and Cuno Amiet, in the 20th. The Impressionists are covered from Manet through Monet, the Nabis by Bonnard. Picasso bridges the gap between Toulouse-Lautrec and Braque; Kirchner, Kandinsky, and Klee represent German expressionism through Blauer Reiter to Bauhaus. Mondrian and Meret Oppenheim round out the 20th century; temporary exhibits often take it from there. ⊠ *Hodlerstr. 8–12, City Center* ☎ *031/3280944* ⊕ *www.kunstmuseumbern.ch* 🕮 *7 SF* ☉ *Tues. 10–9, Wed.–Sun. 10–5.*

⓫ **Münster** (Cathedral). Master Builder Matthäus Ensinger already had Strasbourg's cathedral under his belt when he drew up plans for what became the largest and most artistically important church in Switzerland. The city broke ground in 1421 on the site of a smaller church that was dismantled once the cathedral's choir could accommodate Sunday worshippers, and work continued, with minor interruptions, for about 180 years. The finishing touch, the tip of the open, octagonal, 328-foot **steeple,** was added almost 200 years after that, in 1893. Today Switzerland's highest church tower houses two Towerkeepers (in an apartment below the spire) and presents wraparound views of Bern and the surrounding mountains.

Fodor'sChoice
★

8

The Reformers dismantled much of the Catholic Münster's interior decoration and paintings (dumping them in the Münsterplattform, next door), but the exterior 15th-century representation of the Last Judgment above the **main portal** was deemed worthy and spared. The Archangel Michael stands between ivory-skinned angels with gilt hair (heaven) on the left and green demons with gaping red maws (hell) on the right; painted images of the Annunciation and the Fall of Man flank the carved figures as you pass through the doors. Elaborately carved pews and choir stalls, within, are crowned by 15th-century **stained glass** windows that show an easy mix of local heraldry and Christian iconography. The organ, above the main entrance, is often used for concerts. ⊠ *Münsterpl. 1, Altstadt* ☎ *031/3120462* ⊕ *www.bernermuenster.ch* 🕮 *Steeple 4 SF* ☉ *Easter–Oct., Tues.–Sat. 10–5, Sun. 11:30–5; Nov.–Easter, Tues.–Fri. 10–noon, 2–4, Sat. 10–noon, 2–5, Sun. 11:30–2 (tower closes 30 min before church).*

❼ Nydeggkirche (Nydegg Church). A plaque on the outside wall of the church indicates where vestiges of Duke Berchtold's 12th-century Nydegg Castle (destroyed about 1270) still poke through the landscape; the church itself was begun in 1341 and its wooden pulpit dates from 1566. ⊠ *Nydegghof 2, Altstadt* ☎ *031/3525829* ⊕ *www.nydegg.ch* ☉ *Apr.–Oct., daily 9–5; Nov.–Mar., daily 9–noon, 2–5.*

★ ☉ ❾ Rosengarten (Rose Garden). The lower Altstadt's hilltop cemetery was converted to a public park in 1913. Today, its lawns, arbors, playground, and formal gardens draw leisurely couples and families with young children. The gardens are planted with azaleas, irises, rhododendron, and rose varieties such as Ingrid Bergman (deep velvet red), Maria Callas (bright magenta), Christopher Columbus (peach), Cleopatra (red tips, orange interior), and Lady Di (small, pink). ⊠ *Alter Aargauerstalden/ Laubeggstr.* ☎ *031/3281212* ⊕ *www.rosengarten.be* ⊠ *Free.*

> **NEED A BREAK?**   Open from early March to late November, the **Restaurant Rosengarten** (⊠ Alter Aargauerstalden 31b, ☎ 031/3313206) serves dishes such as salmon tartare with crème fraîche and wasabi, Tandoori chicken kababs, veal saltimbocca, and brie sandwiches against a backdrop of panoramic Altstadt views.

☉ ⓮ Zentrum Paul Klee (Paul Klee Center). Engaged creativity are the watchwords in this undulating, light-filled complex inspired by the life and art of Paul Klee and designed by Renzo Piano. The permanent collection is the world's largest of works by Klee (about 200 are on display at any given time); temporary exhibits focus on his artistic environment and legacy. The Ensemble Paul Klee performs regular, varied, and colorful short concerts in the auditorium; guest artists from the worlds of theater and dance present productions, readings, and workshops (in German)

Fodor's Choice ★

> **WORD OF MOUTH**
>
> "Zentrum Paul Klee fabulous. Amazing architecture (Renzo Piano); even if you don't like Klee, the building—inside and out—and the grounds are worth it. Exhibition is great and we were entranced by the children's area with plenty of hands-on . . . and workshops. Of course, everyone checks email at the free internet set-ups in the museum."
>
> —escargot

with a pictorial slant. The Kindermuseum Creaviva, a sunny, paint-spattered area visible from the Restaurant Schöngrün on the north end of the interior Museum Street, is open to children over four and anyone else who would like to make art. A sculpture garden, free Internet terminals, and multilingual (audio) tours of the permanent collection round out the possibilities—come early and plan to spend the day. All signage is in English. ⊠ *Monument im Fruchtland 3, Schöngrün* ☎ *031/3590101* ⊕ *www.zpk.org* ⊠ *14 SF (collection only)* ☉ *Collection Tues., Wed., and Fri.–Sun. 10–5, Thurs. 10–9; Museum Street Tues., Wed., and Fri.–Sun. 9–6, Thurs. 9–9.*

★ ❺ Zytglogge/Zeitglockenturm (Clock Tower). Though its exterior dates from 1771, the internal walls of Bern's first western gate reach back to

Bern's Artistic Son

It's ironic that expressionist painter Paul Klee (1879-1940), one of Switzerland's most prolific and talented artists, wasn't a Swiss citizen during his life. Though he was born near Bern and spent most of his life in the country, his nationality was determined by the lineage of his father, who was German.

Born into a family of musicians, Klee played with chalk as a toddler and filled his schoolbooks with caricatures and images copied from magazines. At age 19 he left Bern to study drawing in Munich, but he couldn't support himself with his art and returned to his parents in 1902. Four years later he had saved enough from his work as a violinist with the Bern Music Society to marry pianist Lily Stumpf and move to Munich, where they lived until 1926.

A trip to Tunisia in 1914 clarified Klee's artistic calling. "Color has taken possession of me," he wrote, upon encountering desert light. "I am a painter." His signature became color-rendered in oil, watercolor, ink, or all three—and almost childlike paintings with a highly developed sense of poetry, music, and dreams. Recognition followed in the 1920s, with exhibitions in Paris and New York and a teaching postion at the Bauhaus from 1921. In 1933, the Nazis labeled him a degenerate, his academic position in Düsseldorf was terminated, and he and Lily emigrated to Switzerland. The apartment they took the following year in Bern's Elfenau district became his studio for the rest of his life.

In 1935 Klee began to show symptoms of severe fatigue and what was misdiagnosed as the measles turned out to be (determined after his death) scleroderma. He continued to paint, however, and produced more than 1,000 works the year before his death in the Ticino, where he had gone to convalesce. His ashes are buried in Bern's Schosshalde cemetery, next to today's Zentrum Paul Klee.

the 12th century and represent the city's core. The calendar clock on the Kramgasse side began keeping Bern's official time in 1530; the gilded rooster to the left of the mechanical figures crows four minutes before every hour to begin the sequence of marching bears, fools, and gilded knights who strike the bells. The astronomical clock to the rooster's right keeps track of the day, the month, the zodiac, and the moon. Tours of the horological masterpiece behind it all are conducted in English. ✉ *Kramg. at Hotelg., Altstadt* ☏ *031/3281212* ⊕ *www.berninfo.com* 🎫 *Tour 10 SF* ☉ *Tours May–Oct., daily 2:30; Nov.–Apr., by request.*

Museum District

Kirchenfeld is a quiet, leafy neighborhood due south of the Altstadt, with radial streets and unexpected vistas. It was constructed in 1881 according to a district plan and quickly filled with embassies, consulates, and the bulk of Bern's museums.

A GOOD WALK

Begin at Casinoplatz and dip downhill onto the Kirchenfeldbrücke. Far below on your left is the Matteschwelle, a weir almost as old as the city that steers river water around and through the Matte district (most of the time—in August 2005 the entire neighborhood flooded up to the first floor). On your right is a panoramic view of the Bundeshaus and the less precarious Marzili area.

Keep left as you come off the bridge and duck inside the **Kunsthalle Bern** ⑮ ☞ to check the pulse of contemporary art, then cross the street and aim to the left of the building labeled Schulwarte; a little farther along its facade on the right is the entrance to the **Schweizerisches Alpines Museum** ⑯. Return to the corner with a new appreciation for the art of mapping mountains and cross Helvetiaplatz to the castlelike

Bernisches Historisches Museum ⑰. The self-consciously epic statue in the middle of the square commemorates the advent of telegraphic communication in Europe. Exit the museum when you've exhausted Bernese history and follow its walls in either direction, to the left down Bernastrasse for the low-key **Naturhistorisches Museum** ⑱ or to the right down Helvetiastrasse for the interactive **Museum für Kommunikation** ⑲. From Helvetiaplatz cross the Kirchenfeldbrücke back to the Altstadt.

TIMING

You can fill a rainy day wandering from Alpine masks to Burgundian tapestries to the history of postal buses; if the weather is fine, an afternoon trip up the Gurten (see Off the Beaten Path below) will prevent overload.

What to See

⑰ **Bernisches Historisches Museum** (Historical Museum of Bern). Indonesian shadow puppets, Japanese swords, Polynesian masks, Indian figurines, and Celtic jewelry fill the ground floor and the Islamic collection is exquisite, but head to the basement for the real focus: Bern and its place in Swiss history. Armor and arms, lavish church treasure (including sculptures from the Münster), magnificent silver, tapestries "acquired" in 1476–77 when the Bernese pushed Charles the Bold back into France, and several of Hans Gieng's original fountain statues lead the charge. The top floor is devoted to Einstein; major signage is in English. ⊠ *Helvetiapl. 5, Kirchenfeld* ☎ *031/3507711* ⊕ *www.bhm.ch* 🖼 *13 SF* ☉ *Tues.–Sun. 10–5.*

OFF THE BEATEN PATH

GURTEN – Bern's very own hill presents a delightful alternative to the city on clear afternoons. The view moves from the Jura mountains in the west to the Alps in the east by way of Bern itself; multiple lawns, terraces, and restaurants allow for picnics, cafeteria service, or formal dining as you gaze. The bright red funicular to the top takes three minutes; head left to the east for a diagram labeling more than 200 distant peaks or right for a 360-degree view from the top of the Gurtenturm.

You can also walk up from Wabern. ⊠ *Wabern, tram number 9, stop Gurtenbahn* ☎ *031/9703333* ⊕ *www.gurtenpark.ch* ⊠ *Funicular 9 SF round-trip, 5 SF one-way* ⊙ *Funicular Mon.–Sat.* 7 AM–11:40 PM, *Sun.* 7 AM–10 PM.

▶ ⑮ **Kunsthalle Bern** (Bern Art Gallery). A completely different animal from the Kunstmuseum across town, this groundbreaking contemporary art venue built in 1918 by and for artists (among them Kirchner, Klee, and Giacometti père) seeks to confront, provoke, and engage viewers with the artistic phenomena of today. This translates each year to between six and seven exhibits of work by living artists; they become part of a history that includes Vassily Kandinsky, Henry Moore, Jasper Johns, Sol LeWitt, Bruce Nauman, Christo, and Grandma Moses. ⊠ *Helvetiapl. 1, Kirchenfeld* ☎ *031/3500040* ⊕ *www.kunsthalle-bern.ch* ⊠ *8 SF* ⊙ *Tues.* 10–7, *Wed.–Sun.* 10–5.

★ ☾ ⑲ **Museum für Kommunikation** (Museum of Communication). This resolutely interactive museum keeps its focus on the act of communication rather than the means. Exhibits examine body language across cultures, the views of Switzerland's minority populations, the history of the Swiss postal service, and the evolution of telecommunication through to the Internet. The world's largest collection of postage stamps is also here. All signage is in English. ⊠ *Helvetiastr. 16, Kirchenfeld* ☎ *031/3575555* ⊕ *www.mfk.ch* ⊠ *9 SF* ⊙ *Tues.–Sun.* 10–5.

☾ ⑱ **Naturhistorisches Museum** (Museum of Natural History). The biggest draw here is the stuffed body of Barry, a St. Bernard who saved more than 40 people in the Alps between 1800 and 1812, but start with the Alpine minerals, diamonds, and fossils in the basement, working up to wild animals in the city. Birds' nests, skeletons large and small, interactive temporary exhibits, and more than 200 wildlife dioramas round out the highlights. Basic signage is in English. ⊠ *Bernastr. 15, Kirchenfeld* ☎ *031/3507111* ⊕ *www.nmbe.ch* ⊠ *8 SF* ⊙ *Mon.* 2–5, *Tues., Thurs., and Fri.* 9–5, *Wed.* 9–6, *weekends* 10–5.

★ ⑯ **Schweizerisches Alpines Museum** (Swiss Alpine Museum). A slideshow overview of Switzerland's relationship with its mountains acts as an introduction to this detailed museum. Exhibits include massive topographical models and relief maps; audiovisual consoles covering topics such as the Roman introduction of viticulture, power generation, and global warming; Alpine farming implements, toys, and skis; frank descriptions of mountain life; ceremonial masks; and Hodler's seven-part mural of the Matterhorn's conquest. You'll leave with a hearty appreciation for Swiss tenacity. All signage is in English. ⊠ *Helvetiapl. 4, Kirchenfeld* ☎ *031/3500440* ⊕ *www.alpinesmuseum.ch* ⊠ *9 SF* ⊙ *Mon.* 2–5:30, *Tues.–Sun.* 10–5:30.

WHERE TO EAT

Traditional dining in Bern is a pretty grounded affair, characterized by Italian home cooking and German-style meat and potatoes. Two particular local favorites are the *Bernerplatte*—great slabs of salt pork, beef tongue, smoked bacon, pork ribs, and mild pork sausage cooked down in broth then heaped on top of juniper-scented sauerkraut, green beans, and boiled potatoes—and *Berner rösti*, shredded potatoes pan-fried with onions, butter, and chunks of bacon. Other—healthier—options include creative vegetarian cuisine, refined gastronomic delicacies, fresh fish, and ethnic foods. Most menus change with the seasons, featuring asparagus in spring, berries in summer, and wild game in fall; food presentation can be unexpectedly sophisticated; and service is almost universally friendly. Be sure to make reservations, especially if you want to eat outside in summer—the city abandons its dark, often underground winter quarters (though they stay open) as soon as the weather permits.

WHAT IT COSTS In Swiss francs				
	$$$$	**$$$**	**$$**	**$**	**¢**
Main Course	over 60 SF	40 SF–60 SF	25 SF–40 SF	15 SF–25 SF	under 15 SF

Prices are per person for a main course at dinner.

$$$$ ✕ **Meridiano.** The curved gold ceiling, white baby grand, brown suede bench nooks, and sweeping view of the Altstadt complete with operatic Alpine backdrop make this chic, contemporary space a wonderful spot for romance. And the complex, vibrant Mediterranean menu more than holds its own. Chef Fredi Boss oversees the kitchen; ask for a seat on the terrace in summer. ⊠ *Hotel Allegro, Kornhausstr. 3, Kornhausbrücke* ☎ *031/3395500* ⊟ *AE, DC, MC, V* ⊘ *Closed Sun. and Mon. No lunch Sat.*

$$–$$$$ ✕ **Jack's Brasserie.** Time moves a little slower here amid the civilized elegance of lazy cigarette smoke and china teapots. Picture windows face the train station; gilt ceiling details, grapevine motifs, and leopard-print banquettes warm up the wood paneling; and the day's papers hang from lampposts at discreet intervals between tables. The menu changes every week but the classic French theme is constant—expect tartares and minestrone in summer, cassoulet or veal liver in winter, and chateaubriand year-round. There's an excellent selection of Swiss wines and expensive but top-flight French reds. ⊠ *Bahnhofpl. 11, City Center* ☎ *031/3268080* ⊟ *AE, DC, MC, V.*

$$–$$$ ✕ **Schwellenmätteli.** A chest-high glass barrier stands between you and white water at the tip of this sun-soaked, airy restaurant–lounge and bar. Built like a ship's prow past the edge of the Matteschwelle weir, this unique establishment maintains a hip, beachlike atmosphere with its chaises longues, teak bar stools, and cushioned wicker chairs. The dining area, inside or beneath a retractable roof, serves Mediterranean-inspired dishes like lemongrass-cream soup, rhubarb-strawberry chutney with baked Vacherin, red snapper with lemon risotto and grilled vegetables, and *cabillaud* (cod) saltimbocca with saffron potatoes. ⊠ *Dalmaziquai 11, Schwellenmätteli* ☎ *031/3505001* ⊟ *AE, MC, V.*

★ **$$–$$$** ✕ **Verdi.** Music is a leitmotif along walls studded with opera posters, paintings, programs, scores, photos, and clippings; there are also low ceilings, wooden beams, gilt mirrors, velvet drapes, stone walls, and a balcony overlooking a huge working fireplace. The real star, however, is the menu, which sees truffles, cream, and polenta transition to tomatoes, basil, fennel, and lemon soup with salmon ravioli as the weather warms up. Spicy spaghetti alla Scarpara and sliced steak on a bed of arugula with Parmesan are year-round favorites. The wine cellar, visible through glass doors off the dining room, ranges all over Italy. ⊠ *Gerechtigkeitsg. 5, Altstadt* ☎ *031/3126368* ▭ *AE, DC, MC, V.*

★ **$$–$$$** ✕ **Zimmermania.** A deceptively simple local favorite and one of the most typically French bistros in Bern, this cultural transplant tucked away on a back street near the Rathaus has been serving classics like *rognons de veau* (veal kidneys) in mustard sauce, *Kalbsleber* (calves' liver), and lamb with ratatouille since 1848. In a city that celebrates the onion, this is a good place to try onion soup. Lunch specials cost a mere 17.50 SF; wines come from Switzerland, Italy, and France. ⊠ *Brunng. 19, Altstadt* ☎ *031/3111542* ▭ *MC, V* ☉ *Closed Sun. and Mon.*

$$–$$$
Fodor'sChoice
★
✕ **Zum Zähringer.** The owner made his fortune in Napa, the cook is from London, the herbs in your salad hail from the garden out back, and your fish was pulled from the Aare across the street at this simply elegant restaurant. Candlelit rooms and wildflower arrangements provide a warm setting for dishes such as delicate pumpkin ravioli, veal shank with a subtle wine sauce, buckwheat crêpes filled with summer vegetables, and warm berries in balsamic vinegar. ⊠ *Badg. 1, Matte* ☎ *031/3113270* ▭ *MC, V* ☉ *Closed Sun. No lunch Sat. and Mon.*

$–$$$
Fodor'sChoice
★
✕ **Della Casa.** Probably the ultimate place to sample a Bernerplatte, luscious veal liver with rösti, superlative game (in season), or hearty oxtail stew with fried macaroni, this institution beloved of Swiss politicians is affectionately nicknamed "Delli" and has been operating nearly as long as the Federal parliament building, down the street. The yellowed "säli" on the ground floor and the wood-paneled restaurant upstairs share the same big, generous kitchen; the veteran waitresses shepherd you through the menu; and there's no need to rush—your second portion awaits on a warming table nearby. ⊠ *Schauplatzg. 16, City Center* ☎ *031/3112142* ▭ *AE, DC, MC, V* ☉ *Closed Sun. year-round; Apr.–Sept., no dinner Sat.*

$–$$$ ✕ **Harmonie.** Plain wooden chairs, blue tablecloths, warm orange trim, and the telltale whiff of cheese all indicate, correctly, that this family-run establishment within sight of the Zytglogge does Swiss cuisine well. Whether classic (Gruyère), *moitié-moitié* (half Gruyère, half Vacherin), or gussied up with truffles and champagne, fondue will arrive trailing copious amounts of bread and, ideally, a *pot* of Vaudois white. *Käseschnitte* (open-face sandwiches with melted cheese), *Chäshörnli* (macaroni and cheese), traditional pork sausage, veal, beef, rack of lamb, and sides of crispy brown Rösti or *Spätzli* (dumplings) complete the picture of a nation well fed. ⊠ *Hotelg. 3, Altstadt* ☎ *031/3131141* ▭ *AE, DC, MC, V* ☉ *Closed weekends.*

CASANOVA WAS HERE

The history of Zum Zähringer dates back to the time when Badgasse (Bath Street) was Bern's red-light district and the inn on the corner was a favorite with Giacomo Casanova.

$-$$$ ╳ **Kornhauskeller.** Entering the Kornhauskeller is like entering a cathedral, except that the stunning vaulted ceilings and frescoes are underground and the lounge-bar in the gallery stocks 92 whiskeys, 30 rums, 15 bourbons, and a selection of Cuban cigars. The building has focused on food throughout its long life, first as a wine cellar/granary, then as a beer hall, now as a classy, popular restaurant where crostini, carpaccio, lemon risotto, and gnocchi with artichoke occupy the same menu as calves' liver, veal schnitzel, and a regal Bernerplatte. ⊠ *Kornhauspl. 18, Altstadt* ☎ *031/3277272* ☐ *AE, DC, MC, V* ☉ *No lunch Sun.*

★ **$-$$$** ╳ **Lorenzini.** If Bern were Italian, every place might look like this one. Cushioned brown benches and black wooden chairs surround white-clad tables with silver bread bowls. Eclectic photos, prints, and paintings adorn the walls and marble statues stand tucked in alcoves. The staff exudes the barest hint of attitude, and Tuscany and Piedmont jostle for space on the wine list. The kitchen presents mouthwatering homemade pastas and desserts, with a signature dish of escalope of veal with ham, sage, and saffron risotto. The open-air atrium, crammed with tables and summer diners, is decorated with olive trees, grape vines, and pink geraniums. And, there are two bars. ⊠ *Theaterpl. 5/Hotelg. 8, Altstadt* ☎ *031/3117850* ☐ *AE, DC, MC, V* ☉ *Closed Sun.*

$-$$ ╳ **Altes Tramdepot.** The cavernous, stripped-down barn space, voluminous outdoor seating with leafy views of the Altstadt, and hints of Munich in the menu all underline the fact that your Bernerplatte with homemade spätzli, cordon bleu, weisswurst, or warm pretzel filled with ham would be incomplete without a house beer. Dark, light, and "normal" varieties are brewed in copper vats behind the bar and specialty beers appear at Easter, in October, or during the full moon. The kitchen stays open from 11 AM to midnight every day of the year. ⊠ *Grosser Muristalden 6, Bärengraben* ☎ *031/3681415* ☐ *AE, DC, MC, V.*

$-$$ ╳ **Gartenrestaurant Marzilibrücke.** Red-and-yellow pillows punctuate the white benches and wood tables inside this bohemian spot on the Marzili side of the river; the shaded gravel garden out front and the gourmet pizza zone around back more than double the restaurant's size in summer. The staff may seem casual, but the menu's sweep of Indian curries, lentils, and naan; local fish; Thai curry; pasta; schnitzel; and Caesar or Greek salad is presented with timely flair. Italian and Spanish wines dominate; Sunday brunch is served from 10 to 2. ⊠ *Gasstr. 8, Marzili* ☎ *031/3112780* ☐ *AE, DC, MC, V* ☉ *No lunch Sat.*

¢-$$ ╳ **Markthalle.** The name says it all: the global food court you see today—in which Japanese, Turkish, Indian, and tapas eateries rub shoulders with a gelato stand and a white-linen formal restaurant—was once a market hall full of produce and independent vendors. The wine shop does tastings; the tea-and-herbs emporium brews cups from China, India, Japan, South-Africa, and Sri Lanka; and stand-up bars keep things animated late into the evening. ⊠ *Bubenbergpl. 9, City Center* ☐ *AE, MC, V.*

¢ ╳ **Tibits.** Everything on the menu can be ordered to go, and its integration into the train station building makes this airy space a favorite with travelers. But linger in the wicker chairs or spread books across the long tables; the children's corner has toys, storybooks, a blackboard, and high chairs. The food is 100% vegetarian and sold by weight from a buffet that can yield three courses; homemade sandwiches and soups such as

Fodor'sChoice
★

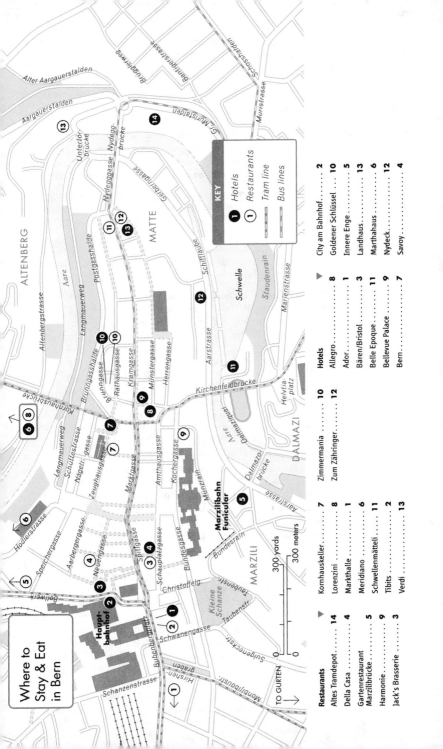

Where to Stay & Eat in Bern

KEY

1 Hotels
① Restaurants
Tram line
Bus lines

Restaurants

Altes Tramdepot. **14**
Della Casa **4**
Gartenrestaurant
Marzilibrücke. **5**
Harmonie **9**
Jack's Brasserie **3**
Kornhauskeller. **7**
Lorenzini **8**
Markthalle **1**
Meridiano **6**
Schwellenmätteli **11**
Tibits **2**
Verdi **13**
Zimmermania **10**
Zum Zähringer. **12**

Hotels

Allegro **8**
Ador **1**
Bären/Bristol **3**
Belle Epoque **11**
Bellevue Palace **9**
Bern **7**
City am Bahnhof. **2**
Goldener Schlüssel . . . **10**
Innere Enge **5**
Landhaus **13**
Marthahaus **6**
Nydeck **12**
Savoy. **4**

300 yards
300 meters

TO GURTEN →

pumpkin, lentil, or green pea with peppermint fill in the gaps. To drink: fresh fruit and vegetable juices, organic wine, flavored coffee, herbal tea, and cocktails such as Rooibos Vodka. ⊠ *Bahnhofpl. 10, City Center* ☎ *031/3129111* ⊟ *No credit cards.*

WHERE TO STAY

Bern has plenty of quality, if sometimes generic, hotels, but book in advance—music festivals, trade conventions, markets, sports events, and parliamentary sessions (March, June, September, and December) can fill rooms fast. ■ TIP→ Rates drop on weekends, when there is less demand.

WHAT IT COSTS In Swiss francs				
$$$$	**$$$**	**$$**	**$**	**¢**
Double Room	over 350	250–350	175–250	100–175	under 100

Prices are for two people in a standard double room in high season, including tax and service.

$$$$ 🏨 **Bellevue Palace.** A pretension-free mix of Belle Epoque elegance and
Fodor'sChoice contemporary ease defines this impeccable hotel, built in 1913 to ac-
★ commodate government visitors. Intricate moldings, golden beige brocade, crystal chandeliers, and Art Nouveau stained glass lure political
events and weddings here. Rooms are outfitted with warm yellows, reds,
and blues; granite bathrooms with heated floors; wireless Internet access; and occasional flat-screen TVs. The fifth floor has sleek modern
lines, glass showers, and sloped ceilings. The elegant Bellevue Grill, with
a terrace, uses seasonal ingredients to create artful dishes and menus.
Outdoor diners and any room facing south enjoy unobstructed Alpine
views. ⊠ *Kocherg. 3–5, Altstadt, CH-3001* ☎ *031/3204545* 🖷 *031/*
3114743 ⊕ *www.bellevue-palace.ch* 🛏 *117 rooms, 13 suites* ♿ *Restau-*
rant, room service, in-room safes, minibars, cable TV with movies, in-
room data ports, Wi-Fi, bar, concierge, business services, meeting rooms,
parking (fee), no-smoking floor ⊟ *AE, DC, MC, V* ⊙ *BP.*

$$$ 🏨 **Bären/Bristol.** The joint occupants of a full city block, halfway be-
tween the Hauptbahnhof and the Bundeshaus, these business-class, Best
Western Siamese twins are favorites with parliament officials and
bankers—and perfectly placed at the heart of Bern's commercial district.
Clean, modern, and functional, the rooms are outfitted with sleek curved
wood, round glass tables, starched white duvets, and free wireless In-
ternet access. ⊠ *Bären: Schauplatzg. 4, City Center, CH-3011* ☎ *031/*
3113367, 800/780–7234 in U.S. 🖷 *031/3116983* 🛏 *57 rooms* ⊕ *www.*
baerenbern.ch ⊠ *Bristol: Schauplatzg. 10, City Center, CH-3011*
☎ *031/3110101, 800/780–7234 in U.S.* 🖷 *031/3119479* ⊕ *www.*
bristolbern.ch 🛏 *92 rooms* ♿ *Snack bar, in-room safes, minibars, cable*
TV, in-room data ports, Wi-Fi, sauna, bicycles, bar, laundry facilities,
business services, no-smoking rooms ⊟ *AE, DC, MC, V* ⊙ *BP.*

★ **$$$** 🏨 **Belle Epoque.** Pay close attention to the walls in this boutique gem,
they're furnished entirely with Belle Epoque originals: Steinlen graces
the bathrooms and breakfast area, Hodler and Klimt spice up suites named
for them, and the bar has photos of Toulouse-Lautrec standing next to

the Moulin Rouge poster behind you. There's no air-conditioning but windows are triple-glazed for silence, bathrooms have vanities, closets disguised as traveling trunks hide televisions, and period consoles pick up BBC World Service Radio. Each of the three suites has

> ## OH, BELLE EPOQUE!
>
> Original works of art by Steinlen, Hodler and Klimt grace the walls of the Belle Epoque hotel.

a DVD player, Dolby Surround Sound, and original LPs. Extras like sunflower seeds and green tea characterize breakfast. ⊠ *Gerechtigkeitsg. 18, Altstadt, CH-3011* ☎ *031/3114336* 🖷 *031/3113936* ⊕ *www.belle-epoque.ch* 🛏 *14 rooms, 3 suites* ⏛ *Restaurant, fans, in-room safes, minibars, cable TV, in-room data ports, Wi-Fi, bar, no-smoking floors; no a/c* ☲ *AE, DC, MC, V.*

$$$ 🖵 **Hotel Allegro.** In a town renowned for its antiquity, the Allegro stands out as thoroughly modern. Styles range from the interior Atrium rooms, with one-way glass windows, flat-screen TVs, and backlit smoked-glass headboards to penthouse suites with private balconies, panoramic city and Alpine views, rounded leather furniture, and Jacuzzis. There is an ice machine on every floor, a stiff formality to the staff, and wireless Internet access everywhere. The modern Chinese restaurant Yù has a wall of falling water. ⊠ *Kornhausstr. 3, Kornhausbrücke, CH-3000* ☎ *031/ 3395500* 🖷 *031/3395510* ⊕ *www.allegro-hotel.ch* 🛏 *167 rooms, 4 suites* ⏛ *3 restaurants, café, in-room safes, minibars, cable TV with movies, in-room broadband, in-room data ports, Web TV, Wi-Fi, health club, bicycles, bar, beer garden, casino, concert hall, business services, meeting rooms, airport shuttle, parking (fee), no-smoking rooms* ☲ *AE, DC, MC, V.*

$$$ 🖵 **Hotel Savoy.** Halogen-lighted hallways lead to pleasant rooms with rose carpets, yellow walls, sleek wood, and white bedcovers in this neatly tailored hotel across the street from the Stauffacher bookstore. The Hauptbahnhof and Bern's markets are just a block away. Most of the doubles have two sinks, the fourth floor has rooftop views, suites have extra seating areas, and any room facing the *hof* (inner courtyard) will be absolutely quiet. ⊠ *Neueng. 26, City Center, CH-3011* ☎ *031/ 3114405* 🖷 *031/3121978* ⊕ *www.zghotels.ch* 🛏 *50 rooms, 6 suites* ⏛ *Café, in-room safes, minibars, cable TV, in-room data ports, Wi-Fi, no-smoking rooms; no a/c in some rooms* ☲ *AE, DC, MC, V* ⧉ *BP.*

$$$ 🖵 **Innere Enge.** Exposed beams, Art Nouveau accents, pristine Alpine views, and jazz memorabilia from greats like Lionel Hampton, John Lewis, Hazy Osterwald, and Clark Terry punctuate the spacious, sunny rooms in this half-timbered inn that dates to the early 1700s. The parklike setting, five minutes by bus from the Hauptbahnhof, provides a tranquil alternative to city streets; Marians Jazzroom warms things up in the basement during the school year. Napoléon's beloved Josephine once had lunch in the Park Pavilion. ⊠ *Engestr. 54, Innere Enge, CH-3012* ☎ *031/3096111* 🖷 *031/3096112* ⊕ *www.zghotels.ch* 🛏 *11 rooms, 15 suites* ⏛ *Restaurant, in-room safes, minibars, cable TV, in-room data ports, Wi-Fi, free parking, no-smoking rooms; no a/c in some rooms* ☲ *AE, DC, MC, V* ⧉ *BP.*

8

$$–$$$ 🏨 **Bern.** The somewhat monolithic facade, on a busy street behind the Kornhaus, contrasts totally with the clean, modern lines inside this energetic establishment. Rooms have colorful block carpeting, curved light fixtures, chairs shaped like punctuation marks, and the occasional architectural flourish such as rounded windows or sloping eaves. Most of the clientele are businesspeople but the hotel is equally suited to children (who stay free in their parents' room). ⊠ *Zeughausg. 9, City Center, CH-3011* ☎ *031/3292222* 🖷 *031/3292299* ⊕ *www.hotelbern.ch* ↘ *100 rooms* ⟡ *3 restaurants (1 seasonal May–September), room service, in-room safes, refrigerators, cable TV, in-room broadband, Wi-Fi, no-smoking floor; no a/c* ⊟ *AE, DC, MC, V* |⊙| *BP.*

★ **$$** 🏨 **City am Bahnhof.** Giant portholes flank the bottom-lighted, smoked-glass bridge that leads guests over pebbled water into the reception area, where Bernese sandstone and blue leather armchairs create a modern Asian feel. Wicker chairs with thin black legs, light-wood café tables, and simple gray-green banquettes give the spot-lighted buffet-breakfast floor a touch of style. Rooms have peach sponge-painted walls, crisp white linens, wicker chairs, smoked-glass desks, and bathrooms that filter in natural light. Mirrors are used strategically throughout. ⊠ *Bubenbergpl. 7, City Center, CH-3011* ☎ *031/3115377* 🖷 *031/3110636* ⊕ *www.fassbindhotels.com* ↘ *58 rooms* ⟡ *In-room safes, minibars, cable TV with movies, in-room data ports, Wi-Fi, laundry service, Internet, no-smoking floors; no a/c* ⊟ *AE, DC, MC, V.*

$$ 🏨 **Hotel Ador.** Functional, if a bit spartan, and located to the west of the Hauptbahnhof near tram stops and a movie theater, this boxy hotel is well placed for access to Daniel Liebeskind's angular, modern, retail-and-leisure development, WESTside, set to open in 2008. The stone lobby sparkles and vending machines on each level replace in-room minibars; rooms have modular furniture, dark parquet floors, and white-tile baths. ⊠ *Laupenstr. 15, City West, CH-3001* ☎ *031/3880111* 🖷 *031/3880110* ⊕ *www.hotelador.ch* ↘ *52 rooms* ⟡ *Restaurant, in-room safes, cable TV, in-room data ports, Wi-Fi, dry cleaning, laundry service, Internet room, meeting room, parking (fee), no-smoking rooms; no a/c* ⊟ *AE, DC, MC, V* |⊙| *BP.*

$ 🏨 **Goldener Schlüssel.** The address is within earshot of the Zytglogge bells, the solidly popular restaurant serves rib-sticking favorites like bratwurst with Rösti, and the reception is in that little alcove past the elevator under the stairs. Rooms are functional and sturdy, with floral duvet covers and medieval-rooftop views on the top floors; some share a bath. ⊠ *Rathausg. 72, Altstadt, CH-3011* ☎ *031/3110216* 🖷 *031/3115688* ⊕ *www. goldener-schluessel.ch* ↘ *29 rooms, 21 with bath* ⟡ *Restaurant, Stübli, cable TV; no a/c* ⊟ *MC, V* |⊙| *BP.*

$ 🏨 **Landhaus.** The river views are idyllic and the wood floors creak authenticity in this airy young hostel with a Fussball console by the reception, live jazz in the laid-back restaurant, communal kitchen space, and a grocery store. Rooms range from dorm-style cubicles (for 30 SF) with sold-separately linens and breakfast to all-inclusive doubles with shower. Every room has modern stainless steel bed frames and a sink. ⊠ *Altenbergstr. 4–6, Altenberg, CH-3013* ☎ *031/3314166* 🖷 *031/3326904* ⊕ *www.landhausbern.ch* ↘ *6 rooms, 2 with bath, 2 dormitories*

           🛁 *Restaurant, kitchen, grocery, cable TV in some rooms, Internet, Wi-Fi; no a/c, no elevator, no smoking* ⊟ *AE, DC, MC, V* ⑩| *BP.*

$ ▭ **Nydeck.** Mirrors work magic in this small, tidy corner hotel near the Nydeggbrücke; light-wood parquet floors, sage-green headboards and upholstery, white-striped duvet covers, pink geraniums, and medieval city views complete the job. Compact white-tile bathrooms have glass showers, hair dryers, and vanities; double-glazed windows keep street noise at bay. The Junkere bar, downstairs, spills into a delightful sidewalk terrace in summer. ⊠ *Gerechtigkeitsg. 1, Altstadt, CH-3011* ☎ *031/3118686* ⎙ *031/3122054* ⊕ *www.hotelnydeck.ch* ⇋ *12 rooms* 🛁 *Cable TV, Wi-Fi, bar, no-smoking rooms; no a/c, no elevator* ⊟ *AE, DC, MC, V* ⑩| *BP.*

¢–$ ▭ **Marthahaus.** Bright, sunny rooms have light wood, white walls, sinks, and up to five beds; the reception is open round the clock; breakfast can be served from 4:30 AM; and the staff will do your laundry at this quiet, comfortable turn-of-the-century pension north of Bern's Altstadt. Mixed-sex dormitory space costs about 40 SF; cooking facilities, bicycles, and Internet access are free. ⊠ *Wyttenbachstr. 22a, Lorraine, CH-3013* ☎ *031/3324135* ⎙ *031/3333386* ⊕ *www.marthahaus.ch* ⇋ *40 rooms, 4 with shower, 6 dormitories* 🛁 *Kitchen, cable TV, Internet room, Wi-Fi, bicycles, laundry service, parking (fee); no a/c, no smoking* ⊟ *MC, V* ⑩| *BP.*

NIGHTLIFE & THE ARTS

Twice a year, Bern Tourismus publishes and widely disseminates *Bern Guide,* a free, pocket-size, bilingual (German/English), and comprehensive guide to what's on in the city (exhibits, nightlife, festivals, shopping, excursions, and useful telephone numbers). The Web site *www.berninfo.com* fills in any remaining gaps.

Nightlife

The Bernese like to party, and nightlife options accordingly run the gamut from plush velvet seating and Belle Epoque refinement to jazz lounges, casual sidewalk bars, and plugged-in clubs where DJs spin the latest. Bärenplatz and Kornhausplatz bubble over with revelers on summer evenings; many restaurants transition into bars as the night wears on.

Bars

Adriano's (⊠ Theaterpl. 2, Altstadt ☎ 031/3188831 ⊕ www.adrianos.ch) is a friendly, glassed-in coffee bar that serves fresh croissants from 7 AM (10 AM on Sunday), sandwiches throughout the day, and wine or beer to a sidewalk crowd come nightfall. Exquisite Belle Epoque paintings and outdoor jazz grace the **Bar Toulouse-Lautrec** (⊠ Hotel Belle Epoque). Well-heeled travelers come to see and be seen at the indoor–outdoor **Bellevue Bar** (⊠ Hotel Bellevue Palace). The wood-paneled weinstube dates from 1635 and the owners are traditionally single blonde women at the **Klötzlikeller** (⊠ Gerechtigkeitsg. 62, Altstadt ☎ 031/3117456 ⊕ www.kloetzlikeller.ch), Bern's last true wine cellar beneath the arcades. The Riviera vibe at the outdoor **Terrasse** and indoor **Color-**

Lounge (✉ Dalmaziquai 11, Schwellenmätteli ☎ 031/3505001 ⊕ www.
schwellenmaetteli.ch), both part of the Scwellenmätteli restaurant complex, lure thirtysomething hipsters down to the river.

Casino

All 261 slot machines and 11 gaming tables at the Kursaal's **Grand Casino
Bern** (✉ Kornhausstr. 3, Kornhausbrücke ☎ 031/3395555 ⊕ www.
grandcasino-bern.ch) stay open until 4 AM from Thursday through Saturday.

Dancing

Smart young professionals stop after work for a mellow glass of wine
and stay 'til 4 AM for weekend dance parties at **Du Théâtre** (✉ Hotelg.
10/Theaterpl. 7, Altstadt ☎ 031/3185067 ⊕ www.lorenzini.ch). **Shakira**
(✉ National Hotel, Hirschengraben 24, City Center ☎ 031/3811988
⊕ www.shakira.ch) specializes in Latin music, salsa dancing, and tropical drinks. The Prodigy, Moby, and The Roots all played the sophisticated, musically multitalented **Wasserwerk Club** (✉ Wasserwerkg. 5, Matte
☎ No phone ⊕ www.wasserwerkclub.ch) early in their careers.

The Arts

Bern's three-pronged arts scene covers opera and symphonic classics,
seasonal festivals, and cubbyhole theaters buried underground.

Film

If a film was made in English, Bernese cinemas will generally show it in
English. Local newspapers list screening times (look for "E" to confirm
the language) and most theaters advertise current programs on big
boards underneath the Käfigturm and in the Christoffelunterführung.
The open-air **OrangeCinema** (✉ Grosse Schanze ☎ 0800/078078 ⊕ www.
orangecinema.ch) sets up camp in front of the University each July and
shows recent mainstream favorites through August.

Music & the Performing Arts

The **Berner Symphonie-Orchester** (☎ 031/3282424 ⊕ www.bernorchester.
ch) performs orchestral work and chamber music, primarily in the **Kultur-Casino** (✉ Herreng. 25, Altstadt). The **Stadttheater** (✉ Kornhauspl.
20, Altstadt ☎ 031/3295111 ⊕ www.stadttheaterbern.ch) presents
seven full-scale operas, 10 dramas (in German), and three contemporary dance pieces each year. **Bern Billett** (✉ Nägelig. 1a, Altstadt ☎ 031/
3295252 ⊕ www.bernbillett.ch) handles ticket sales for the Kultur-
Casino and the Stadttheater.

Altstadt streets empty briefly in mid-July as A-list rockers like James Blunt,
Billy Idol, and David Gray draw crowds to the four-day open-air **Gurten
Festival** (⊕ www.gurtenfestival.ch). **Marians Jazzroom** (✉ Engestr. 54, Innere Enge ☎ 031/3096111 ⊕ www.mariansjazzroom.ch) hosts top international jazz, blues, and gospel artists between September and May;
the **International Jazz Festival** (⊕ www.jazzfestivalbern.ch) amplifies that
program for two months starting in March.

Marionettes, stick puppets, hand puppets, shadow puppets, and masks
come to life on stage at the **Berner Puppen Theater** (✉ Gerechtigkeitsg.

31, Altstadt ☎031/3119585 ⊕www.berner-puppentheater.ch). The **Theater am Käfigturm** (✉ Spitalg. 4, City Center ☎ 031/3116100 ⊕ www.theater-am-kaefigturm.ch), three levels below Spitalgasse, presents pantomime, modern dance, avant-garde plays, satires, burlesques (in Swiss German), and the occasional piece aimed at children.

SPORTS & THE OUTDOORS

Bicycling

There are about 300 km (185 mi) of marked trails in and around Bern. Leave ID and a 20 SF deposit with **Bern Rollt** (✉ Bahnhofpl. and Zeughausg., City Center and Altstadt ☎079/2772857 ⊕www.bernrollt. ch) between May and October and you can ride for free from 7:30 AM to 9:30 PM.

Golf

The **Golf and Country Club Blumisberg** (✉ 18 km [11 mi] west of town ☎ 026/4963438 ⊕ www.swissgolfnetwork.ch) has 18 holes and a clubhouse with a restaurant, bar, showers, and swimming pool. Visitors are admitted on weekdays, provided they're members of any golf club with handicaps; it's not possible to rent equipment.

Swimming

Swimmers have headed into the cold, swift Aare just before its U-turn around the Altstadt since Bern was founded. These days a hot Sunday may see scantily clad (or, in certain sections, naked) crowds of more than 10,000 sprawled on beach towels on the grass, swimming laps in the pools, or bobbing happily in the river (a system of handrails projected over the water prevents bathers from traveling too far downstream). Known universally as **The Marzili** (✉ Marzilistr. 29, Marzili ☎ 031/3110046 ⊕ www.aaremarzili.ch), this sunny stretch of riverbank below the Bundeshaus presents a unique, and entirely free, take on the city.

Heated mineral-rich indoor baths, open-air saltwater pools, underwater massage jets, bubble beds, whirlpools, a mushroom fountain, eucalyptus steam baths, and a sauna park are highlights at the sprawling **Solbad Schönbühl** (✉ Mattenweg 30 Schönbühl ☎ 031/8593434 ⊕ www.solbad.ch), open year-round to the north of Bern. Bathing suits and towels can be rented onsite; admission to the baths is 27 SF.

SHOPPING

Bern's official store hours are 9 to 6:30 weekdays and 8 to 4 on Saturday. Thursday hours are extended to 9; stores in the Hauptbahnhof may open on Sunday. Smaller stores, particularly in the Altstadt, may stay shuttered Monday morning, close for lunch, close before 9 on Thursday, and/or open as late as 10.

Department Stores

Quality, stylish, often vibrantly colorful home accessories and cooking gear fill the upper stories at **Globus** (✉ Spitalg. 17–21, City Center ☎ 031/3134040). On the lower levels, luscious hats and scarves, cosmetics, and designer labels give way to foodstuffs—from specialty oils through cheese—in the up-scale supermarket downstairs. **Loeb** (⊠ Spitalg. 47–51, City Center ☏ 031/3207111) sells model trucks, legos, and children's clothing on the top floor, descending through craft supplies, luggage, house wares, and mid-range clothing brands to assorted stationery, hosiery, and Swiss-themed souvenirs on the ground floor.

Markets

The effects of the colorful **Geranienmarkt** (Geranium Market), held on the Bundesplatz, Bärenplatz, and Waisenhausplatz from 7 AM to 3 PM on a Wednesday in mid-May, can quickly be seen on balconies throughout Bern. Some say the best time to browse the annual **Zibelemärit** (Onion Market) is just after it opens at 4 AM on the fourth Monday in November, when stalls are lighted by candles; you may be treated to a predawn dusting of snow, and confetti battles do not yet rage. Throughout December, hot mulled wine adds spice to the arts and crafts, evergreen, and seasonal produce stalls lining Münsterplatz and Waisenhausplatz during the **Weihnachtsmarkt** (Christmas Market), which keeps regular shop hours.

Tuesday and Saturday are Bern's formal year-round market days, with most of the action concentrated in the morning along the Bundesplatz–Bärenplatz–Waisenhausplatz axis through the center of town. The main **fruit, vegetable, and flower market** fills Bundesplatz and Bärenplatz with fresh produce, herbs, and flowers (daily, during shopping hours on Bärenplatz between May and October). Münstergasse hosts a **meat and cheese market.** The **trader's market** on Waisenhausplatz adds late-night hours on Thursday between May and October and forms an awning-covered warren of handmade soaps, antique copper pots, silver jewelry, handmade hammocks, tie-dyed scarves, and incongruous objects like panama hats.

Arts and crafts stalls create a **craft fair** on the Münsterplattform every first Saturday of the month between March and December. The **flea market,** held on Matte's Mühleplatz the third Saturday of the month from May to October, has the look and feel of an antiques-laden tag sale.

Shopping Streets

No street or side alley in downtown Bern is without interest to shoppers, and you never know what fabulous discovery may await at the end of an intriguing passageway or the bottom of cellar stairs. **Spitalgasse** and **Marktgasse** form the City Center's main shopping drag; parallel streets such as **Neuengasse, Aarbergergasse,** and **Amthausgasse**can also be very rewarding. The Altstadt, from **Brunngasse** to **Junkerngasse** by way of **Kramgasse** and **Gerechtigkeitsgasse,** is lined and honeycombed with fine specialty boutiques ranging from oriental carpets to glasses and funky antiques to avant-garde fashion; there are also exclusive artisan jewelers, design and gift stores full of glassware and silk, art galleries, physiological footwear, toys, and specialty foods. **Münstergasse** is noted for its Tibetan, African, and other quality ethnic artifacts.

Books

It is easy to get lost in the sprawling tri-lingual **Stauffacher** (✉ Neueng. 25–37, City Center ☎ 031/3136363) emporium of books, maps, and multimedia, but there are far worse fates. The substantial English Bookshop occupies the third floor of the west wing; regular readings (some in English) are held in the Café Littéraire. At **Thalia** (✉ Spitalg. 47–51, City Center ☎ 031/3202020), a German-language chain lodged in the basement of the Loeb department store, globes, dictionaries, multilingual travel guides, English-language fiction and biographies, a play area for kids, and a sizeable selection of books about Switzerland are highlights.

Chocolate

Chocolate-covered plums and truffles made with Bailey's, Kirsch, or coconut white chocolate lead the charge at **Abegglen** (✉ Spitalg. 36, City Center ☎ 031/3112111). **Beeler** (✉ Spitalg. 29, City Center ☎ 031/3112808) shapes chocolate to look like members of the Federal Council. **Eichenberger** (✉ Bahnhofpl. 5, City Center ☎ 031/3113325) concocts its strong, dark house mix of cacao by hand on the

> ### SUNDAY TEA
>
> Many chocolatiers' shops have tearoom areas at the back and are, therefore, allowed to open on Sunday. If you go, be sure to try the Bernese specialty *Lebkuchen*, a dense, flat spice cake made with hazelnuts, honey, and almonds.

first floor. Orange, strawberry, passion fruit, lime, and dulce de leche are summer flavors at **Meyer** (✉ Marktg. 31, City Center ☎ 031/3105500). The self-styled prince of Bernese chocolatiers, **Tschirren** (✉ Kramg. 73, Altstadt ☎ 031/3111717), has been making its divine assortment of artfully rough-hewn truffles since 1919.

Gifts & Souvenirs

The warrenlike **Boutique Nelli** (✉ Gerechtigkeitsg. 3, Altstadt ☎ 031/3111040) has a whimsical selection of glassware by local artists, candles in rainbow colors, soap shaped like fruit, and imaginative kitchen gadgets. Victorinox, Wenger, and Swiss Military knives dominate the window at **Heimatwerk** (✉ Kramg. 61, Altstadt ☎ 031/3113000), a high-quality emporium of Swiss-made music boxes, toys, handicrafts, textiles, and ceramics. Colorful handmade wooden figures and candelabras, delicate shaved-wood trees, and lacy wooden cutouts pull focus at **Holz Art** (✉ Münsterg. 36, Altstadt ☎ 031/3126666). Most of the fine, often Swiss-themed, embroidery and linens at **Langenthal** (✉ Marktg. 15, City Center ☎ 031/3118786) were made in Switzerland.

Home Accessories

Cachet (✉ Amthausg. 22, City Center ☎ 031/3118466) stocks culturally resonant items such as iron Japanese teapots, colored grass baskets, camel rugs, Turkish lamps, multicolored bottles, whimsical mobiles, and soulful carved-wood furniture from India, Indonesia, and Pakistan. Clean, liveable, often joyously colorful and affordable designs channel faraway locales at **Interio** (✉ Spitalg. 4, City Center ☎ 031/3276380), where you could outfit a house but might settle for satiny cotton sheets, gossamer curtains in bright colors, hammered steel Moroccan bowls, floating candles, silk pillows, or Indian cotton placemats.

Toys

The big, old, red cash register works; colorful minikites twirl out front; child-sized umbrellas have animal handles; and the plush toys range from snow owls to llamas at **Bilboquet** (⊠ Münsterg. 37, Altstadt ☎ 031/3113671). **Chlätterbär** (⊠ Amthausg. 3, City Center ☎ 031/3111196) sells fully stocked wooden kitchens, xylophones, beaded jewelry, drum sets, hand puppets, and wooden dolls' house furniture. The owner of the **Puppenklinik** (⊠ Gerechtigkeitsg. 36, Altstadt ☎ 031/3120771) has a passion for restoration; the result is a huge collection of vintage dolls, toys, teddy bears, and puppets from around the world. There are very few hard edges at **U-Tiger** (⊠ Gerechtigkeitsg. 79, Altstadt ☎ 031/3279091), where cloud sofas, green dragon bean bags, quilted soccer fields, and fuzzy sheep hot water bottles headline the creative selection of room furnishings for children.

BERN ESSENTIALS

Transportation

BY AIR

AIRPORTS & TRANSFERS Bern's small airport, located 9 km (6 mi) south of the city in Belp, has daily connections to Munich and London City. Shuttle bus service between the Hauptbahnhof and the airport is coordinated with arriving and departing flights; the fare each way is 14 SF and the ride takes 20 minutes. A taxi from the airport to the Hauptbahnhof costs about 50 SF.

🛂 **Bern-Belp Airport** ⊠ Belp ☎ 031/9602111 ⊕ www.flughafenbern.ch.

CARRIERS Germany's national airline, Lufthansa, operates flights from Bern-Belp to Munich; the regional carrier Darwin flies direct to London City and Lugano. The Bern-Belp ticketing office handles local queries for both companies.

🛂 **Bern-Belp Ticket Office** ☎031/9602127. **Darwin** ⊕www.darwinairline.com. **Lufthansa** ⊕ www.lufthansa.com.

BY BUS & TRAM WITHIN BERN

Service is extensive and excellent, with fares costing between 1.90 SF and 3.20 SF. Buy tickets from the dispensers placed at every stop by finding the name of the stop closest to your destination on the map, then selecting the fare listed for it. The machines give change. All public transportation is free for holders of a BernCard, which costs 19 SF for 24 hours, 29 SF for 48 hours, or 35 SF for 72 hours and may be purchased from the Hauptbahnhof and Bärengraben tourist information centers, any museum, or any hotel. Swiss Pass holders also travel free.

🛂 **Bernmobil** ⊕ www.bernmobil.ch.

BY CAR
Bern sits squarely on the map of Swiss expressways. The A1 connects the city with Basel and Zürich to the north, with Lac Léman and Geneva to the south, and via Lausanne with the Valais. The A6 to the Berner Oberland runs just east of the city. Downtown pedestrian zones make parking in city garages a virtual necessity; electric signs on major incoming roads post current numbers of empty spaces.

BY TAXI
Bernese taxis are clean and plentiful, but circuitous downtown traffic routing renders them cumbersome and expensive; a ride from the Hauptbahnhof to the Bärengraben costs about 18 SF. Call or find an official taxi stand; they won't respond if hailed.

Bären Taxi ☎ 031/3711111. **Nova Taxi** ☎ 031/3313313.

BY TRAIN
Bern is a train-based city, and the only European capital to have three high-speed connections: the ICE from Berlin takes 8½ hours, the TGV from Paris takes 4½ hours, and the Pendolino from Milan (known in Switzerland as the Cisalpino) takes 3½ hours. There are daily departures for Rome and, between June and August, Barcelona; Bern's Hauptbahnhof is also a major hub for trains within Switzerland. Intercity trains, which make the fewest stops, leave every 30 minutes: count an hour to reach Zürich or Basel, less than two for Geneva, four hours to Lugano. A tight network of local and regional trains keep Bern connected to surrounding communities. Touch-screen consoles (in English) by the main arrival and departures board sell tickets for any destination in Switzerland.

Hauptbahnhof ✉ Bahnhofpl. ☎ 0900/300300 ⊕ www.sbb.ch.

Contacts & Resources

EMERGENCIES
In an emergency, dial ☎ **117** for the police or ☎ **144** for an ambulance.

Hospitals Inselspital ✉ Freiburgstr. 18, Linde ☎ 031/6322111. **Beau-Site Clinic** ✉ Schänzlihalde 11, Kornhausbrücke ☎ 031/3353535.

INTERNET & MAIL
Most hotels, many restaurants, and even shops in Bern are Public Wireless LAN Hotspots administered by Swisscom. Internet cafés are also plentiful, may include a bar area, and may stay open past midnight on weekends; expect to pay about 2 SF per 15 minutes online.

Post Offices in the city center open and close when the shops do; smaller branches may close for lunch or before noon on Saturday. The Swiss Post Web site lists branches throughout the country with their opening hours. Take a ticket when you enter and wait (usually less than five minutes) for your number to be called. Postcards, stationery, packing materials, even printers can be bought onsite.

Internet Cafés Swisscom ⊕ www.swisscom-mobile.ch. **Thalia** ✉ Loeb, Floor , Spitalg. 47–51, City Center ☎ 031/3202020 ⊕ www.thalia.ch.

🚩 Post Offices **Swiss Post** ☎ 084/8888888 ⊕ www.post.ch. 🖂 3000 Bern 7 Bären-platz 🖂 Bärenpl. 8, City Center ☎ 031/3267878. 🖂 3000 Bern 8 Kramgasse 🖂 Kramg. 1, Altstadt ☎ 031/3115298.

TOUR OPTIONS
Bern Tourismus guides lead 90-minute English-language walking tours of the Altstadt at 11 AM daily between April and October, on Saturday for the rest of the year. Upon request they also organize group tours that examine specific themes or historical periods, are conducted by bus, or float down the Aare in rafts. The tourist information center in the Hauptbahnhof takes reservations and sells tickets; the walking tour costs 16 SF.

🚩 **Bern Tourismus** ☎ 031/3281212 ⊕ www.berninfo.com.

VISITOR INFORMATION
Bern Tourismus, based in the Hauptbahnhof, distributes free brochures and maps, organizes tours, publishes Bern Guide, administers www.berninfo.com, and operates a 3-D multimedia history presentation called *Bern Show* at its satellite information center next to the Bärengraben. BernCards, on sale at either counter, grant free access to the permanent collections of most Bernese museums.

🚩 **Bern Tourismus** 🖂 Tourist Center at railway station, City Center, CH-3011 ☎ 031/3281212 🖷 031/3281277 ⊕ www.berninfo.ch.

Berner Oberland

GSTAAD, INTERLAKEN,
LAUTERBRUNNEN, WENGEN

Murren

WORD OF MOUTH

"Now I know what those "Beware: Switzerland is Addictive" posters mean!"

—KalpanaKar

"I didn't know I HAD any knee problems until the Kleine Scheidegg trail. I literally walked down backwards, with my husband calling out course corrections. Great scenery though—even backwards."

—dmcwriter

WELCOME TO THE BERNER OBERLAND

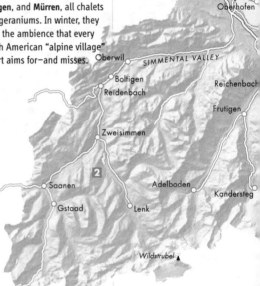

TOP REASONS TO GO

★ **Top of the World:** At 11,400 feet the Jungfraujoch peak isn't the highest place on the planet, but you could probably see it from here.

★ **Twin Peaks:** The upwardly mobile head to the adjacent, mountaintop villages of Wengen and Murren to find the Switzerland of cheese, chalet, and chic cliché.

★ **Shangri-La Found:** The Lauterbrunnen Valley is Yosemite blown up to the nth dimension, complete with 76 cascading waterfalls (among Europe's highest).

★ **Gstaad, Dahling:** Money attracts money, and there's certainly lots of it here. Mere mortals can indulge in exquisite meals, skiing, and overnight stays in paradise.

★ **Old Switzerland, in a Nutshell:** Ballenberg is a delightfully reconstructed Swiss village—à la America's Williamsburg—with traditional crafts on show.

1 Jungfrau Region. A transportation hub, bustling **Interlaken** has upward of 130 hotels and makes the perfect base camp (with a lively nightlife for city mice). A short ride away is the magnificent summit of summits—the Eiger, Münch, and **Jungfrau** (with the highest train station in the world). Nestling below are the villages of **Grindelwald, Lauterbrunnen, Wengen,** and **Mürren,** all chalets and geraniums. In winter, they have the ambience that every North American "alpine village" resort aims for—and misses.

2 Simmental & Gstaad. From **Spiez**, the highway leads southwest into the **Simmental Valley**, where forest gorges hide **Gstaad**, so chic and modish a winter resort Elizabeth Taylor still owns a chalet here.

3 **Thunersee.** This idyllic lake is named for **Thun,** a resort town of medieval dignity. Between bouts of water-skiing and wakeboarding, castle-hop to your heart's content: the shoreline villages of **Spiez, Hilterfingen,** and **Oberhofen** all have fairy-tale-worthy extravaganzas.

GETTING ORIENTED

Blessed with nine valleys, the lovely lakes of Thun and Brienz, jet-set Gstaad, and the ageless grandeur of the Jungfrau, this compact region contains a universe of sights. No wonder Switzerland's tourist industry began here in the early 1800s, with English gentry flocking to gape at this aristocrat of Alpine scenery.

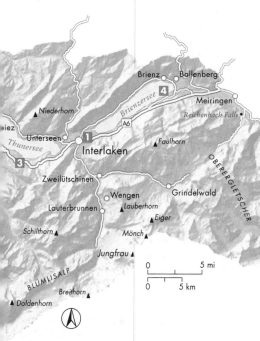

Niederhorn

iez

Unterseen

Thunersee

Interlaken

3

Brienz   Ballenberg

Brienzersee

4

Meiringen

Reichenbach Falls

A6

Faulhorn

Zweilütschinen

Wengen   Grindelwald

Lauterbrunnen   Lauberhorn

Eiger

Schilthorn

Mönch

Jungfrau

OBERERGLETSCHER

BLÜMLISALP

Breithorn

Doldenhorn

| 0 | | 5 mi |
| 0 | | 5 km |

4 **Brienzersee.** In the **Oberland** a wide variety in altitude creates a great diversity of scenery so you can bathe comfortably in **Lake Brienz** after skiing on the **Jungfrau** slopes in July. Waterfront **Brienz** is home to famed wood-carvers and the storybook museum village of **Ballenberg.** Nearby, the plot thickens in **Meiringen**—Sherlock Holmes saw his last here at **Reichenbach Falls.**

BERNER OBERLAND PLANNER

Getting Around

Happily and spectacularly, cars aren't a necessity here, as Mürren, Wengen, and Gstaad are car-free, and rail connections are excellent.

Since the advent of trains and cable cars in the 18th century, the region is lined with narrow-gauge or cog-wheel tracks and aerial cableways—not to mention chairlifts, so you'll often be tempted to join in on a chorus of "Ain't No Mountain High Enough."

If you're planning a circular tour of the region, a car will navigate the valleys a little faster, though.

Direct rail connections from Geneva, Zurich, and Basel run through Bern, from which there is public transportation to every part of the region.

Thun is the hub for Gstaad and Spiez; Interlaken takes you on to Brienz, Lauterbrunnen, and Grindelwald; and hypermagical Lauterbrunnen takes you up to Wengen and Mürren.

Grime Every Mountain

Brrr! What global warming? On Christmas Day, you might not notice any greenhouse effects when standing atop the Jungfrau but, unfortunately, global warming has hit even this region. Acid rain, deforestation erosion, overdevelopment, and burgeoning tourism have all begun to corrode the biggest air-conditioning machine in the world as abnormal heat waves have taken their toll on the erstwhile pristine Swiss Alps. The result? A bit of Switzerland crumbled away on July 13, 2006, with the headline-making rock-fall from the Eiger's notorious north face due to the melting of the rock permafrost (the "glue" that keeps all those cable-car girders in place—hopefully). Little wonder the Swiss remain ever "watch-ful," no more so than the weather-obssessed Bernese Oberlanders (who love to track storms from valley to valley). When nature cooperates, however, the Oberland has four distinct seasons, each more beautiful than the next. Valley springs and summers are perfect for outdoor activities, from hiking and biking to swimming. Falls becomes crisp around October and winter brings snow. Keep in mind that snow can stay as late as May and come as early as August over 6,500 feet. Winter versus summer? Everyone loves the magic of snow but an ermine mantle can easily lend a sameness to all those mountains—something you avoid if you enjoy an Alpine summer. Warm weather, however, brings a global-warmed haze, which can ruin your photos, so be sure to pack your camera's UV filter. And have a care for Mother Nature—as one sign famously put it, "Do Not Hurt the Rocks."

Don't Let Altitude Get You Down

Some excursions here—the Schlithorn and the Jungfraujoch, to name two—should not be attempted by anyone susceptible to mountain sickness, which, though it affects few people, is an unpleasant experience at best and can be dangerous for those suffering from heart trouble, weak lungs, or high blood pressure. Most people simply experience a low-grade headache, so take several aspirins before getting on those cable-cars.

No Wait, not those Kinds of Udders . . .

Cows, cheese, skiing and—Hooters? Of all the gin joints in all the world...a Hooters in Interlaken?

It seems that a couple of lusty Swiss guys went golfing in Florida, stopped in at a local joint for a quick bite and a drink, and came home extremely enthusiastic about a new restaurant concept.

After five years going, business at Höheweg 57 (033/8226512) is brisk, with locals, tourists, families, and surprised North Americans flocking to the establishment.

As a relatively new venture, the establishment is less cynical than in the States (not much silicone to be found here) and has more of an innocent novelty feel about it (picketing feminists having better things to do).

Bottoms up!

Finding a Place to Stay

This is the most-visited region in Switzerland. Translation: book as early as possible.

High season here means winter, with summer making up a second-place high season.

Decide on which experience you want: the townie feel of a place like Interlaken, which has many bars, night clubs, restaurants and movie theaters; the much quieter Grindelwald, with less venues and no movie theaters; or the almost secluded Mürren or Wengen, where you'll be getting most your evening's entertainment from the hotel—usually including meals.

Accommodations in the area range from Gstaad's hyperluxe Palace hotel to Balmer's youth hostel, where you can sleep in a boisterous group tent pitched on the premises in summer.

Swinger Kings and Unspunnen Stones

Newcomers to Switzerland may wonder at headlines proclaiming a new "swinger king" or photos of large brutes throwing massive stones around, but for locals, it's all part of a rural tradition alive and well in these parts.

Schwingen is a Swiss form of wrestling, held annually outdoors on a great big pile of sawdust, with colossal participants attempting to heave each other onto the ground. The winner gets—what else?—a cow.

Based in Interlaken, the Unspunnen Festival—a multiday extravaganza of yodeling, dancing, and traditional costume shows—hosts a competition every 11 years to see who can throw a great big rock the farthest (sorry—the last festival was just held in 2006).

And not just any rock, either: some of the projectiles used date back to the 19th century and are so laden with traditional importance that one has been repeatedly stolen by Jurassic separatists, and is at this writing still missing.

In our increasingly globalized world, it is heartening to see how such festivals are helping to preserve indigenous customs and folk history.

WHAT IT COSTS In Swiss francs

	$$$$	$$$	$$	$	¢
Restaurants	over 60 SF	40 SF–60 SF	25 SF–40 SF	15 SF–25 SF	under 15 SF
Hotels	over 350 SF	250 SF–350 SF	175 SF–250 SF	100 SF–175 SF	under 100 SF

Restaurant prices are per person for a main course at dinner. Hotel prices are for two people in a standard double room in high season, including tax and service.

Updated by
Katrin Gygax

THERE ARE TIMES WHEN THE REALITY of Switzerland puts postcard idealization to shame, surpassing tinted-indigo skies and advertising-image peaks with its own astonishing vividness. Those times happen most often in the Berner Oberland, for this rugged region concentrates some of the best features of rural Switzerland: awesome mountain panoramas, massive glaciers, crystalline lakes, gorges and waterfalls, chic ski resorts, dense pine forests, and charming gingerbread chalets.

After contemplating the Staubbach Falls in 1779, the great German writer Johann Wolfgang von Goethe was moved to write one of his most celebrated poems, "Gesang der Geister über den Wassern" ("Song of the Spirits over the Waters"). After Rousseau spread word of the region's natural phenomena among Paris society, the Romantics began to beat a path to the area, Lord Byron in the lead—it is said he conceived his *Manfred* here in barren, windswept Wengernalp. Shelley followed, then William Thackeray, John Ruskin, the composer Johannes Brahms, and, from America, Mark Twain; British master landscape painter J. M. W. Turner recorded the views; and Queen Victoria herself came, beginning a flood of tourism that permanently changed the Berner Oberland's—and Switzerland's—profile.

Before the onslaught of visitors inspired many locals to switch from farming to inn-keeping, agriculture was the prime industry—this is still true today, evidenced by the frequent sight of brown-and-white cows dotting the hillsides, as though conveniently placed for photo-ops. The houses of the Berner Oberland are classics: the definitive Swiss chalet, whose broad, eaved roofs cover fancifully scalloped and carved gables. Facades are painted with the family dedication on wood, which has weathered to dark sienna. From early spring through autumn, window boxes spill torrents of well-tended geraniums and petunias, and adjacent woodpiles are stacked with mosaiclike precision in readiness for dropping temperatures.

The region is arranged tidily enough for even a brief visit. Its main resort city, Interlaken, lies in green lowlands between the gleaming twin pools of the Brienzersee and the Thunersee, which are linked by the River Aare. Behind them to the south loom craggy, forested foothills, and behind those foothills stand some of Europe's noblest peaks, most notably the snowy crowns of the Eiger (13,022 feet), the Mönch (13,445 feet), and the fiercely beautiful Jungfrau (13,638 feet). Because nature has laid the region out so conveniently, it has become the most popular in Switzerland for tourism, with its excursion and transportation systems carrying enormous numbers of visitors to its myriad viewpoints, overlooks, and wonders. The railroad to the Jungfraujoch transports masses of tour groups to its high-altitude attractions, and on a peak-season day its crowded station can look like the Sistine Chapel in August or the Chicago Board of Trade. But the tourist industry handles the onslaught with ease, offering such an efficient network of boats, trains, and funiculars, such a variety of activities and attractions, and such a wide range of accommodations, from posh city hotels to rustic mountain lodges, that every visitor can find the most suitable way to take in the marvels of the Bernese Alps.

Exploring Berner Oberland

The central, urban-Victorian resort of Interlaken makes a good base for excursions for visitors who want to experience the entire Jungfrau region, which includes the craggy, bluff-lined Lauterbrunnen Valley and the opposing resorts that perch high above it: Mürren and Wengen. Busy Grindelwald, famous for its variety of sporting possibilities, and isolated Kandersteg, ideal for hiking and cross-country skiing, are both easily accessible from Interlaken. Each lies at the dead end of different gorge roads that climb into the heights. Spreading east and west of Interlaken are the Brienzersee and Thunersee, both broad, crystalline lakes, surrounded by forests, castles, and waterfront resorts, including Brienz, Thun, and Spiez. From Spiez, you can head southwest through the forest gorge of the Simmental to the Saanenland and glamorous Gstaad. Connections by rail or car keep most highlights within easy reach.

THE JUNGFRAU REGION

The thriving resort town of Interlaken lies between two spectacularly sited lakes, the Brienzersee (Lake Brienz) and the Thunersee (Lake Thun), and is the gateway to two magnificent mountain valleys, one leading up to the popular sports resort of Grindelwald, the other into Lauterbrunnen and the famous car-free resorts of Wengen and Mürren. Looming over both valleys, the Jungfrau and its partner peaks—the Eiger and Mönch—can be admired from various high-altitude overviews.

Interlaken

▶ ❶ **To & From:** *Interlaken has two train stations (www.sbb.ch), the centrally located Interlaken West, where trains arrive from Bern, Thun and Spiez, and Interlaken Ost (East), which connects you to Brienz and the Jungfrau region. The direct train that comes from Bern every half hour stops at both stations and costs 25 SF each way. Buses to towns nearby leave from the train stations, which both have taxis to help you schlep your luggage to your hotel; there are also carriage rides for the romantically inclined. For departure times and prices for trains and buses for most destinations in this chapter, check with www.sbb.ch—the main Swiss public transportation Web site—or call 0900/300300 (1,19 SF per min). Remember, if you have a Swiss Pass or another rail-discounting card, it also applies to the buses. Interlaken is 58 km (36 mi) southeast of Bern.*

Often touted as a town without character, Interlaken has patiently borne the brunt of being called "the best place in Switzerland to get away *from*"—but this, it turns out, is tribute to the town's nearby location to many of the wonders of the Bernese Alps. As a gateway to the entire Berner Oberland, this bustling Victorian resort town is the obvious home base for travelers planning to visit both the region's two lakes and the mountains towering behind them. And have no fear—there's more than enough character and *gemütlichkeit* to go around.

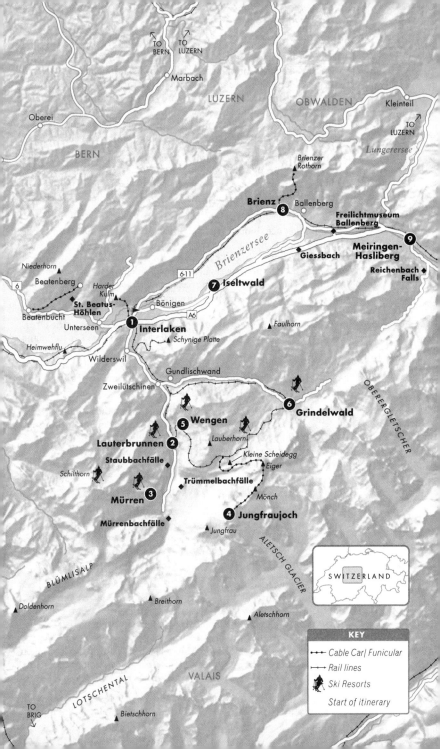

The name *Interlaken* has a Latin source: *interlacus* (between lakes). At 1,870 feet, Interlaken dominates the Bödeli, the branch of lowland between the lakes that Interlaken shares with the adjoining towns of Unterseen, Wilderswil, Bönigen, and Matten. The town's two train stations, Interlaken East and Interlaken West, are good orientation points; most sights are just a few minutes' walk from one of the stations. There are unlimited excursion options, and it is a pleasant, if urban, place to stay put as well, as its setting is spectacular and its ambience genteel.

The **Höheweg** is the city's main promenade, its tree- and flower-lined walkways cutting through the edge of the broad green parklands of the Höhematte. This 35-acre park once provided pasture ground for herds of the Augustinian monastery that dominated medieval Interlaken. Cows still graze in fenced-off areas.

★ Mark Twain once sojourned at the **Grand Hotel Victoria-Jungfrau,** on the Höheweg, designed to take in the view of the snowy Jungfrau that towers above the town. Topped by a magnificent Victorian-style cupola and spire, and lushly appointed with glittering salons, only one room, the mammoth 19th-century Brasserie restaurant, has survived the hotel's numerous renovations. The hotel originated as two humbler inns, the Jungfrau (1864) and the Chalet Victoria (1865), named in honor of the English queen for journeyed here in the 19th century and put the Oberland on the tourist map; these were merged and expanded in 1895, and the facade redesigned and landmark tower added in 1899. Repair here at least once to enjoy drinks in the hotel's many bars and dine on its grassy terrace—this is Interlaken as luxe as it gets. ⊠ *Höheweg 41* ☎ *033/8282828* ⊕ *www.victoria-jungfrau.ch.*

Between the Höheweg and the River Aare, you'll find the beautifully landscaped grounds, complete with a floral clock, surrounding the **Kursaal.** Built in 1859 in a dramatic combination of Oberland-chalet and Victorian styles, the Kursaal (meaning a public room at a resort) was renovated in 1968 and has become once again a social focal point for the city. Plays and concerts are presented here, mostly during the high season, and folklore evenings are held in the adjoining *Spycher* (storehouse).

The **Schlosskirche** (Castle Church) was once the chapel for the Augustinian monastery. All that remains of the monastery, founded in 1133, and the convent that shared its grounds, are a 14th-century chancel and a wing of the cloister. The rest of the convent was incorporated into a private castle in 1745. ⊠ *At end of Höhematte, south of Hotel du Nord.*

☾ Surrounding a geodesic sphere a bit like the one at Epcot, **Mystery Park** is devoted to natural and supernatural events. Designed by extraterrestrial theorist Erich von Däniken—author of that 1970s sci-fi potboiler, *Chariots of the Gods*—the theme park has seven pavilions that explore topics such as the Nazca lines of Peru, the pyramids of Egypt, and the possibility of a space station on Mars. The park is near the Interlaken East train station. ⊠ *Hauptstr. 43* ☎ *033/8275757* ⊕ *www.mysterypark.ch* ⊠ *48 SF* ☾ *Apr.–Oct., daily 10–6; Nov.–Mar., Wed.–Sun. 10–6.*

On the north side of the River Aare is the tiny town of **Unterseen,** with its picturesque Old Town and Marktplatz (Marketplace). Founded in

1279 on land rented from the Augustinians, Unterseen retains some of the region's oldest buildings, including the 17th-century **Stadthaus** (city hall) and the 14th-century **church**, its steeple dating from 1471. The **Schloss Unterseen** (Unterseen Castle), built in 1656 for the reigning Bernese nobleman, stands at the opposite end of the square from these structures, near a medieval arched gateway. You can get here via a 10-minute bus ride from Interlaken's center, or even by walking; it's near the Interlaken West train station.

Fronting on the Unterseen Marktplatz is the **Touristik-Museum der Jungfrau Region,** which traces the history of tourism in the area over the last 200 years. Exhibits include models of early transportation and primitive mountain-climbing and skiing equipment. ⊠ *Obereg. 28* ☎ *033/8229839* 🖃 *5 SF* ☉ *May–mid-Oct., Tues.–Sun. 2–5.*

Fodor's Choice
★

Lovers of Old Swiss style should consider trekking out some 8 km (5 miles) from Interlaken to take in **St. Beatus-Höhlen.** Whether or not you're into natural caverns remains to be seen, but no one could resist St. Beatus's extraordinary entry hillside pavilion: a Hansel and Gretel-esque extravaganza of timbered beams and Alpine gemütlichkeit so picturesque it will practically click your camera for you. Replete with dollhouse-issue waterfall, this is 19th-century Switzerland in excelsius. Beauty is not just skin deep, however, for the deep St. Beatus caves are marvels, too. Their legend goes back to the 6th century, when the missionary St. Beatus arrived on the Thunersee to find the local population terrorized by a dragon who lived in the lake and surrounding grottoes. Exorcised by Beatus, the fleeing dragon fell to his death on the rocks plunging down to the lake. The caves then became the hermit's home; today you can see the stalagmites, stalactites, and pools inside. There's even a replica of Ponzo, the dragon, for children to explore, and a Ponzo-decorated steamship plies the Thunersee. You can reach the caves by taking Bus 21 from the Interlaken West train station or by crossing by boat from Interlaken West station to Sundlaunen, then a quarter-hour hike to the caves. ⊠ *Opposite Interlaken on east coast near Sundlaunen* ☎ *033/8411643* ⊕ *www.beatushoehlen.ch* 🖃 *17 SF* ☉ *Apr.–mid-Oct., daily 10:30–5.*

★

Adorned with a spectacular, turreted, Gothic, chalet-style restaurant, **Harder Kulm** (4,297 feet) can be bested thanks to a 12-minute funicular ride; from there, hike uphill to catch views south over the city, the lakes, and the whole panorama of snowy peaks. The restaurant offers sumptuous meals on a sunny terrace, with views of the surrounding mountains. The funicular runs every 20 to 30 minutes. ⊠ *Funicular station north of River Aare near Interlaken East, across Beaurivagebrücke* ☎ *033/8287339* 🖃 *Funicular round-trip: 24 SF* ☉ *Funicular: May–Oct., Mon.–Sat. 9–6, Sun. 8–6.*

An old-fashioned, red funicular railway leads to the top of the 2,194-foot **Heimwehfluh** mountain, where you will get views over both lakes and an elevated peek at the Jungfrau, the Eiger, and the Mönch. A restaurant and playground have been built at the top, complete with a 985-foot-long bobsled run, and there's a show of model trains every 30 minutes. The funicular station is a five-minute walk from the Interlaken

West station down the Rugenparkstrasse, with a departure every 15 minutes. If you hike to the top, the train show costs just 6 SF. ☎ *033/8223453* 🖼 *16 SF, includes model train show* ☉ *Late Apr.–Oct., daily 10–5:30.*

For the most splendid overview in the region, make the ambitious trip to the 6,445-foot peak of the **Schynige Platte** for a picnic, or wander down any of numerous footpaths, or visit its Alpine Botanical Garden, where more than 520 varieties of mountain flowers grow. A cogwheel train dating from 1893 takes you on the round-trip journey, though you may opt to walk either up or (more comfortably) down. Make sure to specify when you buy your ticket. Trains run from approximately 7:45 AM to 6 PM. To get here, take the six-minute ride on Bernese Oberland Railway from Interlaken East to Wilderswil. ⊠ *Wilderswil* ☎ *033/8287233* 🖼 *One-way 33 SF; round-trip 58 SF* ☉ *Late May or early June–late Oct., daily, depending on snow conditions.*

Where to Stay & Eat

★ **$$–$$$** ✕ **Im Gade.** This welcoming hybrid of carved-wood coziness and sleek formality fills up with appreciative locals who recognize fresh, fine cooking and alert service. Details count here: even that dab of smoky sauerkraut in your crisp mixed salad is made on the premises. Choose seasonal specialties such as salmon with lime mousse and ratatouille, pork fillet with truffles, or veal with oyster mushrooms and fresh noodles in butter. ⊠ *Hotel du Nord, Höheweg 70* ☎ *033/8275050* ⊟ *AE, DC, MC, V* ☉ *Closed mid-Nov.–mid-Dec.*

$$–$$$ ✕ **Krebs.** A sunny, front-porch serving area overlooks the street, but head for the more formal dining room, glassed-in yet still opening onto the main promenade. A classic old-world resort spot, serving upscale Swiss cuisine (such as veal medallions) and homey daily plates (look for the local fish dishes) with starched-collar style, this place has been in Interlaken—and the Krebs family—since 1875. ⊠ *Bahnhofstr. 4* ☎ *033/8227161* ⊟ *AE, DC, MC, V* ☉ *Closed Nov.–Apr.*

★ **$–$$$** ✕ **Alpenblick.** Just 2 km (1 mi) south of Interlaken, this carved wood-and-shingle 17th-century landmark attracts both locals and travelers with its two restaurants. One serves old-style Swiss cuisine (pasta with local wild mushrooms); the other showcases chef Richard Stöckli's renowned international fare, such as octopus carpaccio with tuna, avocado, and wasabi, or chicken curry with pine nuts, raisins, and honeyed herbs. ⊠ *Oberstr. 8, Wilderswil* ☎ *033/8283550* ⊟ *AE, DC, MC, V.*

★ **$–$$$** ✕ **Laterne.** You'll find this unpretentious local favorite, with a sports-bar ambience, a bit off the tourist track, east of the center near the A8 ring road (a 10-minute walk from Interlaken West). The rustic, woodsy setting is a perfect backdrop for the hearty meat dinners and Swiss specialties: seven kinds of Rösti served in iron skillets and eight kinds of cheese fondue. To top it all off, the prices are reasonable. There is live Swiss folk music every other Friday. ⊠ *Obere Bönigstr. 18* ☎ *033/8221141* ⊟ *AE, DC, MC, V.*

$–$$$ ✕ **Schuh.** With a luxurious shady terrace spilling into the Höhematte in summer and mellow piano sounds enhancing the old-fashioned elegance inside, this sweet shop and café-restaurant serves everything from tea to rich, hot Swiss meals. Leave room for the chocolate specialties and pastries, like the glossy strawberry tarts, which you'll also find in the adjoining shop. ⊠ *Höheweg 56* ☎ *033/8229441* ⊟ *AE, DC, MC, V.*

★ **$–$$** ✕ **Stellambiente.** For something nicely out of the ordinary, try this restaurant in the Stella Hotel. The modern, flavorful cuisine includes several vegetarian options with locally grown ingredients, and an extraordinary variety of salads. Order the "surprise" menu and you'll be treated to six inventive courses served on beautiful, individually selected pieces of china. The attractive terrace, complete with fountain, turns summer dining into a garden idyll. ⊠ *Waldeggstr. 10* ☎ *033/8228871* ⊟ *AE, DC, MC, V.*

$$$$ 🏨 **Grand Hotel Victoria-Jungfrau.** Grand says it all. Mark Twain may have
Fodor's Choice slept in this 1865 landmark, but its restoration has taken it firmly into
★ the 21st century, with glitzy postmodern touches such as the burled-wood entryway. The vast Belle Epoque atrium lobby spirals off into innumerable bars, tea salons, and the concierge desks, where the front desk staff may seem frenzied by the awesome demands of 400 occupied beds. There are plenty of facilities, including indoor master golf, and a knock-out spa, which offers everything from reflexology to Clarins Beauty to basic weight-training equipment (the clientele seems beyond buff). The guest rooms are gorgeous, with styles shifting from marble columns to fresh gingham and waxed wood floors. Nearly all take in the obligatory view over the central Interlaken meadow and on to the Cinerama-wide range of Alps, with the snowy peak of the Jungfrau crowning the far distance. A terrific new casual restaurant, La Pastateca, joins the flashy formal dining room, La Terrasse, but don't forget to check out the Brasserie, a mammoth, leaded-glass-and-carved-wood, Victorian concoction almost as delicious as the meals. ⊠ *Höheweg 41, CH-3800* ☎ *033/8282828* 🖷 *033/8282880* ⊕ *www.victoria-jungfrau.ch* ↝ *184 rooms, 28 suites* ♨ *3 restaurants, in-room safes, Wi-Fi, 7 tennis courts, pool, hair salon, spa, billiards, 2 bars, meeting rooms* ⊟ *AE, DC, MC, V.*

★ **$$$–$$$$** 🏨 **Beau Rivage.** This Interlaken old-timer is steeped in luxury. Set well back from the road and surrounded by gardens, it maintains an unruffled calm. Rich in brocades, muted tones, and patterned carpets, the rooms have views of either the mountains or the quiet Aare. Delicate market-fresh cuisine is served in the highly regarded, hearth-warmed restaurant. Try the crab soup with lemon tortellini followed by the chicken in pepper glaze on the enchanting summer terrace. The location, close to the Interlaken East train station, is perfect. ⊠ *Höheweg 211, CH-3800* ☎ *033/ 8267007* 🖷 *033/8267008* ⊕ *www.lindnerhotels.ch* ↝ *89 rooms, 12 suites* ♨ *2 restaurants, in-room safes, minibars, in-room data ports, Wi-Fi, pool, health club, sauna, steam room, bicycles, 2 bars; no a/c* ⊟ *AE, DC, MC, V* ⧉ *BP* ☉ *Closed mid-Nov.–mid-Dec.*

★ **$$$–$$$$** 🏨 **Stella.** This small, family-run gem defies its outdated '60s exterior and residential neighborhood setting. Inside you'll find marvelous, friendly service; innovative, cozy rooms; and special, personal touches such as rose petals strewn across your duvet in welcome. This is a small hotel that truly does try harder—and does so successfully. Its personal touch carries over to the restaurant, the Stellambiente. ⊠ *Waldeggstr. 10, CH-3800* ☎ *033/8228871* 🖷 *033/8226671* ⊕ *www.stella-hotel.ch* ↝ *30 rooms* ♨ *Restaurant, in-room safes, minibars, pool; no a/c* ⊟ *AE, DC, MC, V* ⧉ *BP.*

$$–$$$ ⊡ **Interlaken.** When they say this is the oldest hotel in town, they don't fool around: it's been hosting overnight guests since 1323—first as a hospital, then as a cloister, and by the early 15th century as a tavern-hotel. Felix Mendelssohn and Lord Byron may have once slept here but today the comfortable guest rooms are quite up-to-date, with sleek furnishings and pastel accents. A multicultural air is added by the elaborate Japanese garden, Italian bistro, and excellent Cantonese restaurant. It's a short walk to the Interlaken East train station, making excursions a snap. ⊠ *Höheweg 74, CH-3800* ☎ *033/8266868* 🖷 *033/8266869* ⊕ *www.interlakenhotel.ch* 🖙 *60 rooms* 🛆 *2 restaurants, in-room safes, minibars, sauna, bar, no-smoking rooms* ⊟ *AE, DC, MC, V* ⵏⵏ *BP.*

$–$$$ ⊡ **Royal–St. Georges.** If you are a fan of Victoriana, this impeccably restored grand hotel is a dream come true, with original moldings, built-in furnishings, and fantastical Art Nouveau bath fixtures. In the lobby, you pass beautifully carved columns on your way to the staircase that sweeps you upstairs. The wellness facilities, recently renovated, offer a great retreat after a long day of sightseeing. ⊠ *Höheweg 139, CH-3800* ☎ *033/8227575* 🖷 *033/8233075* ⊕ *www.royal-stgeorges.ch* 🖙 *89 rooms, 6 suites* 🛆 *Restaurant, Wi-Fi, hot tub, sauna, steam room, bar; no a/c* ⊟ *AE, DC, MC, V* ⵏ *Closed Nov.–Jan.* ⵏⵏ *BP.*

$$ ⊡ **Chalet Oberland.** With its city-crossroads position and its storybook exterior bristling with mansard windows and stucco trim, this downtown hotel occupies both sides of the street and keeps expanding. The main hotel offers guest rooms with old-world dimensions and a heavy-on-the browns decor; the newer wing across the pedestrian alley (in a building pierced by a life-size statue of a cow) has '80s modern rooms, with warm wood tones and funkily designed bathrooms. Personality challenged these may be but they are comfortable and quiet, two real pluses in this crowded city. The hotel restaurant is extremely popular—a stage-set of faux trees and timber beams, it offers the usual Swiss suspects but the chef has a deft hand and most dishes go beyond yum to yum-yum. Folklore performances are held on Tuesday. ⊠ *Postg. 1, CH-3800* ☎ *033/8278787* 🖷 *033/8278770* ⊕ *www.chalet-oberland.ch* 🖙 *137 rooms, 23 suites* 🛆 *2 restaurants, pizzeria, in-room safes, minibars, bar; no a/c* ⊟ *AE, DC, MC, V* ⵏⵏ *BP.*

$–$$ ⊡ **Splendid.** Location is key here: you can't get more central to shopping and nightlife. It's a modest, family-run Victorian dwelling with some woodsy rooms and the occasional spindle bed enlivening the decor. The back rooms overlook a quiet street; the corner bays are prettiest. The proprietor is a hunter, so game in season is fresh and local. ⊠ *Höheweg 33, CH-3800* ☎ *033/8227612* 🖷 *033/8227679* ⊕ *www.splendid.ch* 🖙 *35 rooms* 🛆 *Restaurant, in-room safes, minibars, pub; no a/c* ⊟ *AE, MC, V* ⵏ *Closed Nov.–Dec. 24* ⵏⵏ *BP.*

★ $ ⊡ **Alphorn.** Comfortably old-fashioned, this lovely family-run Victorian bed-and-breakfast sits on a quiet side street between Interlaken West and the Heimwehfluh. Some rooms have tapestry wallpaper, waxed parquet floors, and original plaster moldings; florals and other patterns abound. Service is warm and welcoming. ⊠ *Rugenaustr. 8, CH-3800* ☎ *033/8223051* 🖷 *033/8233069* ⊕ *www.hotel-alphorn.ch* 🖙 *10 rooms* 🛆 *Bar; no a/c* ⊟ *AE, DC, MC, V* ⵏⵏ *BP.*

★ ¢ 🎬 **Balmer's.** This popular youth hostel gives families and young travelers bare-bones rooms at rock-bottom prices. Kitchen access, washers and dryers, videos, two fireplaces, a convenience store, and self-service suppers add to the lively, collegiate-party atmosphere. The English-speaking staff can help find the cheapest deals for all outdoor activities. Rooms, all with sinks, are available with one to five beds; you can also go for an even cheaper bed in the massive group tent pitched at the edge of town roughly from June through September. Checkout is at 10 AM; there are no lockers or day storage. ⊠ *Hauptstr. 23–25, CH-3800* ☎ *033/8221961* 🖨 *033/8233261* ⊕ *www.balmers.com* ⇆ *50 rooms* △ *Bar, library, laundry facilities; no a/c* ⊟ *AE, MC, V* ⦿⏐ *BP.*

Nightlife & the Arts

BARS At the Happy Inn Lodge, you'll always find a lively, mixed crowd at **Brasserie 17** (⊠ Rosenstr. 17 ☎ 033/8223225). **Buddy's Pub** (⊠ Höheweg 33 ☎ 033/8227612), at Hotel Splendid, is a popular spot where locals and visitors actually mingle. Feeling homesick? Believe it or not, there's actually a **Hooters** (⊠ Höhenweg. 57 ☎ 033/8226512) here, offering tongue-in-cheek American ambience—somewhat surprisingly, you'll find families here soaking up the vibe.

CASINO The **Casino Kursaal** (☎ 033/8276210) has American and French roulette, as well as 124 slot machines; it's open Sunday–Thursday, noon–2 AM, Fridays and Saturday, noon–3 AM. Las Vegas it's not, but a congenial atmosphere prevails.

DANCING In the Hotel Metropole, the dance club **Black & White** (⊠ Höheweg 37 ☎ 033/8236633) attracts an upscale crowd. **High-Life** (⊠ Rugenparkstr. 2 ☎033/8221550), near Interlaken West, brings back easygoing oldies. **Johnny's Club** (⊠ Höheweg 92 ☎ 033/8260160), in the Hotel Carlton, has been the definitive after-hours club for years. Don't get here too early, as the place comes alive at midnight. **The Metro Bar** (⊠ Hauptstr. 23–25 ☎ 033/8221961), in the Balmers youth hostel, attracts painfully young people.

THEATER For a real introduction to the local
Fodor'sChoice experience, don't miss the **Tell-**
★ **freilichtspiele,** an outdoor pageant presented in Interlaken every summer by a cast of Swiss amateurs. Wrapped in a rented blanket—which you'll need, since evenings can be chilly, even from June to September—and seated in a 2,200-seat sheltered amphitheater that opens onto illuminated woods and a permanent "medieval" village set, you'll see 250 players in splendid costumes acting out the epic tale of

9

STEPPIN' OUT

For groups of 10 or more, dinner folklore shows—yodeling and all—are presented at the Kursaal in the Folklore-Spycher (Off Höheweg, 033/8276100). Call ahead; if another group has booked, individuals can join the party. With dinner only; shows start at 7. At the breathtaking, sky-high restaurant at Harder Kulm (033/8223444), reached by funicular, on Friday only from June through September you can hear typical Ländler (traditional dance) music—and not only the tourists participate. Go ahead, try a few steps yourself.

Swiss hero Wilhelm Tell. The text is Schiller's famous play, performed in German with the guttural singsong of a Schwyzerdütsch accent—but don't worry; with galloping horses, flower-decked cows, bonfires, parades, and, of course, the famous apple-shooting climax, the operatic story tells itself. Tickets range from 26 SF to 48 SF and are available through the **Tellbüro** (✉ Bahnhofstr. 5A ☎ 033/8223722 ⊕ www.tellspiele.ch). Travel agents and hotel concierges can also secure tickets.

Sports & the Outdoors

MOUNTAIN CLIMBING Contact **Alpin Center Interlaken** (✉ Wilderswil ☎ 033/8235523 ⊕ www.alpincenter.ch) to join tours led by accredited mountain guides.

SAILING Lake Thun offers the area's best sailing. From April through October, Interlaken's **Von Allmen Sailing School** (☎ 033/8225693) offers courses and boat rental.

Lauterbrunnen

❷ **To & From:** *The Bernese Oberland Railway (BOB) runs hourly trains*
Fodor'sChoice *from Interlaken Ost station to the village of Lauterbrunnen; the trip takes*
★ *about a half hour and stops in such hamlets as Wilderswil and Isenfluh. Lauterbrunnen is 10 km (6 mi) south of Interlaken.*

Acclaimed by Lord Tennyson as "the stateliest bit of landstrip," the Lauterbrunnen valley is often ranked as one of the five most beautiful places in Switzerland (we give it the number one spot). A Swiss Shangri-la, it encloses a nearly perfect setpiece of earth, sky, and water. The mountains here seem to part like the Red Sea as two awesome, bluff-lined rockfaces line the vast valley, where grassy meadows often lie in shadow as 1,508-foot rocky shoulders rise on either side. What really sets this mountaineous masterpiece apart are the nearly 70 waterfalls (Lauterbrunnen means "only springs") that line the length of the 2-mi-long valley. Some plummet from skyhigh crags, others cascade out of cliff-face crevasses, while many are hidden within the rocks themselves; the largest, the Staubbach Falls, were once immortalized by Göethe, Wordsworth, and Lord Byron who described them as "the tail of a white horse blowing in the breeze." For scenery supreme, Lauterbrunnen clearly can't be topped.

The relentlessly picturesque panorama opens up as you get off the train. This tidy town of weathered chalets also serves as a starting point for the region's two most famous excursions: to the Schilthorn and to the Jungfraujoch. Super-efficient parking and a rail terminal allow long- and short-term parking for visitors heading for Wengen, Mürren, the Jungfraujoch, or the Schilthorn. Consider choosing this valley as a home base for day trips by train, funicular, or cable, thereby saving considerably on hotel rates.

THE SKY'S NO LIMIT!

If you have the stomach for it, hop on a breathtaking heilicopter tour of the amazing mountain ranges from Air Glaciers (at the Heliport, south of town off the main road, 033/8560560); the truly intrepid like riding the many valley thermals here and go paragliding—inquire at the tourist office about Gleitschirmfliegen.

HERO OF 1,001 TRAVEL POSTERS

Shadowed by the Eiger, Mönch, and the Jungfrau peaks, the vista of the Lauterbrunnen Valley has been captured in innumerable books and postcards. If you wanted to bag this panoramic photo, you used to head to mountaintop Wengen but it is now so overbuilt you can't get That View. Instead head for the Panorama Spazierweg trail: take the underpass at Lauterbrunnen's train station to exit on the left side of the village and find the Stocki Road and take the left turn up the hillside. The entire hike to Wengen takes 1½ hours but the most picturesque part is reached in 15 minutes. Here, in a section lined with cow gates and little barns, case out the right meadow (you may have to hike through thigh-high grass to do so) to get the best vantage spot. Another 15 minutes on the trail deposits you at a tiny hut with benches and a cross. Get some more great shots from here, then return to the valley floor. Sir Edmund Hillarys can continue up to Wengen–an hour-long very steep hike.

But don't ignore its own wealth of hiking options through some of the most awe-inspiring scenery in Europe. Several famous trails line the valley, including the **Panorama Spazierweg,** which connects Lauterbrunnen with Wengen: get a map of it (and lots of brochures) from Lauterbrunnen's tourist office, set just across from the train station on Bahnhofplatz.

Magnificent waterfalls adorn the length of the Lauterbrunnen Valley, the most famous being the 984-foot **Staubbachfälle** (Staubbach Falls), which are illuminated at night and visible from town. These falls draw you like a magnet through the village of Lauterbrunnen itself, past a bevy of roadside cafés and the town center (marked by a church and a small Museum of the Lauterbrunnen Valley) and they are found just opposite a centuries-old, flower-bedecked graveyard. At the other of the valley is the Mürrenbachfälle, which at 250 meters (820 feet) are among the tallest in Europe (the tourist office has a brochure outlining a hike to the top 10 waterfalls). Five minutes beyond the Staubbachfälle are the spectacular **Trümmelbachfälle** (Trümmelbach Falls), a series of 10 glacier waterfalls hidden deep inside rock walls at the base of the Jungfrau, which you can access by underground funicular. Approach the departure point via a pretty, creek-side walkway and brace yourself for some steep stair climbing. Be sure to bring along a light jacket—the spray can be more than refreshing in the cool Alpine air. ✉ *Follow signs from town* ☎ *033/8553232* ⊕ *www.truemmelbach.ch* 🎫 *11 SF* ☉ *Apr.–June and Sept.–early Nov., daily 9–5; July and Aug., daily 8:30–6.*

Where to Stay & Eat

★ **$–$$** ✕🔲 **Silberhorn.** Though across from the train station and next to the cogwheel train to Mürren, this family-owned hotel, set in a lovely garden, is surprisingly quiet and a wonderful option. Knotty *Arvenholz* (pine) panels the spic-and-span guest rooms. On clear days you may want to chill out in one of the wicker chairs on the sunny porch. The dependable restaurant ($–$$$) offers satisfying meals of Rösti and meat fondues in a swanky woodlined salon; the more casual Gastshube overlooks a truly soigné fireplace room, replete with cathedral ceiling, exposed timbers, and lots of happy guests. ⊠ *CH-3822* ☎ *33/8562210* 🖷 *033/8554213* ⊕ *www.silberhorn.com* ⇨ *30 rooms* ⚷ *Restaurant, sauna, bar, free parking; no a/c* ⊟ *AE, DC, MC, V* ⧖ *BP.*

¢–$ 🏨 **Staubbach.** Located just across from the famous Staubbach Falls and not far from Lauterbrunnen's main street—handily lined with cafés—is this excellent option. Young owners have turned this local landmark into a stylish hotel, with modern guest rooms that shimmer with teak and pine woods. Al-

though the emphasis is on keeping the prices low, there's no skimping on personal warmth and charm. Needless to say, the views of the falls are astounding and, consequently, most people ask for a south-facing room. The fact that this side also faces the main road (which has its share of roaring buses) means you should also consider the three other directions of the compass. ⊠ *Hauptstrasse, CH-3822* ☎ *033/8555454* 🖷 *033/8555484* ⊕ *www.staubbach.ch* ⇨ *31 rooms* ⚷ *Laundry facilities; no a/c* ⊟ *MC, V* ⊙ *Closed Nov.–mid-Dec.* ⧖ *BP.*

¢ 🏨 **Matratzenlager Stocki.** Set on one of the most enviable patches of real estate in the Bernese Alps—it occupies what might be called a front-and-center orchestra seat to the Lauterbrunnen valley spectacular—this adorable hostel welcomes you with a Hansel-and-Gretel châlet exterior on a quaint residential village street just steps from the Panorama Spazierweg trail. The million-euro views here at the "Mattress Warehouse" (which is the name's translation), however, are enjoyed not by the rich but by pennypinchers—this is a full-fledged hostel, replete with communal baths and beds (the dorms are lined with 10 double-decker beds all pushed together—get ready to sleep a few inches away from total strangers). Lending an eminently civilized touch to it all is Greti Graf-Feuz, the gray-haired manager who speaks perfect English and has the bearing of a grande dame. Reservations are made by phone or by contacting Lauterbrunnen's tourist office. The hostel closes every year from early November until the first snowfall of the season. All in all, a fabulous option. ⊠ *Stocki Rd., CH–3822* ☎ *033/8551754* ⇨ *30 beds* ⚷ *No a/c* ⊟ *No credit cards* ⧖ *BP.*

FodorsChoice
★

CLOSE UP

Moo

IT'S DIFFICULT TO GROW more than grass on the steep slopes of the Alps, so much of the area has traditionally been used to graze sheep, goats, and, of course, cattle, who supply fresh milk to the cheese and chocolate industries that makes up such an important part of the country's agricultural economy. The Brown Swiss cow, said to be the oldest breed in the world, has been a reliable producer of dairy products for centuries. Browns are highly prized in the region, as they adapt to all kinds of weather, have strong feet and legs, and produce more milk (which also happens to be higher in protein than that from other cows). Their robust nature has made them increasingly popular throughout the world, resulting in a current global population of about 7 million.

The seasonal movement of livestock from lowland pastures to Alpine meadows is a tradition that goes back to ancient times. In spring, herders in regional costume spruce up their animals with flowers and embroidered bell collars and move them up to the grazing areas in a ceremony known as the *Alpaufzug* (Alpine ascent). In fall they come down the same way in the *Alpabfahrt* (Alpine descent). All cows are fitted with bells to help make them easier to find if they wander away from the rest of the herd, and the collective clang can echo through an entire valley. If you're driving along during one of the ceremonies, be prepared to pull over for a half hour or more while the cows lumber on past, taking up the entire road.

Mürren

3

Fodor's Choice

★

To & From: *Access is via the cable car from Lauterbrunnen (connect-ing with the Grütschalp Berg Bahn) or the cable cars up to the Schilthorn departing from Stechelberg village. Mürren is 7 km (4 mi) southwest of Lauterbrunnen, 16 km (10 mi) south of Interlaken, plus a 5-minute cable-car ride from Stechelberg.*

Like Wengen, this Noah's Ark village is perched on a mountaintop shelf so high up—5,413 feet, to be precise—that you may feel like James Stewart starring in *Vertigo* (or Cary Grant swinging atop Mt. Rushmore in *North by Northwest*). The Hollywood reference is apropos as these two villages have always lured the rich and famous. Birthplace of downhill and slalom skiing (in the 1920s), Mürren offers extraordinarily peaceful mountain nights and an unrivaled panorama of the Jungfrau, Mönch, and Eiger, all set so close you feel you can almost reach out and touch them. Skiers may want to settle here for daredevil year-round skiing at the top (the annual Inferno Race in January is the longest downhill in the world); hikers can combine bluff-top trails with staggering views. This is a car-free resort, so no parking lots spoil the scenery. You'll have to get upwardly mobile in other ways. Mürren is usually accessed from the center of Lauterbrunnen village by an aerial cablecar and Bergbahn cogwheel rail (round-trip 25 SF) from Grütschalp, but these

LICENSED TO THRILL

Atop Mount Schilthorn perches an amazing sight: the flying-saucer-like lair of Ernst Blofeld, the bald-headed villain from *On Her Majesty's Secret Service* (and the model for Austin Powers's arch-nemesis, Dr. Evil). Or at least that is what it was in the 1969 Bond movie. As eyepopping as granite-featured George Lazenby and the over-the-top plot (Blofeld means to use beautiful women as carriers for a lethal ecovirus), the "Piz Gloria" was ultimately blown-up in the film but the "hideout" was so memorable that it kept its stage name and became Europe's first revolving restaurant, still famous for its James Bond breakfast (no martinis, however), which allows you to watch the sun come up over the peaks. According to Joanna Lumley, one of the Bond Girls in the film: "Ringed by range after range of mountains, the view was unparalleled, perfect; too perfect—it looked like a painted backcloth. A props man was given the task of enticing birds to fly around to show it was real."

can be shut for maintenance (global warming's permafrost melt has increased closings); alternatively, take the bus to Stechelberg—located at the far end of the valley—where two even more dizzying cable cars (round-trip 35 SF) have you reaching for the sky in no time. Upon arrival, Mürren splays out along a long mountain ridge road lined with hotels, restaurants, shops, a few historic châlets, and a large **Sportzentrum** sports center. The village is not overly picturesque but having your *käffee und küchen* on a nearly levitating restaurant terrace will give you that top-of-the-world feeling.

Mürren boasts some of the longest downhill runs because it is at the foot of the **Schilthorn** (9,742 feet) mountain, famed for its role in the James Bond thriller *On Her Majesty's Secret Service*. The peak of this icy Goliath is accessed by a four-stage cable-lift ride past bare-rock cliffs and stunning slopes. At each level, you step off the cable car, walk across the station, and wait briefly for the next cable car. At the top is the much-photographed revolving restaurant, **Piz Gloria,** where you can see clips of the film thriller in the Touristorama—if you can tear yourself away from the restaurant panorama, which slowly rolls past your window (sit here for 50 minutes and you'll go full circle). The cable car station is in the town of Stechelberg, near the spectacular Mürrenbachfälle (Mürrenbach Falls). ⊠ *Stechelberg* ☎ *033/829007* ⊕ *www.schilthorn. ch* 🖃 *Round-trip cable car Stechelberg–Schilthorn 96 SF; 72 SF 7:25–8:55 or after 3:25 in May and mid-Oct.–mid-Nov.* ☉ *Departures daily yr-round, twice hourly 6:25 AM–4:25 PM; last departure from the top 6:03 PM in summer, 5:03 PM in winter.*

A more affordable way to Mürren is the **aerial cable car** built in 2006, whose station sits across the street from Lauterbrunnen's train station. You then connect to the cogwheel rail from Grütschalp, which runs along the cliff and affords some magnificent views. The whole trip takes about 30 minutes and drops you at the Mürren rail station, at the opposite end of town from the cable car stop. There are departures every 15 to 20 minutes. As you ascend, point your binoculars at the gleaming dome on the Jungfraujoch across the valley: you can almost hear the winds howling off the Aletsch Glacier. ⊠ *Lauterbrunnen* ☎ *0900/300300* ⊕ *www.sbb.ch* ⊡ *25 SF.*

Skiing

Mürren provides access to the **Schilthorn,** where you'll find a 15-km (9-mi) run that drops all the way through Mürren to Lauterbrunnen. At 5,413 feet, the resort has one funicular railway, two cable cars, seven lifts, and 65 km (40 mi) of downhill runs. A one-day pass covering the Schilthorn region costs 56 SF; a seven-day pass costs 265 SF.

For lessons, contact Mürren's **Swiss Ski & Snowboard School** (☎ 033/8552022), at Chalet Louise, opposite the Hotel Bellevue.

Where to Stay

$$$–$$$$
Fodor'sChoice
★
🏨 **Eiger.** Set on a hilly flank just to the right of the Bergbahn station and—more importantly—with a front-row perch directly across from the Eiger, Mönch, and Jungfrau, this is the most stylish hotel in Mürren. With one five-story wing dating back to the 1920s and an even larger and snazzier wing from the early 1990s, this is also one of the largest, allowing most rooms to flaunt balconies with "peak" views. In addition, the hotel has room for an impressive spa, replete with an indoor pool with staggering views of the ermine-mantled mountains. Inside, all is *gemütlichkeit*-elegant: the main dining is graced by Alpine paintings, the adorable Táchibar Bar has a big fireplace hood and looks like a Hollywood set, while regular guest rooms come with elegant pine wainscotting and suites can go all out with exposed timber beams and gorgeous fabrics. If you want to enjoy the high life—in more ways than one—head here. ⊠ *CH-3825* ☎ *033/8565454* 🖷 *033/8565456* ⊕ *www.hoteleiger.com* ⬧ *49 rooms* ⬧ *Restaurant, Stübli, bar, pool, gym; no a/c* ⊟ *AE, D MC, V* ⧖ *BP.*

★ **$$**
🏨 **Bellevue.** Distinguished by its lovely yellow-brick-and-shutter facade, this older landmark, with welcoming owners, presents itself as a traditional ski lodge with full modern comforts. Each room has a tiny balcony and the decor is fresh pine and gingham. The main dining room is suave in Swedish woods while the casual Jägerstübli is set around a big fireplace and—those with delicate constitutions beware—hunting trophies. ⊠ *CH-3825* ☎ *033/8551401* 🖷 *033/8551490* ⊕ *www.muerren.ch/bellevue* ⬧ *16 rooms* ⬧ *Restaurant, café, in-room data ports, sauna, Internet room, no-smoking rooms; no a/c* ⊟ *MC, V* ⊗ *Closed Easter–early June* ⧖ *BP.*

★ **$**
🏨 **Alpenruh.** Clad in time-burnished pine, fitted out with picturesque gables, and adorned with some great gingerbread wood trim, the Alpenruh is as picturesque a hotel as you can get in Mürren. Its perch is spectacular, nearly cantilevered over the vast valley and with reach-out-and-touch vistas of the great Jungfrau and Eiger across the way. As for restaurants, no place in Mürren has such a fetching and gorgeous dining terrace. Because the prices here are on the gentle side, the guest rooms are on the plain side. The only drawback: this is the first hotel up from the cable-

9

car stop (some distant girders may mar some room views) but that actually may turn out to be a plus—the owners also run the Mürren cablecar up to the Schilthorn and you can trade in the hotel's buffet for breakfast atop the revolving Piz Gloria. During key weeks—Christmas, for example—room rates are upped to include board. ⊠ *CH-3825* ☎ *033/8568800* 🖷 *033/8568888* ⊕ *www.muerren.ch/alpenruh* 🖙 *28 rooms* ↳ *Restaurant, Stübi, sauna; no a/c* ▤ *AC, DC, MC, V* ⦅◌⦆ *BP.*

Jungfraujoch

❹ **To & From:** *The long slog uphill starts at Interlaken Ost; change in Lauter-*
FodorsChoice *brunnen and also in Kleine Scheidegg (don't worry about missing your*
★ *stop—everyone else is going there, too). A round-trip costs 172.60 SF. Contacts: 033/8287111, www.jungfraubahn.com. Jungfraujoch is ½-day cog railway excursion out of Interlaken, Lauterbrunnen, or Grindelwald.*

The granddaddy of all high-altitude excursions, the famous journey to the Jungfraujoch, site of the highest railroad station in the world, is one of the most popular destinations in Switzerland. From the station at Lauterbrunnen you take the green cogwheel Wengernalp Railway nearly straight up the wooded mountainside, and watch as the valley and the village shrink below. From the hilltop resort of **Wengen** the train climbs up steep grassy slopes past the timberline to **Kleine Scheidegg**, a tiny, isolated resort settlement surrounded by vertiginous scenery. Here you change to the **Jungfraubahn,** another train, which tunnels straight into the rock of the Eiger, stopping briefly for views out enormous picture windows blasted through its stony face.

The **Jungfraujoch terminus** stands at an elevation of 11,400 feet; you may feel a bit light-headed from the altitude. Follow signs to the Top of Europe restaurant, a gleaming white glass-and-steel pavilion. The expanse of rock and ice you see from here is simply blinding.

If you're not sated with the staggering views from the Jungfraujoch terminus, you can reach yet another height by riding a high-tech 90-second elevator up 364 feet to the **Sphinx Terrace:** to the south crawls the vast Aletsch Glacier, to the northeast stand the Mönch and the Eiger, and to the southwest—almost close enough to touch—towers the tip of the Jungfrau herself. Note: even in low season you may have to wait in line for the elevator.

More than views are offered to the hordes that mount the Jungfraujoch daily. You can sign up for a be-

---

FATAL ATTRACTION

Landmarked by its famous "White Spider" (the conjunction of snowy crevasses), the Eiger's notorious north face was first climbed in summer in 1938, but it was not until 1961 that the first group of climbers successfully conquered the almost vertical rock face. As you look up from the comfort of the Jungfrau Railway train, the surprise is not that more than 45 people should have lost their lives on the north face, but that anyone should have succeeded. Legend has it that when a climbing party tackles the north face, townspeople below make bets to see who will succeed and who will not.

ginner's ski lesson or a dogsled ride, or tour the chill blue depths of the **Ice Palace**, a novelty reminiscent of a wax museum, full of incongruous and slightly soggy ice sculptures. Admission to the attraction is included in the price of the excursion.

A few things to keep in mind for the Jungfraujoch trip: take sunglasses, warm clothes, and sturdy shoes; even the interior halls can be cold and slippery at the top. Some sensitive individuals may experience fatigue or headaches while at the top from the high altitude, which usually disappears on the train ride down. Return trains, especially toward the end of the day, can be standing-room only. To save money, take a guided tour with English commentary (called Jungfrau Tour, as opposed to *Jungfrau individuel*), which costs less. Tours leave once a day from Interlaken West, with stops at Interlaken East, Wilderswil, Lauterbrunnen, and Wengen before climbing to Kleine Scheidegg; the return trip is via Grindelwald. You can get to Lauterbrunnen or Grindelwald on your own steam, but you'll have to return the way you came and miss the full round-trip tour. ☎ 033/8287233 🚈 *Round-trip Interlaken East–Lauterbrunnen–Wengen–Jungfraujoch (back via Grindelwald) 173 SF ⊙ May–Oct., daily 6:30 AM (first train up)–6 PM (last train down). The schedule is weather-dependent in winter: call ahead.*

Wengen

❺ *To & From: ½-hour cog railway ride from Lauterbrunnen. Cars cannot drive to Wengen and the only transport is provided by the Wengernalp Mountain Railway—or Wengernalpbahn—which has trains that connect the two towns every quarter hour, with departures as early as 6 AM and as late as 11:30 PM (depending on the season; www.jungfraubahn.ch).*

Lord Byron, Consuelo Vanderbilt (when Duchess of Marlborough), and other social "climbers" put Wengen on the map, spreading the word about its incomparable eagle's-nest perch on a plateau over the Lauterbrunnen Valley. Few places offered such magnificent panoramas, such elegant hotels, and because of its setting, its *Alpenglöh* was said to be the glowiest in Switzerland. Alas, success breeds its own problems. Today, you can barely drink in the famous view 4,068 feet over the

> **IT'S ALL DOWNHILL FROM HERE**
>
> For a handy Web site about winter sports in the region, log on to www.jungfrau.inter.ch.

valley, as hundreds of châlets now elbow each other to get out of the way. Innerwengen, the town center, is crowded with large buildings and shops with plate-glass windows. But once up on your hotel balcony—the higher the better, of course—you may experience the wonder of yore. The "upwardly" mobile still head here because the town is home to some of the Oberland's most challenging skiing (which connects with the trail network at Grindelwald), chicest hotels, and pinkest sunsets. In summer it's a wonderful place to hike and be inspired. For Wengen is not just about legs, it's about heads: get out onto those forest trails and you may understand why Byron was inspired to compose *Manfred* when he hiked to nearby Wengernalp in 1816, kick-starting the 19th-century Romantic movement in the process. You can aim for centrally located upscale hotels, near shopping and nightlife options, or head downhill to pleasant, more isolated lodgings, all artfully skewed toward the view. Half board is just short of obligatory, as only a few restaurants are not attached to a hotel. It's a car-free town; most hotels have porters that meet the trains.

Skiing

Just over the ridge from Grindelwald, **Wengen** (4,265 feet–11,316 feet) nestles on a sheltered plateau high above the Lauterbrunnen Valley; from there, a complex lift system connects to Grindelwald, Kleine Scheidegg, and Männlichen. Wengen has six funicular railways, one cable car, 31 lifts, and 250 km (155 mi) of downhill runs. The Lauberhorn run is tough; it's used for the World Cup Ski Races in January. One-day lift tickets for Kleine Scheidegg–Männlichen cost 57 SF. A two-day pass costs 107 SF. Lift passes for the Jungfrau–Top-Ski-Region are available only for two or more days. A two-day ticket costs 123 SF; a three-day ticket, 169 SF; and a seven-day, 326 SF. For a handy Web site about winter sports in the region, log on to: ⊕ *www.jungfrau.inter.ch.*

Where to Stay & Eat

$$$$ ✕ ▥ **Regina.** It's all about atmosphere in this genteel Victorian hotel.
Fodor'sChoice With its frou-frou trim, Art Nouveau colors, and nestled mountain-
★ side setting, this is the most gracious hotel in Wengen. Thanks to the Meyer family, a genuinely familial mood is palpable, which you sense immediately upon entering the plush and handsome lobby, glowing with sconce lighting and a massive baronial fireplace. Most large guest rooms have balconies and are done in mauve and rose with a very elegant touch; rooms under the eaves have loft beds. Paintings and rustic antiques (such as a huge wooden sled) are scattered throughout. The emphasis is on half board, and it's a treat; the conservatory-like dining room, which serves exceptionally creative seasonal fare, shares the chef with the hotel's popular restaurant, Chez Meyer's ($$–$$$$), adorned with vintage family photos and serving a creative seasonal menu—try the chestnut soup, the zucchini flowers filled with mushrooms, or lobster ravioli with ginger sauce. ⊠ *CH-3823* ☎ *033/8565858* ⊟ *033/8565850* ⊕ *www.wengen.com/hotel/regina* ⇘ *90 rooms* ⌂ *2 restaurants, gym, hair salon, sauna, steam room, bar; no a/c* ⊟ *AE, DC, MC, V* ☉ *Closed Nov.* |⊙| *BP.*

$$$$ ▥ **Park Hotel Beausite.** Grandly situated on the hill above Wengen (more than a bit of a hike from the town center, but that may be a virtue), this hotel offers the kind of views that made Wengen world-famous—a Cinerama vista of mountain majesty with the buildings of the town nearly hidden by trees. Set in a large hotel lined with balconies, the Beausite encourages pampering in its new leisure area, which includes a lovely indoor pool. Relax with a massage followed by a steam bath or sauna. The restaurant is done in dull baby blue, the bar is out of Austin Powers, but the guest rooms are spacious, mostly modern but some have elegant brass beds and a more traditional, rustic style. For a leisurely look at the view, sink into one of the couches in the front lounge off the lobby. Near the cable car station, the hotel is a 10-minute walk from the village. ✉ *CH-3823* ☎ *033/8565161* 📠 *033/8553010* ⊕ *www.beausite-park-hotel.ch* ⇨ *46 rooms, 7 apartments* ⚐ *Restaurant, in-room safes, minibars, in-room data ports, indoor pool, outdoor pool, massage, sauna, piano bar; no a/c* ⊟ *AE, DC, MC, V* ⧦ *BP*.

★ **$$$–$$$$** 🏨 **Alpenrose.** Wengen's first lodging, this welcoming inn has been run by the same family for more than a century. The decor is homey, with knotty pine, painted wood, and skirted lamp shades. Rooms with south-facing balconies are slightly more expensive and well worth it. It's downhill and away from the center, with an emphasis on good half-board meals. The restaurant is for guests only. ✉ *CH-3823* ☎ *033/8553216* 📠 *033/8551518* ⊕ *www.alpenrose.ch* ⇨ *50 rooms* ⚐ *Dining room; no a/c* ⊟ *AE, DC, MC, V* ⊘ *Closed Easter–mid-May and early Oct.–Christmas* ⧦ *BP*.

$–$$ 🏨 **Eden/Eddy's Hostel.** A shingled Victorian jewel box joins forces with an unpretentious crash pad—the Eden Hotel provides marvelous southern views, comfortable rooms with or without bathrooms, and pretty gardens, while Eddy's Hostel has no-frills dorm rooms and a shower down the hall. The terrific proprietress will help organize hikes. There are plenty of occasions to mix with other guests at barbecues, over drinks, or at one of many summertime live music events. ✉ *CH-3823* ☎ *033/8551634* 📠 *033/8553950* ⇨ *18 rooms, 6 with bath, 6 dorms* ⚐ *Restaurant, café; no a/c* ⊟ *AE, DC, MC, V* ⊘ *Closed Nov.–mid-Dec.* ⧦ *BP*.

$–$$ 🏨 **Schweizerheim.** It's worth the hike to this family-run pension nestled
Fodor'sChoice well below the beaten path for the flawless full-valley views, the pris-
★ tine gardens, and the terrace picnic tables balancing precariously over the Lauterbrunnen Valley. The rooms are a dated mix of wood paneling, Formica, linoleum, and carpet, but the experience is welcoming and fun—and the owner is a Swiss hand-organ celebrity. The restaurant serves guests only. ✉ *CH-3823* ☎ *033/8551112* 📠 *033/8552327* ⇨ *24 rooms* ⚐ *Dining room, bar; no a/c* ⊟ *MC, V* ⧦ *BP*.

$–$$ 🏨 **Zum Bären.** This chalet-style lodging just below the center of town is straightforward and bright, with good views and low rates. Rooms are done in blues, yellows, and pale wood; the watercolors are painted by the owner's mother. For extra-cheap sleeps (about 35 SF, including breakfast), you can stay in one of the two camp-style dorm rooms, each filled with 10 beds. ✉ *CH-3823* ☎ *033/8551419* 📠 *033/8551525* ⊕ *www.baeren-wengen.ch* ⇨ *14 rooms* ⚐ *Restaurant, café; no a/c* ⊟ *AE, DC, MC, V* ⊘ *Closed mid-Oct.–mid-Dec. and for 2 wks after Easter* ⧦ *BP*.

Nightlife & the Arts

DANCING Hit **Tiffany** (✉ Hotel Silberhorn ☎ 033/8565131) for a good mix of locals and tourists.

Sports & the Outdoors

ICE SKATING Wengen has a **Natureisbahn** (outdoor ice rink) and a partially sheltered indoor rink. For hours of operation contact the **tourist office** (☎ 033/8551414).

Grindelwald

❻ To & From: *Bernese Oberland Railway (www.jungfraubahn.ch) trains frequently run the 35-minute route between Grindelwald and the Interlaken Ost station. Grindelwald is 27 km (17 mi) southeast of Interlaken.*

Grindelwald (3,445 feet) may be surrounded by the peaks of the Wetterhorn, Schreckhorn, Mönch, and Jungfrau but it is best known as the "Eiger village"—it faces front and center the terrifying north face of the peak that has claimed so many mountain climbers' lives. In the summer of 2006, the Eiger almost claimed Grindelwald itself as its newest victim: headlines around the world described the large chunk of rockface, which broke off (due to global warming) and plummeted down the mountainside, covering Grindelwald in dust for several days. Not counting its sheer Alpine beauty, the town remains among the most popular in the Berner Oberland for the simple reason that it is the most accessible of the region's mountaintop resorts. Strung

ALL IN A DAY'S CLIMB

With the Eiger taunting all climbers within sight, get up close and personal by taking the dandy one-day hike offered by the Bergsteigerzentrum Grindelwald (033/8531200, www.grindelwald.ch/bergsteigerzentrum). After a train ride from Grindelwald to Eigergletscher, you'll hike along the foot of the Eiger's fabled north face, with the guide providing stories of "sheer" excitement. The group then returns to Alpiglen for grilled cheese sandwiches and back to Grindelwald by train. Contact the tourist office at Grindelwald's Sportszentrum on Hauptstrasse for info.

along a mountain roadway with two convenient train stations, it makes an excellent base for skiing, shopping, and dining—if you don't mind a little traffic. Once you get off the main road, there are gorgeous Alpine hikes in all directions.

From Grindelwald you can drive, take a postbus, or hike up to the **Oberergletscher,** a craggy, steel-blue glacier—act fast though, it has already melted by 30% since 1963, and forecasts have it shrinking another 20% by 2030. You can approach its base along wooded trails, where there's an instrument to measure the glacier's daily movement. For an equally fascinating experience, travel down into the valley to Grund, below Grindelwald, and visit the **Gletscherschlucht** (Glacier Gorge). There you can walk along a trail through tunnels and over bridges about 1 km (½ mi) into the gorge itself. Although you can't see the glacier itself while walking along the edges of the spectacular gorge it sculpted, you'll get a powerful sense of its slow-motion, inexorable force. 7 SF ☉ Late May–mid-Oct.

Perhaps the greatest attraction in Grindelwalk is the **Firstbahn,** a 30-minute gondola ride that is one of Europe's longest lifts and offers lovely views of the **First** ski area (7,095 feet). A garden flourishes within easy walking distance (it's even wheelchair accessible). Here, you can see early summer flowers such as gentians, edelweiss, anemones, and Alpine asters.

Skiing

An ideal base for the Jungfrau ski area, **Grindelwald** provides access to the varied trails of Grindelwald First and Kleine Scheidegg–Männlichen. Grindelwald has eight funicular railways, three cable cars, 22 lifts, and 165 km (103 mi) of downhill runs. Some long runs go right down to the village; there are special areas for snowboarders and beginning skiers. One-day lift tickets for Kleine Scheidegg–Männlichen and First each cost 57 SF. A two-day pass costs 107 SF.

Where to Stay & Eat

$–$$ ✕ **Memory.** A no-fuss, family-style chalet restaurant, this welcoming place is known for its cheese and potato dishes, which extend beyond seven kinds of Rösti to include gratins with meat and potato-garlic soup. ✉ *Eiger Hotel* ☎ *033/8543131* ▭ *AE, DC, MC, V.*

★ **$–$$** ✕ **Onkel Tom's Hütte.** This tiny pizza parlor, set in a rustic A-frame cabin on the main drag, is as cozy as they come. Rough wooden floors ac-commodate ski boots, and eight wooden tables share space with a huge iron cookstove, where the young owner produces fresh pizzas in three sizes (the smallest of which is more than enough). There are also gen-erous salads, freshly baked desserts, and a surprisingly large international wine list. Its popularity outstrips its size, so enjoy the delicious smells while you wait. ✉ *Across from Firstbahn* ☎ *033/8535239* ▭ *MC, V* ☾ *Closed Mon. and Nov. and June.*

★ **$$$$** ✕▣ **Schweizerhof.** Behind a dark-wood, red-shuttered Victorian-chalet fa-cade dating from 1892, this big, comfortable hotel attracts a loyal clien-tele. Wing chairs and bookcases in the lobby lounge and dining rooms are inviting on rainy days. Guest rooms are decorated in carved pine and have tile baths. Service is attentive, unhurried, flexible, and extremely friendly. The "Schmitte" restaurant, aglow with decorative wall paintings and lilac hues, ($–$$$) serves nouvelle Swiss cuisine—try duck breast with oys-ter mushrooms and shallots, or something from their vegetarian selections. For more casual fare, repair to the sweet, *Heidi*-worthy Gaststübli. Break-fasts are generous and are offered until 11:30 AM (a rarity in these parts). ✉*CH-3818* ☎*033/8545858* 🖷*033/8545859* ⊕*www.hotel-schweizerhof. com* ➦*41 rooms, 9 suites* ♺ *Restaurant, Stübli, in-room safes, minibars, pool, health club, hair salon, bowling; no a/c* ▭ *AE, DC, MC, V* ☾ *Closed Easter–late May and Oct.–late Dec.* ⍦ *BP.*

★ **$$$–$$$$** ✕▣ **Belvedere.** As you wind your way into Grindelwald, this large, pink structure, precariously perched above the road, comes into view. Suites are tastefully designed: the Salon Louis Philippe, for instance, has period 19th-century furniture and wood-inlay games tables, while oth-ers blend a Swiss traditional touch with modern elegance. Regular rooms suffer a drop in decor but there are great views of the Eiger and surrounding peaks from almost every chamber. The staff and manage-ment radiate genuine warmth and absolute professionalism; the owner takes groups of guests skiing, hiking, and golfing weekly. At the bright and glossy restaurant ($–$$$), the fresh, creative menu includes vege-tarian wild mushroom crepes or the classic tournedos with goose liver topping. Ask about the special rates for Fodor's users when making reser-vations. ✉ *CH-3818* ☎ *033/8545757* 🖷 *033/8535323* ⊕ *www.*

9

belvedere-grindelwald.ch 🛏 55 rooms ⚴ Restaurant, Stübli, Wi-Fi, pool, gym, hot tub, sauna, piano bar, recreation room; no a/c ⊟ AE, DC, MC, V ⊗ Closed late Oct.–mid-Dec. �†⊙⺄ BP.

★ **$–$$$** ✕⊞ **Fiescherblick.** A multistory, flower-box-crazy "chalet," this is the place to eat in Grindelwald, whether as a hotel guest or day-tripper: the same outstanding chef oversees the serious cuisine in the intimate restaurant and the more casual bistro ($–$$$). The seasonal menu might include roast scallops in pepper sauce and black risotto, or guinea fowl in an herb glaze with basmati rice. As for rooms, try to nab one of the "superior" ones, which are bright and spacious, if more expensive. While standard rooms tend to be on the unexciting functional-brown-decor side, guests have called it a "great place to relax after a hard day's skiing." ⊠ *CH-3818* ☎ *033/8545353* 📠 *033/8545350* ⊕ *www.fiescherblick.ch* 🛏 *25 rooms* ⚴ *2 restaurants, in-room safes, minibars, in-room data ports; no a/c, no TV in some rooms* ⊟ *AE, DC, MC, V* ⊗ *No lunch. Closed Easter–mid-May and mid-Oct.–mid-Dec.* ⊙⺄ *BP.*

$$–$$$ ⊞ **Gletschergarten.** Built in archetypal chalet architecture—though it's so large it seems to have grown like topsy—this hotel has been in the same family for three generations. Fittingly, the interior radiates welcome, from heirloom furniture and paintings (by the grandfather) to tea roses cut from the owner's garden. There's heraldry in the leaded-glass windows, a ceramic stove with built-in seat warmer, and a cozy lounge paneled in wood taken from an old Grindelwald farmhouse. All rooms have balconies, some with glacier views, others overlooking the emerald-green hills. Ask for a corner room, as the angle views are especially pleasing. ⊠ *CH-3818* ☎ *033/8531721* 📠 *033/8532957* ⊕ *www.hotel-gletschergarten.ch* 🛏 *26 rooms* ⚴ *Restaurant, sauna, steam room, billiards, Ping-Pong, bar, laundry facilities; no a/c* ⊟ *AE, DC, MC, V* ⊙⺄ *BP.*

$ ⊞ **Wetterhorn.** Overlooking the magnificent ice-blue upper glacier—as well as the sprawling parking lot where hikers leave their cars—this pretty, wood-trimmed inn offers generous lunches outdoors, with full glacier views, and good regional dining inside its comfortable restaurant. The adjoining Gletscherstübli attracts locals as well as the hordes of tourists and hikers who come to marvel at its namesake. Up the creaky old stairs are simple, tidy, aged-pine rooms—some have glacier views—with sink and shared bath. A dormitory with 30 beds is also available. ⊠ *CH-3818* ☎ *033/8531218* 📠 *033/8535818* ⊕ *www.hotel-wetterhorn.ch* 🛏 *9 rooms, 1 dormitory* ⚴ *Restaurant, café, Stübli; no a/c* ⊟ *AE, DC, MC, V* ⊙⺄ *BP.*

¢ ⊞ **Mountain Hostel.** This welcoming hostel sits at the foot of the Eiger in Grund, 2 km (1½ mi) from Grindelwald. The beds, offered with or without linens, are set up in bunk-bed rooms for two to six people. Showers and toilets are down the hall. The owners take groups out on hikes, and there are outdoor barbecues in summer. It's just a couple of minutes on foot from the Grund train station. ⊠ *CH-3818* ☎ *033/8543838* 📠 *033/8543839* ⊕ *www.mountainhostel.ch* 🛏 *20 rooms* ⚴ *Restaurant; no a/c* ⊟ *MC, V* ⊙⺄ *BP* ⊗ *Closed Nov.*

Nightlife & the Arts

DANCING **Challi** (⊠ Hotel Kreuz ☎ 033/8545492) has a DJ who is happy to play requests. **Gepsi** (⊠ Eiger Hotel ☎ 033/8543131) is open late; there's a fun crowd and weekly live music. A self-styled "ethno disco" (decorated with cows and alphorns), the **Plaza Club** (⊠ Sunstar Hotel ☎ 033/8547777) plays music that is strictly modern (no yodeling here). **Regina** (⊠ Grand Hotel Regina ☎ 033/8548600) offers live music nightly.

BRIENZERSEE

Reputedly the cleanest lake in Switzerland—which surely means one of the cleanest in the world—this magnificent bowl of crystal-clear water mirrors the mountain-scape and forests, cliffs, and waterfalls that surround it. Along the lake shore are some top attractions: the woodcarving center of Brienz, the wonderful open-air museum village of Freilichtmuseum Ballenberg—Switzerland's "Williamsburg"—and Meiringen, where Sherlock Holmes met his untimely end at Reichenbachfälle falls. You can cruise alongside Lake Brienz at high speed on the A8 freeway or crawl along its edge on secondary waterfront roads; or you can cut a wake across it on a steamer, exploring each stop on foot, before cruising to your next destination.

Iseltwald

❼ *9 km (6 mi) northeast of Interlaken.*

Set on a lovely and picturesque peninsula jutting out into the quiet waters of the lake, Iseltwald has a bevy of cafés, rental chalets, and hotels (including the noted 19th-cenurty extravaganza, the Grand Hotel Giessbach) clustered at the water's edge. Every restaurant prides itself on its fish dishes, of course. From the village edge you may want to take off on foot; an idyllic forest walk of about 1½ hours brings you to the falls of the **Giessbach,** which tumbles in several stages down rocky cliffs to the lake. You can also get to the falls by taking the Brienzersee steamer, a classic lake excursion, which departs from the landing in Brienz. By land, the most scenic route to Iseltwald from Interlaken is via the southshore road; follow the black-and-white ISELTWALD signs. You can also take the A8 expressway, following the autoroute signs for Meiringen.

Where to Stay & Eat

$$–$$$$
Fodor'sChoice
★

✕⌂ **Grandhotel Giessbach.** The scenery is breathtaking from almost any vantage point in this turreted, 19th-century Belle Epoque haven overlooking the famed Giessbach Falls, across the lake from Brienz. The lobby has high, chandeliered ceilings and period furnishings in golds, yellows, and soft pinks—stucco angels, full-length oil portraits of Swiss beauties, and other Proustian touches all cast their spell and will have you feeling like an off-duty H.R.H. in no time. Guest rooms are comfortable and spacious. The Parkrestaurant ($–$$$) has a glorious "orangerie" overlooking the falls, while Chez Florent is a serious gourmand affair. The official address for this hotel is Brienz. ⊠ *Am Brienzersee, CH-3855* ☎ *033/9522525* 📠 *033/9522530* ⊕ *www.giessbach.ch* 🛏 *66 rooms, 4 suites ₵ 2 restaurants, tennis court, pool, hiking, bar, library, playground, meeting rooms; no a/c* ⊟ *AE, DC, MC, V* ⊙ *Closed late Oct.–late Apr.*

9

Brienz

★ ❽ **To & From:** *Brienz is on the direct rail line with Interlaken with very frequent train connections. Brienz is 12 km (7 mi) northeast of Iseltwald, 21 km (13 mi) northeast of Interlaken.*

The romantic waterfront village of Brienz, world renowned as a wood-carving center, is a favorite stop for people traveling by boat as well as by car. Several artisan shops display the local wares, which range in quality from the ubiquitous, winningly simple figures of cows to finely modeled nativity figures and Hummel-like portraits of Wilhelm Tell. Brienz is also a showcase of traditional Oberland architecture, with some of its loveliest houses (at the west end of town, near the church) dating from the 17th century. Once an important stage stop, Brienz hosted Goethe and Byron at its 17th-century, landmark Hotel Weisses Kreuz; their names are proudly displayed on the gable.

Switzerland's last steam-driven cogwheel train runs from the center of Brienz, at the waterfront, up to the summit of **Brienzer-Rothorn,** 7,700 feet above the town. The ride takes one hour. Trains depart at least once an hour, but to avoid long waits at peak times, purchase your ticket for a particular train in advance on the day you will make the trip; they do not accept reservations. ☎ *033/9522222* ⊕ *www.brienz-rothorn-bahn. ch* 🎟 *72 SF round-trip* ☉ *June–Oct., daily; 1st train up Mon.–Sat. 8:30, Sun. 7:30; last train up 3:40, last train down 4:45.*

Fodor'sChoice
★ Just east of Brienz, a small road leads to the magnificent **Freilichtmuseum Ballenberg.** Time-channeling centuries gone by, Switzerland's "Williamsburg" (although Old Sturbridge Village may be more like it), this outdoor museum village is adorned with 80 characteristic Swiss houses from 18 cantons. Dotting the meadows are 19th-century barns, gorgeous pastel-shuttered houses, antique lace-making shops, old Swiss haberdashers, and plenty of lovely old chalets. Most have been carefully reconstructed. Even the gardens and farm animals are true to type. Old handicrafts and trades like spinning, forging, and lace making are demonstrated using original tools, and many of the "re-enactors" are in period costume. The settlement—found between the villages of Hofstetten and Brienzwiler—ranges over many acres and you can easily spend a half day here. On the other hand, it's not often you come across such a collection of magnificent old relics and abodes, so spend the day at what visitors have called "the perfect family outing." Via public transport, train to the Brienz station and then transfer to municipal bus. ☎ *033/9521030* ⊕ *www.ballenberg.ch* 🎟 *18 SF* ☉ *Mid-Apr.–Oct., daily 10–5.*

At Brienz you may want to try your hand at **wood carving.** During a two-hour lesson at the atelier of Paul Fuchs you can learn to carve the typical Brienzer cow. Make a reservation through the tourist office in Brienz or directly with Mr. Fuchs. You'll be placed in a class of a dozen or more. His workshop is in Hofstetten, between Brienz and Ballenberg. ✉ *Scheidweg 19D, Hofstetten* ☎ *033/9511418* 🎟 *25 SF* ☉ *Apr.–Oct.*

CLOSE UP

A Meiringer By Any Other Name

According to local legend, meringues were invented in 1720 in the Bernese Oberland town of Meiringen by a Swiss confectioner named Gasparini. The popularity of the fluffy deserts was so great that they soon spread to neighboring France, where Marie Antoinette apparently was so taken with them that she was said to actually make them herself regularly at the Trianon. From the palaces of France the dish spread to the rest of the world, and it is the French angle that led to the name change: from the original meiringer to the more common meringue. Melt-in-your-mouth meringues are still a local specialty in Meiringen, where they are sold in dozens of pastry shops. To make them yourself, whip two parts egg whites together with one part sugar until the mass is light and fluffy. Bake for three hours at low heat, then let cool. Serve with a generous dollop of fresh whipped cream. Afterward, you might want to make an appointment with your personal trainer.

Where to Stay & Eat

★ $-$$$$ ✕**Steinbock.** After being almost completely destroyed by a mudslide in 2005, this carved-wooden chalet dating from 1787 was reconstructed from the ground up; it's old style, but all new. Sit out on the broad flower-lined terrace and try to choose from no fewer than 11 interpretations of Lake Brienz whitefish and perch. The menu also has a range of veal classics. ⊠ *Hauptstr. 123* ☎ *033/9514055* ▤ *AE, DC, MC, V* ⊘ *Closed Tues. and Feb.*

$-$$ ✕**Weisses Kreuz.** Generic modern improvements have erased some of the fine origins of this structure, built in 1688 and host to Goethe and Byron, but the idea of its antiquity and the hallowed names on the gable may be allure enough. The pine-lined restaurant offers omelets and *Käseschnitte* (cheese and bread baked in its own whey) as well as lake fish, steaks, and strudel. The sunny lake-view terrace café draws locals and tourists fresh off the boat. ⊠ *Hauptstr. 143* ☎ *033/9522020* ▤ *AE, DC, MC, V.*

★ $-$$ ▦ **Lindenhof.** In a 1787 lodge high above the lakefront, families settle in for a week or two of evenings by the immense stone fireplace, in the panoramic winter garden, or on the spectacular terrace. The grounds are vast and beautifully manicured, the atmosphere familial and formal at once. At the popular restaurant, families with small children can dine together by the fire, apart from other guests. ⊠ *Lindenhofweg 15, CH-3855* ☎ *033/9522030* 🖷 *033/9522040* ⊕ *www.hotel-lindenhof.ch* ⤳ *40 rooms, 4 suites* ⌂ *Restaurant, café, kitchenettes, pool, sauna, bar; no a/c* ▤ *AE, MC, V* ⊘ *Closed Jan. and Feb.* ⦿ *BP.*

Shopping

Brienz is the place for good selections of local wood carvings—everything from cows to plates to nativity figures. The wood carvings at **H. Huggler-Wyss** (⊠ Brunng. 17 ☎ 033/9521000) make it worth stopping by. For mountain crystals, fossils, and stone jewelry, go to **Bergkristalle** (⊠ Hauptstr. 25 ☎ 033/9512625).

9

Meiringen–Hasliberg

9 **To & From:** *Frequent trains run the 45-minute route between Meiringen and Interlaken. Meiringen-Hasliberg is 12 km (7 mi) east of Brienz, 35 km (22 mi) northeast of Interlaken.*

Set apart from the twin lakes and saddled between the roads to the Sustenpass and the Brünigpass, Meiringen is a resort town with 300 km (186 mi) of marked hiking trails and 60 km (37 mi) of ski slopes at the Hasliberg ski region. Historically, its main claim to fame was the place where meringue was invented—it seems the resident chef had too many egg whites left over and decided to do something different for visiting celeb, Napoléon. But there is little history left here and, today, Meiringen is merely a pleasant town, whose main street is lined with shops proffering all sorts of kitschy Swiss merchandise (don't laugh—this stuff is hard to find in many parts of the country). Meiringen's one showstopper is the famous **Reichenbachfälle** (Reichenbach Falls), where Sir Arthur Conan Doyle's fictional detective Sherlock Holmes and his archenemy, Professor Moriarty, plunged into the "cauldron of swirling water and

> ### THE PLOT THICKENS
>
> While Sherlock Holmes met his destiny at the Reichenbach Falls, the faithful will also remember that it was at nearby Rosenlaui that Holmes spent the night before his fateful struggle with Dr. Moriarty. Certain historians have put forward the theory that Conan Doyle modeled Moriarty on the famous, but somewhat sinister, German philosopher Nietzsche. Part of the evidence comes from the hotel register at Rosenlaui, which shows that Nietzsche had a holiday there in 1877, and that Doyle visited the hotel when he came to the falls a few years later.

seething foam in that bottomless abyss above Meiringen" at the climax of the "last" Holmes story, *The Final Problem* (the uproar over the detective's untimely end was such that Doyle was forced to resurrect his hero for further ficitional adventures). The falls, set 2,730 feet up a mountain a little way outside of town can be visited via a funicular. ☎ *033/9714048* 🎫 *7 SF* ⊙ *Funicular: every 10 min daily, 8:30–11:45, 1–6.*

Buffs of the famous detective will delight in the **Sherlock Holmes Museum** in the center of town. Housed in a small chapel, it contains an "authentic" replica of the fictional sleuth's front room at 221B Baker Street. ✉ *Bahnhofstr. 26* ☎ *033/9714141* ⊕ *www.sherlockholmes.ch* 🎫 *4 SF* ⊙ *May–Sept., Tues.–Sun. 1:30–6; Oct.–Apr., Wed.–Sun. 4:30–6:00.*

Sports & the Outdoors

HIKING   A private, 20-km (12½-mi) road to Grindelwald prohibits cars but provides a beautiful, seven-hour Alpine hike. To obtain maps of other local hiking trails, visit the tourist office.

THUNERSEE

If you like your mountains as a picturesque backdrop and prefer a relaxing waterfront sojourn, take a drive around the Thunersee (Lake Thun) or crisscross it on a leisurely cruise boat. More populous than Lake Brienz, its allures include the marina town of Spiez and the large market town of Thun, spread at the feet of the spectacular Schloss Zähringen (Zähringen Castle). There are other castles along the lake, and yet another high-altitude excursion above the waterfront to take in Alpine panoramas—a trip up the Niederhorn.

Spiez

⓾ To & From: *19 km (11¾ mi) west of Interlaken. A rail line connects Spiez, Thun, and Interlaken.*

Spiez is a summer lake resort with marinas for water-sports enthusiasts. Its enormous waterfront castle, **Schloss Spiez,** was home to the family Strättligen and, in the 13th century, its great troubadour, Heinrich. The structure spans four architectural epochs, starting with the 11th-century tower; its halls contain beautiful period furnishings, some from as long ago as Gothic times. The early Norman church on the grounds is more than 1,000 years old. ☎ *033/6541506* ⊕ *www.schloss-spiez.ch* 🖾 *7 SF* ⊙ *Mid-Apr.–June and Sept.–mid-Oct., Mon. 2–5, Tues.–Sun. 10–5; July and Aug., Mon. 2–6, Tues.–Sun. 10–6.*

Where to Stay & Eat

$–$$ ✕🖾 **Seegarten Hotel Marina.** With a pizzeria in one wing and two dining rooms that stretch comfortably along the marina front, this is a pleasant, modern family restaurant ($–$$$). The lake fish specialties are excellent. Spiez Castle looms directly behind you, unfortunately out of sight. The rooms upstairs are spare and modern. ⊠ *Schachenstr. 3, CH-3700* ☎ *033/6556767* 🖷 *033/6556765* ⊕ *www.seegarten-marina. ch* 🖘 *42 rooms* ⚭ *Restaurant, café, pizzeria, minibars, bar; no a/c* 🖃 *AE, DC, MC, V* ⦿l *BP.*

$$–$$$$ 🖾 **Strandhotel Belvedere.** This graceful old mansion has beautiful lawns and gardens, and its manicured waterfront, a five-minute walk away down the hill, offers secluded swimming. Rooms are done in blue and rose, with homey touches such as canopy beds. Corner and lakeside rooms are worth the higher price. On the restaurant's excellent seasonal menu, look for pumpkin ravioli or succulent local chicken. Guests have free access to the city's heated outdoor pool. ⊠ *Schachenstr. 39, CH-3700* ☎ *033/6556666* 🖷 *033/6546633* ⊕ *www.belvedere-spiez.ch* 🖘 *33 rooms* ⚭ *Restaurant, in-room safes, minibars, in-room data ports, spa, beach; no a/c* 🖃 *AE, DC, MC, V* ⦿l *BP.*

Thun

⓫ To & From: *10 km (6 mi) north of Spiez, 29 km (18 mi) northwest of Interlaken. A rail line connects Thun, Spiez, and Interlaken.*

Built on an island in the River Aare as it flows from Lake Thun, this picturesque market town is laced with rushing streams crossed by wooden bridges, and its streets are lined with arcades. On the Old Town's main shopping thoroughfare, pedestrians stroll along flowered terrace sidewalks built on the roofs of the stores' first floors and climb down stone stairs to visit the "sunken" street-level shops.

★ From the charming medieval Rathausplatz (Town Hall Square), a covered stairway leads up to the great **Schloss Thun** (Thun Castle), its broad donjon cornered by four stout turrets. Built in 1191 by Berchtold V, Duke of Zähringen, it houses the fine **Schlossmuseum Thun** (Thun Castle Museum) and provides magnificent views from its towers. The Knights' Hall has a grand fireplace, an intimidating assortment of medieval weapons, and tapestries, one from the tent of Charles the Bold; the Hall is often the imposing venue for concerts. Other floors display local Steffisburg and Heimberg ceramics, 19th-century uniforms and arms, and Swiss household objects, including charming Victorian toys. ⊠ *Schlossberg 1* ☎ *033/2232001* ⊕ *www.schlossthun.ch* ⌛ *7 SF* ⊙ *Apr.–Oct., daily 10–5; Nov.–Dec. 24 and Jan. 3–end of Jan., Sun. 1–4; Dec. 25–Jan. 2 daily 1–4; Feb. and Mar., daily 1–4.*

The **Vaporama Swiss Steam Engine Museum** has gotten under way in the lakeside neighborhood of Schadau. Among a comprehensive collection of stationary steam engines is the cruising star exhibit, the completely restored 1906 steamer *Blümlisalp.* Call ahead for hours. ⊠ *Seestr. 34/ 38* ☎ *033/2332324.*

Where to Stay & Eat

$$–$$$ ✕▣ **Krone.** Positioned directly on the lovely Town Hall Square, this landmark has some fine river views. Although the exterior is classic, the airy interior is generally modern, except for the two lovely tower rooms—round, with bay windows and marble and gilt-edged decor—that are worth requesting. There are two eateries on the premises, one serving a broad range of Chinese dishes and an upscale bistro ($–$$$) that whips up chic versions of regional specialties. ⊠ *Obere Hauptg. 2, CH-3600* ☎ *033/ 2278888* 🖷 *033/2278890* ⊕ *www.krone-thun.ch* 🛏 *27 rooms* ♨ *2 restaurants, in-room safes, minibars, Wi-Fi; no a/c* ▤ *AE, DC, MC, V.*

$ ▣ **Zu Metzgern.** At the base of the castle hill, this shuttered and arcaded *Zunfthaus* (guildhall) overlooks the Town Hall Square. The grand old building has clean, comfortable rooms (bathrooms down the hall). There's atmospheric, traditional Swiss dining, too, whether in the wood-and-linen restaurant or on the intimate little terrace, tucked behind an ivy-covered trellis. ⊠ *Untere Hauptg. 2, CH-3600* ☎ *033/2222141* 🖷 *033/2222182* ⊕ *www.zumetzgern.ch* 🛏 *10 rooms* ♨ *Restaurant, café; no a/c* ▤ *MC, V.*

Shopping

A good spot for traditional pottery in Thun is **Töpferhaus** (⊠ Obere Hauptg. 3 ☎ 033/2227065).

Hilterfingen

★ ⑫ *5 km (3 mi) southeast of Thun.*

Lake Thun is famous for its waterside castles and Hilterfingen and Oberhofen, a little farther along the shore, have two of the best. Hilterfingen's castle, **Schloss Hünegg,** was built in 1861 and furnished over the years with a bent toward Jugendstil and Art Nouveau. The stunning interiors have remained unchanged since 1900. Outside is an idyllic parkland. ✉ *Staatsstr. 52* ☎ *033/2431982* ⊕ *www.schlosshuenegg.ch/* 🖼 *8 SF* ⊙ *Mid-May–mid-Oct., Mon.–Sat., 2–5, Sun. 11–noon, 2–5.*

Oberhofen

★ ⑬ *2 km (4 mi) southeast of Hilterfingen.*

Even Walt Disney would have a hard time topping Schloss Oberhofen for sheer storybook, fairytale splendor. The jewel in the crown of Oberhofen village, this is a delightful hodgepodge of towers and spires on the waterfront. Begun during the 12th century, it was repeatedly altered over a span of 700 years. Inside, a historical museum has a display of the lifestyles of Bernese nobility, along with salons done up in the plushest 19th-century style, plus a Turkish "smoking room," a display of magical medieval stained glass, and a 13th-century chapel with noted Romanesque frescoes. ☎ *033/2431235* ⊕ *www.oberhofen.ch* 🖼 *8 SF* ⊙ *May 15–Oct. 15, Mon. 2–5, Tues.–Sun. 11–5.*

> **YOU NEVER KNOW**
>
> In the castle's Seetuermchen—a small tower on the lake—is a lovely, candlelit chamber where all eyes are drawn to an extraordinary carved-wood Mermaid chandelier, one of the best examples of a kind that became quite common in the 18th century. Those in the know touch the mermaid's belly for good luck.

SIMMENTAL & GSTAAD

Separate in spirit and terrain from the rest of the Berner Oberland, this craggy forest gorge follows the Lower Simme into the Saanenland, a region as closely allied with French-speaking Vaud as it is with its Germanic brothers. Here the world-famous resort of Gstaad has linked up with a handful of neighboring village resorts to create the almost limitless outdoor opportunities of the Gstaad "Super-Ski" region. From Gstaad, it's an easy day trip into the contrasting culture of Lake Geneva and the waterfront towns of Montreux and Lausanne. From Interlaken, take A8 toward Spiez, then cut west on A11 toward Gstaad. The forest gorges of the Simmental Valley lead you through Zweisimmen to the Saanenland and Gstaad.

Gstaad

⑭ **To & From:** *If you're not flying in on a private helicopter, there are twice-hourly (mornings and afternoons) and hourly train connections from Bern; change in Spiez and Zweisimmen (38 SF one-way). There's also a narrow-gauge train from Montreux every hour that costs 23 SF one-way. Gstaad is 49 km (30 mi) southwest of Spiez, 67 km (42 mi) southwest of Interlaken, 68 km (43 mi) northwest of Montreux.*

The four fingerlike valleys of the Saanenland find their palm at Gstaad, the Berner Oberland's most glamorous resort. Linking the Berner Oberland with the French-speaking territory of the Pays-d'Enhaut of canton

Vaud, Gstaad-Saanenland blends the two regions' natural beauty and their cultures as well, upholding Pays-d'Enhaut folk-art traditions such as *papier découpage* (paper silhouette cutouts) as well as decidedly Germanic ones (cowbells, wood carvings, and alphorns). Even Rösti and fondue cohabit comfortably.

However, in Gstaad neither culture wins the upper hand. During high season, the folksy *Gemütlichkeit* (homeyness) of the region gives way to jet-set international style. Although weathered-wood chalets are the norm (even the two tiny supermarkets are encased in chalet-style structures), the main street is lined with designer boutiques. Prince Rainier of Monaco, Roger Moore, and Elizabeth Taylor have all owned chalets in Gstaad (Liz still does), as well as the late Yehudi Menuhin, who founded his annual summer music festival here. (The Menuhin festival takes place from mid-July through early September, and hotels fill quickly then— as they do for the Swiss Open tennis tournament, held every July.)

Gstaad is a see-and-be-seen spot, with equal attention given to its plentiful skiing and its glamorous gatherings—après-ski, après-concert, après-match. The Christmas–New Year's season brings a stampede of glittering socialites to rounds of elite soirees. But you can escape the social scene. There are several unpretentious inns, hotels, and vacation apartments, and dozens of farmhouses that rent rooms, either in Gstaad itself, or in one of the nearby Saanenland hamlets (Gsteig, Feutersoey, Lauenen, Turbach, Schönried, Saanenmöser, Saanen). What paradoxically defies and maintains Gstaad's socialite status is its setting: richly forested slopes, scenic year-round trails, working dairy farms, and, for the most part, stubbornly authentic chalet architecture keep it firmly anchored in tradition. The center of Gstaad is reserved for pedestrians. You can leave your car at the parking facilities at either end of the main street.

The oldest building in the region, the **Saanen Church** was built between the 10th and 11th centuries. Just off Saanen's main street, the church is open daily for visits unless a service is being held. This Romanesque structure was renovated in the 20th century to reveal portions of medieval frescoes on the interior walls. On Saanen's main street next to and behind the Heimatwerk (handcrafts shop), the tiny **Museum der Landschaft Saanen** (Saanenland Museum) traces the history of the area through tools, transport, costumes, furniture, and decorative pieces. ☎ *033/7447988* ⊕ *www.museum-saanen.ch* 🕿 *6 SF.* 🕙 *Mid-May–mid-Oct. and mid-Dec.–Easter, Tues.–Sun. 2–5. Closed mid-Oct.–mid-Dec.*

Skiing

Gstaad-Saanenland does not hesitate to call itself a "Super-Ski" region, and the claim is not far from the truth. With the building of the one-track railroad from Montreux at the beginning of the 19th century, Gstaad-Saanenland became increasingly popular, both for its ideal location at the confluence of several valleys and for the sunny mildness of its slopes, which, starting at 3,608 feet and soaring to 7,217 feet, stay relatively toasty compared with those of other resorts (except for the Diablerets Glacier).

Skiing in Gstaad-Saanenland is, in terms of numbers, the equivalent of Zermatt: 66 lifts can transport more than 50,000 skiers per hour to its network of 250 km (155 mi) of marked runs. In fact, these lifts are spread across an immense territory, 20 km (12 mi) as the crow flies, from Zweisimmen and St-Stefan in the east to Château-d'Oex in the west, and 20 km (12 mi) to the Diablerets Glacier in the south.

Gstaad's expansive area means that most of its lifts are not reachable on foot, and since parking is in short supply, public transport, either by the train or the postauto, is the best option. The flip side is that, except in very high seasons (Christmas and February) and in certain places, such as the lift for the Diablerets, waits for lifts are tolerable. A one-day ticket costs between 29 SF and 55 SF, depending on the sector; a six-day pass costs 299 SF. The **Gstaad Ski School** (☎ 033/7441865) gives lessons in downhill, snowboarding, and cross-country skiing (there are more than 50 km [30 mi] of well-groomed cross-country trails).

Where to Stay & Eat

$$$–$$$$
Fodor'sChoice
★
✕ **Die Chesery.** Lobster cappuccino, brie stuffed with truffles, le pigeon "royal": with such showstoppers as these award-winning chef Robert Speth scales the summits of culinary excellence. He masterfully marries exotic flavors, such as ginger or mango, with *cuisine de marché* local ingredients and his results have foodies and millionaires fighting for reservations; book way ahead in high season. Set in a decorator-perfect chalet (originally built by Prince Sadruddin Aga Khan), this has been a Gstaad landmark ever since it opened in December 1962. Have your dessert—perhaps the signature hot chocolate cake with kumquats—in the piano bar, which lends the place a lively late-night dining scene. An elegant little casino in the cellar adds that James Bond touch. ⊠ *Lauenenstr.* ☎ *033/7442451* ⊕ *www.chesery.ch* ➡ *AE, DC, MC, V* ⊗ *Closed Mon. and Tues.*

★ **$$$$**
✕⊞ **Olden.** At the eastern end of the main thoroughfare, this charming Victorian-style inn has an elaborately painted facade and intricately carved woodwork in every interior niche. Rooms are folksy and atmospheric, but have such modern details as lighted closets. The places to see and be seen are the hotel's bar and restaurant ($$$–$$$$). Offerings at the elegant establishment might include lobster bisque or lamb in an olive crust. A more economic way of scoping the Gstaad scene is to sip a coffee on the Olden's sidewalk terrace. Travelers on Fodor's Talk Forum consider this venue "definitely worth a detour." ⊠ *CH-3780* ☎ *033/7484950* 📠 *033/7484959* ⊕ *www.hotelolden.com* ➪ *16 rooms* ⚹ *2 restaurants, café, bar; no a/c* ➡ *AE, DC, MC, V* ⊗ *Closed mid-Apr.–mid-May and Oct.–mid-Nov.* ⦿ *BP.*

$$$$
Fodor'sChoice
★
✕⊞ **Palace.** Towering over tiny Gstaad like Mad Ludwig's castle, this fantasyland burlesque packs a wallet-wallop. Although it cozily refers to itself as a family "pension" (albeit the largest in Switzerland), it has an indoor swimming pool with underwater music and water-jet massage, chauffeured Rolls-Royces, and oxygen cures, among other amenities. An indoor-outdoor swimming pool (with a glass floor placed on top for dancing on winter nights), tennis weeks in summer, and an elaborate health club are but a few of many compelling amenities. Consci-

9

entious travelers worried about missing out on the local experience, rest assured: The rooms are lavished with appropriately rustic touches, though you could play hockey in the sprawling tiled baths. The kitchen serves four lavish restaurants ($$$$), with renowned guest chefs conducting weeks of special cuisines from around the world. Be prepared for the steep 15-minute walk uphill. ⊠ *CH-3780* ☎ *033/7485000, 800/745–8883 in U.S.* 🖷 *033/7485001* ⊕ *www.palace.ch* ⇆ *71 rooms, 6 suites, 1 apartment* ⚘ *4 restaurants, in-room safes, minibars, in-room broadband, 4 tennis courts, indoor-outdoor pool, health club, squash, ice-skating, lobby lounge, piano bar, nightclub; no a/c* ⊟ *AE, DC, MC, V* ⊘ *Closed late Mar.–mid-June and mid-Sept.–mid-Dec.* ⑂ *MAP.*

$$$–$$$$ ⤬⊡ **Le Grand Chalet.** On a hill just a 10-minute walk from the center of Gstaad, Le Grand Chalet commands a spectacular view of the surrounding mountains and village below. The spacious, comfortable rooms exude an informal elegance, with pale wood and fresh white curtains throughout. An open central fireplace separates the cozy lounge from La Bagatelle ($$–$$$$), the hotel's popular restaurant favored for its nouvelle Swiss cuisine. Try the pepper steak, baby chicken with tarragon, game in season, and marvelous local cheeses. Easy walking trails depart from the hotel's doorstep. ⊠ *Neueretstr., CH-3780* ☎ *033/7487676* 🖷 *033/7487677* ⊕ *www.grandchalet.ch* ⇆ *20 rooms, 4 suites* ⚘ *Restaurant, in-room safes, minibars, pool, gym, sauna, bar; no a/c* ⊟ *AE, DC, MC, V* ⊘ *Closed mid-Oct.–mid-Dec. and Apr.–early June* ⑂ *BP.*

★ $$–$$$ ⤬⊡ **Posthotel Rössli.** This comfortable inn, the oldest in town, combines down-home knotty-pine decor with soigné style. Despite the mountain-cabin look, the clientele is young and chic, and the café, a local-landmark watering hole, draws crowds. The restaurant ($–$$$), full of linens and candlelight, serves good Swiss fare at reasonable prices. ⊠ *CH-3780* ☎ *033/7484242* 🖷 *033/7484243* ⊕ *www.posthotelroessli. ch* ⇆ *18 rooms* ⚘ *Restaurant, café, minibars; no a/c* ⊟ *AE, DC, MC, V* ⑂ *BP.*

★ $$$$ ⊡ **Grand Hotel Park.** A little bit of Vail comes to the Alps in this enormous modern hotel, which opened in May 1990 and seems bent on helping wealthy Americans make a seamless transition between two cultures. Its 1910 predecessor on the site destroyed, this all-new structure refers to the old style in its deep mansard roofs and rows of arched windows but there the homage ends: the interiors are all new, and the look is an opulent mix of chalet-modern and Spanish grandee, with a lot of flowered wallpaper, waxed wooden furniture, and wardrobes painted with Swiss folk-art scenes mixed in. The impression is opulent yet cheerful. The Park offers some of the best health facilities in the Saanenland, including an antistress program, aerobics and gymnastic classes, and an indoor saltwater pool. Treatment weeks offer an irresistible mix of glamour and virtue. ⊠ *CH-3780* ☎ *033/7489800* 🖷 *033/7489808* ⊕ *www.grandhotelpark.ch* ⇆ *88 rooms, 11 suites* ⚘ *3 restaurants, in-room safes, minibars, in-room DVD, Wi-Fi, tennis court, 2 pools (1 indoor), hair salon, sauna, steam room, 2 bars* ⊟ *AE, DC, MC, V* ⊘ *Closed late Sept.–mid-Dec. and Apr.–early June* ⑂ *BP.*

Nightlife & the Arts

BARS **Pinte** (☎ 033/7443444), in the Hotel Olden, is where people gather after a day on the slopes. Belly up to the beautiful wooden bar or huddle around the stone fireplace.

CONCERTS The **Menuhin Festival Gstaad** (✉ Postfach 65, CH-3780 ☎ 033/7488338 🖷 033/7488339 ⊕ www.menuhinfestival.com) hosts a series of world-class concerts from mid-July to early September. **Les Sommets Musicaux de Gstaad** (✉ 36 rue de Montchoisy, case postale 1207, CH-1211 Geneva ☎ 022/7386675 🖷 022/7368505 ⊕ www.sommets-musicaux. com) presents two weeks of classical music from late February to early March. Information for the festivals is available several months in advance, direct or from the Gstaad tourist bureau.

DANCING **Club 95** (☎ 033/7484422), in the Sporthotel Victoria, is popular with a younger crowd. **GreenGo** (☎ 033/7485000), a disco in the Palace Hotel, is open only in winter. There are two crowded bars, but the focal point is the massive dance floor fitted over the hotel's pool.

Sports & the Outdoors

MOUNTAIN CLIMBING Great treks and climbs are a stone's throw from Gstaad. **Alpinzentrum Gstaad** (☎ 033/7484161) can supply you with mountain guides and snowsports teachers. **Beats Adventure** (☎ 033/7441521) aims its tough sports excursions at very fit people. **Experience Gstaad** (☎ 033/7448800) is the place to go for guides for off-trail skiing, ice climbing, and snowshoe trekking.

BERNER OBERLAND ESSENTIALS

Transportation

BY AIR

Belp Airport in Bern brings you within an hour via train of Interlaken, the hub of the Berner Oberland. Near Basel, EuroAirport (across the border in France) is 2¼ hours by train. The Unique Zürich Airport is 2½ hours away. Geneva's Cointrin is less than three hours away.

🛈 Airport Information **Belp** ☎ 031/9602111. **Cointrin** ☎ 022/7177111. **EuroAirport** ☎ 061/3252511. **Unique Zürich Airport** ☎ 0900/300313.

BY BOAT & FERRY

Round-trip boat cruises around Lake Thun and Lake Brienz provide an ever-changing view of the craggy foothills and peaks. The round-trip from Interlaken to Thun takes about four hours; the trip to Spiez takes about two hours and includes stopovers for visits to the castles of Oberhofen, Spiez, and Thun. A round-trip from Interlaken to Brienz takes around 2½ hours, to Iseltwald about 1¼ hours. These boats are public transportation as well as pleasure cruisers; just disembark whenever you feel like it and check timetables when you want to catch another. Tickets are flexible and coordinate neatly with surface transit: you can cruise across to Thun and then take a train home for variety. Buy tickets and catch boats for Lake Thun at Interlaken West station. For Lake Brienz, go to Interlaken East. The official boat company for both lakes is Schiffsbetrieb BLS Thuner- und Brienzersee.

Boat & Ferry Information **Schiffsbetrieb BLS Thuner- und Brienzersee** ☎ 033/3345211.

BY BUS

Postbuses (called postautos or postcars) travel into much of the area not served by trains, including most smaller mountain towns. **Swiss Rail** (☎ 0900/300300 ⊕ www.sbb.ch) is the leading company, and even offers private motor-coach tours to many points of interest. **Gray Line Switzerland** (☎ 044/3831705) has a wide range of routes.

BY CAR

Swift and scenic roads link both Bern and Zürich to Interlaken. From Bern, the autoroute A6 leads to Spiez, then A8 continues as the highway to Interlaken. From Zürich, the planned autoroute link with Luzern (Lucerne) is incomplete; travel by Highway E41 south, then pick up the autoroutes A4 and A14 in the direction of Luzern. South of Luzern, pick up the A4 again in the direction of Interlaken. From Geneva, the autoroute leads through Lausanne and Fribourg to Bern, where you catch A6 south, toward Thun. A long, winding, scenic alternative: continue on the autoroute from Lausanne to Montreux, then to Aigle; then, head northeast up the mountain on A11 from Aigle through Château-d'Oex to Gstaad and the Simmental.

Driving in the Berner Oberland allows you the freedom to find your own views and to park at the very edges of civilization before taking off on foot or by train. If you are confining yourself to the lakefronts, valleys, and lower resorts, a car is an asset. But several lovely resorts are beyond the reach of traffic, and train, funicular, and cable car excursions take you to places ordinary tires can't tread; sooner or later, you'll leave the car behind and resort to public transportation. Remember that Wengen, Mürren, and Gstaad are all car-free.

BY TRAIN

Trains from Bern to Interlaken run once an hour between 6 AM and 11 PM, some requiring a change at Spiez. From Zürich, a direct line leads through Bern to Interlaken and takes about 2½ hours, departing hourly; a more scenic trip over the Golden Pass route via Luzern takes about two hours. From Basel trains run twice an hour via Olten (approximately a 2½-hour trip). Trains run hourly from Geneva (a 2¾-hour ride). Trains stop at the Interlaken West station first. Next stop is Interlaken East. West is the more central, but check with your hotel if you've booked in advance: some of the town's fine hotels are clustered nearer the East station, and all Brienzersee boat excursions leave from the docks nearby. For train information in Interlaken, ask at Interlaken West.

The Berner Oberland is riddled with federal and private railways, funiculars, cogwheel trains, and cable lifts designed with the sole purpose of getting you closer to its spectacular views. A Swiss Pass lets you travel free on federal trains and lake steamers, and gives reductions on many private excursions. If you're concentrating only on the Berner Oberland, consider a 15-day Regional Pass, which offers 450 km (279 mi) of free rail, bus, and boat travel for any five days of your visit, with half fare for the remaining 10 days, as well as discounts on some of the most spectacular (and pricey) private excursions into the heights. The price is 316 SF (first class) and 265 SF (second class). A seven-day pass allows you three days of travel for 263 SF (first class) and 220 SF (second class). These regional passes also grant a 50% discount for travel to Luzern, Zermatt, and Brig. With a Family Card (20 SF), children who are under 16 and accompanied by at least one parent travel free. Discount passes pay for themselves only if you're a high-energy traveler; before you buy, compare the price à la carte for the itinerary you have in mind.

🚆 Train Information **Swiss Rail** ☎ 0900/300300 ⊕ www.sbb.ch.

Contacts & Resources

CAR RENTAL
🚆 Major Agencies **Avis** ✉ Waldeggstr. 34a, Interlaken ☎ 033/8221939. **Hertz** ✉ Harderstr. 25, Interlaken ☎ 033/8226172.

EMERGENCIES
🚆 **Dental referrals** ☎ 1811. **Medical emergencies** ☎ 144. **Pharmacist referrals** ☎ 1811. **Police** ☎ 117.

INTERNET & MAIL
In smaller towns, ask your hotel concierge if there are any Internet cafés nearby.

🚆 Internet & Mail Information A network of Wi-Fi **Hotspots** is rapidly growing throughout Switzerland. ⊕ www.hotspots.ch ⊕ www.swisshotspots.ch. **Kikireon** ✉ Postgasse 6, Interlaken ☎ 033/8233232. **Spacegate** ✉ Bälliz 49, Thun ☎ 033/2215000. **Die Post main post office** ✉ Marktgasse 1, Interlaken. **Die Post mainpost office** ✉ Bahnhofpl. 778F, Gstaad.

TOUR OPTIONS
Auto AG Interlaken offers guided coach tours and escorted excursions within the Berner Oberland. There are bus tours to Mürren and the Schilthorn (including trips on the cable car), to Grindelwald and Trümmelbach Falls, to Kandersteg and the Blausee, and to Ballenberg. Guests are picked up at either the Interlaken West or East train stations or at the Metropole or Interlaken hotels. Some tours are available with English commentary. The tourist office is the best source of information.

If you're traveling without either a Swiss Pass or a Regional Pass, remember that guided tours to the Jungfraujoch or to the Schilthorn, arranged through the railway and cable companies themselves, cost less than independent round-trip tickets.

For a nostalgic tour of the streets of greater Interlaken by horse-drawn carriage, line up by the Interlaken West train station.

🚆 Fees & Schedules **Oberland Tours Grindelwald** ☎ 033/8281717 for reservations. **Horse-drawn carriage** ✉ Charles Wyss Kutschenbetrieb ☎ 033/8222403.

VISITOR INFORMATION

Berner Oberland Tourismus dispenses tourist information for the entire region. It's not oriented toward walk-ins, so write or call ahead. The Interlaken Tourist Office, at the foot of the Hotel Metropole, provides information on Interlaken and the Jungfrau region. Arrange your excursions here.

🛈 Local Tourist Offices Brienz ✉ CH-3855 ☎ 033/9528080 ⊕ www.alpenregion.ch. **Grindelwald** ✉ CH-3818 ☎ 033/8541230 ⊕ www.grindelwald.ch. **Gstaad** ✉ CH-3780 ☎ 033/7488181 ⊕ www.gstaad.ch. **Kandersteg** ✉ CH-3718 ☎ 033/6758080 ⊕ www.kandersteg.ch. **Meiringen** ✉ Bahnhofstr. 22, CH-3860 ☎ 033/9725050. **Spiez** ✉ CH-3700 ☎ 033/6542020 ⊕ www.spiez.ch. **Thun** ✉ Bahnhof, CH-3600 ☎ 033/2259000 ⊕ www.thuntourismus.ch. **Wengen-Mürren-Lauterbrunnen** ✉ CH-3822, Lauterbrunnen ☎ 033/8568568 ⊕ www.wengen-muerren.ch.

🛈 Regional Tourist Offices Berner Oberland Tourismus ✉ Jungfraustr. 38, CH-3800 Interlaken ☎ 033/8283737 🖷 033/8283734 ⊕ www.berneroberland.ch. **Interlaken Tourist Office** ✉ Höheweg 37, CH-3800 ☎ 033/8265300 🖷 033/8265375 ⊕ www.interlaken.ch. **Meiringen-Hasliberg** ✉ Bahnhofstr. 22, CH-3860, Meiringen ☎ 033/9725050 🖷 033/9725055 ⊕ www.alpenregion.ch.

Valais

CRANS-MONTANA, VERBIER, LEUKERBAD,
ZERMATT

Matterhorn

WORD OF MOUTH

"It's Matterhorn-pricey but it's hard to beat the variety and snow quality at Zermatt, plus being able to ski to Italy (a trip which is fine for intermediates) is a treat."　　　　　　　　　—repete3

"The mountains around Saas-Fee are absolutely staggering because they rise about 9,000 feet above the valley almost vertically. I am not sure I would classify them as beautiful, but they are dramatic and awesome."　　　　　　　　　—BBrown

WELCOME TO THE VALAIS

TOP REASONS TO GO

★ **The Matterhorn:** Shutter-snap this glorious enigma from all angles, be it a luxury hotel room at its base or the sky-high Gornegrat–Monte Rosa Bahn.

★ **Be a Downhill Racer:** Get to know your snow at fabled ski resorts like Crans-Montana and Verbier (and the nearby lovely lift villages).

★ **Cantonal Capitol:** Presided over by the castle of Tourbillon, Sion is a fortified link in the giant web of precipitous passes.

★ **Going to the Dogs:** Credited with saving so many lives, the revered St. Bernards still accept thanks at their Col du Grand St-Bernard hospice.

★ **Zermatt.** Worship the cult of the Matterhorn from this posh resort, where chic boutiques and raclette restaurants keynote the *high* life.

1 **Val d'Entremont.** If you have to pick one Valais wild valley to explore, this one also allures with the civilizing pleasures of the St-Maurice abbey and **Martigny's** ancient Roman treasure trove. Head east to **Verbier**, second to none for its ski facilities, or make a great exit south at the famous Col du Grand St-Bernard pass.

Main shopping street in Zermatt

2 **Sion.** The canton's capitol is marked by two rocky hills that materialize in front of you like a fairytale landscape, one crowned by the Tourbillon castle. The town has been a bishopric for 1,500 years and has a wealth of architectural delights from a Gothic cathedral to a 17th-century town hall.

- Eiger
- Mönch
- Jungfrau
- Gletsch
- Münster
- Aletschhorn
- Eggishorn
- Fiesch
- Bietschhorn
- LÖTSCHENTAL
- Leuk
- Brig
- Turtmann
- Visp
- VISPERTAL
- ITALY
- MATTERTAL
- SAASTAL
- Zinal
- Längfluh
- Weisshorn
- Alphübel
- Allalinhorn
- Piz d'Andolla
- Zermatt
- Unterrothorn
- Matterhorn 4,478m
- Gornergrat
- Trockener Steg
- Klein Matterhorn
- Breithorn
- Dufourspitze
- Monte Rosa 4,634m

0 —— 10 mi
0 —— 10 km

GETTING ORIENTED

Born in the heights above the Gletsch Glacier, the mighty River Rhône dominates this region of southern Switzerland. Its silty torrent carves out the valley of the upper Rhône, around which chic ski resorts like Zermatt and Crans-Montana are groomed into gnarls of stone and ice.

3 Conversion de la Valle. The adjoining modern ski resorts of Crans-Montana are attractively perched 5,000 feet up on a sunny plateau among woods, grasslands, and small lakes. In nearby **Val d'Anniviers,** tiny villages are noted for their folkloric mazots (small wooden barns balanced on stone disks and columns).

4 Alpine Zentrum. Feast your eyes on the **Matterhorn** (and your belly on some great fondue) in glamorous Zermatt, where you can catch your breath strolling the car-less streets before taking a lift or train to even higher elevations. Allow a half a day to get here and back, enjoying spectacular views from the train en route. Nearby is Saas-Fee, famed for its glacier skiing.

Bettmeralp

10

VALAIS PLANNER

How's the Weather?

The Valais is at its sunny best in the high summer and midwinter; foggy dampness overwhelms in late autumn and spring. Mountain weather is impetuous, embracing with its warmth one day and obliterating views and trails the next.

Take your cues from local forecasts and mountain operators who have an experienced sense about shifting patterns. Cloud layers and storms move up and down elevations hovering atop cool valley floors, following the flow of riverbeds, and are sometimes snagged on mountain ridges.

Misty banks move away in short order opening up the path or vista for those who are patient.

Some of the best skiing and hiking can be had in March and September when crowds are the lightest and the sun is at the perfect arc.

Because of its radiant orientation, the Valais is a particularly favored destination for Swiss and other Europeans who vacation here year-after-year and for weeks at a time.

And remember: May and June plus November to mid-December are renovation, repair, and get away times for locals.

Facilities rotate closing periods so you will always find a fluffy bed and good meal, but not always in the one you may prefer.

Finding a Place to Stay

The most appealing hotels in Valais seem to be old. That is, historic sites have maintained their fine Victorian ambience; postwar inns, their lodgelike feel. Most of those built after about 1960 popped up in generic, concrete-slab, balconied rows to accommodate the 1960s ski boom. They are solid enough but, for the most part, anonymous, depending on the personality and dedication of their owners.

Valais is home to some of Switzerland's most famous resorts, and prices vary widely between top-level Zermatt lodgings and simple, wayside auberges (inns) in humbler towns. The price categories below have been equally applied, so the standards in a $$$-rated hotel in expensive Zermatt may be moderate compared with those in nonresort towns, and even the best hotels do not have air-conditioning. Often included in the price, demipension (half board)—also called Modified American Plan (MAP)—includes breakfast and a hot meal, either lunch or dinner; rates may be listed per person. There are sometimes enormous differences between high- and low-season prices, but, although some places offer low-season savings, others simply close their doors. If you're planning a vacation for fall or spring, remember that many resorts shut down altogether during the lulls in May and from November to mid-December and schedule their renovations and construction projects for these periods.

Over Hill, Over Dale

As skiing is to winter, hiking is to summer in Valais, and the network of valleys that radiate north and south of the Rhône provides almost infinite possibilities. Sociable hikers can join the crowds on trails out of the big resorts—especially outside Saas-Fee and Zermatt, where the mountain peaks and glaciers are within tackling distance—but don't overlook wilder, more-isolated alternatives in the less-developed Val d'Anniviers. Skilled trekkers opt for multiday hut-to-hut excursions into the higher elevations, skirting mountain peaks that fail to recognize official borders with France and Italy.

Loosen Those Belts

For Valaisans, the midday meal remains the mainstay. Locals gather at a bistro for a hearty *plat chaud* (warm meal) that includes meat, vegetable or pasta, and salad for under 20 SF. Baskets of crusty *pain Valaisan* (bread made of wheat and cereal grains) freshly cut from thick loaves, never presliced, circulate around the table.

The evening meal is lighter, perhaps comprising an *assiette* (platter) of cheese and cold cuts shared by the table, accompanied by another bread basket and fruit. For the time-pressed, sandwiches and quick meals can be picked up at a corner boulangerie or supermarket (Manor, Migros, or Coop), where food halls have buffets and inexpensive sit-down options.

Dress and atmosphere are understated even at top-dollar restaurants, which eschew worn jeans but seldom require a jacket. Keep in mind that most eateries do not offer continuous service; lunch winds down around 2 and dinner does not begin before 6. Unless a host greets you or you have a reservation, it is fine to take a seat at an open table.

Multiple dining options can share the same entrance and kitchen. A brasserie or Stübli is the homey casual section just inside the doorway, with paper place mats, straightforward dishes, and lively conversation. The quieter *salle à manger* (dining room) has tables dressed in linen and a *carte* (menu) of multicourse meals and more complicated preparations. If cheese specialties are served, a *carnotzet,* a cozy space in the cellar or a corner away from main dining, is designated to confine the aroma and foster conviviality.

Wine is a standard companion whether *vin ouvert* (open wine) poured from small pitchers or bottles selected from cellar holdings. The pace of eating is leisurely, and the server will not bring a check until you request it.

Getting Around

An exceptional network of rail and bus service links even the most remote Valais hamlets carved into valley walls and anchored atop tapered passes. Main thoroughfares and highways are easy to navigate, but it takes skill and courage to tackle the twisted and graded (sometimes single-track and without guardrail) roads that spur off them.

Many travelers prefer to cover these distances by train or on one of the bright yellow postal buses, which cover the terrain multiple times a day.

These same comfortable coaches pick you up at designated roadside stops or post offices and are a good option when the hiking trail terminates or your legs are too weary to carry you farther.

Martingy, Sion, and Visp are main rail transfer hubs. Schedules are synchronized so that you step off one transport onto the other by walking from platform to parking lot.

If you must travel by car, check with the destination as resorts like Zermatt and Saas-Fee require that you leave your vehicle in a garage or lot on the outside of town adding parking fees to vacation costs. And guess what? Some hotels reserve space for your car along with your bed.

10

WHAT IT COSTS In Swiss francs

	$$$$	$$$	$$	$	¢
Restaurants	over 60 SF	40 SF–60 SF	25 SF–40 SF	15 SF–25 SF	under 15 SF
Hotels	over 350 SF	250 SF–350 SF	175 SF–250 SF	100 SF–175 SF	under 100 SF

Restaurant prices are per person for a main course at dinner. Hotel prices are for two people in a standard double room in high season, including tax and service.

Updated by
Kay
Winzenried

THIS IS THE BROAD UPPER VALLEY OF THE MIGHTY RHÔNE, a river born in the heights above Gletsch (Glacier), channeled into a broad westward stream between the Bernese and the Valaisan Alps, lost in the depths of Lac Léman (Lake Geneva), and then diverted into France, where it ultimately dissolves in the marshes of the Camargue. The region is still wild, remote, beautiful, and slightly unruly. Its *mazots* (typical little Valais barns balanced on stone disks and columns to keep mice out of winter food stores) are romantically tumbledown, its highest slopes peopled by nimble farmers who live at vertiginous angles. More than 500 km (310 mi) of mountains and glaciers span the Bietschhorn, Aletsch, and Jungfrau summits. In 2001 UNESCO named this area a World Heritage site, joining such other natural wonders as the Galapagos Islands, Yellowstone National Park, and the Serengeti desert.

The birthplace of Christianity in Switzerland, Valais was never reformed by Calvin or Zwingli, nor conquered by the ubiquitous Bernese—one reason, perhaps, that the west end of Valais seems the most intensely French of the regions of the Suisse Romande.

Its romance appeals to the Swiss. Longing for rustic atmosphere, they build nostalgic Valais-style huts in their modern city centers so they can eat raclette (melted cheese with potatoes and pickles) under mounted pitchforks, pewter pitchers, and grape pickers' baskets. For vacations, the Swiss come here to escape, to hike, and, above all, to ski. The renowned resorts of Zermatt, Saas-Fee, Crans-Montana, Verbier, and Leukerbad are all in the Valais, some within yodeling distance of villages barely touched by modern technology.

Exploring Valais

Valais is an L-shape valley with Martigny at its angle. Its long (eastern) leg, a wide, fertile riverbed flanked by bluffs, is the most characteristic and imposing. It's fed from the north and south by remote, narrow valleys that snake into the mountains and peter out in Alpine wilderness or lead to the region's most famous landmarks—including that Swiss superstar, the Matterhorn. Not all of Valais covers Alpine terrain, however. The western stretch—between Martigny and Sierre—comprises one of the two chief sources of wine in Switzerland (the other is in Vaud, along Lac Léman). Valaisan wines come from vineyards that stripe the hillsides flanking the Rhône.

The Val d'Entremont leads southward down an ancient route from Lac Léman to the Col du Grand St-Bernard (Great St. Bernard Pass), traversing the key Roman crossroads at Martigny. Up the Rhône Valley, past the isolated eagle's-nest village of Isérables, two magnificent castle-churches loom above the historic Old Town at Sion. From Sion, the Val d'Hérens winds up into the isolated wilderness past the stone Pyramides d'Euseigne (Pyramids of Euseigne) and the Brigadoon-like resorts of Évolène and, even more obscure, Les Haudères. The Val d'Anniviers, the valley winding south from Sierre, leads to tiny, isolated skiing and hiking resorts such as St-Luc and Grimentz. The most famous southbound valley, the Mattertal, leads from Visp to the stellar resort of Zermatt and its mascot

A WINE & CHEESE PARTY

Though the French influence in the western portion of this region means a steady diet of cuisine bourgeoise, leading newcomers to think entrecôte with peppercorn sauce is a native dish, the elemental cuisine of Valais is much simpler. In a word: cheese.

The most popular way to enjoy this regional product is raclette, an exclusive invention of this mountain canton (though the French of Haute-Savoie embrace it as their own).

Ideally, the fresh-cut face of a half wheel of Orsières (a mild cheese produced in the high pastures near Martigny) is melted before an open wood fire, the softened cheese scraped onto a plate and eaten with potatoes (always in their skins), pickled onions, and tiny gherkins.

Nowadays, even mountain carnotzets with roaring fires depend on electric raclette heaters that grip the cheese in a vise before toasterlike elements.

Fondue, of course, is omnipresent and is often made with a blend of the local Bagnes and Orsières.

Its consumption is generally held to the cold months, although locals casually request raclette *à discrétion* (as much as you want) on a cool summer's eve.

The beverage of choice to accompany your raclette is a crisp, bubbly, fruity Fendant (a local white wine), but there are other regional favorites.

Appellations and vintner names aren't as prominent in the Valais; it's the name of the grape that holds the spotlight.

Winemakers welcome tasting guests most times of the year except harvest (late September through early October).

A true Valaisan wouldn't enjoy a fine meal without a ruby red Dôle (pinot noir and gamay blend) swirled in a stemmed *ballon* (glass) or a sparkling white Fendant poured into a shot-size glass.

On your way through the region follow custom and give a toast: *Santé*.

Cheese isn't the region's only culinary treasure, however.

Valais rivals Graubünden in its production of *viande séchée* (air-dried beef), a block of meat marinated in herbs, pressed between planks until it takes on its signature bricklike form, and then dried in the open air.

Shaved into thin, translucent slices, it can be as tender as a good prosciutto *crudo*—or as tough as leather. The flavor is concentrated, the flesh virtually fat-free.

mountain, the Matterhorn. A fork off that same valley leads to spectacular Saas-Fee, another car-free resort in a magnificent glacier bowl. From Brig, back at the Rhône, a valley mounts southward to the Simplon Pass and Italy, and the river flows from the northeast and its glacier source, Gletsch, near the Furka Pass, which leads out of the region.

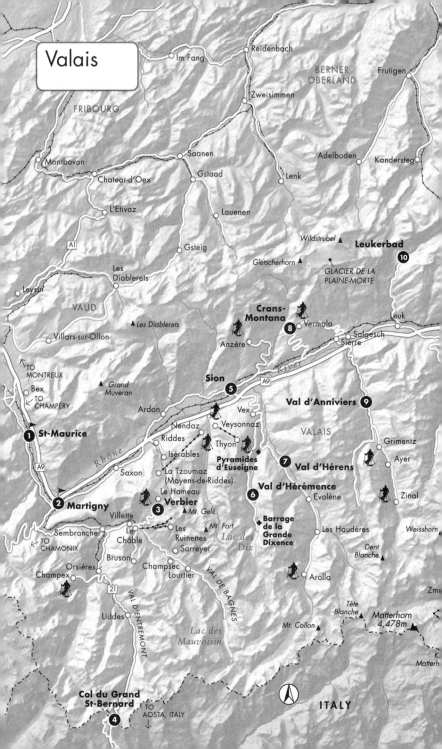

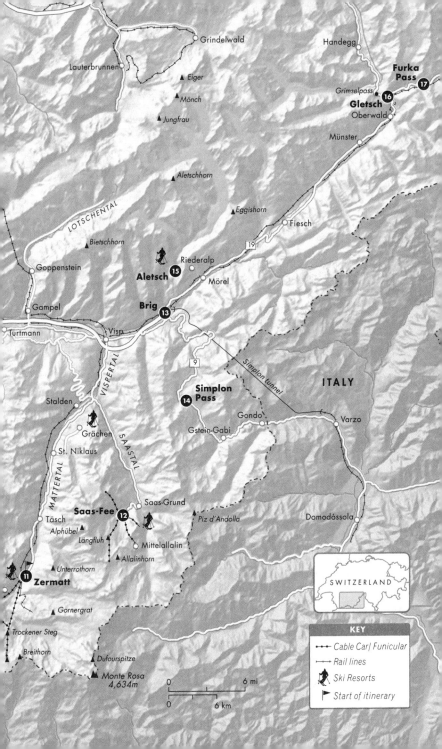

SCALING THE HEIGHTS

You'll feel unsated if you miss Switzerland's most photographed icon, the Matterhorn, so strike out on the most direct route to Zermatt. Allow a half day to get there and back, enjoying spectacular views from the train en route (you can't drive to the town of Zermatt itself). If the weather is clear when you arrive, hustle to the end of the village to see the mountain. Then split your day of exploring between taking a lift or the train to higher elevations and strolling the narrow streets and shops, being sure to stop at one of the local restaurants for raclette.

To experience Valais, it's not necessary to explore every wild valley that ribs out from the Rhône; better to choose one region and spend a few days hiking, driving, or skiing. Enter from Lac Léman and visit the Gianadda museum in Martigny. Spend the night and next

day exploring the citadel and Old Town of Sion. Other Alpine resort options—Saas-Fee, Verbier, and Crans-Montana—are also magnificently sited. If you prefer wilderness and old-fashioned retreat, shun the famous spots, and make an excursion up the Val d'Hérémence, Val d'Hérens, or Val d'Anniviers.

Whatever locales you choose, staying three or four nights enables you to settle in and fully explore the facilities. From these valleys, you can exit Valais via the Simplon Pass or the Furka Pass. If you opt for the Furka route, take the aerial cable car from Fiesch for stunning views of the Bernese and Valaisan Alps and glaciers that make up the World Heritage site. Whenever time and road conditions permit, opt for the slow switchback crawl over the mountain passes rather than the more efficient tunnels.

VAL D'ENTREMONT

At Villeneuve the Rhône broadens deltalike into a flat valley that pours into Lac Léman. But head upriver (south), crossing from the canton of Vaud into Valais, and the valley and the river change character. The mountains—the Dents du Midi in the west and the Dents de Morcles to the east—begin to crowd in. The Rhône no longer flows placidly but gives a taste of the mountain torrent it will become as you approach its source. And at the Martigny elbow, the most ancient of Alpine routes leaves the Rhône and ascends due south to 8,098 feet at the Col du Grand St-Bernard before descending into Italy's Valle d'Aosta.

St-Maurice

▶ ❶ **To & From:** *For departure times and prices for trains and buses for most destinations in this chapter, check with www.sbb.ch—the main Swiss public transportation Web site—or call 0900/300300 (1,19 SF per minute). Remember, if you have a Swiss Pass or another rail-discounting card, it also applies to the buses. St-Maurcie is 46 km (28 mi) west of Sion, 56 km (35 mi) southeast of Lausanne.*

Pushed up against a stern, gray rock face, this village is quiet and peaceful, with patrician homes lining its Grand-rue. Once a customs station along the Roman route over the Col du Grand St-Bernard, in the 3rd century it witnessed the massacre of a band of Christian soldiers, the Theban Legion, and their chief, Maurice, who had refused to worship the Roman deities.

★ At the end of the 4th century the first bishop of the Valais built a sanctuary over Maurice's tomb, and in 515 the **Abbaye de Saint-Maurice** (St. Maurice Abbey) was founded. Its treasury contains a stellar collection of religious offerings, with precious Romanesque and Gothic objects given in honor of the martyrs. Contemplate both sides of the stunning bronze doors with inscriptions honoring martyrs from around the world. Excavations near the baroque **église abbatiale** (abbey church) have revealed the foundations of the original building. ☎ *024/4860404* ⊕ *www. abbaye-stmaurice.ch* ✉ *Church free; guided tour 6 SF* ☉ *Guided tours May–June, Sept., and Oct., Tues.–Sat. at 10:30, 3, 4:30, Sun. at 3 and 4:30; July and Aug., Tues.–Sat. at 10:30, 2, 3:15, 4:30, Sun. at 2, 3:15, 4:30; Nov.–Apr., Tues.–Sun. at 3.*

Where to Stay & Eat

$ ×🏠 **Le St-Christophe.** Time your entry into the Valais to stop at this stone *relais* (inn), hewn of boulders from the gorge that separates Bex and St-Maurice. It's an unlikely location for a gourmet kitchen ($$–$$$), but the place has been operating successfully for decades. Two options await: the less-expensive, three-table anteroom turned bistro and the open dining room, where contemporary paintings soften the walls and enliven the atmosphere. Updated classics use ideas as refreshing as the art—puffy lardon-seasoned crispies on the salad, morel-filled ravioli with Parmesan cream sauce. Reserve one of the upper-level rooms, and you can stay put after dinner. ⊠ *Rte. St- Maurice (exit Bex, direction Lavey) CH-1880* ☎ *024/4852977* 📠 *024/ 4852445* ⇆ *12 rooms* ⚹ *Restaurant, café, minibars, cable TV, free parking* ▤ *AE, DC, MC, V* ☉ *Closed Sun. and Mon.* ⦶⧉ *CP.*

Martigny

⏵❷ **To & From:** *Martigny is the transportation hub for the Lower Valais. Trains often stop at its rail station on the line running between Lausanne (25 SF, 50 min) and Brig (25 SF, 1 hr). Post buses connect all the towns of the Lower Valais. Inquire about special bus passes for the region, including the Martigny Pass and the Valais Central Pass through the auspices of TMRSA (Transports de Martigny et Régions) at www. tmrsa.ch. Martigny is 17 km (11 mi) south of St-Maurice, 23 km (14 mi) southwest of Sion.*

Fodor'sChoice
★ At the foot of the Col du Grand St-Bernard, Martigny has long been a commercial crossroads. Testimony to this past are the Gallo-Roman ruins discovered in 1976 by engineer

> **DOUBLE IDENTITY**
>
> You may spot posters for concerts by international classical stars such as Cecilia Bartoli or Itzhak Perlman at the Fondation Pierre Gianadda–it doubles as a concert hall.

10

Leonard Gianadda. When Gianadda's brother Pierre died in a plane crash, Leonard created a cultural center in his memory. The **Fondation Pierre Gianadda** now rises in bold geometric shapes around the ruins. Inside are three separate collections, and the foundation itself sponsors high-profile, themed art exhibits. Recent temporary exhibitions have spotlighted works by Felix Vallonton, Claudel and Rodin, and Henri Cartier-Bresson. Its permanent holdings include works by Van Gogh, Cézanne, and Picasso. The **Musée Gallo-Romain** displays Gallo-Roman relics excavated from a 1st-century temple: striking bronzes, statuary, pottery, and coins. A marked path leads through the antique village, baths, drainage systems, and foundations to the fully restored 5,000-seat amphitheater, which dates from the 2nd century. In the gracefully landscaped garden surrounding the foundation, a wonderful **Parc de Sculpture** displays works by Rodin, Brancusi, Miró, Calder, Moore, Dubuffet, and Max Ernst. There's also a sizable **Musée de l'Automobile,** which contains some 50 antique cars, all in working order. They include an 1897 Benz, the Delauneay-Belleville of Czar Nicholas II of Russia, and a handful of Swiss-made models. ⊠ *59 rue de Forum* ☎ *027/7223978* ⊕ *www.gianadda. ch* 🖃 *15 SF* ⊙ *June–Oct., daily 9–7; Nov.–May, daily 10–6.*

☺ Story boards and films at the **Musée et Chiens du St-Bernard à Martigny** praise the lifesaving work of a breed of dogs that has come to symbolize the Alpine zone straddling Switzerland and Italy. Tended for centuries by the monks of the Order of St. Augustine, who live in service on the Col du Grand St-Bernard, care has shifted to a private foundation. The animals are no longer used for rescue in the desolate reaches that surround the hospice, so they are brought down in autumn to the **Chenil à Martigny (kennel at Martigny),** located in a restored arsenal adjacent to the Roman amphitheater where they are groomed for visitations. Exercised, trained, and sired to keep the blood line perpetuated, these cuddly, brave canines return to their mountain home in summer. Le Collier d'Or (Gold Collar), a terraced café and gift shop expand the museum services.(⇨ *See* Col du Grand St-Bernard *below.*) ⊠ *34 rte. du Levant* ☎ *027/7204920* ⊕ *www.musee-saint-bernard.ch* 🖃 *10 SF* ⊙ *Museum daily 10–6.*

Where to Stay & Eat

$–$$ ✕🖼 **Hôtel du Forum.** Martigny is something of a one-street town, but if it suits your itinerary to stop over, then this is a convenient choice. Though the pine-decorated rooms are comfortable, the real draw is the hotel's top-rated chef, who oversees both the more formal restaurant, Le Gourmet ($$$$), and a brasserie, l'Olivier ($$). The menu's temptations could include crayfish gazpacho and pigeon with an arabica-infused sauce. Take Bus 13 from the railway station to the Le Bourg stop. ⊠ *74 av. de Grand-St-Bernard, CH-1920* ☎ *027/7221841* 🖷 *027/7227925* 🛏 *29 rooms* ♨ *2 restaurants, cable TV* 🖃 *AE, DC, MC, V* ⊠◯ *CP.*

Verbier

❸ **To & From:** *Verbier is a compact resort with excellent shuttle service between hotels, chalets, and the lifts. In the high season unless there is parking space at your lodging, a car will be an additional expense and* *nuisance. Access to Verbier requires two transfers—a combination rail and bus. From Martigny, take the St. Bernard Express train bound for Orsières, its bright red rail cars emblazoned with the region's famous mascot. Change in Sembrancher (15 min.) where the line splits into two separate valleys. A connecting train waits on the parallel track for the 10-minute run to La Châble. A yellow postal bus meets passengers outside the station for the 30-minute ride to the post office in the center of Verbier. If you are traveling light, there is a gondola that departs from this base station. In all, the trip from Martigny will take an hour and cost 20 SF. Another option is to drive to La Châble and leave the car in the large parking lot, then transfer to the resort using the bus or cableway. Verbier is 28 km (18 mi) east of Martigny (exit at Sembrancher), 58 km (36 mi) southwest of Sion. For departure times and prices for trains and buses for most destinations in this chapter, check with www.sbb.ch—the main Swiss public transportation Web site—or call 0900/300300 (1,19 SF per min). Remember, if you have a Swiss Pass or another rail-discounting card, it also applies to the buses.*

It's the skiing on sunny slopes that draws committed sports lovers to Verbier, a high-tech, state-of-the-art sports complex that links Quatre Vallées (four valleys) and multiple ski areas, including Thyon, Veysonnaz, Nendaz, and La Tzoumaz. Verbier has a huge aerial cableway, with a cabin that accommodates 150, plus 89 smaller transportation installations. There is plenty of vertical drop, as the extreme ski and snowboard competitions can attest. Summer sports are equally serious: hiking, mountain biking, and hang gliding and its variations compete with golf as the principal sports. Perched on a sunny shelf high above the Val de Bagnes, with wraparound views and the 10,923-foot Mont-Fort towering above, Verbier is protective of its picturesque wooden chalet architecture, yet stays current with modern amenities and comforts. Thanks to its compact layout and easygoing locals, the town has a friendlier feel than the traffic-snarled sprawl of Crans-Montana or hotel-packed Zermatt. Rail and cable car connections from Le Châble are an alternative to driving switchback roads to the resort. Once here, you can easily navigate the village on foot or by shuttle bus, and all hotels are clearly signposted.

10

Les Musées du Val de Bagnes is a collection of six installations, some within easy walking distance of each other, in the villages and hamlets of La Châble, Villette, Champsec, Lourtier, Sarreyer, and Le Hameau. Most open their doors only in July and August for a historical perspective of life in this isolated area. A restored home, blacksmith forge, grain and logging mill, soapstone masonry, alpine memorabilia, and contemporary art gallery make up the eclectic displays. Open days and hours vary; check the brochure available from the Tourist Office. ☎ 027/7761525 ⊕ *www.museedebagnes.ch.*

Skiing

At 4,921 feet, Verbier is the center of Switzerland's famous transit network, **Televerbier** (⊕ www.televerbier.ch)—which consists of 12 gondolas, five cable cars, 32 chairlifts, and 44 other ski lifts giving access to 410 km (253 mi) of marked pistes. From this hub an immense complex of resorts has developed—some more modest, others more exclusive—

covering four valleys in an extended ski area whose extremities are 15 km (9 mi) or so apart as the crow flies and several dozen kilometers apart by way of winding mountain roads.

Les Ruinettes gives access to Verbier's entire upper ski area, which culminates at **Mont-Fort**, at 10,923 feet. This is reached by an aerial tram, *Le Jumbo,* equipped with a cab that accommodates 150. La Chaux Express, a chondola (combination chair lift and gondola on the same cable) sweeps skiers to the upper station. You decide whether to keep your skis or snowboard on for the chair, or take them off to enter the gondola. This entire sector is crisscrossed by a dense network of astonishingly varied pistes. There are several strategic passes, including **Les Attelas, Chassoure, Col des Gentianes,** and **Tortin.** Swiss freestyle snowboarder Alex Zillio assisted with the design of the jumps, rails, and pipes at **1936 Neipark** at La Chaux. One-day lift tickets for all four valleys cost 67 SF; six-day passes, 319 SF. If you ski only Verbier, Bruson, or Savoleyres/La Tzoumaz, expect to save 12% to 35%. Automated ski passes streamline the lift check-in process; free tickets and discounts for children are available.

If you're looking for a private instructor to fine-tune your ski or snowboard technique, stop in at the **Ecole Suisse de Ski** (☎ 027/7753363 ⊕ www/verbiersportplus.ch), or at one of the two **Adrenaline** (☎ 027/7717459 ⊕ www.adrenline-verbier.ch) locations in the **Hardcore** and **Ski Adventure** stores.For a different alpine experience, rent a sled at any of the village sports outlets and take a run down the 10 km (6 mi) track from Savoleyers to La Tzoumaz.

Where to Stay & Eat

$–$$$ ✕ **L'Ecurie.** Locals and chalet dwellers in-the-know gather at this central location beneath the Ermitage hotel. Choose between the no-frills, rough-wood-tables corner, and the linen-and-candelight section set off by amber glass panels. Wood fire grill specialties and pastas are staples, but there are always a few daily specials that are equally tempting. In a region where chicken is difficult to find, the poussin with fries is a treat. ✉ *pl. Centrale* ☎ *027/7712760* ☐ *AE, DC, MC, V.*

$–$$$ ✕ **La Grange.** To eat cheese or not to eat cheese will be the question here. In keeping with the traditional decor, you can sample regional specialties, such as fondue or dried beef, or you can go for more lofty epicurean choices from the open grill, such as emicé de veau (veal) with curry or liver pâté with plum sauce. The wine list includes an excellent selection of local vintages. ☎ *027/7716431* ☐ *AE, DC, MC, V* ⊗ *Closed May–June and mid-Sept. to mid–Dec.*

$–$$$ ✕ **Le Millénium/El Toro Negro.** Bask in the sun on the terrace during lunch at this combination restaurant–grill house. The prawn salad with ginger sauce and the brochettes of teriyaki beef with Asian vegetables are both flawless. Head downstairs to the steak house for a menu heavy with meat and hearty side dishes. ✉ *Carrefour Centrale* ☎ *027/7719900* ☐ *MC, V.*

★ **$$$$** ✕▥ **Chalet d'Adrien.** Named for the owner's grandfather, a baron, who discovered the village in the early 1900s, this luxury inn passes on the baron's aristocratic taste. Antiques and collectibles from old farmhouses and châteaux, and a large number of suites contribute to the private ski mansion feel. Rooms, outfitted with hand-carved headboards and richly textured fabrics, are named for wildflowers. South-facing rooms (many with a balcony) look out on the French Alps backlit by the afternoon sun. To work out those après-ski kinks, visit the spa's infinity pool that takes in the same breathtaking view. The epicurean menu at Apartement ($$$–$$$$) has imaginative dishes like lamb with a ratatouille canneloni, while the more classic Grenier ($–$$$) serves hearty stews and cheese dishes. ⊠ *rte. des Creux, CH-1936* ☎ *027/7716200* 🖷 *027/7716224* ⊕ *www.chalet-adrien.com* ⇄ *13 rooms, 17 suites* ⌂ *2 restaurants, in-room safes, minibars, cable TV, in-room data ports, indoor-outdoor pool, gym, hot tub, sauna, spa, steam room, billiards, bar, video game room, free parking, no-smoking rooms* ⊟ *AE, DC, MC, V* ⊘ *Closed late Apr.–early July and late Sept.–early Dec.*

★ **$$$$** ✕🖳 **Rosalp.** The rustic-chic pine decor of Pierroz ($$$$), the main restaurant here, sets a warm tone for one of Switzerland's best menus. Chef Roland Pierroz has earned an international following for such dishes as grilled salmon with leek cream and truffles. For simpler, less pricey, but equally creative food, try La Pinte ($$–$$$). An outstanding cellar makes Rosalp the place to sample rare regional vintages. Reservations are essential. If you plan to stay overnight, ask for one of the newer rooms, which have marble baths. Upper rooms are smaller but quieter and have better views. ⊠ *rte. de Médran, CH-1936* ☎ *027/7716323* 🖷 *027/7711059* ⊕ *www.rosalp.ch* ⇄ *25 rooms, 5 apartments* ⌂ *2 restaurants, in-room safes, minibars, cable TV, in-room data ports, gym, hot tub, sauna, Turkish bath, massage, bar* ⊟ *AE, DC, MC, V* ⊘ *Closed late Apr.–early July and late Sept.–early Dec.* ⍫⊙l *CP.*

$$$$ 🖳 **Hotel Montpelier.** This classy, chalet-style lodge sits apart from the town hub. Generously sized rooms with balconies are brightened with honey-colored wood and blue stenciled decorations. The half board is far from a hardship, as the cuisine is excellent; if you'd like a change of scenery, though, the owners will book you a table at their restaurant in the upper village. ⊠ *37 rue de Centre Sportif, CH-1936* ☎ *027/7716131* 🖷 *027/7714689* ⊕ *www.hotelmontpelier.ch* ⇄ *46 rooms, 24 suites, 1 apartment* ⌂ *2 restaurants, minibars, cable TV, in-room DVD, indoor pool, sauna, steam room, mountain bikes, bar, free parking, parking (fee), no-smoking rooms* ⊟ *AE, DC, MC, V* ⊘ *Closed May and Nov.* ⍫⊙l *MAP.*

$$–$$$$ 🖳 **Central Hotel.** Finding this hotel is easy; you'll see exterior signage on the honey-colored building standing on the traffic circle. Locating the up-stairs, side entrance, however, is more difficult; especially when it's ob-scured by vacationers filling TBar, the hotel's indoor-outdoor hot spot for breakfast, light meals, and drinks. In the guest rooms, sliding glass pan-els separate the bedroom from a Jacuzzi tub bath. Chocolate color woods and leather seating contrast with stark white walls, accented with chrome lighting and a plasma-screen TV. Draped windows buffer the noise from the animated crowd circulating below, but don't count on soundproof-ing. ⊠ *pl. Central, CH-1936* ☎ *027/7715007* 🖷 *027/7715011* ⊕ *www. verbiercentralhotel.com* ⇄ *8 rooms* ⌂ *In-room data ports, in-room safes, minibars, cable TV* ⊟ *AE, DC, MC, V* ⍫⊙l *CP.*

10

$$–$$$ ⚇ **Ermitage.** Centrally located, this traditional mainstay features compact rooms with south facing balconies that offer views of the Combin mountains. (Be sure to request one because rooms on the north side of the building look out at the slow crawl of cars and people along the main street.) A hospitible family member welcomes you in a lobby filled with plush cushioned furniture and an Internet corner—a gathering place for guests as there is no seating en chambre. Shower-and-tub baths have been recently renovated. ⊠ *18 Carrefour Central, CH-1936* ☎ *027/7716477* 🖷 *027/7715264* ⊕ *www.ermitage-verbier.ch* ⇨ *25 rooms* ⚇ *Restaurant, minibar, cable TV, Internet, bar, free parking* ⊟ *AE, DC, MC, V* ⊘ *Closed mid-Sept. to mid-Oct., and mid-Apr.–mid-May* ⧖ *CP.*

> ## ON THE CALENDAR
>
> For more than two weeks overlapping July and August, the **Verbier Festival & Academy** (☎ 027/7718282 🖷 027/9259068 ⊕ www.verbierfestival.com) hosts an impressive classical music festival of performances and master classes. Musical director James Levine assembles youth performers and celebrated guests such as Maxim Vengerov, Evgeny Kissin, and Martha Argerich to play together under a sprawling tent.

Nightlife & the Arts

DANCING The popular **Crok No Name** (⊠ rte. des Creux ☎ 027/7716934) has live music or DJs nightly. If you don't plan to hit the slopes early, you can party into the wee hours at Moroccan-themed **Casbah** (⊠ Hôtel Farinet, pl. Centrale ☎ 027/7716626). The **Farm Club** (⊠ Rhodania Hotel, rue de Verbier Station ☎ 027/7716121) is the place to be seen in Verbier. Apparently it's not fashionable to turn up before 1 AM. The club is closed Sunday. If you're looking for someplace unpretentious, head to **IceBox** (⊠ rue de la Poste ☎ 079/4489790), where the music doesn't stop until 4 AM.

Sports & the Outdoors

Verbier offers a variety of summer and winter high-altitude sports, ranging from rock and ice climbing to rafting and snow tubing, all led by specialist outfitters.

BICYCLING Trails and routes (250 km [188 mi]) for the enthusiast range from difficult distance rides across the passes to simpler runs closer to town. **Médran Sports** (☎ 027/7716048), on the other side of the village, offers a choice of equipment and gear at competitive rates. Twice a week, free guided tours depart from the Tourist Office and there is a bike park with jumps and ramps plus a variety of training camps to improve technique.

The pros at **No Bounds** (☎ 027/7715556) will help you plan your entire outing plus rent standard or high-performance bikes, helmets, and shells.

GOLF Concentrating on your drive may be difficult with the Combin and Mont Blanc ranges backdropping the shot. Verbier has two 18-hole courses open to the public. **Les Esserts** (☎ 027/7715314) is adjacent to the upper settlement of Hameau. Closer to the main village, **Les Moulins** (☎ 027/7717693), a compact golf course, is a challenge at par 54.

HIKING &
CLIMBING
Randonnées and trails thread from ridgeline to valley floor in 400 km (300 mi) of pathways that cross nature reserves, highland streams, and historical villages. Sign up at **La Fantastique** (☎ 027/7714141 ⊕ www.lafantastique.com) or **Verbier Sport**+ (☎ 027/7753363 ⊕ www.verbiersportplus.ch) for hut-to-hut trekking tours of the Mont Blanc region, or technical rock climbing and rappelling sessions. Closer to town **Sentier Suspendu,** an outdoor climbing wall and network of rope bridges operated by Verbier Sport+, gives beginners an introduction.

SPORTS CENTERS
Verbier's **Centre Sportif** (☎ 027/7716601) is a hub for the active, with indoor skating, swimming, curling, climbing, beach volleyball, tennis, and squash; as well as whirlpools, saunas, and a solarium. There's even a backpackers' dorm and Internet café.

Col du Grand St-Bernard

★ ❹ To & From: *The opening of the Col du Grand St-Bernard, the pass connecting Switzerland and Italy, is weather dependent. This high mountain crossing is closed during the winter months while the tunnel remains open year round. Don't be deceived: the roadway can be shut down in summer due to random snowfalls. On a clear day the drive on narrow twisting roads that thread in and out of avalanche breaks is unforgettable. The traffic on the approach to the pass dramatically reduces once vehicles driving through to Aosta (Italy) leave the highway at the tunnel entrance. During summer, public transport to the Hospice Grand St-Bernard is available from Martigny. The journey starts with train service to the village of Orsières, terminus of the rail line, and then switches to coach. It's a one hour drive by car; add an additional half hour for the rail-bus connection. Col du Grand St-Bernard is 40 km (25 mi) south of Martigny, 69 km (43 mi) southwest of Sion.*

Breasting the formidable barrier of the Alps at 8,101 feet, this pass is the oldest and most famous of the great Alpine crossings, and the first to join Rome and Byzantium to the wilds of the north. Used for centuries before the birth of Christ, it has witnessed an endless stream of emperors, knights, and simple travelers—think of Umberto Eco's *The Name of the Rose,* with its two friars crossing on donkey back in howling winter winds. Napoléon took an army of 40,000 across it en route to Marengo, where he defeated the Austrians in 1800.

10

You'll have an easier time crossing today. If you simply want to get to Italy quickly, take the tunnel, which opens on the other side above the Valle d'Aosta. But by skipping the tiny winding road over the top, you'll miss the awe-inspiring, windswept moonscape at the summit and the hospice that honors its namesake. In 1038, the story goes, Bernard of Menthon, bishop of Aosta, came to clear the pass of brigands. When he reached the top, he found a pagan temple, which he covered with his chasuble. The shrine immediately crumbled to dust and, by the same power, the brigands were defeated. Bernard established his hospice there.

L'Hospice du Grand St. Bernard served international travelers throughout the Middle Ages. Kings and princes rewarded the hospice by showering estates upon the order. Today, a dwindling number of residents—

Augustinian canons—still train as mountain guides and ski instructors and host seasonal retreats that include outdoor excursions. Within the hospice there is a multilevel museum with exhibits about the history of the pass and the devoted monks of the Order of St. Augustine who have lived here. Displays of church treasures—chalices, crosses, and altar clothes in gold, silver, and jewels—are on view in another wing. The fresco bedecked chapel remains open for daily prayers.Behind the hospice is **Chenil au Col du Grand St-Bernard,** a kennel full of the landmark's enormous, furry namesakes: the famous St. Bernard dogs, who for centuries helped the monks find travelers lost in the snow. They supposedly came to Switzerland with silk caravans from central Asia and were used by Romans as war dogs; today they're kept more for sentimental than functional reasons. In winter the dogs are boarded in Martigny (*see* Musée et Chiens du St-Bernard à Martigny *above*). The most famous was Barry, who saved more than 40 people in the 19th century and today stands stuffed in Bern's Naturhistorisches Museum (Museum of Natural History). Souvenir stands sell plush versions of St. Bernards and there are a handful of dining options on either side of the pass. ☎ *027/ 7871236* ⊕ *www.gsbernard.ch* ✉ *Museum and kennel 7 SF* ☽ *June and Sept., daily 9–11:30 and 1–5:30; July and Aug., daily 9–6:30.*

SION & ENVIRONS

The Rhône Valley is most fertile just east of Martigny, its flatlands thick with orchards and vegetable gardens, its south-facing slopes quilted with vineyards. The region nurtures a virtual market basket of apples, pears, apricots, and delicate white asparagus, a specialty of early spring. The local blue-blood crop, however, is grapes: this is one of the primary wine-producing regions in the country, and the fruity Fendant and hearty red Dôle appear on lists throughout the area. Lesser known local varietals include Petite Arvine, Amigne, Cornalin, and Humagne. Once Valais wines were poured from hinged-lid tin or pewter pitchers called *channes*; reproductions are sold throughout the region. Also from the orchards come potent, intensely perfumed eaux-de-vie (or schnapps), especially *abricotine* (from apricots) and *williamine* (from pears).

This patch of Valais demonstrates the region's dramatic contrasts. Over the fertile farmlands looms the great medieval stronghold of Sion, its fortress towers protecting the gateway to the Alps. High up in the bluffs and valleys to the south are scores of isolated eagle's-nest towns, including Évolène and Isérables. The latter, set on a precarious slope that drops 3,280 feet into the lowlands, has narrow streets that weave between crooked old stone-shingle mazots. Since the arrival of the cable car, Isérables has prospered and modernized itself. Yet the inhabitants of this village still carry the curious nickname *Bedjuis*. Some say it's derived from "Bedouins" and that the people are descended from the Saracen hordes who, after the battle of Poitiers in 732, overran some of the high Alpine valleys.

Excursions to the sights and villages of these *haute vallées* (high valleys) can be accomplished in a day, with plenty of time to hike and explore before returning to the city. Keep in mind that narrow roads twist up and down steep grades and require additional time to navigate. Above the town of Vex, the road splits: to the west is the Val d' Hérémence, which terminates at the base of the Barrage de la Grande Dixence (Grande Dixence Dam); to the east is the Val d'Hérens, which begins near the Pyramides d'Euseigne and pushes toward the Dent Blanche. Expanses of wilderness are broken by clusters of chalets and small cultivated plots. Accommodations and services are modest and limited. The tourist office in Sion can assist with reservations for overnight stays or multiday hiking trips.

Sion

❺ **To & From:** *Sion is a main stop on the railway running between Lausanne (30 SF, 1 hr) and Brig (19 SF, 50 min); many post buses threading the region stop at the train station. Sion is 6 km (10 mi) northeast of Verbier.*

Rearing up in the otherwise deltalike flatlands of the western Valais, two otherworldly twin hills flank the ancient city of Sion. The two hills together are a powerful emblem of the city's 1,500-year history as a bishopric and a Christian stronghold. From the top of either hill are dramatic views of the surrounding flatlands and the mountains flanking the valley. The town itself can be comfortably explored on foot in an afternoon, unless you lose yourself in one of its museums or labyrinthine antiques shops. In summer a trolley called Le P'tit Sédunois shuttles between the train station, main plaza, and elevated sights.

Sion folk are fiercely proud and independent, as reflected in the fanatical support for their soccer team and their dogged attempts to host the Winter Olympics. (There was bitter disappointment when they lost the bid for the 2006 games to rivals across the border in Turin, Italy.) A shortage of high-quality hotels gives the impression that the town is not as hospitable to travelers as the tourist-oriented ski resorts, but don't be deterred; there are ample reasons to spend time here. For example, the city walking tour offered in summer includes a wine tasting.

★ Crowning Tourbillon, the higher of Sion's hills, the ruined **Tourbillon château** was built as a bishop's residence at the end of the 13th century and destroyed by fire in 1788. If you take the rugged walk uphill, try to time it for a visit to the tiny chapel with its ancient, layered frescoes. 🔳 *Free* ⊙ *Mid-Mar.–mid-Nov., Tues.–Sun. 10–6.*

★ On Valère, Sion's lower hill, the **Église-Forteresse de Valère** (Church-Fortress of Valère) is a striking example of sacred and secular power combined—reflective of the Church's heyday, when it often subjugated rather than served its parishioners. Built on Roman foundations, the massive stone walls enclose both the **château** and the 11th-century **Église Notre-Dame de Valère** (Church of Our Lady of Valère). This structure stands in a relatively raw form, rare in Switzerland, where monuments are often restored to perfection. Over the engaging Romanesque carvings, 16th-century fresco fragments, and 17th-century stalls painted with scenes of the Passion, there hangs a rare **organ**, its cabinet painted with two fine medieval Christian scenes. Dating from the 14th century, it's the oldest playable organ in the world, and an annual organ festival celebrates its musical virtues.

The château complex also houses the **Musée Cantonal d'Histoire** (History Museum), which displays a wide array of medieval sacristy chests and religious artifacts. Expanded exhibits trace daily life and advances in the canton from these early centuries to present day, including soccer championships. Explanations are in three languages, including English. Guided tours are conducted from March through October at quarter past the hour. ☎ 027/6064670 ⬚ *Church 3 SF; museum 6 SF; combination ticket 7 SF* ⊘ *Church June–Sept., Tues.–Sat. 10–5, Sun. 2–5. Museum June–Sept., Tues.–Sun. 11–6; Oct.–May, Tues.–Sun. 11–5.*

The **Old Town,** down rue de Lausanne (take a left when leaving the tourist office on the place de la Planta), is a blend of shuttered 16th-century houses, modern shops, and a host of sights worth seeing.

> ## WORTH THE EFFORT
>
> To reach the Musée Cantonal d'Histoire, you'll have to trek up uneven stone walkways and steep staircases, but you won't regret it.

The grand old **Maison Supersaxo** (House of Supersaxo), tucked into a passageway off rue Supersaxo, was built in 1505 by Georges Supersaxo, the local governor, to put his rivals to shame. This extravagantly decorated building includes a Gothic staircase and a grand hall, whose painted wood ceiling is a dazzling work of decorative art. ⬚ *passage Supersaxo* ⬚ *Free* ⊘ *Weekdays 2–5.*

The imposing **Hôtel de Ville** (Town Hall) has extraordinary historic roots: though it was built in the 1650s, it has transplanted stones in the entrance bearing Roman inscriptions, including a Christian symbol from the year AD 377. The 17th-century doors are richly carved wood, and the tower displays an astronomical clock. Upstairs, the **Salle du Conseil** (Council Hall) is also adorned with ornate woodwork. The only way to visit the Hôtel de Ville is by taking a guided walking tour of the town, which costs 8 SF and leaves from the Sion tourist office. Tours are held from July to the end of August on Tuesday, Thursday, and Saturday mornings plus Wendesday afternoon. ⬚ *rue de Conthey and rue du Grand-Pont* ⬚ *Free with walking tour.*

NEED A BREAK?

It's a tight squeeze to get into Old Town's popular *vinotek* (wine store–tasting room) Le Verre à Pied (⬚ 29 rue du Grand-Pont ☎ 027/3211380), where 150 regional vintages are poured. For a few francs you can join winemakers and enthusiasts who swill and sip.

The **Musée Cantonal d'Archéologie** (Museum of Archaeology) displays a collection of excavated pieces, including fine Roman works found in Valais. The narrow, cobbled rue des Châteaux, which leads up toward the twin fortifications, passes graceful old patrician houses, among them the museum. ⬚ *12 rue des Châteaux* ☎ 027/6064670 ⬚ *4 SF* ⊘ *June–Sept., Tues.–Sun. 1–6; Oct.–May, Tues.–Sun. 1–5.*

The cathedral, **Notre-Dame du Glarier** (Our Lady of Glarier), is dominated by its Romanesque tower, built in the Lombard, or Italian, style and dating from the 12th century. The rest of the church is late Gothic in style. ⊠ *Rue de la Cathédrale.*

Just across from the cathedral, the **Tour des Sorciers** (Sorcerers' Tower) is the last remnant of the walls that once ringed the town. ⊠ *rue de la Tour.*

Where to Stay & Eat

$–$$$ ✕ **L'Enclos de Valère.** If you've worked up an appetite climbing the Tourbillon, you may want to stop in this Old Town eatery on your way back down. Unfussy service, fine regional cuisine, and a rustic-cottage setting make it a sentimental favorite. Seasonal items—mushrooms, asparagus, shellfish, and game—lend variety to the upscale menu. When it's not mealtime, drop in for a coffee or a *channe* (pitcher) of wine. ⊠ *18 rue des Châteaux* ☎ *027/3233230* ⚐ *Reservations essential* ⊟ *AE, DC, MC, V* ⊘ *Closed Sun. evening and Mon. and Oct.–Apr.*

$–$$ ✕ **Au Cheval Blanc.** Set on one of Old Town's cobblestone streets, this congenial bistro is bustling around noon, when locals take their midday meal accompanied by a glass of gamay or Walliser (beer). *Entrecôte avec frites* (steak and fries) and *moules à la marinière* (mussels in white wine and parsley butter) hold top billing with such traditional dishes as *civet de chevreuil* with spaetzle (venison stew served with dumplings). ⊠ *23 rue du Grand-Pont* ☎ *027/3221867* ⊟ *AE, DC, MC, V* ⊘ *Closed Sun. and Mon. and last 2 wks of Dec.*

$–$$ ⊞ **Hôtel des Vignes.** For a hotel with character, head a few kilometers east of Sion to the village of Uvrier to find this sienna-color palazzo flanked by vineyards. The welcoming lobby has a central fireplace and a fountain; guest rooms are done in warm peach. ⊠ *9 rue du Pont, CH-1958 Uvrier* ☎ *027/2031671* ⊟ *027/2033727* ⊕ *www.hoteldesvignes.ch* ⊋ *33 rooms, 10 suites* ⚐ *Restaurant, tea shop, cable TV, driving range, 2 tennis courts, indoor pool, sauna, Turkish bath, bar, laundry service, helipad, free parking* ⊟ *AE, DC, MC, V* ⊘ *Closed end of Dec.–mid-Jan.* ⦿ *BP.*

$ ⊞ **Du Rhône.** The reception area of this cinder block property has a dated feel, with brown furniture and tired accents. The guest rooms are livelier, done in red, green, and blue with exhibition posters from the Fondation Pierre Gianadda. Operating under the Best Western flag, the lodging is located at the edge of Old Town and is handy to the castle walks. Consider it a comfortable, no-frills base. ⊠ *10 rue de Scex, CH-1950* ☎ *027/3228291* ⊟ *027/3231188* ⊕ *www.bestwestern.com* ⊋ *44 rooms* ⚐ *Restaurant, in-room safes, minibars, cable TV, in-room data ports, bar, parking (fee), no-smoking rooms* ⊟ *AE, DC, MC, V* ⦿ *BP.*

Nightlife & the Arts

Sion attracts world-class musicians and scholars to its festivals celebrating the medieval organ in its church-fortress. The **Festival International de l'Orgue Ancien Valère** (International Festival of the Ancient Valère Organ ☎ 027/3235767) takes place from July through late August.

Val d'Hérémence

16 km (10 mi) south of Sion.

❻ Across Route 9 and past Vex, a right fork takes you up a narrow mountain road and into the Val d'Hérémence. Here you'll find the **Barrage de la Grande Dixence,** a gargantuan monolith of concrete built in the mid-1960s at the improbable altitude of 7,754 feet. Only the Swiss could have accomplished such a feat of Alpine engineering—an achievement that brings them millions of kilowatt-hours of electricity every year. You can walk the rim of the dam and view the pristine lake either by taking a cable car or by hiking to the top on the marked trail. Sturdy trekkers can take the ibex trail, a four-hour loop through the region's watershed. There is a museum with exhibits explaining the construction and a tour down to operating sections of the dam. ☎ *027/3284311* ⊕ *www. grande-dixence.ch* ✉ *Museum 10 SF, cable car 7 SF, combination 15 SF* ☯ *Mid-June–Sept., daily. Museum 9–6; cable car every 10 min 9:30–12:15 and 1:15–6:25; tours 11:30,1:30, 4:30.*

Val d'Hérens

28 km (14 mi) southeast of Sion.

❼ If you take the left (east) fork south of Vex, you'll drive up the Val d'Hérens, where the road transforms into a rural byway often edged in solid rock. As you wind farther into the valley's confines, passing an oncoming car can require precision gauging. Here are the **Pyramides d'Euseigne,** a group of bizarre geological formations: stone pillars formed by the debris of glacial moraines and protected by hard-rock caps from the erosion that carved away the material around them. The effect is that of enormous, freestanding stalagmites wearing hats. A car tunnel has been carved through the bases of three of them.

In a broad, fertile section of the valley sits **Évolène,** a town of ramshackle mazots and wooden houses edged with flower-filled window boxes that provide a picturesque setting for vacationers—mostly French—and mountaineers, who tackle nearby Mont-Collon and the Dent Blanche. If you're lucky, you'll see some of the older women villagers in the traditional dress of kerchiefs and flowered cottons they still favor. Travel farther into the valley to **Les Haudères,** little more than a scattering of chalets in a spectacular, isolated mountain valley. For those seeking a total retreat into the Alpine reaches, continue into the Val d'Arolla, where the road ends in the tiny resort village of **Arolla** (6,555 feet), home to mountain guides and skiers.

CONVERSION DE LA VALLÉE

Secured above the plateau north of Sierre and Leuk are the ski towns of Crans and Montana and the hot springs resort of Leukerbad, each with a different personality. Crans-Montana offers expansive skiing, pricey boutiques, and clubby restaurants. Though Leukerbad also has first-class hotels and ski runs (albeit fewer), it is the restorative pools and spas and authentic Alpine village that attract visitors here. Along this stretch of the Rhône, the switchback of language and culture begins. The Valais, as it is referred to by French speakers, is called Wallis by locals with Germanic ties. To the south the remote Val d'Anniviers offers a glimpse of a simpler life before high-speed lifts and Internet cafés.

Crans-Montana

❽ To & From: *Operators of SMC (Sierre Mollens Crans-Montana), the funicular and bus service that connects the city of Sierre with the famous ski and golf villages of Crans-Montana make it a snap to find the funicular departure point for a speedy ascent to the sunny communities. Once outside the rail station, cross the street and look for the red lines designating the pathway. Follow the colored stripes for the five-minute walk through the central business district to the funi. The ride (12 min) in roomy red and white cabins delivers passengers to the Montana side of town where free shuttle buses disperse guests to hotels and chalets. If this transfer seems too cumbersome, board the SMC motor coaches waiting in the parking area adjacent to the station for a half hour switchback ride through vineyards and forest (12 SF). Log on to www. cie-smc.ch for funicular and bus schedules. Crans-Montana is 12 km (7 mi) northwest of Sierre, 19 km (12 mi) northesast of Sion.*

This well-known twin sports center rises above the valley on a steep, sheltered shelf at 4,904 feet. It commands a broad view across the Rhône Valley to the peaks of the Valaisan Alps, and its grassy and wooded plateau gets the benefit of Sierre's sunshine. Behind the towns, the **Rohrbachstein** (9,686 feet), the **Gletscherhorn** (9,653 feet), and the **Wildstrubel** (10,637 feet) combine to create a complex of challenging ski slopes. The most direct route to Crans-Montana is from Sierre, just southeast, either by car, postbus, or funicular.

The resort towns themselves are highly developed and uncaptivating, lacking the regional color and grace of Zermatt. The streets are lined with designer boutiques and hotels. Car traffic is almost always heavy, so it's best to get around on foot or shuttle bus. As in other resorts, signs point the way to the hotels. The crowds are young, wealthy, and international, roving in cocoons of the fit, fun-loving, and fashionable.

10

Skiing

The pearl of the region is the **Plaine Morte,** a flat glacier 5 km–6 km (3 mi–3½ mi) long, which is perched like a pancake at an elevation of 9,840 feet and has snow year-round. A cross-country ski trail (watch out for your lungs at this altitude) of 10 km–12 km (6 mi–7½ mi) is open and maintained here seven months of the year. The ascent on the gondola from **Violettes Plaines-Morte,** virtually under assault by crowds during the high season and in good weather, will in itself justify your

SEPTEMBER SWINGS

Every September, the 18-hole golf course at Crans-Montana is the site of the annual European Masters, a period the locals describe as "party week."

stay in Crans-Montana. Expert skiers may prefer the **Nationale Piste**, site of previous world championships. The incredibly steep-pitched **La Toula** is a challenge for pros. The eastern section of the ski area connects to Aminona, where a park for snowboarders and a bobsled run drop from **Petit Bonvin**, at 7,874 feet. A one-day lift ticket costs 57 SF; a six-day pass costs 279 SF, permitting access to 160 km (100 mi) of runs and more than 30 ways to ride to the top. There are several classic cross-country ski circuits atop the golf courses and around the village lakes.

Where to Stay & Eat

$–$$ ✕ **Le Chalet.** On the shopping promenade in Crans, an adorable stucco cottage trimmed in carved wood and stenciling holds one of the village's favorite spots for specialty fondues and raclette au feu de bois (on the wood fire). It's so popular with locals that it doesn't close between seasons. All is not cheesy as the grill turns out exceptional meat and fish dishes. A large sunny terrace (also heated) holds diners even on the coldest days. ⊠ *rte. du Prado* 🕾 *027/4810505* 🖃 *AE, DC, MC, V.*

¢ ✕ **Taillens.** Regardless of which side of town you're on, these overflowing sibling coffee shops with exquisite pastries are a must-stop before or after an activity packed day. Light meals—salads, soups, and sandwiches—keep service clipping along at a fast pace. Toss aside the calorie counter and peruse the desert cases for a decadent concoction of chocolate, sugar, and whipped cream. ⊠ *ave. de la Gare Montana* 🕾 *027/4817361* ✉ *Grand Pl. Crans* 🕾 *027/4854082* 🖃 *MC, V.*

$$$$ ✕🖃 **L'Hostellerie du Pas de l'Ours.** In a town known for blocklike tow-
Fodor'sChoice ers, this petite auberge with its preserved wooden facade stands out. Plush
★ and rich with amenities, the roomy suite-apartments have polished wood floors, stucco walls, balconies, fireplaces, and Jacuzzis. The restaurant ($$$–$$$$) draws a chic crowd, thanks to superb French cuisine such as almond-roasted lamb with apricot reduction; book well in advance for a table. Spa L'Alpage is a prime spot to rejuvenate after a day of skiing or hiking the trails. ⊠ *rue du Pas de l'Ours, CH-3963 Crans* 🕾 *027/4859333* 🖷 *027/4859334* ⊕ *www.pasdelours, ch* 🛏 *9 suites* ♨ *Restaurant, café, in-room safes, minibars, cable TV, in-room data ports, indoor-outdoor pool, sauna, steam room, gym, spa, bar, free parking* 🖃 *AE, DC, MC, V* ☺ *Closed May and Nov.* ¶◎ *CP.*

$$$–$$$$ ✕🖃 **Aïda-Castel.** This warm and welcoming complex has kept pace with the times. Its moderately isolated hillside, though quiet, requires a shuttle or uphill walk to activities. Public areas have carved or aged wood, stone, and stucco; the rooms, sturdy Alpine furniture, wrought iron, and stenciling. South-facing balconies fill with afternoon sun worshippers. The very popular public restaurant, La Hotte ($$–$$$$), serves Italian fare, some prepared on the open grill, as well as raclette made at the fireside—it's so good, reservations are essential. ⊠ *rue du Béthania, CH-3963 Montana* 🕾 *027/4854111* 🖷 *027/4817062* ⊕ *www. aida-castel.ch* 🛏 *56 rooms, 4 suites* ♨ *3 restaurants, minibars, cable TV, pool, exercise equipment, massage, sauna, Turkish bath, bar, free parking* 🖃 *AE, DC, MC, V* ¶◎ *MAP.*

★ $$$–$$$$ ✕🖃 **Hôtel LeTerminus.** Travelers bound for the uphill resorts detour to Chef-hotelier Didier de Courten's contemporary conversion in the center of Sierre. One of the country's highest-rated chefs fills the tables of his gourmet atelier and upscale brasserie with food and wine enthusiasts who admire his creativity in dishes like peppered venison medallions with red cabbage and spiced pear marmalade. Sleek design elements from the restaurant are repeated behind the red door guest rooms outfitted with crisp white-on-white linens and colorful leather seating. L'Ampelos, the wine bar, offers an extensive sampling of top Swiss and international vintages. Reserve a table and room in advance, this is a popular stand alone destination. ⊠ *rue du Bourg 1, CH-3960 Sierre* ☎ *027/4551351* 🖨 *027/4534491* ⊕ *www.hotel-terminus.ch* 🛏 *18 rooms, 2 suites ♨ 2 restaurants, Wi-Fi, in-room safes, minibars, cable TV, pool, bar, free parking, no-smoking rooms* ⊟ *AE, DC, MC, V* ⭫⭐ *CP* ⊙ *Closed Christmas–mid–Jan.*

$$$$ 🏨 **Alpina & Savoy.** A third generation of the Mudry family oversees this rambling hotel on convenient middle ground between the two villages. Secluded in a hilltop park, it is buffered from the main thoroughfare by enormous evergreens. A shuttle service offers links in both directions, and the Crans-Cry-d'Err cable car is a five-minute walk uphill. Rooms, outfitted with familiar heavy furnishings and damask coverlets, undergo seasonal spruce-ups but remain homey, luring repeat guests. Activity areas, though a bit worn, are full of options, from games to workout equipment to a pool. An in-house spa is a plus, and the demipension meal plan means you won't have to vie for a reservation in town. ⊠ *rte. du Rawyl, CH-3963 Crans* ☎ *027/4850900* 🖨 *027/4850999* ⊕ *www.alpinasavoy.ch* 🛏 *45 rooms, 5 suites ♨ Restaurant, Stübli, minibars, cable TV, indoor pool, exercise equipment, sauna, spa, steam room, billiards, Ping-Pong, piano bar, video game room, free parking* ⊟ *AE, DC, MC, V* ⊙ *Closed mid-Sept.–mid-Dec. and mid-Apr.–mid-June* ⭫⭐ *MAP.*

$$$$ 🏨 **Grand Hôtel du Golf.** This grand, genteel, blue-blooded oasis offers urbane taste with few of life's nicks and scrapes. Built by English golfers in 1907, it feels like a country clubhouse—gold and burgundy with a dash of floral, tassels, and fringe. The hotel has been modernized outside and attentively tended within, with finely turned-out rooms done in teal and rose. In addition to a formal dining salon there is a casual restaurant option serving Lebanese cuisine. Manicured grounds adjoin 9- and 18-hole golf courses, and a spa adds pampering and beauty treatments. In addition to the Dabliù Beauty Farm, there is a medical oriented spa, the Swiss Health Center, that pampers and treats guests. ⊠ *rte. du Rawyl, CH-3963 Crans* ☎ *027/4854242* 🖨 *027/4854243* ⊕ *www.grand-hotel-du-golf.ch* 🛏 *76 rooms, 8 suites, 2 apartments ♨ 2 restaurants, Wi-Fi, cable TV with movie, in-room VCRs, indoor pool, gym, hair salon, sauna, spa, Turkish bath, piano bar, concierge, Internet, business services, free parking* ⊟ *AE, DC, MC, V* ⭫⭐ *BP.*

$$–$$$ 🏨 **Mirabeau.** Done in pastels straight out of suburbia, this attractive midtown property keeps working at self-improvement, expanding activity areas and fluffing guest quarters. Views (of the street and other hotels) aren't spectacular, but the hotel *is* at the hub of the downtown dining and shopping scene, enabling you to park in the garage and leave your car until departure. After a day on the trails, pick up a game of pool in the lounge or soothe tired muscles in the sauna. ⊠ *CH-3962 Montana*

10

☎ *027/4802151* 🖷 *027/4813912* ⊕ *www.hotel-mirabeau.ch* ↩ *40
rooms, 10 apartments* ⌂ *Restaurant, in-room safes, minibars, cable TV,
Wi-Fi, gym, hot tub, sauna, billiards, bar, business center, parking (fee)*
⊟ *AE, DC, MC, V* ⦿ *CP.*

$–$$$ 🏨 **Hôtel de l'Etrier.** A sweeping roofline, stone entry, and larch trim have
an appropriately Alpine feel. Inside the butterscotch colored walls and
raised hearth fireplace warm the lobby, which boasts floor-to-ceiling win-
dows that frame golf course greens and southern mountains. Generous-
size guest rooms are uninspired, furnished with traditional heavy furniture
and white duvets. Amenities like a heated pool, spa, and multiple din-
ing options are shared with the property's stylish sister hotel Pas de l'Ours.
⊠ *rte. Pas de l'Ours, CH-3963 Crans* ☎ *027/4854400* 🖷 *027/4817610*
⊕ *www.hoteletrier.ch* ↩ *50 rooms, 9 suites* ⌂ *3 restaurants, Stübli, in-
room safes, in-room data ports, minibars, cable TV, indoor-outdoor pool,
sauna, spa, steam room, bar, video game room, Internet, free parking;
no a/c* ⊟ *AE, DC, MC, V* ⦿ *CP.*

$ 🏨 **Le Mont-Paisible.** One of the hotel directors, an architect, lent his de-
sign expertise and eye for interiors to this lookout lodge, which takes
in the sweep of Valaisan mountains. Slate floors, colorful stenciled fur-
niture, and a raised-hearth fireplace set a sophisticated yet rustic mood.
Paneled rooms with built-in furniture and a small sitting area are well
thought out. The terrific location is away from the village hubbub but
near the Violettes cable car station. ⊠ *chemin du Mont-Paisible, CH-
3962 Montana* ☎ *027/4802161* 🖷 *027/4817792* ⊕ *www.montpaisible.
ch* ↩ *40 rooms* ⌂ *Restaurant, Stübli, in-room safes, cable TV, in-room
data ports, Wi-Fi, sauna, tennis court, bar, free parking* ⊟ *AE, DC, MC,
V* ⦿ *BP.*

Nightlife

BARS & DANCING If you've ever wondered what Salvador Dalí would have produced if
he'd illustrated a vodka ad, then head for poster-filled **Absolut** (☎ 079/
2136139), a Crans nightclub where martini-swilling and swaying don't
get started until after 11 PM. Book a table online at ⊕ www.absolutclub.
ch. The dance floor buzzes at **Le Barocke** (☎ 079/2211635), around the
corner from Absolut, in Crans. If music, videos, and shots à Gogo in-
terest you, **Monk's** (☎ 079/4093285), in Crans, is a hot, primate-theme
venue with noshes. Up in Montana, the small but convivial **Amadeus**
(☎ 027/4812985), beneath the Olympic Hotel, is a popular après-ski
venue. **Le Tirbouchon** (☎ 027/4802608) is a chummy little blue-and-
gold trimmed wine bar in Montana where you can catch up on regional
vintages.

CASINO Roulette, blackjack, poker, and an abundance of slot machines are
among the games you can play at the high-stakes **Casino Crans-Montana**
(☎ 027/4859040), in Montana. You can also just stop in for a drink or
dinner, as there is no pressure to play. The casino is open 10 AM–4 AM;
you'll need your passport for admission.

Sports & the Outdoors

BICYCLING The Tour de Suisse and other top-name bike competitions pass through
the streets during racing season. Serious amateur mountain bikers can
test the obstacle course set up in the parking lot of the Crans-Cry-d'Err

cable car or the downhill practice run. Cycling enthusiasts find a full range of clothing and bike rentals at **Avalanche Pro Shop** (✉ Montana ☏ 027/4802424). **Montana Sports** (☏ 027/4812288) is a convenient shop, providing bikes for rent and information about the 16 marked trails that radiate from the resort. They can also tell you which lifts to use to gain altitude without pedaling. For a different orientation on downhill, try one of the big-wheel, monster 4X4 bikes.

BOATING **Lac Grenon and Lac Moubra,** two crystalline lakes near the connected villages, are filled with pedal boats and windsurfers on long summer days. Rentals are available at shoreside kiosks. Wakeboarding and waterskiing services are available on **Lake Etang.**

GOLF With four in-town courses (one 18-hole, three 9-hole), Crans-Montana is a golfer's destination. One of the 9-hole courses was designed by Jack Nicklaus; the full course, designed by and named for Severiano Ballesteros, is a challenge. A driving range and video simulator help even the best handicappers improve their strokes. For more information, contact **Golf Club Crans** (☏ 027/4859797), the organization that oversees all the golf courses in town.

HIKING Networks of well marked trails (280 km [215 mi]) branch out from both villages, sometimes intersecting but more often leading in opposite directions. Unless you want to scale higher peaks, all that is needed is a good pair of boots and a map to guide you to signed pathways through open terrain, forests, or along the bisses (irrigation channels). Keep an eye out for fast paced nordic walkers (power hikers using ski poles). If it's an extreme challenge you're looking for, contact the pros at **Bureau Officiel des Guides** (☏ 027/4811480) for gear and guidance.

SWIMMING If your hotel doesn't have a swimming pool or wellness center, head over to **Club Hotel Valaisia** (✉ Montana ☏ 027/4812612). The lower-level complex, open to the public, has a large saltwater pool with jets and currents, hot tubs, and cold plunges. Additional services include sauna, steam, and massage.

TENNIS **Centre de Congrès & Sports** (✉ Crans ☏ 027/4811615) has five indoor and two outdoor tennis courts as well as squash courts. **Centre de Tennis** (✉ Montana ☏ 027/8415014) calls itself the largest tennis center in the Alps, with five indoor and six outdoor clay courts. Both centers offer private and group lessons.

Shopping

At times, the streets of stylish Crans can feel like a fashion runway, with the leather and fur-trimmed crowd hidden behind logo sunglasses and cashmere hats. This tiny village has assembled the most high-end shops and designer boutiques in the entire region—many only open in season. Don't be deceived by its name, at **Alex Sports** (✉ rue du Prado ☏ 0274614061) you'll find labels such as Bogner, Escada, Ralph Lauren, and Zegna. And, yes, you can buy a down jacket or rent a pair of skis. Around the corner **Attitude** (✉ rue Central ☏ 027/4812080), a women's specialty shop, houses equally notable names including Burberry, Gucci, and Prada. If it's jewelry or watches you're looking for, you'll find them in the storefronts of rue du Prado tucked in between Hermès, Chanel, and Louis Vuitton.

EN
ROUTE
Split between the towns of Sierre/Siders and Salquenen/Salgesch, the **Musée Valaisan de la Vigne et du Vin** (Valaisan Vine and Wine Museum) offers a two-part discovery of grape growing and wine making. To follow the process in order, start at the Zumofenhaus, a winemaker's home, in Salgesch and conclude at Château Villa, a merchant's villa, in Sierre. A walking path through the vineyards connects the two exhibits. The Villa also houses a restaurant and tasting shop. ⊠ *Château de Villa, 4 rue Ste-Catherine, Sierre* ☎ *027/4551986* ⊠ *Zumofenhaus, Salgesch* ☎ *027/4564525* ⊕ *www.museevalaisanduvin.ch* ⊠ *5 SF* ☉ *Villa daily 10:30–1 and 4:30–8:30; Zumofenhaus Apr.–Nov., Tues.–Fri. 2–5.*

Val d'Anniviers

25 km (16 mi) south of Sierre.

❾ If you drive east of Sierre and south of the Rhône, following signs for Vissoie, you enter a wild and craggy valley called Val d'Anniviers. The name is said to come from its curious and famous (among anthropologists, at least) nomads, known in Latin as *anni viatores* (year-round travelers). If you don't have time to follow the lengthy gorge to its end, climb the switchback road to the tiny village of **St-Luc** for a taste of rural life and celestial viewing at the observatory. In summer you can continue down a narrow forest road to **Grimentz**, with the Weisshorn dominating the views. With a population of 370, this ancient 13th-century village has preserved its weathered-wood houses and mazots in its tiny center. **Zinal**, farther into the valley, is another isolated mountaineering center with well-preserved wood houses and mazots. A stopover in any one of these windswept mountain hideouts to walk, climb, ski, or relax by the fire is a reward. In late September when the herds are brought down from the mountians, there is a seasonal celebration and sporting event featuring fighting cows.

Where to Stay & Eat

★ **$$–$$$$** ✕🏨 **Bella Tola.** Stepping stones lead to the wrought iron entry of this stately, multistory mansion perched above the main road. A mountain retreat since the late 1800s, the designer setting mixes antiques and collectibles, with sepia photos, rippled mirrors, orchids, and fur pillows—the handiwork of the wife of the genial hotelier team. Floors creak and window frames sigh in cozy guest quarters that have hung on to their character through various updates. Gourmet dining (à la carte or demi-pension) is part of the top drawer ambience as is an ultramodern, grottolike pool and spa. ⊠ *CH-3961 St-Luc* ☎ *027/4751444* 🖷 *027/ 4752998* ⊕ *www.bellatola.ch* 🛏 *32 rooms* ♨ *2 restaurants, cable TV, in-room data ports, indoor pool, hot tub, massage, sauna, steam room, bar, lobby lounge, no-smoking rooms* ☰ *AE, DC, MC, V* ⊙Ⅼ *MAP* ☉ *Closed mid-Apr.–mid-June and mid-Oct.–mid-Dec.*

$ ✕🏨 **De Moiry.** This family-run country inn is draped in a profusion of geraniums in summertime and bundled in snowbanks in winter. Rooms are walled in pine and larch, with carved furniture and mounds of white

CLOSE UP

A Trail of Two Cultures

THE LINE BETWEEN FRENCH and German settlements in the Valais (also known as Wallis) is imperceptible. At a restaurant a server may speak French to one group of diners and German to the next. It's called "bilingue." Locals drop in and out of languages at the drop of a chapeau (or *Hut*), even if one language prevails as their native tongue.

On the wine trail that's called the *sentier viticole* at one end and the *rebweg* at the other, you cross that imaginary boundary somewhere between the Walliser Reb und Weinmuseum and the Musée Valaisan de la Vigne et du Vin, which comprise a museum dedicated to wine and wine growing. The two parts of this museum complement each other and the two cultures, as do the towns in which they are located: Salquenen and Sierre in French, Salgesch and Siders, respectively, in German. (You may choose to start at either end of the trail, though to follow the wine-growing and winemaking processes in order, you'll have to begin your journey in Salgesch/Salquenen.)

Germanic roots are visible in the converted farmhouse museum, the Zumofenhaus, in Salgesch. The multilevel, double-gabled structure has low rooms and is built of stucco and worn timbers in a style found in Bernese villages on the other side of the mountains. The size and comfort of the vineyard owner's home—including a basement press and cave and upper and lower family quarters—indicates that he was successful. Exhibits here focus on the agriculture of the vineyard, including the *terroir* (soil), cultivation techniques, and seasonal chores.

Outside the museum a well-marked trail (6–7 km [4 mi]) leads past current growers' homes into the vineyard. Here panels explain the grape varieties in the long rows of vines, which are shored up by trellises and stone walls. Traditional varietals Pinot Noir, Chasselas, and Gamay, long the mainstays of Valaisan wine production, are being eased out by Humagne Rouge, Humagne Blanche, Petite Arvine, Amigne, Syrah, and lesser-known Malvoisie, Cornalin, and Marsanne Blanche.

The path dips downhill into a forested nature preserve along the Gorge Raspille, filled with boulders brought down from jagged ridgelines. Unusual pyramidlike formations emerge on a chalky wall, and a network of channels used to feed the hot vineyard floor fans out from the streambed.

The turreted entry and architecture of Château de Villa is decidedly French. It's an estate home of grand proportions with gardens and salons converted into a restaurant that serves typically Valaisan dishes. The actual wine museum is housed in the manor's outbuildings. At this end of the trail, the focus is on winemaking.

10

The whole experience takes about three or four hours, two of which are spent on the walk. In that short period, you will have made the transition from German to French culture without knowing exactly where you crossed the invisible border. Since wine is the universal language, a tasting at L'Oenotheque (the wine store) is the perfect conclusion. Santé or Gesundheit, whichever toast you prefer.

linen on the beds. Hikers and skiers gather on the porch or near the stone hearth in the dining room ($–$$) for raclette bubbling off the open fire. Ask the owner, who's an experienced mountain guide and photographer, to show you some of his work; it will leave you breathless. ⊠ *CH-3961 Grimentz* ☎ *027/4751144* 🖷 *027/4752823* ⊕ *www.hoteldemoiry.ch* 🗷 *16 rooms* ⚗ *Restaurant, cable TV, Wi-Fi, no-smoking rooms* ⊟ *AE, DC, MC, V* ⋈ *CP.*

HIKING   Walk through the universe on an astronomically themed 6 km (4 mi) trail called **Le Chemin des Planètes.** Integrity in size and distance has been maintained in planetary stations set along a pathway that begins at the base of the **Observatoire François-Xavier Bangoud** (☎ 027/4755808 ⊕ www.ofxb.ch). Explanations about scientific elements and planet relationships are in French. The Tignousa funnicular delivers you to the starting point at 2,200 meters (7,218 feet). Allow two hours to make the ascent from there, past the Hotel Weishorn. Celestial viewing using the reflecting and refracting telescopes plus camera are held at the mountaintop observatory.

Leukerbad

 21 km (13 mi) northeast of Sierre.

At 4,628 feet, Leukerbad is Europe's highest spa village; travelers have been ascending to this Alpine retreat for centuries to take the curative waters and fill their lungs with cleansing mountain air. With 90 km (43 mi) of downhill and cross-country runs of varying difficulty, including some used for World Cup training and testing, Leukerbad is a pleasant alternative to the larger resorts and its rejuvenating hot mineral pools are soothing for après-ski. The Torrent gondola whisks skiers to slopes; a one-day ski pass including a visit to one of the public spas is 62 SF; a six-day pass is 314 SF. Without the spa visit, ski passes cost 44 SF and 223 SF, respectively.

Summer brings hikers who love the combination of trekking and soaking. High-altitude crossings via the Gemmi Pass go back to 500 BC. The ancient connection between the Valais and the Berner Oberland can be traversed easily in a day.

Calcium sulphite hot springs flow beneath the village, filling stone troughs with warm vapor, keeping thoroughfares free of snow, and circulating to private tubs and public pools daily. In the late 1960s an arthritis and rheumatism treatment facility was established, but it has since been overshadowed by upscale wellness hotels and sports clinics.

The two largest bath facilities in Leukerbad are Burgerbad and Alpentherme. Both have pools, fountains, whirlpools, jets, and sprays of thermal waters at a temperature of 35°C (100°F). Towels and robes can be rented at the reception desk.

> **DRINK TO YOUR HEALTH**
>
> Don't forget to drink a glass of water from the tap in Leukerbad—it's touted to have added health benefits.

The multilevel **Burgerbad,** with both indoor and outdoor pools, resembles an aqua park and is often packed with families clad in multicolor swim gear. The facility also has exercise rooms, a sauna, solarium, and snack bar. ✉ *Rathausstr.* ☎ *027/4722020* ⊕ *www.burgerbad.ch* 💶 *22 SF* ☉ *Daily 8–10.*

★ Sporting expansive Palladian windows set in marble, the **Lindner Alpentherme** looks like a temple perched on the hill. It has facilities similar to the Bugerbad but in a more sophisticated setting. Annexes contain a beauty center, medical complex, and shopping arcade that includes a pharmacy specializing in natural remedies, *confiserie* (pastry shop), and juice bar. The unique spa treatment here is the *Bain Romano-Irlandais* (Roman-Irish bath), a two-hour succession of hot and cold soaks and vapor treatments. Massage, herbal wraps, scrubs, and medical consultations are also on the menu. Children under six aren't allowed at this spa. ✉ *Dorfpl.* ☎ *027/4721010* 💶 *25 SF* ☉ *Daily 8–10.*

Where to Stay & Eat

$–$$$$ ✕▥ **Lindner Alpenhof.** Two hotels, Maison Blanche and the Hotel de France, are merged under one banner. The more regal Maison Blanche, which hosts reception for both, has guest rooms and salons that take a contemporary approach, using the colors of wheat and sage to create a soothing mood. Across the plaza the Hotel de France imitates the village's Alpine roots with knotty woods and gingham checks. Alpentherme, the village's posh bath and spa complex, is under the same ownership, and an underground walkway permits you to tread to your appointment in robe and slippers. Packages include admission and treatments. Restaurant choices follow the ambience of each location: glitzy hotel dining room ($$$–$$$$) and convivial brasserie, Sacré Bon($–$$$). ✉ *Dorfpl., CH-3954* ☎ *027/4721000* 🖷 *027/4721001* ⊕ *www.lindnerhotels.ch* 🛏 *123 rooms, 12 suites* ⚖ *2 restaurants, in-room safes, minibars, cable TV, 2 tennis courts, indoor-outdoor pool, health club, spa, piano bar, parking (fee)* ▭ *MC, V* ⦿ *CP.*

★ ¢–$$ ✕▥ **Waldhaus Grichting.** This is the prototypical *relais de campagne* (country inn): honey-color wood, cheerful rooms, and a vivacious proprietress. Set on a forested hillside convenient to both the Alpentherme and the Torrent station, this expanded chalet seems more like a private home than a hotel. The Stübli ($–$$) attracts locals for raclette and the daily special, and hotel guests are treated to a six-course meal in the dining room ($$–$$$), included in the price of the room. Pool and spa facilities are shared with a nearby sister hotel. ✉ *On Promenade, CH-3954* ☎ *027/4703232* 🖷 *027/4704525* ⊕ *www.grichting-hotels.ch* 🛏 *16 rooms* ⚖ *Restaurant, Stübli, cable TV, bar, parking (fee)* ▭ *MC, V* ⦿ *MAP.*

10

ALPINE ZENTRUM

Immediately east of Sierre, you'll notice a sharp change: *vals* become *tals,* and the sounds you overhear at your next pit stop are no longer the mellifluous tones of the Suisse Romande but the lilting, guttural Swiss-German dialect called Wallisertiitsch, a local form of Schwyzerdütsch.

Welcome to Wallis (*vahl*-is), the Germanic end of Valais. This sharp demographic frontier can be traced back to the 6th century, when Alemannic tribes poured over the Grimsel Pass and penetrated as far as Sierre. Here the middle-class cuisine changes from steak frites to veal and *Rösti* (hash brown potatoes).

Zermatt

▶ **⑪** **To & From:** *Zermatt, the world's most famous car-free Alpine village,*
Fodor'sChoice *requires that residents and guests leave their vehicles in the village of*
★ *Täsch. Shuttle service (12 min,13 SF) is provided by train via a state-of-the-art station with adjacent decks of covered parking. Access to the commuter trains that run every 20 minutes is eased with ramps and luggage carts that roll onto the passenger cars. Five-star hotels like those in the Seiler group have separate valet terminals plus private transfer that can be booked with your room reservation. In addition, there are open lots where the rates are less expensive, but plan to add 8–14 SF per day to your vacation expenses. If you don't want to make the half-hour drive on mountain roads into the Mattertal Valley, use rail service that connects through Visp. The scenic ride will take about an hour; a first class ticket costs 53 SF. Zermatt is 28 km (18 mi) south of Visp, plus a 10 km (6 mi) train ride from Täsch.*

Despite its fame—which stems from that mythic mountain, the Matterhorn, and from its excellent ski facilities—Zermatt is a resort with its feet on the ground. It protects its regional quirks along with its wildlife and its tumbledown mazots, which crowd between glass-and-concrete chalets like old tenements between skyscrapers. Streets twist past weathered-wood walls, flower boxes, and haphazard stone roofs until they break into open country that slopes, inevitably, uphill. Despite the crowds, you're never far from the wild roar of the silty river and the peace of a mountain path.

In the mid-19th century, Zermatt was virtually unheard of; the few visitors who came to town stayed at the vicarage. The vicar and a chaplain named Joseph Seiler persuaded Seiler's little brother, Alexander, to start an inn. Opened in 1854 and named the Hotel Monte Rosa, it's still one of five Seiler hotels in Zermatt. In 1891, the cog railway between Visp and Zermatt took its first summer run and began disgorging tourists with profitable regularity—though it didn't plow through in wintertime until 1927. Today the town remains a car-free resort (there's a reason for those carriages). If you're traveling primarily by car, you can park it in the multistory terminal connected to the station in Täsch, where you catch the train into Zermatt.

Fodor'sChoice Hordes of package-tour sightseers push shoulder to shoulder to get yet
★ another shot of the **Matterhorn** (14,685 feet). Called one of the wonders of the Western world, the mountain deserves the title, though it has become an almost self-parodying icon, like the Eiffel Tower or the Empire State Building. Its peculiar snaggletooth form, free from competition from other peaks on all sides, rears up over the village, larger than life and genuinely awe-inspiring. As you leave the train station and weave

through pedestrian crowds, aggressive electric taxi carts, and aromatic horse-drawn carriages along the main street, Bahnhofstrasse, you're assaulted on all sides by Matterhorn images—on postcards, sweatshirts, calendars, beer steins, and candy wrappers—though not by the original, which is obscured by resort buildings (except from the windows of pricier hotel rooms). But break past the shops and hotels onto the main road into the hills, and you'll reach a slightly elevated spot where you'll probably stop dead in your tracks. There it is at last, its twist of snowy rock blinding in the sun, weathered mazots scattered romantically at its base. Surely more pictures are taken from this spot than from anywhere else in Switzerland.

It was Edward Whymper's spectacular—and catastrophic—conquest of the Matterhorn, on July 14, 1865, that made Zermatt a household word. Whymper stayed at the Hotel Monte Rosa before his departure and there named his party of seven for the historic climb: Michel Croz, a French guide; old Peter Taugwalder and his son, young Peter, local guides; Lord Francis Douglas, a 19-year-old Englishman; Douglas Hadow; the Reverend Charles Hudson; and Whymper himself. They climbed together, pairing "tourists," as Whymper called the Englishmen, with experienced locals. They camped at 11,000 feet and by 10 AM had reached the base of the mountain's famous hook. Wrote Whymper of the final moments:

The higher we rose the more intense became the excitement. The slope eased off, at length we could be detached, and Croz and I, dashing away, ran a neck-and-neck race, which ended in a dead heat. At 1:40 PM, the world was at our feet, and the Matterhorn was conquered!

Croz pulled off his shirt and tied it to a stick as a flag, one that was seen in Zermatt below. They stayed at the summit one hour, then prepared for the descent, tying themselves together in an order agreed on by all. Croz led, then Hadow, Hudson, Lord Douglas, the elder Taugwalder, then the younger, and Whymper, who lingered to sketch the summit and leave their names in a bottle.

I suggested to Hudson that we should attach a rope to the rocks on our arrival at the difficult bit, and hold it as we descended, as an additional protection. He approved the idea, but it was not definitely decided that it should be done.

They headed off, "one man moving at a time; when he was firmly planted the next advanced," Whymper recalled.

Croz . . . was in the act of turning around to go down a step or two himself; at this moment Mr. Hadow slipped, fell against him, and knocked him over. I heard one startled exclamation from Croz, then saw him and Mr. Hadow flying downward; in another moment Hudson was dragged from his steps, and Lord Douglas immediately after him. All this was the work of a moment. Immediately we heard Croz's exclamation, old Peter and I planted ourselves as firmly as the rocks would permit; the rope was taut between us, and the jerk came on us both as on one man. We held; but the rope broke midway between Taugwalder and Lord Fran-

cis Douglas. For a few seconds we saw our unfortunate companions slid-ing downward on their backs, and spreading out their hands, endeav-oring to save themselves. They passed from our sight uninjured, disappeared one by one, and fell from precipice to precipice on to the Matterhorn glacier below, a distance of nearly 4,000 feet in height. From the moment the rope broke it was impossible to help them. So perished our comrades!

A "sharp-eyed lad" ran into the Hotel Monte Rosa to report an avalanche fallen from the Matterhorn summit; he had witnessed the deaths of the four mountaineers. The body of young Lord Douglas was never recov-ered, but the others lie in little cemeteries behind the park near the vil-lage church, surrounded by scores of other failed mountaineers, including an American whose tomb bears the simple epitaph I CHOSE TO CLIMB.

In summer the streets of Zermatt fill with sturdy, weathered climbers, state-of-the-art ropes and picks hanging at their hips. They continue to tackle the peaks, and climbers have mastered the Matterhorn literally thousands of times since Whymper's disastrous victory.

It's quite simple to gain the broader perspective of high altitudes with-out risking life or limb. A train trip on the **Gornergrat–Monte Rose Bahn** functions as an excursion as well as ski transport. Part of its rail system was completed in 1898, and it's the highest open-air rail system in Europe (the tracks to the Jungfrau-joch, though higher, bore through the face of the Eiger). It connects out of the main Zermatt train station and heads sharply left, at a right angle to the track that brings you into town. Its stop at the **Riffel-berg,** at 8,469 feet, offers wide-

> **DID YOU KNOW?**
>
> Zermatt lies in a hollow of mead-ows and trees ringed by moun-tains—among them the broad **Monte Rosa** and its tallest peak, the **Dufourspitze** (at 15,200 feet, the highest point in Switzerland)—plus 36 others that tower above 13,000 feet—of which visitors hear relatively little, so all-consuming is the cult of the Matterhorn.

open views of the Matterhorn. Farther on, from **Rotenboden,** at 9,246 feet, a short downhill walk leads to the **Riffelsee,** which obligingly pro-vides photographers with a postcard-perfect reflection of the famous peak. At the end of the 9-km (5½-mi) line, the train stops at the summit sta-tion of **Gornergrat** (10,266 feet), and passengers pour onto the obser-vation terraces to take in the majestic views of the Matterhorn, Monte Rosa, Gorner Glacier, and an expanse of scores of peaks and 24 other glaciers. Make sure to bring warm clothes, sunglasses, and sturdy shoes, especially if you plan to ski or hike down. ⊠ *Zermatt station* ☎ *027/ 9214711* 🖭 *72 SF round-trip, 36 SF one-way* ☉ *Departures daily every 24 min, 7–6.*

🔾 To get a sense of life in this high-altitude region and climber's risks, visit the **Matterhorn Museum,** a sunken village of chalets, mazots, and dwellings depicted as an archaeological site, which visitors walk through, expe-riencing different periods of time along the way. The personal accounts

of local docents liven up the displays of antiquated equipment, clothing, and historical documents about those who lived and climbed here.
There is a farmer's cottage, hotel, and church interior, plus stuffed and
mounted animals. A multimedia film takes you atop the Matterhorn for
dramatic climate changes; an Internet center enables you to research questions on your own. ☎ *027/9674100* 🎞 *10 SF* ☉ *June–Oct., daily
10–noon and 3–6; Nov.–May, Mon.–Sat. 4–7.*

Climb the winding pathway behind the ski and snowboard school to
the white church on the hill, **St. Peter's** (The English Church). Anglican
services are still held in the tiny sanctuary established by the British who
ignited a climbing fervor to conquer the Matterhorn and other towering peaks in the region. Take time to pause in the cemetery that holds
the graves of those who were not fortunate enough to return safely and
others who remained in this beloved community to live out their lives.

Skiing
Zermatt's skiable terrain lives up to its reputation: the 63 lift installations are capable of moving well above 50,000 skiers per hour to reach
its approximately 313 km (194 mi) of marked pistes—if you count
those of Cervinia in Italy. Among the lifts are the cable car that carries
skiers up to an elevation of 12,746 feet on the Matterhorn Glacier Paradise (previously known as Klein Matterhorn), the small Gornergrat-
bahn that creeps up to the Gornergrat, and a subway through an
underground tunnel that gives more pleasure to ecologists than it does
to sun-loving skiers.

The skiable territory on this royal plateau was once separated into three
separate sectors, but the installation of a gondala to Riffelberg has linked
the three together. The first sector is **Sunegga-Blauherd-Rothorn**, which culminates at an elevation of 10,170 feet. **Gornergrat-Stockhorn** (11,155
feet) is the second. The third is the region dominated by the **Matterhorn
Glacier Paradise (MGP),** which goes to Italy. The best way to prioritize your
ski day is still to concentrate on one or two areas, especially during high
season. Thanks to snowmaking machines and the eternal snows of the
Klein Matterhorn Glacier, Zermatt is said to guarantee skiers 7,216 feet
of vertical drop no matter what the snowfall—an impressive claim. Grav-
ity Park, a snowboarding center on Theodul glacier below the MGP, has
pipes, kickers, and rails to thrill. A one-day lift ticket costs 68 SF; a six-
day pass costs 336 SF; if you want to ski to Italy it costs 76 SF and 379
SF. Ask for the hands-free "Smart Card" or "Swatch Access Key" with
computer chip gate activation and billing. A **ski and snowboard school**
(✉ Skischulbüro, Bahnhofstr. ☎ 027/9662466) operates seven ski schools
from mid-December until April and in July and August.

Where to Stay & Eat
Many Zermatt hotels, especially larger ones, decide on a year-by-year
basis to close during low season, which lasts from "melt-down" (anywhere from late April to mid-June) until "preseason" (November through
mid-December). If you plan to travel during the low season, be sure to
call ahead. Summer can be more popular than the winter ski season,
with rates and availability to match.

$–$$$$ ✕ **Elsie's Bar.** This tiny log cabin of a ski haunt, directly across from the Zermatt church, draws an international crowd as soon as it opens its doors at 4 o'clock. They come to select from an extensive list of aged scotches and mixed cocktails. Light meals include cheese dishes, oysters, escargots, and would you believe spaghetti with caviar and crème fraîche? ⊠ *Kirchepl. 16* ☎ *027/9672431* ▭ *AE, DC, MC, V* ◷ *Closed May, June, Oct., and Nov.*

$–$$$ ✕ **Findlerhof.** This mountain restaurant is ideal for long lunches be-
Fodor'sChoice   tween sessions on the slopes or for a panoramic break on an all-day hike.
★   It's perched in tiny Findeln, between the Sunnegga and Blauherd ski areas; the Matterhorn views are astonishing. The food is decidedly fresh and creative. Franz and Heidi Schwery tend their own Alpine garden to provide lettuce for their salads and berries for vinaigrettes and hot desserts. The fluffy *Matterkuchen,* a bacon and leek quiche, will fortify you for the 30- to 40-minute walk down to the village. ⊠ *Findeln* ☎ *027/9672588* ▭ *MC, V* ◷ *Closed May–mid-June and mid-Oct.–Nov.*

$–$$$ ✕ **Grill-Room Stockhorn.** The moment you step across the threshold into this low-slung, two-story restaurant decked with mountaineering memorabilia, tantalizing aromas of cheese melting and meat roasting on the open grill should sharpen your appetite. This is a great place for regional dishes. The service and the clientele are equally lively. ⊠ *Hotel Stockhorn, Riedstr. 22* ☎ *027/9671747* ▭ *AE, MC, V* ◷ *Closed mid-May–mid-June and Oct.*

★ **$–$$** ✕ **Zum See.** In a hamlet (little more than a cluster of mazots) of the same name, this restaurant turns out inventive meals that merit acclaim. Although it's in the middle of nowhere, it overflows until late afternoon with diners sunning on the terrace or packed into the 400-year-old log house. (The quickest way to get here is to walk or ski down from Furi.) Hosts Max and Greti Mennig masterfully prepare such daily specials as venison salad with wild mushrooms and handmade tortelloni with spinach ricotta filling. The selection of wines and brandies sets skiers aglow. ⊠ *Zum See* ☎ *027/9672045* ⌒ *Reservations essential* ▭ *MC, V* ◷ *Closed mid-Apr.–June and Oct.–mid-Dec. No dinner.*

★ **$** ✕ **Whymperstube.** At this little restaurant in the Hotel Monte Rosa, plates of melted raclette and bubbling pots of fondue are delivered to tightly packed tables by an agile waitstaff. Imagine the climbers' stories that must have echoed within these walls. In the winter season, the place stays open until 1 AM. ⊠ *Bahnhofstr. 80* ☎ *027/9672296* ▭ *AE, DC, MC, V.*

$$$$ ✕▥ **Julen.** The decor here happily shuns regional kitsch. Instead, rooms have a Bavarian style: century-old spruce-wood decor paired with primary-color carpets and silk curtains. Each suite is equipped with a green-tile stove and sitting area. A three-floor wellness center includes an elaborate Roman bath where you can indulge in various therapies. The main restaurant ($$–$$$) offers international cuisine, and the welcoming Stübli ($–$$) serves unusual dishes prepared with lamb from local family-owned flocks. ⊠ *Riedstr. 2, CH-3920* ☎ *027/9667600* 🖷 *027/9667676* ⊕ *www.zermatt.ch/julen* ↬ *27 rooms, 5 suites* ⌂ *2 restaurants, Stübli, minibars, cable TV, in-room data ports, indoor pool, gym, sauna, Turkish bath, spa* ▭ *AE, DC, MC, V* ⊠│ *MAP.*

★ **$$$$** ✕⌂ **Mont Cervin Hotel Palace.** Part of the Seiler dynasty, this luxurious, urbane hotel isn't grandiose in either scale or attitude. Built in 1852, it's unusually low-slung for a grand hotel. Rooms are decorated with tasteful stripes and plaids in primary colors; many have Matterhorn views. The Residence, across the street, offers spacious apartments. The main restaurant ($$$) has a light, modern ambience with dishes to match, including seabass with white tomato mousse on lemon risotto. There's also a more casual dining option ($–$$), plus dine-around options at the hotel's sister properties. Reserve covered parking and transportation from Täsch. The wellness and spa facilities are exceptional. ⊠ *Bahnhofstr. 31, CH-3920* ☏ *027/9668888* 🖷 *027/9668899* ⊕ *www.seilerhotels.ch* 📑 *87 rooms, 31 suites, 15 apartments* ♨ *2 restaurants, in-room safes, minibars, cable TV, in-room data ports, indoor-outdoor pool, gym, sauna, spa, piano bar, concierge, no-smoking rooms* ☰ *AE, DC, MC, V* ⊘ *Closed May–mid-June, Oct. and Nov.* ⎐ *MAP.*

$$–$$$$ ✕⌂ **Hotel Mirabeau.** The best of old and new merge at this two-part hotel with a traditional main building and contemporary new addition. Standard rooms in the main building are smartly furnished, but its the newer addition that is the attention-getter with elements of old chalets combined with sleek bedding and open Jacuzzi baths. An epicurean restaurant, Corbeau d'Or ($$–$$$$), attracts outsiders for refined, fresh cuisine like fillet of wild rockfish, roasted with lavender butter and served with fennel couscous. It's best to reserve a table before check-in. The spa center and popular wine lounge (Josef's) are bonuses in a location set apart from the hub of the village. ⊠ *Untre Mattenrstr. 12–14, CH-3920* ☏ *027/9662660* 🖷 *027/9662665* ⊕ *www.hotel-mirabeau.ch* 📑 *44 rooms, 18 suites* ♨ *2 restaurants, in-room safes, minibars, cable TV, WiFi, indoor pool, hot tub, sauna, spa, steam bath, bar, wine bar, no-smoking rooms* ☰ *AE, DC, MC, V* ⎐ *MAP.*

$$–$$$ ✕⌂ **Pollux.** This modern, small-scale hotel is simple and tidy, with straightforward rooms trimmed in pine and leatherette. Though none of its windows looks onto the Matterhorn, its position directly on the main pedestrian shopping street puts you in the heart of resort activities. The restaurant ($$) is based on a village square, with garden furniture and a central fountain; an appealing, old-fashioned *pinte* ($–$$) draws locals for its low-price lunches, snacks, and Valaisan cheese dishes. Its popular T-Bar disco is always packed. ⊠ *Bahnhofstr. 28, CH-3920* ☏ *027/9664000* 🖷 *027/9664001* ⊕ *www.reconline.ch/pollux* 📑 *33 rooms* ♨ *Restaurant, Stübli, in-room safes, minibars, cable TV, sauna, hot tub, bar, dance club* ☰ *AE, DC, MC, V* ⎐ *CP.*

10

$$$$ ⌂ **Apartmenthotel Zurbriggen.** Sleeping under the roof of Olympic medalist Pirmin Zurbriggen's six-unit apartment house may not make you a better skier, but the view will elicit dreams of starting gates and downhill races. Flexible configurations with fully stocked kitchenettes can sleep a couple or expand to include a pack of friends. Near the cable car to Matterhorn Glacier Paradise, this ultramodern glass structure has plenty of tech-amenities: flat-screen TV, ISDN lines, CD players, and so on. ⊠ *Schulhmattstr. 68, CH-3920* ☏ *027/9663838* 🖷 *027/9663839* ⊕ *www.zurbriggen.ch* 📑 *6 apartments* ♨ *In-room safes, kitchenettes,* *minibars, cable TV, in-room data ports, indoor pool, hot tub, sauna* ☰ *AE, DC, MC, V* ❧❘ *CP.*

$$$$ 🏨 **Hotel Monte Rosa.** Alexander Seiler founded his first hotel in the core of this historic building, expanding it over the years to its current size. (This was the home base of Edward Whymper when he conquered the Matterhorn in 1865.) Behind its graceful, shuttered facade you'll find an ideal balance between modern convenience and history in the burnished pine, flagstone floors, original ceiling moldings, fireplaces, and Victorian dining hall. The beige room decor is impeccable; southern views go quickly and cost more. The bar is an après-ski must. The pool and health facilities are shared with Mont Cervin and guests can take advantage of the hotel group's dine-around plan. ✉ *Bahnhofstr. 80, CH-3920* 🕿 *027/9660333* 🖷 *027/9660330* ⊕ *www.seilerhotels.ch* ❧ *43 rooms, 3 suites* ♨ *Restaurant, in-room safes, minibars, cable TV, bar, meeting room* ☰ *AE, DC, MC, V* ☉ *Closed mid-Apr.–mid-June and late Oct.–mid-Dec.* ❧❘ *MAP.*

★ **$$$$** 🏨 **Omnia.** A glass-and-steel tower juts out of the hillside above the church square, its only concession to local architecture the wooden panels that cap each end. Part engineering marvel, the rest 21st-century chic, the hotel is a standout in a village of traditional hoteliers. A private tunnel leads to the secure elevator where you are whisked to the reception platform, a contemporary lobby with stone fire box and Mies Van Der Rohe-like furnishings. Rooms are lettered not numbered, a tip of the hat to personalization. The staggered level arrangement with three-sided glass elevator that accesses guest quarters is a bit confusing, but once inside your aesthetically cool room all is serene, from the Bose sound system to slate baths with designer toiletries. Decks and balconies maximize views in all directions. For a jaw-dropping wake-up call push back the curtains to see the sun cast its red flare on the Matterhorn. The restaurant and bar are equally sleek places to sip and dine; the wellness area with multiple steam applications and a contoured tile relaxation room adds solitude. ✉ *auf dem Fels, CH-3920* 🕿 *027/9667171* 🖷 *027/9667100* ⊕ *www.the-omnia* ❧ *18 rooms, 12 suites* ♨ *Restaurant, in-room data ports, in-room safes, minibars, in-room VCRs, indoor pool, gym, hot tub, massage, sauna, steam room, Turkish bath, bar, lobby lounge, library, concierge, Internet, no-smoking rooms* ☰ *AE, DC, MC, V* ☉ *Closed late Apr.–late May, Oct. and Nov.* ❧❘ *CP.*

★ **$$$$** 🏨 **Riffelalp Resort 2222.** This grand mountaintop hotel, at 7,288 feet, has a stunning location amid fields and Alpine forest. Its direct views of the Matterhorn are especially breathtaking in the orange glow of early morning. The expansive complex includes a wine cellar with tastings and a converted chapel for concerts. The sumptuous rooms have Jacuzzi tubs and Bose sound systems. Even transit is made memorable, as you can ride a private restored tram to and from the train station. (Rail transfer for arrival and departure plus special night train service from the village is included.) For those who prefer to be away from the village hub-bub this remote location is heavenly; others might chafe at having to synchronize with the rail schedule. The spa center offers comprehensive services from chilling footbaths to an organic sauna. ✉ *CH-3920* 🕿 *027/9660555* 🖷 *027/9660550* ⊕ *www.seilerhotels.ch* ❧ *65 rooms, 5 suites,*

2 apartments ⟋ 3 restaurants, in-room safes, cable TV, in-room DVD, in-room data ports, Wi-Fi, indoor-outdoor pool, sauna, Turkish bath, billiards, bowling, ski storage, piano bar, cinema, concierge, meeting room, helipad ⊟ AE, DC, MC, V ⊘ Closed mid-Apr.–late-June and mid-Oct.–mid-Dec. |O| MAP.

$–$$ ▦ **Hotel Admiral.** Easy going, anglophone owners make it a snap to check-in at this fastidious lodging along the river promenade. Rooms are ship-shape and done in dark blue, honey, and russet with lookouts to the mountains. The Sunnegga cableway is just across the way so access to the slopes couldn't be easier. Skiers warm themselves at the raised hearth fireplace in the lobby lounge and gather on the outdoor deck. ⊠ *Matterstr. 23, CH-3920* ☎ *027/9669000* 🖷 *027/9669090* ⊕ *www.hotel-admiral.ch* ⟋ *24 rooms, 1 suite ⟋ Restaurant, in-room safes, cable TV, Wi-Fi, hot tub, sauna, steam bath, bar, Internet, no-smoking rooms ⊟ AE, DC, MC, V |O| CP.*

$–$$ ▦ **Romantica.** Among the scores of anonymously modern hotels along the Zermatt plain, this modest structure offers an exceptional location directly above the town center, no more than a block up a narrow, mazot-lined lane. Its tidy, bright gardens, game trophies, and granite stove give it personality, and the plain rooms benefit from big windows and balconies. You can also stay in one of the two *Walliserstadel*, tiny (but charming), 200-year-old huts in the hotel's garden. Keep in mind that this is a *garni* hotel (no restaurant), so only breakfast is served. ⊠ *Churm 21, CH-3920* ☎ *027/9662650* 🖷 *027/9662655* ⊕ *www.reconline.ch/romantica* ⟋ *13 rooms, 1 apartment, 2 cabins ⟋ Cable TV, bar ⊟ AE, DC, MC, V |O| CP.*

$–$$ ▦ **Touring.** Reassuringly traditional architecture, sunny rooms full of pine, and an elevated position apart from town, with excellent Matterhorn views make this an appealing, informal alternative to the chic downtown scene. Hearty daily menus are served to pension guests in the cozy dining room (the same menu is available in the Stübli). ⊠ *Riedstr. 45, CH-3920* ☎ *027/9671177* 🖷 *027/9674601* ⊕ *www.touring.buz.ch* ⟋ *20 rooms ⟋ Restaurant, Stübli, cable TV, hot tub, sauna, steam room, bar, playground ⊟ MC, V |O| CP.*

¢–$ ▦ **Alpenhotel.** If steep resort prices don't suit your budget, stay downhill in the village of Täsch. Train connections to Zermatt are easy, though you'll have to compete with guests required to leave their cars in nearby lots. This Best Western standard has tidy rooms with blond modular furniture and tile showers, plus an on-premises bakery. ⊠ *CH-3929, Täsch* ☎ *027/9662644* 🖷 *027/9662645* ⊕ *www.bestwestern.ch/alpenhof* ⟋ *29 rooms ⟋ Restaurant, cable TV, gym, sauna, steam room, bar ⊟ AE, DC, MC, V |O| CP.*

Nightlife

GramPi's Bar (☎ 027/9677788), located on the Bahnhofstrasse in what locals call the Bermuda Triangle because of the concentration of nightspots, is a lively bar, where you can get into the mood for dancing downstairs with a Lady Matterhorn cocktail. Across the cobblestones is the multifaceted **Pöstli** (☎ 027/9671931), with **The Pink,** a live concert hall; **Village Dance Club,** where a DJ spins tunes for late night revelers; **Broken Bar,** a grotto dance floor with a different beat; and **Papa**

10

Caesar Lounge, for those who prefer to sit and sip whiskey and smoke a cigar. Venues rotate openings depending on the season. The final point in the trefoil is the **Hexen Bar** (☎ 027/9675533), which is decorated in witch memorabilia and serves cocktails and cognacs into the wee hours.

At **Vernissage** (☎ 027/9676636) you can see old and current films in the screening room, have a drink at the bar, or check out the art scene at the gallery. For an excellent choice in wines served with a modern flair head down the pathway beside the Hotel Mirabeau to **Josef's Wine Lounge** (☎ 027/9662560). A double dose of folklore song and dance can be had at the **Schwyzer Stübli** (☎ 027/9676767), in the Hotel Schweizerhof; be prepared for rowdy sing-alongs and accordion music.

Sports & the Outdoors

HIKING   With 400 km (248 mi) of marked trails available, you'll have plenty of options for exploring the mountains on foot. Outfitted with scarred boots, rucksacks, and walking sticks, trekkers strike out in all directions for daylong excursions ranging from easy to exhausting. Maps and route guides are available at the tourist office. Be sure to pack rain gear and a warm jacket along with sunscreen, as the weather changes quickly. Multiday lift passes will ease the way up and leave some change in your pocket for an after-hike beer.

MOUNTAIN   Mountain biking is closely monitored by Zermatt authorities to prevent
BIKING   interference with hiking on trails. To keep pace with other resorts, about 25 km (15 mi) have been set aside for dedicated downhill tracks with challenging features. A map is available at the tourist office. Bikes can be rented at **Slalom Sport** (☎ 027/9662366).

MOUNTAIN   The Matterhorn is one of the world's most awe-inspiring peaks, and many
CLIMBING   visitors get the urge to climb it. However, this climb must be taken seriously; you have to be in top physical condition and have climbing experience to attempt the summit. You also need to spend 7–10 days acclimatizing once in the area. Less-experienced climbers have plenty of alternatives, though, such as a one-day climb of the Riffelhorn (9,774 feet) or a half traverse of the Breithorn (13,661 feet). For those wanting a challenge without such extreme altitudes, try a guided trip across the rugged Gorner gorge. For detailed information, advice, instruction, and climbing guides, contact the **Zermatt Alpin Center** (✉ Bahnhofstr. 58 ☎ 027/9662460 ⊕ www.alpincenter-zermatt.ch).

Shopping

Zermatt may be Switzerland's souvenir capital, offering a broad variety of watches, knives, and logo clothing. Popular folk crafts and traditional products include large, grotesque masks of carved wood, and lidded channes in pewter or tin, molded in graduated sizes; they're sold everywhere, even in grocery stores.

You'll see lots of stores offering state-of-the-art sports equipment and apparel, from collapsible grappling hooks for climbers to lightweight hiking boots in brilliant colors to walking sticks—pairs of lightweight, spiked ski poles for hikers to add a bit of upper-body workout to their climb. **Bayard** (✉ Bahnhofpl. 2 ☎ 027/9664950 ✉ Bahnhofstr. 35

☏ 027/9664960) has sporting-goods shops scattered throughout the village, including these two main branches. **Glacier Sport** (✉ Bahnhofstr. 19 ☏ 027/9681300) specializes in ski and climbing equipment and accessories.

Saas-Fee

⑫ To & From: *Car-free Saas-Fee is on bus lines connecting with Brig (18 SF, 1 hr) and Visp (15 SF, 45 min); train here from Brig by transferring at Visp or connect with Zermatt by rail with a transfer at Stalden-Saas. Saas-Fee is 36 km (22 mi) south of Visp.*

At the end of the switchback road from Saas-Grund lies a parking garage where visitors must abandon their cars for the length of their stay in Saas-Fee. But even by the garage you'll be amazed, for the view on arriving at this lofty (5,871 feet) plateau is humbling. (In true Swiss-efficient fashion, you can drop off your bags curbside and call an electric shuttle that will arrive to fetch you in the time it takes to park your car.)

Saas-Fee is at the heart of a circle of mountains called the Mischabel, 13 of which tower to more than 13,120 feet, among them the **Dom** (14,908 feet), the highest mountain entirely on Swiss soil. The town lies in a deep valley that leaves no doubt about its source: it seems to pour from the vast, intimidating **Fee Glacier,** which oozes like icy lava from the broad spread of peaks above. *Fee* can be translated as "fairy," and although Saas-Fee itself is a tourist-saturated resort, the landscape could illustrate a fairy tale.

★ Carved into the deep ice of the Fee Glacier at 11,482 feet, an **Eis Pavillon** (ice cave), considered the largest in the world, combines fascinating construction with a dash of kitsch. Twenty-six feet below the ice pack, the cavernous facility provides an impressive view of the surreal, frozen environment inside glacial formations. There are ice sculptures, exhibits on glaciology and crevasse rescue, and even a chapel-like room for meditation, concerts, and art shows. A special collaboration with global adventurer Mike Horn simulates elements of his polar expedition in film and interactive displays. The ticket for the cable car and underground funicular is pricey, but if you are up on the mountain, spring for the entrance fee and have a look below the frozen surface of the earth. ✉ *Mittelallalin* ☏ 027/9573560 💳 5 SF ⊙ *Daily 8:30–4.*

Skiing

The first glacier to be used for skiing here was the **Längfluh** (9,414 feet), accessed by gondola, then cable car. The run is magnificent, sometimes physically demanding, and always varied. From the Längfluh you can take a lift to reach *the* ski area of Saas-Fee, the **Felskinn-Mittelallalin** sector (9,840–11,480 feet). Felskinn harbors its own surprise: in order to preserve the land and landscape, the Valaisans have constructed a subterranean funicular, the Métro Alpin, which climbs through the heart of the mountain to Mittelallalin, that is, halfway up the Allalinhorn (13,210 feet). Tourists debark in a rotating restaurant noted more for the austere grandeur of its natural surroundings than its food. Felskinn-

Mittelallalin's exceptional site, its high elevation, its runs (15 km [9 mi]), and its ample facilities (cable car, funicular, and three ski lifts) have made Saas-Fee the number one summer-skiing resort in Switzerland. It's also one of two official European snowboard centers sanctioned by the International Snowboard Federation. Lifts don't connect with other resorts in the valley—Saas-Almagell, Saas-Balen, or Saas-Grund. However, good days of skiing can be found a bus ride away, and hiking trails open in winter and summer link all four valleys. A one-day lift ticket costs 69 SF; a six-day pass costs 341 SF and includes ski bus to valley lifts. A special excursion plan to Zermatt is available, as is a savings program for parents who buy six-day passes, which allows discounted skiing for children under 16.

Where to Stay & Eat

¢–$ ✕ **Restaurant Skihütte.** During high season, you'll have to be quick in order to snag a table on the sun-filled deck of this traditional restaurant on the main drag. A great location at the bottom of the lift and good Walliser favorites hold you for another beer and a few more rays. ☎ 027/9589280 ▭ AE, MC, V.

$$$$ ✕▦ **Beau-Site.** A proud family with unyielding standards tends this elegant hotel. Interiors of patinated wood, stacked stone, and leaded glass give the look of a respected manor house. Guest rooms have baths with modern fixtures; furnishings tastefully mix antiques with the more modern. The refined main restaurant ($$–$$$) rates as one of the most romantic around. Intimate dining of a different type can be found at La Ferme ($–$$), a low-slung, elegantly rustic restaurant with a central woodstove and farmhouse detail. ⊠ CH-3906 ☎ 027/9581560 ▭ 027/9581565 ∰ www.beausite.org ⤳ 15 rooms, 3 suites, 16 apartments ⚏ 3 restaurants, Stübli, in-room safes, minibars, cable TV, indoor pool, hot tub, massage, sauna, bar ▭ DC, MC, V ⍅⍅ MAP.

★ $$$$ ✕▦ **Waldhotel Fletschhorn.** Once a customhouse, this quiet, sophisticated *Landgasthof* (country inn) is set apart from the resort at the end of a forested lane. Pine paneling, antiques, and serene views mellow the rooms' ultramodern fittings and contemporary art. The restaurant's ($$–$$$$) innovative French cuisine, which won Chef Markus Neff chef-of-the-year distinction, is based on local products; savor choices such as Alpine lamb with herbed potatoes and kohlrabi. Lunch is a great time to sample the gourmet team's talents at a favorable price. The expansive wine cellar matches the cuisine's high style. Reservations are essential. ⊠ CH-3906 ☎ 027/9572131 ▭ 027/9572187 ∰ www.fletschhorn.ch ⤳ 15 rooms ⚏ Restaurant, cable TV, Wi-Fi, hot tub, sauna ▭ AE, DC, MC, V ⊗ Closed late Apr.–early June and mid-Oct.–early Dec. ⍅⍅ CP.

$$–$$$$ ✕▦ **Hotel du Glacier.** One of the original hotels in the village, this veteran shows no signs of its age. The owners are seasoned travelers and have added touches of their own globetrotting to the decor and restaurant offerings. Modular furniture and spotless baths are accented with primary colors. The downstairs restaurant, Feeloch (¢–$$$), is a popular spot for grill and cheese dishes. The eclectic menu includes tandoori chicken, T-bone steaks, raclette, and fondue. Spa facilities and the Ice Box Bar are great spots to recoop after a day on the mountain. ⊠ CH-

3906 ☎ 027/9581600 ⊟ 027/9581605 ⊕ *www.duglacier.ch* ⇆ *36 rooms, 4 suites* ⚇ *Restaurant, Stübli, in-room data ports, in-room safes, cable TV, hot tub, sauna, Turkish bath, bar, no-smoking rooms* ⊟ *AE, DC, MC, V* ⎮◯⎮ *MAP.*

$$$$ 🏨 **Dom Hotel.** Follow the snowboarders who flock to Popcorn, the wildly popular on-site bar and gear boutique, to find this contemporary hotel—a place where a traditional exterior belies a funky interior. Modern furnishings in vibrant colors and unusual shapes fill the lobby lounge. The amply sized rooms with modular furniture all have TV-stereo combinations loaded with Sony PlayStations. ✉ *CH-3906* ☎ *027/9587700* ⊟ *027/9587701* ⊕ *www.uniquedom.com* ⇆ *40 rooms* ⚇ *Restaurant, cable TV, Wi-Fi, sauna, 2 bars, Internet room* ⊟ *AE, DC, MC, V* ⎮◯⎮ *CP.*

$$$$ 🏨 **Ferienart Resort & Spa.** Located in the center of town, the two-part hotel offers some of the best views and an abundance of entertainment options. Refurbished and traditional rooms have mixed amenities—generous seating areas in some, tight built-in nooks in others; whirlpool baths versus standard tub and shower—so quiz the reservationist to ensure you get the room you want. An expansive breakfast buffet and multi-course dinner are served in the stylish main dining room that pays tribute to Càsar Ritz, noted hotelier from the region. Their three-quarter pension plan includes a light lunch or afternoon sweets along with morning and evening meals. The wellness area with chandelier and mock grotto pool plus waterfall has a segmented "textile free" environment with a series of unique steam and spa treatments. ✉ *CH-3906* ☎ *027/9581900* ⊟ *027/9581905* ⊕ *www.ferienart.ch* ⇆ *83 rooms, 5 suites, 4 apartments* ⚇ *4 restaurants, café, in-room safes, minibars, cable TV, in-room data ports, pro shop, pool, gym, massage, sauna, spa, piano bar, nightclub* ⊟ *AE, DC, MC, V* ⎮◯⎮ *MAP.*

$$ 🏨 **Wellness Hotel Pirmin Zurbriggen.** Move into the valley without compromising quality at this upscale guesthouse, owned and run by a local world champion and his equally athletic wife. Tucked back on a country lane across from the Saas-Almagell lift, the lodge commingles ultramodern public and spa areas with traditional rooms. Enjoy an aperitif in front of the trophy laden glass case while pondering your next downhill run. ✉ *CH-3905, Saas-Almagell* ☎ *027/9572301* ⊟ *027/9573313* ⊕ *www.zurbriggen.ch* ⇆ *5 rooms, 2 suites, 1 apartment* ⚇ *Restaurant, in-room data ports, in-room safes, minibars, cable TV, indoor pool, hot tub, massage, sauna, steam bath, bar, no-smoking rooms* ⊟ *AE, DC, MC, V* ⎮◯⎮ *MAP.*

Nightlife & the Arts

BARS & DANCING A popular dance zone, **Vernissage** (☎ 027/9581904) is located at the Ferienart Walliserhof hotel. The **Metropol Hotel** (☎ 027/9571001) hosts late-night revelers with mixed music sets at **Crazy Night Disco** and offers spirits at **John's Pub.** People often squeeze into **Nesti's** (☎ 027/9572112), a perennial après-ski favorite. Snowboarders and a younger crowd congregate for brews at **Popcorn** (☎ 027/9574006) at the Unique Hotel Dom. **The Living Room Bar** (☎ 027/9575101) is another hot spot at the Unique Hotel Dom.

MUSIC   Like other resorts, Saas-Fee is not without echoes of symphonies and chorus groups during its summer months. The **International Alpine Music Festival** and **Summer Festival** please audiences in July and August with
Philharmonic orchestra performances and chamber music concerts. Bookings and ticket information are available through the tourist office.

Sports & the Outdoors

HIKING   Larch forests, flower and herb-filled meadows, and glacial zones offer
a huge variety of trails (350 km [218 mi]) at all levels of difficulty. Historical routes cross passes into Italy and extend outbound along ridgelines toward the Rhône River. Bus and lift services make it easy to
return to the village in time for dinner. Most hotels will pack a lunch
for the outing or you can stop at buvettes (snack bars) scattered along
the trails. **Sentier des Chapelles (Trail of the Chapels)** is a time-worn pilgrimage from Saas-Fee to Saas-Grund featuring 15 shrines with costumed
wooden statues strung along the path like beads on a rosary.

MOUNTAIN   The **Bergfürerbüro** (☎ 027/9574464) conducts daily guided forays year-
CLIMBING   round; you can rent season-appropriate equipment. Another popular activity is gorge crossing, which uses safety cables and pulleys to traverse
the valley's deep divide. There are also a few via ferrata (iron way), preset routes with ladders and cables secured in place to challenge climbers
at all stages of competence.

SLEDDING   Your stay won't be complete without a few runs on the **Feeblitz** (☎ 027/
9573111), the curved and looped track of the *rodelbobbahn* (bobsled)
near the Alpin Express cable car station.

SPORTS CENTER   The **Bielen Recreation Center** (☎ 027/9572475) has a four-lane swimming
pool, children's pool, whirlpools, steam baths, sauna, solarium, table
tennis, billiards, badminton, and two indoor-tennis courts.

BRIG & THE ALPINE PASSES

This region is the Grand Central Station of the Alps. All mountain
passes lead to or through Brig, as traffic and rail lines pour in from Italy,
the Ticino, central Switzerland, and the Berner Oberland. It is also a transit link for Paris, Brussels, London, and Rome. The Simplon, Nufenen,
Grimsel, and Furka passes provide exit options and stunning vistas dependent on destination. Northeast of this critical junction, the spectacular Aletsch Glacier, the largest in Europe, straddles the cantons of
Valais and Bern. The Rhône River becomes increasingly wild and silty
until it meets its source in Gletsch, at the end of the valley called Goms.

Brig

🔞 **To & From:** *Brig is a main stop on the Glacier Express railway between
Zermatt and St. Moritz. Brig is 19 km (12 mi) southeast of Leukerbad.*

A rail and road junction joining four cantons, this small but vital town
has for centuries been a center of trade with Italy. Often overlooked as
merely a transit point, the town has a legacy that can be appreciated in
a couple of hours: a restored core with cobblestone streets, shops, cafés,
and the main attraction, the elegant merchant's castle.

The fantastical **Stockalperschloss,** a massive baroque castle, was built between 1658 and 1678 by Kaspar Jodok von Stockalper, a Swiss tycoon who made his fortune in Italian trade over the Simplon Pass. Topped with three gilt onion domes and containing a courtyard lined by elegant Italianate arcades, it was once Switzerland's largest private home and is now restored. Group tours in English are available upon request. To get here from the station walk up Bahnhofstrasse to Sebastienplatz; then turn left onto Alte Simplonstrasse. ⊠ *Alte Simplonstr. 28* ☎ *027/ 9216030* ✆ *7 SF* ☉ *May–Sept., Tues.–Sun., guided tours at 9:30, 10:30, 1:30, 2:30, 3:30, and 4:30. Oct. no tour at 4:30.*

Simplon Pass

⑭ *23 km (14 mi) southeast of Brig.*

Beginning just outside Brig, this historic road meanders through deep gorges and wide, barren, rock-strewn pastures to offer increasingly beautiful views back toward Brig. At the summit (6,593 feet), the **Hotel Bellevue Simplon-Kulm** shares the high meadow with the **Simplon Hospitz** (Simplon Hospice), built 150 years ago at Napoléon's request and now owned by the monks of St. Bernard. Just beyond stands the bell-towered **Alt Spital,** a lodging built in the 17th century. Beyond the pass, the road continues through Italy, and it's possible to cut across the Italian upthrust and reenter Switzerland in the Ticino, near Ascona.

> **VIEWS OF THE PAST**
>
> From the summit of Simplon Pass you can still see parts of the old road used by traders and Napoléon, and it's easy to imagine the hardships travelers faced at these heights. Look north toward the Bernese Alps to see a portion of the massive Aletsch Glacier.

OFF THE BEATEN PATH

SIMPLON TUNNEL – If you'd rather ride than drive, you can hop aboard (or load your car on) the train through this tunnel, which starts above the eastern outskirts of Brig and runs nearly 20 km (12 mi) before ending in Italian daylight. The first of the twin tunnels—the world's longest railway tunnels—was started in 1898 and took six years to complete.

Aletsch

⑮ **To & From:** *Car-free alpine villages are often at the terminus of a rail line. Riederalp's transportation link to the Rhone River Valley is a giant gondola that lifts passengers from the village of Mörel to the hamlet above. Commuters with shopping bags, workman lugging tool boxes, and travelers with wheeled-suitcases and skis fill the cabin, which holds 80. The Aletsch Riederalp Bergbahn is located across the street from the Mörel train station, a stop on the Matterhorn Gornergrat line. The seven-minute ride covers nearly 2,000 meters stopping at the middle station for a handful of residents who board using a silolike elevator. Electric carts from hotels meet the half-hourly arrivals and departures. The round-trip fare is 18 SF. More transfer information can be found on www. riederalpbahnen.ch. Aletsch is 13 km (8 mi) north of Brig.*

Fodor's Choice ★

10

All About Aletsch

EUROPE'S LONGEST GLACIER –24 km (15 mi)–was at its longest 150 years ago but now recedes 100–165 feet a year. Concern about the recession of the earth's ice formations has made preserving the Aletsch Glacier internationally significant. So UNESCO designated a 250-square-km (97-square-mi) area around the glacier, shared between the cantons of Valais (77%) and Bern (23%), as a protected site. Generations ago, the Swiss sensed the need to safeguard the area and began placing parts in conservationist hands.

The glacier's starting point, Concordia Platz, is the confluence of three ice masses that move down from the Bernese Alps. Here the ice has been measured as deep as 2,952 feet–over twice as tall as the Empire State Building. Another magnificent formation, the Mäjelensee is a lake with icebergs floating on top, carved into the glacier field with walls of ice and stone. As the glacier's ice recedes, nature reclaims the land, first with moss and small plants, then forest. Pro Natura, the conservation organization that oversees the region, describes the process as "forest emerging from ice." Though some of the area's pine and larch are 600–700 years old, extreme conditions keep them short. Animals thought to be extinct thrive here; chamois, marten, badgers, lizards, and birds have adapted to the elevation and temperature.

Cable cars ferry tourists to ridge tops above Ried and Fiesch, where 360-degree views of the sweep of ice are framed by extraordinary peaks. You can see the Bernese Alps, including the Sphinx station on the Jungfraujoch called the "Top of Europe"; the Valaisan Alps; and even into Italy and France. Hiking trails lead to the glacier's edge, and guides take trekkers across parts of the ice field. All around are places to admire nature's grandeur and be grateful for its protection.

Ice-capped peaks with small mountain resorts staggered up their spines rim the Aletsch, a glacier that shares its name with the area surrounding it, paralleling the valley floor. A variety of ecological zones—from deep, frozen expanses in the center to forests emerging at the fringes—are part of a wilderness region that is now firmly in the hands of conservationists, protected as a UNESCO international nature site. In contrast to these extreme expanses, sunny south-facing slopes are active with skiers and hikers staying in the villages of Riederalp, Bettmeralp, and Fiescheralp.

Villa Cassel, a turn-of-the-20th-century mansion, was considered a wealthy Englishman's folly when the tudor-style structure was installed on the rugged pass above the village of Ried. It has weathered time well and is now the headquarters for **Pro Natura Zentrum Aletsch**, an environmental education center. The naturalist organization offers guided tours, glacier walks, and expeditions to spot marmots and eagles. In addition, the center offers self-directed paths, an Alpine garden, a tearoom, and even dorm and private rooms for overnight stays. Some information is available in English; prices vary according to the activity. To access the facility, take the cable car from Morel to Riederalp. From the village station it's a 30-minute walk, but more appealing and challenging is the hike from Moosfluh (an additional gondola ride) where you can catch views of the glacier rimmed by its old-growth Alpine forest. ⊠ *CH-3987, Riederalp* ☎ *027/9286220* ⊕ *www.pronatura.ch/aletsch* ⊠ *8 SF* ⊘ *Mid-June–mid-Oct., daily 9–6; mid-Dec.–mid-Apr., Wed. 2–4:30.*

Skiing

The three resorts of **Riederalp, Bettmeralp,** and **Fiescheralp** are connected by trails, lifts, and shuttle buses. There are 33 lifts and 83 km (52 mi) of runs, a quarter of which are expert and peak at 9,415 feet. A one-day lift ticket for access to the whole Aletsch ski area costs 46 SF; a six-day pass costs 228 SF. All of the essentials are in place in these picture-book villages, but don't expect lots of amenities, varied dining choices, or glitzy nightlife. Riederalp is best known as the home of Art Furrer, who became famous in the United States as one of the pioneers of freestyle skiing. His ski school, the **Skischule Forum Alpin** (☎ 027/9284488 ⊕ www.artfurrer.ch) is still up and running. You will see his name on everything from hotel placards to the weather Web cam.

Where to Stay

$–$$ 🏨 **Wellness Resort Alpenrose.** Ski legend Art Furrer returned to his village and became the recreational and hospitality backbone of the community; this hotel is the most upscale in his portfolio. Perched on a ledge with views shared by Swiss and Italians, the multibuilding complex combines a traditional hotel with newer structures connected by covered walkways. Standard rooms located above the lobby and busy dining venues show their age, while modern rooms in the adjacent lodges are fresh and untrodden. The pizzeria is a popular draw for oven-fired pies; more formal areas satisfy demi-pension and à la carte diners. The spa—with pool, sauna, and massage options—shares spectacular vistas. ⊠ *CH-3987, Riederalp* ☎ *027/9284545* 🖷 *027/9274555* ⊕ *www.artfurrer.ch* ➫ *35 rooms, 15 suites* ⊘ *2 restaurants, pizzeria, in-room data ports, in-room safes, cable TV, hot tub, massage, sauna, bar, no-smoking rooms* ⊟ *AE, DC, MC, V* ⊘ *Closed Easter–early July and Nov.–mid-Dec.* ⊠ *CP.*

EN ROUTE If the day is clear, grab the chance for a spectacular ride to the top of one of the lofty peaks that shadows the roadway by taking the **Fiesch cable car** (☎ 027/9712700) up to Eggishorn (9,303 feet). The panoramic views of Alps and glaciers will leave you breathless. As the cable car rotates 360 degrees, you can tick off famous Bernese and Valaisan peaks. The Jungfrau, Eiger, Matterhorn, and Dom are clearly visible, as are peaks that lie across the border in Italy and France.

10

Gletsch

🔟 *48 km (30 mi) northeast of Brig.*

Summer travelers may want to go the distance of the remote Goms region to the tiny resort of Gletsch, named for its prime attraction: the glacier that gives birth to the Rhône. From this aerie crossroad, the views of ice fields and mountain peaks are magnificent, but accommodations are scarce. Make an exit by descending into the Bernese Oberland over the scenic Grimsel Pass (7,101 feet), or continue higher to the Furka Pass (7,975 feet) to the central and western parts of the country.

If you want to go the old-fashioned way, take the **Furka Cogwheel Steam Railway.** After more than 20 years in storage, the Realp/Gletsch steam engine once again pulls itself up to the Gletsch glacier cog by cog, passing through fantastic Alpine scenery, over bridges, and through tunnels as it crosses the Furka Pass. A one-way trip takes an hour and a half. Board at Realp or Gletsch; you can return via shuttle bus for a change of pace (included in the round-trip ticket). ☎ 084/8000144 ⊕ *www. furka-bergstrecke.ch/eng* 🖃 *154 SF round-trip ⊗ July and Aug., daily; Sept., Fri.–Sun., depending on weather; departures from Gletsch at 11:10 and 2; Realp 10:40 and 2.*

Furka Pass

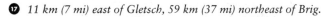 *11 km (7 mi) east of Gletsch, 59 km (37 mi) northeast of Brig.*

Making the final ascent of Valais by way of the Furka Pass, travelers have a choice to drive the stunning alpine highway or take the train. Be aware that even in summer, adverse weather can close this thoroughfare. From Oberwald, the rail line cuts through the heights with a 15-km (9-mi) tunnel to Realp before leading down to central Switzerland. Passengers and cars are loaded at this base, offering an attractive alternative for reluctant and weary drivers and those trying to save time. Transit time once on board the train is approximately 15 minutes.

Whether from a lookout point or train window, the views are spectacular. Stark moonscapes are punctuated by the occasional Spielbergian military operations—white-clad soldiers melting out of camouflaged hangars carved deep into solid-rock walls. Should you choose to drive, the sleek, broad highway that snakes down toward Andermatt shows Swiss Alpine engineering at its best.

VALAIS ESSENTIALS

Transportation

BY AIR

For international arrivals you can choose between two airports when flying to Valais: Geneva Cointrin or Unique Zürich. Geneva Cointrin recieves few international flights directly from the United States, but connecting service through London and Paris makes it preferrable for those heading to the west (French) end of Valais; it's about two hours away by train or car. Unique Zürich brings passengers closer to the east (German) side, but the Alps are in the way; you must connect by rail tunnel or drive over one of the passes which will take three to four hours. Commuter and private jet service is available into Sion.

🖪**Cointrin Airport** ☎022/7177111 ⊕www.gva.ch. **Unique Zürich Airport** ☎043/8618600 ⊕ www.zurich-airport.com. **Aéroport de Sion** ☎ 027/3290600 ⊕ www.sion.ch.

BY BUS

As in other parts of the country, an efficient network of postal buses covers the region, even to the most remote hamlets, at least once a day. The bright yellow coaches pick up and deliver passengers at main rail stations like Martigny, Sion, Sierre, Visp, and Brig and transport them to higher destinations. Many travelers prefer the convenience of being dropped off in carless resorts and not having to navigate narrow, torturous roadways especially in icy and snowy conditions, not to mention paying additional parking fees at lots and garages. Schedules are available online and at all tourist offices. The buses are easily hailed at their regular stops marked with signage along the roadway or at village post offices. They are also a convenient way to return to starting points from long-distance hikes. Resorts like Verbier, Crans-Montana, and Saas-Fee with its contingent valleys have free shuttles that loop a circuit for skiers and snowboarders, as well as for summer guests.

In Sierre, in addition to the 12-minute funicular connecting the town with Crans-Montana there is bus service on the **SMC** (**Sierre Mollens Crans-Montana**) that winds its way through villages on east and west routes from the train station. It will add a half hour to your arrival. Access to St-Luc and Grimmentz is made via Sierre by switching to the postbus at the station.

A similar train–bus transfer takes place in the valley station of Leuk to get to the thermal village of Leukerbad. The **LLB** (**Leuk Leukerbad**) schedule is synchronized with SBB arrivals and departures and takes about a half hour. The fares and schedules for all of these connections are available through the SBB.

🚌 **PostBus** ☎ 084/8888888 ⊕ www.swisspost.ch. **SMC** ☎ 027/4813355 ⊕ www.cie-smc.ch. **LLB** ☎ 027/4702052 ⊕ www.llbreisen.ch.

BY CAR

Valais is something of a dead end by nature: a fine expressway (A9) carries you in from Lac Léman, but to exit—or enter—from the east end, you must park your car on a train and ride through the Furka Pass tunnel to go north or take the train through the tunnel under the Simplon Pass to go southeast. (The serpentine roads over these passes are open in summer; weather permitting; the Simplon road stays open all year.) You also may cut through from or to Kandersteg in the Berner Oberland by taking a car train to Goppenstein or Brig. A summer-only road twists over the Grimsel Pass as well, heading toward Meiringen and the Berner Oberland or, over the Brünig Pass, to Luzern.

If you want to see the tiny back roads—and there's much to be seen off the beaten path—you'll need a car. The A9/9 expressway from Lausanne turns into a well-maintained highway at Sierre that continues on to Brig. Additional tunnels and expanded lanes are being carved out of existing highways, but don't count on making good time in this end of the valley. Distances in the north and south valleys can be deceptive: apparently short jogs are full of painfully slow switchbacks and distractingly beautiful views. Both Zermatt and Saas-Fee are car-free resorts, though you can drive all the way to a parking lot at the edge of Saas-Fee's main

10

street. Zermatt must be approached by rail from Täsch, the end of the line for cars (there's a central, secure rail terminal and garage).

BY TRAIN

There are straightforward rail connections to the region by way of Geneva/Lausanne to the west and Brig/Brigue to the east. The two are connected by one clean rail sweep that runs the length of the valley. In winter a special extension of the high-speed train from France, TGV Neige, terminates in Brig. (Information is available through the SBB.) The run to main connections mid-valley takes about two hours. Add on another hour to arrive at mountain destinations. Routes into smaller tributary valleys are limited, although most resorts are served by cheap and reliable postbuses running directly from train stations.The Mont Blanc/St. Bernard Express with its signature red and white cars emblazened with a picture of the country's beloved canine, passes through La Châble for connections to Verbier on its way from Martigny to Chamonix. In La Châble take the cableway or bus for the 10 to 20 minute ride. To travel to the Grand St-Bernard Pass, you will have to switch to the company's bus line in Orsières for an hour's drive to the pass or through the tunnel to Aosta, Italy.The Matterhorn Gottard Bahn ferries passengers from Visp to Zermatt and operates frequent shuttle service from Täsch to the village on a private railway system. It also connects with the famous panoramic Glacier Express that runs between Zermatt and St. Moritz. Once in Zermatt, another arm of the network, the Gornergrat Bahn takes over to sweep skiers and day-trippers to the Gornergrat. The SBB provides 24-hour information about all rail service, but you may want to consult local schedules for commuter service.

🔗 **SBB Information** ☎ 090/0300300 ⊕ www.rail.ch. **Matterhorn Gottard Bahn** ☎ 027/9277474 ⊕ www.mgbahn.ch. **Gonergrat Bahn** ☎ 027/9214711 ⊕ www.gornergrat. ch. **Mont Blanc/St. Bernard Express** ☎ 027/7216840 ⊕ www.momc.ch.

Contacts & Resources

EMERGENCIES

There are standardized telephone numbers throughout Switzerland for emergencies.

🔗 **Ambulance** ☎ 144. **Fire** ☎ 118. **Late-night Pharmacies** ☎ 111. **Police** ☎ 117. **Roadside Assistance** ☎ 140.

INTERNET & MAIL

INTERNET CAFÉS Connecting to the Internet gets easier every season with dedicated terminals in most lodging and Wi-Fi connections at cafés. A number of hotels offer complimentary laptops that you take to your room. Tourist offices have listings of spots where you can log on.

🔗 **Internet Cafés Centre Sportif** ✉ rue du Centre Sportif Verbier ☎ 027/7717542 ⊕ www.verbier-sport.ch. **Restaurant Le Farinet** ✉ rue Louis-Antille 7 Montana ☎ 027/4813615. **Stoked** ✉ Hofmattstr. 7 Zermatt ☎ 027/9677020 ⊕ www.stoked.ch.

POST OFFICES Rail stations and bus transfer points are where you also will find most post offices. City postal centers remain open all day; village outposts close over lunch. General hours are 8–6 weekdays, 8–noon Saturday, closed Sunday except in urban hubs.

🔗 **Post Offices SION** ✉ 1 pl. de la Gare.

TOUR OPTIONS

Guided coach tours of Valais, including lodging and dining packages, are offered by Valais Tourism. Sion's Air-Glaciers has several itineraries out of Sion for groups of four or six who want a bird's-eye view of Valais—from a helicopter. Prices start at 360 SF for 10 minutes.

🏠 **Air-Glaciers** ☎ 027/3291415.

VISITOR INFORMATION

The main tourist office for Valais is in Sion, but there are also local offices in other Valaisan towns.

🏠 Local Tourist Offices **Bettmeralp** ✉ CH-3992 ☎ 027/9286060 ⊕ www.bettmeralp. ch. **Brig** ✉ Train station, CH-3900 ☎ 027/9216030 ⊕ www.brig.ch/tourismus. **Crans-Montana** ✉ CH-3963 ☎ 027/4850404 ⊕ www.crans-montana.ch. **Leukerbad** ✉ CH-3954 ☎ 027/4727171 ⊕ www.leukerbad.ch. **Martigny** ✉ 9 pl. Centrale, CH-1920 ☎ 027/7212220 ⊕ www.martignytourism.ch. **Riederalp** ✉ CH-3987 ☎ 027/9286050 ⊕ www.riederalp.ch. **Saas-Fee** ✉ CH-3906 ☎ 027/9581858 ⊕ www.saas-fee.ch. **Sierre and Val d'Anniviers** ✉ CH-3960 ☎ 027/4558535 ⊕ www.sierre-salgesch.ch. **St-Maurice** ✉ 1 ave. des Terreaux, CH-1890 ☎ 024/4854040 ⊕ www.st-maurice.ch. **Sion** ✉ pl. de la Planta, CH-1950 ☎ 027/3277727 ⊕ www.siontourism.ch. **Verbier** ✉ pl. Centrale, CH-1936 ☎ 027/7753888 ⊕ www.verbier.ch. **Zermatt** ✉ CH-3920 ☎ 027/9668100 ⊕ www.zermatt.ch.

🏠 Regional Tourist Office **Valais Main Cantonal Tourist Office** ✉ 6 rue Pré-Fleuri, CH-1951 Sion ☎ 027/3273570 🖨 027/3273571 ⊕ www.valaistourism.ch.

SUGGESTED TOURS THROUGH VAUD

If time is limited and let's say you only have three days, fly into Geneva Cointrin and drive the shore highway through Coppet—site of Madame de Staël's famous chateau—to Nyon to visit its Roman museum and medieval castle. Overnight in one of the lake's smaller towns before taking a full day to immerse yourself in the sights, shops, and streetside cafés of the region's largest city, Lausanne. On the next day, set out for the winding Corniche de la Vaud, visiting a *vignoble* (vineyard) or two in Cull. You'll end up at the lakefront town of Montreux, with its fabled Château de Chillon.

If you have five days to tour the region, start with two days savoring Lausanne and its Old Town, museums, and hyperactive waterfront. Lunch at one of the region's top restaurants will consume hours but is lighter on your wallet than dinner. On your third day, follow the Corniche route east as it winds through the vineyards of Lavaux. Stop for photos (pull-offs are strategically interspersed), walk a section of the wine trail, and definitely taste a glass of white wine. The harbor-front town of Vevey deserves a leisurely visit, especially its older section. A night's rest here or in Montreux will ready you to take in the glitzy, Riviera-like city's highlights before touring the Château de Chillon. Hop a late train from Montreux, or take the half-hour winding drive for a good night's sleep in the brisk mountain air of Villars-sur-Ollon, where chalet architecture contrasts with contemporary museums and estate homes. Break in the new day with an Alpine walk before heading back down the steep canyon to the main roads that speed you west to Nyon for a last afternoon learning about the Roman influence.

If you can go the Grand Tour route with ten days at your disposal, spend more time outside the cities in wine villages and mountain resorts. After launching your tour with a few days in Lausanne, go west along the Route du Vignoble to Morges and Nyon, which you can use as a base to explore this part of Vaud, including a side trip to Coppet. (Lake steamers can serve as alternative transportation for town-hopping.) Backtrack east past Lausanne, and pick up the Corniche road for stops in Cully and St-Saphorin to taste local wines. If you arrive in Vevey on a Saturday, you may need a few extra hours to peruse the market, and if fatigue is creeping in, a spa appointment will remedy it.

Next stop: the resort town of Montreux paired with a visit to the Château de Chillon. Leaving the lake behind, zigzag your way into the Alpes Vaudoises, which have been staring over your shoulder for days. Spend a couple of nights in Villars-sur-Ollon to hike, ski, or bask on a sunny balcony. In winter, if the passes are closed by snow, return to Montreux to board the Montreux-Oberland-Bernois Railroad (MOB), a spectacularly panoramic train ride.

Vaud

LAUSANNE, MONTREUX, LES ALPES VAUDOISES

Château d'Aigle

WORD OF MOUTH

"If you only have one day as a day trip from Paris, my vote would be for Lausanne, as we found it to be most charming, with a lovely waterfront district, Ouchy, where one takes the steamboat to Château de Chillon. We found Lausanne just very pretty, elegant, and slow paced."

—Maribel

"If you prefer beautiful views to small European cities, stay in Montreux, not Geneva."

—LynFrance

WELCOME TO VAUD

TOP REASONS TO GO

★ **Montreux's Promenade du Lac.** Walk three magical miles along Lac Léman to the Chateau de Chillon, Switzerland's most beautiful castle.

★ **Tramping with Charlie Chaplin:** Vevey commemorates its celebrated citizen in bronze at its lake rose garden and will open a new museum in his honor in 2008.

★ **Lausanne's Table for Two:** Acolyte of superchef Fredy Giradet, Phillipe Rochat is now a master culinary king in his own right.

★ **The Grape Escape:** From La Côte to Chablais, vineyards and wine cellars allow you to sip vintages that seldom make it beyond the border.

★ **Palatial pursuits:** Grand dames of luxury, the Beau Rivage Palace and Montreux Palace hotels even synchronize their gilded awnings to the sun's daily tour over the lake.

1 **La Côte.** Studded with wine villages, this region is famed for its chateaux—**Coppet's** housed Madame de Staël, **Prangins** displays Swiss history, and **Morges** has 10,000 miniature lead soldiers in residence. But don't miss waterside **Nyon**, founded by Julius Caesar.

2 Lausanne. Not quite the city it was when Voltaire, Rousseau, and Victor Hugo waxed passionate about its beauty, **Lausanne** is largely a modern maze, but here and there you'll enjoy a burnt-orange jumble of medieval rooftops, shuttered windows with flower boxes, and misty **Lac Léman** and the Alps. Happily, the art and nightlife scenes are lively.

Lausanne on Lake Geneva

3 **Les Alpes Vaudoises.** This high-altitude, ear-popping Alpine forgetaway is a well-kept secret to most but **Villars-sur-Ollon** and **Les Diablerets** are names whispered by the best skiers.

In the region of les Diablerets

GETTING ORIENTED

From Lord Byron to Audrey Hepburn, beauty-lovers have always been attracted to the crescent-shaped, glacier-fed Lac Léman (aka Lake Geneva). Beyond its dockside villages and vineyards, more urban desires can be sated by Lausanne's cathedral architecture, modern art, and fine dining.

LAVAUX VIGNOBLES A9
Lausanne
Cully
St-Saphorin
Vevey **4**
Montreux
Villeneuve
St-Gingolph
Dent d'Oche ▲

Châtel-St-Denis
A12
Dent de Lys ▲
Montbovon

Vanil Noir
Chateau-doex

LES ALPES VAUDOISES

Col des Mosses
3
Les Diablerets
Col de la Croix
Les Diablerets ▲
Villars-sur-Ollon

Aigle
A9
Monthey
St-Maurice

Grand Muveran ▲

FRANCE

4 **Lavaux Vignobles & Riviera.** Set amid wine villages, the gorgeously picturesque Corniche de la Vaud heads toward **Vevey**, home to Nestlé chocolates. Globetrotters have always loved this romantic town—Rousseau, Henry James, and Hemingway are just a few who loved taking walks here. More modern is **Montreux**: spilling down the hill to a sunny bay, this usually tranquil city goes hot-cool when the Jazz Festival takes over in July.

View of Rivaz

VAUD PLANNER

Getting Around

Excellent rail and bus service links towns, depositing commuters and travelers at clean, well-lit stations and shopping hubs in the heart of everything.

If you must drive, rent the smallest car your physique and luggage will allow. Negotiating narrow lanes in wine villages and parking in cities is a headache.

To access wineries in La Côte and Chablais and to traverse the Corniche road of the Lavaux a car is essential.

Intercity trains stopping in Nyon, Morges, Lausanne, Vevey, and Montreux dovetail their schedules for transfers to local S-trains and buses.

The best of the region—whether city or countryside—can easily be experienced on foot, supplemented by an occasional taxi or public transit when the grade becomes too steep or the traveler too weary.

How's the Weather?

The lake sparkles and clouds lift from Mont Blanc from spring to fall; November tends to be drizzly gray, and then winter brightens things up above the plain (as they call the flatter terrain surrounding the lake). Crowds monopolize Montreux and Chillon year-round but overwhelm it in July (jazz festival time) and August (Europe-wide vacations). It's worth aiming for concert and dance season in Lausanne: from September through May. Prime ski time in the Alpes Vaudoises is from late December through Easter, and prices go up accordingly. Remember that at these latitudes summer daylight extends until 9 PM, allowing you to pack a lot into one day; the reverse is true in winter.

Making the Most of Your Time

To experience the highlights of lake and mountain, reserve five days. Spend two savoring Lausanne and its Old Town, museums, and hyperactive waterfront. Dine at one of the region's top restaurants; lunch will leave more funds in your travel budget than an evening meal.

The Corniche route winds its way through the vineyards and hamlets of the Lavaux. Pull-offs are strategically interspersed for photo-ops and to steady the nerves of drivers not used to narrow, cantilevered roadways. Get out and walk a section of the wine trail and definitely taste a glass of white wine. A few hours in the harbor-front town of Vevey, especially its older section, and the glitzy, Riviera-like city of Montreux will suffice.

A visit to the region would be incomplete without a chateaux tour of Chillon; while heavily touristed it is exemplary of life within a walled fortress. It's the location that inspired Lord Byron to pen his famous poem, "Prisoner of Chillon." For a good night's sleep in the brisk mountain air, hop a train from Montreux or take the winding drive to Villars-sur-Ollon, where chalet architecture contrasts dramatically with contemporary museums and estate homes of the low lands. Break in the new day with an Alpine walk before doubling back down the steep canyon for connections to Nyon for a dose of Roman history.

Finding a Place to Stay

It's a pleasure unique to Vaud to wake up, part floor-length sheers, and look out over Lac Léman to Mont Blanc. A series of 19th-century grand hotels with banks of balconied lakeview rooms were created to offer this luxury to such grand-tourists as Strauss, Twain, Stravinsky, and Henry James. Yet there's no shortage of charming inns offering similar views on an intimate scale. Up another 3,936 feet you'll find the antithesis to an airy lakefront inn: the cozy, honey-gold Alpine chalet, with down quilts in starched white envelopes, balustrade balconies with potted geraniums, and also panoramic views.

The hotels of Lausanne and Montreux are long on luxury and grace, and low prices are not easy to find. Especially at peak periods—Christmas–New Year's and June–August—it's important to book ahead. These days, in-room Internet connections, safes, and business centers are the rule rather than the exception. Small auberges in the villages along the lake and the vineyards offer traditional dishes and simple comforts. Up in the Pays-d'Enhaut and the Alps southeast of the lake, there are comfortable mountain hotels in all price ranges—though rates are naturally higher in the resorts themselves. At the cantonal tourist office Web site, www.lake-geneva-region.ch, you can scan hotel facilities and rates, then click to reserve.

Pampered Pooches

In this posh part of the country, animal lovers should remember that the Swiss take their dogs everywhere—out to lunch, for a ride on the bus, to visit relatives (both two and four-legged ones), even on vacation. Of course, some hotels charge extra for canine guests and unless the owner wants to order special meals from room service, it is expected they will pack their pet's favorite food (surely Louis Vuitton has a piece of luggage specially designed for this purpose).

In Search of the Perfect Lunch

Because of its sunny, scenic position, the Lac Léman shore draws weekenders and car tourists who speed along the waterfront highway, careening through cobbled wine towns in search of the perfect meal.

As in all great wine regions, *dégustation* (wine tasting) and *haute gastronomie* (refined cuisine) go hand in hand.

In inns and auberges throughout La Côte and Lavaux (the two stretches of vineyard-lined shore) you'll dine beside ascoted oenophiles who lower their half lenses to study a label and order a multicourse feast to complement their extensive tastings.

To experience Vaud's best cuisine, look for *déjeuners d'affairs* (business lunches), plats du jour, and prix-fixe menus, which can offer considerable savings over à la carte dining.

Of course, you will be spoiled for choice by the quality of Lausanne's restaurants. Prices–like quality–can be high, but if you wander through the back streets you will see that the less affluent in Lausanne eat well, too. Even some department stores have excellent inexpensive restaurants and cafés.

WHAT IT COSTS In Swiss francs

	$$$$	$$$	$$	$	¢
Restaurants	over 60 SF	40 SF–60 SF	25 SF–40 SF	15 SF–25 SF	under 15 SF
Hotels	over 350 SF	250 SF–350 SF	175 SF–250 SF	100 SF–175 SF	under 100 SF

Restaurant prices are per person for a main course at dinner. Hotel prices are for two people in a standard double room in high season, including tax and service.

Updated by
Kay
Winzenried

IN JUST ONE REGION, you can experience a complete cultural, gastro-nomic, and scenic sweep of Switzerland. Vaud (pronounced Voh) has a stunning Gothic cathedral (Lausanne) and one of Europe's most evoca-tive châteaux (Chillon), palatial hotels and weathered-wood chalets, so-phisticated culture and ancient folk traditions, snowy Alpine slopes and balmy lake resorts, simple fondue, and the finesse of some of the world's great chefs. Everywhere there are the roadside vineyards with luxurious rows of vines and rich, black loam.

This is the region of Lac Léman (Lake Geneva), a grand body of water graced by Lausanne and Montreux. The lake's romance—Savoy Alps looming across the horizon, steamers fanning across its surface, palm trees rustling along its shores—made it a focal point of the budding 19th-century tourist industry and an inspiration to the arts. In a Henry James novella, the imprudent Daisy Miller made waves when she crossed its waters unchaperoned to visit Chillon; Byron's Bonivard languished in chains in the fortress's dungeons. From their homes outside Montreux, Stravinsky wrote *The Rite of Spring* and Strauss his transcendent *Four Last Songs*. There are resorts, of course—Leysin, Villars, Château-d'Oex—but none so famous as to upstage the region itself.

Throughout the canton, French is spoken, and the temperament the Vau-doise inherited from the Romans and Burgundians sets them apart from their Swiss-German fellow citizens. It's evident in their humor, their style, and—above all—their love of their own good wine.

Exploring Vaud

Lac Léman is a graceful swelling in the Rhône River, which passes through the northern hook of the Valais and channels between the French and Vaudoise Alps before breaking into the open at Bouveret, west of Villeneuve. The lake is shared by three of Switzerland's great French cities, grandes dames of the Suisse Romande: Lausanne, Mon-treux, and Geneva. Though the lake's southern shore lies in France's Haute-Savoie, the green hillsides of the north portion and the cluster of nearby Alps that looms over its east end are all part of the canton of Vaud.

LA CÔTE

Just northeast of Geneva, La Côte (the shore) of Lac Léman has been settled since Roman times, with its south-facing slopes cultivated for wine. It is thus peppered with ancient waterfront and hillside towns, castles, and Roman remnants. Train and bus service connects most towns and villages, but a car is a must if you want to wind through tiny wine vil-lages. Do get out and walk—if only to hear the trickling of any num-ber of Romanesque trough fountains and to saunter along a lakefront promenade. Be willing to traverse a few times from the slopes to the wa-terfront and back if you're determined to cover all the region's charms; sticking exclusively to either the diminutive Route du Vignoble or the shore road deprives you of some wonderful sights.

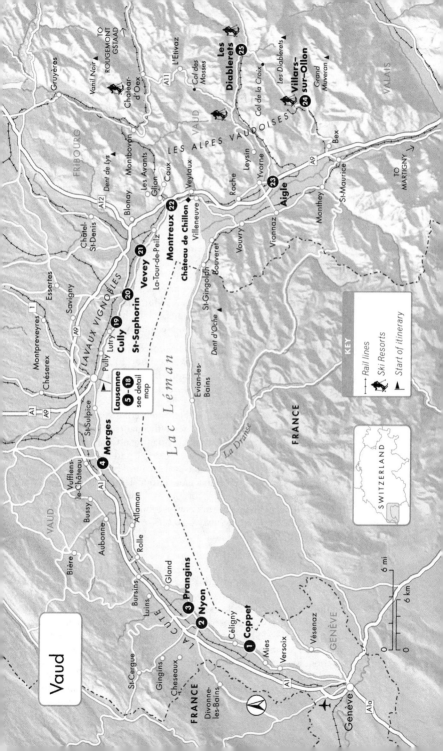

Coppet

▶ ❶ **To & From:** *Coppet is but the first of many towns that rim Lac Léman and are strung along a main rail line in synchronized links approximately 20 minutes apart. Main stations like Morges, Nyon, Lausanne, Vevey, and Montreux are served by all trains (regional and inter-regional) allowing multiple arrivals and departures every hour; Coppet, Rolle, Lutry, Cully, St-Saphorin by the local S-trains every half hour. Ticket prices vary with short runs costing 3–5 SF and longer ones 10–15 SF. For departure times and prices for trains and buses for most destinations in this chapter, check with www.sbb.ch—the main Swiss public transportation Web site—or call 0900/300300 (1,19 SF per minute). Remember, if you have a Swiss Pass or another rail-discounting card, it also applies to the buses. Coppet is 9 km (6 mi) south of Nyon, 46 km (28 mi) southwest of Lausanne.*

Its pretty, arcaded main street, with occasional peeks through to the jettied waterfront, makes Coppet a pleasant stop for a stroll. But it's the
★ **Château de Coppet** that puts this lake village on the map. Enclosed within vast iron gates, the château has been kept in its original 18th-century form, with luxurious Louis XVI furnishings arranged in a convincingly lived-in manner; its grounds, which harbor grand old trees, hidden courtyards, and stone stairs, are equally evocative.

Built in the 1300s, the château was restored when purchased in 1784 by Jacques Necker, a Genevan banker who served as financial minister to France's Louis XVI. The turmoil of the French Revolution and Necker's opposition to Napoléon forced him into exile in this splendid structure, where his remarkable daughter, Madame de Staël, created the most intriguing salon in Europe. Her intellectual sparkle and concern for the fiery issues of the day attracted the giants of the early Romantic period: Lord Byron, the Swiss historian Jean-Charles Sismondi, the German writer August Wilhelm von Schlegel, and British historian Edward Gibbon. Part of the château is still occupied by family descendants, but you can see the interior on a guided tour. The language of the commentary is generally chosen according to the language of the tour participants. Tours in English are not always available. ⊠ *3 chemin des Murs, uphill from waterfront highway* ☎ *022/7761028* ⊕ *www.swisscastles.ch* ☑ *10 SF* ⊙ *Apr.–Oct., daily 2–6.*

Where to Stay & Eat

$$–$$$ ✕⌂ **Hôtel du Lac.** First ranked as a *grand logis* in 1628 to distinguish it from a common roadhouse, this historic inn still feels like an exclusive men's club, catering to power-lunchers and well-heeled travelers. It fronts on the main road and is accessible by boat, with a sycamore-shaded terrace and rooms with exposed beams, niches, and antiques. Its inventive restaurant ($$–$$$) draws a regular clientele for its exquisite open-grill specialties, such as Simmental fillet de boeuf or lamb loin with jus reduction. Reservations for the restaurant are essential. ⊠ *51 Grand-rue, CH-1296* ☎ *022/9608000* 🖷 *022/9608001* ⊕ *www.hoteldulac.ch* ⤳ *12 rooms, 4 suites, 3 apartments* ♿ *Restaurant, some kitchens, minibars, cable TV, bar, some free parking, kennel* ▤ *AE, DC, MC, V* ⦿ *CP.*

11

EN ROUTE

With its lakefront setting, small port, lawns for sunbathing, and pier, the endearing village of **Céligny** provides the best swimming opportunities for miles around. The enclave, 6 km (4 mi) north of Coppet, is wholly charming: rows of vineyards, a historic (but private) château and church, and a village square adorned with flowers and a stone fountain. Richard Burton made his home here during the last years of his life. You can visit the village cemetery where you'll find Burton's simple grave in the smaller area, hugging the edge of the forest.

Nyon

➋ *10 km (6 mi) north of Coppet, 27 km (17 mi) southwest of Lausanne.*

Lovely Nyon, with its waterfront drive, shops, museums, and a castle dominating its cliff-top Old Town, was founded by Julius Caesar around 45 BC as a camp for war veterans. The Romans called it Noviodunum and developed the entire region for miles around. Lovely views can be had from the château-museum's terrace and the town's waterfront promenade, where boats and swans bob in the waves.

★ Flanked by a statue of Caesar, the **Musée Romain** (Roman Museum) contains an attractively mounted collection of sumptuously detailed architectural stonework, fresco fragments, statuary, mosaics, and earthenware. The museum was built atop foundations of a 1st century AD basilica; a pristine miniature model inside and an excellent trompe l'oeil palace on an outside wall evoke the remarkable original structure. A complete listing of the exhibits in English is available upon request, as are guided tours. ✉ *rue Maupertuis* ☎ *022/3617591* ⊕ *www.mrn.ch* 💶 *6 SF includes Musée du Léman* ☉ *Apr.–June, Sept., and Oct., Tues.–Sun. 10–noon and 2–6; July and Aug., daily 10–noon, 2–6; Nov.–Mar., Tues.–Sun. 2–6.*

Dominating Nyon's hilltop over the waterfront is **Le Château de Nyon,** a magnificent 12th-century multispire fortress with a terrace that takes in sweeping views of the lake and Mont Blanc. Its spacious rooms hold the collection of the **Musée Historique,** which traces the history of the castle inhabitants from residence by the Dukes of Savoy (1293–1536), through occupation by the Bernese (1536–1798), to reclamation by the canton following the Vaud revolution. The upper floors held prisioners until 1979 while the city council and courts met in chambers here until 1999. Exhibits throughout highlight the city's position as a renowned porcelain center. Modern day conversions include a marriage salon and a *caveau des vignerons* (wine cellar), featuring wines of local growers. ✉ *pl. du Château* ☎ *022/3638351* ⊕ *www.chateaudenyon.ch* 💶 *Free* ☉ *Apr.–Oct., Tues.–Sun. 10–5; Nov.–Mar., Tues.–Sun. 2–5.*

Nestled in a charming floral park that parallels the water, the **Musée du Léman** exhibits models of lake steamers, crew sculls, and private yachts as well as sizable lake-water aquariums, housed in a shuttered 18th-century hospital. ✉ *8 quai Louis-Bonnard* ☎ *022/3610949* ⊕ *www. museeduleman.ch* 💶 *6 SF includes Musée Romain* ☉ *Apr.–Oct., Tues.–Sun. 10–5; Nov.–Mar., Tues.–Sun. 2–5.*

CHÂTEAUX COUNTRY

Home to magnificently restored Chillon, the most visited if not the best château in Switzerland, Vaud offers a variety of smaller draws as well, including Nyon, Coppet, Prangins, Rolle, Allaman, Aubonne, and Aigle. Their salons and gardens tell stories of a grand life often interrupted by hardship. As you travel main highways and back roads, you will see similar compounds appropriated by or constructed anew for rock stars and corporate chieftains. The most legendary house was the Villa Diodati, which still stands in the Geneva suburb of Cologny.

Here, on one stormy night in the summer of 1816, Byron, Shelley, and Shelley's wife, Mary Wollstonecraft Shelley, all competed to think of the most terrifying horror story. While *The Vampyre*—history's very first fictional vampire story—was dreamed up here, it was Mrs. Shelley's *Frankenstein*, which she later fashioned as a novel, that took the prize. Scandalously, the municipality auctioned off the historic decor of the 18th-century house a few years ago, and the house was sold to a private owner.

Where to Stay & Eat

¢–$$ ✕ **Café du Marché.** Away from the activity of the castle plaza, this delightful eatery near the market square has umbrella-shaded tables that spill out onto the cobblestones. Italian influences accent pasta, lake fish, and produce that may have been plucked from one of the nearby open-air stalls. ✉ *3 rue du Marché* 🕾 *022/3623500* 🖃 *MC, V* ☾ *Closed Sun.*

¢–$ ✕ **Auberge du Château.** This traditional restaurant, just steps from Nyon's château, serves straightforward Swiss fare, well-priced plats du jour, and specialty items like shrimp and vegetables on a pillow of saffron cream. In fall the menu expands to include an assortment of game. A big terrace lets diners study the château; in winter, broad windows take in the comings and goings on the municipal plaza. ✉ *8 pl. du Château* 🕾 *022/3616312* 🖃 *AE, DC, MC, V.*

$$–$$$ 🏠 **Hôtel Real.** This contemporary white box stands out on the lower plaza across from the lake promenade. A sleek reception area with adjacent bar and seating has stone floors, leather furniture, and novel lighting. Bleached wooden furniture and crisp white linens give guest accommodations a refreshing feel, especially when lake breezes blow through open balcony doors that frame stunning views of sailboats and mountains. Le Grand Café, the hotel's Italian restaurant, is a meeting place for locals and day-trippers drawn to the active waterfront. ✉ *1 pl. de Savoie, CH-1260* 🕾 *022/3658585* 🖷 *022/3658586* ⊕ *www.hotelrealnyon.ch* ↪ *29 rooms, 1 suite* ♦ *Restaurant, minibars, cable TV, in-room VCRs, in-room data ports, bar, some free parking* 🖃 *AE, MC, V* ⦿ *CP.*

$–$$$ 🏠 **Hôtel Ambassador.** Terra-cotta stucco and peaked dormers set off this petite hotel on Nyon's main thoroughfare. Request one of the "under the roof" rooms; these have hand-hewn dark wooden beams, floral bedding, and compact modern baths. The quiet garden terrace with its view of the castle (which is illuminated at night) is an exquisite spot for a glass of wine or a light meal. ✉ *26 rue St-Jean, CH-1260* ☎ *022/9944848* 🖷 *022/9944860* ⊕ *www.hotel-ambassador-nyon.ch* ⇆ *20 rooms* ⅋ *Restaurant, minibars, cable TV, in-room data ports, bar; no a/c* ▤ *AE, DC, MC, V* ℠ *CP.*

Prangins

❸ **To & From:** *Take a train to the Nyon station and switch to local bus service that picks up passengers outside the main entrance. The No. 31 or 32 routes (2.80 SF) take 6 minutes to the village stop; from there it is a 3-minute walk to the château. Prangins is 3 km (2 mi) northeast of Nyon.*

You'll see the elegant hillside chateau that's home to the national museum before you reach this little commune, where the pace of life moves gently between the boulangerie, post office, and café. The 18th-century

★ **Château de Prangins** is the Suisse Romande branch of the **Musée National Suisse** (Swiss National Museum). The castle estate once had land holdings that stretched all the way to Rolle. Its four floors detail (in four languages, including English) Swiss life and history in the 18th and 19th centuries. Surrounded by parks and gardens (take note of the extensive culinary plantings set according to ancient documents), the museum is also a major venue for cultural events and regional celebrations. A café with terrace is open for lunch and refreshments. ☎ *022/9948890* ⊕ *www.musee-suisse.com* ✉ *7 SF* ⊙ *Tues.–Sun. 11–5.*

NEED A BREAK? After strolling the galleries and gardens of the National Museum, head to **Rapp Chocolatier** (✉ 6 rue des Alpes ☎ 022/3617914 ⊙ Closed Sun.), a petite chocolate shop in the heart of town. Here handmade confections are stacked in perfect pyramids, and a school and demonstration kitchen are adjacent, so if your timing is right you'll see artisans shaping molten cocoa and plying their forms with heavenly fillings. The family also has a *confiserie* (sweet shop) on the place Bel-Air in Nyon and in Gland.

Where to Stay & Eat

$$–$$$ ✕🏠 **La Barcarolle.** Hidden in a parklike setting off the lake road, this mustard-color complex is a modern *relais* (inn) amid historic châteaux and country homes. The hotel's name and musical theme reflect its owner's fondness for great classical composers. Guest rooms with lawn and lake views contain painted furniture and floral furnishings in red and gold. Spacious baths have granite countertops, separate tub and shower, and towel warmers. The bright breakfast room and fine dining area ($$–$$$$) spill onto a wide terrace. French cuisine dominates the menu, which ranges from regional fish specialties to guinea fowl in a honey-ginger sauce. ✉ *rte. de Promenthoux, CH-1197* ☎ *022/3657878* 🖷 *022/3657800* ⊕ *www.labarcarolle.ch* ⇆ *36 rooms, 3 suites* ⅋ *Restaurant, minibars, cable TV, Wi-Fi, pool, lake, marina, bar, free parking, no-smoking floor* ▤ *DC, MC, V* ℠ *CP.*

EN ROUTE Twelve kilometers (7 mi) northeast of Nyon, the lakefront village of **Rolle** merits a detour for a look at its dramatic 13th-century **château,** built at the water's edge by a Savoyard prince. While in town, you can visit the

Moinat Antiques and Decoration shop for a sample of what it takes to furnish a grand country home.

Route du Vignoble

36 km (22 mi) between Nyon and Lausanne.

Parallel to the waterfront highway, threading through the steep-sloping vineyards between Nyon and Lausanne, the Route du Vignoble (Vineyard Road) unfolds a rolling green landscape high above the lake, punctuated by noble manors and vineyards. **Luins,** home of the flinty, fruity white wine of the same name, is a typical pretty village. Just up the road, the village of **Vinzel** develops its own white wines on sunny slopes and sells them from the *vin-celliers* (wine cellars) that inspired its name.

> **LOCAL TREATS**
>
> The village of Vinzel is the best source for a very local specialty, the malakoff. These rich, steamy cheese-and-egg beignets have always been a favorite of the Vaudois, but after the Crimean Wars they were renamed after a beloved officer who led his army of Vaud-born mercenaries to victory in the siege of Sebastopol.

The route continues through **Bursins,** home of an 11th-century Romanesque church, and goes all the way to Morges. The road is clearly signposted throughout.

NEED A BREAK? While driving the Route du Vignoble, you can sample the local wine and munch a few rich *malakoffs* (egg-and-Gruyère fritters) at **Au Coeur de la Côte** (⊠ Vinzel ☎ 021/8241141) or **Auberge de Luins** (⊠ Luins ☎ 021/8241159). Usually there is a cluster of villagers gathered at the community table debating the quality of the latest vintage or regional politics.

Morges

❹ *23 km (14 mi) northeast of Prangins, 8 km (5 mi) west of Lausanne.*

On the waterfront just west of the urban sprawl of Lausanne, Morges is a pleasant lake town favored by sailors and devotees of its **Fête de la Tulipe** (Tulip Festival), held annually in April and May. The town's castle, built by the duke of Savoy around 1286 as a defense against the bishop-princes of Lausanne, now houses the **Musée du Château,** which combines three collections: weapons, military uniforms, and 10,000 miniature lead soldiers. In the Salle Général Henri Guisan, you'll find memorabilia of this World War II general, much honored for keeping both sides happy enough to leave Switzerland safely alone. ☎ 021/3160990 🖾 7 SF ⊙ Feb.–June and Sept.–mid-Dec., weekdays 10–noon, 1:30–5, weekends 1:30–5; July and Aug., Tues.–Sun. 10–5.

In the heart of town, a 15th-century courtyard-centered mansion, once home to renowned engraver Alexis Forel, displays the holdings of the **Musée Alexis Forel.** Although most of Forel's exceptional engravings are in the Musée Jenisch, in Vevey, here you can experience his home surroundings. Thick-beamed salons filled with high-back chairs, stern por-

CLOSE UP

Wild About Wine

11

AS ONE OF THE MAIN wine-producing regions in Switzerland, Vaud is best savored when sampling the local vintages.

If you're only tangentially interested, check the blackboard listings in any café for local names of *vins ouvert* (open wines), sold by the deciliter: the fruity whites of Épesses and St-Saphorin of Lavaux (between Lausanne and Montreux); the flinty Luins, Vinzel, and other La Côte variations (between Lausanne and Geneva); or the flowery Yvorne and Aigle, the best-known names from Le Chablais (between Villeneuve and Bex). You'll be tasting the previous season's harvest (local vintages are not aged).

If time allows, drive down narrow, fountain-studded stone streets in tiny wine villages, where inns and *vignobles* (vineyards) offer tastings. Keep an eye peeled for hand-painted signs announcing CAVEAU OUVERT or DÉGUSTATION; this indicates that a cellar owner or cooperative is pouring wine. (Do designate a driver; laws are strict.)

Local vintners welcome visitors year-round, except during harvest, which is usually in October. Some vineyards have sophisticated tasting rooms; at others, a family member gathers guests around a tasting barrel within the working cellar. You may share a barrel top or slot at the bar with locals, as these are communal gathering spots. If there is a particular winemaker you want to visit, phone ahead for an appointment. Most cellars charge for tasting, and if you occupy the winemaker's time beyond a casual pour, it is appropriate to buy a bottle unless you find the label not to your liking.

In July and August you can head for a Saturday market in Vevey, where, for the price of a commemorative glass, winemakers and tasters move from booth to booth. To boost your knowledge of wine cultivation, processing, and labeling, go to the Château d'Aigle's Musée de la Vigne et du Vin.

Interconnected hiking trails (signposted in several languages, including English, and full of informative tidbits) span the length of the shore from Ouchy to Chillon, traversing vineyards and traffic arteries from the lakefront to hillside villages. Walking the entire 32-km (19-mi) *parcours viticole* (wine route) takes about 8½ hours, but you can also break it into smaller segments, allowing time for wine tastings and meals at local restaurants. Tourist offices can provide a copy of the specialized map that identifies the route and cellars open for tastings. (If you're doing a portion of the trail, you can easily catch a train back to your starting point, as there are hourly stops in every village along the lakefront.) Speaking of trains, if the distance and grade of the trails seem too much, you can take the bright yellow coaches of the Train des Vignes (vineyard train) through the rows of pinot noir, gamay, and chasselas vines. The train starts from Vevey's station, near the waterfront, and ends more than 2,000 feet above sea level in the village of Puidoux-Chexbres; its timetable is part of the regular CFF schedule.

traits, and delicate china remain as they were in the 1920s, when musicians and writers such as Stravinsky, Paderewski, and Rolland gathered for lively discussions and private concerts. An attic room has a selection of 18th-century puppets and porcelain dolls. ☒ *54 Grand-rue* ☎ *021/8012647* ☒ *7 SF* ☉ *Apr.–early Dec., Tues.–Sun. 2–6.*

The oar-powered warships of the Greeks, Romans, and Phoenicians once crossed the waters of Lac Léman. Now you can follow in their wake on *La Liberté,* a reconstruction of a 17th-century galley. This brainchild of historian Jean-Pierre Hirt is part public works project, part historical re-creation. Unemployed workers helped handcraft the 183-foot vessel. Christened in 2001, the ship sails the lake twice a day mid-May to mid-October; the $1^{1}/_{2}$ tour costs 27 SF, the two-hour 38 SF. You must book space in advance. ☒ *45 rue de Lausanne* ☎ *021/8035031* ☒ *Shipyard 5 SF* ☉ *Daily 10–6.*

OFF THE
BEATEN
PATH **VUFFLENS-LE-CHÂTEAU –** This village, 2 km (1 mi) northwest of Morges, is known for its namesake château, a 15th-century Savoyard palace with a massive donjon and four lesser towers, all trimmed in fine Piedmont-style brickwork. It's privately owned, but the grounds are open to the public.

Where to Stay & Eat

$$$–$$$$ ✕⊞ **L'Ermitage des Ravets.** A multicourse gastronomic treat awaits at the restaurant ($$$$; closed Sunday and Monday) of this 17th-century farmhouse, set beneath old, draping trees and edged by overflowing garden beds. Chef Bernard Ravet serves the classics with creative twists, such as four styles of duck and goose foie gras, saddle of venison with truffles and chanterelles, or sea bream in leek papillotte (pouch). Reservations are essential and the business lunch a gem. Chic rooms trimmed in dark green and burgundy are furnished with polished antiques and *canard* (duck) accessories to create a country setting that begs you to stay for more than just one superb meal. ☒ *26 rte. du Village, CH-1134 Vufflens-le-Château* ☎ *021/8046868* 🖨 *021/8022240* ⊕ *www.ravet.ch* ⇆ *6 rooms, 3 suites* ♨ *Restaurant, in-room safes, minibars, cable TV, Wi-Fi, bar, free parking* ⊟ *AE, MC, V* ☉ *Closed late Dec. and Aug.* ⦿ *CP.*

$$–$$$ ✕⊞ **Hotel Fleur du Lac.** As the draperies are pulled back from south-facing windows, sun-splashed Mont Blanc comes into direct view. This lakefront retreat, just outside town on the main route to Lausanne, is surrounded by abundant seasonal plantings and stately old trees. Rooms are filled with a mix of antique and modern furniture. The terrace and dining room ($–$$$) are the big draws. Fresh perch, a regional favorite, tastes even better when served lakeside. Book well in advance, as their guest return rate is unusually high. ☒ *70 rue de Lausanne, CH-1110* ☎ *021/8815811* 🖨 *021/8115888* ⊕ *www.fleur-du-lac.ch* ⇆ *31 rooms, 7 suites* ♨ *Restaurant, minibars, cable TV, Wi-Fi, bar, free parking; no a/c* ⊟ *AE, DC, MC, V* ⦿ *EP.*

LAUSANNE

"Lausanne is a block of picturesque houses, spilling over two or three gorges, which spread from the same central knot, and are crowned by

GETTING AROUND

You will exhaust yourself if you attempt to walk the hillsides of Lausanne from Ouchy (at the lakefront) to Old Town. So do what the locals do and use the "tl" (Transports Publics de la région Lausannoise), a subway, rail, and bus network. The Métro subway line is under renovation and expansion until 2008 so its underground stops have been replaced with tandem buses that depart from a stop across the street from the main train station. The automated ticket machines can be confusing as they list all routes. Short runs will get you anywhere you want to go in the heart of the city in 10 minutes and should cost about 2.50 SF. For schedules and fares go to www.t-l.ch. Lausanne serves as gateway to the region and connector for the east-west routes across the Alps to Milan (3 hrs) and the TGV to Paris or Avignon (4 hrs). Trains coming from the north (Zurich-Bern) make an eastern turn stopping in Lausanne before continuing to Morges, Nyon, and Geneva; to travel west (Vevey, Montreux) a switch often on the adjacent platform is necessary.

a cathedral like a tiara. . . . On the esplanade of the church . . . I saw the lake over the roofs, the mountains over the lake, clouds over the mountains, and stars over the clouds. It was like a staircase where my thoughts climbed step by step and broadened at each new height." Such was Victor Hugo's impression of this grand and graceful tiered city. Voltaire, Rousseau, Byron, and Cocteau all waxed equally passionate about Lausanne—and not only for its visual beauty. It has been a cultural center for centuries, the world drawn first to its magnificent Gothic cathedral and the powers it represented, then to its university, and during the 18th and 19th centuries to its vibrant intellectual and social life. Today the Swiss consider Lausanne a most desirable city in which to live.

Lausanne's importance today stems from its several disparate roles in national and world affairs. Politically, it is the site of the Tribunal Fédéral, the highest court of appeals in Switzerland. Commercially, although it is by no means in the same league as Zürich or Bern, it figures as the headquarters for many multinational organizations, corporations, and sports federations. On a major international rail route and at a vital national junction 66 km (41 mi) northeast of Geneva, Lausanne serves as a trade center for most of the surrounding agricultural regions and the expanding industrial towns of Vaud. This prosperity spills over into the arts; there's a surprising concentration of dance companies—including that of Maurice Béjart—as well as several theaters, jazz cellars, and a pair of excellent orchestras. Thousands of students come for the top-notch universities, private academies, and technology centers. Lausanne is also the world's Olympic capital; the International Olympic Committee has been based here since 1915 (its founder, Baron Pierre de Coubertin, is buried nearby at Montoie Cemetery).

The balance of old and new has not always been kept. The first 20 years after World War II saw an immense building boom, with old buildings and whole neighborhoods pulled down to make way for shining contemporary office and apartment buildings—an architectural exuberance that has given Lausanne a rather lopsided air.

Exploring Lausanne

Rising in tiers from the lakeside at Ouchy (1,181 feet) to more than 2,000 feet, the city covers three hills, which are separated by gorges that once channeled rivers. The rivers have been built over, and huge bridges span the gaps across the hilltops. On one hill in particular, modern skyscrapers contrast brutally with the beautiful proportions of the cathedral rising majestically from its crest. Atmospheric alleys and narrow streets have mostly been demolished, yet the Old Town clustered around the cathedral has been painstakingly restored.

Below the Old Town spreads the commercial city center, and in the bottom of the hollow between avenue Jules Gonin and rue de Genève is the Flon, a neighborhood with plenty of nightspots. Still farther south, along the lake, is the separate township of Ouchy, an animated resort area dominated by the Château d'Ouchy, with a tower dating from the Middle Ages.

What to See

❾ Cathédrale de Notre-Dame (Cathedral of Our Lady). A Burgundian
Fodor'sChoice Gothic architectural treasure, this cathedral, also called the Cathédrale
★ de Lausanne, is Switzerland's largest church—and probably its finest. Begun in the 12th century by Italian, Flemish, and French architects, it was completed in 1275. Pope Gregory X came expressly to perform the historic consecration ceremony—of double importance, as it also served as a coronation service for Rudolf of Habsburg as the new Holy Roman Emperor. Rudolf brought his wife, eight children, seven cardinals, five archbishops, 17 bishops, four dukes, 15 counts, and a multitude of lesser lords to watch in the church's exquisitely proportioned nave.

Viollet-le-Duc, a renowned restorer who worked on the cathedrals of Chartres and Notre-Dame-de-Paris, brought portions of the building to Victorian Gothic perfection in the 19th century. His repairs are visible as paler stone contrasting with the weathered local sandstone. Streamlined to the extreme, without radiating chapels or the excesses of later Gothic trim, the cathedral wasn't always so spare; in fact, there was brilliant painting. Zealous Reformers plastered over the florid colors, but in so doing they unwittingly preserved them, and now you can see portions of these splendid shades restored in the right transept. The dark and delicate choir contains the 14th-century tomb of the crusader Otto I of Grandson and exceptionally fine 13th-century choir stalls, unusual for their age alone, not to mention their beauty. The church's masterpiece, the 13th-century painted portal, is considered one of Europe's most magnificent. Constant repairs and renovations often shroud parts of the structure in scaffolding.

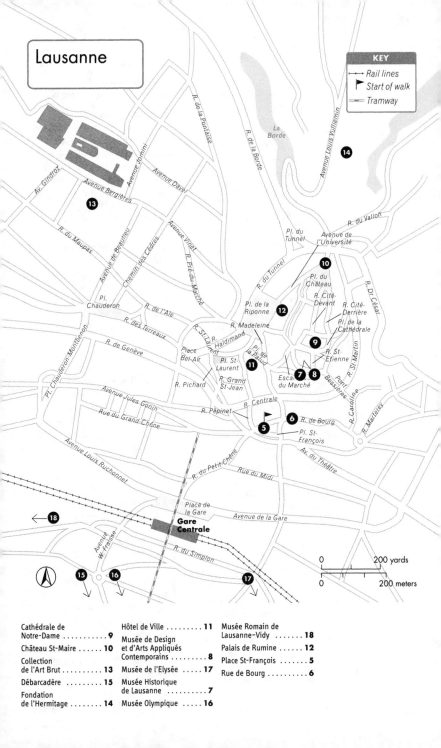

Lausanne

KEY

- ⊢┼┼ Rail lines
- ▶ Start of walk
- ══ Tramway

A GOOD WALK: LAUSANNE

Begin in the commercial hub of the city, the **place St-François** ⑤ ▶ (nicknamed Sainfe by the Lausannois), where you'll see the former Franciscan Église St-François. Behind the church, take a near hairpin turn right onto the fashionable main shopping street, the ancient **rue de Bourg** ⑥. At the top of rue de Bourg, rue Caroline leads you left and left again over the Pont Bessières, where you can see the city's peculiar design spanning gorges and covered rivers.

Crossing the bridge and bearing right brings you up into the Old Town. On your left, the imposing palace of the Old Bishopric now houses the **Musée Historique de Lausanne** ⑦. Adjacent is the **Musée de Design et d'Arts Appliqués Contemporains** ⑧ known as the Mudac to locals. Straight ahead, at the top of rue St-Étienne, towers the tremendous **Cathédrale de Notre-Dame** ⑨, which is on par with some of Europe's finest churches.

With the cathedral on your left, walk up the narrow passage of rue Cité-Derrière to the place du Château and its eponymous monument, the **Château St-Maire** ⑩. As you face the château, turn left and walk down the rue Cité-Devant. As you pass the cathedral again, veer right toward a flight of wooden steps that leads down to the dramatic Escaliers du Marché, a wood-roof medieval staircase and the place de la Palud and the **Hôtel de Ville** ⑪, the seat of the municipal and communal councils. Turning right, just up rue Madeleine, you will come upon the

place de la Riponne and the imposing **Palais de Rumine** ⑫.

A long hike up avenue Vinet, northwest of the Old Town, will take you to the **Collection de l'Art Brut** ⑬, an unusual museum of fringe art across from the Beaulieu convention center. To view the works of more classical, well-known painters, visit the **Fondation de l'Hermitage** ⑭, a 15-minute bus ride from the Old Town. Take Bus 3 from the Gare Centrale (central train station) or Bus 16 from place St-François. South of the Old Town, Ouchy's **Débarcadère** ⑮ has typical quayside attractions—vendors and people strolling on a promenade. It can be easily reached by the steep subway Métro; there are stations across from the Gare Centrale and under the rue du Grand-Chêne in the Flon. (There's also a large underground parking garage, a boon in this space-pressed city.) Just east of Ouchy, on a hillside overlooking the lake, the dramatic **Musée Olympique** ⑯ tells about the history and sports of the Olympic Games. It's less than half a mile from the Débarcadère along the quai de Belgique, which turns into the quai d'Ouchy. Uphill and connected by garden pathways, the **Musée de l'Elysée** ⑰ is a photography museum housed in a restored 18th-century *campagne* (country manor home). West of Ouchy at Vidy is the **Musée Romain de Lausanne-Vidy** ⑱, where you can see a reconstructed private Roman home. Like the Musée Olympique, this is easy to get to on foot or bus; it's just under a mile from the Débarcadère.

Protestant services (the cathedral was reformed in the 16th century) exclude nonworshipping visitors on Sunday at 10 AM and 8 PM. You may want to come instead for the evening concerts given on an almost-weekly basis in spring and autumn; call ahead for a precise schedule. Guided tours are given July to mid-September. ⊠ *pl. de la Cathédrale, Old Town* ☎ *021/ 3167161* ☉ *Apr.–Oct., weekdays 7–7, weekends 8–7; Nov.–Mar., weekdays 7–5:30, weekends 8–5:30.*

> **BEHIND THE SCENES**
>
> A self-portrait of Viollet-le-Duc, renowned restorer of the Cathédrale de Notre-Dame, appears in the face of King David, harp and scroll in hand, to the right of the main portal.

⑩ Château St-Maire. The fortresslike elements of this 15th-century stone cylinder certainly came into play. The castle was built for the bishops of Lausanne; during the 16th century, the citizens wearied of ecclesiastical power and allied themselves with Bern and Fribourg against the bishops protected within. Before long, however, Bern itself marched on Lausanne, put a bailiff in this bishops' castle, and stripped the city fathers of their power. The Bernese imposed Protestantism on the Lausannois, and their Catholic churches and cathedral were ransacked to fill the coffers of Bern. Today the Château St-Maire is the seat of the cantonal government. ⊠ *pl. du Château, Old Town.*

★ ⑬ Collection de l'Art Brut. This singular museum focuses on the genre of fringe or "psychopathological" art, dubbed *l'art brut* (raw art) in the 1940s by French artist Jean Dubuffet. His own collection forms the base of this ensemble of raw material from untrained minds—prisoners, schizophrenics, or the merely obsessed. Strangely enough, the collection is housed in the Château de Beaulieu, a former mansion of Madame de Staël, she of the sophisticated salons. The exhibits range from intricate yarn and textile pieces to a wall full of whimsical seashell masks. One of the most affecting works is a panel of rough carvings made by an asylum patient in solitary confinement; it was shaped with a broken spoon and a chamber-pot handle. You can get here by walking up avenue Vinet or by taking Bus 2 from place St-Laurent in the direction of Le Désert. ⊠ *11 av. des Bergières, Beaulieu* ☎ *021/3152570* ⊕ *www.artbrut.ch* ▣ *8 SF, free the first Sat. of month* ☉ *July and Aug., daily 11–1, 2–6; Sept.–June, Tues.–Sun. 11–1, 2–6.*

☾ ⑮ Débarcadère (Wharf). In fine weather, the waterfront buzzes day and night—strollers, diners, concertgoers, in-line skaters, artisans selling their wares—while the white steamers that land here add to the traffic. It's as if sedate Lausanne lifts her skirts a bit at the shoreline. ⊠ *pl. du Port, Ouchy.*

⑭ Fondation de l'Hermitage. A 15-minute bus ride from the Old Town takes you to this beautifully set 19th-century country home. The estate is now an impressive art gallery with a fine permanent collection of Vaudois artists and headline-grabbing, yet seriously presented, blockbuster shows. Exhibits have included the works of Picasso, Giacometti, and the American impressionists. Details of the elegant villa have been preserved, including intricate moldings, carved fireplaces, and multipatterned parquet floors. Allow time for a walk on the grounds and a coffee or light meal at **L'esquisse,** the café backdropped by the outlying orangerie. Call ahead to check the museum's hours, since it shuts down during transition periods between exhibits and for private events. To get here, take Bus 3 from Gare Centrale to the Motte stop or Bus 16 from place St-François to Hermitage. ⊠ *2 rte. du Signal, Sauvabelin* ☎ *021/3125013* ⊕ *www.fondation-hermitage.ch* 🖼 *15 SF* ⊙ *Tues., Wed., and Fri.–Sun. 10–6, Thurs. 10–9.*

⓫ **Hôtel de Ville** (Town Hall). Constructed between the 15th and 17th centuries, this is the seat of municipal and communal councils. A painted, medieval **Fontaine de la Justice** (Justice Fountain) draws strollers to lounge on its heavy rim. Across the street, you can watch the modern **animated clock,** donated to the city by local merchants; moving figures appear every hour on the hour. A street market is held in the square every Wednesday and Saturday morning. ⊠ *2 pl. de la Palud, city center* ☎ *021/ 3152223* 🖼 *Free.*

❽ **Musée de Design et d'Arts Appliqués Contemporains** (Museum of Contemporary Design and Applied Arts). A museum of contemporary design seems amiss in this ancient quarter of the city and in the restored Maison Gaudard yet it demonstrates the passion for art in everyday life. Temporary and permanent installations feature glassworks, textiles, and graphics. Creative and performing arts merge in multimedia shows. ⊠ *6 pl. de la Cathédrale, Old Town* ☎ *021/3152530* ⊕ *www.mudac. ch* 🖼 *6 SF* ⊙ *Tues.–Sun. 11–6.*

⟲ ⓱ **Musée de l'Elysée.** Stark white walls and parquet floors form an inviting backdrop for the changing array of contemporary photography assembled by this museum in an 18th-century country manor. Recent shows have included "Chaplin in Pictures" and "reGeneration: Fifty Photographs of Tomorrow." Wander the rooms, cellar, and attic spaces to view multiple exhibitions—some interactive and designed especially for children. The park surrounding the estate is a quiet place to find a shaded bench and critique the current show. ⊠ *18 ave. de l'Elysée, Ouchy* ☎ *021/3169911* ⊕ *www.elysee.ch* 🖼 *8 SF* ⊙ *Daily 11–6.*

❼ **Musée Historique de Lausanne** (Lausanne Historical Museum). The Ancien-Évêché (Old Bishopric) holds a wealth of both temporary and permanent historical exhibits about the city. Don't miss the 250-square-foot scale model of 17th-century Lausanne, with its commentary illuminating the neighborhoods' histories. Also look for the re-created 19th-century shop windows. ⊠ *4 pl. de la Cathédrale, Old Town* ☎ *021/ 3154100* ⊕ *www.lausanne.ch/MHL* 🖼 *8 SF* ⊙ *July and Aug., daily 11–6; Sept.–June, Tues.–Thurs. and Sat. 11–6, Fri. and Sun. 11–5.*

⟲ ⓰ **Musée Olympique** (Olympic Museum). With high-tech presentation and touching mementos, this complex pays tribute to the athletic tradition in ancient Greece, to the development of the modern Games, to the evolution of the individual sports, to Paralympic competitions, and to the

FodorśChoice
★

athletes themselves. There are art objects—an Etruscan torch from the 6th century BC, Rodin's *American Athlete*—as well as archival films and videos, interactive displays, photographs, coins and stamps, and medals from various eras throughout Olympic history. A museum shop, a lovely café overlooking the lake and sculpture park, and occasional Sunday-afternoon classical concerts complete this ambitious, world-class endeavor. Brochures and guided tours are available in English. ⊠ *1 quai d'Ouchy, Ouchy* ☎ *021/6216511* ⊕ *www.museum.olympic.org* 💲 *15 SF* ⊗ *May–Sept., daily 9–6; Oct.–Apr., Tues.–Sun. 9–6.*

⑱ Musée Romain de Lausanne–Vidy (Lausanne-Vidy Roman Museum). Two Roman communities, Lousonna and Vidy, flourished near the lakefront from 15 BC into the 4th century; excavations of their ruins have brought these ancient settlements to light. A reconstructed private home serves as the museum's headquarters, where displays include a small treasure trove of coins, votive figures, mosaics, and objects from daily life—carved combs, toga pins, jewelry. On request you can get guided tours in English of the museum and the vast archaeological sites. The museum is west of Ouchy, just off the Lausanne-Maladière exit from E25/A1. Bus 1 stops at Maladière. ⊠ *24 chemin du Bois-de-Vaux, Vidy* ☎ *021/3154185* ⊕ *www.lausanne.ch/MRV* 💲 *8 SF* ⊗ *Tues., Wed., and Fri.–Sun. 11–6, Thurs. 11–8.*

⊗ ⑫ Palais de Rumine. Built at the turn of the last century, this enormous neo-Renaissance structure houses several museums, all with a local spin. The **Musée Cantonal de Géologie** (Cantonal Geology Museum ☎ 021/6924470 💲 4 SF ⊗ Tues.–Thurs. 11–6, Fri.–Sun. 11–5) has an excellent fossil collection, including a mammoth skeleton. Besides its collection of regional fauna, the **Musée Cantonal de Zoologie** (Cantonal Zoology Museum ☎ 021/3163460 💲 4 SF ⊗ Tues.–Thurs. 11–6, Fri.–Sun. 11–5) has a rare collection of comparative anatomy. The top exhibit at the **Musée Cantonal d'Archéologie et d'Histoire** (Cantonal Archaeology and History Museum ☎ 021/3163430 💲 4 SF ⊗ Tues.–Thurs. 11–6, Fri.–Sun. 11–5) is the gold bust of Marcus Aurelius discovered at nearby Avenches in 1939. The **Musée Cantonal des Beaux-Arts** (Cantonal Museum of Fine Arts ☎ 021/3163445 💲 10 SF ⊗ Tues. and Wed. 11–6, Thurs. 11–8, Fri.–Sun. 11–5) has an enlightening collection of Swiss art, not only by the Germanic Hodler and Anker but also by Vaud artists—especially Bocion, whose local landscapes are well worth study during a visit to this region. Each museum has some descriptions or an abbreviated guide in English. There are no combination entrance tickets, but all museums offer free admission the first Sunday of each month. ⊠ *6 pl. de la Riponne, city center.*

▶ ⑤ Place St-François (St. Francis Square). The stone-paved square is dominated by the massive post office and the former Franciscan **Église St-François** (Church of St. Francis), built during the 13th and 14th centuries. From 1783 to 1793, Gibbon lived in a house on the site of the post office and there finished his work on *The Decline and Fall of the Roman Empire*. In those days, the square, now reserved for pedestrians, was a popular riding circuit. ⊠ *St-François.*

NEED A
BREAK? Le Saint François (⊠ 5 pl. St-François ☎ 021/3202751), a see-and-be-seen gathering spot opposite the church, serves decadent pastries and inventive light meals in a sleek blond-wood setting or outside on the plaza. Just behind the restaurant is an epicurean boutique chock-full of gourmet items, including private-label products from regional gastronomic star Philippe Rochat.

❻ Rue de Bourg. Once a separate village isolated on a natural ridge, this is now Lausanne's fashionable main shopping street. Narrow and cobblestoned, it's lined with platinum-card stores such as Hermès and Louis Vuitton plus home-furnishings emporiums and jewelry salons.

> **TO MARKET, TO MARKET**
>
> On Wednesday and Saturday, a fresh-produce market sets up on Rue de Bourg.

Boutiques have been built into the centuries-old buildings, though some have added fittingly modern facades. ⊠ St-François.

Where to Stay & Eat

$$$$ ✕ **Restaurant de l'Hôtel de Ville–Philippe Rochat.** Secure in his position as
Fodor'sChoice heir to the legendary chef Fredy Girardet, Philippe Rochat reigns as culi-
★ nary don of the region. It's a quick drive west from Lausanne to his understated manse. Service and presentation are spectacular, and the food is absolutely stellar. For these finely orchestrated prix-fixe menus, the ingredients are key—lamb raised in the Pyrenees, cardoons (an artichoke-like vegetable) grown in the village. Pace yourself, reserving time and room for selections from the immense cheese cart or celestial desserts. Make reservations as far ahead as possible—lunch may be your only option. ⊠ 1 rue d'Yverdon, Crissier, 7 km (4 mi) west of Lausanne ☎ 021/6340505 ⚫ Reservations essential ▭ AE, MC, V ☯ Closed Sun. and Mon. and late July–mid-Aug.

$–$$$$ ✕ **Louis, Villa, et Dépendances.** This multilevel, multivenue industrial restoration has brought new daytime action to late-night-oriented Flon. Brainchild of international restaurateur Luigi Godio, the building houses a fast-paced bistro and vinothéque (wine bar) on the first floor ($–$$), with seating that expands onto outdoor decking. Upstairs, L'Atelier Gourmand ($$–$$$$) is an elegant epicurean salon complete with an exhaustive wine cellar and cheese cave. Preparations range from updated bistro dishes on the ground floor to dazzling tasting menus on the second. A cigar-cognac lounge and nightclub complete the complex. ⊠ pl. de l'Europe, Flon ☎ 021/2130300 ▭ AE, MC, V ☯ No lunch Sat. Atelier closed Sun. and Mon.

★ **$$–$$$** ✕ **Café Beau-Rivage.** As if turning its back on Michelin-starred sibling, La Rotonde, and the aristocratic Beau-Rivage Palace, which shelters both, this young, lively brasserie-café faces the lake and the Ouchy waterfront scene. Its flashy brass-and-Biedermeier dining area and bar fill with smart Lausannois and internationals enjoying trendy cuisine du marché. Despite the brasserie atmosphere, there are no paper place mats: linen, silver, and monogrammed damask set the tone. In summer the pillared terrazzo terrace (protected from embarcadero traffic by rose gardens) is the place go; dine on lamb tajine with apricot coriander compote or sea bream with niçoise potatoes. ⊠ *17–19 pl. du Port, Ouchy* ☎ *021/ 6133330* ⚲ *Reservations essential* 🖃 *AE, DC, MC, V.*

$–$$$ ✕ **Café Restaurant du Théâtre.** Locals come here for smoky, oven-fired individual-size pizza, but the home-style pasta and risotto are also robust and flavorful. The stucco-walled dining room is tight and toasty in winter; in summer there is nothing more delightful than sitting under the garden's sprawling trees and umbrellas. Entrances connect to a theater complex, making it a natural for pre- and postperformance dining. ⊠ *12 av. du Théâtre, city center* ☎ *021/3515115* 🖃 *AE, MC, V* ⊘ *Closed Sun.*

¢–$$$ ✕ **À la Pomme de Pin.** Behind the cathedral, this winsome *pinte* (wine pub)—one of Lausanne's oldest—produces an eclectic menu ranging from French to Italian to Swiss (rabbit and Rösti, anyone?) along with reasonable plats du jour, served both in the casual café and the adjoining linen-decked restaurant. ⊠ *11–13 rue Cité-Derrière, Old Town* ☎ *021/ 3234656* 🖃 *AE, MC, V* ⊘ *Closed Sun. No lunch Sat.*

¢–$$ ✕ **Bleu Lézard.** A cross section of Lausanne urbanites—hip artists, yup-
★ pies, shoppers, university students—fights for tables at this stylish restaurant. Dishes such as yakitori chicken brochette or duck with figs, plus an array of vegetarian offerings are available at remarkably low prices. A tongue-in-cheek decor of found-object art and easygoing waiters dressed in whatever they found near the bed that morning add to the laid-back ambience. Mixed drinks and live music draw a nocturnal clientele downstairs. ⊠ *10 rue Enning, city center* ☎ *021/3123830* 🖃 *AE, MC, V.*

★ **¢–$$** ✕ **Café Romand.** All the customers seem to know each other at this vast, smoky dining institution, where shared wooden tables and clattering china create the perfect ambience for fondue feasts, mussels, *choucroûte* (sauerkraut), or a sausage plate. Prominent members of Lausanne's arts community swarm here after rehearsals and concerts as service continues until 10 PM, late by Swiss standards. ⊠ *2 pl. St-François, St-François* ☎ *021/3126375* 🖃 *MC, V* ⊘ *Closed Sun.*

¢–$ ✕ **Manora.** If you're fed up with heavy Vaud cheese dishes and local sausage, this cheery self-service outpost on the top floor of the city's popular Manor department store offers startlingly inexpensive options. Stir-fries sizzle in huge woks under silent no-smoke hoods; there are also iced pitchers of fresh-squeezed fruit juices, assemble-your-own salads, a fruit bar, a pasta station, and a dessert buffet. No one dish costs more than 20 SF, and the no-smoking dining section is a lifesaver in this city of chain-smokers. It's also a great place for morning coffee and a croissant, plus the free newspaper. ⊠ *7 rue St-Laurent, city center* ☎ *021/ 3213699* ⚲ *Reservations not accepted* 🖃 *No credit cards.*

★ **$$$$** 🏨 **Beau-Rivage Palace.** Of the scores of luxury hotels in Switzerland, this gleaming grande dame stands apart, its neoclassical structure seamlessly restored to period opulence, its vast waterfront grounds manicured like a country estate. Every inch of marble, crystal, and polished mahogany sparkles like new. Rooms have many modern touches—remote light controls, towel heaters, wireless connections. The hotel has a pair of first-class restaurants: the romantic La Rotonde (jacket required) and the Café Beau-Rivage (see above) plus an uber-restorative spa, Cinq Mon-des. Umbrella canopied terraces, footpaths, and a hovering staff make it easy to understand why some guests stay the season. ⊠ *17–19 pl. du Port, Ouchy, CH-1006* ☎ *021/6133333* 🖷 *021/6133334* ⊕ *www.brp.ch* ⇨ *155 rooms, 20 suites* ⚴ *2 restaurants, in-room safes, minibars, cable TV with movies, Wi-Fi, 2 tennis courts, indoor-outdoor pool, gym, sauna, spa, Turkish bath, 2 bars, babysitting, laundry service, concierge, parking (fee), no-smoking rooms* ▭ *AE, DC, MC, V.*

$$$$ 🖬 **Hôtel de la Paix.** Anchored hillside in the center of town, this upscale turn-of-the-20th-century hotel has some of the city's best views and is near corporate addresses, shopping, and nightlife. No wonder so many business types are repeat visitors. The fresh-market bistro buzzes with multilingual conversations, while the adjacent Benjamin Bar fills to overflowing for mid-morning espressos and after work glasses of wine. Cheery rooms are decked out in creamy tones accented with blond wood and tailored furnishings. ⊠ *5 av. Benjamin-Constant, St-François, CH-1003* ☎ *021/3107171* 🖷 *021/3107172* ⊕ *www.hoteldelapaix.net* ⇨ *109 rooms, 6 suites* ⚴ *Restaurant, café, in-room safes, minibars, cable TV with movies, in-room data ports, piano bar, laundry service, concierge, business services, parking (fee), no-smoking rooms* ▭ *AE, DC, MC, V* ⦿ *CP.*

★ $$$$ 🖬 **Lausanne Palace & Spa.** This Edwardian landmark, distinctly urban in setting and style, stands on a hill high over the lake, with layers of city scenery draped behind. It faces a city street, so to take advantage of its views you need a back room. Rooms have Empire reproduction decor with period details such as inlaid wood and dramatic art deco baths. The sleek, calming Ayurveda spa offers a wide array of treatments and classes. You are likely to spot International Olympic Committee officials exiting the meeting areas; the city's influential professionals entertain clients at the gastronomic La Table d'Edgard or at the casual but polished Brasserie du Grand Chêne. ⊠ *7–9 rue du Grand-Chêne, city center, CH-1002* ☎ *021/3313131* 🖷 *021/3232571* ⊕ *www.lausanne-palace.ch* ⇨ *121 rooms, 31 suites* ⚴ *3 restaurants, in-room safes, minibars, cable TV with movies, in-room data ports, indoor pool, health club, sauna, spa, Turkish Bath, 2 bars, nightclub, shops, babysitting, laundry service, concierge, business services, parking (fee), no-smoking rooms* ▭ *AE, DC, MC, V* ⦿ *EP.*

★ $$$–$$$$ 🖬 **Hôtel Angleterre & Résidence.** Within four graceful 18th- and 19th-century villas and a historic hotel near the waterfront, this small complex has been modernized without ruffling its gentility or disturbing its graceful stone arches, marble floors, or discreet gardens. The hotel, where Lord Byron penned *The Prisoner of Chillon*, anchors the compound. A private courtyard with glass pavilion receives guests and dispenses them to quarters furnished in styles ranging from contemporary historical to garden-party floral. A meal taken on the terrace of L'Accademia, the quay-facing Italian bistro, provides a glimpse of lakefront lifestyle. It's the best of both worlds: small-hotel attentiveness plus access to the facilities of the grand Beau-Rivage Palace next door. ⊠ *11 pl. du Port, Ouchy, CH-1006* ☎ *021/6133434* 🖷 *021/6133435* ⊕ *www.angleterre-residence.ch* ⇨ *62 rooms, 12 suites* ⚴ *2 restaurants, in-room safes, minibars, cable TV with movies, in-room data ports, pool, bar, laundry service, parking (fee), no-smoking rooms* ▭ *AE, DC, MC, V* ⦿ *EP.*

$$–$$$ ⛶ **Nash Carlton.** A quiet tree-lined street in one of Lausanne's nicest neighborhoods masks this lodging's close proximity to the train station. Rococo-style architecture is emphasized by embossed wallpapers, textured upholstery, and sweeping draperies in guest rooms and dining areas. Relax with a glass of wine in the French-influenced Nash Bar, knowing you are minutes from the Métro and the lakefront promenade. ⊠ *4 av. de Cour, CH-1007* ☎ *021/6130707* 🖷 *021/6130710* ⊕ *www.nashcarlton. com* ➳ *38 rooms, 6 suites* ⚹ *Restaurant, in-room safes, minibars, cable TV, in-room data ports, bar, free parking* ⊟ *AE, MC, V.*

$$ ⛶ **Hôtel Regina.** Owners at this friendly lodging spent more than a decade in the United States, so the language barrier is nonexistent. Guest rooms are neatly squared away with color-coordinated carpets and upholstery, most with shower-baths. Some have panoramic views of the cathedral, while others look out onto red-tile rooflines. Rooms on the top floor are modern multilevel spaces with bleached-plank ceilings and cherrywood furniture. The hotel is well situated in a pedestrian zone with parking access. ⊠ *18 rue Grand-St-Jean, city center, CH-1003* ☎ *021/3202441* 🖷 *021/3202529* ⊕ *www.hotel-regina.ch* ➳ *36 rooms* ⚹ *In-room safes, minibars, cable TV, in-room data ports, laundry service, Internet, free parking, no-smoking floors; no a/c* ⊟ *MC, V* ⫶⊙⫶ *CP.*

¢ ⛶ **Lausanne Guest House.** This tidy 19th-century town house not far from the train station is run by a brother-and-sister team. Rooms are spread over five floors—some private with baths, others dorm-style with shared showers and toilets. You can prepare meals in the community kitchen or on the outdoor grill, or get caught up at the Internet corner with multiple terminals. The guesthouse is ecologically conscious, using solar heating and a special ventilation system, which makes smoking off-limits. ⊠ *4 Epinettes, CH-1007* ☎ *021/6018000* 🖷 *021/6018001* ⊕ *www. lausanne-guesthouse.ch* ➳ *25 rooms, 6 with bath* ⚹ *Picnic area, BBQs, bicycles, laundry facilities, Internet, parking (fee); no a/c, no room phones, no room TVs, no smoking* ⊟ *AE, DC, MC, V* ⫶⊙⫶ *EP.*

Nightlife & the Arts

Nightlife

BARS Pints and pitchers of international beers, giant-screen sports broadcasts, dueling pianos, and waiters in kilts make the **King Size Pub** (⊠ 16 Port Franc, Flon ☎ 021/6190650) a larger-than-life, rowdy, English-style watering hole. It's part of a cinema complex. One of the city's choicest and liveliest gathering spots is **Le Bar** (⊠ Beau-Rivage Palace, Ouchy ☎ 021/6133330). There's a sophisticated armchair-filled lounge and a tiny wine bar inside the hotel's lower lobby entrance, where you can sip your favorite cocktail or wine. Upstairs sibling **The Bar Anglais** offers spectacular lake views from its clubby setting and terrace chaises. The Lausanne Palace serves the after-hours crowd in the stately **Le Bar du Palace** (⊠ city center ☎ 021/3313131); the hotel's stylish, pared-down **LP Bar** is just a corridor away. Tapas and exotic cocktails make the bilevel restaurant-lounge **Minuit Soleil** (⊠ 23 rue Central, city center ☎ 021/3235364) a popular evening stop. The mood is coastal Mediterranean with DJ selections to match. To explore the vintages of the country, drop in at the **Swiss Wine Bar** (✉ 9 rue St-Laurent, Old Town ☎ 021/3230133) where they pour over 400 different wines and host tasting events.

DANCING   Since most nighttime activity is centered on the Flon and place St-François areas, it's easy to sample several hot spots. If you pass a crowded club where the music is to your taste, duck in. It may be one of the happening locations too new or ephemeral to list here. On the west side of town, **Amnesia** (✉ 9 av. E. Jacques-Dalcroze, Vidy ☎ 021/6190650) fills four levels with themes ranging from beach party to R&B Soul. A 20 SF cover for nonmembers puts a damper on the party mood.Latin and tropical music fill **Atelier Volant** (✉ 12 rue des Côtes-de-Montbenon, Flon ☎ 021/3235280). Inside the **D! Club** (✉ 4 rue du Grand-Pont, city center ☎ 021/3213847), there's a mix of film, fashion, and music. Special-effect lighting and video screens lend tech appeal at **Loft Electroclub** (✉ 1 pl. de Bel-Air, Flon ☎ 021/3116400), whose multiple floors and bars come to life Wednesday through Saturday. Clubbers come from as far away as Zürich and Basel for trance concerts and live performances at **MAD** (✉ 23 rue de Genève, Flon ☎ 021/3116400). On Sunday night the club hosts a gay crowd.

JAZZ CLUBS   In a city with its own jazz music school, look for a range of styles at the clubs that fill quickly with diehard fans. **Le Chorus** (✉ 3 av. Mon Repos, city center ☎ 021/3232233) has a renowned jazz cellar and also serves food and drinks. For acoustic jazz, drop in at **Pianissimo Onze** (✉ Foyer du Théâtr'Onze, 11 rue des Deux-Marchés, city center ☎ 021/3120043).

The Arts

Lausanne is one of Switzerland's arts capitals. Event seasons generally run from September to May, though summer brings outdoor concerts and more casual events. A listing of free and ticketed offerings can be found in *Allons-y*, while monthly updates appear in *Reg'art* (in French). Check out the daily newspaper *24 Heures* for listings as well. Tickets for many performances can be purchased through **Ticket Corner** (☎ 084/8800800 ⊕ www.ticketcorner.ch). Or look online at **Billetnet** (⊕ www.billetnet.ch).

The **Opéra de Lausanne** (✉ 12 av. du Théâtre, city center ☎ 021/3101600) stages classics in its eponymous hall. The riveting experiments of the **Maurice Béjart** ballet company take the stage at the **Salle Métropole** (✉ 1 pl. Bel-Air, city center ☎ 021/3111122), which is also home to the **Orchestre de Chambre de Lausanne**. The **Théâtre de Beaulieu** (✉ 10 av. des Bergières Beaulieu ☎ 021/6432111), right across from the Collection de l'Art Brut, hosts full-scale musical performances like those of the **Orchestre de la Suisse Romande,** which Lausanne shares with Geneva. **Théâtre Kléber-Méleau** (✉ 9 chemin de l'Usine-à-Gaz, Lausanne-Malley ☎ 021/6258400) offers a variety of French-language theater, old and new. **Théâtre-Municipal Lausanne** (✉ 12 av. du Théâtre, city center ☎ 021/3126433), an underground fortification in the heart of Lausanne, is one of the city's key performance venues for concerts, plays, and dance. **Théâtre Vidy-Lausanne** (✉ 5 av. Émile-Jacques-Dalcroze, Vidy ☎ 021/6194545) presents classical and contemporary theater in French.

Sports & the Outdoors

Bicycling

Gare CFF de Lausanne (train station ✉ 5a pl. de la Gare city center ☎ 051/2242162) rents bikes. You must make a reservation at least one day in advance; in summer three days is recommended. For a lakefront ride, check out a set of wheels at **Guy Delessert** (✉ 4 pl. du Vieux Port, Ouchy ☎ 021/6170928).

Ice-Skating

Open-air ice-skating rinks in the Lausanne area operate from October to March. **Patinoire de Montchoisi** (✉ 30 av. du Servan, outside city center ☎ 021/3154963) has 35,000 square feet of ice surface. **Patinoire de la Pontaise** (✉ 11 rte. Plaines-du-Loup, outside city center ☎ 021/ 3154933) attracts urban crowds. Rental skates are available at both rinks.

Swimming

Bellerive (✉ 23 av. de Rhodanie, Ouchy ☎ 021/3154860) has access to the lake and three pools, one Olympic-size, plus generous lawns and a self-service restaurant. The indoor pool at **Mon-Repos** (✉ 4 av. du Tribunal-Fédéral, city center ☎ 021/3154888) stays open from late August through June. The pool at **Piscine de Montchoisi** (✉ 30 av. du Servan, outside city center ☎ 021/3154962) makes artificial waves; it's open from May through August.

Shopping

The main shopping circle centers on **place St-François, rue St-François, rue de Bourg,** and **rue du Grand-Pont.** Less-expensive shopping is along **rue St-Laurent** and **rue de l'Ale.**

Books

For magazines, travel guides and other books, and music, **FNAC** (✉ 6 rue Genève, Flon ☎ 021/2138585) is *the* superstore; it even has a hyperactive coffee bar and ticket kiosk.

Department Stores

Bon Génie (✉ 10 pl. St-François, St-François ☎ 021/3452727) has clusters of designer areas on several levels. **Globus** (✉ rue Centrale at rue du Pont, city center ☎ 021/3429090) is a large upscale department store with a splendid basement food hall. Value-priced **Manor** (✉ 7 rue St-Laurent, city center ☎ 021/3213699) stocks a full range of merchandise, including logo items and souvenirs. It has bountiful food offerings, too.

Markets

There are fruit and vegetable markets in Lausanne along **rue de l'Ale, rue de Bourg,** and **place de la Riponne** every Wednesday and Saturday morning. **Place de la Palud** adds a flea market to its Wednesday and Saturday produce markets and is the site of a handicrafts market the first Friday of the month from March through December. A weekly flea market sets up on Thursday on **Place Chauderon.** Seasonal additions include summer produce found Sunday along the **Allée Bacounis** in Ouchy, and the *Marché Noel* (Christmas Market) in December on the transformed **Place St-François.**

Watches

Most watch shops are in the St-François neighborhood. **Bucherer** (✉ 1 rue de Bourg ☎ 021/3123612) sells Rolex and Baume & Mercier; **Junod** (✉ 8 pl. St-François ☎ 021/3128366) sells Blancpain. If you are searching for Ebel go to **Guillard** (✉ 1 pl.du Palud ☎ 021/3126886). Large Swatch boutiques are located in Globus and Manor (above).

LAVAUX VIGNOBLES & RIVIERA

To the east of Lausanne stretches the Lavaux, a remarkably beautiful region of vineyards that rise up the hillsides all the way from Pully, on the outskirts of Lausanne, to Montreux—a distance of 24 km (15 mi). Brown-roof stone villages in the Savoy style, old defense towers, and small baronial castles stud the green-and-black landscape. The vineyards, enclosed within low stone walls, slope so steeply that all the work has to be done by hand. Top soil, fungicides, and manure are carried in baskets, and containers are strapped to workers' backs. In early October pickers harvest the fruit, carrying the loads to the nearest road and driving them by tractor to the nearest press. Some Lavaux vintages are excellent and in great demand, but unfortunately, as with so much of Switzerland's wine, the yield is small, and the product is rarely exported. Throughout the year, especially on weekends, winegrowers' cellars and some of the private châteaux-vignobles open for tastings (and, of course, sales). A listing of cave open hours, festivals, and eateries can be found at ⊕ www.lavaux.ch.

Fodor'sChoice The scenic **Corniche de la Vaud** stretches some 17 km (10 mi) through
★ Lavaux, threading above the waterfront from Lausanne to Vevey, between the autoroute and the lakeside Route 9. This is Switzerland at its most Franco-European, reminiscent in its small-scale way of the Riviera or the hill towns of Alsace. You'll careen around hairpin turns on narrow cobbled streets, with the Savoy Alps glowing across the sparkling lake and the Dents du Midi looming ahead. Stop to gaze at the scenery from roadside overlooks or wander down a side lane into the fields of Riex, Épesses, Rivaz, or the Dézaley, the sources of some of Switzerland's loveliest white wines and typically magical little Vaudois villages.

Cully

⑲ *9 ½ km (6 mi) southeast of Lausanne.*

The cluster of businesses, homes, barns, and cellars in Cully epitomizes the Lavaux lifestyle. Although it's not as picturesque as some lakeside or hill towns, as you pass through this narrow crossroads you can get a glimpse of what a vintner's life is really like, full of hard work and good eating. From the waterfront where the whistle of lake steamers marks the time of day, the community moves upward through a narrow clutch of shops and cafés until it reaches vineyard terraces banked against the rail line and highway. The *caveau* (cellar operated by local winegrowers), just off the main street on the walkway to the boat landing, opens for tastings on Thursday, Friday, and Sunday evenings except during the winter months of January and February. On summer weekends a miniature train connecting Cully and Lutry travels along grape-growers' paths through the heart of these appellations. In March the commune swells with jazz enthusiasts who come for a weeklong festival that some find more authentic than the world-famous one in Montreux.

Where to Stay & Eat

$$$–$$$$ ×⌷ **Auberge du Raisin.** Fashionably dressed families, romantic couples, and international business teams gather here to celebrate birthdays, weddings, and deal closings. In the center of the animated dining room ($$$$), rotisserie hooks and spits twirl in a raised-hearth grill, as the chef seasons, times, and dispatches meats to the servers (side dishes are synchronized in the kitchen). In the auberge's guest rooms, puffy spreads cover the draped four-posters, and the brightly painted armoires and chests are a change from the usual fruitwoods; some of the large baths have skylights. Reservations are essential for the restaurant. ⌧ *1 pl. de l'Hôtel de Ville, CH-1096* ☎ *021/7992131* 🖷 *021/7992501* ⊕ *www. relaischateaux.com* ⟳ *7 rooms, 2 suites* ♨ *Restaurant, in-room data ports, Wi-Fi, bar, free parking* ═ *AE, DC, MC, V* ⦿⦿ *CP.*

EN ROUTE   For a more modern take on sampling the appellations, stop in the hamlet of Rivaz. Here **Bacchus** (☎ 021/9461113), a petite wine bar that's open Thursday through Sunday from March to October from 5–9, is carved out of a stone building on the steeply graded main street. Parking, halfway between the lake and church, is in an underground garage camouflaged by the vineyards.

St-Saphorin

★ ⑳   *5½ km (3.5 mi) southeast of Cully, 15 km (9 mi) southeast of Lausanne.*

At the end of the Cornich Road, just west of Vevey, St-Saphorin is perched above the water. With its impossibly narrow, steep cobbled streets and ancient wine makers' houses crowded around fountains and crooked alleys, this is a village that merits a stop. It lies along the ancient Roman highway, and its small church sits atop Roman Foundations. There's a tiny **museum** of Roman artifacts (including a sizeable millstone) in the church. Go through the low door near the altar; you can see the museum whenever the church is unlocked and services are not being held. The explanations are all in French, but it's easy to chart the church's expansion through its ruins.

For additional vineyard explorations accompanied by jaw-dropping vistas, take the vertical grade uphill—on foot or by car—to Chexbres. Be attentive as the close, walled-street relies on tight pull-offs to pass oncoming vehicles. The reward is a different orientation on the working wine village complete with rail connections to wisk you back down to the active waterfront via Vevey.

Where to Stay & Eat

★ **$–$$**   × **Auberge de l'Onde.** Once the main *relais* (stagecoach stop) between the Simplon Pass and Geneva, this vineyard inn is out of central casting, groaning with history and heady with atmosphere: Igor Stravinsky and Charlie Chaplin were among the artists loyal to its charms. The ambience is equally seductive in its tiny wood-paneled pinte (café), where winemakers come to read the daily papers with a pitcher of St-Saph, as they call it, and devour the plat du jour. In the adjacent, white-table-cloth salons or upstairs in the attic beamed grill room, the staff hovers with a bottle of local or imported vintage while day-tripping connoisseurs and repeat faithfuls sniff and roll perfumed wine over their tongues, and savor a fillet with black truffles or gingered veal with lemongrass. Additional features—a wine bar, music lounge, and fondue cave—keep things lively on all levels. ⊠ *Centre Ville, CH–1071* ☎ *021/9254900* ☐ *MC, V* ⊙ *Closed Tues. and Wed. lunch; 2 wks in Aug.*

$$ ✕🔳 **L'Hôtel Baron Tavernier.** Lodging high up on the Corniche Road yields superlative views with elegant comfort. Named for 17th-century author and adventurer, Jean-Baptiste Tavernier, the entry of the inn is stocked with stained glass, porcelain, and metal works similar to the trove brought back from his travels to Persia, Africa, and the Orient. Guest rooms assume a modern appearance, clad in honey and green with marbled bathrooms and private balconies. Le Deck ($$), an expansive terrace bar and alfresco eatery connected by crosswalk, is tethered above the lake like a hot air balloon. When there is a chill in the air, take to the warm, wood-paneled pinte ($–$$) for mets du terroir (regional specialties), or move into the stately dining room ($$$) for a multicourse extravaganza. There is garage parking tucked into the curve on the adjacent hillside; a car is needed to access this location. ⊠ *rte. de la Corniche, Chexbres, CH-1071* ☎ *021/9266000* 🖷 *021/9266001* ⊕ *www.barontavernier.ch* ⇥ *11 rooms, 8 suites* ♻ *Restaurant, café, in-room data ports, minibars, bar, free parking, no smoking rooms; no a/c,* ☐ *AE, DC, MC, V* ⦿I *CP.*

Vevey

㉑ **To & From:** *The 7-minute regional and local S-trains linking the adjacent cities Vevey-Montreux have departures every 10 to 15 minutes, but the trolley bus that snakes along the lake road is more scenic (and it prevents you from climbing up hill to Montreux's rail station)—its route extends from Villenuve to the Vevey Funnicular and is the best way (other than by car) to reach Château de Chillon. Depending on how many zones you cross, the fare is about 3 SF. There is a map and fare chart on the automated ticket machine located in the back of the bus or you can find them on www.vmcv.ch. Vevey is 9.5 km (6 mi) east of Cully, 19 km (12 mi) east of Lausanne.*

This soigné waterfront town was the setting for Anita Brookner's evocative 1985 novel *Hotel du Lac*, about a woman retreating to a lake resort to write; her heroine was attracted to the site, in part, because of its slightly stuffy 19th-century ways. In the 1870s Henry James captured this mood of prim grace while writing (and setting) *Daisy Miller* in the Hôtel des Trois Couronnes. Indeed, despite its virtual twinning with glamorous Montreux, Vevey retains its air of isolation and old-world gentility. Loyal visitors have been returning for generations to gaze at the Dent d'Oche (7,288 feet), across the water in France, and make sedate steamer excursions into Montreux and Lausanne. Today there are some who come just to see the bronze statue of Charlie Chaplin, in a rose garden on the lakefront quay, and to take the funicular or mountain train up to Mont Pèlerin. Vevey is also a great walking town, with more character in its shuttered Old Town; better museums, landmarks, and shops; and more native activity in its wine market than cosmopolitan Montreux can muster. By following an excellent brochure–map published by the tourist office, you can travel "On the Trail of Hemingway"— and to the homes and haunts of some 40 other luminaries.

> ## CELEBRITY SIGHTINGS
>
> Among the notables who have been drawn to Vevey are Graham Greene, Victor Hugo, Jean-Jacques Rousseau (who set much of his *Julie, ou la Nouvelle Héloïse* here), Fyodor Dostoyevsky, Gustave Courbet, Oskar Kokoschka, Charlie and Oona Chaplin (buried in the cemetery at Corsier), and Swiss native Édouard Jeanneret, known as Le Corbusier.

★ Le Corbusier's **Villa le Lac,** a single-story white house built directly on the Vevey waterfront, was constructed for his parents in 1923. It remains unaltered, with his original furnishings and details preserved within. Shingled in corrugated sheet metal, with a white-metal railed balcony looking over the water and a "birdhouse" chimney in molded concrete, it is typically sculptural and, in a modest way, visionary. ⊠ *rte. de Lavaux 21, Corseaux* ☎ *021/9254011* ⚏ *5 SF* ☉ *Self-guided tours Apr.–Oct., Wed. 1:30–5:30.*

☉ The Nestlé Foundation, a dynamic force in the region, sponsors an unconventional museum, the **Alimentarium.** A sculpture of an apple at the entrance of the 19th-century lakefront mansion symbolizes the museum's purpose: the celebration and study of food. In a stainless-steel kitchen chefs demonstrate their skills, and displays on food preparation cover everything from the campfire to futuristic equipment. Other sections focus on merchants, supermarkets, food presentation, and marketing; you can also stroll through herb and vegetable gardens. The exhibits have material in English; some are interactive. ⊠ *quai Perdonnet* ☎ *021/9244111* ⊕ *www.alimentarium.ch* ⚏ *10 SF* ☉ *Tues.–Sun. 10–6.*

The **Musée Jenisch** owes its considerable inventory of the works of the expressionist Oskar Kokoschka to his retirement on Vevey's shores. If it's strictly the Kokoschkas you want to see, you may need to plan ahead. His works are not always on display, but advance arrangements can be made to view the holdings in the archives. The museum's partner wing, the **Cabinet Cantonal des Estampes** (Cantonal Print Collection) contains a rich assortment of engravings, including some by Dürer and Rembrandt. ⊠ *2 av. de la Gare* ☎ *021/9212950* ⊕ *www.museejenisch.ch* ⚏ *12 SF* ☉ *Daily 11–5:30.*

The **Musée Historique du Vieux Vevey** (Historical Museum of Old Vevey) occupies a grand 16th-century manor house, briefly home to Charlotte de Lengefeld, wife of Friedrich von Schiller. It retains some original furnishings as well as collections of arms, art, keys, and winemaking paraphernalia. The first floor serves as headquarters for the Brotherhood of

Winegrowers, the organization that stages the mammoth Fêtes des Vignerons (Winegrowers' Festival). The festival is held roughly every 25 years; you can get a taste of the most recent celebration (1999) from the costumes, photographs, and memorabilia on display. ✉ *2 rue du Château* ☎ *021/ 9210722* ⊕*www.museehistoriquevevey.ch* 🖼*6 SF* ⊙*Mar.–Oct., Tues.–Sat. 10:30–noon and 2–5:30, Sun. 11–5; Nov.–Feb., Tues.–Sat. 2–5:30.*

The **Musée Suisse de l'Appareil Photographique** (Swiss Camera Museum) displays an impressive collection of cameras, photographic equipment, and mounted work. It also hosts *Images,* a biennial multimedia show held in the fall of even-numbered years. ✉ *99 Grande-pl.* ☎ *021/ 9252140* ⊕ *www.cameramuseum.ch* 🖼 *8 SF* ⊙ *Tues.–Sun. 11–5:30.*

Resting on a shelf above Vevey, **The Charlie Chaplin Heritage Site** (scheduled to open sometime in 2007) has taken over Manoir de Ban, a compound in a wooded area on the outskirts of Corsier. It was here that the world-famous comedian and his family lived as private citizens. The manor and outbuildings have been converted into display centers for memorabilia and private papers. Walk the hallways of this retreat; pause in front of the showcase housing Mr. Chaplin's signature bowler hat and three-piece suit to reflect on the enormous character who defined comedy for the 20th century. Reels of film from the silent era run in the 200-seat movie theater while an outdoor stage is the set for current day theatrics. The gardens offer quiet spaces enjoyed by the individual whose work continues to bring laughter to the world. ✉ *Corsier-sur-Vevey* ⊕ *www.chaplinmuseum.com.*

NEED A BREAK?

Pause for a glass of a local or imported vintage at the storefront wine bar **Les Dix Vins** (✉ 24 rue des Deux-Marchés ☎ 021/9223033), on a side street between market plazas. The owner's friendly enthusiasm adds to the pleasure of time spent toasting, chatting, or people-watching. If sweets are more your mood, pick a luscious pastry from the case at **Poyet** (✉ 8 rue du Théâtre ☎ 021/9213737), on the pedestrian walkway near the tourist office, or join the ladies for a light lunch in the adjacent dining room.

Just east of town, the **Musée Suisse du Jeu** (Game and Toy Museum) fills a 13th-century castle. Games of strategy and chance, ranging from dice to video games, are represented in displays spanning centuries. Its excellent gift shop is stocked with Legos, puzzles, and board games. Tours and notes are available in English. The courtyard eatery, L'Oubliette serves snacks and light meals. ✉ *1½ km (1 mi) east of Vevey on rte. 9, au Chateau, La Tour-de-Peilz* ☎ *021/9772300* ⊕ *www.museedujeu.com* 🖼 *6 SF* ⊙ *Mar.–Oct., Tues.–Sun. 11–5:30; Nov.–Feb., Tues.–Sun. 2–5.*

OFF THE BEATEN PATH

BLONAY–CHAMBY RAILROAD – From Vevey and Montreux, a number of railways climb into the heights, which in late spring are carpeted with an extravagance of wild narcissi. If you like model railroads, you will especially enjoy a trip on the Blonay–Chamby Railroad, whose real steam-driven trains alternate with electric trains. You can depart from either end (parking is more plentiful in Blonay); trains make a stop at a small museum of railroad history in between. The trip takes about 20 minutes each way, not including a browse in the museum. ⊠ *Case Postale 366, CH-1001 Lausanne* ☎ *021/9432121* ⊕ *www.blonay-chamby.ch* 🚂 *Round-trip ticket 16 SF* ⊗ *May–Oct., weekends 10–6:30.*

Where to Stay & Eat

$–$$ ✕ **À la Montagne.** This elegant, intimate restaurant is set in a restored home in the wine village of Chardonne. Perched on a sunny shelf high above the Nestlé corporate complex, it offers a view of the lake (from part of the dining room) that is worthy of a champagne toast. Traditional French preparations like beef medallions and rack of lamb are straightforward, smartly garnished, and paired with fresh herbs and vegetables. A well-composed wine list of Swiss and international selections offers breadth to match. Those who like a stroll before and after dinner can take the mostly flat five-minute walk to the funicular, an easy way to access these upper reaches. ⊠ *21 rue du Village, Chardonne* ☎ *021/9212930* ⊟ *AE, DC, MC, V* ⊗ *Closed Sun. and Mon. and July.*

$–$$ ✕ **National.** The crowd is mixed across ages at this popular west side location. A frequently changing menu combines fresh ingredients with a twist on standards like lake fish or a bowl of penne. Seating under the twinkling lights of the patio provides a respite from the serious smoking crowd. Extended service hours and proximity to the cinema attract late diners. ⊠ *9 rue du Torrent* ☎ *021/9237625* ⊟ *MC, V.*

¢–$ ✕ **Charly's Café.** Enter the multilevel casual eatery from the lakefront or cobblestone plaza near the main marketplace. Upstairs seating catches the breeze; lower level tables spill out on to the fountain-filled pedestrian zone. Friendly servers deliver mugs of steaming latte with crusty croissants to the morning crowd, and neatly stacked club sandwiches surrounded by a heap of fries late into the evening. Plated specials of fresh fish or pasta are pleasing and well-priced. ⊠ *45 rue du Lac* ☎ *021/9215006* ⊟ *MC, V* ⊗ *Closed Dec.–Feb.*

¢–$ ✕ **Le Mazot.** Offerings at this tiny pinte are limited. Regulars favor the tender steak—entrecôte of beef or *cheval* (horse)—accompanied by an overflowing plate of fries or a half-moon of crispy Rösti. After years of overseeing bubbling pots of fondue, the other popular draw, hand-painted murals and mirrors set in dark frames have a smoky patina. The narrow room is crowded with scarred booths and bare tables, which can be moved together in long chains. It's a casual neighborhood place where local wines are poured from pewter pitchers and the people at the next table eavesdrop. ⊠ *7 rue du Conseil* ☎ *021/9217822* ⊟ *MC, V* ⊗ *Closed Wed. No lunch Sun.*

★ **$$$–$$$$** ✕🏨 **Hôtel des Trois Couronnes.** Honeycombed by dramatic atrium stairwells that look down on marble columns and gleaming floors inlaid with golden coronets, this regal landmark was Henry James's home base when he wrote (and set here) the novella *Daisy Miller*. A vast lakefront terrace with pool overlooks the pollards, the promenade, and the steamers plying the lake. Burgundy brocade with floral swags and coverlets contrast boldly with neutral striped wallpaper in generously sized guest rooms. The spa, called Puressens (Pure Senses), offers a full range of restorative services that are a relaxing extension to time spent in the lower-level pool. A jacket is not required in the formal Louis XV-style restaurant, but you will want to spiff up for the French gastronomic experience. ⊠ *49*

Fond of Fondue

THOUGH FONDUE IS DE RIGUEUR in any Alpine setting, Vaud is a fanatical stronghold. In the Pays-d'Enhaut (Highlands), cattle head uphill in summer, and production of local cheeses—the firm, fragrant Gruyère and L'Etivaz—soars. They are sold at various stages: young and mild, ripe and savory, or aged to a heady tang. Take a guided hike from Chateaux-d'Oex to the highland pastures to see all aspects of cheese making and then share a bubbly pot of perfection.

Fondue is simply cheese melted together with white wine, garlic, and a dash of kirsch. Aficionados debate the perfect blend of cheeses and whether to include mushrooms, tomatoes, and even chunks of potatoes. Most restaurants serve a blend of Gruyère, Emmental, and Appenzeller; others have their own recipe. The especially popular *moitemoite* (half and half) is half Gruyère

and half bold l'Etivaz or creamy Vacherin.

Diners dip chunks of bread on long forks into the bubbling mixture. Many restaurants serve fondue in an adjoining *carnotzet* or *Stübli* (French and German versions of a cozy pub)—both to re-create a rustic Alpine experience and to spare fellow diners the fierce aromas of cheese, garlic, and the fuel that keeps the fondue melted. It's a dish best suited to winter.

Appropriate accompaniments are a fruity white wine or plain black tea—never red wine, beer, or cola—and the traditional *coup du milieu* (shot in the middle), a reviving midmeal shot of kirsch. The salty cheese will make you yearn for water; go light and never with ice. Custom dictates that if you lose your bread in the caquelon, women must kiss the host or nearest man, while men buy another round.

rue d'Italie, CH-1800 ☎ 021/9233200 🖨 021/9233399 ⊕ www. hoteldestroiscouronnes.com 🛏 45 rooms, 10 suites ♨ Restaurant, café, in-room safes, minibars, cable TV, in-room data ports, indoor pool, health club, hair salon, spa, bar, business services, free parking ▤ AE, DC, MC, V.

$$$–$$$$ ✕🖽 **Le Mirador Kempinski.** On a ledge above Vevey, this combination spa resort and elite conference center is set among the meadows and modest villages of Mont-Pèlerin. Breathtaking panoramic views of lake, Alps, and vineyards can be had from elegant guest rooms trimmed in marble, parquet, and brocade. The luxurious Givenchy spa has a broad treatment menu, from jet-lag relief to cosmetic pampering. La Trianon ($$$–$$$$), the fine-dining restaurant, ranks as one of the best haute tables and wine cellars in this gastronomic region. Not to fear, the calorie-conscious are accommodated in all dining venues. ✉ *5 chemin du Mirador, CH-1801 Mont-Pèlerin ☎ 021/9251111 🖨 021/9251112 ⊕ www.mirador.ch 🛏 74 rooms, 19 suites ♨ 3 restaurants, in-room safes, minibars, cable TV with movies and video games, in-room data ports, 3 tennis courts, indoor-outdoor pool, health club, hair salon, spa, bar, concierge, business services, helipad, free parking, no-smoking rooms ▤ AE, DC, MC, V.*

¢–$ ⊞ **Des Négociants.** Handy to the market and near the lake, this comfortable and lively lodging is in the Old Town. Rooms have bright colors and modular blond-wood furniture, and bathrooms have showers only. The arcaded restaurant and terrace have a vivacious hum at mealtimes, courtesy of the guests who gather for Alsatian specialties and homemade desserts. ⊠ *27 rue du Conseil, CH-1800* ☎ *021/9227011* 🖷 *021/9213424* ⊕ *www.hotelnegociants.ch* 🛏 *23 rooms* ♿ *Restaurant, cable TV, in-room data ports, free parking; no a/c* ▭ *AE, DC, MC, V* ⊙ *CP.*

Nightlife

Despite its quiet, small-town appearance, Vevey has gathering spots where the music is loud and revelers dance until dawn. At **Epsilon** (⊠ 30 av. General Guisan ☎ 021/9212196), people warble karaoke Monday through Wednesday before full-throttle clubbing takes over for the weekend. For dance, concerts, and jam sessions, head over to the multivenue complex **Les Temps Modernes** (⊠ 6 rue des Deux Gares ☎ 021/9222721). **National** (⊠ 9 rue du Torrent ☎ 021/9237625), just off the place du Marché, combines music and late food.

Sports & the Outdoors

As you drive along the highway you will see sunbathers lounging on rocks jutting out into the lake and swimmers playing on the stony beaches. It's difficult to tell if they are on private property or have public access. There *are* swimming areas open to everyone that include a mix of facilities—toilets, showers, changing cabins, and snack bars—but lifeguards are only at the pools, so be careful. Slippery rocks, drop-offs, and water traffic on the lake require special attention. ☼ **Jardin Doret** (⊠ Off pl. du Marché ☎ 021/6178131) provides access to the lake, a generous lawn with play area, and a snack bar. The indoor pool at **Piscine les Mousquetaires** (⊠ 13 pl. des Anciens-Fossés, La Tour-de-Peilz ☎ 021/9770307) is open most of the year; there's also a beach at the port. The **Vevey/Corseaux Plage** (⊠ 19 av. de Lavaux, Corseaux ☎ 021/9212368), west of Nestlé headquarters, has both lake swimming and two large pools (indoor and outdoor).

Shopping

Boutiques and galleries in the Old Town east of place du Marché deserve attentive shopping. **L'Air du Temps** (⊠ 25 rue des Deux-Marchés ☎ 021/9222303) carries gifts for the home plus wine accessories. Next door is the town's best cheese shop, **La Grenette** (⊠ 27 rue des Deux-Marchés ☎ 021/9212345). **Saint-Antoine** (⊠ 1 ave. Général-Guisan), a modern, multilevel complex diagonally across from the train station, clusters large and small retailers within its glass panels. An extra bonus: its underground parking is a smart alternative to the cramped, restricted parking in the Old Town.

Tuesday and Saturday bring neighbors, politicians, and foodies to the center of Old Town for an open air bazaar where wagons circle and stalls fill tidy rows; each piled high with produce from nearby farms, meats cut to order, or seafood netted at dawn. Handicrafts, flower stands, and assorted wares round out the mix and add to the convivial atmosphere of friendly banter and vendor exchanges. As Vevey is a marketing center for regional wines, the local white is sold in summer at the Saturday market, adding to the spirit of a folkloric festival; you buy your own glass and taste *à volonté* (at will).

Montreux

 4 km (2 mi) southeast of Vevey, 21 km (13 mi) southeast of Lausanne.

Montreux could be called the Cannes of Lac Léman—though it might raise an eyebrow at the slur. Spilling down steep hillsides into a sunny south-facing bay, its waterfront thick with magnolias, cypresses, and palm trees, the historic resort earns its reputation as the capital—if not the pearl—of the Swiss Riviera. Unlike the French Riviera, it has managed, despite overwhelming crowds of conventioneers, to keep up appearances. Its Edwardian-French deportment has survived considerable development, and though there are plenty of harsh modern high-rises with parking-garage aesthetics, its mansarded landmarks still unfurl yellow awnings to shield millionaires from the sun.

The site where Stravinsky composed *Petrouchka* and *Le Sacre du Printemps* and where Vladimir Nabokov resided in splendor, Montreux and its suburbs have attracted artists and literati for 200 years: Byron, Shelley, Tolstoy, Hans Christian Andersen, and Flaubert were drawn to its lush shoreline. When its casino opened in 1883, tourism began in earnest. Even rock star Freddie Mercury came under the resort's spell; a statue of the late Queen singer stands on the quay. But the resort is best known for its annual jazz festival, which lately has strayed from its original focus to include rock, R&B, Latin, and hip-hop. Each July, Montreux's usually composed promenade explodes in a street festival of food tents, vendor kiosks, and open band shells, which complement standing-room-only concert hall venues.

Above the train station, a complex of 17th-century homes once belonging to the town's successful winemakers is now the **Musée du Vieux-Montreux** (Museum of Old Montreux). This historical museum traces regional development from the time when Roman coins were used as tender, focusing on agricultural life and the shift to tourism. Profiles of famous residents and visitors who lived and worked in the area are highlighted. The museum's cellar restaurant is a good place to sample typical cuisine. ⊠ *40 rue de la Gare* ☎ *021/9631353* ⊕ *www.museemontreux. ch* ⊠ *6 SF* ☉ *Apr.–Nov., daily 10–noon, 2–5.*

Montreux's cultural center, the **Maison Visinand,** is housed in a restored mansion in the Old Town. Its calendar of events mixes exhibitions and performances with classes and studios for painting, photography, and dance. ⊠ *32 rue du Pont* ☎ *021/9630726* ⊕ *www.centreculturelmontreux.ch* ⊠ *Free* ☉ *Wed.–Sun. 3–6.*

| NEED A BREAK? | The lunch-and-tearoom set (ladies with poodles, Brits in tweeds, fashion plates in Gucci) regularly descends on Zurcher (⊠ 45 av. du Casino ☎ 021/9635963), the irresistible confiserie on Montreux's main drag. A green salad, the potage du jour (soup of the day), and a chocolate-striated torte make a great quick meal. The café is closed on Monday. |

Fodor'sChoice
★ Certainly the greatest attraction at Montreux and one of Switzerland's must-sees is the **Château de Chillon,** the awe-inspiring 12th-century castle that rears out of the water at Veytaux, down the road from and within sight of Montreux. Chillon was built on Roman foundations under the direction of Duke Peter of Savoy with the help of military architects from Plantagenet England. For a long period it served as a state prison, and one of its shackled guests was François Bonivard, who supported the Reformation and enraged the Savoyards. He spent six years in this prison, chained most of the time to a pillar in the dungeon, before being released by the Bernese in 1536.

While living near Montreux, Lord Byron visited Chillon and was so transported by its atmosphere and by Bonivard's grim sojourn that he was inspired to write his famous poem "The Prisoner of Chillon." He charts the prisoner's despair and brief moments of hope, culminating in the realization on release that "these heavy walls to me had grown/A hermitage—and all my own!/ . . .So much a long communion tends/To make us what we are:—even I/Regain'd my freedom with a sigh." Like a true tourist, Byron carved his name on a pillar in Bonivard's still-damp and chilly dungeon; his graffito is now protected under a plaque.

In high season visitors to Chillon must now file placidly from restored chamber to restored turret, often waiting at doorways for entire busloads of fellow tourists to pass. Yet the restoration is so evocative and so convincing, with its tapestries, carved fireplaces, period ceramics and pewter, and elaborate wooden ceilings, that even the jaded castle hound may become as carried away as Byron was. While you're waiting your turn, you can gaze out the narrow windows over the sparkling, lapping water and remember Mark Twain, who thought Bonivard didn't have it half bad. Proceeds from the purchase of a bottle of Clos de Chillon, the white wine from estate vineyards, goes to restoration activities. ⊠ *Veytaux, less than 3 km (2 mi) south of Montreux* ☎ *021/9668910* ⊕ *www.chillon.ch* ☑ *10 SF* ☼ *Mar. and Oct., daily 9:30–5; Apr.–Sept., daily 9–6; Nov.–Feb., daily 10–4.*

OFF THE BEATEN PATH

LES AVANTS – The Montreux–Oberland–Bernois (MOB) railroad leads to the resort village of Les Avants (3,181 feet) and then on to Château-d'Oex, Gstaad, and the Simmental. Noël Coward bought his dream home in Les Avants, at No. 8 route de Sonloup. Ernest Hemingway wrote to his family and friends of the village's fields of daffodils—and, more in character, of its bobsled track. A more easternly spur of the MOB ascends above Caux to a ridgeline called **ROCHERS-DE-NAYE,** also known as *marmot's paradise,* where these playful creatures are headliners in an alpine zone with 360-degree views. Winter brings beginner-level skiers; summer hikers and hang gliders.

Where to Stay & Eat

$$$$
Fodor'sChoice
★
✕ **Le Pont de Brent.** Tucked on a hillside next to its namesake bridge in the suburb of Brent, this small but elegant establishment ties with Philippe Rochat's restaurant for the honor of best table in the region. Who would guess that the pale stone exterior of this unassuming building screens showstopping cuisine? Norman chef Gérard Rabaey performs

alchemy with local ingredients to turn out dishes almost too pretty to eat, such as Breton lobster and crayfish with lemongrass or veal kidneys with black truffles. All is warm here, from the ocher walls to the welcome and service. The four-course business lunch is a well-priced sampler of the chef's talents. ⊠ *rte. de Brent, 7 km (4½ mi) northwest of Montreux, Brent* ☎ *021/9645230* ⌂ *Reservations essential* ▭ *MC, V* ⊘ *Closed Sun. and Mon., last 3 wks of July, and late Dec.–early Jan.*

$-$$$ ✕ **La Vieille Ferme.** Follow the winding road into the village of Chailly. Past the fountain and across the street, you'll see the stone facade of a 14th-century farmhouse restored to rustic elegance and said to be the oldest in the region. Dining rooms that were once stalls and family quarters have stucco and wooden beams. The owner's philosophy—*A BON MANGER, BON BOIRE* (good food and good drink)—is carved above the raised fireplace that doubles as a grill. The cuisine is true to the heritage of the homestead: lamb chops prepared with herbs, chicken simmered in honey and lemon. If it's a fondue or raclette you prefer, a separate carnotzet serves these cheese specialties. ⊠ *rue de Bourg, Chailly-sur-Montreux* ☎ *021/9646465* ▭ *AE, MC, V* ⊘ *Closed Mon. and Tues.*

$-$$ ✕ **La Pinte de Veytaux.** It's not easy to spot this tiny bistro in the crook of an uphill residential street and even tougher to snag a parking spot, but the stone-walled dining room has been a launch pad for several of the region's luminary chefs. The one in residence now has trained alongside a master and brings his own creativity (and favorable pricing) to the dishes, like fillet of red fish with couscous and balsamic reduction, or thyme infused rack of lamb accompanied by a cherry tomato compote. ⊠ *11 rue Bonivard, Veytaux* ☎ *021/9633151* ▭ *MC, V* ⊘ *Closed Sun. and Mon.*

¢-$$ ✕ **La Rouvenaz.** If it's an oven-fired pizza or plate of pasta you have been pining for there's no place more convivial or convenient than this trattoria on the main drag. The atmosphere is warmed by terra-cotta walls with bold blue accents and endless pitchers of wine. Seafood is fresh and a specialty of the house whether atop a pie crust or mound of linguine. There is a satellite location serving light fare and desserts across the street on the lakefront promenade. ⊠ *1 rue du Marché* ☎ *021/9632736* ▭ *MC, V* ⊘ *Closed Mon.*

★ $$-$$$ ✕🏨 **L'Ermitage.** Freestanding on its own waterfront-garden grounds, this genteel, intimate retreat offers top-drawer haute gastronomie and a few luxurious rooms upstairs. The guest rooms are lightened with fresh flowers, lacquered cane furniture, and lake views; many rooms have balconies. Chef Étienne Krebs's exceptional menu may include cod fillet with confit of candied onions and red peppers or cannelloni of rabbit stuffed with foie gras. A bit less formal than the dining room is the canopied terrace, open daily in summer for alfresco dining. ⊠ *75 rue du Lac, CH-1815 Clarens* ☎ *021/9644411* 🖷 *021/9647002* ⊕ *www.ermitage-montreux. com* ⇨ *4 rooms, 3 suites* ⌂ *Restaurant, minibars, cable TV, in-room data ports, free parking* ▭ *AE, DC, MC, V* ⊘ *Closed late Dec.–late Jan.* ⦿ *CP.*

$$$$ 🏨 **Grand Hôtel Suisse Majestic.** It's not unusual to mistake similar Belle Epoch architecture and repeating yellow awnings for the Palace down the street. Half the size and less ritzy, the Majestic has a gracious ambience of its own plus the convenience of being across the street from the train station and in the heart of shopping and dining. Rooms have crown molding and fireplaces; lake views are definitely worth the extra charge. At the lively terrace restaurant, you can dine perched above the hubbub; the station-side café is great for people watching. ⊠ *45 ave. des Alpes, CH-1820* ☎ *021/9663333* 🖶 *021/9663300* ⊕ *www.suisse-majestic.ch* 🛏 *140 rooms* ☾ *Restaurant, café, minibars, cable TV with movies, bar, business services, parking (fee)* ▤ *AE, DC, MC, V.*

$$$–$$$$
Fodor's Choice
★

✕🖵 **Le Montreux Palace.** Silver mansards and yellow awnings flag this vast institution as a landmark, though its aristocratic interiors are now filled with cell-phone-chatting travelers. This colossal Belle Epoque folly of stained glass, frescoes, and flamboyant molded stucco opened in 1906 and counts Vladimir Nabokov among its notable residents (a bronze of the author stands in the lakeside gardens). Updated facilities do not compromise the allure of this grand hotel. You can be cyber-connected from any corner or secluded in a massage suite at the Amrita wellness center. Guest rooms have fruitwood furniture, bold accessories, and Jacuzzis trimmed in granite and marble. For an American cocktail or sandwich, Harry's Bar ($–$$) sates your appetite while the posh restaurant, Jaan ($$$$), soars to French starred status. ⊠ *100 Grand-rue, CH-1820* ☎ *021/9621212* 🖶 *021/9621717* ⊕ *www.montreux-palace.com* 🛏 *185 rooms, 50 suites* ☾ *4 restaurants, cable TV with movies, in-room data ports, tennis court, 2 pools, health club, hair salon, spa, 2 bars, nightclub, concierge, convention center, parking (fee), no-smoking rooms* ▤ *AE, DC, MC, V.*

$–$$
🖵 **Masson.** If you enjoy being away from the downtown resort scene, look up this demure little inn on a hillside in Veytaux, between Chillon and Montreux. Since it was built in 1829, it has had only four owners, and the current family takes pride in its genteel period decor and the personalized attention that attracts repeat guests season after season. You'll find floral prints, brass beds, pristine linens, buffed parquet, and expansive lake views from the numerous balconies. The breakfast buffet is generous, with homemade breads and jams. ⊠ *5 rue Bonivard, Veytaux CH-1820* ☎ *021/9660044* 🖶 *021/9660036* ⊕ *www.hotelmasson.ch* 🛏 *33 rooms* ☾ *Restaurant, in-room safes, minibars, cable TV, hot tub, sauna, free parking; no a/c* ▤ *AE, MC, V* ☾ *Closed Oct.–Apr.* ⦿ *CP.*

Nightlife & the Arts

Montreux's famous festivals and arts events are listed in a seasonal booklet published by the tourist office; tickets are sold from its booth at the waterfront. The renowned **Montreux Jazz Festival** takes place every July in the ultramodern **Auditorium Stravinski** (⊠95 Grand-rue) and other lakeside venues. For tickets to these popular events, it's easiest to monitor the schedule (not released until late April or May) on the Web site ⊕ www.montreuxjazz.com. Popular events sell out in hours so be ready to purchase online. The **Ticket Corner** (☎900/800800 ⊕www.ticketcorner.com) also sells tickets. In summer Montreux offers a variety of free outdoor concerts from its bandstand on the waterfront near the landing stage.

BARS The swank **Harry's New York Bar** (⊠ 100 Grand-rue ☎ 021/9621200), at the Montreux Palace, has a pianist after 5. Adjacent to a popular Italian restaurant (La Rouvenaz), the eclectic **Il Baretto** (⊠ 1 rue du Marché

☎ 021/9621212) is the smallest bar in town. An urbane, designer-clad crowd flocks to the **Mayfair Café** (✉ 52 Grand-rue ☎ 021/9667979) to take in the afternoon sun and make plans for the evening.

CASINO   The **Casino Barrière** (✉ 9 rue du Théâtre ☎ 021/9628383) has dancing, slot machines, table games, and multiple dining venues. Revised gambling regulations have upped the betting limits, making it a major gaming center. Be sure to bring your passport, as no other ID will get you in. Table games don't begin until 4 PM. The casino is open from 11 AM to 3 AM, Friday and Saturday to 4 AM.

DANCING   A DJ spins at the **Copy Cat** (✉ 100 Grand-rue ☎ 021/9633444), the Montreux Palace's hot spot for dancing. Funk, techno, and Latin sounds lure the young set at **Ned** (✉ 19 rue du Marché ☎ 021/9612540), where weekend partying goes until 3 AM. The sound takes a salsa turn at the **Tropical Bar** (✉ 5 rue d'Auberge ☎ 021/9638888).

Sports & the Outdoors

BOATING   Pedal boats are popular along Montreux-Vevey's waterfront. Rentals are available by the convention center and at the quai du Casino. **Ecole de Voile de Montreux** (✉ Clarens ☎ 021/4691338), the local sailing club, gives sailing lessons. The **Ski-Nautique Club** (✉ Clubhouse du Casino ☎ 021/9634456) can be hired by first timers or experts for runs on the lake. Montreux offers its hotel guests free and supervised use of its waterfront facilities for windsurfing and waterskiing.

SWIMMING   **La Maladaire** (✉ Clarens ☎ 021/9645703) has an Olympic-size indoor pool. The **Casino Barrière** (✉ 9 rue du Théâtre ☎ 021/9628383) has a pool on an outdoor terrace with a bar.

Shopping

Souvenir shops, tony boutiques, and jewelry stores are interspersed randomly along the Grand-Rue. The **Forum** (✉ quai de la Rouvenez), a modern complex, is anchored by grocery giant Migros and topped with shops, restaurants, and expensive condominiums. Underground parking is connected to the **Place du Marché**, a large covered pavilion where the weekly open-air food market is held every Friday morning. The pavilion also doubles as the hub for festivals, concerts, and the famous Marche Noël (Christmas Market).

LES ALPES VAUDOISES

At the eastern tip of Lac Léman, the Alps on the French and Swiss sides close in on the Rhône, and the lakefront highways begin a gradual, ear-popping ascent as the scenery looms larger and the mountains rise around you. The high-altitude Alpine resorts of Villars, Leysin, and Les Diablerets each have their charms for winter-sports fans and summer hikers; a visit to any one of the three would suffice for a mountain retreat. On the other hand, the Pays-d'Enhaut, over the Col des Mosses, is a rustic, lower-altitude region surrounded by rocky ridges and velvet hillsides sprinkled with ancient carved-wood chalets; either Château-d'Oex or Rougemont would serve well as home base for a sojourn in this gentle resort area. You can make a beeline from one to another, but rail

EATING WELL IN THE VAUD

The marvelous culinary delights of the region range from the *cuisine marché* (cuisine based on fresh market produce) of top-drawer chefs to the simplest fare: *papet Vaudois* (a straightforward stew of leeks, potatoes, and cream served with superb local sausages), delicate *filets de perche* (local perch fillets, sautéed or fried), and even *malakoffs* (egg-and-Gruyère fritters), which hark back to the days when the soldiers of La Côte fought in the Crimean Wars. Fondue, the Swiss national dish, can be ordered in any season, but locals prefer chillier months or cooler climes before gathering around a *caquelon* (earthen pot) of bubbling cheese.

A generation of acolytes from the kitchen of renowned chef Fredy Girardet are now master performers in their own right, showcasing their culinary talents in villages scattered along the lake. Season after season, they fill their high-end dining rooms with scores of obsessed restaurant habitués and locals celebrating milestone events. Eating well does not mean you have to raise your credit card limit or book a table months in advance. There is hardly a village without a white-tablecloth dining area. It could be a nook of half a dozen tables or a carefully orchestrated salon, the space and the menu set apart. Your host has stocked the cellar with top-quality vintages from neighboring wineries as well as global selections, and the staff is aptly qualified to pair them with the *menu du jour.*

Be adventurous and stop when you see a sign or lace-curtained window you find inviting. There is probably an exceptional meal to be had—one that is in harmony with the character of the wines produced down the lane and appreciative of each head of sun-sweetened lettuce.

connections are cumbersome and driving often challenging; you'd do well to choose one dreamy spot and stay put—by the fireplace or on the balcony—for as many days as your itinerary allows.

The resorts of the Alpes Vaudoises, although anything but household words to most ski buffs, offer the bonus of a transportation linkup and lift-ticket package with the sprawling Gstaad "Super-Ski" region. This skiing mecca takes in the entire Saanen Valley from Zweisimmen to Château-d'Oex and even dovetails with the parallel valley resorts of Adelboden and Lenk, justifying a visit for skiers who want to cover a lot of territory during their stay.

Aigle

23 **To & From:** *Connections to the ski and hiking resorts of Les Diablerets, Villars-sur-Ollon, and Leysin all radiate from the town of Aigle. Most regional trains departing from Lausanne stop at this transfer station, but not all. Brightly painted coaches with only second-class seating wind their way to mountain villages on opposite sides of the valley ar-*

riving at Leysin in an hour, Les Diablerets in one and a half. The fastest way to get to Villars (1 ¼ hour), is to switch to the No. 10 bus, but you can use train service (1 ½ hour) available from Bex, the next stop on the line. Like Aigle, not all trains service this station. Round-trip tickets to all will cost 50 SF. Aigle is 17 km (10 mi) south of Montreux, 38 km (24 mi) southeast of Lausanne.

On a smooth plain flanked by the sloping vineyards of the region of Le Chablais, Aigle is a scenic wine center. Its spired and turreted **Château de Savoie,** originally built in the 13th century, was almost completely destroyed—and then rebuilt—by the 15th-century Bernese.

★ At the **Château d'Aigle,** both the novice and wine aficionado can get a close-up look at wine-making history and promotion. First peruse display casks, bottles, presses, and winemakers' tools within the wood-beamed chambers of the **Musée de la Vigne et du Vin** (Museum of Viticulture and Wine), in the chateau. Some living quarters are reproduced, and there's even a collection of costumes worn over the centuries at the local Fête des Vignerons. The separate **Musée de l'Étiquette** (Museum of Wine Labels), in a timbered attic in an adjacent warehouse called the Maison de la Dîme, chronicles the history of prestigious vintages through a collection of labels representing more than 50 countries and dating back 200 years. You need go no farther for a tasting: the Pinte du Paradis wine bar is just downstairs, overlooking the vineyards. The château is closed for renovations until the first half of 2007. ☎ 024/4662130 ⊕ *www. chateauaigle.ch* ⊠ *9 SF ☉ Apr.–June, Sept. and Oct., Tues.–Sun. 10–12:30 and 2–6; July and Aug., daily 10–6; Nov.–Mar., tours by appointment.*

Lance Armstrong devotees and other cycling enthusiasts will find the **Centre Mondial du Cyclisme** (World Cycling Center) a fascinating stop. Headquarters of the UCI, cycling's international sports federation, the contemporary silver-tone facility has an exhibition hall, athlete training facility, and indoor velodrome—all state-of-the-art and used by world-class competitors. The track is open to the public in the off-season, and guided tours can be arranged. Both require advance booking. ⊠ *chemin de la Mêlée* ☎ *024/4685885* ⊕ *www.cmc-aigle.ch* ⊠ *Free ☉ Weekdays 8–6.*

Shopping

Chasselas grapes are cultivated on the steep shale and sandstone terraces by Aigle and Yvorne; these local wines flare with exuberance. Generations of the Badoux family have tended the land around Aigle held by *murailles* (stone walls), producing a signature wine identified by the lizard on the label. **La Boutique du Lézard** (⊠ 18 av. du Chamossaire ☎ 024/ 4688888), a lovely wineshop, is just the place to scout a local find. Browse the shelves for select vintages, etched decanters, and corkscrews.

Villars-sur-Ollon

❷ *15 km (9 mi) southeast of Aigle, 53 km (33 mi) southeast of Lausanne.*

At 4,264 feet, this welcoming ski center spreads comfortably along a sunny terrace, the craggy peaks of Les Diablerets (10,528 feet) behind it and before it a sweeping view over the Rhône Valley all the way to Mont Blanc.

Balanced along its ridge and open to the vast space below, the busy little downtown—sports shops, cafés, resort hotels—tapers off quickly into open country. Though it's thriving with new construction, Villars retains a sense of coziness and tradition, and some of its family-owned hotels have preserved the feel of mountain lodges that's rare these days in Switzerland. What Villars lacks in glitz, it amply compensates for with unpretentious good cheer. A network of lifts connecting with Les Diablerets makes this a good choice for skiers or hikers who want to experience Suisse Romande relatively unspoiled. The boarding schools headquartered in the area keep the town animated with teen adrenaline, backing sports such as snowboarding, mountain biking, in-line skating, and rock climbing.

> ## SKI, FLOAT AND SURF ALL IN ONE DAY
>
> The Alpes Vaudoises allows you to experience all levels of skiing difficulty. Summer opens trails and high-altitude passes for hikers and mountain bikers. Well-marked paths in every direction give proof that the Swiss adore an outing, especially with the requisite rest stop at a *buvette* (snack bar). You can also take on a more unusual activity, such as strenuous river-gorge expeditions, breathtaking paragliding and hot-air ballooning, and even mountain surfing (zipping downhill on a skateboardlike scooter with handlebars).

Skiing

Villars nicely balances sophistication and Alpine isolation, thanks to a compact village, 36 lifts, and 100 km (67 mi) of downhill runs. The main ski area above the village can be reached easily either by cable car to **Roc d'Orsay** (6,560 feet) or by cog railway from the center to **Bretaye** (5,925 feet); either site allows access to the lifts that fan out over a sunny bowl riddled with intermediate runs and off-trail challenges. From Bretaye, you can also take lifts up to **Grand Chamossaire** (6,954 feet) for gentle, open runs. Trails from Chaux Ronde are easy enough for beginners, but the more advanced can find jumps and trees enough to keep them more than alert. Just beyond Villars, the linking resort of **Gryon**, with runs that pitch off **Les Chaux,** presents a few more options and a change of scenery, again with trails for all levels of skill. For serious skiers, the link to **Les Diablerets Glacier** provides stepped-up challenges in vertical territory that is used for training professionals. One-day lift tickets without glacier access cost 47 SF. If you are going to ski for six days, purchase the region's all-inclusive pass for 265 SF, which provides access to Glacier 3000 at Les Diablerets, Leysin, and Mosses. There are also 50 km (31 mi) of cross-country trails plus sledding and snowshoeing.

Where to Stay & Eat

¢–$ ✕ **Le Refuge de Frience.** Detour off the scenic route from Villars to Gryon at Barboleuse to get to this 18th-century Heidi-esque chalet in the highland pastures. It combines the grist of Alpine legend with good, honest food. Three cheery rooms glowing with log fires under low, beamed ceilings give way to unfettered views of the mountains. You won't see many tourists here; it's a word-of-mouth place that packs in locals and weekend expats in the know. They go for the fondue and raclette, river trout, and plates of fresh regional mushrooms—and wine spouting from an old *fontaine,* a wrought-iron contraption rarely seen in restaurants. ⊠ *4½ km (3 mi) from Villars, Alpe des Chaux* ☎ *024/4981426* ⊟ *MC, V* ⊗ *Closed Tues., Apr.–May, and mid-Nov.–mid-Dec.*

$$$–$$$$ 🏨 **Grand Hôtel du Park.** You can't sleep any closer to the slopes than this upscale lodge at the base of the mountain, which has been run by the same family for generations. Its park setting is enjoyable in all seasons, and the honey-colored wood interior says ski chalet. Themed culinary weeks feature round-the-world cuisine, a delightful change from regional dishes. ⊠ *rue Centrale, CH-1884* ☎ *024/4962828* 🖷 *024/4953363* ⊕ *www.parcvillars.ch* ⇌ *60 rooms* ⚹ *4 restaurants, minibars, cable TV, bar, free parking; no a/c* ⊟ *AE, DC, MC, V* ⊗ *Closed Nov.* ⫟⊙⫠ *CP.*

$$–$$$ 🏨 **Le Bristol.** This resort hotel, one of the poshest in town, rose from the ashes of an older landmark. Despite the Colorado-condo exterior with balconies that jut from every room, it is furnished with a light, bright, and convincingly regional touch. Interiors are mostly white with mauve accents and carved blond pine, and picture windows are angled to take in the views. There are good fitness facilities and a choice of attractive restaurants, including one on a terrace above the valley. ⊠ *rue Centrale, CH-1884* ☎ *024/4963636* 🖷 *024/4963637* ⊕ *www.bristol-villars.ch* ⇌ *87 rooms, 23 suites* ⚹ *2 restaurants, minibars, cable TV, indoor pool, gym, hot tub, massage, sauna, steam room, bar, free parking; no a/c* ⊟*AE, DC, MC, V* ⫟⊙⫠ *CP.*

$–$$ 🏨 **Écureuil.** Although there's a restaurant downstairs and a carnotzet for fondue, many rooms in this warm family-run inn have a kitchenette, so you can make yourself at home mountain cabin–style. Opened in 1947 and now run by the son of the founder, the hotel has lots of homey touches: books and magazines, swing sets, and a piano parlor. An older stone-base chalet on the grounds offers bigger rooms; both buildings stand across the street from the Bristol and therefore don't have direct access to those Villars views. ⊠ *rue Centrale, CH-1884* ☎ *024/4963737* 🖷 *024/4963722* ⊕ *www.hotel-ecureuil.ch* ⇌ *27 rooms* ⚹ *Restaurant, Stübli, in-room safes, some kitchenettes, cable TV, in-room data ports, Ping-Pong, Internet, free parking; no a/c* ⊟ *MC, V* ⫟⊙⫠ *CP.*

Sports & the Outdoors

HIKING There are 300 km (186 mi) of hiking trails in the region. Most only require a map (pick one up at the tourist office) and a good pair of hiking shoes. If you would like to tackle more difficult routes or add mountaineering to your outing, **Villars Experience** (⊠ rue Centrale ☎ 024/4954138 ⊕ www.villars-experience.ch) has guides and equipment.

SPORTS CENTERS The **Centre des Sports** (⊠ chemin de la Gare ☎ 024/4951221 ⊠ rte. du Col de la Croix ☎ 024/4953030) has two locations. One has an indoor skating rink (skates available for rent) and an indoor pool, whereas the other offers an extensive range of activities—from badminton to wall climbing—as well as an outdoor pool.

Les Diablerets

 19 km (12 mi) northeast of Aigle, 59 km (37 mi) southeast of Lausanne.

This small resort (3,806 feet) lies at the base of the 10,525-foot peak of the same name—which sheds the dramatic namesake 9,840-foot glacier. The village was named after a folklore tale of devils who played skittles among the desolate glacier peaks. A compact handful of hotels, shops, and steep-roof chalets are strung along a winding road. The valley brightens only when sun finds its way over crags and crests, which may be why skiing is guaranteed year-round and the Swiss team trains here in summer. To get here from Villars during those warm months, car travelers can cut along spectacular heights on a tiny 13%-grade road over the Col de la Croix (5,832 feet). Keep an eye out for packs of mountain bikers pushing their way across the pass. Train travelers have to descend to Bex and backtrack to Aigle.

Fodor'sChoice ★ The ride on **Glacier 3000,** an aerial cableway strung from its station at Col du Pillon 7 km (4 mi) outside the resort village to a shelf at Scex-Rouge, is a thrill and well worth the steep fare. Vistas of Alpine peaks, vast meadows, and clusters of sloping-roof farmhouses extend to Lac Léman and the Jura mountains. The 20-minute ascent is done in two segments, ending at the metallic, jewel box–shaped restaurant designed by world-famous architect Mario Botta. In warm weather, skiers share the glacial zone with snowcat (motorized vehicle) and dogsled tours. ☎ *024/4923377* ⊕ *www.glacier3000.ch* ✉ *55 SF* ☉ *July–Oct., daily 9–4:50; Nov.–Apr., daily 9–4:30.*

Skiing

The connection of Les Diablerets' ski facilities with those of Villars adds considerably to ski options—including summer skiing on the glacier itself. The lift to **Meilleret** (6,394 feet), the peak that lies directly above the village of **Les Diablerets** (3,806 feet), serves as the aerial linchpin with Villars. A cable car from another station in the village lifts skiers to **Isenau,** which has intermediate and expert runs cascading from the peak of **Floriettaz** (6,956 feet). But it is the glacier—and the dramatic peak-top pistes at **Quille du Diable** and **Scex-Rouge** that many come to ski. Take a bus to Col du Pillon, where a series of gondolas ascends along the sheer wall to mountaintop ski stations. From Scex-Rouge, a popular run carries you around the top of the **Oldenhorn** and down to **Oldenegg,** a wide-open intermediate run through a sheltered valley. For an additional adrenaline rush, there's one gravity-defying expert slope, directly under the gondola, from **Pierre-Pointes** back to the valley.

Before purchasing your tickets, study ski maps carefully and assess your stamina and skill level. Lift rates are often priced in combinations. A one-day pass for Les Diablerets/Villars is 47 SF; Isenau is 40 SF. Adding Glacier 3000 takes the cost up to 55 SF, but you will have 74 lifts and 200 km (137 mi) of runs from which to choose. (Reduced family prices are available.)

Cross-country skiers can explore 45 km (27 mi) of trails, some tracking through woods and meadows. There are also runs specifically designed for sledding and snow tubing.

Where to Stay & Eat

$ ✕⌂ **Auberge de la Poste.** The Pichard family, keepers of this weathered centuries-old inn, holds dear the inn's heritage of lodging stagecoach passengers and Alpine enthusiasts. The rustic chalet has carved eaves with hand-painted designs, creaky floors, and old, rippled, handblown-glass windows. The simplicity of this relais has attracted celebrities from Stravinsky to David Bowie. The restaurant (¢–$$) has heavy wood furniture and serves hearty fare, including fondue and platters of air-dried meats and cheese with crusty bread. Some rooms share toilet and shower facilities. ⊠ *rue de la Gare, CH-1865* ☎ *024/4923124* 🖷 *024/ 4921268* ⊕ *www.aubergedelaposte.ch* ⤶ *12 rooms* ⌂ *Restaurant, cable TV, free parking; no a/c* ▤ *MC, V* ⊗ *Closed Nov.* ⦿ *CP.*

$$ ⌂ **Hôtel des Diablerets.** Carved wooden eaves and ornate balconies frame this chalet-style hotel. It practically breathes Alpine ambience, from the heavy, carved blond-wood furniture to the starched white mile-high duvets. The café and brasserie are true to type, serving traditional Alpine dishes. The hotel is just minutes from the lifts—and it has outstanding, inspiring views. ⊠ *chemin du Vernex, CH-1865* ☎ *024/4920909* 🖷 *024/4922391* ⊕ *www.hoteldesdiablerets.ch* ⤶ *54 rooms, 5 suites* ⌂ *Restaurant, minibars, cable TV, indoor pool, sauna, steam room, bar, parking (fee); no a/c* ▤ *AE, DC, MC, V* ⊗ *Closed late Apr.–June, Oct., and Nov.* ⦿ *CP.*

Sports & the Outdoors

You can satisfy your taste for adventure with activities ranging from leisurely to extreme. **Centre ParAdventure** (⊠ rue de la Gare ☎ 024/ 4922382) can take you hang gliding, canyoning, sledding, dirt biking, and zorbing (rolling down the mountainside in a huge plastic ball). **Mountain Evasion** (⊠ pl. de la Gare ☎ 024/4921232 ⊕ www.mountain-evasion. ch) organizes luge, snowshoeing, canyoning, rock climbing, and dirt-biking excursions, among others. Both have English-speaking guides. **Parc des Sports** (⊠ Centre Ville ☎ 024/4923988) is the hub of summer and indoor athletics from archery to tennis, swimming to wall climbing.

For a real tobogganing experience, try the 7-km (4.5-mi) run from **Vioz-Mazots,** accessible from the Meilleret lift, at night. You can rent sleds at any of the village sports stores; the ticket to the top costs 11 SF. Alternatively, you can book an all-inclusive excursion (transportation, equipment, and hot cider après sled run) with Mountain Evasion or Center ParAdventure. Evening outings start with a delicious fondue dinner followed by a torchlit race to the bottom.

EN ROUTE From the switchback highway A11, a small mountain road leads up to **Leysin,** a family resort with easy skiing and a spectacular, sunny plateau looking directly onto the Dents du Midi. The crowd, many of whom spill out of nearby boarding schools, is young and athletic. Snowboarding hot shots and mountain bikers swarm the trails—home to qualifying training runs and championship competition. The best views are from Kukulos, a revolving restaurant in the glass tower on Berneuse, a peak 6,720 feet above the village.

VAUD ESSENTIALS

11

Transportation

BY AIR

Geneva's Cointrin is the second-busiest international airport in Switzerland, servicing flights from European and international destinations on Swiss as well as other international carriers. From Cointrin, Swiss connects to secondary airports throughout the country. Low-cost carrier easyJet also serves a number of European destinations. Both airports have rail stations connected by sky bridges in adjacent terminals making it a snap to transit to all major towns in the region.

🛈 Airlines & Contacts **easyJet** ☎ 084/8888222 ⊕ www.easyjet.com. **Swiss** ☎ 084/9700700 toll free within the country ⊕ www.swiss.com.

🛈 Airport Information **Cointrin** ✉ 55 km (34 mi) southwest of Lausanne ☎ 022/7177111 ⊕ www.gva.ch.

BY BOAT & FERRY

Like all fair-size Swiss lakes, Lac Léman is crisscrossed with comfortable and reasonably swift steamers. In summer they sometimes run more often than the trains that parallel their routes. With a Swiss Pass you travel free. You can embark and disembark freely at ports along the way. The trip from one end of the lake to the other will take the better part of a day as routes are designed to serve a third of the lake per circuit, connecting towns on both the French and Swiss sides. Shorter trips like the one from Lausanne to Vevey will take an hour; the crossing to Evian les Bains in France is only 30 minutes. For boat schedule and docking information contact Compagnie Générale de Navigation or pick up a timetable in any tourist office.

🛈 **Compagnie Générale de Navigation** ☎ 084/8811848 ⊕ www.cgn.ch.

BY BUS

A useful network of postbus routes covers the region for the resourceful traveler (with plenty of time) who desires connections to outlying villages and hamlets; some routes are covered only once or twice a day. The signature yellow buses pick up at rail stations and drop off at rural post offices harkening back to the day when they were the main source of mail delivery. Schedules are available from tourist offices and rail stations; in smaller towns at the post office.

Lausanne has an excellent city bus network called the *tl* (Transports Publics de la région Lausannoise) that includes the Metro (a subway that runs uphill through the city from the port of Ouchy), and commuter rail lines that bring passengers in from near suburbs. At the moment, the multi-tunnel track of the Metro is *hors service* (out of service) for several years of renovation and expansion; its circuit is replaced by a special bus. Fares depend on how many zones you transit—tickets start at 2.40 SF for single trip or 7 SF all day; *Mobilis,* a pass that combines all rail and bus services starts at 7 SF. If you plan to stay out late club hopping, a *pajama service* runs on most lines until 2 AM.

Throughout the Riviera, bus service is provided by *VMCV* (Vevey-Montreux-Chillon-Villeneuve). The Line 1 trolley bus parallels the lake-front and is the most heavily used. Spur routes to the villages of Corsier, Blonay, and others are part of the network, while separately operated funiculars from Vevey and Territet take passengers to the hill towns of Mt. Pelerin and Glion. Tickets on all transportation lines are purchased at automated machines either located at the stop or once on board (at the rear not from the driver). If you have a Swiss Pass, you can travel free on city buses and funiculars in the country and access all national museums.

🚍 **Bus Information PostBus** ☏ 084/8888888 ⊕ www.swisspost.ch. tl ☏ 090/0564900 toll call ⊕ www.t-l.ch. **VMCV** ☏ 021/9891811 ⊕ www.vmcv.ch.

BY CAR

There are two major arteries leading to Lac Léman, one entering from the north via Bern and Fribourg (A12), the other arcing over the north shore of Lac Léman from Geneva to Lausanne (A1), then to Montreux and on south through the Alpes Vaudoises toward the Col du Grand St-Bernard (A9) in Canton Valais. They are swift and often scenic expressways, and the north-shore artery (A1 and A9) traces a route that has been followed since before Roman times. Secondary highways parallel the expressways, but this is one case where, as the larger road sits higher on the lakeside slopes, the views from the expressway are often better than those from the highway. Be sure, however, to detour for the Corniche road views between Lausanne and Montreux.

PARKING   Parking within cities and major towns is difficult and zone restricted. Although expensive, opt for public garages that are clearly signed whenever possible. Take the ticket with you after entry, as payment is made via automated machines at the pedestrian entrance; many locations accept credit cards. The ticket returned after payment is your access card to exit.

BY TRAIN

Lausanne lies on a major train route between Bern and Geneva, with express trains connecting from Basel and Zürich. From Geneva, trains take about 30 minutes and arrive in Lausanne up to four times an hour; from Bern, they take a little more than an hour and arrive twice an hour. TGVs (high-speed trains) run to and from Paris in about four hours and have 10 schedule options. The Cisalpino train to Milan and to Venice has at least four daily departures, plus connecting service via Brig. From June to September extra trains are scheduled. There is also a Euronuit (night sleeper) connection to Italian cities. The ICE, the German high-speed train, has departures to northern destinations with only one change in Basel or Bern. The SBB provides information on international trains.

Regional trains along the waterfront, connecting major lake towns, are frequent and swift unless you board one of the S-trains that stops at every village. Travel time between centers like Geneva and Nyon, or Lausanne and Vevey is about 15 minutes; count on doubling that on an S-train. There are no conductors on the local lines to check tickets, but be assured there are random audits and stiff fines for those on board without paying. Tickets for all rail services can be purchased at automated machines on the station platforms.

There are also several private rail systems leading into small villages and rural regions, including the Montreux–Oberland–Bernois (MOB) Railroad, which climbs sharply behind Montreux and cuts straight over the pre-Alps toward Château-d'Oex and the Berner Oberland. Reserve space in one of their glass dome, panoramic cars and take in the countryside with food and beverage service brought to your seat. The historic Blonay–Chamby Railroad has steam-powered seasonal excursions as does the Rochers-de-Naye line. From Nyon, the red and orange cars of the Nyon–St-Cergue-Morez Railroad deliver passengers to St-Cergue in 30 minutes, before going on to the border town of La Cure and into France. To access the ski resorts of Villar-sur-Ollon and Les Diablerets, separate lines operated by Transports Publices du Chablais (TPC) connect through Bex and Aigle take an hour. The Swiss Pass is accepted on these private lines, but there may be an additional fee for panoramic excursions. Inquire at local tourist offices or train stations about a regional pass that combines rail, boat, bus, and cable car excursions on these private transports at a reduced fee.

⚑ Train Information Blonay–Chamby Railroad ☎ 021/9432121 ⊕ www.blonay-chamby.ch. **Montreux–Oberland–Bernois Railroad** (MOB) ☎021/9898181 ⊕www.mob.ch. **Nyon-St-Cergue-Morez Railroad** (NStCM) ⊕www.tprnov.ch/fr/pages/nstcm. **Transports Publices du Chablais** (TPC) ☎ 024/4680330 ⊕ www.tpc.ch. **SBB** ☎ 090/0300300 (toll call) ⊕ www.rail.ch.

Contacts & Resources

EMERGENCIES

There are standardized telephone numbers throughout Switzerland for emergencies.

⚑ Ambulance ☎ 144. **Fire** ☎ 118. **Late-night pharmacies** ☎ 111. **Police** ☎ 117. **Roadside Assistance** ☎ 140.

INTERNET & MAIL

Internet terminals and Wi-Fi connections are becoming commonplace in hotel guest rooms and lobbies in even the smallest villages. Tourist offices have listings of storefronts where you can log on; many within easy access to their offices, rail stations, and bus transfer points (which is where you also will find most post offices). City postal centers remain open all day; village outposts close over lunch. General hours are weekdays, 8–6 and Saturday, 8-noon (closed Sunday except urban hubs). Lines are cued with an electronic numbering system so be sure to pull a ticket at the dispenser when you walk in. Mailing envelopes, packing supplies, and gift items are for sale, too.

⚑ Internet Cafés Centre de Langues ✉ 10 rue du Simplon Lausanne ☎ 021/6014280. **Cyber World** ✉ 14 rue du Torrent Vevey ☎ 021/9237833. **Cyber World** ✉ 90 Grand - rue Montreux ☎ 021/9635152.

⚑ Post Offices Lausanne ✉ 1 pl. de la Gare. **Vevey** ✉ ave. Général-Guisan. **Montreux** ✉ ave. des Alpes 70. **Nyon** ✉ pl. Bel-Air 5.

TOUR OPTIONS

BUS TOURS The two drop-by branches of the Lausanne tourist office run a daily two-hour coach trip into the Old Town, including a visit to the cathedral and an extended city coach tour that takes in the Lavaux vineyards.

🚍 **Lausanne tourist office** ✉ Gare Centrale, 9 pl. de la Gare ✉ Ouchy pl. de la Navigation.

WALKING TOURS Walking tours led by local historians in Lausanne, Vevey, and Montreux are increasingly popular. They are organized by the town's tourist office and are given daily between April and September. English-speaking guides are often available, but you should call in advance to check. Most local tourist offices offer daily general tours in summer to Gruyères, to Chamonix and Mont Blanc, to the Alps by coach, and to Les Avants and Château-d'Oex by the Montreux–Oberland–Bernois Railroad line's panoramic train. There is also a chocolate excursion to the Nestlé factory in Broc. To ensure a tour with English commentary, reserve in advance.

VISITOR INFORMATION

The Office du Tourisme du Canton de Vaud has general information on the region.

🚩 Local Tourist Offices **Aigle** ✉ 5 rue Colomb, CH-1860 ☎ 024/4663000 ⊕ www.aigle.ch. **Lausanne** ✉ 2 av. de Rhodanie, CH-1006 ☎ 021/6137373 ⊕ www.lausanne-tourisme.ch ✉ Gare Centrale, 9 pl. de la Gare ✉ Ouchy, pl. de la Navigation. **Les Diablerets** ✉CH-1865 ☎024/4923358 ⊕www.lesdiablerets.ch. **Lutry** ✉quai Gustav-Doret, CH-1095 ☎ 021/7914765 ⊕ www.lutry.ch. **Montreux-Vevey** ✉ 5 rue du Théâtre, CH-1820 Montreux ☎ 084/8868484 ⊕ www.montreux-vevey.com ✉ pl. de l'Eurovision, Montreux ✉ 29 Grand-pl., Vevey. **Morges** ✉ 2 rue du Château, CH-1110 ☎ 021/8013233 ⊕ www.morges.ch. **Nyon** ✉ 8 av. Viollier, CH-1260 ☎ 022/3656600 ⊕ www.nyon.ch. **Villars** ✉ rue Centrale, CH-1884 ☎ 024/4953232 ⊕ www.villars.ch.

🚩 Regional Tourist Office **Office du Tourisme du Canton de Vaud** ✉ 60 av. d'Ouchy, CH-1000 Lausanne ☎ 021/6132626 🖷 021/6132600 ⊕ www.lake-geneva-region.ch.

Geneva

The Bol d'Or Rolex regatta on Lake Geneva

WORD OF MOUTH

"You can't go wrong anywhere in Switzerland. We always tell people Geneva's a great place to stop for a few days and relax between, say, Paris and Florence. Meander through Old Town, shop, enjoy a promenade by the lake, and have afternoon tea."
—pmccallum

"And stop at one of the cafés near the Jet d'Eau for some ice cream and enjoy the scenery!"

—Mollie8

WELCOME TO GENEVA

TOP REASONS TO GO

★ **Falling Water:** The feathery Jet d'Eau, Geneva's iconic harbor fountain and the ultimate public shower, is visible for tens of miles in every direction.

★ **Time on Your Hands:** According to statistics, it is ten-to-one you'll leave this city of watchmakers with a new timepiece—for glorious old ones, visit the Patek Philippe Museum.

★ **City of God:** Perhaps as a backlash against the city's rich beauty, John Calvin's fiery Reformation left so many monuments here.

★ **Block Party!** The Fétes de Geneve gives the city a mid-summer break by turning the Rade into a 10-day smorgasbord of international foods.

★ **Exclusive Baubles:** A stroll along the shops of the Rue du Rhône is like walking the catalog of the world's finest jewels—only here they're all home-grown.

1 The Waterfront. La Rade, the 3-mile-long necklace along which Geneva is strung, is woven of parkland, tree-lined promenades, and working marinas, with Mont Blanc and the Horloge Fleurie both posing for your camera.

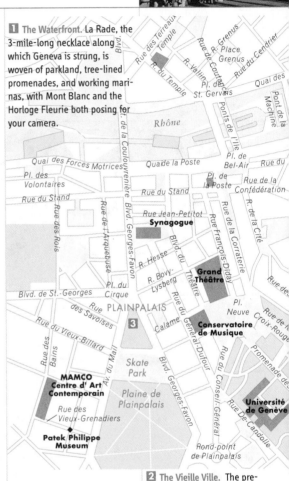

The Rues Basses

2 The Vieille Ville. The pre-Roman Celts who settled this strategically perfect hill could not have imagined it would grow into a renegade religious fortress, a center of government, or the gentrified soul of a large city. Museum central, the Old Town has no less than three historic Reformation sites.

GETTING ORIENTED

A postcard waiting to happen, Geneva lies at the southwestern end of Lac Léman. Presided over by Mont Blanc—the crown jewel of the French Alps—the city is almost entirely surrounded by French territory (lunch in Lyon, anyone?), underscoring its role as a crossroads of culture.

3 Plainpalais. A newcomer and a workhorse, Plainpalais is also a shape-shifting free spirit. Contemporary Art has colonized one-time factories along Rue des Bains; University students amble to class at Uni Mail, while the Swiss National Circus sets up shop on the plaine de Plainpalais.

4 International Area. United Nations security may give these broad, leafy avenues a sense of danger, but crowds always flock to the Red Cross Museum and Palais des Nations here. The villas and diplomatic compounds around them house a community with its finger firmly attached to the world's pulse.

The Nations Palace

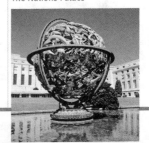

GENEVA PLANNER

How's the Weather?

Hot and sunny with a slight breeze in summer, crisp and clear in spring and autumn, rainbow-prone in June—Geneva's weather, when it's good, is spectacular.

The Alps glow pink and the Jura fade to silhouette at the end of the day; restaurants set tables outside from March through October.

Contrary to belief, summers in Geneva can be very hot, and when it is the city's Pâquis-Plage swimming area is jammed.

There are other days—whole weeks of them in winter—when stratus clouds coagulate between the mountains and grey out everything in sight.

But relief comes from La Bise, the often bitingly cold north wind that blows in off the lake, clears away *la grisaille*, and reveals sparkling snow-covered peaks.

Finding a Place to Stay

Weekend deals make Geneva's luxury palaces affordable, 24 hour kitchens produce everything from Four Seasons perfection to afternoon tea, and tasteful, centrally located rooms with a view may be had in all price ranges. Hotel sniffiness is a problem, however, in this conference and convention-driven town; genuinely gracious service (like free wireless Internet access and breakfast in bed) remains vexingly confined to the professionally trained top and family-run bottom of the rate structure.

Getting Around

The Rhône River divides Geneva into two parts: the *Rive Gauche* (Left Bank) and the *Rive Droite* (Right Bank). The Rive Gauche, to the south, comprises the *Vielle Ville* (Old Town), the Jardin Anglais, the university, and the Pleine de Plainpalais. The Rive Droite includes the *quartier international* (International Area), the train station, St-Gervais district, the quai du Mont-Blanc, the important parks, and the luxury waterfront hotels. Pont du Mont-Blanc, the main bridge, connects the two areas. Geneva has an extensive public transportation system, but you won't need it to see most sights. If you want to take buses or trams, vending machines at each stop spit out tickets good for one hour; All-day tickets are available from agents listed on the signs at the stops.

All this noted, pedestrians have an almost sacred right of way in Geneva—crossing the street in designated places can bring four lanes of traffic to a screeching halt—and walking is by far the most (cost-)effective way to discover quayside promenades, parks, shopping areas, and car-free cobblestone alleys. Street parking demand outstrips supply, meter maids are zealous, and taxis expensive; public transport, meaning buses, trams, trains, and shuttle boats, is clean, punctual, cheap, and ubiquitous. Count 15 minutes on foot from the main train station of Gare Cornavin—on the northern edge of town, between place de Cornavin and rue de Montbrilliant—to either place du Bourg-de-Four or place Neuve.

Making the Most of Your Time

A curious tension exists in Geneva between dour intellectual concepts and breathtaking physical beauty, and you will probably find yourself torn between the urge to wander the quays and the sense that you ought to hit the museum trail. Don't choose: try to divide whatever time you have in the city equally between an extended stroll along the waterfront and a thorough exploration of the Vieille Ville.

Make time for the International Area if it interests you—never mind if it doesn't. Do not, however, skip the creative, convivial Carouge, one of Geneva's loveliest districts. Do try to see some specialist collections (the Fondation Bodmer and the Patek Philippe Museum are stars), do check out the Rues-Basses shopping scene, and make sure that you go somewhere—Port Noir, the tip of the Jet d'Eau jetty, the cathedral towers, La Perle du Lac, Cologny—where you can see distance: Geneva genuinely does look equally good from up close and far away.

Here's a three-day Grand Tour studded with the kind of sights that should be on any traveler's Santa Claus list. Spend your first morning exploring the downtown waterfront, with its boats, swans, 15-foot-wide flowered clock face, and feathery Jet d'Eau.

Then window-shop your way along the Rues-Basses and up into the Vieille Ville. Have lunch on place du Bourg-de-Four, and investigate the Espace St-Pierre, an umbrella term for the starkly beautiful Cathédrale St-Pierre and the Musée International de la Réforme. Don't forget the contemplative Auditoire de Calvin; the Monument de la Réformation sums it all up.

The next day head for the International Area. Spend the morning at the Palais des Nations and the Musée International de la Croix-Rouge, have lunch at the Château de Penthes, and spend the afternoon wandering the Jardin Botanique.

On your third morning, head back to the Vieille Ville for some museum-hopping at the Maison Tavel, Musée Barbier-Mueller, Musée Rath, and Patek Philippe Museum. Then take a break and spend the afternoon riding the waves of Lac Léman on a Compagnie Générale de Navigation (CGN) paddle steamer.

Shop-'til-You-Drop Alert

12

Calvin created watchmakers out of less-utilitarian jewelers and goldsmiths, but the urge to create beautiful baubles never died in Geneva.

Teams of expert craftsmen still toil steadily behind chic shop walls, and Geneva watchmakers are rightfully known for unparalleled excellence. But great shopping is not confined to timepieces. Handmade chocolates are an art form here.

Stores just off the beaten path can be extraordinarily vibrant, and the Vieille Ville has no shortage of antiques shops.

Geneva is also a city of markets; chatty fruit and vegetable vendors, taciturn flea-market regulars, and craftspeople clustered in designated squares continue the legacy of the medieval trade fairs once held along the department-store-lined Rues-Basses.

As for the main shops in Geneva's main shopping district around the Rue duRhône, the dazzling window displays will prove an irresistible magnet for even the most budget-conscious tourist.

Updated
by Jennifer
McDermott

THE COSMOPOLITAN, GRACEFUL SOUL OF SWITZERLAND'S FRENCH-SPEAKING TERRITORY, Geneva exudes a Gallic hauteur. Grand, mansarded mansions stand guard beside the Rhône river, yachts bob, gulls dive, and Rolls-Royces purr past manicured promenades. The combination of Swiss efficiency and French savoir faire gives Geneva a chic polish; the infusion of international blood from the UN adds a heterogeneity rare in a city of only 180,000. Of course, foreigners have long been drawn to the city. In recent centuries, the Big-League international organizations were established here: the International Red Cross was founded in 1864; Woodrow Wilson gave Geneva the League of Nations in 1919 and the roll call also includes the World Health Organization (WHO) and the World Trade Organization (WTO). More than 150 countries maintain permanent missions to the United Nations Office in Geneva, 40% of the local population is not Swiss, and the World Wide Web was invented here at CERN, the European Center for Nuclear Research. But none of this seems to faze the Genevois: the world has mingled in their postcard-perfect city for millennia.

One main reason has been the city's reputation for enlightened tolerance. It gave refuge to the writers Voltaire, Victor Hugo, Alexandre Dumas, Honoré de Balzac, and Stendhal, as well as the religious reformers John Calvin and John Knox. Lord Byron, Percy Bysshe and Mary Shelley, Richard Wagner, and Franz Liszt all fled from scandals elsewhere into Geneva's sheltering arms.

The narrow austerity and bigotry of 16th-century Calvinism—whose namesake reformed the city that sheltered him, preaching fire and brimstone and stripping the cathedral of its papist icons—did, however, cause nonbelievers to leave Geneva even as masses of Protestants fled to it. The English fled Bloody Mary, Protestant Italians the wrath of the pope, Spaniards the Inquisition, French Huguenots the oppressive French monarchy—and Geneva flourished. Philosopher (and Geneva native) Jean-Jacques Rousseau first left the country as a Roman Catholic convert, then returned years later to reenter the Protestant church.

To this day the conservative Genevois seem to hear Calvin task-taking in their ears as they hurry by some of the world's most expensive stores and palatial hotels; it is the urbane foreigners who seem to indulge themselves the most. Stories still abound about oil-rich sheikhs taking over whole hotels for month-long shopping sprees in the 1970s,

AN OPEN INVITATION

Nothing is too insignificant, it would seem, to be feted in Geneva: the city enthusiastically supports a stream of celebrations, including wine-harvest, jazz, and cinema-arts festivals. The three-day Fête de la Musique marks the summer solstice with more than 500 open-air concerts; the Fête de l'Escalade rolls back the clock to 1602 each December. The flamboyantly raunchy Lake Parade grinds its way along the quays in July. The 10-day Fêtes de Genève fills the waterfront each August with Ferris wheels, open-air discos, international foods, and a massive display of fireworks set to music.

and you'll find many of the world's wealthy still head here to bid at the jewelry auctions Sotheby's holds at the Beau-Rivage and to dine in restaurants with dry-mouth high prices. But there is something to delight everyone here—particulary when it comes to museums. Geneva's are a big draw because they offer a wide-open perspective on history and culture: you can visit a military exhibit up the hill from the Red Cross's examination of the horrors of war; weigh the extremes of ancient and contemporary ceramics; browse archaeological finds from Egypt and the Far East; compare pre-Christian primitive art with its modern incarnation; relive the Reformation; or explore the fruits of human thought and creativity as expressed on paper, in science, and inside the case of a tiny pocket watch. The Palais des Nations forms the ultimate living (and working) museum of 20th-century history. To make things easier, seven of the private institutions have developed a Passeport Musées, a "passport" that cuts chunks off their entrance fees. Geneva's historic feast takes a special twist every December 11, when the city lets its elegant chignon down to celebrate the Escalade, a 17th-century battle that ended with a pot of soup dumped on the enemies' heads.

EXPLORING GENEVA

The *République et Canton de Genève* (Republic and Canton of Geneva) commands sweeping views of the French Alps and the French Jura from its fortuitous position at the southwestern tip of *Lac Léman* (Lake Geneva). The water flows straight through the city center and into the River Rhône en route to Lyon and the Mediterranean, leaving museums, shops, restaurants, and parks to jostle for space on its history-laden south shore, known as *Rive Gauche* (Left Bank). Busy shopping streets underline the hilltop *Vieille Ville* (Old Town), the Plaine de Plainpalais lies to its west, and Eaux-Vives stretches along the quays to the east. The *quartier international* (International Area), the *Gare Cornavin* (main train station), and sumptuous waterfront hotels dominate the north shore, or *Rive Droite* (Right Bank). St-Gervais, just north of the ponts de l'Ile, was once a watchmaking quarter. Les Pâquis, an unruly mix of artists, ethnic communities, and scrappy pleasure-seekers, extends north from the pont du Mont-Blanc. The International Area, on the outer edge of the city, is a short tram ride from the station; all other neighborhoods are easily toured on foot.

Numbers in the text correspond to numbers in the margin and on the Geneva map.

The Waterfront

Geneva is centered on water. The city's quays line the downtown area, link the well-groomed Right and Left Banks, and form a horseshoe-shape continuum of scrupulously tended parkland, historical sites, grand hotels, monuments, and breathtaking views.

What to See

❸ **Beau-Rivage.** Jean-Jacques Mayer's descendants still own and operate the hotel he built in 1865. It has discreetly witnessed the birth of a na-

A GOOD WALK

From Gare Cornavin, take Bus 1 to the Sécheron stop and walk through the gate labeled RESTAURANT LA PERLE DU LAC. The second paved path to your left after the parking lot leads to the Villa Bartholoni, home of the **Musée d'Histoire des Sciences ❶** ☛, housed in an elegant Neoclassical mansion.

Turn right as you exit the museum, and make your way down to the water. On a clear day, **Mont Blanc** floats above the hills on the far side of the lake like a sugar-dusted meringue. Keep the water to your left as you head past the Mouettes Genevoises landing dock, La Perle du Lac, and spectacular seasonal flower beds.

Continue straight along quai Wilson as the traffic curls down to meet you. The stately **Palais Wilson ❷**, on your right, housed the League of Nations from its creation after World War I until 1936. Follow the manicured lawns and ornate town houses around a sharp curve to the right. The Bains des Pâquis, hugely popular public baths with protected space to swim and sunbathe, occupy most of the jetty extending to your left. The Palace Hilton, a bit farther along to your right, opens the Right Bank parade of grand hotels.

Keep walking past the Port des Mouettes and the Hotel d'Angleterre. The slender statue of Sissi, Empress Elisabeth of Austria, on your left, was erected in 1998 to mark the centennial of her death; she was stabbed as she left the **Beau-Rivage ❸** to board one of the paddle steamers docked alongside the quay. Detour briefly out to the end of the jetty for a close-up view of the boats and the city center. Then cross the street in front of the Beau-Rivage and angle left to the elaborate **Monument Brunswick ❹**.

Cross back to the quay at the far end of the block, head right past the plaque marking the spot where Sissi was stabbed, and take the last staircase before the pont du Mont-Blanc down to the left. Continue straight under the bridge. When you surface in front of the Hotel des Bergues, make two lefts onto the pedestrians-only pont des Bergues. The **Ile Rousseau ❺**, halfway across, harbors a statue of its locally contentious namesake. The **Temple de la Fusterie ❻**, on the far side of the bridge, was Geneva's first custom-built Calvinist church.

Turn left when you reach dry land, and follow the quay under the pont du Mont-Blanc a second time. Turn left at the top of the ramp, then right toward the statue commemorating the union of Geneva and the Swiss Confederation on September 12, 1814. Keep to the left of the statue, follow the path as it arcs to the right, and keep walking until the **Horloge Fleurie ❼** comes into view on the left. Continue past the floral clock face and through the Jardin Anglais, toward its graceful 19th-century fountain, then rejoin the quay where it veers to the left by the bust of Gustave Ador.

Take the steps down and angle left toward *La Neptune* ❽, the only original boat of its kind still in service on Lac Léman. Sticking out of the water to its right are the

12

Pierres du Niton, two glacial erratics deposited during the last Ice Age. Geneva's Guillaume-Henri Dufour designated the larger one as the base reference point (1,222 feet above sea level) for all altitude measurements taken during the 19th-century land survey that produced the first map of Switzerland.

Return to the upper promenade by the next set of stairs, continue to your left past more flower beds, and veer back to the lower level where rue du 31-Décembre meets quai Gustave-Ador. The **Jet d'Eau** ❾, Europe's tallest fountain, gushes straight up from the lake halfway along the stone jetty before you; it also produces spray that feels like the mother of all sprinklers. The lighthouse at the end of the jetty has an unmatched view of the Centre Ville.

Return to the quay and continue to the left past the city's main marina. Look back for a great view of the cathedral just before you reach the statue of La Bise (the North Wind). Then turn right when the asphalt ends and cross the street opposite **Parc La Grange** ❿.

Have a peek at the park and return to the quay, or wander through the rose garden on the left inside the gates, make your way into the neighboring Parc des Eaux-Vives, and return to the quay farther down the road. Regardless of which park exit you use, cross the street and continue to the right past parallel beds of roses and terrific Jura, lake, and city views. At Port Noir, where the formal quay ends, a simple nautical monument commemorates the June 1, 1814, landing of Swiss troops sent to guarantee Geneva's

safety in the aftermath of Napoléon's rule.

If you're feeling energetic and time permits, continue past Port Noir, cross the street at the traffic light, and follow the steep, leafy rampe de Cologny about 1 km (½ mi) up to the hilltop village of Cologny, where Byron's guest, Mary Shelley, wrote *Frankenstein*. Continue straight through the small traffic circle and head left to the end of the Auberge du Lion d'Or parking lot for sweeping views of the Palais des Nations, lake, and Jura; turn right at the traffic circle toward the **Fondation Martin Bodmer** ⓫ if the sweeping vista of human thought is more your style.

Retrace your steps or take the peaceful pedestrian chemin du Righi, just below the museum, back down the hill, then head left to Port Noir. If the sun is setting, stay awhile and watch the city lights flicker on; in July and August, opt for an open-air film at Cinélac. When you're ready to head home, cross the street and take Bus 2 (direction Bernex) to the Métropole stop. From there you can take Bus 8 (direction OMS) or walk across the pont du Mont-Blanc to the train station. ☹ TIMING TIPS➔ Discounting its final uphill loop through Cologny, this walk covers 5 km (3 mi) of largely flat, paved promenade—the perfect way to spend a leisurely day following the sun. Wear sunscreen and comfortable shoes, bring a book and binoculars if you have them, and give yourself at least a few hours to stroll and linger—there are always boats coming in, swans to feed, benches to rest on, and people to watch.

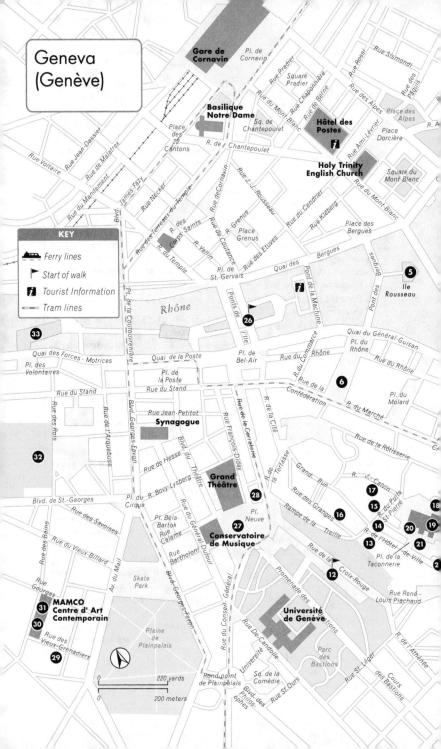

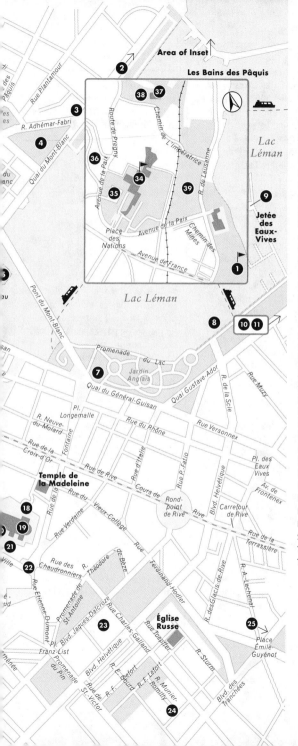

GENEVA THROUGH THE AGES

Geneva's identity as a crossroads dates from about 500 BC, when the Celtic Allobroges built a settlement on raised ground between the Rhône and Arve rivers and policed the only bridge over the Rhône north of Lyon. Julius Caesar arrived rather suddenly in 58 BC, burned the bridge to prevent the Helvetians from migrating south, and ushered in five centuries of Pax Romana. Rome handed off to the Burgundians around AD 460, Charlemagne convened his army commanders here in 773, and in 1032 Geneva caught the eye of the territorially ambitious House of Savoy. Geneva's existing rulers, bishop-princes subordinate to the Holy Roman Emperor, sparred with Savoy for control of the "merry city" for the next five hundred years.

The Genevois, meanwhile, took care of business: the city developed its highly profitable trade fairs, exacted a Magna Carta–like agreement from its bishop in 1387, and defied Savoy's efforts to strangle its economy by concluding treaties of friendship with Bern and Fribourg in 1477. As overland trade routes declined in the Age of Discovery, Geneva reinforced its ties with Bern, overthrew its bishop, and set the stage for seismic change.

By May 1536, Bern's evangelical emissary, Guillaume Farel, had persuaded the young Republic that it would be advantageous to adopt the Reformation. Two months later he also persuaded Jean Calvin, a trained lawyer, skilled orator, and Protestant refugee passing through the city, to stay and shepherd its implementation. Calvin spent the rest of his life preaching a Reformed gospel that fundamentally altered Geneva in look, spirit, and character—by the time of his death in 1564 it had become the dour, bookish, and heavily fortified Protestant Rome.

Savoy's efforts to stamp out the Reformation and reclaim Geneva for Catholicism were decisively thwarted during the Escalade victory of 1602, and waves of diligent, educated, highly skilled Protestant refugees poured into the city from around Europe. French Huguenots, in particular, introduced printing, textile manufacturing, watchmaking, enameling, and banking industries that restored economic prosperity; Jean-Jacques Rousseau was born in and based many of his revolutionary ideas on Geneva, then left for good in 1762 when the increasingly corrupt and conservative city government burned his books. Napoléon arrived in 1798.

Geneva rather gingerly became part of Switzerland in 1814, when the Congress of Vienna required post-Napoleonic France to cede a narrow strip of lakeshore linking its territory to Vaud. A newly liberal city government voted to tear down Calvin's walls in 1850, and the city as it looks now dates from that period. It also still shares more than 96% of its border, as well as its language, with France.

tion (Czechoslovakia, in 1918), the death of an empress (Empress Elisabeth of Austria, in 1898), the sale of royal treasure (the Duchess of Windsor's jewels, in 1987), and the passage of crowned heads from around the world. Sotheby's commandeers its conference rooms for jewelry auctions twice a year. ⊠ *13 quai du Mont-Blanc, Les Pâquis* ☎ *022/ 7166666* ⊕ *www.beau-rivage.ch.*

⓫ **Fondation Martin Bodmer** (Martin Bodmer Foundation). The library that
Fodor'sChoice sources this humbling (and rotating) exhibition of original texts—from
★ cuneiform tablets, papyrus scrolls, and parchment to a first edition of
Ulysses—maps the development of history by tracking human thought. Dramatic displays of bas-reliefs and dimly lighted Egyptian books of the dead give way to handwritten Gospels according to Matthew and John; a perfectly preserved Gutenberg Bible; Martin Luther's *Ninety-Five Theses;* Dante's *Divine Comedy;* Shakespeare's complete works (published 1623); first editions of *Paradise Lost, Don Quixote, Oliver Twist,* and the *Communist Manifesto;* a handwritten score by Mozart; Homer's *Iliad;* Copernicus's *Revolutions of the Celestial Orbs;* and *Alice in Wonderland.* A comprehensive printed guide is available in English; the hilltop views are superb. ⊠ *19-21 route du Guignard, Cologny* ☎ *022/ 7074433* ⊕ *www.fondationbodmer.org* ⊠ *15 SF* ☉ *Tues.–Sun. 2–6.*

➐ **Horloge Fleurie** (Flower Clock). The city first planted this gigantic, and accurate, floral timepiece in 1955 to highlight Geneva's seminal role in the Swiss watchmaking industry. Some 6,500 plants are required each spring and fall to cover its 16-foot-wide surface. ⊠ *Corner quai du Général-Guisan and pont du Mont-Blanc, Centre Ville.*

➎ **Ile Rousseau.** Jean-Jacques Rousseau, the son of a Genevois watchmaker, is known to history as a liberal *French* philosopher in part because Geneva's conservative government so thoroughly rejected his views. His statue on this former city bastion, erected reluctantly in 1835 (57 years after his death), was surrounded by trees and deliberately hidden from view until the 1862 construction of the pont du Mont-Blanc gave Rousseau the last laugh. ⊠ *Off pont des Bergues, Centre Ville.*

☾ ➒ **Jet d'Eau** (Water Jet). The direct descendant of a late-19th-century hy-
Fodor'sChoice droelectric safety valve, Europe's tallest fountain shoots 132 gallons of
★ water 390 feet into the air every second at 120 mph (wind conditions permitting). The water is aerated on the way up by a special nozzle, making it white. ⊠ *Off quai Gustave-Ador, Eaux-Vives.*

NEED A BREAK? The ice-cream maestros at **Gelateria Arlecchino** (⊠ 1 rue du 31-Décembre, Eaux-Vives ☎ 022/7367060), across the street from the Jet d'Eau, crank out more than 40 homemade flavors, including ginger-lime, tiramisu, *pannacotta* (cream custard), rhubarb, gingerbread, licorice, and three options for diabetics.

➑ *La Neptune.* Old photos of Geneva show scores of black masts and graceful, cream-color lateen sails crowding the lake. Now the only authentic traditional barge still in existence is hired out for day sails. Built in 1904 and restored twice, in 1976 and 2005, she hauled stone and sand between far-flung construction sites until 1968. ⊠ *Off quai Gustave-Ador, Eaux-Vives* ☎ *022/7322944.*

★ **Mont Blanc.** At 15,767 feet, Mont Blanc is the highest mountain in Europe and the crown jewel of the French Alps. Geneva's Right Bank—particularly its waterfront parkland—has a front-row view framed by three less-lofty acolytes: Les Voirons, to the left; Le Môle, in the center; and Le Salève, to the right.

❹ **Monument Brunswick.** Charles d'Este-Guelph, the famously eccentric (and deposed) duke of Brunswick, died in Geneva in 1873 and left his vast fortune to the city on condition that his tomb, a replica of the 14th-century Scaligeri mausoleum in Verona, be given prominence. No one is sure why his sarcophagus faces inland. ⊠ *Bounded by rue des Alpes, quai du Mont-Blanc, and rue Adhémar-Fabri, Les Pâquis.*

★ ⌐ ❶ **Musée d'Histoire des Sciences** (Museum of the History of Science). Walk-around glass cases display age-old sundials and astrolabes, microscopes and telescopes, barometers, and ornate globes that collectively document (in English) the evolution of modern science; there's a small room full of harrowing medical implements upstairs. The Neoclassical Italianate jewel that houses the collection, the Villa Bartholoni, dates from 1830. ⊠ *128 rue de Lausanne, International Area* ☎ *022/4185060* ⊕ *mah. ville-ge.ch* ⊠ *Free* ☉ *Wed.–Mon. 10–5.*

❷ **Palais Wilson.** Inaugurated in 1875 as the Hotel National, the largest of Geneva's grand palaces, this dignified structure leapt to international prominence on April 28, 1919, when the peace negotiators in Paris chose Geneva to host the newborn League of Nations. Hotel rooms were converted to offices, 700 international civil servants began work here in November, 1920, and the building was renamed in honor of U.S. President Woodrow Wilson in 1924.

By 1936, the faltering League had run out of space and moved to the custom-built Palais des Nations. Ten years later it was dismantled. The Palais Wilson was gutted by fire in 1987, meticulously restored in 1998, and now houses the headquarters of the United Nations High Commissioner for Human Rights (HCHR). It is not open to the public. ⊠ *51 rue des Pâquis, Les Pâquis.*

NEED A BREAK? The crowded and casual cafeteria at **Bains des Pâquis** (⊠ 30 quai du Mont-Blanc, Les Pâquis ☎ 022/7322974) serves hearty lunchtime plats du jour by the water in summer; look for champagne fondue with a harbor backdrop on winter evenings.

☝ ❿ **Parc La Grange.** The Orangerie and the Théâtre de Verdure stage performances and open-air concerts through the summer months; new varieties of roses compete for prizes each June; and the remnants of a first-century Roman villa crown the hillside in this gracious, sun-dappled park, once the private grounds of an 18th-century villa overlooking the lake. William Favre's bequest of his family's domain to the city in 1917 stipulated that the park be made available to the public during the day and closed at night. It is still the only green space in Geneva to be locked when the sun goes down. ⊠ *quai Gustave-Ador, Eaux-Vives.*

❻ Temple de la Fusterie. Designed by Huguenot refugee Jean Vennes and completed in 1715, Geneva's first specifically Calvinist church was built to accommodate the flood of French Protestants that followed the 1685 revocation of the Edict of Nantes. The plain, Baroque facade blended into the secular landscape around it; the well-lighted and whitewashed galleries within allowed 750 people to hear every word the minister said. ✉ *pl. de la Fusterie, Centre Ville.*

12

Vieille Ville

Geneva's Old Town (Vieille Ville), a tight cluster of museums, boutiques, historical sites, and sidewalk cafés capped by the cathedral, represents the city's core. The cantonal government's executive, legislative, and judicial branches operate within its walls; the Left Bank radiates out from its slopes.

What to See

⓮ Ancien Arsenal. (Old Arsenal). Designed as a granary on the site of a Roman marketplace and converted to a gunpowder depot after l'Escalade, this municipal storage space has sustained Geneva through the ages. The current 1636 structure stocks history: murals on the inner wall and frescoes along the outer rim of the arcade tell the town's story from Julius Caesar to 1848; records in the State Archives date back to 1387. Scholars and officials use this institution, not the general public. ✉ *Intersection of rue de l'Hôtel-de-Ville and rue du Puits-Saint-Pierre, Vieille Ville.*

㉑ Auditoire de Calvin (Calvin's Lecture Hall). Reformed services in English, Italian, Spanish, Dutch, and German made this simple Gothic structure, built in the 15th century on the site of two prior churches and originally called the New Church of Our Lady, a potent international gathering place for 16th-century Protestant refugees. The Scots reformer John Knox preached here from 1556 to 1559 while he translated the Bible into English; Calvin and his successors used the space to teach theology and train missionaries into the 18th century. Today the Auditoire hosts the Church of Scotland, the Dutch Reformed Community, and the Waldensian Church of Italy; the Church of Scotland welcomes visitors to its Sunday-morning service at 11. ✉ *1 pl. de la Taconnerie, Vieille Ville* ▭ *Free* ☉ *Religious services only.*

★ ⓳ Cathédrale St-Pierre (St. Peter's Cathedral). A stylistic hybrid scarred by centuries of religious upheaval and political turmoil, this imposing cathedral somehow survived the ages with its dignity intact. The massive Neoclassical facade was an 18th-century addition meant to shore up 12th-century Romanesque-Gothic walls; stained-glass windows, the Duke of Rohan's tomb, a few choir stalls, and the 15th-century **Chapel of the Maccabees** hint at lavish alternatives to Calvin's plain chair. Fifteenth-century bells and bird's eye city views reward those who climb the **north tower.** ✉ *Cour St-Pierre, Vieille Ville* ☎ *022/3117575* ⊕ *www.saintpierre-geneve.ch* ▭ *North tower 4 SF* ☉ *June–Sept., Mon.–Sat. 9:30–6:30, Sun. noon–6:30; Oct.–May, Mon.–Sat. 10–5:30, Sun. noon–5:30.*

A GOOD WALK

Begin at place Neuve, Geneva's musical hub, and walk straight through the gates of the Parc des Bastions. The Université de Genève, on your right, is descended from Calvin's ground-breaking Academy; the enormous **Monument de la Réformation** ⑫ ☛ spreads 150 years of Protestant history along the park wall to your left. Climb the steps to the right of the Monument, ascend the ramp, cross rue de la Croix-Rouge, and zigzag up a second ramp to the mercifully flat promenade de la Treille.

Catch your breath on the world's longest bench beside Geneva's *Marronnier Officiel* (Official Chestnut Tree), then turn to the **Hôtel de Ville** ⑬, seat of Geneva's cantonal government. Follow the promenade to the statue of Charles Pictet de Rochemont, Geneva's and ultimately Switzerland's delegate to the Congress of Vienna, and head right through the 18th-century portico. Make a U-turn to the right into No. 2 rue de l'Hôtel-de-Ville to see the arcaded inside of the government complex. Exit through either door and cross the street to the city's 17th-century **Ancien Arsenal** ⑭, now home to the State Archives. The **Maison Tavel** ⑮, on the far side of the arcade, has a huge scale model of Geneva in 1850, before the city walls came down, lodged in its attic.

Turn right when you leave the museum, right again at the top of the hill, and head straight into the Grand-Rue. The Espace Jean-Jacques Rousseau, a 25-minute audiovisual overview (in English) of the philosopher's life, occupies No. 40, where Rousseau was born;

Ferdinand Hodler kept a painting studio across the street at No. 33.

Turn left into ruelle du Sautier by No. 28, former residence of Jorge Luis Borges, and loop left around the quietly soulful **Eglise Saint-Germain** ⑯. Turn right into rue des Granges, duck into the church as you pass its entrance, and continue straight past the back of the 18th-century facades overlooking place Neuve. The Fondation Zoubov has recreated a sumptuous 18th-century salon at No. 2.

Continue through place du Grand-Mézel, Geneva's Medieval meat market and 15th-century Jewish ghetto, and detour briefly to the left when you reach the 19th-century fountain crowned with dolphins. The ornate sides of the Grand Théâtre loom over rue de la Tertasse; rue de la Cité connects the city with its ancient river crossing.

Head back up the Grand-rue and turn left down rue de la Pélisserie. The road curves past a plaque noting George Eliot's visit to the city and becomes rue Jean-Calvin. The **Musée Barbier-Mueller** ⑰ presents thematic exhibits of primitive art across from No. 11, where Calvin and his family lived in a previous building from 1541 until his death in 1564.

Turn right at the fountain, then left into rue Otto-Barblan. The cour de Saint-Pierre, home to the Espace Saint-Pierre—an umbrella term for the **Musée International de la Réforme** ⑱, the **Cathédrale St-Pierre** ⑲, and the underground **site archéologique** ⑳—has been Geneva's spiritual center since the time of Celtic goddesses. You can

12

tour the Espace in any order; what follows here is the scenic route.

Head straight into rue du Cloître, past the spot where Geneva made its single biggest collective decision, and follow it to the museum entrance. Turn left upon leaving with a full appreciation of the Reformation's legacy and make a right into rue de l'Evêché. This becomes rue Guillaume-Farel when you reach the back of the cathedral; the sober, contemplative chapel straight ahead is the **Auditoire de Calvin** ㉑. Peek inside if the doors are open, then continue straight back to the cour de Saint-Pierre. The entrance to the site archéologique is the wrought-iron gate to your immediate right; finish with the view from the cathedral towers.

When you've exhausted the Espace Saint-Pierre, return to rue de l'Evêché and either follow it to the steep, covered passage des Degrés-de-Poules behind the cathedral or take rue des Barrières down to your right. In the latter case, continue straight, up a few stairs, past mythical mosaics of the Rhône, the Arve, and Neptune, and toward the edge of the Terrasse d'Agrippa d'Aubigné. Look back for terrific views of the cathedral's north tower; the 15th-century Temple de la Madeleine and a contemporary flea market with merry-go-round frame a vista straight ahead that extends past the Rues-Basses to the lake and the Bains des Pâquis.

Follow the terrace wall to the right and down the ramp to rue de la Fontaine, then head right past the Lutheran Church and the bottom of the passage des Degrés-de-Poules to **place du Bourg-de-Four** ㉒.

Continue past the Palais de Justice to the crest of the hill, then dip straight down the other side to rue Etienne-Dumont.

Continue straight to place Franz-Liszt—the composer lived in the corner house on the right—and turn left onto promenade de Saint-Antoine. Descend the second set of steps marked *site archéologique* for a stroll through the massive remains of Geneva's defense walls (and the Vieille Ville parking garage), then ride the elevator back up and cross the bridge on your right to the wide-ranging **Musée d'Art et d'Histoire** ㉓.

Turn right when you exit the museum, cross the bridge, and veer left into rue Rodolphe-Toepffer. Six gilt cupolas crown the 19th-century Eglise Russe, around the corner; its ancient Muscovite interior is filled with gold and silver icons. Take either road marked rue François-Le-Fort away from the church, cross rue Charles-Galland, and head left a block later on rue Munier-Romilly. The **Collections Baur** ㉔, a serene private museum of Asian ceramics, jade, and lacquerware, is the last door on the right.

Angle straight away from the museum, take any of the roads linking rue du Mont-de-Sion with boulevard des Tranchées, and turn left. The **Muséum d'Histoire Naturelle** ㉕ is the modern black-and-white building shrouded by trees on the far side of route de Malagnou. Bus 8 (direction OMS) leaves from here for the Right Bank; Rive and the waterfront are a short walk down the hill.

㉔ Collections Baur (Baur Collections). Alfred Baur's lovingly preserved collection of Far East Asian art, Switzerland's largest, packs more than 10 centuries of Chinese ceramics and jade, Japanese smoking paraphernalia, prints, netsuke, lacquerware, and sword fittings into a tranquil 19th-century townhouse on the edge of the Vieille Ville. Thematic temporary exhibits occupy the basement; general texts in English introduce each room. ⊠ *8 rue Munier-Romilly, Centre Ville* ☎ *022/7043282* ⊕ *www.collections-baur.ch* ☜ *5 SF* ☉ *Tues.–Sun. 2–6.*

⑯ Eglise Saint-Germain (Saint-Germain Church). The second chapel on the left maps a structural lineage that began in AD 400 and the steeple dates from the 14th century; the rest of this pristine 15th-century sanctuary served as a Protestant temple, a butcher's warehouse, a foundry, and a government meeting hall before Napoléon's troops returned it to Catholicism in 1803. Allocated to the Old Catholics since 1873, its whitewashed walls, strategic lighting, and 20th-century stained glass frame weekly classical music concerts in summer. ⊠ *9 rue des Granges, Vieille Ville* ⊕ *www.concerts-st-germain.ch* ☜ *Free* ☉ *Tues.–Sat. 2–5.*

⑬ Hôtel de Ville (City Hall). Sixteen countries signed the first Geneva Convention in the ground-floor **Alabama Hall** on August 22, 1864, making it the birthplace of the International Red Cross, and the League of Nations convened its first assembly here, on November 15, 1920. The canton's executive and legislative bodies meet here; until 1958 city functionaries lived here. But the history of this elegant vaulted compound begins in 1455, when the city built a large fortified tower, the **Tour Baudet**, to house the State Council Chamber. Its circular ramp, an architectural anomaly added during the Reformation, was used by at least one lawmaker to reach the second-floor meeting place without dismounting his horse. ⊠ *2 rue de l'Hôtel-de-Ville, Vieille Ville* ☎ *022/3272118* ⊕ *www.geneve.ch* ☜ *Free* ☉ *Daily; information booth weekdays 8:30–noon, 2–5.*

⑮ Maison Tavel (Tavel House). Vaulted cellars and ground-floor kitchens display medieval graffiti, local coins, 15th-century tiles, and a guillotine in Geneva's oldest house, now a museum focused on life in the city from 1334 to the 1800's. Seventeenth-century ironwork, doors, and other fragments of long-demolished houses fill the first floor; a bourgeois home complete with 18th-century wallpaper is re-created on the second. The enormous Magnin Model (which depicts Geneva as it looked before its elaborate defense walls came down in 1850), is housed in the attic; temporary exhibits rotate through the basement. ⊠ *6 rue du Puits-St-Pierre, Vieille Ville* ☎ *022/4183700* ⊕ *mah.ville-ge.ch* ☜ *Free* ☉ *Tues.–Sun. 10–5.*

▶ **⑫ Monument de la Réformation** (Wall of the Reformers). Conceived on a grand
Fodor's Choice scale and erected between 1909 and 1917, this solemn 325- by 30-foot
★ swath of granite pays homage to the 16th-century religious movement spearheaded by Guillaume Farel, Jean Calvin, Théodore de Bèze, and John Knox. Smaller statues of major Protestant figures, bas-reliefs, and inscriptions connected with the Reformation flank the lifelike giants as they hover over Bern, Geneva, and Edinburgh's coats of arms; Oliver Cromwell is surrounded by Pilgrims praying on the deck of the *Mayflower* and the 1689 presentation of the Bill of Rights to King William and Queen Mary by the English Houses of Parliament. The Reformation's—and

Geneva's—motto, *Post Tenebras Lux* (After Darkness, Light), spreads over the whole. ⊠ *Parc des Bastions, Centre Ville.*

★ ⑰ **Musée Barbier-Mueller.** Josef Mueller began acquiring fine primitive art from Africa, Oceania, Southeast Asia, and the Americas in 1907. Today his family's vast, inspired collection of sculpture, masks, shields, textiles, and ornaments spans six continents and seven millennia. A small selection is on view at any given time, displayed like jewels in warm, spotlighted vaults of scrubbed stone. Basement galleries focus consistently on pre-Columbian America, Africa, and Southeast Asia. ⊠ *10 rue Jean-Calvin, Vieille Ville* ☎ *022/3120270* ⊕ *www.barbier-mueller.ch* ⊠ *5 SF* ☉ *Daily 11–5.*

㉓ **Musée d'Art et d'Histoire** (Museum of Art and History). The city has based its huge archaeology, fine art, and applied art collections in this custom-built museum since 1910. They include, notably, Switzerland's largest concentration of Egyptian art, Escalade-era weapons, Alpine landscapes from both ends of the 19th century, and substantial contemporary art. The 15th-century *Miracle of the Fishes,* in which Christ paces the waters of Lac Léman, keeps things focused locally; temporary exhibits range much farther afield. ⊠ *2 rue Charles-Galland, Vieille Ville* ☎ *022/ 4182600* ⊕ *mah.ville-ge.ch* ⊠ *Free* ☉ *Tues.–Sun. 10–5.*

⑱ **Musée International de la Réforme** (International Museum of the Reformation). Engaging audiovisuals, period artifacts, and carefully preserved documents explain the logic behind the Protestant Reformation, explore its impact as a religious, cultural, and philosophical phenomenon, and trace its roots from the early 16th century through today in this sophisticated, modern, and remarkably friendly museum. The sparkling 18th-century premises, on the site where Geneva voted to adopt the Reform, connect by underground passage to the *site archéologique*; all signage and audioguide material is in English. ⊠ *2 rue du Cloître, Vieille Ville* ⊕ *www.musee-reforme.ch* ⊠ *10 SF, 16 SF with cathedral towers and site archéologique* ☉ *Tues.–Sun. 10–5.*
Fodor'sChoice ★

㉕ **Muséum d'Histoire Naturelle** (Museum of Natural History). Large, evocative wildlife dioramas complete with sound effects cover most major animal types; large quantities of fossils and a multimedia display on plate tectonics lead to human evolution, gigantic crystals, precious stones, exotic birds, coral reefs, and a case full of polyhedrons in this spacious museum swarming with local school groups. Swiss geology, the history of the solar system, and thematic temporary exhibits round out the collection; most labels are in French. ⊠ *1 rte. de Malagnou* ☎ *022/ 4186300* ⊠ *Free* ☉ *Tues.–Sun. 9:30–5.*

★ ㉒ **Place du Bourg-de-Four.** Ancient roads met in this layered Vieille Ville square before heading south to Annecy and Lyon, east to Italy and the Chablais, north to the Rues-Basses, and west through the center of town to the bridge. Once a Roman cattle market, later flooded with refugees, it's still the quintessential Genevois crossroads where shoppers, lawyers, workers, and students all meet for drinks around an 18th-century fountain. ⊠ *Intersection of rue de la Fontaine, rue Verdaine, rue des Chaudronniers, rue Etienne-Dumont, rue Saint-Léger, and rue de l'Hôtel-de-Ville, Vieille Ville.*

NEED A BREAK? | **La Clémence** (✉ 20 pl. du Bourg-de-Four, Vieille Ville ☎ 022/3122498), an old and much-loved café named for the largest of the cathedral bells, serves most of its breakfast *tartines* (baguettes with butter and jelly) in the middle of the square.

☼ ⑳ **Site archéologique.** Archaeologists found multiple layers of history underneath the Cathédrale St-Pierre when its foundations began to falter **FodorśChoice** in 1976. Excavations have so far yielded remnants of two 4th-century ★ Christian sanctuaries, mosaic floors from the late Roman Empire, three early churches, and an 11th-century crypt. The first Romanesque cathedral on the site was built in 1000; today audio guides in English and careful lighting help navigate the (reinforced) underground maze that remains. ✉ *cour St-Pierre, Vieille Ville* ☎ *022/3117574* 🎫 *8 SF* ☉ *Tues.–Sun. 10–5.*

Plainpalais

Reclaimed from the swamps that formed the confluence of the Rhône and Arve rivers as recently as 1850, the area centered on the diamond-shaped Plaine de Plainpalais is now home to contemporary art galleries, traveling circuses, weekly flea markets, local and regional media, the sprawling Université de Genève, and remnants of a late-19th-century industrial past.

What to See

㉝ **Bâtiment des Forces Motrices** (Driving Energy Building). A fine example of 19th-century industrial architecture moored in the middle of the river, Geneva's second opera house was built in 1886 by engineer Théodore Turrettini to supply drinking water, harness the river's energy for local industry, and keep the lake level steady. Restored and converted to a 985-seat theater in 1997, it now hosts the overflow from the Grand Théâtre as well as classical concerts by the famed Orchestre de la Suisse Romande and traveling productions. The cavernous L-shaped lobby has retained two of its original 18 turbines. ✉ *2 pl. des Volontaires, Plainpalais* ☎ *022/3221220* ⊕ *www.bfm.ch.*

㉚ **Centre d'Art Contemporain** (Center for Contemporary Art). Andy Warhol, Cindy Sherman, Nan Goldin, Pippilotti Rist, Thomas Scheibitz, and Shirana Shabhaz are some of the pioneering international artists who have presented work here since 1974, when Geneva's Kunsthalle (art institute) began showing the art of tomorrow today. The Centre's seven annual exhibits tend to be transdisciplinary and shocking in their quest to examine the practice of art in a cultural context. ✉ *10 rue des Vieux-Grenadiers, Plainpalais* ☎ *022/3291842* ⊕ *www.centre.ch* 🎫 *5 SF* ☉ *Tues.–Sun. 11–6.*

㉜ **Cimetière de Plainpalais** (Plainpalais Cemetery). Originally part of a 15th-century hospital complex built on dry land outside the city to isolate victims of the plague, these verdant 7 acres bordering the city's tax office hold the mortal remains of Jean Calvin, Simon Rath, Guillaume-Henri Dufour, William Favre, Jorge Luis Borges, and Sergio Vieira de Mello (the United Nations Special Representative killed in Iraq in 2003),

A GOOD WALK

Begin by facing the mid-river tourist information booth on pont de la Machine. Follow either walkway around the building, cross the footbridge, and keep to the left of the Ile de la Cité. A plaque on the side of the **Tour de l'Ile** 26 ▶, to your right when you reach place de Bel-Air, notes the passage of Julius Caesar in 58 BC.

Head left across the bridge Caesar burned and continue straight through rue de la Monnaie and the heart of the ancient market crossroads. Turn right at the fountain commemorating Geneva's Escalade victory, follow the tram lines to the left onto rue de la Corraterie, and continue past city walls that bore the brunt of the 1602 Savoyard attack. To your immediate right when you reach **place Neuve** 27 is the **Musée Rath** 28. The Grand Théâtre, to its right, is modeled on the Opéra Garnier in Paris. At the far end of the square is the Italianate Conservatoire de Musique, built—as is everything that follows—on reclaimed land.

Follow rue Alexandre-Calame to the right of the Conservatoire, keep the Maison des Arts du Grütli (Grütli Arts Center) on your right, and turn right when you reach boulevard Georges-Favon. Cross at the traffic light, veer left past the fountain, and stay to the right of the park. Cross all three segments of rue Harry-Marc, and continue straight under the trees. The Plaine de Plainpalais, Geneva's all-purpose open space and fairgrounds, stretches beyond the skateboard park and boccie pitches to your left and hosts a constant stream of outdoor markets, fun fairs, circuses, and exhibitions.

Cross the busy street where the Plaine veers left, double back a block, and turn left down rue des Vieux-Grenadiers. Take time to explore the art of watchmaking and enameling at the **Patek Philippe Museum** 29; the combined entrance to the **Centre d'Art Contemporain** 30 and **Mamco (Musée d'Art Moderne et Contemporain)** 31 lies across the street at the end of the block.

Leave the world of contemporary art by the door through which you entered it and U-turn to the right onto rue des Bains. Keep going for three blocks, cross boulevard de Saint-Georges, and continue straight down rue des Rois to the peaceful **Cimetière de Plainpalais** 32.

Follow rue des Rois to its end, then turn left onto rue de la Coulouvrenière. The entrance to the imposing **Bâtiment des Forces Motrices** 33, a 19th-century hydroelectric plant turned opera house, lies to the right across place des Volontaires. Detour briefly to the left of the building, where the Barrage du Seujet maintains the river level, generates hydroelectricity, and lets fish and boats through separate sets of locks; then either follow the quai to the end of the BFM and cross the footbridge or take the narrow wooden walkway around the outside of the theatre to the narrow, terraced mid-river park.

12

Swords & Soup

The Fête de l'Escalade commemorates a watershed military victory. By 1602 Geneva had gained the upper hand in its long conflict with Savoy, and the Duke decided that this upstart, independent Reformed citadel must be destroyed. He cried wolf for a while to dull Geneva's defences, assembled a secret army behind the Salève, and marched on the sleeping city during the longest night of the year (recorded in Geneva as December 11). His advance guard scaled the outer walls with ladders (*l'Escalade*) and were about to let the larger army in through the town gates when a sentry raised the alarm. Geneva defended itself so well that by morning Savoy had retreated and within months renounced all claims to the city. Today period costumes, parades, torches, cannon fire, fife-and-drum bands, roast boar with lentils, and hot soup turn back the clock in the Vieille Ville; chocolate *marmites* (cauldrons) stuffed with marzipan vegetables recall one townswoman's unique choice of weapon.

as well as many of the people whose names grace street signs all over town. The relative paucity of tombstones reflects a turbulent history of flooding and neglect, not lack of use; funeral monuments were introduced in the 19th century. ⊠ *10 rue des Rois, Plainpalais* 🎫 *Free* 🕓 *Daily 8–5:30.*

Mamco (Musée d'Art Moderne et Contemporain) (Museum of Modern and Contemporary Art). Concrete floors and fluorescent lighting set the tone for this gritty collection of stark, mind-stretching, post-1960 art that shares its former factory compound with separate centers for contemporary photography and publishing. The industrial surroundings help juxtapose aesthetic approaches; temporary exhibits add current artists to the mix. ⊠ *10 rue des Vieux-Grenadiers, Plainpalais* 🕾 *022/3206122* ⊕ *www.mamco.ch* 🎫 *8 SF* 🕓 *Tues.–Fri. noon–6, weekends 11–6.*

Musée Rath. Switzerland's original fine arts museum, inaugurated in 1826 and named for its late benefactor, Simon Rath, housed Geneva's growing collections of art and archaeology until they overflowed to the Musée d'Art et d'Histoire in 1910. Now the Rath hosts two major temporary exhibitions each year; they range in focus from archaeology to contemporary art. ⊠ *pl. Neuve, Centre Ville* 🕾 *022/4183340* ⊕ *mah.ville-ge.ch* 🎫 *9 SF* 🕓 *Tues. and Thurs.–Sun. 10–5, Wed. noon–9.*

Patek Philippe Museum. Geneva's renown as a center for watchmaking and enameling, sustained since the 16th century, finds full justification in this breathtaking private collection of delicate gold watch cases, complicated watch innards, lifelike portrait miniatures, and softly lighted enameled fans, pens, pocket knives, snuffboxes, telescopes, and vanity pistols that shoot singing birds. Most of the objects displayed in this former watchmaking workshop are hundreds of years old; many were created in Geneva by Patek Philippe, one of the city's most venerable watchmaking companies. Meticulously restored workbenches, audiovisual displays, classical music, and a horological library complete the

FodorsChoice
★

picture; the 2½-hour guided tour (in English at 2:15 on Friday) puts it all in context. All signage is in English. ⊠ *7 rue des Vieux-Grenadiers, Plainpalais* ☎ *022/8070910* ⊕ *www.patekmuseum.com* 🖃 *10 SF* ⊙ *Tues.–Fri. 2–5, Sat. 10–5.*

27 **Place Neuve.** Aristocratic town houses now overlook Geneva's opera house, the Musée Rath, the Conservatoire de Musique, and the gilded wrought-iron entrance to the Parc des Bastions, but until 1850 this wide-open space was the city's heavily fortified main southern gate. The equestrian statue at the center of the square honors Guillaume-Henri Dufour, the first general of Switzerland's federal army and the first person to map the country. The large bust of Henry Dunant, founder of the International Red Cross, marks the spot where public executions once took place. ⊠ *Intersection of blvd. du Théâtre, rue de la Corraterie, rue de la Croix-Rouge, and rue Bartholoni, Centre Ville.*

> **TRIP TIP**
>
> Entrance fees at seven of Geneva's private collections are substantially reduced for holders of the Passeport Musées, a little booklet that, when stamped at the door like a passport, allows one free entrance each to the Collections Baur, Fondation Martin Bodmer, Musée des Suisses dans le Monde, Musée Barbier-Mueller, Musée International de la Croix-Rouge et du Croissant-Rouge, Musée International de la Réforme, and Patek Philippe Museum. Tourist information booths, many hotels, and the museums themselves sell the booklets; they are valid for three months, cost 20 SF, and can be handed off to a friend.

➤ **26** **Tour de l'Ile.** The lone surviving fragment of a 13th-century castle built by Bishop Aymon de Grandson to protect Geneva from attack via the bridge and demolished in 1677, this carefully preserved lookout tower now houses the Banque Safdié. It is not open to the public. ⊠ *rue de la Tour-de-l'Ile, Centre Ville.*

International Area

The Palais des Nations, 10 minutes north of the Gare Cornavin by tram, is the focal point of Geneva's humanitarian and diplomatic zone. Modern structures housing UN agencies dominate streets leading to it; embassies, 19th-century villas full of nongovernmental organizations, and museums surround them.

What to See

★ ☾ **39** **Jardin Botanique** (Botanical Garden). Sixty-nine peaceful acres of winding paths and streams, mountain views, and Alpine rock gardens bear witness to Geneva's early-19th-century fascination with botany. They also include tropical and Mediterranean hothouses, beds of irises, classic rose gardens, an aviary, a deer park, a garden of scent and touch, a living catalog of economically useful and medicinal plants, a seed bank, and a formidable research institute. Several of the trees predate 1700. ⊠ *1 chemin de l'Impératrice, International Area* ☎ *022/4185100* ⊕ *www.ville-ge.ch/cjb* 🖃 *Free* ⊙ *Apr.–Sept., daily 8–7:30; Oct.–Mar., daily 9:30–5.*

A GOOD WALK

Take Tram 13 or 15 from the Gare Cornavin to the end of the line (Nations), and disembark onto the pedestrian promenade des Nations. To your left are the world headquarters of the International Telecommunications Union (ITU) and the World Intellectual Property Organization (WIPO); to your right, past an honor guard of flags from member countries, sits the rarely used ceremonial entrance to the **Palais des Nations** ③④ ☞.

Angle right across the promenade, cross the street, and curve up avenue de la Paix. The domed palace set back from the road on your right is the **Musée Ariana** ③⑤, home to Geneva's considerable ceramics and glassware collections. The **Musée International de la Croix-Rouge et du Croissant-Rouge** ③⑥, a fiercely moving look at the history of humanitarian assistance, lies directly opposite the visitors' entrance to the Palais.

Avenue de la Paix becomes route de Pregny as it continues up the hill. You'll pass the Pregny campus of the International School of Geneva, on the right, and the American Mission to the UN, on the left. Turn right into chemin de l'Impératrice,

keep the parking lot on your left, and head straight through the green wrought-iron gates of the Domaine de Penthes. The **Musée des Suisses dans le Monde** ③⑦ fills the ivy-covered Château de Penthes with tales of Swiss people who left Switzerland; the **Musée Militaire Genevois** ③⑧ traces local military history in a converted stable.

Stroll through the Domaine's Arcadian grounds past perfectly framed mountain views, and rejoin chemin de l'Impératrice as it winds down under the train tracks to the **Jardin Botanique** ③⑨. Enter by the main gate, on the right, and wander past pink flamingos, sweeping lawns, huge trees, and burbling waterfalls to the exit gate at place Albert-Thomas. Keep the Centre William Rappard, headquarters of the World Trade Organization, on your left as you cross all four segments of avenue de la Paix; Bus 1 (direction Rive) leaves from here for the Gare Cornavin. ⊘ **TIMING TIPS→** Try to devote a full day to this part of town—there's lots of territory, both literal and figurative, to cover. Wear good walking shoes, pace yourself, and leave time to absorb the scenery.

③⑤ **Musée Ariana.** An architectural anachronism when it was completed in 1887 and stocked with Gustave Revilliod's immense collection of ceramics, sculpture, furniture, textiles, coins, books, and silverware, this serene Italianate structure ceded its parkland to the Palais des Nations in 1928 and now houses the **Musée Suisse de la Céramique et du Verre** (Swiss Museum of Ceramics and Glass). Stoneware, earthenware, porcelain, and glass covering 700 years of East-West exchange populate the upper floors; contemporary work rotates through the basement. ✉ *10 av. de la Paix, International Area* ☎ *022/4185450* ⊕ *mah.ville-ge.ch* ▢ *Free* ⊘ *Wed.–Mon. 10–5.*

③⑦ Musée des Suisses dans le Monde (Museum of Swiss Citizens in the World). Books, audio guides in English, and 19th-century rooms full of models, paintings, documents, and objects highlight the considerable achievements of Swiss people outside Switzerland in this dense little museum surrounded by parkland. Swiss Guards and military men give way to artists, bankers, explorers, doctors, writers, archaeologists, chocolatiers, and inventors as the centuries progress; many, like Albert Gallatin, were surprisingly prominent. ⊠ *18 chemin de l'Impératrice, International Area* ☎ *022/7349021* ⊕ *www.penthes.ch.* ⊠ *5 SF* ⊙ *Jan.–Mar., Wed.–Fri. 2–5, weekends 10–noon, 2–5; Apr.–Dec., Tues.–Sun. 10–noon, 2–6.*

NEED A BREAK?

Have a generous plat du jour or a slice of homemade fruit tart on the summer terrace at **Le Cent Suisses** (⊠ 18 chemin de l'Impératrice, International Area ☎ 022/7344865), a lunch-only spot on the grounds of the Château de Penthes.

③⑥ Musée International de la Croix-Rouge et du Croissant-Rouge (International Red Cross and Red Crescent Museum). Powerful mute statues speak to the need for human kindness in the face of disaster, and balanced but often grim exhibits trace the history of the struggle to provide it in this carefully nonjudgmental museum buried in the hillside beneath the world headquarters of the International Committee of the Red Cross.

Fodor'sChoice ★

Audiovisuals show the postbattle horrors at Solferino that moved Henry Dunant to form the Red Cross; endless aisles of file boxes hold 7 million records of World War I prisoners. Good deeds are dramatized, from the proverbial Samaritan's to Clara Barton's. There's a replica of a 6½-foot by 6½-foot concrete cell in which Red Cross workers discovered 17 political prisoners; the **Mur du Temps** (Wall of Time), a simple time line punctuated by armed conflicts and natural disasters in which more than 10,000 people died, puts the overall story into sobering perspective. Good news, in the form of disaster-relief kits and snapshots used to reunite Rwandan families after the 1994 genocide, is also on display, however; signage and audio guides are in English. ⊠ *17 av. de la Paix, International Area* ☎ *022/7489525* ⊕ *www.micr.org* ⊠ *10 SF* ⊙ *Wed.–Mon. 10–5.*

③⑧ Musée Militaire Genevois (Geneva Military Museum). The humble setting adds authenticity to this detailed look at a neutral but thoroughly competent military force. Uniformed models, weapons, prints, and documents proceed in chronological order through the eventful history of *la Garde Genevoise* from 1814 to the present, including a Napoleonic officer's outfit, Guillaume-Henri Dufour's personal effects, and a full-scale re-creation of a Genevois border post during World War II. ⊠ *18 chemin de l'Impératrice, International Area* ☎ *022/7344875* ⊕ *www. museemilitaire-ge.com* ⊠ *Free* ⊙ *Late Jan.–late Dec., Tues.–Sat. 2–5, Sun. 10–noon, 2–5.*

★ ▶ ③④ Palais des Nations (Palace of Nations). Built between 1929 and 1936 for the League of Nations, this monumental compound became the European office of the United Nations in 1946 and quickly evolved into the largest center for multilateral diplomacy in the world. Today it hosts some 9,000 conferences and 25,000 delegates each year; it is also the largest nexus for United Nations operational activities after New York.

Security is tight: be prepared to show your passport and join a tour to see the interior. Points of particular interest include the **Assembly Hall,** the largest of 34 conference rooms, where the UN General Assembly and scores of world leaders have met, and the ornate **Council Chamber,** home to the Conference on Disarmament, which glows with allegorical murals. Tours last about an hour and are conducted in English. There are no set starting times. ⊠ *14 av. de la Paix, International Area* ☎ *022/9174896* ⊕ *www. unog.ch* ✆ *10 SF* ⊗ *Jan.–Mar. and Nov.–mid-Dec., weekdays 10–noon, 2–4; Apr.–June, Sept., and Oct., daily 10–noon, 2–4; July and Aug., daily 10–5.*

> **SHINING AGAIN**
>
> The design of the Palais des Nations's original wing was determined by an architectural competition in 1926; the group of five architects who won followed a style that has, ironically, come to be known as Fascist. The building remains a superb example of the severe blend of Art Deco and stylized classicism that Mussolini and Hitler idealized. Its details—bronze torchères, gleaming marble—and many of its decorations (including some famous allegorical murals by Catalan artist José Maria Sert in the ornate Council Chamber) from the interwar period have been preserved practically untouched.

WHERE TO EAT

Genevois menus tend to follow the seasons, changing three or four times a year on average. Fast food consists of complex salads, fresh sandwiches, and warm quiche to go; lunchtime plats du jour and bakeries with tearooms are delicious budget options. Many restaurants close on weekends, so be sure to call ahead.

$$$$
Fodor'sChoice
★
✕ **Domaine de Châteauvieux.** Philippe Chevrier's expansive kitchen, out in the heart of Geneva's wine country, draws inspiration and the culinary equivalent of spun gold from local and regional foods (many of which are sold on-site in a little *épicerie*). Fitted out in the ancient *dependences* of a 16th-century château (itself destroyed by French Revolutionary troops), ancient beams, antique winepresses, 18th-century tapestry-lined armchairs, and silk flowers make an incomparably romantic and sumptous dining area. Outside, weathered stone, a kitchen garden beside a small chapel, and a leafy summer terrace complete the utterly unpretentious country setting amid vineyards and sylvan dells. Prix-fixe menus—ranging from 300 SF to 600 SF—cover six or seven courses; exquisite seasonal dishes transform asparagus in spring, game come October, and truffles in winter. The tongue is constantly dazzled as it moves from one showstopper—grilled langoustines de St-Guénolé with truffle risotto and lobster crème, caramelized warm soup of bananas with mangoes rosé, pigeon in mushrooms—to another. Prices are housemorgaging: appetizers are usually around 100 SF, main courses, 134 SF.

The cellar houses top Swiss and French wines and there's a humidor off the bar. Take a boat up the Rhône to Peney, train it to Satigny (where a restaurant van can pick you up), or drive 20 minutes from Geneva to Peney, about 16 km (10 mi) from the city. ✉ *16 chemin de Châteauvieux, Peney-Dessus, Satigny* ☎ *022/7531511* ⊕ *www.chateauvieux. ch* ⌖ *Reservations essential* ▭ *AE, DC, MC, V* ⊗ *Closed Sun. and Mon.*

12

★ **$$$$** ✕ **Le Lion d'Or.** On the lakeside bluff of Cologny—the Beverly Hills or Neuilly of Geneva—the summer terrace of this culinary landmark is a little paradise, with an overwhelming view of the bay and the UN. Jet-setters, artists, writers, and celebrities—ski champion Jean-Claude Killy, singer Charles Aznavour, actress Sophia Loren, *comme ça*—have dined here. Burnished-silk walls and picture windows frame the sun setting over the lake and Jura mountains; the upstairs lounge looks south toward the city. Though the chic decor is strictly Louis XV–Louis XVI, the cuisine is modern, light, sophisticated, and of the highest gastronomic level. Local celebrity chefs Gilles Dupont and Tommy Byrne create refined dishes that complement the cellar of great Bordeaux and Burgundies. Don't miss the famous bouillabaisse, enormous, savory, and an echo from the days of chef Henri Large. Dupont and Byrne roast their line-caught sea bass to perfection, serve cardons au gratin with truffles, and grow herbs in the garden below the terrace. The bistro next door shares the restaurant's kitchen, not its prices—grab a cab and come for lunch. ✉ *5 pl. Pierre-Gautier, Cologny* ☎ *022/7364432* ⊕ *www.liondor.ch* ⌖ *Reservations essential* ▭ *AE, DC, MC, V* ⊗ *Closed weekends.*

★ **$$$–$$$$** ✕ **Le Chat Botté.** One of the more famous names in Geneva dining is the culinary outpost of the soigné Beau-Rivage hotel. Historic as the hotel is, the dining salon—unfortunately—is comprised of the usual suspects: polished wood Biedermeier-esque chairs, beige walls, framed prints, and low ceilings. Any fireworks here come out of Dominique Gauthier's kitchen, as the noted chef tweaks the details of his menu every few months. The menu is ambitious and ranges from classics, like the fillets of Austrian venison with quince and cinnamon compote, or the roast Scottish woodcock served up with sweet chestnuts and ceps from the Voirons to the nouvelle: scampis roasted in Kadaïf, citrus vinaigrette, and basil chiffonade. From May to September, you can opt for a seat on the balcony-terrace, with a lovely view of the Jet d'Eau. The wine cellar, Geneva's largest, has 40,000 hand-picked bottles. ✉ *Beau-Rivage Hotel, 13 quai du Mont-Blanc, Les Pâquis* ☎ *022/7166920* ⌖ *Reservations essential* ▭ *AE, DC, MC, V.*

★ **$$$–$$$$** ✕ **Il Lago.** Risotto with lobster and basil, risotto with calamari and champagne, and tortelli with cheese, lemon, and mint are some of the northern Italian creations Carrara native and unabashed lover of pasta Marco Garfagnini has road-tested on diners then added to his menu. The green and blue-tinted dining room, split in half by gilt French doors, is decorated with brocades, chandeliers, and sweeping hand-painted scenery—if seared scallops with wild mushrooms in a shellfish reduction or braised veal cheek with semolina gnocchi and asparagus were served at Versailles, this is what it might be like. ✉ *Des Bergues Hotel, 33 quai des Bergues, Centre Ville* ☎ *022/9087000* ▭ *AE, DC, MC, V* ⌖ *Reservations essential.*

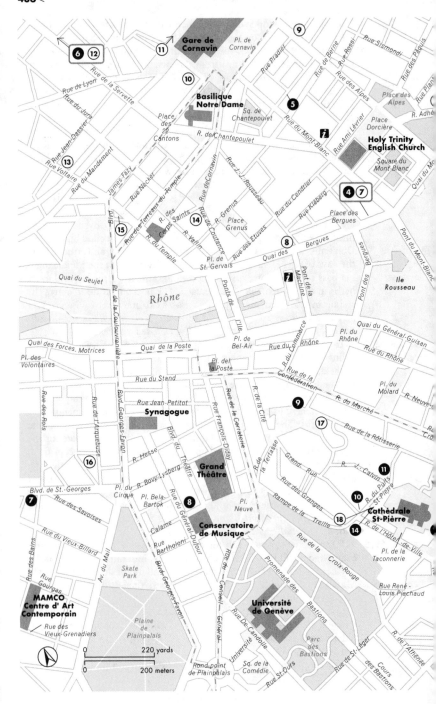

Gare de Cornavin

Pl. de Cornavin

Rue Sismondi

Rue des Pâquis

Rue Pradier

Rue de Berne

Rue des Rossi

Rue des Alpes

Place des Alpes

R. Adhé

R. Plant

Rue de Lyon

Rue de la Servette

Basilique Notre Dame

Sq. de Chantepoulet

Rue du Mont-Blanc

Place Dorcière

Rue du Jura

Place des 22 Cantons

R. de Chantepoulet

Rue Ami Lévrier

Holy Trinity English Church

Rue Jean-Dassier

James Fazy

Rue du Mandement

Rue Nécker

Rue de Cornavin

Rue J.-J.-Rousseau

Rue du Cendrier

Rue Kléberg

Square du Mont-Blanc

Quai du Mo

Rue Voltaire

Rue des Terreaux du Temple

R. des Corps Saints

R. Grenus

Place Grenus

Place des Bergues

Pont du Mont-Blanc

R. Vallin

Rue de Coutance

Rue des Étuves

Bergues

Pont des

Rue du Temple

Pl. de St. Gervais

Quai des

Bergues

Ile Rousseau

Quai du Seujet

Rhône

Pont de la Machine

Ponts de l'Île

Quai des Forces. Motrices

Quai de la Poste

Pl. de Bel-Air

Quai du Général-Guisan

Pl. du Rhône

Pl. des Volontaires

Pl. de la Poste

Rue du Commerce

Rhône

Rue du Rhône

Rue du Stand

Rue de la Confédération

R. du Marché

Pl. du Molard

R. Neuve

Rue des Rois

Rue de l'Arquebuse

Rue Jean-Petitot

Rue François-Diday

Rue de la Corraterie

R. de la Cité

R. du Marché

Synagogue

Rue de la Rôtisserie

R. Cro

Blvd. Georges-Favon

R. Hesse

Blvd. du Théâtre

R. Bovy-Lysberg

Grand Théâtre

R. de la Terrasse

Grand-Rue

R. J.-Calvin

St-Pierre

Pl. du Cirque

Pl. Bela-Bartók

Pl. Neuve

Rue des Granges

R. du Puits-

Cathédrale St-Pierre

Blvd. de St.-Georges

Rue des Savoises

Calame

Rue du Général-Dufour

Rampe de la Treille

R. de l'Hôtel-de-Ville

Rue des Vieux-Billard

Rue Bartholoni

Conservatoire de Musique

Pl. de la Taconnerie

Rue des Bains

Skate Park

Blvd. Georges-Favon

Rue de la Croix-Rouge

Rue René-Louis Piachaud

Rue Gourgas

Rue des Vieux-Grenadiers

MAMCO Centre d'Art Contemporain

Av. du Mail

Plaine de Plainpalais

Rue De-Candolle

Université de Genève

Promenade des Bastions

Parc des Bastions

R. de l'Athénée

Rue St-Léger

Cours des Bastions

Rue du Conseil

Rue Général-

Université

Rond point de Plainpalais

Sq. de la Comédie

Rue St-Ours

0   220 yards

0   200 meters

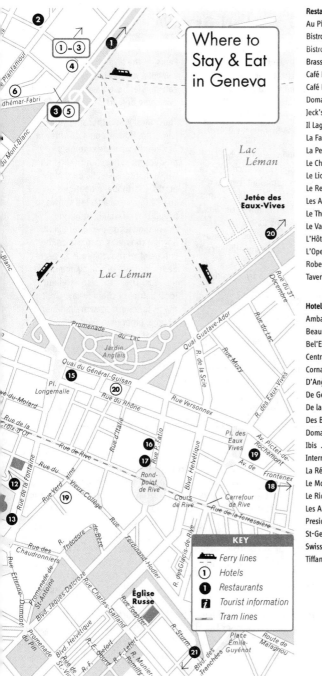

Where to
Stay & Eat
in Geneva

Lac
Léman

Jetée des
Eaux-Vives

Lac Léman

Restaurants ▼

Au Pied-de-Cochon **13**
Bistrot du Boeuf Rouge **2**
Bistrot du Boucher **18**
Brasserie Lipp **9**
Café Léo **17**
Café Lyrique **8**
Domaine de Châteauvieux **6**
Jeck's Place **5**
Il Lago **4**
La Favola **11**
La Perle du Lac **1**
Le Chat Botté **3**
Le Lion d'Or **20**
Le Relais de l'Entrecôte **15**
Les Armures **14**
Le Thé **7**
Le Vallon **21**
L'Hôtel-de-Ville **10**
L'Opera Bouffe **19**
Roberto **16**
Taverne de la Madeleine **12**

Hotels ▼

Ambassador **8**
Beau-Rivage **5**
Bel'Espérance **19**
Central **17**
Cornavin **10**
D'Angleterre **4**
De Genève **15**
De la Cloche **3**
Des Bergues **7**
Domaine de Châteauvieux **12**
Ibis **13**
International et Terminus **9**
La Réserve **1**
Le Montbrillant **11**
Le Richemond **6**
Les Armures **18**
President Wilson **2**
St-Gervais **14**
Swissôtel Métropole **20**
Tiffany **16**

KEY

🚢 Ferry lines
① Hotels
❶ Restaurants
🛈 Tourist information
▭ Tram lines

EATING WELL IN GENEVA

Geneva's many restaurants teem with innovative, experimental menus and chefs with lofty pedigrees, but its traditional cooking is simple, earthy, full of flavor, and solidly middle class. *Cardon* (cardoon, a locally grown vegetable related to the artichoke and available in winter) is baked with cream and Gruyère cheese. Lac Léman yields abundant fish—perch, trout, *féra* (related to salmon), and *omble* (char)—in summer. *La chasse* (wild game) turns up on menus between late September and mid-December. The culinary influence of Lyon, 150 km (94 mi) to the southwest, can be felt year-round in dishes such as *pieds de cochon* (pigs' feet), *longeole* (unsmoked pork sausage stuffed with cabbage and fennel), *petit salé* (salt pork), *fricassée de porc* (simmered pork), *abats* (organ meats), *andouillettes* (chitterling sausages), and *boudin noir* (rich, rosy-brown blood pudding, best eaten in cold weather). Potatoes (often served au gratin) are a favorite side dish. Pears, in the form of a spiced compote, a delicate tart, or a light eau-de-vie, have a well-established role come dessert.

Think local when choosing your wine. The Romans planted vines in Geneva; by now area vintners produce red, white, and sparkling wines that consistently earn high marks. (Bartholie, a boutique sparkling wine, has been known to trump French champagnes in international competition.) Small, ancient chasselas grapes lead the charge of whites; the round, generous taste of gamay dominates the reds. There are also excellent local bottles of chardonnay, pinot blanc, pinot gris, gewürztraminer, Aligoté, pinot noir, Gamaret, and cabernet sauvignon. The hilly area around Satigny, Dardagny, and Russin (known for its annual harvest festival) is by far the canton's most productive.

★ **$$–$$$** ✕ **La Favola.** Lace curtains, embroidered tablecloths, antique silver, a sponge-painted ceiling, and a vertiginous spiral staircase strike a delicate balance between rustic and fussy in this wood-paneled dollhouse down the street from Calvin's residence. Often hailed as Geneva's finest Italian restaurant, it's especially packed on weekends. The food echoes the picturesque decor: part country-simple, part city-chic. Homemade pastas melt on the tongue, the carpaccio is paper-thin, and the tiramisu is divine. Seasonal risottos, creamy polenta, and regional wines reflect the Ticinese chef's roots in Ascona, near Locarno. ⊠ *15 rue Jean-Calvin, Vieille Ville* ☎ *022/3117437* ⊕ *www.lafavola.com* ▭ *No credit cards* ♨ *Reservations essential* ☉ *Closed weekends June–Aug., Sat. lunch and Sun. Sept.–May.*

$$–$$$ ✕ **La Perle du Lac.** A beloved Right Bank landmark, La Perle stays open from February to December but this sprawling chalet-style former guesthouse in the midst of Geneva's Mon Repos waterfront park comes dramatically into its own in summer. Set with pink tablecloths and plants, the large covered terrace looks straight out over the lake at Mont Blanc;

the Mouettes Genevoises water taxis dock directly in front. Inside, the Grand Salon is all romantic woodwork and candlelight, while L'Orangerie is a plate-glass, light-filled festive room. The French-accented seasonal menu highlights fish such as *rouget barbet* (red mullet), sole, sea bass, and trout, but there are also unique creations, such as the Noix de Saint-Jacques (scallops) with sweet potatoes and sea-urchin cream. The wine list is exhaustive. ⊠ *126 rue de Lausanne, International Area* ☎ *022/9091020* ⊕ *www. laperledulac.ch* ⊟ *AE, DC, MC, V* ⊘ *Closed Mon. and Jan.*

★ **$$–$$$** ✕ **Le Vallon.** A rosy facade, snappy green awnings, and hanging grapevines set the scene at this century-old village restaurant, where you can choose between two cozy dining rooms—nearly wallpapered with oil sketches, Victorian mirrors, and 19th-century posters—or sit out back on the terrace. Creative, seasonal dishes run the gamut from *boudin blanc* (white sausage) at Christmas to delicate fish in summer and *cuisses de grenouilles* (frogs' legs) year-round; the prix-fixe *menu découverte* gives a three- or four-course taste of whatever is current. Set in the village of Conches, a suburb of Geneva, this is part of the noted Domaine de Châteauvieux family. ⊠ *182 rte. de Florissant, Conches* ☎ *022/3471104* ⊕ *www. chateauvieux.ch* ⊟ *AE, DC, MC, V* ⊘ *Closed weekends.*

$$–$$$ ✕ **Roberto.** Roberto Carugati, still spry in his nineties, attempts to "stay out of the way" these days and let his daughter, Marietta, oversee the red-gold dining room he opened in 1945, but don't be surprised to see him drop in. The easy formality he perfected continues to lure lawyers, bankers, politicians, and fashionable Italians for melt-in-the-mouth gnocchi with butter and sage, grilled sole, vitello tonnato, and risotto *au scampi* (with shrimp) served from shining copper and silver pots. Unusual and rare Italian wines keep conversation flowing into the night. ⊠ *10 rue Pierre-Fatio, Centre Ville* ☎ *022/3118033* ⊟ *AE, MC, V* ⊘ *Closed Sun. No dinner Sat.*

$$ ✕ **Bistrot du Boeuf Rouge.** Despite the Belle Epoque decor—a contrived
Fodor'sChoice send-up of a Lyonnais bistro, jam-packed with kitschy ceramics and Art
★ Nouveau posters—this cozy, popular spot delivers the real thing: rich, unadulterated Lyonnais cuisine, from the bacon-egg-and-greens salade Lyonnaise and the homemade boudin blanc to the sausage with lentils, the duck pâté, and the authentic tarte tatin. Many of the rillettes, foie gras, terrines, *quenelles de brochets* (pike soufflé), andouillettes, pistachio-filled sausages, and *gratins dauphinois* (baked cream and potatoes covered with melted cheese) are made in-house. The tender filet de boeuf barely requires a knife. And while the ambience is relaxed, the service is flamboyant: all dishes are presented on a flower-crowded tray before they're served at tableside. Dine late to avoid crowds of sauce-on-the-side Americans and their political chatter, which can be so aggressive you feel you're in Georgetown. Desserts include silky flan au caramel and chestnut mousse. ⊠ *17 rue Alfred-Vincent, Les Pâquis* ☎ *022/7327537* ⊕ *www.boeufrouge.ch* ⊟ *AE, DC, MC, V* ⊘ *Closed weekends.*

★ **$$** ✕ **Bistrot du Boucher.** Aperitifs are on the house, steak tartare is mixed to your taste, and waiters wear long aprons and solemn expressions as they bring out the *côte de boeuf* (rib steak) to be viewed before it's carved. Cheeky cow posters, figurines, and paintings add a sly hilarity to the Art Nouveau woodwork and stained-glass ceiling; the homemade chocolate-pear tart is decadently serious. ✉ *15 av. Pictet-de-Rochemont, Eaux-Vives* ☎ *022/7365636* 🖃 *AE, MC, V* ⊘ *Closed Sun. No lunch Sat.*

★ **$$** ✕ **Brasserie Lipp.** "Années Folles" 1920s decor—green-and-white tiles, mustard-yellow ceilings, warm wood, and busy waiters in ankle-length aprons—busily channel Paris as Genevois diners of all stripes tuck into *choucroute* (sauerkraut), tuna carpaccio, couscous, *magret de canard* (breast of duck), pumpkin cream soup with pine nuts, and heaping platters of seafood. The dining room expands to a delightful summer terrace at the foot of the Vieille Ville. The kitchen stays open from noon to 12:30 AM. ✉ *Confédération-Centre, 8 rue de la Confédération, Centre Ville* ☎ *022/3111011* ⊕ *www.brasserie-lipp.com* 🖃 *AE, DC, MC, V.*

$$ ✕ **Le Relais de l'Entrecôte.** It is rare to find a line of people waiting for a table anywhere in Geneva, so the fact that it's commonplace outside this bustling wood-paneled Parisian import means the tender strips of grilled steak drenched in herb-based *sauce maison* (house sauce) are a true cut above. A crisp green salad sprinkled with walnuts, robust house wine, and thin, golden fries complete the only option on the menu; don't worry, there's a second portion on the way. ✉ *49 rue du Rhône, Centre Ville* ☎ *022/3106004* ⌕ *Reservations not accepted* 🖃 *MC, V* ⊘ *Closed July.*

Fodor'sChoice
★

$–$$ ✕ **Au Pied-de-Cochon.** Low ceilings, whitewashed beams, white tile, and a worn zinc bar give context to simple regional dishes like cassoulet, longeole, choucroute, *émincé de veau* (veal strips in a cream reduction), filets de perches, and the namesake pigs' feet (served grilled or stuffed). The crowd can be noisy and smoky; table service can be gruff. But the Bourg-de-Four terrace makes for great people-watching. ✉ *4 pl. du Bourg-de-Four, Vieille Ville* ☎ *022/3104797* ⊕ *www.pied-de-cochon.ch* 🖃 *AE, DC, MC, V.*

★ **$–$$** ✕ **Café Léo.** Trendy locals descend for lunch, then linger over coffee at this tiny, smoky, sunny corner bistro whose highlights include avocado and Roquefort salad, homemade ravioli, veal *piccata* with mustard sauce, and a noteworthy *tarte au citron* (lemon tart). ✉ *9 cours de Rive, Centre Ville* ☎ *022/3115307* ⊕ *www.cafeleo.com* 🖃 *MC, V* ⊘ *Closed Sun. No dinner Sat.*

$–$$ ✕ **Café Lyrique.** Black-and-white floor tiles offset warm yellow walls, high wedding-cake ceilings, and portraits of Beethoven, Verdi, Strauss, and Liszt; the menu starts with salads and carpaccio, moves on to *suprême de volaille* (chicken in cream sauce), and ends with desserts that taste as good as they look. Time your arrival carefully, as pre- and postopera crowds sweep through this relaxed corner brasserie opposite the Grand Théâtre; an alternative is afternoon tea. ✉ *12 blvd. du Théâtre, Centre Ville* ☎ *022/3280095* 🖃 *AE, DC, MC, V* ⊘ *Closed weekends.*

$–$$ ✕ **Jeck's Place.** Even by Genevois standards, this unassuming little restaurant near the train station presents a staggering mix of cultures. Owner Jeck Tan, a native of Singapore and Swiss hotel-school graduate, greets his guests warmly in English and presents a menu written in Malay, Chinese, Thai, and French. The food—whether smooth, deep-fried bean curd with peanut sauce, chicken in green curry, fried *mee hoon* vermicelli, or roast duck *au diable*—keeps the international clientele coming back for more. ✉ *14 rue de Neuchâtel, Les Pâquis* ☎ *022/7313303* 🖃 *AE, DC, MC, V* ⊘ *No lunch weekends.*

12

$-$$ ✕ **Les Armures.** Dark beams, wrought iron, medieval arms, stained glass, and a robust Swiss menu that covers fondue, raclette, *Schübling* (sausage), and *Rösti* (hash browns) make this Vieille Ville institution a magnet for local street sweepers, foreign heads of state, and everyone in between. The kitchen serves until 11:30 PM (11 on Sunday) and the risk-averse can order pizza. ✉ *1 rue du Puits-St-Pierre, Vieille Ville* ☎ *022/3103442* ⊟ *AE, DC, MC, V.*

$-$$ ✕ **L'Hôtel-de-Ville.** It's hard to get more Genevois than this: filets de perches, longeole, choucroute, and game dominate the menu; service can be somewhat frank; the dining room transfers to the sidewalk in summer; and the location, at the political heart of the Vieille Ville, guarantees a loyal, smoky crowd of civil servants. Choose the *Dégustation Genevois* menu for a guided culinary tour with wine; the kitchen closes at 11:30 PM. ✉ *39 Grand-rue, Vieille Ville* ☎ *022/3117030* ⊟ *AE, DC, MC, V.*

$-$$ ✕ **L'Opéra Bouffe.** The mood is casual-chic and friendly, with wine bottles stacked floor to ceiling, large framed mirrors, classical music in the background, and opera posters on the walls. The Syrian chef rolls out subtle updates of traditional bistro fare and overhauls the menu once a month; there would be a riot if he stopped making warm tarte Tatin with Gruyère cream. ✉ *5 av. de Frontenex, Eaux-Vives* ☎ *022/7366300* ⊕ *www.operabouffe.ch* ⊟ *AE, DC, MC, V* ☾ *Closed Sun. No lunch Sat.*

¢-$ ✕ **Taverne de la Madeleine.** The sunny, elevated stone terrace looks across at the 15th-century Temple de la Madeleine, homemade fruit tarts sell for 3 SF per slice between 3 and 6 PM, and the lunch-only kitchen in this big, plain, friendly canteen serves wholesome plats du jour, choucroute (in winter), filets de perche, and chocolate or citrus mousse. The city's temperance league owns and operates the Taverne, so it serves no wine or beer. ✉ *20 rue Toutes-Âmes, Vieille Ville* ☎ *022/3106070* ⊟ *AE, DC, MC, V* ☾ *Closed Sun. No dinner.*

★ ¢ ✕ **Le Thé.** Almost everything on the menu in this microscopic piece of China, whether succulent rice-flour crepes stuffed with shrimp, dim sum, steamed bread, wobbly cubes of tapioca cake, or rare, scented, and little-known teas, is steamed. The delicate red-clay teapots lining the walls are for sale, the front door is easy to miss, and the nine tiny tables fill up fast—call ahead or drop by after 1:30 for lunch. ✉ *65 rue des Bains, Plainpalais* ☎ *079/4367718* ⊟ *No credit cards* ☾ *Closed Sun.*

WHERE TO STAY

The many conferences and high-profile events held in Geneva have defined the city's hotel scene in three ways. Great-value weekend deals and group rates are easy to secure (rack rates are comparable to those in most European capitals). Large events can suddenly fill entire hotels (book as early as you can). And the city is particularly well endowed with luxury establishments, all of which have excellent restaurants and most of which are right downtown. Plan carefully and you could wake up to gorgeous views, breakfast in bed, and terrific value for money.

$$$$ ▥ **Beau-Rivage.** Boasting more history than plenty of venerable towns,
Fodor'sChoice this grand dame of a hotel witnessed no less than the assasination of
★ Empress Elisabeth of Austria (1898; upon being stabbed by an Italian

anarchist she returned to the hotel and died in the arms of Fanny Mayer, the hotel owner's wife), the treaty creating the Republic of Czechoslovakia (1918), and the fabled auction of the jewels of the Duchess of Windsor (1987). But this beloved landmark has many more strings to its bow: 19th-century frescoes, marble columns, and a murmuring fountain set the scene and add up to a pervading sense of romance at this hushed, genteel, and family-owned Victorian palace. Its showpiece remains the five-story atrium replete with gilt chairs, gleaming pillars, and Pompeian-style paintings. As for guest rooms, period details—from tiles and lithographs to chandeliers—frame front views of the harbor and mountains beyond; plasma screen TVs, triple phone lines, glassed-in showers, plush bathrobes, and lots of space keep all rooms resolutely up to date. Too bad the Chat-Botte restaurant has such standard-issue decor; the menu is much more ambitious (raviolis of hen pheasant with sweet chestnut mousse and a tempura of Vallorbe frogs' haunches are two dazzlers). If it is stylish decor you want, head to Patara, the hotel's Thai eatery, a vision in teakwood and pink orchids. Breakfast is served outdoors on the first-floor terrace in summer and soigné drinks are to be had in L'Atrium, the exquisitely elegant bar. Outside the front door is a busy, shop-laden street but front rooms have grand views of the Right Bank. ⊠ *13 quai du Mont-Blanc, Les Pâquis, CH-1201* ☎ *022/7166666* 🖷 *022/7166060* ⊕ *www.beau-rivage.ch* 🛏 *82 rooms, 11 suites* ♧ *2 restaurants, room service, in-room safes, minibars, cable TV with movies, Wi-Fi, gym, piano bar, laundry service, concierge, parking (fee), no-smoking rooms* ⊟ *AE, DC, MC, V.*

$$$$ 🏨 **D'Angleterre.** What a past! From King Leopold II of Belgium (who infamously colonized the Congo and often stayed here—with mistresses in tow) to Michael Jackson (yes, this was the hotel where he dangled his child from a window), the D'Angleterre has given Geneva's larger palace-hotels a run for their money. Waving the banner "small is beautiful," this boutique hotel flaunts its impeccable taste and a tangible passion for detail: thematic decoration stretches from African to Baroque, desks are equipped with office supplies, breakfast can be tailored to your needs, and room service includes afternoon tea. Guest rooms are done in beige on brown and give off a masculine and sophisticated vibe: the opulent suites go the Louis Seize route and are breathtakingly pretty. Downstairs, the Leopard Room bar has a working fireplace, Cuban cigars, and live music Tuesday through Saturday; Windows, the quayside winter-garden restaurant, serves creative French cuisine with a fine view of the Jet d'Eau and Mont Blanc. ⊠ *17 quai du Mont-Blanc, Les Pâquis, CH-1201* ☎ *022/9065555* 🖷 *022/9065556* ⊕ *www.dangleterrehotel. com* 🛏 *39 rooms, 6 suites* ♧ *Restaurant, room service, in-room safes, minibars, cable TV with movies, in-room data-ports, Wi-Fi, gym, sauna, bar, laundry service, concierge, parking (fee), no-smoking rooms* ⊟ *AE, DC, MC, V.*

$$$$ 🏨 **Des Bergues.** A Wedgewood-blue color scheme, lights that follow the
Fodor's Choice   sun, and unpretentious, friendly service give the first Four Seasons in
★   Switzerland and the oldest, least self-conscious of Geneva's grand hotels an inner glow. Louis-Philippe opulence, ornamental stucco, and Portuguese marble mesh seamlessly with modern comforts like flat-screen

TVs that turn toward you, luxuriously thick mattresses, in-room spa treatments, and breakfast menus that stretch from Asia to the Alps. Risotto is a specialty at the northern Italian restaurant, Il Lago, and the dining rooms recall Versailles. A landmark that has hosted everybody from Emperor Franz-Josef to Jean Cocteau, the Des Bergues reigns over the lakefront—what magical views of the Jet d'Eau!—in this swooningly impressive palace. Rooms booked for children have pint-sized bathrobes and slippers, milk and cookies, and a smorgasbord of toys. ✉ *33 quai des Bergues, Centre Ville, CH-1201* ☎ *022/9087000* 🖷 *022/9087090* ⊕ *www.hoteldesbergues.com* ⬢ *68 rooms, 35 suites* ⚭ *Restaurant, room service, in-room safes, minibars, cable TV with movies, in-room DVD, in-room broadband, Wi-Fi, gym, massage, bar, laundry service, concierge, parking (fee), no-smoking floors* ⊟ *AE, DC, MC, V.*

$$$$ ☷ **La Réserve.** The richest people in the world and some of the most historic hotels fight to have Jacques Garcia—France's most regal interior decorator—do their decor. La Réserve lucked out, but in this case Monsieur Garcia left his usual passementeries, Louis Quinze sofas, and over-the-top luxe back home in Paris. Instead, he adopted a "modern" scheme, tinged with strong Asian and African accents (which makes you wonder why the hotel or the designer bothered). Giraffe, butterfly, and rabbit topiary dot the 10-acre park, a baby elephant (sculpture) guards leopard-print carpets and colorful parrot cut-outs, and the indoor heated pool, lighted by glowing jellyfish lamps, has an underwater soundtrack at this ochre bungalow-style hotel facing the Alps north of Geneva. Most rooms have a balcony, terrace, or private patio; bathrooms have two sinks, frosted-glass doors, and mosaic marble floors; and pillow menus let you customize your linens. There's a treefort for children and authentic Chinese cuisine at the acclaimed Tsé Fung restaurant while Le Loti offers Mediterranean dishes that are delights. The huge, full-service spa creates individual multiday packages. ✉ *301 rte. de Lausanne, CH-1293 Bellevue* ☎ *022/9595959* 🖷 *022/9595960* ⊕ *www.lareserve.ch* ⬢ *85 rooms, 17 suites* ⚭ *3 restaurants, room service, in-room safes, minibars, cable TV, in-room DVD, in-room broadband, in-room data ports, Wi-Fi, 2 tennis courts, 2 pools (1 indoor), health club, hair salon, spa, beach, dock, waterskiing, bar, lounge, library, babysitting, children's programs (ages 6 months–13 years), laundry service, taxi boat, helipad, free parking, dog sitting, no-smoking rooms* ⊟ *AE, DC, MC, V.*

$$$$ ☷ **Le Richemond.** Back in the many decades when the fabled Armleder family ran this landmark, Fodor's described it thus: "Its atmosphere marries the exclusiveness of a private club with the glamour of a theater, touched with a hint of backstage mystery." Alas. Rocco Forte Hotels has now finished a roots-up overhaul of this prominent 19th-century property and they made a point of replacing, rather than updating, the classic stage-set opulence that has hosted Walt Disney, Charlie Chaplin, Luciano Pavarotti, and Tom Cruise. The decor has tossed out all the moiré and crimson satin and gone corporate-modern: flawlessly tasteful but if-you've-seen-one-modern-room-you've-seen-them-all (literally: the Rocco Forte people pulled the same number at Rome's erstwhile opulent Hotel de Russie). Of course, we're talking the best that money can buy: rich carpets, expensive drapes, and well-tailored furniture have re-placed the congenial cornucopia of elegant furnishings that once distin-guished this hotel. Still and all, the spacious rooms, flat-screen TVs, unassuming service, spa facilities that include a small pool, a large fit-ness center, an Italian restaurant, and balconies overlooking the Mon-ument Brunswick keep the Rolls-Royces angling for space outside. ✉ *Jardin Brunswick, Les Pâquis, CH-1201* ☎ *022/7157000* 🖷 *022/ 7157001* ⊕*www.roccofortehotels.com* ⮐*74 rooms, 33 suites* ⚙*2 restau-rants, room service, in-room safes, minibars, cable TV with movies, Wi-Fi, indoor pool, gym, hair salon, spa, bar, lounge, laundry service, concierge, business services, meeting rooms, parking (fee), no-smoking rooms* ⊟ *AE, DC, MC, V.*

$$$$ 🏨 **Les Armures.** Original 17th-century stonework, frescoes, painted beams, and tapestries adorn the lobby and some rooms in this low-key luxury hotel near the cathedral; others have clean modern lines and rest-ful deep-brown accents. Cobblestone views, a sense of peace, and sur-prising amounts of natural light frame glowing glass-and-tile baths, fresh flowers, thick bathrobes, and flat-screen TVs throughout; two very quiet rooms give onto a tiny inner courtyard. ✉ *1 rue du Puits-St-Pierre, Vieille Ville, CH-1204* ☎ *022/3109172* 🖷 *022/3109846* ⊕*www. hotel-les-armures.ch* ⮐ *28 rooms, 4 suites* ⚙ *Restaurant, room serv-ice, in-room safes, minibars, cable TV, in-room DVD, in-room broad-band, Wi-Fi, bar, laundry service, concierge, business services, meeting room, car rental, parking (fee), pets allowed, no-smoking rooms* ⊟ *AE, DC, MC, V* ⭐ *BP.*

$$$$ 🏨 **President Wilson.** Huge, fragrant flower arrangements punctuate the public areas of this expansive hotel (yes, named for Woodrow); 17th-century tapestries, colorful paintings, and Greco-Roman stonework balance green marble floors and sleek wood throughout. The heated out-door pool faces the sunrise and many of the streamlined, modern rooms have sweeping views of the lake, Cologny, or the French Alps. Le Spice's restaurant serves modern Asian and Indian cuisine. ✉ *47 quai Wilson, Les Pâquis, CH-1211* ☎ *022/9066666* 🖷 *022/9066667* ⊕ *www. hotelpwilson.com* ⮐ *197 rooms, 33 suites* ⚙ *3 restaurants (1 sea-sonal), room service, in-room safes, minibars, cable TV with movies, in-room broadband, Wi-Fi, pool, gym, hair salon, spa, lobby lounge, piano bar, shops, laundry service, parking (fee), no-smoking floors* ⊟ *AE, DC, MC, V.*

$$$$ 🏨 **Swissôtel Métropole.** Massive scrubbed-stone arches, swirled wrought-iron sconces, brass accents, warm colors, lush carpets, and the imme-diate proximity of high-voltage rue du Rhône shopping give this 1854 Left Bank palace an air of urban gentility and center-city bustle. Rooms have espresso machines, broad stripes, and triple-glazed windows; bath-rooms in executive rooms and suites each have a TV perched in a wa-tertight alcove. The wraparound view from the roof is much envied during Fêtes de Genève fireworks. ✉ *34 quai du Général-Guisan, Centre Ville, CH-1204* ☎ *022/3183200* 🖷 *022/3183300* ⊕ *geneva.swissotel.com* ⮐ *111 rooms, 16 suites* ⚙ *2 restaurants, room service, in-room safes, minibars, cable TV with movies, in-room DVD, in-room data ports, Wi-*

Fi, gym, massage, piano bar, babysitting, laundry service, parking (fee), no-smoking rooms ⊟ *AE, DC, MC, V.*

12

$$$ 🏨 **Ambassador.** The multiyear renovation working its way down all seven floors is adding generous closet space, red and purple accents, flat-screen TVs, and a contemporary aesthetic to rooms that already have double-paned windows, rose-and-yellow carpeting, white-tile bathrooms, and lots of natural light. Many of the huge doubles would be called suites elsewhere; corner rooms have a separate alcove for kids. Top floor views of the Vieille Ville are superb. Now if they can only do something about that airport-lounge lobby. ⊠ *21 quai des Bergues, St-Gervais, CH-1211* ☎ *022/9080530* 🖷 *022/7389080* ⊕ *www.hotel-ambassador.ch* ➷ *79 rooms* ♙ *Restaurant, in-room safes, minibars, cable TV with movies, in-room data ports, Wi-Fi, lobby lounge, laundry service, business services, meeting rooms, parking (fee), no-smoking floors* ⊟ *AE, DC, MC, V.*

$$$ 🏨 **Cornavin.** The comic-book character Tintin made this hotel famous with *L'Affaire Tournesol* (*The Calculus Affair*) in 1956. Now the nine-story clock pendulum in the lobby, the deft manipulation of frosted glass and natural light on the top two floors, the spectacular glassed-in breakfast hall, and panoramic views compete for attention. Fourteen large triples and six interconnecting doubles easily accommodate families; double-glazed windows keep things quiet. ⊠ Gare de Cornavin, Centre Ville, CH-1201 ☎022/7161212 🖷022/7161200 ⊕www.fhotels.ch ➷160 rooms, 4 suites ♙ In-room safes, minibars, cable TV with movies, Wi-Fi, lobby lounge, laundry service, business services, meeting rooms, no-smoking rooms ⊟ AE, DC, MC, V.

★ $$$ 🏨 **Tiffany.** The designers of this intimate Belle Epoque jewel near the Plaine de Plainpalais took their cue from the restored ceiling painting by the side entrance, then got all the details right. Stained-glass lamps, ivy-clad wall sconces, period paintings, and curved wood accent the rose-and-green public areas. Guest rooms have blue-and-yellow stenciling, art nouveau bath tiles, fluffy bathrobes, and Crabtree & Evelyn bath products; those on the top "Attic" floor are vast and often have mansard roofs and exposed wood beams. The clublike bar has mahogany paneling, leather chairs, and cigars but the headliner here is the hotel restaurant, a Jugendstil knockout gleaming in lime-greens and cobalt-blue, swagged with Art Nouveau garlands, and glowing under 19th-century lamp globes—a true work of art. ⊠ *1 rue des Marbriers, Plainpalais, CH-1204* ☎ *022/7081616* 🖷 *022/7081617* ⊕ *www.hotel-tiffany.ch* ➷ *44 rooms, 2 suites* ♙ *Restaurant, room service, in-room safes, minibars, cable TV with movies, in-room broadband, Wi-Fi, massage, bar, lounge, laundry service, Internet room, car rental, parking (fee), no-smoking rooms* ⊟ *AE, DC, MC, V.*

$$–$$$ 🏨 **Le Montbrillant.** Exposed stone walls and massive wooden beams channel mountain huts in the lobby of this busy family-run hotel behind the Gare Cornavin. Rooms have clean lines, rosy wallpaper, white satin duvets, blue-gray trim, flat-screen TVs, ceiling fans, and double-glazed windows; those facing forward also have a terrific view of the TGV as it arrives from Paris. Studio apartments on the fifth floor have kitchenettes, dormer windows, cathedral ceilings, air-conditioning, and

monthly rates. ✉ *2 rue de Montbrillant, Les Grottes, CH-1201* ☎ *022/ 7337784* 🖷 *022/7332511* 🌐 *www.montbrillant.ch* 🛏 *58 rooms, 24 studios* 🕭 *2 restaurants, room service, fans, in-room safes, minibars, cable TV with movies, Wi-Fi, massage, bar, lobby lounge, laundry service, free parking, no-smoking floor; no a/c in some rooms* ☰ *AE, DC, MC, V* ⍟ *BP.*

$$ 🏨 **Domaine de Châteauvieux.** Delicate stenciling, marble sinks, and bright
Fodor'sChoice calico reflect a happy marriage of good taste and warm country spirit
★ at this hilltop complex, once part of a venerable château. Bicycles make the countryside accessible and after a ride through all the flowers, vineyards, and rolling green mountain nothing will please like the *chambre romantique*'s hot tub. Guest rooms are countryish yet cultured; the "suite" is a duplex apartment. Breakfast includes homemade bread and pastries, local honey, and jams made in-house from local fruit. ✉ *16 chemin de Châteauvieux, Peney-Dessus, CH-1242 Satigny* ☎ *022/ 7531511* 🖷 *022/7531924* 🌐 *www.chateauvieux.ch* 🛏 *12 rooms, 1 suite* 🕭 *Restaurant, in-room safes, minibars, cable TV, in-room data ports, bicycles, bar, laundry service, free parking, no-smoking rooms* ☰ *AE, DC, MC, V* ⍟ *BP.*

$–$$ 🏨 **International et Terminus.** The leafy outdoor terrace, soft yellow facade, and peach-paneled lobby impose civility on this modest hotel's central but chaotic location on a busy street opposite the Gare Cornavin. Rooms have marbled tile bathrooms, sleek wood furniture, double-glazed windows, and restful rose, green, and raspberry color schemes. The multilingual, uniformed staff is on duty round the clock. ✉ *20 rue des Alpes, Les Pâquis, CH-1211* ☎ *022/9069777* 🖷 *022/9069778* 🌐 *www.international-terminus.ch* 🛏 *60 rooms* 🕭 *Restaurant, fans, in-room safes, minibars, cable TV with movies, in-room data ports, Wi-Fi, dry cleaning, parking (fee); no a/c* ☰ *AE, DC, MC, V* ⍟ *BP.*

$ 🏨 **Bel'Espérance.** Rooftop views of Lake Geneva, bright yellow-and-blue
Fodor'sChoice rooms, tile baths, impeccable upkeep, and a graceful Louis-Philippe–style
★ breakfast salon put this family-run former *foyer pour dames* (ladies' boarding house) on a par with much pricier hotels. Large doubles connect to form "suites" for parents and children, the communal kitchen has a fridge with lockers, the whole hotel is off limits to smokers, and place du Bourg-de-Four is right up the hill. ✉ *1 rue de la Vallée, Vieille Ville, CH-1204* ☎ *022/8183737* 🖷 *022/8183773* 🌐 *www.hotel-bel-esperance.ch* 🛏 *37 rooms, 3 studios* 🕭 *Fans, in-room safes, kitchen, cable TV, lobby lounge, piano, laundry facilities, Internet room; no a/c, no smoking* ☰ *AE, DC, MC, V* ⍟ *BP.*

★ **$** 🏨 **Central.** Warm Indonesian wood, intense pastel greens and blues, sponge-painted terra-cotta, and exotic flowers reflect the Gangsted family ties to Bali in this low-cost hotel wedged into the top of a Left Bank shopping street. Flexible sleeping configurations include budget rooms with a bunk bed and shower, expansive apartments for six, and everything in between. Most rooms have balcony views, about half are air-conditioned, and all come with movies, free wireless access, and breakfast in bed. ✉ *2 rue de la Rôtisserie, Centre Ville, CH-1204* ☎ *022/8188100* 🖷 *022/8188101* 🌐 *www.hotelcentral.ch* 🛏 *30 rooms, 1 suite, 8 apart-*

ments ☆ *Room service, fans, some kitchenettes, cable TV, some in-room DVDs, some in-room VCRs, in-room broadband, Wi-Fi, lounge; no a/c in some rooms* ☰ *AE, DC, MC, V* ⍼ *BP.*

★ $ 🏨 **De Genève.** Rustic stone, carved wood, and a thoroughly cozy chalet-style lobby give way to cheery rooms full of eclectic modern and antique furnishings, original art, and delicate stenciling in this family-run establishment housed in a block-long Belle Epoque building. Corner doubles with bay windows and parquet floors face the 15th-century Temple de Saint-Gervais, double-glazing ensures silence, and breakfast comes with a backdrop of plane trees. ✉ *1 pl. Isaac-Mercier, St-Gervais, CH-1201* ☏ *022/7323264* 🖷 *022/7328264* ⊕ *www.hotel-de-geneve.ch* ⇌ *39 rooms* ☆ *Fans, cable TV, Wi-Fi, lounge, library, laundry facilities, laundry service, Internet room, pets allowed, no smoking floor; no a/c* ☰ *AE, DC, MC, V* ⍼ *BP.*

$ 🏨 **Ibis.** Breakfast starts at 4 AM (on demand), the reception is staffed 24/7, and the train station is five minutes away, making this cheerful chain hotel ultraconvenient if you're arriving late or departing early. Smooth wood and apricot accents add warmth to green pinstripes; the bright, well-appointed rooms are spotless; and the reception will loan you a safe. ✉ *10 rue Voltaire, St-Gervais, CH-1201* ☏ *022/3382020* 🖷 *022/3382030* ⊕ *www.ibishotel.com* ⇌ *65 rooms* ☆ *Cable TV, some Wi-Fi, bar, no-smoking floors* ☰ *AE, DC, MC, V.*

$ 🏨 **St-Gervais.** Red tartan carpeting and clean white linens warm some of the garretlike rooms in this old Right Bank inn; others have transitioned to blue walls and accents, parquet floors, and modular wooden desks. Fluffy white towels, hair dryers, and friendly service are common to all; breakfast is served in the wood-paneled bar–café on the ground floor. ✉ *20 rue des Corps-Saints, St-Gervais, CH-1201* ☏ *022/7324572* 🖷 *022/7314290* ⊕ *www.stgervais-geneva.ch* ⇌ *26 rooms, 2 with bath* ☆ *Fans, cable TV, Wi-Fi, bar; no a/c* ☰ *AE, DC, MC, V* ⍼ *BP.*

★ ¢–$ 🏨 **De la Cloche.** Flocked wallpaper, creaky parquet floors, chandeliers, fireplaces, ornate ceilings, Jet d'Eau views, and breakfast in bed serve as reminders that this kindly budget hotel one block from the lake was once a plush private apartment. Today all eight rooms have light yellow walls and light blue duvets, five have modular bathrooms with shower, and two overlook a quiet courtyard. Owner Christian Chabbey doubles as an informal concierge. ✉ *6 rue de la Cloche, Les Pâquis, CH-1201* ☏ *022/7329481* 🖷 *022/7381612* ⊕ *www.geneva-hotel.ch/cloche* ⇌ *8 rooms, 5 with shower* ☆ *Fans, cable TV, Wi-Fi; no a/c* ☰ *AE, DC, MC, V* ⍼ *BP.*

NIGHTLIFE & THE ARTS

Genève Agenda publishes weekly English and French listings of concerts, performances, temporary exhibits, restaurants, and clubs. The bilingual monthly *Genève Le Guide* (⊕ www.le-guide.ch) profiles current films, dance events, theatrical performances, and restaurants outside the city center. Free copies of both are available from tourist information booths and hotels.

Nightlife

A successful night out in Geneva—whether exclusive, trendy, or pub-based—can hinge on understanding that you are not in a major metropolis. Though bars and clubs have lots of life, much of it English-speaking, it may not be possible to party till dawn.

Bars

Whiskey, grappa, cognac, and little-known wines from well-known places flow freely around communal tables laid with regional tapas at **Boulevard du Vin** (⊠ 3 blvd. Georges-Favon, Plainpalais ☎ 022/3109190 ⊕ www.boulevard-du-vin.ch). **La Clémence** (⊠ 20 pl. du Bourg-de-Four, Vieille Ville ☎ 022/3122498 ⊕ www.laclemence.ch) fills with university students and explodes into the street. **Mr. Pickwick Pub** (⊠ 80 rue de Lausanne, Les Pâquis ☎ 022/7316797 ⊕ www.mrpickwick.ch) serves full English breakfasts, shows European League soccer, and staves off homesickness in British expats. The Guinness is on tap and the accents are robustly Irish at **Mulligan's** (⊠ 14 rue Grenus, St-Gervais ☎ 022/7328576 ⊕ www.ireland.ch). The **Roi Ubu** (⊠ 30 Grand-rue, Vieille Ville ☎ 022/3107398) draws a lively, young international crowd. Classic pub comfort, American bartenders, and large-screen TVs draw crowds to the **Spring Bros. Pub** (⊠ 23 Grand-rue, Vieille Ville ☎ 022/3101040).

Clubs

Expect to wait in line at the ultrachic **B'Club—Le Baroque** (⊠ 12 pl. de la Fusterie, Centre Ville ☎ 022/3110515 ⊕ www.lebaroque.com), where the jet-set party moves downstairs after 11 PM. **Bypass** (⊠ 1 carrefour de l'Etoile, Acacias ☎ 022/3006565 ⊕ www.bypass-geneve.ch) lures cosmopolitan twenty- and thirty-somethings to the outer edge of Carouge. Up-and-coming musicians from around the world perform live at the small, relaxed, and affordable **Chat Noir** (⊠ 13 rue Vautier, Carouge ☎ 022/3434998 ⊕ www.chatnoir.ch). Generations of St-Tropezesque celebrity guests have kept **Griffin's Club** (⊠ 36 blvd. Helvétique, Eaux-Vives ☎ 022/7351218 ⊕ www.griffins-club.com) on the map. Local fashionistas and a genuine Big-City vibe make **Javaclub** (⊠ Palace Hilton Hotel, 19 quai du Mont-Blanc, Les Pâquis ☎ 022/9089088 ⊕ www.javaclub. ch) the place to see and be seen. **Macumba** (⊠ 403 rte. d'Annecy, St. Julien-en-Genevois, France ☎ 0033/450492350 ⊕ www.macumba.fr), to the south, in France, fills six throbbing dance floors and a karaoke bar with techno, house, reggae, disco, salsa, classic rock, and hits from the 1980s. **Moa Club** (⊠ 22 chemin des Batailles, Vernier ⊕ www.moaclub.com) has a popular vibe and a dance-party schedule loaded with techno. The cocktails are potent and the dance hits current at **Shakers** (⊠ 4 rue Arnold-Winkelried, Centre Ville ☎ 022/3105598 ⊕ www.shakers.ch).

The Arts

Geneva's legacy as a cultural crossroads has produced an unusually rich arts scene for a city of its size: most performance spaces in town are roadhouses through which flow a steady stream of foreign as well as Swiss artists. Tickets remain on sale from theater box offices up to the day of

La Cité Sarde

Greenwich Village, these days, to Geneva's Upper East Side, Carouge (from *quadruvium*,) began life in the Roman era as a crossroads next to a bridge over the river Arve. It remained a mere hamlet until 1754, when the Duke of Savoy, by then also King of Sardinia, annexed it with intent to create a rival commercial hub for Geneva. That never happened, courtesy of the French Revolution, but the town grew so fast that the royal planners in Turin drew up five separate development plans between 1772 and 1783; their harmonious architecture, plazas, and courtyard gardens still recall Mediterranean ways unheard of in Geneva. Colorful shop windows, sidewalk cafés, friendly restaurants, hole-in-the-wall galleries, tree-lined fruit-and-vegetable markets (on Wednesday and Saturday), open doors, and working artists infuse rue St-Joseph, rue Ancienne, rue St-Victor, and place du Marché with vibrant creative energy; don't miss the outdoor street fairs in early September and mid-December.

performance, but it's wise to book ahead. The Service Billetterie at **FNAC Rive** (⊠ 16 rue de Rive, Centre Ville ☎ 022/8161256 ⊕ www. FNAC.ch) manages sales for a huge, ever-changing list of events. The third-floor ticket booth at **Globus** (⊠48 rue du Rhône, Centre Ville ☎022/ 3195583) handles concerts and theatrical performances throughout the Lac Léman region; note that it does not accept credit cards.

Film

English-language films are always screened undubbed somewhere in town—check local newspaper listings for the initials *v.o.*, short for *version originale* (original version). The **CAC Voltaire** (⊠ 16 rue du Général-Dufour, Centre Ville ☎022/3207878 ⊕ www.ville-ge.ch/grutli) organizes ongoing, undubbed classic film minifestivals in the basement of the Grütli Arts Center. **Cinélac** (⊠ Port-Noir, Cologny ☎ 022/3196111 ⊕ www.orangecinema.ch) screens a different film outside by the lake every night from July through August.

Music & Dance

Classical music, opera, contemporary dance, and the occasional film festival cycle through the **Bâtiment des Forces Motrices** (⊠ 2 pl. des Volontaires, Plainpalais ☎ 022/3221220 ⊕ www.bfm.ch). The **Grand Théâtre** (⊠ pl. Neuve, Centre Ville ☎ 022/4183130 ⊕ www.geneveopera.ch) stages eight full-scale operas, five ballets, and six recitals each season (September to June). **Victoria Hall** (⊠ 14 rue du Général-Dufour, Centre Ville ☎ 022/4183500 ⊕ www.ville-ge.ch/vh/), Geneva's classical concert venue, is home to the world-famous **Orchestre de la Suisse Romande** (☎ 022/8070017 ⊕ www.osr.ch). The AMR musical association stocks the program at **Sud des Alpes** (⊠ 10 rue des Alpes, Les Pâquis ☎ 022/7165630 ⊕ www.amr-geneve.ch) with nervy improvisation and contemporary jazz.

Theater

The creative, colorful children's theater **Am Stram Gram** (⊠ 56 rte. de Frontenex, Eaux-Vives ☎ 022/7357924 ⊕ www.amstramgram.ch) draws inspiration from myth, folktales, lyric poetry, Shakespeare, and contemporary writing. Anne Bisang's **Comédie de Genève** (⊠ 6 blvd. des Philosophes, Plainpalais ☎022/3205001 ⊕www.comedie.ch) stages modern drama and international classics. The experimental **Théâtre du Grütli** (⊠ 16 rue du Général-Dufour, Centre Ville ☎ 022/3289868 ⊕ www. grutli.ch) fills its spare, flexible space with contemporary Swiss and foreign plays. All three theaters' productions are in French.

SPORTS & THE OUTDOORS

Skiing

Geneva is surrounded by terrific downhill skiing, most of it in the French Alps. Special daily ski buses to Chamonix and weekend buses to Flaine and Morzine-Avoriaz depart the **Gare Routière de Genève** (⊠ pl. Dorcière, Les Pâquis ☎ 0900/320230 ⊕ www.gare-routiere.com) throughout the season (generally early December to mid-April). Trips take 1½–2 hours, and the 65–80 SF fare includes a ski-lift pass.

Swimming

The Genevois love their beaches, which open in May and stay crowded through September. Lac Léman water quality is closely monitored by the **Etat de Genève** (⊕ www.geneve.ch/plages) and regularly re-certified clean and safe for swimmers. A laid-back and popular concrete sunbathing area surrounds a protected mid-harbor swim zone and casual restaurant at **Bains des Pâquis** (⊠ 30 quai du Mont-Blanc, Les Pâquis ☎ 022/7322974 ⊕ www.bains-des-paquis.ch). **Genève-Plage** (⊠ Port Noir, Cologny ☎ 022/7362482 ⊕ www.geneve-plage.ch) has green lawns, an Olympic outdoor pool, lake access, multilevel diving boards, basketball and volleyball courts, Ping-Pong tables, a canteen, and a water slide.

SHOPPING

Official store hours are Monday to Wednesday from 9 to 7, Thursday from 9 to 9, Friday from 9 to 7:30, and Saturday from 9 to 6. Smaller shops may open later Monday, close earlier Thursday and Saturday, or close for lunch.

Auctions

As a jewelry capital rivaled only by New York, and an international center for Swiss watchmakers, Geneva regularly hosts high-profile auctions by the major houses. **Antiquorum** (⊠ 2 rue du Mont-Blanc, Centre Ville ☎ 022/9092850) focuses on antique timepieces. **Christie's** (⊠ 8 pl. de la Taconnerie, Vieille Ville ☎ 022/3191766) auctions off wine and cigars as well as mega-glamorous jewelry and watches twice a year. **Sotheby's** (⊠ 13 quai du Mont-Blanc, Les Pâquis ☎ 022/9084800) displays lots of spectacular jewelry and watches in May and November before they are sold.

Department Stores

Bon Génie (✉ 34 rue du Marché, Centre Ville ☎ 022/8181111) stocks floor after hushed floor with designer clothing and cosmetics. **Globus** (✉ 48 rue du Rhône, Centre Ville ☎ 022/3195050) forms a physical link between the Left Bank shopping arteries and excels at home accessories, kitchen paraphernalia, hosiery, men's and women's clothing, and food.

Markets

Halle de Rive (✉ 17 rue Pierre-Fatio/29 blvd. Helvétique, Centre Ville ⊕ www.halle-de-rive.com) sells fresh cheeses, meats, pasta, fish, flowers, wine, and chocolate all day Monday through Saturday. A vibrant seasonal fruit-and-vegetable market fills **boulevard Helvétique** on Wednesday and Saturday mornings. Arts-and-crafts vendors crowd **place de la Fusterie** every Thursday. Flea market stalls move into position around the **Plaine de Plainpalais** on Wednesday and Saturday, replacing the Tuesday and Friday morning fruit-and-vegetable stands.

Shopping Streets

Geneva's principal shopping streets, known collectively as the **Rues-Basses** (Low Streets), run parallel along the Left Bank. **Rue du Rhône,** closest to the river, marks the epicenter of luxury shopping. One block in is the more popular thoroughfare known variously as **rue de la Confédération, rue du Marché, rue de la Croix-d'Or,** and **rue de Rive.** Galleries, antiques shops, home-accessories emporia, and chic boutiques line the **Grand-Rue** as well as streets radiating out from **place du Bourg-de-Four. Rue du Mont-Blanc** represents the frenetic hub of Right Bank shopping.

Specialty Stores

Antiques

Antiquités Scientifiques (✉ 19 rue du Perron, Vieille Ville ☎ 022/3100706) buys, sells, and assesses telescopes, barometers, microscopes, binoculars, sundials, and cameras. Head to **Librairie Ancienne** (✉ 20 Grand-Rue, Vieille Ville ☎ 022/3102050) for leather-bound and gilt first editions (not in English). **Montparnasse** (✉ 40 Grand-Rue, Vieille Ville ☎ 022/3116719) deals in pristine original books, prints, maps, and paintings from the 19th- and early-20th century Ecole Suisse. Well-polished English furniture fills the **Regency House** (✉ 3 rue de l'Hôtel-de-Ville, Vieille Ville ☎ 022/3103540). **Rue des Belles Filles** (✉ 8 rue Etienne-Dumont, Vieille Ville ☎ 022/3103131) buys and sells vintage jewelry, clothing, linens, crystal, silver, china, and paintings.

Books

French giant **FNAC** (✉ 16 rue de Rive, Centre Ville ☎ 022/8161220) holds readings and devotes its block-length first floor to current French (and a few English) titles. **Librairie Archigraphy** (✉ 1 pl. de l'Ile, Centre Ville ☎ 022/3116008) sells art, design, and architecture books in a setting worthy of its subjects. **Librairie Bernard Letu** (✉ 2 rue Jean-Calvin, Vieille Ville

☎022/3104757) carries an inspired range of multilingual art and photography titles. French-language books about Geneva form the tip of the proverbial (and dusty) iceberg at the venerable old **Librairie Jullien** (✉ 32 pl. du Bourg-de-Four, Vieille Ville ☎ 022/3103670). **L'Oreille Cassée** (✉ 9 quai des Bergues, St-Gervais ☎ 022/7324080) serves devotees of hardcover, secondhand, and vintage *bandes dessinées* (Franco-Belgian comic books). **Off the Shelf** (✉15 blvd. Georges-Favon, Plainpalais ☎ 022/3111090) lures English-speaking browsers with a sunny space and a hand-picked selection. The English Bookshop within the commercial chain **Payot** (✉5 rue de Chantepoulet, Les Pâquis ☎ 022/7318950) keeps abreast of current U.S. and U.K. trends.

Chocolate

Silky, handmade white-chocolate truffles top the winter selection at **Arn** (✉ 12 pl. du Bourg-de-Four, Vieille Ville ☎ 022/3104094). Local cobblestones inspired Henri Auer's *pavés glacés,* creamy bite-size delicacies that have become Genevois classics; his descendants at **Auer** (✉ 4 rue de Rive, Centre Ville ☎ 022/3114286) maintain the tradition. **Du Rhône** (✉ 3 rue de la Confédération, Centre Ville ☎ 022/3115614) has sold bittersweet hot chocolate since 1875. **Merkur** (✉ 32 rue du Marché, Centre Ville ☎ 022/3102221 ✉ Galerie marchande de Cornavin, Les Pâquis ☎ 022/7324182) stocks Swiss-theme gift boxes, individual bars, and huge champagne truffles. **Rohr** (✉ 3 pl. du Molard, Centre Ville ☎ 022/3116303 ✉ 4 rue d'Enfer, Centre Ville ☎ 022/3116876) models its smooth, rich signature truffles after old Geneva garbage cans. Don't be fooled; it's the best chocolate in town.

Gifts & Souvenirs

Helvès (✉ 14 rue Etienne-Dumont, Vieille Ville ☎ 022/3113462) sells folkloric Swiss dolls and embroidered linens, lace, blouses, and handkerchiefs. Carved wooden castles, train sets, stilts, hammocks, and puppets make **Pinocchio** (✉ 10 rue Etienne-Dumont, Vieille Ville ☎ 022/3104047) fun for all ages. Quality kitchen gadgets and every major configuration of Swiss army knife line the walls at **Riethmüller** (✉ 19 pl. Longemalle, Centre Ville ☎ 022/3124052).

Home Accessories

Color, whimsy, and solid craftsmanship define the dishes, candles, glassware, and sofas at **Duo sur Canapé** (✉ 10 rue Verdaine, Vieille Ville ☎022/3112241). **La Maison** (✉ 49 rue Ancienne, Carouge ☎ 022/3433032) surrounds Esteban incense products with iron teapots, soapstone figurines, colorful baskets, and printed Asian or African textiles. Hollow-wax candleholders lead to tealights that smell like champagne, licorice, and bitter-orange chocolate at **Tout Feu Tout Flamme** (✉ 6 rue de la Tour-Maîtresse, Centre Ville ☎ 022/3101390). Graceful iron teapots, porcelain tea sets, and a multipage menu of exotic brews are highlights at **Tschin-Ta-Ni** (✉ 5 rue Verdaine, Vieille Ville ☎ 022/3116500).

Jewelry

Bucherer (✉ 45 rue du Rhône, Centre Ville ☎ 022/3196266 ✉ 22 rue du Mont-Blanc, Les Pâquis ☎ 022/7327216) sells luminous pearls and diamonds of all sizes. **Bulgari** (✉ 30 rue du Rhône, Centre Ville ☎ 022/3177070) favors heavy gold necklaces and rings crusted with jewels. **Cartier** (✉ 35 rue du Rhône, Centre Ville ☎ 022/8185454) famously renders feline grace in diamonds, rubies, and emeralds. **Chopard** (✉ 8 rue de la Confédération, Centre Ville ☎ 022/3113728 ✉ 27 rue du Rhône, Centre Ville ☎ 022/3107050) creates icelike necklaces out of in-laid diamonds. **Gilbert Albert** (✉ 24 rue de la Corraterie, Centre Ville ☎ 022/3114833) lets nature inspire interchangeable stones wrapped in curvaceous, coral-like gold.

Paper Goods

Clean lines and vibrant color define the writing paper and fabric-bound photo albums at **Bookbinders** (✉ 15 rue de la Fontaine, Vieille Ville ☎ 022/3016450). **Brachard** (✉ 10 rue de la Corraterie, Centre Ville ☎ 022/8170555) has art and office supplies in the basement, specialty pens next door, wrapping paper and calendars on the first floor, and exquisite (books of) Italian, French, and Nepali paper in between. Spiral and perfect-bound notebooks, photo albums, and monochromatic cards form tall swathes of color at **Ordning&Reda** (✉ 20 rue de Rive, Centre Ville ☎ 022/8101020).

Watches

Bucherer (✉ 45 rue du Rhône, Centre Ville ☎ 022/3196266 ✉ 22 rue du Mont-Blanc, Les Pâquis ☎ 022/7327216) is Geneva's one-stop shop for prestigious, indestructible Rolex models. **Franck Muller** (✉ 1 rue de la Tour-de-l'Ile, Centre Ville ☎ 022/8180030) creates complicated modern timepieces. **Patek Philippe** (✉ 41 rue du Rhône, Centre Ville ☎ 022/7812448) occupies the 1839 building where Antoine Norbert de Patek invented the winding mechanism inside all watches. **Piaget** (✉ 40 rue du Rhône, Centre Ville ☎ 022/8170200) wraps its ultraflat tourbillons in sleek white gold. **Vacheron Constantin** (✉ 1 rue des Moulins, Centre Ville ☎ 022/3161740), the oldest watch company in Geneva, sold its first sober design in 1755.

GENEVA ESSENTIALS

Transportation

BY AIR

British Airways, easyJet, and Swiss fly direct between London and Geneva; Swiss and Continental operate direct service from New York. Swiss also schedules frequent connections to its hub in Zürich.

CARRIERS ✈ Airlines & Contacts **British Airways** ☎ 0848/801010 ⊕ www.ba.com. **Continental** ☎ 022/4177280 ⊕ www.continental.com. **easyJet** ☎ 0848/888222 ⊕ www.easyjet.com. **Swiss** ☎ 0848/852000 ⊕ www.swiss.com.

AIRPORTS Cointrin International Airport, Switzerland's second-largest, lies 5 km (3 mi) northwest of downtown Geneva.

✈ Airport Information **Cointrin** ☎ 022/7177111 ⊕ www.gva.ch.

AIRPORT TRANSFERS The No. 10 bus runs regularly between the airport departure level and downtown Geneva. The ride lasts about 20 minutes and the fare is 3 SF. Taxis are plentiful but expensive: expect to pay 35 SF or more to reach the city center, plus 1.50 SF per bag. Multilingual limousine services provide buses, minivans, or Mercedes sedans; Privilège has a stretch Rolls-Royce. Trains run about every 15 minutes between Cointrin and the Gare Cornavin, Geneva's main train station, from 6 AM to midnight; the six-minute trip costs 3 SF each way.

✈ Limousine Services **Globe** ☎ 022/7310750 ⊕ www.globelimousines.ch. **Privilège** ☎ 022/7383366 ⊕ www.privilegelimousine.ch.

BY BIKE

Bike lanes, indicated by a yellow line and a yellow bicycle symbol on the pavement, are ubiquitous downtown. Yellow signs indicate routes elsewhere in the canton. Genèv'Roule rents out bicycles from May to October in all of their locations; Les Grottes stays open year-round. Pay a deposit of 50 SF and return the bike by 9:30 PM between May and October, and you "rent" the bike for free.

✈ Bike Rentals **Genèv'Roule** ✉ 17 pl. Montbrillant, Les Grottes ☎ 022/7401343 ⊕ www.geneveroule.ch ✉ Bains des Pâquis, Les Pâquis ✉ pl. du Rhône, Centre Ville ✉ Plaine de Plainpalais, Plainpalais.

BY BOAT & FERRY

The Compagnie Générale de Navigation operates steamship connections between Geneva and Nyon, Lausanne, Vevey, Montreux, and assorted smaller lake towns in Switzerland, as well as Yvoire, Thonon-les-Bains, and Evian-les-Bains, in France. Swiss Pass holders travel free; those with a Swiss Boat Pass pay half price. Smaller-scale lake travel, including a shuttle service across Geneva's harbor, is entrusted to the Mouettes Genevoises; the M1-4 lines are covered by the standard 3 SF city-bus fare.

✈ Boat & Ferry Information **Compagnie Générale de Navigation** (CGN) ☎ 0848/811848 ⊕ www.cgn.ch. **Mouettes Genevoises** ✉ 8 quai du Mont-Blanc, Les Pâquis ☎ 022/7322944 ⊕ www.mouettesgenevoises.ch.

BY BUS & TRAM

The Gare Routière de Genève, Geneva's central bus station, lies hidden behind the English Church off rue du Mont-Blanc and handles buses arriving from or departing for points across Europe. Local buses and trams operate every few minutes on all city routes from 5 AM to midnight, when, on Friday and Saturday, the Noctambus night-bus service kicks in. Buy a 3 SF ticket from the UNIRESO vending machine at the stop before you board (instructions are given in English) and use the system, transferring at will between buses, trams, airport-bound trains, and the Mouettes Genevoises harbor shuttles, for one hour. Day passes, known as *cartes journalières,* are available from the vending machines or the Transports Publics Genevois (TPG) booths at the train station and rond-point de Rive, and come in two forms. Unlimited city-center travel between 9 AM and midnight costs 7 SF; 10 SF will buy you a 24-hour period that begins when the ticket is purchased and allows two people to travel for the price of one on weekends. The Geneva Transport Card costs 20 SF for 48 hours or 30 SF for 72 hours, covers two people on weekends, grants discounts at museums and tourist attractions, and must be stamped by a hotel reception or at a TPG booth. Holders of the Swiss Pass travel free.

⊞ Bus & Tram Information Gare Routière de Genève ✉ pl. Dorcière, Les Pâquis ☎ 0900/320230 ⊕ www.gare-routiere.com. **Transports Publics Genevois** (TPG) ☎ 0900/022021 ⊕ www.unireso.com.

BY CAR

Geneva's long border with France makes for easy access from all points French. Paris (to the northwest) is six hours away; Dijon (to the north), Lyon (to the southwest), Grenoble (to the south), and Chamonix (to the southeast) are all within two hours' drive on the French A40 expressway (l'Autoroute Blanche). The French south shore of Lac Léman gives access to the Valais via Evian-les-Bains. The Swiss A1 expressway, along the north shore, connects Geneva to the rest of Switzerland by way of Lausanne. Traffic along the quays clogs easily and parking in town is both restricted and expensive; look for electric signs on major incoming roads that note the whereabouts of (immaculate) municipal parking garages and their current number of empty spaces.

BY TAXI

Taxis are clean and drivers are polite, but be prepared to pay a 6.30 SF minimum charge plus 3.20 SF per km (about ½ mi) traveled. In the evening and on Sunday the rate climbs to 3.80 SF per km. Cabs won't stop if you hail them; go to a designated taxi stand (marked on the pavement in yellow) or call. More and more drivers accept credit cards.

⊞ Taxis Taxi-Phone ☎ 022/3314133 ⊕ www.taxi-phone.ch.

BY TRAIN

Express trains from most Swiss cities arrive at and depart from the Right Bank Gare Cornavin every hour. Bern is about two hours away, Zurich and Basel roughly three. The French TGV leaves seven times a day for Paris (five times on weekends) and arrives 3½ hours later; the Cisalpino makes the four- to five-hour journey to Milan twice each morning. Regional trains leave every 15 minutes en route to Nyon and Lausanne. Touch-screen consoles (in English) in the main ticket hall sell tickets for any destination in Switzerland.

⊞ Train Information Gare Cornavin ✉ 7 pl. Cornavin ☎ 0900/300300 ⊕ www.cff. ch.

Contacts & Resources

EMERGENCIES

Dial ☎ **117** for the police, ☎ **118** in case of fire, or ☎ **144** for an ambulance. Call ☎ **1811 or 144** for directions to 24-hour pharmacies (*Pharmacies de garde*).

🔳 Doctors **AMGE—Emergency Doctors at Home** ☎ 022/3222020. **SOS Médecins à domicile (SOS Doctors at Home)** ☎ 022/7484950.

🔳 Hospitals **Hôpital Cantonal de Genève** ✉ 24 rue Micheli-du-Crest, Plainpalais ☎ 022/3723311 or 022/3823311 ⊕ www.hug-ge.ch. **Hôpital de la Tour** ✉ 3 ave. J-D Maillard, Meyrin ☎ 022/7196111 ⊕ www.latour.ch.

INTERNET & MAIL

Wireless Internet access is common in Geneva; free wireless access is rare. Internet cafés are scarce and usually shoehorned into a larger (shop) context, but always crowded. They charge about 2 SF per 15 minutes online and may close well before midnight. Post offices open and close about an hour earlier than shops do; smaller branches may close for lunch or before noon on Saturday. The Swiss Post Web site lists individual branch opening hours. Take a ticket when you enter and wait (usually less than five minutes) for your number to be called; postcards, stationery, and packing materials are sold on-site.

🔳 Internet Cafés **F.Sys Informatique** ✉ 18 rue du Conseil-Général, Plainpalais ☎ 022/3282444. **Open Vidéo Club** ✉ 19 rue des Alpes, Les Pâquis ☎ 022/7311321.

🔳 Post Offices **Swiss Post** ☎ 0848/888888 ⊕ www.post.ch. **Genève 1 Mont-Blanc** ✉ 18 rue du Mont-Blanc, Les Pâquis ☎ 022/7392084. **Genève 3 Rive** ✉ 3 rue du Vieux-Collège, Centre Ville ☎ 022/8186121.

TOUR OPTIONS

BOAT TOURS The Compagnie Générale de Navigation boards passengers on both sides of the pont du Mont-Blanc and serves multicourse meals aboard special Belle Epoque steamship cruises. Separate, hour-long CGN loops of the lower lake point out local sights. Swissboat and the Mouettes Genevoises jointly operate smaller-scale guided tours that take in castles, famous homes, ports, and parkland along the lake every day from April to October. Trips last anywhere from 40 minutes to two hours; recorded commentary is in English. The boats leave from two spots on the quai du Mont-Blanc—opposite the Monument Brunswick (Swissboat) and opposite the Hotel Palace Hilton (Mouettes Genevoises)—as well as from the Eaux-Vives waterfront between the Jet d'Eau and the Jardin Anglais. The Mouettes Genevoises also operate nearly three-hour natural-history tours of the Rhône. Live commentary is in English, and the boats depart from place de l'Ile.

🔳 Fees & Schedules **Compagnie Générale de Navigation** (CGN) ☎ 0848/811848 ⊕ www.cgn.ch. **Mouettes Genevoises** ✉ 8 quai du Mont-Blanc, Les Pâquis ☎ 022/7322944 ⊕ www.mouettesgenevoises.ch. **Swissboat** ✉ 4 quai du Mont-Blanc, Les Pâquis ☎ 022/7324747 ⊕ www.swissboat.com.

BUS TOURS Key Tours conducts two-hour bus-and-minitrain tours of the International Area and the Vieille Ville, leaving place Dorcière daily at 2 PM as well as at 10 AM May–October and 3:15 PM July and August. Each circuit costs 45 SF, and recorded commentary is in English. Between May and October you can also opt to catch the minitrain (independent of the bus tour) at place du Rhône for a trip around the Vieille Ville. Between March and October, a second minitrain leaves from the quai du Mont-Blanc for a tour of the International Area and Right Bank parks, and a third departs the Jardin Anglais for a ride along the Left Bank quays. Each loop lasts between 30 and 75 minutes; the cost is 7–19 SF. Afternoon bus tours of the Geneva countryside are also available May–October. A KeyPass, good for 24 or 48 hours for either 49 SF or 98 SF, grants free access to bus and minitrain tours, public transport, and all museums that have entrance fees.

🚹 Fees & Schedules **Key Tours** ✉ 7 rue des Alpes, Les Pâquis ☎ 022/7314140 ⊕ www. keytours.ch.

WALKING TOURS English-speaking guides linked to Genève Tourisme lead a two-hour walk through the Vieille Ville every Saturday at 10 AM. Additional weekday circuits at 10 AM, as well as 6:30 PM outings on Tuesday and Thursday, take place between June and late September. The cost is 15 SF. Unscheduled thematic tours for five or more people cost 40 SF per person and trace the history of watchmaking, Henry Dunant's legacy, literary Geneva, or one of 17 other subjects. English-language audio guides to the Vieille Ville last 2½ hours and cost 10 SF plus a 50 SF deposit. The map, CD, and player must be returned within four hours.

🚹 Fees & Schedules **Genève Tourisme** ✉ 18 rue du Mont-Blanc, Les Pâquis ☎ 022/ 9097000. **Service des Guides** ✉ 18 rue du Mont-Blanc, Les Pâquis ☎ 022/9097030.

VISITOR INFORMATION

Genève Tourisme is headquartered inside the large Post Office building halfway between the pont du Mont-Blanc and the Gare Cornavin. Additional information booths serve the airport and, from June through September, the train station. The mid-river Arcade d'information de la Ville de Genève, an excellent, multilingual source of information about all things Geneva, is run by the city; Genève Tourisme sends a representative on weekday afternoons.

🚹 Tourist Information Booths **Airport** ✉ Cointrin Arrivals ☎ 022/7178083. **Right Bank** ✉ 18 rue du Mont-Blanc, Les Pâquis ☎ 022/9097000. **Train Station** ✉ Gare Cornavin ☎ 022/9097050. **Arcade d'information de la Ville de Genève** ✉ 1 pont de la Machine, Centre Ville ☎ 022/3119970 (Ville de Genève) ☎ 022/3119827 (Genève Tourisme). 🚹 Tourist Office **Genève Tourisme** ✉ 18 rue du Mont-Blanc, Case Postale 1602, CH-1211 Genève 1 ☎ 022/9097070 🖶 022/9097075 ⊕ www.geneve-tourisme.ch.

UNDERSTANDING
SWITZERLAND

THE GOOD, THE BAD & THE TIDY

UP IN THE HOARY, windswept heights and black fir forests of the Alps, an electric eye beams open a glistening all-glass door—and reveals the honey-gold glow of wood, the sheen of copper, the burnt-chocolate tones of ancient wooden rafters. Candles flicker; Sterno radiates blue-white flames under russet pots of bubbling fondue. The cheery *boomp-chick boomp-chick* of an accordion filters down from high-tech stereo speakers cleverly concealed behind oversize cowbells. Waitresses in starched black dirndls and waiters in spotless white ties scuttle briskly from kitchen to table, table to kitchen, while platters of gravy-laden veal, sizzling *Rösti* (hash brown potatoes), and rosy entrecôte simmer over steel trivets—preheated, electrically controlled—ready to be proudly, seamlessly served.

Coziness under strict control, anachronism versus state-of-the-art technology: strange bedfellows in a storybook land. Nowhere else in Europe can you find a combination as welcoming and as alien, as comfortable and as remote, as engaging and as disengaged as a glass cable car to the clouds. This is the paradox of the Swiss, whose primary national aesthetic pitches rustic Alpine homeyness against high-tech urban efficiency. Though they're proud, sober, self-contained, independent culturally and politically, disdainful of the shabby and the slipshod, painfully neat, rigorously prompt—the Swiss have a weakness for cuteness, and they indulge in incongruously coy diminutives: a German *Bierstube* (pub) becomes a *Stübli,* *Kuchen* (cake) becomes *Küchli, Wurst* becomes *Würstli,* and a *coupe* (glass) of champagne becomes a *Cüpli.*

It is lucky for travelers, this dichotomy of the folksy and the functional. It means your trains get you to your firelit lodge on time. It means the cable car that sweeps you to a mountaintop has been subjected to grueling inspections. It means the hand-woven curtains are boiled and starched, and the high-thread-count bed linens are turned back with a chocolate at night. It means the scarlet geraniums that cascade from window boxes on every carved balcony are tended like prize orchids. It means the pipe smoke that builds up in the Stübli at night is aired out daily, as sparkling clean double-glazed windows are thrown open on every floor, every morning, to let sharp, cool mountain air course through hallways, bedrooms, and fresh-bleached baths.

Yet there is a stinginess that peeks around the apron of that rosy-cheeked efficiency. Liquor here is measured with scientific precision into glasses marked for one centiliter or two, and the local wines come in carafes reminiscent of laboratory beakers. Despite the fine linens and puffs of down that adorn each bed, double beds have separate mattresses with sheets tucked primly down the middle, sometimes so tightly you have to lift the mattress to loosen the barrier. And if you wash out your socks and hang them loosely on the shower rod in the morning, you may return at night and find them straightened, spaced, toes pointing the same direction, as orderly as little lead soldiers.

Nevertheless there is an earthiness about these people, as at ease with the soil as they are appalled by dirt. A banker in Zürich may rent a postage-stamp parcel of land in a crowded patchwork outside town, sowing tight rows of cabbages and strawberries, weeding bright borders of marigolds, and on Sunday he may visit his miniature estate, pull a chair out from the tidy toolshed, and simply sit and smoke, like Heidi's Alm-Uncle surveying his Alpine realm. An elderly woman may don knickers and loden hat and board a postbus to the mountains and climb steep, rocky trails at a brisk clip, cheeks glowing, eyes as icy bright as the glaciers above her.

There's a 21st-century counterpoint to this: the high-tech, jet-set glamour that splashes vivid colors across the slopes at St. Moritz, Gstaad, Zermatt, Verbier. Step out of a bulbous steel-and-glass cable car onto a concrete platform at 6,560 feet and see Switzerland transformed, its workers' blue overalls and good wool suits exchanged for ski suits. Wholesome, healthy faces disappear behind mirrored goggles and war-paint sunblock, and gaudy skis and poles bristle militarily, like the pikes and halberds in the Battle of Sempach.

The contradictions mount: while fur-clad socialites raise jeweled fingers to bid at Sotheby's on Geneva's quai du Mont-Blanc, the women of Appenzell stand beside the men on the Landsgemeindeplatz and raise their hands to vote locally—a right not won until 1991. While digital screens tick off beef futures in Zürich, the crude harmony of cowbells echoes in velvet mountain pastures. While a Mercedes roars down an expressway expertly blasted through solid rock, a horse-drawn plow peels back thin topsoil in an Alpine garden plot, impossibly steep, improbably high.

And on August 1, the Swiss national holiday, while spectacular displays of fireworks explode in sizzling colors over the cities and towns, the mountain folk build the bonfires that glow quietly, splendidly, on every hillside of every Alp, uniting Swiss citizens as they celebrate their proud independence, their cultural wealth, and above all their diversity. It's that diversity and those quirky contradictions that make Switzerland a tourist capital—the folksy, fiercely efficient innkeeper to the world.

—Nancy Coons

SKIING SWITZERLAND

AFTER TWO CABLE CAR RIDES, we sit in a mountain restaurant thousands of feet above the resort village of Verbier. On the table in front of us are two cups of hot chocolate, and one tiny glass of bubbly white Fendant wine from Sion. Our legs are tired from a long day of skiing. We catch our breath before the evening run, while the slopes below empty themselves of skiers and fill up with evening light. Outside, Mont Blanc is an island of ice rising out of a sea of summits along the Franco-Swiss border. Peaks and passes stretch as far as the eye can see, an art director's Alpine fantasy in late light.

Verbier skiing is one reason I've returned to Switzerland in winter, faithfully, for the past 25 years. This is a giant of a ski area in a region of giant ski areas, perched high in the French-speaking southwest of Switzerland, draped over four mountain valleys, embracing six villages, a labyrinth of interconnected lifts (more than 100), interlaced slopes (too many to count)—a ski area you can't explore in a week or even exhaust in a season.

For passionate skiers every trip to Switzerland is a homecoming. All our skiing archetypes originate here. White sawtooth horizons point to the sky, picture-postcard chalet roofs poke up under great white hats of snow, necklaces of lifts and cable cars drape themselves over the white shoulders of fairy-tale mountains, and runs go on forever.

These are big mountains, with vertical drops twice the length of those of the Rockies. In the Alps you can often drop 4,000, 5,000, or 6,000 vertical feet in one run. Here runs are so long that halfway down you need a break—which you'll find at a little chalet restaurant in the middle of nowhere, where the views are as exhilarating as the schnapps that's so often the drink of choice.

These are pure white mountains, too, whiter than we're used to. In the Alps, the tree line is low, often only 6,000 feet above sea level, and many ski areas stretch upward from there. The skier's playing field is white on white; marked pistes are white rivers of groomed snow snaking down equally white but ungroomed flanks of Alpine peaks. There are more treeless bowls than you can hope to ski in several skiers' lifetimes.

When European skiers tell you that the western Alps are higher and more glaciated, more likely to have good snow in a dry year, and that the eastern Alps are lower in elevation but full of charm, with more intimate, more richly decorated villages, they are usually referring to the difference between the French Alps and Austria. In fact, they could just as well be talking about the mountains and ski resorts of southwest Switzerland versus those of eastern Switzerland, Graubünden, and the Engadine; for Switzerland, with its many cantons, is a microcosm that mirrors the diversity of skiing all across the greater Alps. You can test your credit card limits at the Palace Hotel in worldly St. Moritz, ride the cog railways of modest Kleine Scheidegg, or ponder the hearty existence of mountain farmers among the peaks of Valais—but always, the local mountain culture will be part of your ski experience.

As varied as the regions are the people who ski them. The ski pistes of Switzerland are the polyglot crossroads of Europe, where stylish Parisians in neon outfits rub elbows with Brits in navy blue, Munich businessmen in Bogner suits, and Swedish students with punk haircuts. And yet, when you're surrounded by mountains that will outlast fashions, lifetimes, and languages, such differences fade, and the mountains are all you can see.

We walk uphill through knee-deep powder toward the summit of the Allalinhorn—the friendliest of Canton Wallis's many 13,120-foot peaks. Early-morning sunshine rakes the corniced ridges around us; the village of Saas-Fee still hides in shadow below. With climbing skins glued to the bottom of our skis, we've shuffled up the Feegletscher to earn a morning's bliss in deep untracked snow. This glacier highway is taking us above the domain of passes and ski lifts and groomed slopes, into a world of icy north walls, pure knife-edge ridges, undulating mile-long coverlets of fresh powder, summits of whipped meringue, and snow crystals sparkling at our feet. Munching cheese and chocolate as we climb, thinking that we must look like silhouettes in one of Herbert Matter's prewar Swiss travel posters, breathing deeply, climbing slowly, we daydream our way to the top. Our tracks, like zippers in the snow, stretch up to a vanishing point in the midnight-blue sky above.

* * *

IT'S A SOFT APRIL MORNING AT LES DIABLERETS, a ski area on the frontier between francophone Vaud and the German canton of Bern. It's already 11 AM and the frozen corn snow is only now softening up on the wide glacier beneath the dark, thumblike peak of the Oldenhorn. From the topmost lift we can see west toward Lake Geneva, south toward the giant peaks of the Valais, and northeast toward the dark brooding peaks of the Berner Oberland. An observation deck on the roof of the Alps reveals mountains filling space to its farthest corners, to the hazy horizon. On the deep valley flanks below Les Diablerets, winding west toward the Rhône Valley, the slopes are greening up with no respect for commonsense color—pastures of eye-dazzling kelly green under dark forests and crags. Only a few miles away, down the eastern German-speaking side of the mountains, the chic resort of Gstaad seems deserted; its jet-set winter guests have already hung up their skis and headed for the Mediterranean. The mountains are ours for a day.

At the top of the lift we break through the clouds. A sea of fog fills the Rhône Valley below us, a fluffy false plain, punctured only by snowy peaks, stretching to the horizon. Somewhere under these clouds is Lake Geneva, and far across, Les Dents du Midi ("The Teeth of Noon") rise out of the clouds like ice-sheathed knuckles. Villars-Gryon is a ski resort so small most American skiers have never heard of it, even though it's bigger than half the ski areas in Colorado. Alone, we ski along the edge of the piste, where the slope steepens and drops away in a succession of rocky ledges. Just over the border that separates the skier's world from the mountaineer's, we see a lone ibex, posing on a rock outcrop against the clouds, scimitar-shape horns swept back in wide twin arcs. We christie to a stop, stand in awe wishing we had cameras, and realize eventually that the ibex is not going to bolt. These are its Alps, its domain; we are the newcomers, birds of passage, intruders. It feels like a privilege to share the roof of Europe with this ibex, a privilege that our Swiss hosts have slowly earned over 700 years by farming basically unfarmable mountainsides, by making this land their domain. We push off, the cold snow squeaking under our skis. Behind our backs the ibex still stares off into the distance.

These images stay with me, indelible as the Alps themselves. Say the word *Switzerland* and I see the gentle slopes of the Plateau Rosa above Zermatt, perforated by the dotted lines of T-bars, peppered with tiny bright-color skiers, slopes lapping in white waves against the base of the Matterhorn. Near St. Moritz I see the blue-green crevasses of the Morteratsch Glacier, a frozen white-water rapid, spilling down from the ski area.

That Switzerland has some of the best skiing in the world goes without saying. In the end, though, it's not the skiing I remember, or the runs. It's the mountains I remember. And so will you.

—Lito Tejada-Flores

BOOKS & MOVIES

Books

Wilhelm Tell, by Friedrich von Schiller, is the definitive stage version of the dramatic legend. "The Prisoner of Chillon," by Lord Byron, is an epic poem inspired by the sojourn of François Bonivard in the dungeon of Chillon. *A Tramp Abroad,* by Mark Twain, includes the author's personal impressions—and tall tales—derived from travels in Switzerland. *Arms and the Man,* by G. B. Shaw, was the source of Oscar Straus's Viennese operetta *The Chocolate Soldier;* both are about a Swiss mercenary with a sweet tooth.

Novels set at least partially in Switzerland include *Daisy Miller,* by Henry James (Lac Léman, Chillon); *Tender Is the Night,* by F. Scott Fitzgerald; *A Farewell to Arms,* by Ernest Hemingway; Thomas Mann's *The Magic Mountain* (Davos); Albert Cohen's *Belle du Seigneur* (Geneva); *Hotel du Lac,* by Anita Brookner (Vevey); Katharine Weber's *Objects in Mirror Are Closer Than They Appear* (Geneva); John le Carré's *The Night Manager* (Zürich); and Patricia Highsmith's *Small g: A Summer Idyll* (Zürich). A couple of fine contemporary Swiss authors, whose works reflect 20th-century Switzerland and are found in good English translations, are Max Frisch (*I'm Not Stiller*) and Friedrich Dürrenmatt (*End of the Game* and *The Visit*).

The best-known children's book set in Switzerland is, of course, *Heidi,* by Johanna Spyri (Maienfeld). Newbery Medal–winning *The Apple and the Arrow,* by Mary and Conrad Buff, tells the story of Wilhelm Tell from the point of view of his son. *Banner in the Sky,* by James Ramsey Ullman, is a powerful children's book about a boy's attempt to climb Switzerland's most challenging mountain.

La Place de la Concorde Suisse, by John McPhee, was developed from a series of *New Yorker* pieces the author wrote after traveling with members of the Swiss army.

Heidi's Alp, by Christine Hardyment, a first-person account of a family traveling in a camper-van in search of the Europe of fairy tales, includes an adventure with a latter-day alm-uncle in a cabin above Maienfeld. *Terminal,* by Colin Forbes, is a murder-mystery tale with fantastic descriptions of Swiss cities.

There's no shortage of spellbinding mountain-climbing accounts. In *The Climb Up to Hell,* Jack Olsen details the dramatic 1957 Eiger expedition. Heinrich Harrer's *The White Spider: The Classic Account of the Ascent of the Eiger,* covering his successful 1938 ascent, was recently reprinted. *A Guide to Zermatt and the Matterhorn,* Edward Whymper's memoirs of his disastrous climb up the Matterhorn, is out of print, but it may be available in a library (excerpts appear in this guide's chapter on the Valais).

Movies

Heidi is undoubtedly the best-known film to be shot in Switzerland. Make sure you see the 1937 version directed by Allan Dulan, starring Shirley Temple (most filmed on Hollywood backlots). Swiss air must agree with James Bond; several films have Swiss scenes in them, including *Goldfinger* (1964) and *Goldeneye* (1995); *On Her Majesty's Secret Service* (1969) shows dazzling ski scenes of the Schilthorn in central Switzerland. You can also get glimpses of Swiss scenery in the 1994 version of *Frankenstein. Trois Couleurs Rouge (Three Colors Red),* the last in director Krzysztof Kieslowski's trilogy, and a big hit in Europe, is set in Geneva's Old Town, and Peter Greenaway's 1993 *Stairs* shows Geneva through the director's unique artistic vision. Gstaad and its Palace Hotel are featured in Peter Sellers's *Return of the Pink Panther.* The ultimate Swiss film? *The Eiger Sanction,* the Clint Eastwood thriller from 1975 , filmed all over the Bernese Oberland.

VOCABULARY

	English	French	Pronunciation
Basics			
	Yes/no	Oui/non	wee/no
	Please	S'il vous plaît	seel voo **play**
	Thank you	Merci	mare-**see**
	You're welcome	De rien	deh ree-**enh**
	Excuse me	Pardon	pahr-**doan**
	Hello	Bonjour	bohn-**zhoor**
	Goodbye	Au revoir	o ruh-**vwahr**
Numbers			
	One	Un	un
	Two	Deux	deuh
	Three	Trois	twa
	Four	Quatre	**cat**-ruh
	Five	Cinq	sank
	Six	Six	seess
	Seven	Sept	set
	Eight	Huit	weat
	Nine	Neuf	nuf
	Ten	Dix	deess
Days			
	Today	Aujourd'hui	o-zhoor-**dwee**
	Tomorrow	Demain	deh-**menh**
	Yesterday	Hier	yair
	Morning	Matin	ma-**tenh**
	Afternoon	Après-midi	ah-pray-mee-**dee**
	Night	Nuit	nwee
	Monday	Lundi	**lahn**-dee
	Tuesday	Mardi	**mahr**-dee
	Wednesday	Mercredi	**mare**-kruh-dee
	Thursday	Jeudi	**juh**-dee
	Friday	Vendredi	**vawn**-dra-dee
	Saturday	Samedi	**sam**-dee
	Sunday	Dimanche	**dee**-mawnsh

*Prevalent Swiss-German dialect

German	German Pronunciation	Italian	Italian Pronunciation
Ja/nein	yah/nine	Sí/No	see/no
Bitte	**bit**-uh	Per favore	pear fa-**voh**-reh
Danke	**dahn**-kuh	Grazie	**grah**-tsee-ay
Bitte schön	**bit**-uh **shern**	Prego	**pray**-go
Entschuldigen Sie *Äxgüsi	ent-**shool**-de-gen-zee **ax**-scu-see	Scusi	**skoo**-zee
Guten Tag *Grüezi *Grüss Gott	**goot**-en **tahk** **grit**-zee groos got	Buon giorno	bwohn **jyohr**-noh
Auf Widersehen *Ufwiederluege *Tschüss (*familiar*)	Auf **vee-der**-zane oof-**vee-der**-lawgah choohs	Arrivederci	a-ree-vah-**dare**-chee
Eins	eints	Uno	**oo**-no
Zwei	tsvai	Due	**doo**-ay
Drei	dry	Tre	tray
Vier	fear	Quattro	**kwah**-troh
Fünf	fumph	Cinque	**cheen**-kway
Sechs	zex	Sei	say
Sieben	**zee**-ben	Sette	**set**-ay
Acht	ahkt	Otto	**oh**-to
Neun	noyn	Nove	**no**-vay
Zehn	tsane	Dieci	dee-**eh**-chee
Huete	**hoi**-tah	Oggi	**oh**-jee
Morgen	**more**-gehn	Domani	do-**mah**-nee
Gestern	geh-**shtairn**	Ieri	ee-veh-ree
Morgen	**more**-gehn	Mattina	ma-**tee**-na
Nachmittag	nahkt-**mit**-ahk	Pomeriggio	po-mer-**ee**-jo
Nacht	nahkt	Notte	Noh-teh
Montag	**mohn**-tahk	Lunedì	**loo**-neh-dee
Dienstag	**deens**-tahk	Martedì	**mahr**-teh-dee
Mittwoch	**mit**-vohk	Mercoledì	**mare**-co-leh-dee
Donnerstag	**doe**-ners-tahk	Giovedì	**jo**-veh-dee
Freitag	**fry**-tahk	Venerdì	**ven**-air-dee
Samstag	**zahm**-stahk	Sabato	**sah**-ba-toe
Sonntag	**zon**-tahk	La Domenica	lah doe-**men**-ee-ca

	English	French	French Pronunciation

Useful Phrases

	English	French	French Pronunciation
	Do you speak English?	Parlez-vous anglais?	par-lay-vooz awng-**gleh**
	I don't speak French/German/Italian.	Je ne parle pas français.	juh nuh parl pah fraun-**seh**
	I don't understand.	Je ne comprends pas.	juh nuh kohm-prawhn **pah**
	I don't know.	Je ne sais pas.	juh nuh say **pah**
	I am American/British.	Je suis américain/anglais	jhu sweez a-may-ree-**can**/awn-**glay**
	I am sick.	Je suis malade.	juh swee ma-**lahd**
	Please call a doctor.	Appelez un docteur s'il vous plâit.	a-pe-lay uhn dohk-**tore** seel voo **play**
	Have you any rooms?	Est-ce que vous avez une chambre?	Ehskuh vooz ah-vay-oon **shahm**-br
	How much does it cost?	C'est combien?	say comb-bee-**enh**
	Do you accept . . . (credit card)	Est-ce que vous acceptez . . .	Ehskuh voo zahksehptay . . .
	Too expensive	Trop cher	troh **shehr**
	It's beautiful.	C'est très beau.	say tray boh
	Help!	Au secours!	o say-**koor**
	Stop!	Arrêtez!	a-ruh-**tay**

Getting Around

	English	French	French Pronunciation
	Where is . . .	C'est où . . .	say oo
	The train station?	la gare?	la gahr
	The post office?	la poste?	la pohst
	The hospital?	l'hôpital?	lo-pee-**tahl**
	Where are the restrooms?	Où sont les toilettes?	oo sohn lay **twah**-let
	Left	A gauche	a **gohsh**
	Right	À droite	a **drwat**
	Straight ahead	Tout droit	**too drwat**

Dining Out

	English	French	French Pronunciation
	Waiter/Waitress	Monsieur/Mademoiselle	muh-**syuh**/mad-mwa-**zel**
	Please give me . . .	S'il vous plait, donnez-moi . . .	see voo **play** doh nay **mwah**

*Prevalent Swiss-German dialect

German	German Pronunciation	Italian	Italian Pronunciation
Sprechen Sie Englisch?	Shprek-hun zee **eng**-glish	Parla inglese?	**par**-la een **glay**-zay
Ich sprech kein Deutsch.	ihkh **shprek**-uh kine doych	Non parlo italiano.	non **par**-lo ee-tal-**yah**-no
Ich verstehe nicht.	ihkh fehr-**stay**-eh nikht	Non capisco.	non ka-**peess**-ko
Ich habe keine Ahnung.	ihkh hah-beh kine-eh **ah**-nung	Non lo so.	non lo **so**
Ich bin Amerikaner(in). Engländer(in).	ihkh bin a-mer-i **kah**-ner(in)/**eng**-glan-der(in)	Sono americano(a)/ Sono inglese.	**so**-no a-may-ree-**kah**-no(a)/**so**-no een-**glay**-zay
Ich bin krank.	ihkh bin **krahnk**	Sto male.	sto **ma**-lay
Bitte rufen einen Arzt.	**bit**-uh **roof**-en ine-en **ahrtst**	Chiami un dottore per favore.	kee-**ah**-mee oon doe-**toe**-ray pear fah-**voh**-reh
Haben sie ein Zimmer?	**Ha**-ben zee ine **tsimmer**	C'e una camera libera?	chay **oo**-nah **cam**-er-ah **lee**-ber-eh
Wieviel kostet das?	**vee**-feel **cost**-et dahs	Quanto costa?	**kwahn**-toe-**coast**-a
Nehmen Sie . . .	**nay**-men zee . . .	Posso pagare . . .	**pohs**-soh pah-**gah**-reh . . .
Es kostet zu viel.	es **cost**-et tsu feel	Troppo caro	**troh**-poh **cah**-roh
Das ist schön.	dahs is **shern**	É bello(a).	eh **bell**-oh
Hilfe!	**hilf**-uh	Aiuto!	a-**yoo**-toe
Halt!	hahlt	Alt!	ahlt

Wo ist . . .	**vo** ist	Dov'è . . .	doe-**veh**
Der Bahnhof?	dare **bahn**-hof	la stazione?	la sta-tsee-**oh**-nay
Die Post?	dee **post**	l'ufficio postale?	loo-**fee**-cho po-**sta**-lay
Das Krankenhaus? *Das Spital?	dahs **krahnk**-en-house dahs shpee-**tahl**	l'ospedale?	lo-spay-**dah**-lay
Wo ist die Toilette?	vo ist dee twah-**let**-uh	Dov'è il bagno?	doe-**vay** eel**bahn**-yo
Links	links	a sinistra	a see-**neess**-tra
Rechts	rechts	a destra	a-**des**-tra
geradeaus	geh-**rod**-uh ouse	Avanti dritto	a-**vahn**-tee **dree**-to

Herr Ober/ Fraülein	hehr **oh**-ber **froy**-line	Cameriere(a)	kah-meh-**ryeh**-reh(rah)
Bitte geben sie mir . . .	**bit**-uh gay behn zee-**meer**	Mi dia pear-fah-**voh**-reh . . .	mee **dee**-a

English	French	French Pronunciation
The menu	La carte	la cart
The bill/check	L'addition	la-dee-see-**ohn**
A fork	Une fourchette	ewn four-**shet**
A knife	Un couteau	uhn koo-**toe**
A spoon	Une cuillère	ewn kwee-**air**
A napkin	Une serviette	ewn sair-vee-**et**
Bread	Du pain	due penh
Butter	Du beurre	due bur
Milk	Du lait	due lay
Pepper	Du poivre	due **pwah**-vruh
Salt	Du sel	due sell
Sugar	Du sucre	due **sook**-ruh
Coffee	Un café	uhn kahfay
Tea	Un thé	uhn tay
Mineral water *carbonated/still*	De l'eau minéral *gazeuse/non gazeuse*	duh loh meenehrahl gahzuhz/noh(n) gahzuhz
Wine	Vin	venh
Cheers!	A votre santé!	ah vo-truh sahn-**tay**

German	German Pronunciation	Italian	Italian Pronunciation
Die speisekarte	dee **shpie**-zeh-car-tuh	Il menù	eel may-**noo**
Die Rechnung	dee **rekh**-nung	Il conto	eel **cone**-toe
Eine Gabel	**ine**-eh-**gah**-buhl	Una forchetta	oona for-**ket**-a
Ein messer	I-nuh-**mess**-ehr	Un coltello	oon kol-**tel**-o
Einen Löffel	I-nen **ler**-fuhl	Un cucchiaio	oon koo-kee-**ah-yo**
Die Serviette	dee zair-vee-**eh**-tuh	Il tovagliolo	eel toe-va-lee-**oh-lo**
Brot	broht	Il pane	eel **pa**-nay
Butter	**boo**-tehr	Il burro	eel **boo**-roh
Milch	meelch	Il latte	eel **lot**-ay
Pfeffer	**fef**-fehr	Il pepe	eel **pay**-pay
Salz	zahlts	Il sale	eel **sah**-lay
Zucker	**tsoo**-kher	Lo zucchero	loh **tsoo**-ker-o
eine Kaffee	**ine**-eh **kah**-feh	un caffè	oon kahf-**feh**
einen Tee	**ine**-en tay	un tè	oon teh
Mineral wasser *mit gas/ohne gas*	mi-neh-**raal**-**vahs**-sehr mit gahz/**oh**-nuh gahz	L'acqua minerale *gassata/naturale*	l'ah kwa mee-neh-**rah**-leh gahs-**sah**-tah/ nah-too-**rah**-leh
Wein	vine	Il vino	eel **vee**-noh
Zum Wohl! *Proscht	zoom vole prosht	Salute!	sah-**loo**-teh

Switzerland Essentials

PLANNING TOOLS, EXPERT INSIGHT, GREAT CONTACTS

There are planners, and there are those who fly by the seat of their pants. We happily place ourselves among the planners. Our writers and editors try to anticipate all the issues you may face before and during any journey, and then they do their research. This section is the product of their efforts. Use it to get excited about your trip to Switzerland, to inform your travel planning, or to guide you on the road should the seat of your pants start to feel threadbare.

GETTING STARTED

We're really proud of our Web site: Fodors. com is a great place to begin any journey. Scan Travel Wire for suggested itineraries, travel deals, restaurant and hotel openings, and other up-to-the-minute info. Check out Booking to research prices and book plane tickets, hotel rooms, rental cars, and vacation packages. Head to Talk for on-the-ground pointers from travelers who frequent our message boards. You can also link to loads of other travel-related resources.

▌RESOURCES

ONLINE TRAVEL TOOLS

When it comes to Switzerland Web sites, the best is **Switzerland Tourism** (⊕ www. myswitzerland.com), which allows travelers to customize a vacation in Switzerland and even to book it through an interactive travel planner.

All About Switzerland **Go Ski** ⊕ www.goski. com lists the country's top resorts and hosts a skiing-focused forum. **Great Outdoor Recreation Pages** (GORP) ⊕ www.gorp.com has information on trekking and walking in the Alps. **Pro Helvetia** ⊕ www.pro-helvetia.ch, a Swiss arts group, promotes arts events and publishes books and brochures on all aspects of Swiss cultural life. The **Swiss Broadcasting Corporation** ⊕ www.swissinfo.org highlights top news stories involving Switzerland. **Swissart Network** ⊕ www.swissart.ch has links to several museums, city art associations, and galleries; some information is in English. **Swissworld** ⊕ www.swissworld.org posts general information on a host of topics ranging from politics to Christmas carols.

Currency Conversion **Google** ⊕ www. google.com does currency conversion. Just type in the amount you want to convert and an explanation of how you want it converted (e.g., "14 Swiss francs in dollars"), and then voilà. **Oanda.com** ⊕ www.oanda.com also allows you to print out a handy table with the current day's conversion rates. **XE.com** ⊕ www.xe.com is a good currency conversion Web site.

Safety **Transportation Security Administration** (TSA) ⊕ www.tsa.gov.

Time Zones **Timeanddate.com** ⊕ www. timeanddate.com/worldclock can help you figure out the correct time anywhere in the world.

Weather **Accuweather.com** ⊕ www. accuweather.com is an independent weather-forecasting service with especially good coverage of hurricanes. **Weather.com** ⊕ www. weather.com is the Web site for the Weather Channel.

VISITOR INFORMATION

U.S. (nationwide) ☎ 212/757–5944 🖷 212/ 262–6116 ⊕ www.myswitzerland.com. **Anglo-Phone** ☎ 0900/576444 is an English-language information service giving details on hotels, restaurants, museums, nightlife, skiing, what to do in an emergency, and more. Lines are open weekdays 9–noon and 2–7. Calls cost 3.13 SF per minute.

▌THINGS TO CONSIDER

GEAR

In most of Switzerland the dress is casual. City dress is more formal. Men would be wise to pack a jacket and tie if dining in some of the expensive restaurants, even in mountain resorts; otherwise, a tie and sweater are standard at night. Women wear skirts more frequently here than in the United States, though anything fashionable is fine. Except at the most chic hotels in international resorts, you won't need formal evening dress.

Even in July and August the evening air grows chilly in the mountains, so bring a warm sweater. And take along a hat or sunscreen, as the atmosphere is thinner at high altitudes. Glaciers can be blinding in the sun, so be sure to bring sunglasses, which should have side shields especially for high-altitude hiking or skiing. Good walking shoes or hiking boots are a must, whether you're tackling medieval cobblestones or mountain trails.

To ensure comfort, budget travelers should bring their own washcloth and soap, not always standard in one- and two-star-rated Swiss hotels. If you're planning on shopping and cooking, a tote bag will come in handy: most groceries do not provide sacks, but sturdy, reusable plastic totes can be bought at checkout. Coin-operated laundries are rare, so laundry soap is useful for hand washing.

PASSPORTS

Australian, British, Canadian, New Zealand, and U.S. citizens need only a valid passport to enter Switzerland for stays of up to 90 days.

PASSPORTS

■ TIP→ Before your trip, make two copies of your passport's data page (one for someone at home and another for you to carry separately). Or scan the page and e-mail it to some-

one at home and/or yourself. The cost to apply for a new passport is $97 for adults, $82 for children under 16; renewals are $67. Allow six weeks for processing, both for first-time passports and renewals. For an expediting fee of $60 you can reduce this time to about two weeks. If your trip is less than two weeks away, you can get a passport even more rapidly by going to a passport office with the necessary documentation. Private expediters can get things done in as little as 48 hours, but charge hefty fees for their services.

U.S. Passport Information **U.S. Department of State** ☎ 877/487-2778 ⊕ http://travel.state.gov/passport.

BOOKING YOUR TRIP

Unless your cousin is a travel agent, you're probably among the millions of people who make most of their travel arrangements online. But have you ever wondered just what the differences are between an online travel agent (a Web site through which you make reservations instead of going directly to the airline, hotel, or car-rental company), a discounter (a firm that does a high volume of business with a hotel chain or airline and accordingly gets good prices), a wholesaler (one that makes cheap reservations in bulk and then resells them to people like you), and an aggregator (one that compares all the offerings so you don't have to)? Is it truly better to book directly on an airline or hotel Web site? And when does a real live travel agent come in handy?

ONLINE

You really have to shop around. A travel wholesaler such as Hotels.com or Hotel-Club.net can be a source of good rates, as can discounters such as Hotwire or Priceline, particularly if you can bid for your hotel room or airfare. Indeed, such sites sometimes have deals that are unavailable elsewhere. They do, however, tend to work only with hotel chains (which makes them just plain useless for getting hotel reservations outside of major cities) or big airlines (so that often leaves out upstarts like jetBlue and some foreign carriers like Air India). Also, with discounters and wholesalers you must generally prepay, and everything is nonrefundable. And before you fork over the dough, be sure to check the terms and conditions, so you know what a given company will do for you if there's a problem and what you'll have to deal with on your own.

■ TIP→ To be absolutely sure everything was processed correctly, confirm reservations made through online travel agents, discounters, and wholesalers directly with your hotel before leaving home.

Booking engines like Expedia, Travelocity, and Orbitz are actually travel agents, albeit high-volume, online ones. And airline travel packagers like American Airlines Vacations and Virgin Vacations—well, they're travel agents, too. But they may still not work with all the world's hotels.

An aggregator site will search many sites and pull the best prices for airfares, hotels, and rental cars from them. Most aggregators compare the major travel-booking sites such as Expedia, Travelocity, and Orbitz; some also look at airline Web sites, though rarely the sites of smaller budget airlines. Some aggregators also compare other travel products, including complex packages—a good thing, as you can sometimes get the best overall deal by booking an air-and-hotel package.

WITH A TRAVEL AGENT

If you use an agent—brick-and-mortar or virtual—you'll pay a fee for the service. And know that the service you get from some online agents isn't comprehensive. For example Expedia and Travelocity don't search for prices on budget airlines like jetBlue, Southwest, or small foreign carriers. That said, some agents (online or not) *do* have access to fares that are difficult to find otherwise, and the savings can more than make up for any surcharge.

A knowledgeable brick-and-mortar travel agent can be a godsend if you're booking a cruise, a package trip that's not available to you directly, an air pass, or a complicated itinerary including several overseas flights. What's more, travel agents that specialize in a destination may have exclusive access to certain deals and insider information on things such as charter flights. Agents who specialize in types of travelers (senior citizens, gays and lesbians, naturists) or types of trips (cruises, luxury travel, safaris) can also be invaluable.

■ TIP→ Remember that Expedia, Travelocity, and Orbitz are travel agents, not just booking engines. To resolve any problems with a reservation made through these companies, contact them first.

Agent Resources American Society of Travel Agents ☎ 703/739-2782 ⊕ www.travelsense. org.

■ ACCOMMODATIONS

The lodgings we list are the cream of the crop in each price category. We always list the facilities available—but we don't specify whether they cost extra: when pricing accommodations, always ask what's in-

cluded and what costs extra. In addition, assume that all rooms have a private bath unless otherwise noted. Properties indicated by an ✕▥ are lodging establishments whose restaurant warrants a special trip (and will accommodate nonhotel guests). Price charts appear in the planner section of each chapter introduction.

Switzerland is as famous for its hotels as it is for its mountains, watches, and chocolates; its standards in hospitality are extremely high. Rooms are impeccably clean and well maintained, and they are fur-

Online Booking Resources

BOOKING ENGINES		
Cheap Tickets	www.cheaptickets.com	discounter.
Expedia	www.expedia.com	large online agency that charges a booking fee for airline tickets.
Hotwire	www.hotwire.com	discounter.
lastminute.com	www.lastminute.com	specializes in last-minute travel; the main site is for the U.K., but it has a link to a U.S. site.
Luxury Link	www.luxurylink.com	has auctions (surprisingly good deals) as well as offers on the high-end side of travel.
Onetravel.com	www.onetravel.com	discounter for hotels, car rentals, airfares, and packages.
Orbitz	www.orbitz.com	charges a booking fee for airline tickets, but gives a clear breakdown of fees and taxes before you book.
Priceline.com	www.priceline.com	discounter that also allows bidding.
Travel.com	www.travel.com	allows you to compare its rates with those of other booking engines.
Travelocity	www.travelocity.com	charges a booking fee for airline tickets, but promises good problem resolution.
ONLINE ACCOMMODATIONS		
Hotelbook.com	www.hotelbook.com	focuses on independent hotels worldwide.
Hotel Club	www.hotelclub.net	good for major cities worldwide.
Hotels.com	www.hotels.com	big Expedia-owned wholesaler that offers rooms in hotels all over the world.
Quikbook	www.quikbook.com	offers "pay when you stay" reservations that allow you to settle your bill when you check out, not when you book.

nished with comforts ranging from the simplest to the most deluxe. Prices are accordingly high: you will pay more for minimal comforts here than in any other European country. Americans accustomed to spacious motels with two double beds, a color TV, and a bath-shower combination may be disappointed in their first venture into the legendary Swiss hotel: spaces are small, bathtubs cost extra, and single rooms may have single beds. What you're paying for is service, reliability, cleanliness, and a complex hierarchy of amenities you may not even know you need.

Where no address is provided in the hotel listings, none is necessary: in smaller towns and villages, a postal code is all you need. To find the hotel on arrival, watch for the official street signs pointing the way to every hotel that belongs to the local tourist association.

Some things to bear in mind when you check in: the standard double room in Switzerland has two prim beds built together, with separate linens and, sometimes, sheets tucked firmly down the middle. If you prefer more sociable arrangements, ask for a "French bed," or *lit matrimonial*—that will get you a single-mattress double. Some hotels may offer extra beds—for example, to expand a double room to a triple. Also note that air-conditioning is not as prevalent as in the United States; evenings are generally cool, so Alpine air often stands in for air-conditioning. Unfortunately, global warming has had a real impact in Europe and you may discover that even early October can prove hot and sticky in Switzerland; if this poses a major problem for you, spend the extra money to book at a hotel that offers air-conditioning (and, ipso facto, also be sure it will be functioning during the time you are at the hotel).

Most hotels in Switzerland allow children under a certain age to stay in their parents' room at no extra charge, but others charge for them as extra adults; be sure to find out the cutoff age for children's discounts. The Swiss Hotel Association (⇨ Hotels, *below*) has listings of family-friendly hotels throughout the country. Supervised playrooms are available in some of the better hotels, and many winter resorts provide lists of reliable babysitters. For recommended local sitters, check with your hotel.

Particularly in ski resorts or in hotels where you'll be staying for three days or more, you may be quoted a room price per person including *demipension* (half board). This means you've opted for breakfast included and to eat either lunch or dinner in the hotel, selecting from a limited, fixed menu. Unless you're holding out for gastronomic adventure, your best bet is to take half board. Most hotels will be flexible if you come in from the slopes craving a steaming pot of fondue, and they will then subtract the day's pension supplement from your room price, charging you à la carte instead.

Price charts are based on the cost of a standard double room during peak season, including tax, service, and breakfast only. Note that a hotel's prices may vary widely during the rest of the year and that the half board available at many hotels, for only slightly more than our listed room cost, significantly increases the value of these hotel stays. When comparing lodging options, check the hotels' low season rates and meal plans.

Most hotels and other lodgings require you to give your credit-card details before they will confirm your reservation. If you don't feel comfortable e-mailing this information, ask if you can fax it (some places even prefer faxes). However you book, get confirmation in writing and have a copy of it handy when you check in.

Be sure you understand the hotel's cancellation policy. Some places allow you to cancel without any kind of penalty—even if you prepaid to secure a discounted rate—if you cancel at least 24 hours in advance. Others require you to cancel a week in advance or penalize you the cost of one night. Small inns and B&Bs are most likely to require you to cancel far in advance.

■ TIP➔ Assume that hotels operate on the European Plan (**EP**, no meals) unless we specify that they use the Breakfast Plan (**BP**, with full breakfast), Continental Plan (**CP**, continental breakfast), Full American Plan (**FAP**, all meals), Modified American Plan (**MAP**, breakfast and dinner) or are **all-inclusive** (**AI**, all meals and most activities).

BED & BREAKFASTS

You can order brochures and get information about B&Bs from the user-friendly site of Bed & Breakfast Switzerland, ⊕ www.bnb.ch. You can make reservations online through the site.

FARM STAYS

An unusual option for families seeking the local experience: stay on a farm with a Swiss family, complete with children, animals, and the option to work in the fields. Participating farm families register with the Schweizerischer Bauernverband (Swiss Farmers Association), listing the birth dates of their children, rooms and facilities, and types of animals your children can see. Prices are often considerably lower than those of hotels and vacation flats. You should be reasonably fluent in French or German, depending on the region of your stay. More information is available through Switzerland Tourism.

Organizations Schweizerischer Bauernverband (Swiss Farmers Association) ✉ Laurstr. 10, CH-5200 Brugg ☎ 056/4625111 🖷 056/4415348. **Verein Ferien auf dem Bauernhof** (Swiss Holiday Farms Association) ✉ Feierlenhof, CH-8595 Altnau ☎ 071/6952372 🖷 071/6952367 ⊕ www.bauernhof-ferien.ch.

HOTELS

When selecting a place to stay, an important resource can be the Swiss Hotel Association (SHA), a rigorous and demanding organization that maintains a specific rating system for lodging standards. Four

out of five Swiss hotels belong to this group and take their stars seriously. In contrast to more casual European countries, stars in Switzerland have precise meaning: a five-star hotel is required to have a specific staff–guest ratio, a daily change of bed linens, and extended hours for room service. In contrast, a two-star hotel must have telephones in the rooms, soap in the bathrooms, and fabric tablecloths in the restaurant. But the SHA standards cannot control the quality of the decor and the grace of service. Thus you may find a five-star hotel that meets the technical requirements but has shabby appointments, leaky plumbing, or a rude concierge, or a good, family-run two-star pension that makes you feel like royalty.

Some rules of thumb: if you are looking for American-style chain-motel comfort—a big bed, color TV, minibar, safe—you will probably be happiest in four-star business-class hotels. A number of four-star hotels in Switzerland are part of the Best Western chain. If you are looking for regional atmosphere, family ownership (and the pride and care for details that implies), and moderate prices, but don't care about a TV or minibar, look for three stars: nearly all such rooms have showers and toilets. Two stars will get you tidy, minimal comfort with about a third of the rooms having private toilet and bathing facilities. One-star properties are rare: they have only shared facilities and no phone available in-house and generally fall below the demanding Swiss national standard. Several hotels in the SHA are specially rated *Landgasthof* or *relais de campagne,* meaning "country inn." These generally are rustic-style lodgings typical of the region, but they may range from spare to luxurious and are rarely set apart in deep country; some are in the midst of small market towns or resorts. The SHA distinguishes them as offering especially high-quality service, personal attention, and parking.

Many hotels close for a short period during their region's off-season. Closing dates often vary from year to year, so be sure to call ahead and check.

A few useful phrases in French, German, and Italian: a room with a bath (*une chambre avec salle de bain, ein Zimmer mit Bad, una camera con bagno*; a room with a view (*une chambre avec vue, ein Zimmer mit Aussicht, una camera con vista*); a quiet room (*une chambre calme, ein ruhiges Zimmer, una camera tranquilla*).
Swiss Hotel Association ✉ Monbijoustr. 130, CH-3001 Bern ☎ 031/3704111 ⊕ www. swisshotels.ch.

INNS

Travelers on a budget can find help from the *Check-in E & G Hotels* guide (E & G stands for *einfach und gemütlich*: roughly, "simple and cozy"), available through Switzerland Tourism. These comfortable little hotels have banded together to dispel Switzerland's intimidating image as an elite, overpriced vacation spot and offer simple two-star standards in usually very atmospheric inns.

Other organizations can help you find unusual properties: the Relais & Châteaux group seeks out manor houses, historic buildings, and generally atmospheric luxury, with most of its properties falling into the $$$ or $$$$ range. A similar group, Romantik Hotels and Restaurants, combines architectural interest, historic atmosphere, and fine regional food. Relais du Silence hotels are usually isolated in a peaceful, natural setting, with first-class comforts.
Organization Contacts Relais & Châteaux ✉ 15 rue Galvani, 75017 Paris, France ☎ 33/1/45-72-90-00 ⊕ www.relaischateaux.ch. **Relais du Silence** ✉ 17 rue d'Ouessant, 75015 Paris, France ☎ 33/1/44-49-90-00 ⊕ www. silencehotel.com. **Romantik Hotels and Restaurants** ☎ 49/69/661-2340 ⊕ www. romantikhotels.com.

▌ AIRLINE TICKETS

Most domestic airline tickets are electronic; international tickets may be either electronic or paper. With an e-ticket the only thing you receive is an e-mailed receipt citing your itinerary and reservation and ticket numbers. The greatest advantage of an e-ticket is that if you lose your receipt, you can simply print out another copy or ask the airline to do it for you at check-in. You usually pay a surcharge (up to $50) to get a paper ticket, if you can get one at all. The sole advantage of a paper ticket is that it may be easier to endorse over to another airline if your flight is canceled and the airline with which you booked can't accommodate you on another flight.

▌ **TIP →** Discount air passes that let you travel economically in a country or region must often be purchased before you leave home. In some cases you can only get them through a travel agent.

EuropebyAir offers passes for travel that connect Basel, Geneva, and Zürich to other European destinations.
Air Pass Info EuropebyAir ☎ 888/321-4737 ⊕ www.europebyair.com.

▌ RENTAL CARS

When you reserve a car, ask about cancellation penalties, taxes, drop-off charges (if you're planning to pick up the car in one city and leave it in another), and surcharges (for being under or over a certain age, for additional drivers, or for driving across state or country borders or beyond a specific distance from your point of rental). All these things can add substantially to your costs. Request car seats and extras such as GPS when you book.

Rates are sometimes—but not always—better if you book in advance or reserve through a rental agency's Web site. There are other reasons to book ahead, though: for popular destinations, during busy times of the year, or to ensure that you get certain types of cars (vans, SUVs, exotic sports cars).

▌ **TIP →** Make sure that a confirmed reservation guarantees you a car. Agencies sometimes overbook, particularly for busy weekends and holiday periods.

If booked from overseas, rates in Zürich and Geneva begin at around $50 a day and $200 a week for an economy car with air-conditioning, a manual transmission, and unlimited mileage. This does not include the 7.6% tax on car rentals. Try to arrange for a rental before you go; rentals booked in Switzerland are considerably more expensive. European companies like Europcar and Sixt often have better deals.

Eurailpass and Europass (⇨ By Train) both offer discount passes combining rail travel and car rental.

Your own driver's license is acceptable in Switzerland, but an International Driving Permit (IDP)—available from the American and Canadian automobile associations and, in the United Kingdom, from the Automobile Association and Royal Automobile Club—is a good idea in case of emergency. In certain European countries, you may not be able to rent a car without an International Driving Permit, which can be used only in conjunction with a valid driver's license and which translates your license into 10 languages.

Check the AAA Web site for more info as well as for IDPs ($10) themselves. The minimum age is generally 20, and you must have possessed a valid driver's license for at least one year. Note that some agencies do not allow you to drive cars into Italy. In Switzerland, some rental agencies charge daily fees of about 25 SF for drivers under 25. If you wish to pay cash, agencies may request a deposit.

CAR-RENTAL INSURANCE

When driving a rental car you are generally responsible for any damage to or loss of the vehicle. Collision policies that car-rental companies sell for European rentals typically do not cover stolen vehicles. Before you rent—and purchase collision or theft coverage—see what coverage you already have under the terms of your personal auto-insurance policy and credit cards.

Car Rental Resources

LOCAL AGENCIES		
Europcar	0848/808099	www.europcar.ch.
Sixt	0848/884444	www.sixt.ch.
MAJOR AGENCIES		
Alamo	800/522-9696	www.alamo.com.
Avis	800/331-1084	www.avis.com.
Budget	800/472-3325	www.budget.com.
Hertz	800/654-3001	www.hertz.com.
National Car Rental	800/227-7368	www.nationalcar.com.
WHOLESALERS		
Auto Europe	888/223-5555	www.autoeurope.com.
Europe by Car	212/581-3040 in New York or 800/223-1516	www.europebycar.com.
Eurovacations	877/471-3876	www.eurovacations.com.
Kemwel	877/820-0668	www.kemwel.com.

TRANSPORTATION

Switzerland offers perhaps the best transit network in Europe: impeccable expressways studded with emergency phones; trams and buses snaking through city streets; steamers crisscrossing blue lakes; and, of course, the famous trains, whose wheels roll to a stop under the station clock just as the second hand sweeps to 12.

Once at the station, a web of transportation options gets you even closer to those spectacular views: cogwheel trains grind up 45-degree slopes, lifts and gondolas sail silently to vantage points, tiny Alpine Metros bore through granite up to green tundra above 8,000 feet.

Traveling by car is the surest way to penetrate the Swiss landscape, but if you invest in a rail pass, you will not feel cut off. Most Swiss trains intersect with private excursion networks and allow for comfortable sightseeing itineraries without huge layovers. And there's always a sturdy yellow postbus, following its appointed rounds at minimal cost; connections to obscure villages and trails are free to holders of the Swiss Pass.

❚ BY AIR

The entire country of Switzerland is smaller in area than the state of West Virginia, so flying from one region to another is a luxury that, considering how efficient the trains are, few travelers require—unless there's a convenient connection from your intercontinental arrival point (Geneva, Zürich) to a smaller airport (Basel, Bern, Lugano, and Sion).

In Switzerland, you will not usually need to check in more than an hour before boarding. If you are catching a connecting flight, make sure you have at least an hour to transfer, especially on Sunday in Zürich, where delays are frequent. To avoid delays at airport-security checkpoints, try not to wear any metal. Jewelry, belt and other buckles, steel-toe shoes, barrettes, and un-

derwire bras are among the items that can set off detectors. Be sure to check your airline's limit on checked and carry-on luggage; Swiss and other airlines often accept one carry-on item.

For 20 SF per bag round-trip, passengers on Swiss and partner airlines with tickets on Swiss Federal Railways can forward their luggage to their final destination, allowing them to travel unencumbered. The baggage is retrieved from the train station at the final destination. Baggage check-in and airline boarding passes can be arranged at more than 100 train stations around Switzerland. An English-language "Fly-Rail Baggage" brochure is available free of charge from the Swiss Federal Railways.

Note that Swiss and many budget airlines such as easyJet charge for food and drink during flights.

Swiss, which does not allow smoking, stocks Nicorette gum.

Flying time to Geneva or Zürich is just under 2 hours from London, 7 hours from New York, 10 hours from Chicago, 14 hours from Los Angeles, and 23 to 25 hours from Sydney.

In Switzerland, there is no longer a need to reconfirm your flight, though it won't hurt to do so. Swiss and other airlines now send electronic delay messages to passengers who provide cell phone numbers.

Airlines & Airports Airline and Airport Links.com ⊕ www.airlineandairportlinks.com has links to many of the world's airlines and airports.

Airline Security Issues Transportation Security Administration ⊕ www.tsa.gov has answers for almost every question that might come up.

AIRPORTS

The major gateways are the Unique Zürich Airport (ZRH) and Geneva's Cointrin Airport (GVA). Most Swiss flights will fly via Zürich Airport, the airline's hub. Be sure to allot yourself at least an hour to transfer to your connecting flight. Delays are especially common on Sunday. The EuroAirport near Basel is used by many airlines as a stopover. It's proximity to Basel and Zürich make it very convenient. **International Airports** Geneva: **Cointrin Airport** ☎ 022/7177111. Zürich: **Unique Zürich Airport** ☎ 043/8162211. Basel: **EuroAirport Freiburg-Basel-Mulhouse** (MLH) ☎ 0761/1200-3111 from outside Germany 0033/3899-03111 ⊕ www.euroairport.com.

Regional Airports Basel: **EuroAirport** ☎ 061/3253111. Bern: **Belp** ☎ 031/9602111. Lugano: **Aeroporto Lugano-Agno** ☎ 091/6101111. Upper Engadine: **Engadine Airport** ✉ Samedan ☎ 081/8510851.

FLIGHTS

Swiss Air Lines, the national carrier more commonly known as Swiss, flies from Boston, Chicago, Los Angeles, and New York to Zürich, as well as from New York to Geneva. Continental flies from New York to Geneva and Zürich. Swiss flies from London to Geneva and Zürich, as does British Airways. From Australia and New Zealand, connections to Switzerland are available via Frankfurt or Bangkok. Air Canada connects major Canadian cities to Basel, Geneva, and Zürich via Frankfurt or Munich. American and Delta fly from New York, Miami, and Los Angeles to Zürich.

Low-cost airlines flying into Geneva include bmi Baby (from Birmingham and other cities in the United Kingdom), easy-Jet (from London and other European cities), fly Baboo (from Lugano, Florence, Venice, Prague), flybe (from Southampton), Hapag Lloyd Express (from Cologne-Bonn), and Jet 2 (from Leeds-Bradford). If you're headed to Zürich, Helvetic (from London) and Belair (from Mediterranean islands as well as Dubrovnik and other cities) are among the low-cost carriers.

Airline Contacts Aer Lingus ☎ 0845/0844444 in U.K., 0818/365000 in Ireland, 043/2869933 in Switzerland ⊕ www.aerlingus. com. **Air Canada** ☎ 888/247-2262 ⊕ www. aircanada.com. **American Airlines** ☎ 800/433-7300 ⊕ www.aa.com. **British Airways** ☎ 0870/850-9850 in U.K. ⊕ www. britishairways.com. **Continental Airlines** ☎ 800/523-3273 for U.S. and Mexico reservations, 800/231-0856 for international reservations, 043/8009214 in Switzerland ⊕ www. continental.com. **Delta Airlines** ☎ 800/221-1212 for U.S. reservations, 800/241-4141 for international reservations ⊕ www.delta.com to Zürich. **Northwest Airlines** ☎ 800/225-2525 ⊕ www.nwa.com. **Swiss (Swiss International Air Lines)** ☎ 877/359-7947, 0848/852000 in Switzerland ⊕ www.swiss.com. **United Airlines** ☎ 800/864-8331 for U.S. reservations, 800/538-2929 for international reservations ⊕ www.united.com. **USAirways** ☎ 800/428-4322 for U.S. and Canada reservations, 800/622-1015 for international reservations ⊕ www.usairways.com.

Low-Cost Carriers Belair ☎ 043/2118120 in Switzerland ⊕ www.belair-airlines.com. **bmi Baby** ☎ 0870/264-2229 ⊕ www.bmibaby. com. **easyJet** ☎ 0870/600-0000 ⊕ www. easyjet.com. **fly Baboo** ☎ 0848/445445 in Switzerland, 0800/4454-4545 in Europe ⊕ www.flybaboo.com. **flybe** ☎ 0871/700-0535 ⊕ www.flybe.com. **Hapag Lloyd Express** ☎ 0870/606-0519 in U.K., 0848/848553 in Switzerland ⊕ www.hlx.com. **Helvetic** ☎ 0207/026-3464 in the U.K., 043/5579099 in Switzerland ⊕ www.helvetic.com. **Jet 2** ☎ 0871/226-1737 in the U.K., 0848/000016 in Switzerland ⊕ www.jet2.com.

▌ BY BOAT

All of Switzerland's larger lakes are crisscrossed by elegant steamers, some of them restored paddle steamers. Their café-restaurants serve drinks, snacks, and hot food at standard mealtimes; toilet facilities are provided. Service continues year-round but is greatly reduced in winter. Unlimited travel is free to holders of the Swiss Pass. The Swiss Card and the Flexipass (⇨ By Train) may also be used for boat travel.

Tickets can be purchased at ticket booths near the docks before departure; for some shorter boat rides, tickets are also sold at a counter on board before departure. Tourism offices usually have the latest schedules, though it may be better to check with the boat companies. Credit cards are generally accepted, as are Swiss francs and euros.

The Compagnie Générale de Navigation offers excursion boat rides on Lake Geneva for about 20 SF to 65 SF, depending on the distances covered. In the Ticino, the Navigazione Lago di Lugano and Navigazione Lago Maggiore-Bacino Svizzero run frequent daily boat trips. In Zürich, boat rides of 1½ to 7 hours are available in summer. In winter, the number of boat rides dwindles.

Compagnie Générale de Navigation ✉ Rhodanie 17, Lausanne CH-1000 ☎ 0848/811848 ⊕ www.cgn.ch. **Navigazione Lago di Lugano** ✉ Casella Postale 56, CH-6906 Lugano ☎ 091/9715223 ⊕ www.lakelugano.ch. **Navigazione Lago Maggiore-Bacino Svizzero** ✉ Lungolago Motta, CH-6600 Locarno ☎ 091/7511865 ⊕ www.navlaghi.it.

▌ BY BUS

Switzerland's famous yellow postbuses (called *Postautos* or *postcars*), with their stentorian tritone horns, link main cities with villages off the beaten track and even crawl over the highest mountain passes. Both postbuses and city buses follow posted schedules to the minute: you can set your watch by them. You can pick up a free schedule for a particular route in most postbuses; full schedules are included in train schedule books. You can also check the Swiss Post Web site. Watch for the yellow sign with the picture of a bus. Postbuses cater to hikers: walking itineraries are available at some postbus stops.

There's also a special scenic postbus route, the *Palm Express*. This route goes from St. Moritz to Lugano via the Maloja Pass. The buses run daily from mid-June through mid-October and, weather permitting, from late December through mid-June Friday to Sunday. Reservations can be made at any train station or tourist office.

The Swiss Pass (⇨ By Train) gives unlimited travel on the postbuses. You may have to pay a supplement of 5 SF to 10 SF on some of the Alpine routes; check in the timetables or ask the staff.

Be sure to ask whether reservations are required, as is the case for some Alpine pass routes.

Note that information about prices and schedules on the Swiss Post bus system are almost more readily available logging on to the main Swiss train Web site, www.sbb.ch (which covers both national train and bus systems), than to the less comprehensive Swiss Post Web site listed below.

Bus Information Swiss Post ☎ 0900/300300, 1.19 SF per min ⊕ www.swisspost.com.

▌ BY CAR

GASOLINE
If there's one thing that's generally cheaper in Switzerland than elsewhere in Western Europe, it's gasoline. If you are crossing borders, try to fill the tank in Switzerland unless you happen to be driving a diesel, which is cheaper in Austria, France, and Germany, but not Italy. Regular unleaded (*bleifrei* in German, *sans plomb* in French) gas costs just over 1.78 SF per liter. Leaded fuel is no longer available. Prices are slightly higher in mountain areas. Have some 10 SF and 20 SF notes available, as many gas stations (especially in the mountains) have vending-machine pumps that operate even when they're closed. Simply slide in a bill and fill your tank. Many of these machines also accept major credit cards with precoded PIN numbers. You can request a receipt (*Quittung* in German, *quittance* in French) from the machine.

PARKING
Parking areas are clearly marked. In blue or red zones a *disque* (provided in rental

cars or available free from banks, tourist offices, or police stations) must be placed clearly in the front window noting the time of arrival. These zones are slowly being replaced by metered-parking white zones. Each city sets its own time allotments for parking; the limits are posted. Metered parking is often paid for at communal machines that vary from city to city. Some machines simply accept coins and dispense tickets. At others you'll need to punch in your parking space or license plate number, then add coins. The ticket for parking may or may not have to be placed in your car window; this information is noted on the machine or ticket. Parking in public lots normally costs 2 SF for the first hour, increasing by 1 SF every half hour thereafter.

ROAD CONDITIONS

Swiss roads are well surfaced but when you are dealing with mountains they do wind a lot, so don't plan on achieving high average speeds. When estimating likely travel times, look carefully at the map: there may be only 32 km (20 mi) between one point and another—but there may be an Alpine pass in the way. There is a well-developed highway network, though some notable gaps still exist in the south along an east–west line, roughly between Lugano and Sion. In addition, tunnels—notably the St. Gotthard—are at times closed for either repairs or weather conditions, or they become bottlenecks in times of heavy traffic. Road signs throughout the country use a color-coding system, with the official route numbers in white against a colored background. Expressway signs are green and highway signs are blue (unlike in the rest of Europe, where expressway signs are blue and highway signs are green). Signs for smaller roads are light blue. All signage indicates the names of upcoming towns as well, and it is generally easiest to use these names for navigating. A combination of steep or winding routes and hazardous weather means some roads will be closed in winter. Signs are posted at the beginning of the climb.

To find out about road conditions, traffic jams, itineraries, and so forth, you can turn to two places: the Swiss Automobile Club has operators standing by on weekdays from 8 to 5 to provide information in all languages. Dues-paying members of the Touring Club of Switzerland may contact the organization for similar information. Note that neither of these numbers gets you breakdown service. For frequent and precise information in Swiss languages, you can dial 163, or tune in to local radio stations.

Automobile Associations Swiss Automobile Club ☎ 031/3283111. **Touring Club of Switzerland** ☎ 022/4172424. U.S.: **American Automobile Association** (AAA) ☎ 315/797–5000 ⊕ www.aaa.com; most contact with the organization is through state and regional members.

ROADSIDE EMERGENCIES

All road breakdowns should be called in to the central Switzerland-wide emergency number, 140. If you are on an expressway, pull over to the shoulder and look for arrows pointing you to the nearest orange radio-telephone, called Bornes SOS; use these phones instead of a mobile phone because they allow police to find you instantly and send help. There are SOS phones every kilometer (½ mi), on alternate sides of the expressway.

Emergency Services Emergencies ☎ 140.

RULES OF THE ROAD

As in most of the rest of Europe, driving is on the right. Vehicles on main roads have priority over those on smaller roads. At intersections, priority is given to the driver on the right except when merging into traffic circles, when priority is given to the drivers coming from the left. In residential areas in some places—notably Geneva—traffic coming from the right has the right of way. In urban areas the speed limit is 50 kph (30 mph); on main highways, it's 80 kph (50 mph); on expressways, the limit is 120 kph (75 mph). Pass only on the left. It is illegal to make a

REMEMBER

In spite of its laid-back image, Switzerland suffers the bug of aggressive driving as well. Tailgating, though illegal, is a common problem, as is speeding. If you are being tailgated on the highway, just move into the right lane and ignore any high-beam flashing and visible signs of road rage behind you. If you are driving extra slowly, let the people behind you pass you.

Children under age seven are not permitted to sit in the front seat.

Use headlights in heavy rain, in poor visibility, or in tunnels—they are compulsory.

Always carry your valid license and car-registration papers; there are occasional roadblocks to check them.

Wear seat belts in the front- and backseats—they are mandatory.

To use the main highways, you must display a sticker, or *vignette*, on the top-center or lower corner of the windshield. You can buy one at the border or in post offices, gas stations, and garages. A vignette costs 40 SF or 27 (EUR). Driving without a vignette puts you at risk for getting a 100 SF fine. Cars rented within Switzerland already have these stickers; if you rent a car elsewhere in Europe, ask if the rental company will provide the vignette for you.

Traffic going up a mountain has priority except for postbuses coming down. A sign with a yellow post horn on a blue background means that postbuses have priority. On winding mountain roads, a brief honk as you approach a curve is a good way of warning any oncoming traffic.

In winter be sure your car has snow tires and snow chains. The latter are mandatory in some areas and advisable in most. Snow-chain service stations have signs marked SERVICE DE CHAÎNES À NEIGE or SCHNEEKETTENDIENST; snow chains are available for rent.

right-hand turn on a red light. The blood-alcohol limit is 0.05.

▌ BY TRAIN

The Swiss Federal Railways, or SBB/CFF/FFS, boasts one of the world's densest transportation networks; trains and stations are clean and, as you'd expect, service is extremely prompt. The cleanliness extends to restrooms—in some countries these are grim affairs, but in Switzerland's large city stations, look for "McClean" restrooms. They have nothing to do with the red-and-yellow hamburger chain; instead, they're immaculate, sleekly designed spaces, with bathrooms, changing stations, showers, and a toiletries kiosk. Entrance is about 1 SF or 2 SF depending on the extent of your use.

Trains described as Inter-City or Express are the fastest, stopping only in principal towns. *Regionalzug/Train Régional* means a local train. If you're planning to use the trains extensively, get the official timetable ("Kursbuch" or "Horaire") for 16 SF; the portable pocket version is called "Reka" and costs 12 SF. The Swiss Federal Railways also has an excellent Web site allowing you to work out itineraries online, including suburban trains and buses.

In addition to the federal rail lines there are some private rail lines, such as the Montreux-Oberland-Bernois line and the Rhätische Bahn. These private lines generally accept discount rail passes for a surcharge.

If your itinerary requires changing trains, bear in mind that the average connection time is six to eight minutes.

You can rely on the Swiss rail service to provide clean, timely service in both first and second class. If you are eager to read or get some work done on the train, try the Quiet Area compartments available in first and second class on a number of routes in Switzerland. Travelers are asked not to use cell phones, listen to music, or engage in loud conversation. The upper decks of some first-class cars also offer business compartments or seats; they are designated with the laptop icon and are equipped with power outlets.

If Switzerland is your only destination in Europe, there are numerous passes available for visitors. The **Swiss Pass** is the best value, offering unlimited travel on Swiss Federal Railways, postbuses, lake steamers, and the local bus and tram services of 36 cities. It also gives reductions on many privately owned railways, cable cars, and funiculars. And it gives you access to more than 400 museums in the country.

Available from Switzerland Tourism and from travel agents outside Switzerland including Rail Europe and Europe On Rail, the card is valid for four days (250 SF second class; 378 SF first class); eight days (362 SF second class; 543 SF first class); 15 days (440 SF second class; 660 SF first class), 22 days (508 SF second class; 762 SF first class); or one month (558 SF second class; 837 SF first class). There's also the **Flexipass** offering the same for 3 to 8 days in a 30-day period at the user's convenience (240 SF–450 SF second class; 362 SF–675 SF first class). There's an approximately 15% discount on the Swiss Pass and the Flexipass for two or more people. The **STS Family Card** is issued to nonresidents of Switzerland and Liechtenstein, upon request.

Within some popular tourist areas, **Regional Holiday Season Tickets** are available. Their discount offers vary; prices vary widely, too, depending on the region and period of validity. Passes are available from Switzerland Tourism and local tourist boards, but to be on the safe side, inquire well in advance.

The **Swiss Card,** which can be purchased in the United States through Rail Europe, Europe On Rail, and at train stations at the Zürich and Geneva airports and in Basel, is valid for 30 days and grants full round-trip travel from your arrival point to any destination in the country, plus a half-price reduction on any further excursions during your stay (178 SF second

TRAIN TIPS

If you happen to suffer from motion sickness, note that the Swiss ICN trains—and the German ICE, the French TGV, and the Italian Cisalpino—all use "tilt technology" for a less jerky ride. One side-effect, however, is that some passengers might get literally seasick, especially if the track is curvy (as between Biel/Bienne and Geneva). An over-the-counter drug for motion sickness should help. Also close the shades and avoid looking out the window. Consider a first-class ticket only if the extra comfort is worth the price. The principal difference between first and second class is more space, as the first-class cars are less crowded. Seat size is the same, upholstery fancier, and you usually will be delivered to the track position closest to the station.

class; 250 SF first class). For more information about train travel in Switzerland, get the free "Swiss Travel System" or "Discover Switzerland" brochures from Switzerland Tourism.

Switzerland is one of 17 countries in which you can use Eurailpasses, which provide unlimited first-class rail travel, in all of the participating countries, for the duration of the pass. If you plan to rack up the miles, get a standard pass. These are available for 15 days ($605), 21 days ($785), one month ($975), two months ($1,378), and three months ($1,703). If your plans call for only limited train travel, look into a Eurail Selectpass, which costs less money than a Eurailpass. Unlike with Eurailpasses, however, you get a limited number of travel days, in a limited number of countries, during a specified time period. For example, a two-month pass allows between 5 and 15 days of rail travel; costs range between $383 and $850. Keep in mind that the basic Eurail Selectpass is good only in France, Germany, Italy, Spain, and Switzerland, though you have the option of adding two "associate countries" (Austria, Hungary, the Netherlands, Belgium, Luxembourg, Greece, or Portugal). There are numerous other options available, however, especially if you have planned your itinerary carefully—these depend on how many countries you care to visit, and so on. In addition to standard Eurailpasses, ask about special rail-pass plans. Among these are the Eurail Youthpass (for those under age 26), the Eurail and Europass Saverpasses (which give a discount for two or more people traveling together), the Euraildrive Pass and the Europass Drive (which combine travel by train and rental car).

Make seat reservations for trips during rush hours and in high season, especially on international trains.

Swiss Federal Railways ☎ 0900/300300, 1.19 SF per min ⊕ www.rail.ch.

Train Information Abercrombie & Kent ☎ 630/954-2944 or 800/323-7308 ⊕ www.abercrombiekent.com. **Europe On Rail** ☎ 877/667-2457 ⊕ www.europeonrail.com. **Rail Europe** ☎ 914/682-5172 or 800/438-7245 ✉ Ontario ☎ 800/361-7245 ⊕ www.raileurope.com. *Venice-Simplon-Orient Express* ☎ 020/7928-6000 ⊕ www.orient-express.com.

THE CHANNEL TUNNEL

With the Channel Tunnel completing a seamless route, you can leave London around noon on the Eurostar and (thanks to connections via Paris-Lyon on the French *train à grande vitesse*) have a late supper in Geneva. Note that the TGV tracks connecting Geneva and Paris are a bit bumpy, which can be unsettling for sensitive passengers. Also note that the *Venice-Simplon-Orient Express* stops in Luzern between London and Venice-information is available from the tour company Abercrombie & Kent. Many travelers assume that rail passes guarantee them seats on the trains they wish to ride. Not so. You need to book seats ahead even if you are using a rail pass; seat reservations are required on some European trains, particularly high-speed trains, and are a good idea on trains that may be crowded-particularly in summer on popular routes. You will also need a reservation if you purchase sleeping accommodations. Whichever pass you choose, remember that you must purchase your pass before you leave for Europe. The Swiss Federal Railways has a user-friendly site that lets you check fares and schedules. You can also call its hotline, which has information in English. Most rail stations let you purchase tickets from machines that accept cash and major credit cards.

SCENIC ROUTES

Switzerland makes the most of its Alpine rail engineering, which cuts through the icy granite landscape above 6,560 feet, by offering special trains that cross over spectacular passes with panoramic cars. The *Glacier Express*, for example, connects the two glamorous resorts of Zermatt and St. Moritz, crawling over the Oberalp Pass and serving lunch in a burnished-wood period dining car; the *Wilhelm Tell Express* combines a rail crossing of the Saint Gotthard Pass with a cruise down the length of Lake Luzern. The *Golden Pass/Panoramic Express* climbs from the balmy waterfront of Montreux into the Alpine terrain through Gstaad to Interlaken and rolls on to Luzern via the Brünig Pass. (Note this involves several train changes.) The *Bernina Express* ascends from Chur to St. Moritz, then climbs over the magnificent Bernina Pass into Italy, where visitors can connect by postbus to Lugano. These sightseeing itineraries take 4–11 hours' travel time. For information on these and other scenic routes, contact Swiss Federal Railways or Railtour Suisse, Switzerland's largest train-tour company.

Scenic Route Information Railtour Suisse ✉ Chutzenstr. 24, CH-3000 Bern ☎ 031/3780101 🖷 031/3780108 ⊕ www.railtour.ch. **Swiss Federal Railways** ☎ 0900/300300, 1.19 SF per min ⊕ www.rail.ch.

ON THE GROUND

■ COMMUNICATIONS

INTERNET

Some hotels now have in-room modem connections; ask about rates before you plug in (just make sure your computer is Wi-Fi-enabled—if you are using your own computer, you will need an adapter plug and should use a surge protector). You will also find Internet terminals in airports and train stations in many cities and towns. Many hotels and public places have now been turned into Wi-Fi (in Europe: WLAN) "hot spots." Usually you must pay a fee to log on, though some hotels will provide the service for free. Cost is 5 SF for a half-hour, or 19 SF for two hours. Unused portions of your time will not be stored for you. Some cities provide Wi-Fi service for free. **Cybercafes** ⊕ www.cybercafes.com lists more than 4,000 Internet cafés worldwide.

PHONES

The good news is that you can now make a direct-dial telephone call from virtually any point on earth. The bad news? You can't always do so cheaply. Calling from a hotel is almost always the most expensive option; hotels usually add huge surcharges to all calls, particularly international ones. In some countries you can phone from call centers or even the post office. Calling cards usually keep costs to a minimum, but only if you purchase them locally. And then there are mobile phones (⇨ *below*), which are sometimes more prevalent—particularly in the developing world—than land lines; as expensive as mobile phone calls can be, they are still usually a much cheaper option than calling from your hotel.

The country code for Switzerland is 41. When dialing a Swiss number from abroad, drop the initial 0 from the local area code. The country code is 1 for the United States and Canada, 61 for Australia, 64 for New Zealand, and 44 for the United Kingdom.

CALLING WITHIN SWITZERLAND

Dial 111 for information within Switzerland (1.60 SF for two requests 24 hours a day). All telephone operators speak English, and instructions are printed in English in all telephone booths.

Dial the local area code (including the 0) when calling any local number.

There's direct dialing to everywhere in Switzerland. For local area codes consult the pink pages and for international country and city codes, consult the green-banded pages at the front of the telephone book. Include the area code preceded by 0 when dialing anywhere within Switzerland.

To make a local call on a pay phone, pick up the receiver, insert a phone card, and dial the number. A local call costs 0.50 SF plus 0.10 SF for each additional unit. Toll-free numbers begin with 0800. Swisscom phone cards are available in 5 SF, 10 SF, or 20 SF units; they're sold at post offices, train stations, airports, and kiosks. Slip a card into an adapted public phone, and a continual readout will tell you how much money is left on the card. The cost of the call will be counted against the card, with any remaining value still good for the next time you use it. If you drain the card and still need to talk, the readout will warn you: you can either pop in a new card or make up the difference with coins, although very few phones still accept coins. Many phone booths now also accept Visa, MasterCard, and American Express cards, but be sure to have a four-digit PIN code.

CALLING OUTSIDE SWITZERLAND

The country code for the United States is 1.

You can dial most international numbers direct from Switzerland, adding 00 before the country code. If you want a number that cannot be reached directly, dial 1141 for a connection. Dial 1159 for international numbers and information.

Language Regions of Switzerland

GERMANY

FRANCE

Basel

Zürich

AUSTRIA

GERMAN

LIECHTEN-STEIN

Bern

Fribourg

FRENCH

ROMANSH

St. Moritz

ITALIAN

Bellinzona

Sierre

Geneva

ITALY

0   60 miles
0   90 km

(Neighboring countries have their own information numbers: 1151 for Austria; 1152 for Germany; 1153 for France; and 1154 for Italy.) It's cheapest to use the booths in train stations and post offices: calls made from your hotel cost a great deal more. For precise information on the cost of any call, dial 0800/868788. Current rates for calls to the United States, United Kingdom, and Canada are 0.12 SF per minute weekdays and 0.10 SF per minute on weekends and Swiss holidays. Calls to Australia and New Zealand cost 0.25 SF a minute weekdays and 0.20 SF per minute on weekends and Swiss holidays.

Access Codes AT&T Direct ☎ 0800/890011. **MCI WorldPhone** ☎ 800/444-4141. **Sprint International Access** ☎ 800/877-4646 for other areas.

CALLING CARDS

A variety of international phone cards in denominations of 10 to 50 SF are available in newspaper shops. They often offer the cheapest rates. You can use the code on the card until you run out of units.

MOBILE PHONES

If you have a multiband phone (some countries use different frequencies than what's used in the United States) and your service provider uses the world-standard GSM network (as do T-Mobile, Cingular, and Verizon), you can probably use your phone abroad. Roaming fees can be steep, however: 99¢ a minute is considered reasonable. And overseas you normally pay the toll charges for incoming calls. It's almost always cheaper to send a text message than to make a call, since text messages have a very low set fee (often less than 5¢).

If you just want to make local calls, consider buying a new SIM card (note that your provider may have to unlock your phone for you to use a different SIM card) and a prepaid service plan in the destination. You'll then have a local number and can make local calls at local rates. If your trip is extensive, you could also simply buy a new cell phone in your destination, as the initial cost will be offset over time.

■ TIP➔ **If you travel internationally frequently, save one of your old mobile phones or buy a cheap one on the Internet; ask your cell phone company to unlock it for you, and take it with you as a travel phone, buying a new SIM card with pay-as-you-go service in each destination.**

Cellular phones (*natels*) may be rented at either the Geneva or Zürich airports from Rent@phone. You can arrange for a rental on a daily, weekly, or monthly basis. The Rent@phone desks are clearly indicated in each airport.

Cellular Abroad ☎ 800/287-5072 ⊕ www. cellularabroad.com rents and sells GMS phones and sells SIM cards that work in many countries. **Mobal** ☎ 888/888-9162 ⊕ www. mobalrental.com rents mobiles and sells GSM phones (starting at $49) that will operate in 140 countries. Per-call rates vary throughout the world. **Planet Fone** ☎ 888/988-4777 ⊕ www.planetfone.com rents cell phones, but the per-minute rates are expensive. **Rent@phone** ☎ 022/7178263 in Geneva, 043/8165063 in Zürich ⊕ www.rentaphone.ch.

▌CUSTOMS & DUTIES

You're always allowed to bring goods of a certain value back home without having to pay any duty or import tax. But there's a limit on the amount of tobacco and liquor you can bring back duty-free, and some countries have separate limits for perfumes; for exact figures, check with your customs department. The values of so-called "duty-free" goods are included in these amounts. When you shop abroad,

save all your receipts, as customs inspectors may ask to see them as well as the items you purchased. If the total value of your goods is more than the duty-free limit, you'll have to pay a tax (most often a flat percentage) on the value of everything beyond that limit.

Entering Switzerland, a visitor who is 17 years or older and is arriving from Europe may bring in 200 cigarettes or 50 cigars or 250 grams of tobacco; 2 liters of alcohol up to 15 proof and 1 liter over 15 proof; if the visitor arrives from elsewhere, the quantities are doubled. Visitors over 17 may bring gifts valued at up to 100 SF. Medicine, such as insulin, is allowed for personal use only.

Information in Switzerland Federal Customs Administration ⊕ www.ezv.admin.ch/index. html.

U.S. Information U.S. Customs and Border Protection ⊕ www.cbp.gov.

▌EATING OUT

The restaurants we list are the cream of the crop in each price category. Properties indicated by an ✕⊡ are lodging establishments whose restaurant warrants a special trip (and will accommodate nonhotel guests). In regional chapters price charts appear in the dining subsection of the Planner section, which is found near the beginning of each regional chapter. In chapters devoted to a single city, price charts appear in the introductions to the dining section. Please note that the price charts reflect the cost of only the main dish at dinner and that two- and three-course menus are offered in many restaurants, representing a better value than the à la carte price charts would indicate.

MEALS

Breakfast in Switzerland tends to be little more than coffee with bread, butter, and marmalade. If you prefer a lot of milk in your coffee, ask for a *renversé* in French (literally, *upside-down*) or a *Milchkaffee* in German. Increasingly popular in German-speaking Switzerland is the *latte mac-*

TASTY TIPS

Many restaurants close after lunch (as of 3 PM) and reopen for dinner (about 6 PM). In remote regions it may prove difficult to find kitchens open past 9 or 10 PM, so plan ahead. Many restaurants are closed on Sunday and many close for the month of August or even longer. Bars often close at 1 or 2 AM, although clubs continue serving into the wee hours.

For lunch or dinner, most regions offer cheese specialties. Remember when eating these tasty dishes, that you tend to be full before your brain registers the fact, and the fatty cheeses can result in difficult digestion. Fondue (literally, "melted" in French) originated in the western part of Switzerland and comes in regional varieties, of which the Neuchâtel preparation is the most famous (combining equal portions of Gruyère and Vacherin). Bits of white bread are skewered on long, thin forks and twirled in the melted cheese. Anyone losing his or her piece of bread has to perform some small activity as "penance," like singing a song, or paying for the next round. The grilled cheese remaining in the *caquelon* is known as the *religieuse* ("the nun") and is a favorite. The other big cheese specialty is raclette from the Valais canton. Traditionally, the cut surface of half a cheese is exposed to a fire and the melted cheese is consistently scraped off (*racler* means "to scrape") and eaten with baked potatoes, pickled white onions, and other condiments. Another cheesy dish is a *Malakoff*, a chunk of Gruyère that is pressed onto a piece of toast and then deep-fried. You may order only one Malakoff at a time (which may be a blessing in disguise to those who tend to bite off more than they can chew).

A crisp wine as you dine or a shot of kirsch after a meal can help soothe your overtaxed stomach. Some fondue experts recommend washing these heavy cheese dishes down with hot black tea and not drinking too much while eating.

chiato, lots of steamed and foamy milk with a little espresso. The signature Bircher muesli—invented by Dr. Maximilian Oskar Bircher-Benner at his diet clinic at the end of the 19th century—is available in most supermarkets (such as Migros and Coop) and can make a hearty lunch, especially when served with plain or fruit yogurt instead of milk.

There are other fondues that are not so "cheesy." *Fondue bourguignonne* involves dipping bits of meat (veal, beef, chicken, or even horse), fish, and vegetables in hot oil. The lighter "Chinese" variation (*fondue chinoise*) uses bouillon. The boiled or fried tidbits are dipped in condiments. There is even a sweet fondue version, with fruits dipped in hot chocolate sauce.

On a lighter touch, the French-speaking cantons pride themselves on *filets de perche* (fried perch fillets), possibly the most popular dish in the region. A few variations on the theme exist—some with herbs or cognac sauce—but the traditional version is served with lemon and french fries on the side. German-speaking Switzerland made its mark in culinary history with the ubiquitous *Rösti*, a grated potato pancake—often spruced up with herbs, bacon, or cheese—that is served with nearly any meat or fish. Competing with Rösti for most popular side dish, *Spätzli* (egg-flour dumplings) continue to be fashioned according to age-old local traditions (though toss-in-boiling-water-and-serve packets have a strong following). The Ticino, to the south, has preserved its penchant for Italian cuisine with a simple touch that reflects the erstwhile poverty of the region: risotto, gnocchi, polenta, and pasta dishes appear on most menus. Graubünden has its own set of specialties also harking back to its regional history as a canton cut off from the world during the winter months. For descriptions of *capuns, maluns,* and *pizzocheri,* see the chapter on the region.

Besides these staples, you are likely to encounter a variety of stews, organ meats, and sausages. Classics such as *truite me-*

unière (trout rolled in flour, fried in butter, and served with lemon and parsley) are also standard fare.

Children's menus are available in many restaurants around Switzerland; otherwise, you can usually request a child-size portion and the prices will be adjusted accordingly.

Unless otherwise noted, the restaurants listed in this guide are open daily for lunch and dinner.

PAYING

Credit cards are widely accepted, and euros often accepted, especially in areas that border on the European Union. Note that service is included unless indicated on the menu. It is customary to leave a small tip in cash (up to 10% depending on how pleased you are with the service).

For guidelines on tipping *see* Tipping *below.*

RESERVATIONS & DRESS

Regardless of where you are, it's a good idea to make a reservation if you can. We only mention them specifically when reservations are essential (there's no other way you'll ever get a table) or when they are not accepted. For famed restaurants, book as far ahead as you can (often 30 days), and reconfirm as soon as you arrive. (Large parties should always call ahead to check the reservations policy.) We mention dress only when men are required to wear a jacket or a jacket and tie.

WINES, BEER & SPIRITS

Quality and diversity are the hallmarks of Swiss wine, celebrated in annual festivals where everyone samples the year's harvest. They may not be widely exported, but Swiss wines are generally available in restaurants, and you can also get to know them in wine cellars (often with delicious local cheese). All of Switzerland's 23 cantons produce wines, but six areas outdo the rest: the Valais, Vaud, Geneva, the Three Lakes region in western Switzerland, the German-speaking region of eastern Switzerland, and the Ticino. The Chasselas is by far the most successful among white grapes, and pinot noir among the reds. Other top white grape varieties include Müller-Thurgau and Sylvaner; reds feature gamay and merlot. You can get more information from the Swiss Wine Exporters' Association (⊕ www.swisswine. ch).

Switzerland counts more than 120 official active breweries that regularly produce *Lager, Spezialbier* (slightly stronger and a touch more bitter than the lager), and *Festbier* (strong, dark holiday beer produced at Easter and Christmas and sometimes sold as *Bockbier* or *Märzenbier*). Specialty beer includes the amber *Altbier*, the corn-infused *Maisbier,* and *Weizenbier* (wheat beer). A bit of trivia: the strongest beer ever brewed is said to have been the now-retired Samichlaus brand from the Feldschlösschen Brewery; with a whopping 14% alcohol content, it had no head and an aroma akin to molasses.

Switzerland is brimming with spirits. Most notably, *kirsch* (cherry spirit) from Zug and the Lake Luzern region has gained worldwide recognition. Plums are used to make *Zwetschgenwasser.* The tiny damassine plum, reportedly brought back from Damascus by a crusading knight, is distilled into the delightfully fragrant *Damassine,* available in Saignelégier. The many apple spirits include *Träsch* and *Gravensteiner;* pears from the Valais give their spirit to the redolent *Williamine.* A unique variety of grappas are up for grabs in the grottoes of the Ticino; this potent firewater gets its name and taste from the skins of the grape. Now that vodka is gaining popularity among consumers around the globe, the Swiss have begun to promote their own designer spirit: Xellent, which entered the market in its sleek red bottle in 2003.

▌ ELECTRICITY

The electrical current in Switzerland is 220 volts, 50 cycles alternating current (AC); wall outlets take plugs that have two or three round prongs. The two-pronged continental-type plugs can be used throughout the country.

Consider making a small investment in a universal adapter, which has several types of plugs in one lightweight, compact unit. Most laptops and mobile phone chargers are dual voltage (i.e., they operate equally well on 110 and 220 volts), so require only an adapter. These days the same is true of small appliances such as hair dryers. Always check labels and manufacturer instructions to be sure. Don't use 110-volt outlets marked FOR SHAVERS ONLY for high-wattage appliances such as hairdryers.

Steve Kropla's Help for World Traveler's ⊕ www.kropla.com has information on electrical and telephone plugs around the world. **Walkabout Travel Gear** ⊕ www.walkabouttravelgear.com has a good coverage of electricity under "adapters."

∎ EMERGENCIES

Foreign Embassies Embassy ✉ Jubiläumsstr. 93, CH-3001 Bern ☎ 031/3577011, 031/3577344 24-hour emergency hotline. **Consular agency** ✉ Rue Versonnex 7 ☏ CH-1207 Geneva ☎ 022/8405160. **Consular agency** ✉ Dufourstr. 101 ☏ CH-8008 Zürich ☎ 043/4992960.

General Emergency Contacts Police ☎ 117. **Ambulance** ☎ 144.

∎ HEALTH

SPECIFIC ISSUES IN SWITZERLAND

Switzerland's reputation for impeccable standards of cleanliness is well earned. But even at the foot of an icy-pure 6,500-foot glacier, you'll find the locals drinking bottled mineral water; you'll have to insist a little if you want tap water with your meal. This is as much a result of the tradition of expecting beverages in a café to be paid for as it is a response to health questions. If you're traveling with a child under two years old, you may be advised by locals not to carry him or her on ex-

cursions above 6,500 feet; check with your pediatrician before leaving home. Adults should limit strenuous excursions on the first day at extra-high-altitude resorts, those at 5,248 feet and above. Adults with heart problems may want to avoid all excursions above 6,500 feet.

When hiking or skiing in the mountains, be aware of the dangers of altitude sickness, as well as other afflictions such as heat stroke, dehydration, sunstroke, frostbite, and snow blindness. Wear sunglasses with side shields or goggles to avoid snow blindness, especially if you have light-colored eyes. Symptoms of altitude sickness, which occurs in some individuals who ascend rapidly to high altitudes, include numbness, tingling, nausea, drowsiness, headaches, and vision problems. If you experience discomfort, return to a lower altitude as soon as possible. You should wear sunscreen all through the year; many different brands are available at ski shops near the slopes. If you plan to spend extended periods in rural areas, take precautions against ticks, especially in spring and summer. Wear long sleeves, long pants, and boots, and apply insect repellent containing the powerful repellent DEET. Two vaccines against tick-borne infections are available in Europe: TicoVac (also known as FSME Immun) and Encepur, but neither has been approved in the United States. Remove ticks with tweezers, grasping the insect by the head.

OVER-THE-COUNTER REMEDIES
Basic over-the-counter medicines are available from pharmacies (*pharmacie, Apotheke, farmacia*), which are recognizable from afar thanks to signs with green crosses.

▌HOURS OF OPERATION

Most businesses still close for lunch in Switzerland, generally from noon or 12:30 to 1:30 or 2, but this is changing, especially in larger cities, and especially in the German-speaking part of the country. All remain closed on Sunday. Banks are open weekdays from 8:30 to 4:30 or 5. Post offices are generally open limited hours on Saturday.

Gas station kiosks are usually open daily from 6:30 AM until 9 PM. Automatic pumps, which accept major credit cards and Swiss bank notes, are in service 24 hours a day.

Museums generally close on Monday. There is, however, an increasing trend toward staying open late one night a week, usually on Thursday or Friday evening.

Pharmacies are generally open weekdays from 9 to 1 and 2 to 6, and Saturday 9 to 1. In cities, they tend to stay open through the lunch hour. To find out which pharmacy is covering the late-night shift, check listings posted near or on the window of any pharmacy.

Shops are generally open every day except Sunday. They usually close early (4 or 5 PM) on Saturday except in larger cities, where they stay open until 6 on Saturday and often stay open until 8 or 9 one day a week. Smaller stores close for an hour or two for lunch. Stores in train stations in larger cities often open on Sunday (until 9 PM); in the Geneva and Zürich airports, shops are open on Sunday.

HOLIDAYS

National holidays include January 1 (New Year), Good Friday (March or April), Easter Sunday and Monday (March or April), May 1 (Labor Day), Ascension Day (May), Whitsunday and Whitmonday (May), August 1 (Swiss National Holiday), and December 25–26 (Christmas and Boxing Day).

▌MAIL

Airmail letters and postcards generally take two business days to reach the United Kingdom from Switzerland, at least four days to reach the United States, and a few days more to reach Australia and New Zealand.

Mail rates are divided into first-class "A" (airmail) and second-class "B" (surface). Letters and postcards to North America weighing up to 20 grams (about .07 oz) cost 1.80 SF and 1.40 SF; to the United Kingdom, 1.30 SF and 1.20 SF.

If you're uncertain where you'll be staying, you can have your mail, marked *poste restante* or *postlagernd,* sent to any post office in Switzerland. It needs the sender's name and address on the back, and you'll need proof of identity to collect it. You can also have your mail sent to American Express for a small fee; if you are a cardholder or have American Express traveler's checks, the service is free. Postal codes precede the names of cities and towns in Swiss addresses.

▌MONEY

Despite increased competition across Europe, the recent decrease in the Swiss franc's value against other currencies, and the negligible inflation rate over the past several years, Switzerland remains one of the most expensive countries on the Continent for travelers, and you may find yourself shocked by the price of a light lunch or a generic hotel room. If you are traveling on a tight budget, avoid staying in well-known resorts and the most sophisticated cities; Geneva, Zürich, Zermatt, Gstaad, and St. Moritz are especially expensive. One sure way of saving some pennies: in those cities (and others) you can often find a good meal at the cafeterias of the local Migros or Coop supermarket chains, or at the Manor department stores. If you are traveling by car, you have the luxury of seeking out small family hotels in villages, where costs are relatively low. Unless you work hard at finding budget accommodations, you will average more than 150 SF a night for two—more if you stay in business-class hotels.

A cup of coffee or a beer costs about 3.50 SF in a simple restaurant; ordinary open wines, sold by the deciliter ("deci"), start at about 3 SF. All three beverages cost sometimes double that in resorts, city hotels, and fine restaurants. A plain, one-plate daily lunch special averages 14–18 SF. A city bus ride costs between 1.80 SF and 3 SF, a short cab ride 18 SF.

Prices throughout this guide are given for adults. Substantially reduced fees are almost always available for children, students, and senior citizens.

ATMS & BANKS

Your own bank will probably charge a fee for using ATMs abroad; the foreign bank you use may also charge a fee. Nevertheless, you'll usually get a better rate of exchange at an ATM than you will at a currency-exchange office or even when changing money in a bank. And extracting funds as you need them is a safer option than carrying around a large amount of cash.

■ TIP→ PIN numbers with more than four digits are not recognized at ATMs in many countries. If yours has five or more, remember to change it before you leave.

You can withdraw money from ATMs in Switzerland as long as your card is properly programmed with your personal identification number (PIN). For use in Switzerland, your PIN number must be four digits long. If your PIN is longer than four digits, you may want to change it before leaving home. Banks offer good wholesale exchange rates.

CREDIT CARDS

Throughout this guide, the following abbreviations are used: **AE,** American Express; **DC,** Diners Club; **MC,** MasterCard; and **V,** Visa.

It's a good idea to inform your credit-card company before you travel, especially if you're going abroad and don't travel internationally very often. Otherwise, the credit-card company might put a hold on your card owing to unusual activity—not a good thing halfway through your trip. Record all your credit-card numbers—as well as the phone numbers to call if your cards are lost or stolen—in a safe place, so you're prepared should something go wrong. Both MasterCard and Visa have general numbers you can call (collect if you're abroad) if your card is lost, but you're better off calling the number of your issuing bank, since MasterCard and Visa usually just transfer you to your bank; your bank's number is usually printed on your card.

If you plan to use your credit card for cash advances, you'll need to apply for a PIN at least two weeks before your trip. Although it's usually cheaper (and safer) to use a credit card abroad for large purchases (so you can cancel payments or be reimbursed if there's a problem), note that some credit-card companies *and* the banks that issue them add substantial percentages to all foreign transactions, whether they're in a foreign currency or not. Check on these fees before leaving home, so there won't be any surprises when you get the bill.

■ TIP→ Before you charge something, ask the merchant whether or not he or she plans to do a dynamic currency conversion (DCC). In such a transaction the credit-card *processor* (shop, restaurant, or hotel, not Visa or MasterCard) converts the currency and charges you in dollars. In most cases you'll pay the merchant a 3% fee for this service in addition to any credit-card company and issuing-bank foreign-transaction surcharges.

Dynamic currency conversion (DCC) programs are becoming increasingly widespread. Merchants who participate in them are supposed to ask whether you want to be charged in dollars or the local currency, but they don't always do so. And even if they do offer you a choice, they may well avoid mentioning the additional surcharges. The good news is that you *do* have a choice. And if this practice really gets your goat, you can avoid it entirely thanks to American Express; with its cards, DCC simply isn't an option.

Reporting Lost Cards American Express
☎ 800/992-3404 in the U.S., 336/393-1111 collect from abroad ⊕ www.americanexpress. com. **Diners Club** ☎ 800/234-6377 in the U.S., 303/799-1504 collect from abroad ⊕ www.dinersclub.com. **MasterCard** ☎ 800/ 622-7747 in the U.S., 636/722-7111 collect from abroad ⊕ www.mastercard.com. **Visa** ☎ 800/847-2911 in the U.S., 410/581-9994 collect from abroad ⊕ www.visa.com.

CURRENCY & EXCHANGE

■ **TIP➔** Even if a currency-exchange booth has a sign promising no commission, rest assured that there's some kind of huge, hidden fee. (Oh . . . that's right. The sign didn't say no *fee*). And as for rates, you're almost always better off getting foreign currency at an ATM or exchanging money at a bank.

The unit of currency in Switzerland is the Swiss franc (SF), available in notes of 10, 20, 50, 100, 200, and 1,000. Francs are divided into centimes (in Suisse Romande) or rappen (in German Switzerland). There are coins for 5, 10, 20, and 50 centimes or rappen. Larger coins are the 1-, 2-, and 5-franc pieces.

At press time (winter 2007) the Swiss franc stood at 1.16 to the U.S. dollar, 0.94 to the Canadian dollar, and 2.22 to the pound sterling.

In terms of convenience, train stations have the edge; more than 300 stations have currency exchange offices that are open daily, including lunch hours, when many banks are closed. These booths swap currency, buy and sell traveler's checks in various currencies, and cash Eurocheques.

TRAVELER'S CHECKS & CARDS

Some consider this the currency of the cave man, and it's true that fewer establishments accept traveler's checks these days. The convenience of getting hard cash from all those ATM machines makes traveler's checks redundant for the most part. Nevertheless, they're a cheap and secure way to carry extra money, particularly on trips to urban areas. Both Citibank (under the Visa brand) and American Express issue traveler's checks in the United States, but Amex is better known and more widely accepted; you can also avoid hefty surcharges by cashing Amex checks at Amex offices. Whatever you do, keep track of all the serial numbers in case the checks are lost or stolen.

Note that there is a limit (300 SF) on the cashing of Eurocheques drawn on European banks.

American Express ☎ 888/412-6945 in the U.S., 801/945-9450 collect outside of the U.S. to add value or speak to customer service ⊕ www.americanexpress.com.

■ RESTROOMS

Restroom standards are high even for public toilets, such as those in train stations, where you sometimes have to pay a small fee. It is appropriate to buy a drink in a bar when you want to use the facilities. Basel has made waves with its public toilets with one-way glass—no one can see you when you're inside, but you have a view of the entire street.

Find a Loo The Bathroom Diaries ⊕ www. thebathroomdiaries.com is flush with unsanitized info on restrooms the world over—each one located, reviewed, and rated.

■ SAFETY

Switzerland is a very safe country, but not immune to larceny. Use common sense, especially after dark, and particularly in large cities. Walk on well-lit, busy streets. Look alert and aware; a purposeful pace helps deter trouble wherever you go. Store valuables in a hotel safe or, better yet, leave them at home. Keep a sharp eye (and hand) on handbags and backpacks; do not hang them from a chair in restaurants. Carry wallets in inside or front pockets rather than hip pockets. Use ATMs in daylight, at an indoor location when possible.

■ TIP➔ **Distribute your cash, credit cards, IDs, and other valuables between a deep front pocket, an inside jacket or vest pocket, and a hidden money pouch. Don't reach for the money pouch once you're in public.**

SPORTS & THE OUTDOORS

HIKING

The Swiss Alps are riddled with hiking trails; yellow trail indicators are standard all over the country. Hiking is an especially popular pastime in the German-speaking areas, such as the Berner Oberland. For suggested hiking itineraries including lists of huts for overnight stays, contact regional tourist offices or the Fédération Suisse de Tourisme Pédestre (Swiss Hiking Federation); many newspaper stands, kiosks, train stations, and bookstores also carry detailed topographical maps with marked trails.

Fédération Suisse de Tourisme Pédestre (Swiss Hiking Federation) ✉ Im Hirshalm 49, CH-4125 Riehen ☎ 061/6069340 ⊕ www. swisshiking.ch.

SKIING

Switzerland's legendary phenomenal ski slopes are bolstered by excellent transportation networks, plentiful vacation packages, and visitor facilities.

Slope difficulty levels are indicated with color codes. A black slope is the most difficult; red indicates intermediate levels; blue is for beginners. A daily bulletin of ski and weather conditions throughout Switzerland is available by calling ☎ 0900/ 162333 (0.86 SF per min); reports are in the local language.

Serious skiers may want to join the Swiss Alpine Club. Applications should be addressed to Mr. Edmond F. Krieger at the Sektion Zermatt branch. Remember to include a passport-size photo. Excursions involve much climbing. It's not necessary to be fluent in German. For a booklet of mountain-club refuges, contact the Swiss

Alpine Club in Bern. A refuge directory called "Hütten der Schweizer Alpen," complete with color photos, can be ordered for 44 SF from the club's office in Verlag. **Swiss Alpine Club** ✉ Sektion Zermatt, Haus Dolomit, CH-3920 Zermatt ☎☎ 027/9672610 ✉ Monbijoustr. 61, Postfach, CH-3000 Bern ☎ 031/3701880 ☎ 031/3701890 ⊕ www.sac-cas.ch or www.sac-verlag.ch.

■ TAXES

What you see is what you pay in Switzerland: restaurant checks and hotel bills include all taxes.

If your purchases in a shop amount to 400 SF and the goods are exported within 30 days of the purchase date, you may reclaim the V.A.T. (7.6% in Switzerland). This tax is included in the sales price of most items.

When making a purchase, ask for a V. A.T. refund form and find out whether the merchant gives refunds—not all stores do, nor are they required to. Have the form stamped like any customs form by customs officials when you leave the country or, if you're visiting several European Union countries, when you leave the EU. After you're through passport control, take the form to a refund-service counter for an on-the-spot refund (which is usually the quickest and easiest option), or mail it to the address on the form (or the envelope with it) after you arrive home. You receive the total refund stated on the form, but the processing time can be long, especially if you request a credit-card adjustment.

Global Refund is a Europe-wide service with 225,000 affiliated stores and more than 700 refund counters at major airports and border crossings. Its refund form, called a Tax Free Check, is the most common across the European continent. The service issues refunds in the form of cash, check, or credit-card adjustment.

V.A.T. Refunds Global Refund ☎ 800/566-9828 ⊕ www.globalrefund.com.

▮ TIME

Switzerland is six hours ahead of New York, nine hours ahead of Los Angeles, one hour ahead of London, and nine hours behind Sydney.

▮ TIPPING

Despite all protests to the contrary and menus marked *service compris*, the Swiss *do* tip at restaurants, giving quantities anywhere from the change from the nearest franc to 10 SF or more for a world-class meal that has been exquisitely served. Unlike American-style tipping, calculated by a percentage, usually between 10% and 20%, a tip is still a tip here: a nod of approval for a job well done. If, in a café, the waitress settles the bill at the table, fishing the change from her leather purse, give her the change on the spot—or calculate the total, including tip, and tell her the full sum before she counts it onto the tabletop. If you need to take more time to calculate, leave it on the table, though this isn't common practice in outdoor cafés. If you're paying for a meal with a credit card, try to tip with cash instead of filling in the tip slot on the slip: not all managers are good about doling out the waiters' tips in cash. Bartenders are also tipped along these lines. Tipping porters and doormen is easier: 2 SF per bag is adequate in good hotels, 1 SF per trip in humbler lodgings (unless you travel heavy). A fixed rate of 5 SF per bag applies to porter fees at the Geneva and Zürich airports. Tip taxi drivers the change or an extra couple of francs, depending on the length of the drive and whether they've helped with your bags. To tip other hotel personnel, you can leave an appropriate amount with the concierge or, for cleaning staff, with a note of thanks in your room.

GREETINGS

In Switzerland it's polite to say hello and good-bye (*bonjour, au revoir; grüezi, auf Wiedersehen; buon giorno, arrivederci*) to everyone you speak to, from police officers to cashiers. The standard gesture for each is a simple handshake. In the French- and Italian-speaking cantons, it is standard for friends to greet each other with three kisses on the cheek. In the German-speaking areas, kissing is much less common, as is hugging.

DOING BUSINESS

When doing business, use your counterpart's first name only after he or she has used yours. Always shake hands when you greet and say good-bye.

LANGUAGE

One of the best ways to avoid being an Ugly American is to learn a little of the local language. You need not strive for fluency; even just mastering a few basic words and terms is bound to make chatting with the locals more rewarding. Nearly 70% of the population of Switzerland speaks one dialect or another of German; Swiss German can be a far cry from high German, although standard German is generally understood. French is spoken in the southwest, around Lake Geneva, and in the cantons of Fribourg, Neuchâtel, Jura, Vaud, and most of the Valais. Italian is spoken in the Ticino. In the Upper and Lower Engadines, in the canton of Graubünden, the last gasp of a Romance language called Romansh is still in daily use. In the areas most frequented by English-speaking tourists—Zermatt, the Berner Oberland, the Engadine, Luzern—people in the tourist industry usually speak English. See the vocabulary section in this book for helpful words and phrases. *Fodor's French for Travelers, Fodor's German for Travelers, and Fodor's Italian for Travelers* (available at bookstores everywhere) are excellent.

INDEX

PHOTO CREDITS

NOTES

ABOUT OUR WRITERS

Fodor's success in showing you every corner of Switzerland is a credit to our extraordinary writers. Many editions ago, this guide was originally written by Nancy Coons. Since then, our Switzerland-based authors have added much to the book, including the Welcome and Planner sections to each chapter. Although there's no substitute for travel advice from a good friend who knows your style, our contributors are the next best thing—the kind of people you would poll for travel advice if you knew them.

Original author of this guidebook, **Nancy Coons** has been tracing ancestral trails in Switzerland since moving to Europe in 1987. Along the way she wrote several of our guides, including those devoted to Switzerland and Provence, along with our *Escape to Provence* and *Escape to the Riviera*. Based in her 300-year-old farmhouse in Lorraine, she has written on European culture and food for the *Wall Street Journal*, *Opera News,* and *National Geographic Traveler*.

Katrin Gygax was born in Zürich. She moved to California when she was four and to Vancouver when she was six, and she didn't stop traveling for the next 28 years. Now based in Zürich with her own translating business, she writes movie reviews, mystery novels, and sings whenever possible. For this edition, she updated the chapters on Zürich, Eastern Switzerland, Luzern & Central Switzerland, and the Berner Oberland.

Jennifer McDermott moved to Geneva in 1984 and can't quite imagine living anywhere else. Trained as a geographer/anthropologist, she has written about Greek wine, Irish roots, and Geneva's history, opera, and regional museums. She teaches theater at the International School of Geneva, lends her voice to language tapes, and travels whenever she can. For this edition, she updated the chapters on Geneva and Bern.

Marton Radkai, journalist and translator, was born in New York City and raised in France, England, and Switzerland. His enthusiasm for Graubünden dates to a school field trip in 1974; when he laid eyes on the region's gorgeous mountains, it was love at first sight. Marton took up residence in Geneva in 2002, after seven years of living in Bavaria and writing for *Fodor's Germany*. For this edition, he updated the chapters on the Ticino, Graubünden, and Switzerland Essentials.

Sharon-Anne Wilcox has worked as a journalist and editor for a wide-range of popular magazines in the UK and Europe. A Londoner by birth, she enjoys reporting on city life throughout the world. Now settled in Zürich, she's become an aficionado of Switzerland's wonderful mountains and valleys. For this edition, she updated the chapters on Basel and Fribourg & Neuchâtel

Kay Winzenried made her first visit to Switzerland in 1980 and has returned every year since. Now a dual citizen by marriage, she has lived in both the French- and German-speaking regions. She's used the centrally located country as a base for travels throughout Europe and a solo trip around the world, and as a training site for high-altitude trekking. Hiking with friends, exploring vineyards, and dining—be it rustic or haute cuisine—are her pleasures. For this edition, she updated the chapters on Vaud and Valais.

We'd also like to thank the staff of the Swiss regional tourist offices, as well as Erica Loser of the Switzerland Tourism office in New York, for their help with questions big and small.